A Half Century
of Returns on
Stocks and Bonds

A Half Century of Returns on Stocks and Bonds

Rates of Return on Investments
in Common Stocks and
on U.S. Treasury Securities,
1926–1976

Lawrence Fisher
and James H. Lorie

Chicago:
The University of Chicago
Graduate School of Business

1977

Library of Congress Cataloging in Publication Data

Fisher, Lawrence, 1929–
    A half-century of returns on stocks & bonds.

    Bibliography: p.
    1. Stocks—Prices—United States. 2. Bonds—Prices—United States.
I. Lorie, James Hirsch, 1922–   joint author. II. Title.
HG4915.F47   332.6'322'0973   77-76923
ISBN 0-918584-01-9

Printed in the United States of America

Dedication

The publication of this book on rates of return has been made possible in two ways by the support of Merrill Lynch, Pierce, Fenner & Smith Inc. The most important way in which Merrill Lynch helped was in stimulating and financing the founding of the Center for Research in Security Prices, which Merrill Lynch still sponsors, at the Graduate School of Business of the University of Chicago. The Center has been responsible for the first and the most refined measurements of rates of return on common stocks. Merrill Lynch's second way of helping was to provide funds for the publication of this book. The authors, the Center for Research in Security Prices, the Graduate School of Business of the University of Chicago, and, perhaps, the financial community are grateful to Merrill Lynch for its continuing and substantial support of scientific research in the field of investing.

Table of Contents

List of Tables

Table		Page

Foreword

The research for this book, *A Half Century of Returns on Stocks and Bonds: Rates of Return on Investments in Common Stock and on U.S. Treasury Securities, 1926–1976,* was supported by the Center for Research in Security Prices (sponsored by Merrill Lynch, Pierce, Fenner & Smith Inc), Graduate School of Business, the University of Chicago. It is another in a long series of research efforts supported by the Center. This book is of fundamental importance to financial planners, to investors, to those doing research, and to all who are interested in understanding the rewards and the risks of alternative investments. It is useful to continue to try to understand how these changes affect us.

The Center was formed in 1960 with an initial purpose of accurately measuring the returns from investing in common stocks listed on the New York Stock Exchange for the period 1926 to 1960. Since no machine-readable data file existed, it was necessary to build the basic data file to undertake the study. This task, under the competent and careful direction of Lawrence Fisher, took four years, a period in which computer technology was in its infancy. Merrill Lynch gave generous support to this research effort— financial support, information and, most important, encouragement and enthusiasm for the research itself.

Much of the credit for making the Center viable must go to the authors of this book, my colleagues James Lorie and Lawrence Fisher.

Professor Lorie directed the activities and growth of the Center from its inception in 1960 through 1974. He still continues to be active in the Center and still directs the Seminar on the Analysis of Security Prices. He had the foresight to realize that it was important to foster the common interests between the academic community and the financial community in understanding the operations of security markets—that each group would gain from interaction with the other, and important new research would result. To accomplish this goal, three important steps were carried out. Each step had and has as its main purpose the stimulation of research into the operations of the securities markets.

The first step was to establish the Center by undertaking an important study on rates of return on common stock and to establish basic machine-readable data files that could be used by faculty and students to conduct other research projects at reasonable cost. Professor Fisher led this difficult and important effort, and his insights made the development of the data files possible. Many at Merrill Lynch had similar foresight. They supported this activity and have continued to support the Center.

The second step was to develop new data resources and to give direct support to faculty and to students at the Graduate School of Business of the University of Chicago. This led to many important papers and many new insights into the operations of the securities markets. This effort continues to this day. In addition, students and faculty at sixty other universities are using the Center's data files for their research and educational programs.

The third step was to establish a direct link between the academic community interested in financial research and practitioners in the financial community. In 1964, Professor Lorie established the Seminar on the Analysis of Security Prices. Twice a year, in May and November, thirty-six member firms send participants to the Seminar. At each two-day Seminar, academicians and practitioners present their insights and original research findings. These papers are published in a proceedings volume. Most papers are subsequently published in established journals. The Seminar affords participants an important opportunity to exchange ideas and to seek answers to important questions. This interchange stimulates further research and leads to the direct application of research findings.

Professors Fisher and Lorie have produced an important new work. I have learned a lot in reading it, and expect to use their findings in my own research and teaching.

Myron Scholes
Director
Center for Research in Security Prices
(Sponsored by Merrill Lynch, Pierce, Fenner & Smith Inc)

University of Chicago
June 1977

Authors' Preface

Myron Scholes points out in the Foreword that the research we report here has been supported by the Center for Research in Security Prices (CRSP). What he does not point out is that the support has gone far beyond the mere provision of funds to make the calculations. We have had the active participation of the entire CRSP staff.

Professor Scholes updated and expanded the scope of the CRSP stock-market files. Only then could we, in turn, update and expand our earlier studies of rates of return.

C. William Spangler, senior programmer-analyst for CRSP, has been a full professional participant in the updating process. He has also been a constant source of aid in the writing and debugging of the analytical computer programs that we have developed.

Marvin Lipson, who was a programmer-analyst for CRSP from 1964 to 1977, carried out most of the actual coding and running of the programs used in the development of the data file for Government bonds. Mark C. Case did part of the programming and much of the data collection for the bond file.

In the course of almost any empirical study that is carried out in a careful manner, many discrepancies are found in the data that are under consideration. Mrs. Karen Ellsworth, who has performed most of the recent collection and analysis of data from printed sources for CRSP, made it possible to clear up the discrepancies and apparent discrepancies that we found reliably and promptly.

Richard Vaughan's work eased the mechanics of carrying out the study by, among other things, running and rerunning the most time consuming programs so that that work was completed in two nights.

The programs that were used for this study were developed; tested; and, in most cases, run at the Computation Center of the University of Chicago, which uses an IBM 370, model 168 computer.

Mrs. Babu Jones, administrative assistant for CRSP, supervised the preparation of the manuscript. Her work allowed the manuscript to be delivered to the printer within a month after the final analytical results had been obtained. Most of the typing was by Charlesetta Nowells and Sherry Narodick.

Betty McGuire, editor of publications for the Graduate School of Business, coordinated our contacts with the printer; and she and her staff also carried out the copy editing.

Our families willingly put up with the irregularities of our being away from home on many evenings and weekends in order to use the computer and at home on many days while writing and editing the manuscript.

L. F.

Chicago, July 1977

J. H. L.

Chapter 1
Introduction

In this volume we present fifty-one tables that show estimates of rates of return on investments in portfolios of common stocks listed on the New York Stock Exchange (NYSE) and on investments in United States Treasury securities (Governments). The estimates cover the periods beginning on the last business day of each year from 1925 through 1975 and ending on the last business day of every subsequent year from 1926 through 1976—1,326 overlapping time periods in all.

The rates of return take full account of dividends and other distributions as well as capital gains and losses, whether realized or not. The rates have been calculated under a variety of assumptions regarding the initial selection of the portfolio, the reinvestment of dividends, and the liability for the payment of income taxes and brokerage commissions. They are annual rates of return and most are presented twice, in current dollars and after adjustment for changes in the level of the Consumer Price Index.

The book is a reference book whose varied uses cannot be foretold. It contains over 60,000 rates of return or rates of price change. Some of these are interesting in themselves and some derive their interest from analysis and interpretation. Some examples may encourage the reader to undertake the search for insights through the perusal of the numerous numbers.

The rate of return on an equally weighted portfolio of all NYSE stocks that was held from the end of 1925 through the end of 1976 was 9.0

percent per annum compounded annually (Table I). The rate of return on long-term Governments for the same period was 3.4 percent. Both of these calculations are in current dollars.

From the end of 1961 till the end of 1976, the rate of return to an investor who invested in all NYSE common stocks (initial investments proportional to market value, dividends reinvested, higher tax rate, deflated by the Consumer Price Index) was slightly negative (Table XII). This period was by far the longest in the period after World War II with a negative rate. The disappointing result may help explain the net liquidation of mutual fund shares, the decline in the number of individuals investing in stocks, the low rate of net investment in plant and equipment, and the low rate of economic growth in the United States.

From the end of 1929 till the end of 1933, the average annual rate of return (deflated) on the NYSE was −6.6 percent; for the four years ending December 31, 1976, the average annual rate was −6.2 percent (Table VIII). The decline in the stock market from December 31, 1972 till December 31, 1976 was similar in magnitude to the decline during the "great crash."

Since the beginning of World War II, the after-tax rates of return on short-term Governments, deflated, have almost constantly been negative (Table LI).

Bonds are quite risky. During the five years ending December 31, 1969, the average annual rate of return on long-term Governments in

1

current dollars was −1.4 percent; during the next five years, the rate was 8.9 percent (Table XXXIV). For 1969, the rate was −8.4 percent; for 1970, +20.5 percent (Table XXXIV).

Of course, stocks are even riskier. In 1931, the rate of return on NYSE stocks was −48.2 percent; in 1933, +106 percent (Table I).

When the Center for Research in Security Prices was established, under a grant from Merrill Lynch, Pierce, Fenner & Smith Inc in 1960, our primary goal was the compilation of a machine-readable file of data which could be used to compute rates of return on portfolios of all common stocks listed on the NYSE. The estimated rates of return were to take account of brokerage commissions and of federal income taxes. In 1964, we published tables of rates of return for twenty-two time periods during 1926–60.[1] These first refined estimates of rates of return covering all of the common stocks on the largest stock exchange attracted wide attention and continued support. In 1968, we published tables that were similar to those of the first study except that the new tables covered all 820 year-to-year periods during 1926–65.[2] The data file we have worked with now contains information covering more than fifty years. Hence, in this study we report rates of return for 1,326 overlapping periods that range in length from one to fifty-one years.

In addition to the longer time period covered, this study expands the scope of our earlier work in three ways. In the earlier studies, we assumed the use of a single, naïve way of picking stocks for the portfolio. We assumed that each company's stock had the same chance of being picked as that of any other listed company and that the same amount of money was invested in each selected issue. To find the average result of such a policy, each portfolio studied consisted initially of the same number of dollars' worth of every listed company's stock. In this volume, we continue that naïve policy; but, in addition, we estimate rates of return for a selection policy that is somewhat less naïve and is consistent with the aggregate behavior of all investors. We assume that the initial investment in each company is proportional to the market value of that company's common stock. This policy is very nearly the same as assuming that the portfolio consisted of, say, one-tenth of one percent of all of the common shares listed on the NYSE. It also is a good approximation to buying a "market portfolio," which is advocated on sound theoretical grounds by a number of writers. We think that comparison of the results of the two alter-

native policies will prove interesting and instructive.

In the earlier studies, we reported results only on a current-dollar basis. We did not attempt to adjust the results to reflect changes in the purchasing power of money. As we shall discuss in more detail below, we had good reason for not attempting to adjust for such changes. The undeniable inflation since 1965, however, tips the scales the other way. In this volume, most of our results are reported both in terms of current dollars and after deflating all dollar amounts (both receipts and portfolio values) by the Consumer Price Index of the United States Bureau of Labor Statistics.

The third addition in this study is the presentation of rates of return for Government securities. In "Rates (1964)," in comparing Government bonds and common stocks, we relied on the performance of indexes of bond yields rather than on rates of return on investments in particular bonds. At the Center for Research in Security Prices, a comprehensive file of data on the prices and interest payments of U.S. Government securities has recently been compiled.[3] The bond file is comparable in scope to the common-stock file used for this study. We use data from the bond file for the tables of rates of return on long-, intermediate-, and short-term Treasury securities presented in this volume.

The changes in the length of time covered and the addition of "value-weighted" portfolios, deflation by the Consumer Price Index, and of rates of return on Treasury securities more than quadruple the number of statistics in "Rates (1968)."[4]

Inspection of the tables should provide a sense of how much rates of return have varied from one time period to another. Also, during any single period of time, returns among individual stocks vary widely.[5] The tables presented in this volume do not describe the cross-sectional

---

[1] *Lawrence Fisher and James H. Lorie, "Rates of Return on Investments in Common Stocks,"* Journal of Business 37 (January 1964): 1–21, hereafter referred to as "Rates (1964)."

[2] *Lawrence Fisher and James H. Lorie, "Rates of Return on Investments in Common Stocks: The Year-by-Year Record, 1926–65,"* Journal of Business 41 (July 1968): 291–316, hereafter referred to as "Rates (1968)."

[3] *Lawrence Fisher, (compiler),* CRSP Monthly Return File for U.S. Treasury Securities.

[4] *The increase would have been more than ten-fold, but we have omitted a large fraction of the total number of possible tables. Most of the omitted tables would have dealt with the "cash-to-cash" case described below.*

[5] *Even in October 1929, the month of the "great crash," at least three issues rose in price.*

distributions. Our study on variability of returns[6] provides that information for the period 1926–65. We hope to bring that study up to date.

Organization of This Volume

The material in this volume is presented in three main parts and three appendixes.

Part I, The Study as a Whole

Part I deals with the study as a whole. It follows this introductory chapter and contains Chapter 2. In Part I, we discuss the definition of items that are reported for both stocks and bonds and point out the similarities and differences in the assumed investment policies. We describe how income-tax liability has been taken into account, and the relationship between an annual rate of return (compounding annually) and the total gain or loss on the investment in the portfolio. We also suggest some of the uses that may be made of the tables of rates of return. In considering uses, we concentrate on comparisons of rates of return of stocks and Governments.

Part II, Common Stocks

Part II describes the study of and reports the rates of return for common stocks. It contains Chapters 3 through 11.

The results presented are for portfolios that represent an average of the results for individual issues of common stock. Chapter 3 describes the averaging process and compares it with some alternatives: the similar rules used for "Rates (1964)" and "Rates (1968)," the rules for a number of stock-market indexes, and the rules that might be desirable for portfolios that had been managed.

Most of the results for common stock are "cash-to-portfolio" calculations. Brokerage commissions are charged on the initial purchase of the portfolio and on all subsequent purchases to reinvest dividends or for other reasons, and federal income taxes are deducted from all dividends. Commissions on the sale of stock and capital-gain taxes are not taken into account because it is assumed that no stock is sold. Chapter 4 discusses the "cash-to-portfolio" calculations. Chapters 5, 6, and 7 present the rates of return on a "cash-to-portfolio" basis assuming, respectively, that dividends are reinvested, that they are spent on consumer goods as they become available, and that they are ignored. Table I, which shows rates of return with dividends

reinvested, corresponds to the most widely quoted table from our earlier studies.

In our earlier studies, we reported all results on a "cash-to-cash" basis as well as on the "cash-to-portfolio" basis. The former differs from the latter because, in converting a portfolio to cash, it must be sold. Brokerage commissions must be paid and all gains and losses will be realized. The "cash-to-cash" results are reported in Chapter 8, but only two complete tables are presented. With the computer programs used for the earlier studies, finding "cash-to-cash" results in addition to "cash-to-portfolio" results added only a small amount to the total costs. In the present study, changes that have led to improved accuracy make finding both "cash-to-cash" and "cash-to-portfolio" results cost about three times as much as finding only "cash-to-portfolio" results. The effects of brokerage commissions alone may be estimated from the tables in Chapter 9. Then the effects of capital gains taxes may be found from the tables presented.

Our studies, including those in this book, have taken account of brokerage commissions; studies by others have not. In Chapter 9, we present tables of rates of return ignoring both taxes and commissions. With these tables, our results may be compared with results of studies that ignore taxes and commissions. In addition, the tables in Chapter 9 will aid in the estimate of what "cash-to-cash" results would have been for those cases where we have not calculated them.

Chapter 10 presents the results from two of the tables in Chapter 5 in index form, i.e., instead of showing the results in terms of annual rates of return, the tables in Chapter 10 show the total value of one hundred dollars' worth of each starting portfolio at each of the specified ending dates.

Chapter 11 presents year-end values of four other indexes developed at the Center for Research in Security Prices. Two of the indexes may be called Investment Performance Indexes. They recognize the effects of reinvesting cash dividends. The others are price indexes, which ignore cash dividends. In one index of each pair, the returns for all issues are given equal weight; in the other, returns for a month are weighted in proportion to the total market value of each issue at the end of the previous month ("value weighted"). Unlike the rate-of-return calculations, however, the computation of these indexes

[6]*Lawrence Fisher and James H. Lorie, "Some Studies of Variability of Returns on Investments in Common Stocks,"* Journal of Business 43 (April 1970): 99–134, *hereafter referred to as "Variability."*

assumes implicitly that the portfolio is reallocated each month according to the weighting criterion of the index.

Part III, U.S. Treasury Securities

Part III presents rates of return for investments in marketable U.S. Treasury securities. The rate-of-return estimates presented in this study are for the purpose of comparison with returns on common stocks.

The expected rate of return on a common stock may be viewed as the sum of a "pure" interest rate and a risk premium that depends on the uncertainties in the prospects of the company. For the purposes of this study, a "pure" interest rate is the promised yield on a security that has no risk of default and which is taxed at the same rate as dividends. Departures of the actual return from the expected rate are caused both by changes in the cash flow that the stockholder expects to receive and by changes in the expected rate of return. The latter are due to changes in the risk premium and to changes in the "pure" interest rate. By examining rates of return on Treasury securities, we can isolate the effects of changes in the pure interest rate. The view just outlined is presented at greater length in Chapter 12. In Chapter 12, we also discuss the problem of selecting securities whose rates of return will reflect only the appropriate "pure"

interest rate and its changes and not extraneous factors.

Chapters 13, 14, and 15 present rates of return for investments in U.S. Government bonds with at least ten years to maturity or first call; intermediate-term bonds and notes, usually with five-to-ten years to maturity or first call; and on notes, certificates of indebtedness, and Treasury bills with maturities of about one year. These rates of return are intended to be analogous to the rates of return with reinvestment of dividends presented in Chapter 5. That is, the interest received is reinvested in the same portfolio of Governments.

Appendixes

Appendix A describes the data that have been used for the estimates of rates of return reported in this volume.

Appendix B describes the computational procedures that have been used in making the estimates of rates of return.

Appendix C presents two compound-interest tables. Except for internal rates of return (without reinvestment of dividends), all rates of return in this volume were found from an average ratio of the value at the ending date to the investment at the beginning date of a period. This ratio determines the annual rate of return. The rate of return, compounded annually (the "effective" rate) was then found by a process equivalent to using either Table C1 or C2.

Part I
The study
as a whole

Chapter 2
General Methodology

The rates of return that we report in this study have been found by stating an investment policy, assuming that the policy had been applied to the securities under study for a particular period of time, calculating the "income stream" that would have been realized, and finding the single effective rate of interest that would have made the present value of the benefits received equal to the investment and associated costs. For some of the investment policies, we have stated the cost as 100 and benefits available at successive dates as a series of index numbers. In stating costs and benefits, we had to choose a yardstick. We chose two; our results are given with current dollars and dollars deflated by the Consumer Price Index as alternative measures. Finally, we have collected the results into series of tables. Then, it is up to the reader to make appropriate comparisons within and among the tables.

In this chapter, we define the investment policies used in general terms and point out how they differ among tables, from the policies implicit in a number of stock- and bond-market indexes, and also from policies that might, in fact, be desirable.

Elements of Investment Policies

No matter whether it is naïve or sophisticated, any investment policy must have a substantial number of elements specified. In practice, the investor may make decisions on a day-to-day basis as problems arise. For research—especially research using past data—the rules must be stated before computation begins. When the specific time period to be studied has been defined, we must decide how much of each stock to buy at the start of the period, how and when to change the amount held, and what to do with any cash that is received during the period. Also, several "bookkeeping" rules must be made. Are brokerage commissions to be paid out of the portfolio? Are income and other taxes? If so, when?

Time Periods Covered

As noted in the introduction, we cover all possible periods of one or more calendar years from 1926 through 1976.

When the Center for Research in Security Prices was established in 1960, it was recognized that extension of the data files backward in time would be increasingly expensive. Even so, we thought that the files should start at least a full business cycle before the 1929 stock-market crash.[1]

The reasons for covering as long a time period as we can with consistent methods should be obvious at this date. Historical data show the kinds of human experience that have taken place and, perhaps, their relative frequencies. But, each period also has its own special features. To ignore all data from the 1920s, 1930s, and early

---

[1] *The initial date of data in the common stock files has recently been changed from January 30, 1926 to December 31, 1925.*

1940s in estimating the riskiness of investments in common stock—as many did in the late 1960s—now appears to be foolhardy. Older data could be ignored safely only if risk were much better understood.

All periods are multiples of twelve months. Computation costs would have been changed only slightly if we had increased the number of periods during the fifty-one year span of the data files, but the resultant tables would have been hard to use.

Calendar years rather than results on a March-to-March basis, for example, have been used because calendar years are the usual fiscal years in our society. We have heard some criticism of this policy because of the alleged effects of tax-loss selling in December of many years. Even if that activity did affect the distribution of returns for December in a way that made it atypical, it should not have made the distribution of returns for calendar years differ from that for other fiscal years.[2]

How Much to Buy

We assume that on December 31 of any given year the investor decides to buy common stocks listed on the New York Stock Exchange or, alternatively, to buy long-, intermediate-, or short-term Governments. For common stocks and all other investments for which future returns are unknown, a cardinal principle of investment is diversification. We apply two methods to create diversified portfolios. The first assumes that equal amounts are invested in each stock; the second, that the amount invested in each stock is proportional to the total market value of all outstanding shares of that stock. Rates of return on Governments are reported in this study primarily for comparison with common stocks. Governments rather than other bonds have been used because the risk of default can be ignored. Many Government securities, particularly bonds, have features that make them undesirable for measuring returns that are affected only by the level of and by changes in the "pure" interest rate. For that reason, that security least subject to such undesirable features is bought for the bond portfolios.

Common Stocks. We have used two methods of deciding how much stock to buy. We call them *equal weighting* and *value weighting*.

For equal weighting, we buy the same number of dollars' worth of each listed issue of common stock. Both price and the number of shares outstanding are irrelevant. We doubt that any investor has actually followed this policy.

This way of making up the portfolio, however, produces a result (in terms of wealth) that is equal to the average result from a process that many investors could use—simple random sampling of issues. If this method of selection, which is akin to throwing darts at a page of stock-market quotations in a newspaper, is followed, the actual return to any particular portfolio will almost always differ from the value we calculate. However, if a large number of random samples is taken, their average will almost certainly lie close to the calculated value.[3]

The rule of equal weighting is the most naïve one that we can think of for achieving a well-diversified portfolio. Some may not like it for either of two reasons. First, not all investors could follow such a policy simultaneously, because the largest issues on the NYSE are worth more than a thousand times as much as the smallest issues. The largest issues are worth billions of dollars; the smallest, millions. Therefore, the smallest issues would be completely taken up before an appreciable fraction of the largest issues had been absorbed. Second, the policy of equal weighting is not theoretically sound. In the absence of special knowledge about individual stocks, the best available theory asserts that each investor should hold a "market portfolio" of risky assets.[4] In a market portfolio, the investor owns a given fraction of all the shares of each issue. In our value-weighting policy, we allocate an amount of money equal to a given fraction of the total market value of each listed issue. This would result, at least initially, in a "market portfolio" except for two factors, one major and the other trivial.

The major factor is that common stocks listed on the NYSE are only part of the universe of risky assets, and we do not, therefore, have sufficient data to compute the results of buying a true market portfolio.

---

[2] *Kenneth R. Jensen used June-to-June results for a simulation of college endowment funds for 1926–66. However, that distribution hardly differed from the December-to-December distribution ("An Analysis of Various Rules for Determining Expenditures from Endowment Funds," unpublished Ph.D. Dissertation, Graduate School of Business, University of Chicago, 1973). Typically, colleges have June fiscal years.*

[3] *For periods longer than one year, the annual rate of return that we calculate will tend to be larger than the mean of the annual rates for sample portfolios. For portfolios of eight stocks, we think that the bias is of the order of one half of one percent per annum (estimated by comparing medians with means in Table A1 of "Variability"). It is smaller for portfolios containing more than eight stocks.*

[4] *The theory is known as the Capital Asset Pricing Model. It has been derived under a variety of assumptions by a number of authors. The first published version is by William F. Sharpe, "Capital Asset Prices: A Theory of Market Equilibrium under Conditions of Risk,"* Journal of Finance 39 (September 1964): 425–42.

The trivial factor has little effect but does call attention to a problem that is ignored by the theory. We have used the term "value weighted" to make it clear that funds are invested in each issue in proportion to its total market value. If transactions are subject to brokerage commissions, however, there are at least three "prices" that might be used to find an issue's total market value—the quoted price itself; the sum of quoted price and commission, which is what a buyer pays; and the difference between the quoted price and the commission, which is what the seller gets. Since the ratio of commission to price depends on the quoted price per share, the choice of "price" will have an effect, albeit small, on the relative weights of issues. If commissions are ignored, value weighting is the same as holding a given fraction of the shares of each issue. When commissions are taken into account, value weighting and holding a given fraction of shares are not identical. We chose to value at quoted price primarily to minimize the cost of computation. This choice also means that future price changes tend to be weighted according to the price the seller would get, which is his opportunity cost. Here the effects of differences among policies are trivial, but they illustrate the requirement of exact definition of terms.

Bonds. The *CRSP Monthly Return File for U.S. Treasury Securities* contains data on nearly all direct, marketable Treasury issues. We consider long-, intermediate-, and short-term issues separately. For our purposes, long-term issues are Treasury bonds with more than ten years to first call or to maturity if not callable. Intermediate-term issues are Treasury bonds and notes that have between five and ten years to maturity or first call.[5] Short-term issues are Treasury bills, notes, and certificates of indebtedness that have maturities of six to twelve months.

At any time, a "portfolio" of Governments contains only one security. That security is the one that appears to offer a rate of return that seems most likely to reflect only the "pure" interest rate. The tables we present are intended to be directly comparable with the tables for common stocks with dividends reinvested and on a cash-to-portfolio basis. The most important difference between bonds and stocks is that the net payments to be received by bondholders are fixed by the offering circular issued by the Secretary of the Treasury. The issue selected is the one that appears to us to have the most nearly certain income stream. Many issues have had special features that may cause the price to

be substantially higher or lower than the price of a "straight" bond. Bonds that were bad for our research purposes were those that could be called for redemption before maturity, could not be bought by banks (were not "bank eligible"), could be used at par to pay the owner's estate tax ("flower bonds"), or could reasonably be expected to be exchanged in the near future for a new issue that would be worth appreciably more than par. In addition, with our methods of calculation, differences in the definition of capital gains and losses for bank and nonbank bondholders and the possibility of impaired marketability for securities selling at high premiums or deep discounts from par led us to avoid such issues. We also selected bonds that are taxed similarly to stocks whenever we could.

For the purpose of this study, the "pure" interest rate is the promised yield on a security that is free of risk of default, which sells at par value so that the realized return is income for tax purposes, and does not possess the special features just listed. In order of importance, the selection criteria are as follows for long-term issues:

1. Avoid "flower bonds" (goal achieved except for bonds held January 1958–December 1971).

2. Avoid callable bonds (goal achieved 1958–76 only; note that goals (1) and (2) were both achieved only during 1972–76).

3a. 1926–35: Partial tax exemption of interest (achieved).

  b. 1936–76: Fully taxable interest (achieved 1942–76).

4. If goal (1) is achieved, pick the bond with the price closest to par; otherwise, prefer a bond selling at a premium to one selling at a discount.

Altering the Initial Allocation

Common Stocks. All of the common stock portfolios that we have dealt with are, as nearly as possible, buy-and-hold portfolios. For the present study, the buy-and-hold policy implies that, so long as the stock is still traded on the NYSE, all distributions received by the stockholder are reinvested in that stock with the possible exception of cash dividends. If the stock stops being traded because of a merger in which its holders received at least some listed common stock of

---

[5] *In December of 1928 and 1929, there were no Treasury securities that met our definition. We used a bond that was first callable in 1940.*

the successor, the proceeds of the merger are reinvested in the successor. Otherwise, the proceeds are reinvested in a new equally- or value-weighted portfolio, as may be appropriate.

The buy-and-hold policies that we have applied cause the composition of a portfolio at any given date to depend on when it was bought. We used fifty-one different beginning dates in preparing our tables. The buy-and-hold policies caused all fifty-one portfolios to differ from one another on December 31, 1975, for example. Hence, all fifty-one portfolios show different returns for the period December 31, 1975–December 31, 1976.

Bonds. The long- and intermediate-term bonds were selected anew each December, and the short-term instrument was selected anew each June and December. Because of the selection criteria and the special features associated with all of the bonds offered for sale during periods of several consecutive years, this policy has not necessarily resulted in replacement at each opportunity. For example, for many years the Treasury $2^{1}/_{2}$s of September 15, 1967–72, which were issued in 1941, were the only long-term government bonds that had two characteristics that are desirable for research purposes: their interest was fully taxable and they were not acceptable at par in the payment of estate taxes. It was the single long-term issue assumed to be held from December 31, 1941 through December 31, 1957.

Indexes. Indexes of stock and bond prices or of investment performance require periodic changes either in the securities held or in the amounts that are held. For example, since 1928 the Dow-Jones Industrial Average (DJIA) has been based on holding one share of each included issue. Each distribution to stockholders of either cash or stock dividends and each exchange of stock, as in a stock split, change the relative importance of the companies included in the DJIA. Also, there have been changes in the list of thirty stocks included. The CRSP Equally Weighted Indexes require reallocation each month to reflect differences in return during the month and to take account of changes in the NYSE list. The CRSP Value-Weighted Indexes also require reallocation each month, but only to take account of changes in the list.

Some readers may be interested in comparing our indexes with the Standard & Poor's Composite Index (the S&P "500"), the value-weighted index covering the longest period of time. The S&P "500" has had several changes in its method of computation over the period cov-

ered by this study. Currently, it is a value-weighted index and has reallocation similar to the CRSP Value-Weighted Index. However, it includes only the largest stocks within each of several broad industrial classes. From 1926 to 1956, however, only ninety stocks in three classes were included, and the weight of each class was fixed. Differences in return thus required continual reallocation among classes. Moreover, for 1926 and 1927, the S&P "500" is available for only one day per week. The New York Stock Exchange Indexes, which began in May 1965, are value weighted and include all NYSE stocks—both common and preferred.[6] Of the indexes just discussed, only the CRSP Investment Performance Indexes take account of cash dividends.

Use of Cash Received

Stocks. Nearly all cash receipts are for dividends declared by the company. The exception is primarily proceeds from the sale of issues just before a previously announced termination of trading or shortly after an unplanned suspension of trading prior to delisting. Cash dividends received three alternative treatments:

1. Dividends were reinvested in the issue on which they had been paid (Time-Weighted Rates of Return). The cash-flow stream for the investor then had two elements, the initial purchase and an ending value.

2. Dividends were consumed by the investor (Internal Rates of Return). The cash flow then had from 14 to 614 elements, the initial purchase, a smaller ending value, and the dividends for each month during the period.

3. Dividends were ignored (Rates of Change in Price). The cash flow again had two elements, the initial purchase and the ending value.

Cash received from the sale or liquidation of issues that had ceased trading was reinvested using the same rule as for the initial purchase. These funds were allocated among the stocks listed at the end of the month in which the proceeds were received. When the portfolio is thought of as consisting of all NYSE common stocks, that is an obviously appropriate policy. When the portfolio is thought of as providing the expectation for a random sample of stocks (equal initial investment), the policy represents the result of a choice between accurate estimation of the expectation and of statistics that describe

---

[6] *The NYSE reports values of its index back to 1939, but the early values are for a different index covering far fewer stocks.*

the distribution about the mean. Since the latter are not reported in this volume, the choice was easy.

As noted above, whenever an issue has disappeared because of merger with another listed company and the survivor's listed common stock was all or part of the proceeds, the entire investment has been reallocated to the surviving common stock.

Bonds. Interest is assumed to be reinvested at the end of the month in which it is received. For stocks, however, dividends are assumed to be reinvested at the end of the ex-dividend month.[7] The difference in assumptions, taken by itself, produces a small downward bias in returns of bonds vis-à-vis stocks because interest payments have, in fact, been made on the first or fifteenth of the month in question while many of the cash dividends are not paid until after the settlement date for the assumed reinvestment transaction. The magnitude of the bias varies positively with the coupon rate and negatively with the price of the bond. On the other hand, we introduce an offsetting upward bias of about the same magnitude. Most of the bond quotations are from bids and offers made in the over-the-counter market by dealers. The ask (or offering) price includes a markup in lieu of brokerage commissions. However, we assume that all bond transactions take place at a net price equal to the mean of the bid and ask quotations. For the "cash-to-portfolio" case, the net bias is probably less than 0.03 percent per annum (3 basis points). We are not sure of the direction.

Brokerage Commissions

Stocks. Except for the tables in which both taxes and commissions are ignored, we have assumed that brokerage commissions must be paid on the initial investment, on reinvestment of cash dividends, and on reinvestment of the proceeds from liquidation of delisted issues. The rate charged is the "minimum" rate for nonmembers' transactions of 100 shares as specified by the rules of the NYSE on the date in question. The rate for April 30, 1975, when the rules expired, has been used for later transactions.

In the "cash-to-cash" case, commissions were also charged upon liquidations and upon the sale of the portfolio at the end of a period.

Bonds. Commissions and the magnitude of the spread between bid and ask prices have been ignored. As we just noted, omitting transaction costs has approximately offset a bias that was introduced by the assumption about the time when interest was reinvested.

Taxes

To take account of federal income taxes, we have reduced each dividend or other taxable distribution by the amount of tax that had to be paid. Three alternative assumptions have been made about the investor's tax bracket:

1. The investor is tax-exempt.
2. The investor is in a "low" tax bracket.
3. The investor is in a "high" tax bracket.

To determine the tax bracket, we have assumed that the investor's adjusted gross income (plus excluded dividends during 1961–76) was equal to either $10,000 or $50,000 in 1960 and was in approximately the same relative position with respect to median family income or per capita personal income in the other years. The actual assumed income for the lower tax bracket ranged from $1,780 in 1933 to $26,000 in 1976. For the higher tax bracket, the range was from $8,950 to $131,000. The tax rates are the marginal rates that applied to a married couple filing a joint return and claiming the standard deduction. In years that had different rates for property income ("unearned income") and income from personal services ("earned income"), we have assumed that property income was a very small proportion of total income. This results in the smallest possible marginal rate for the property income.

When capital gains or losses are recognized for tax purposes, we have assumed that the holding period was between two years and five years. From 1942 to 1976, this assumption is equivalent to assuming a holding period of at least six months, since all holding periods over six months were "long-term." The tax bracket is found by assuming that the taxable capital gain was very small.

Stocks. In the "cash-to-portfolio" case, income taxes are assumed to be paid on dividends but capital-gain taxes are ignored. In the "cash-to-cash" case, both regular income taxes and capital-gain taxes are assumed to be paid. The latter are paid whenever the entire portfolio is sold and whenever an individual issue is sold or liquidated and the net proceeds are reinvested.

Bonds. Even when bonds are held to final maturity, there are cases in which part of the income is ordinary income and the remainder is a capital gain. The use of a single-bond index makes the matter of exact calculation rather complex. When we wish to compare rates of

---

[7] *The ex-dividend date is the first day on which a dividend paid near the time of a sale belongs to the stock's seller rather than the buyer.*

return on a "cash-to-portfolio" basis, obtaining exactly comparable figures would require tracing a far more complicated investment strategy.[8] Moreover, the complicated strategy would have to be applied to 1,326 separate portfolios for each assumption about tax liability.

As a compromise, we have assumed that each month's return consists of the sum of an expected amount and a windfall. The windfall is analogous to the unrealized and, hence, untaxed capital gain or loss on stocks. It is equal to the difference between the total return for the month and what the return would have been if the promised yield had stayed the same throughout the month. Another name for the windfall is "excess return." Both total and excess return are given in the CRSP File on Governments. Income tax is charged on the difference between total return and excess return each month. An exception is made for Treasury bills. By law, the total return on a Treasury bill is interest income. Such interest was wholly tax-exempt till 1941 and fully taxable thereafter.

Comparability of Tax Rates. From 1926 through 1935, dividends were exempt from "normal" tax but subject to surtax. The long- and intermediate-term bonds that we consider were also "partially tax-exempt." In addition, the interest from the first five-thousand-dollars' worth of bonds owned by the taxpayer was exempt from surtax. From 1926 to 1935, cash dividends were also exempt from normal tax. Hence, for that period, taxes for stocks and bonds were about the same. However, interest on all Treasury bills and on many of the notes and certificates of indebtedness was exempt from all income taxes.

From 1936 through February 1941, dividends were subject to both normal tax and surtax. Moreover, the ratio of dividends to total earnings tended to be high in 1936–38, because the retained earnings of corporations were subject to a special tax. Interest on Governments, including that on new issues, continued to be wholly or partially tax-exempt. Hence, from 1936 through 1941, tax rates are not comparable.

From mid-1942 through July 1954, both dividends on stocks and interest on all of the Governments that we include in this study were taxable as ordinary income. Again, tax rates were comparable.

From August 1954 through 1964, there was a four-percent or two-percent tax credit on dividends but not on interest. The credit was about as large as the benefit of partial tax exemption had been during 1936–41, but in the opposite direction.

Since 1965, both dividends and interest have been taxed as ordinary income for most taxpayers (except for the dividend exclusion of up to $200 for a married couple).

Deflation

We present results under a variety of assumptions about investment and bookkeeping policy. We also present nearly all of our results with calculations in which income streams are stated in terms of current dollars and, alternatively, after deflating all cash flows by the Consumer Price Index of the U.S. Bureau of Labor Statistics (CPI). Tables in which the rates of return are based on deflated figures are recommended for comparing rates of return for different periods. Either set of tables may be used when the effects of altering investment and bookkeeping policies are being examined.

Unfortunately, comparisons of rates of return in current dollars and those based on deflated figures are likely to be misleading unless the reader keeps in mind that there is inherent upward bias through time in the CPI, and, therefore, a downward bias in rates of return computed from deflated data. The true cost of maintaining a given standard of living (in terms of material well-being) does not rise as fast as the CPI.

The CPI is computed by studying the actual expenditures of a sample of urban families to develop an average budget. The items in the budget are in fixed proportions. Then, for a sample of items in the actual budget, price series are collected to make an index of the cost of the components in the standard budget. The component indexes are combined to form the CPI. The budget studies are repeated at intervals of several years; and the weights in the average budget and, hence, in the sample of items are revised. Then the revised weights are used for computing the CPI between the date they are adopted and the date at which the next set of revised weights is adopted. The revision process is both costly and time consuming.[9]

Meanwhile, as prices change relative to one another, consumers will change their budgets by increasing their purchases of items whose prices

[8]*Lawrence Fisher and Roman L. Weil, "Coping with the Risk of Interest-Rate Fluctuations: Returns to Bondholders from Naïve and Optimal Strategies,"* Journal of Business *44 (October 1971): 408–31.*

[9]*For a detailed description of the CPI see publications of the U.S. Bureau of Labor Statistics such as the* BLS Handbook of Methods (BLS Bulletin 1711, *revised 1972*).

have fallen most (or have risen least) and reducing their purchases of items whose prices have risen most.[10] Because of the response of consumers to changes in relative prices, indexes based on weights determined by past data tend to rise, even when the true cost of maintaining a given standard of living remains constant. (Conversely, an index based on weights determined after the prices are collected tends to fall.)[11] The magnitude of the bias in the CPI is unknown, but 1 or 2 percent per annum is considered reasonable. There are other technical problems with broad price indexes. Despite all of the problems, the changes in the CPI over relatively short periods are indications of the relative rates at which prices have changed.

Alternative indexes could have been used, but similar results would have been found. Over the half century of this study, the Wholesale Price Index of the Bureau of Labor Statistics has changed at roughly the same rate as the CPI, i.e., 2.5 percent per annum.

There is another problem that causes price indexes to be biased deflators. That is the problem of changes in the quality of goods and services that are priced. We suspect that most of the time quality improves, but, during periods of price control, there is likely to be deterioration.[12] Hence, all deflated figures should be regarded as approximate.

Changes in Methodology

Some of our computational techniques are more precise than in "Rates (1964)" and "Rates (1968)." Some others, which reflect rare occurrences, have become less reliable. Altogether, the corresponding figures presented here differ little from those of the earlier studies. For a discussion of the computational techniques, see Appendix B.

Uses of the Tables

We think that the data in the tables are interesting in themselves, when results for one time period are compared with those of another, when results in one table are compared with results in another, and also when rates of return on one class of security—common stocks—are compared with rates of return on another—Governments.

We suggest some of the relationships among closely related tables in the part or chapter where they are discussed in detail. Since this is the only chapter that covers both stocks and Governments, we now suggest some of the uses of comparing Tables I–XII with Tables XXXIV–LI. In both groups of tables, we report rates of return assuming reinvestment of income (dividends or interest), i.e., what are described as "time-weighted" rates of return in Chapter 3. Hence, entries in tables that have the same assumptions about income taxes and deflation of data are directly comparable.

The most important comparisons are those of rates of return on stocks with corresponding rates for Governments; for example, figures in Table I compared with corresponding figures in Table XXXIV, XL, or XLVI. One may choose to compare one-year periods with one-year periods, two-year periods with two-year periods, etc.

One important question is how often and by how much rates of return on stocks have been greater than rates of return on long-term Governments. For example, if we compare Table I with Table XXXIV, we see that the realized risk premium on stocks was 5.6 percent per annum for the entire period. However, from the end of 1967 till the end of 1976, the average annual rate of return on bonds exceeded that on stocks by almost 2 percentage points.

What Some Comparisons Show

The market price of a security may be viewed as the present value of what will be, or is expected to be, paid to its holder in the future. For most Governments, the entire schedule of future receipts is known and a promised yield can be calculated.[13] If, over a period of time, the

---

[10] There may be exceptions caused by an actual change in demand, e.g., an increased consumption of natural gas for home heating at sharply higher prices—the shift in demand having been caused by exceptionally cold winter weather.

[11] This argument is a standard proposition of economic theory. The effect of substitution on an index may be illustrated by the following example. Assume that in the base year (when the budget study was done) beef and pork each sold for $1.00 per pound. Assume further that families like to consume both products and also like variety. Let them be equally well off so long as the quantity of beef times the quantity of pork remains constant. Suppose that in the base year 100 pounds of each were consumed on the average. The index for meat prices will be measured by finding the total cost of 100 pounds of each in the year in question, dividing by the cost of 100 pounds of each in the base year, and multiplying the quotient by either 100 or the value of the index in the base year. Hence, if in the next year beef were $2.00 per pound and pork were $0.50, the index would be 125. However, at those prices 200 pounds of pork and 50 pounds of beef could be purchased for the same total outlay as during the base year and they would provide equal satisfaction. Indeed, "Laspeyres" price indexes, such as the CPI, must have upward bias unless all commodities are actually consumed in fixed proportions regardless of relative price.

[12] U.S. Bureau of Labor Statistics, "Report of President's Commission on Cost of Living," Monthly Labor Review 60 (January 1945): 168–74.

[13] At least in money terms and either before taxes or at an assumed tax rate.

realized rate of return which we report in our tables does differ from the promised yield, that difference will be caused by changes in promised yields, i.e., by changes in interest rates during the period.[14] For common stocks there is no promised yield because there are no promises to pay specific sums to the stockholders at specified dates. But, in principle, there is an *expected* return that is frequently thought to be higher than the promised yield on bonds because stocks are riskier. The realized return on a common stock will almost certainly differ from the expected return not only because of changes in promised yields on bonds but also because of two other factors:

1. Expectations about future receipts are almost certain to change.
2. The difference between the expected return on a stock and the promised return on bonds (the "risk premium") may change.

We suspect strongly that changes in expectations of future receipts are far more important than changes in risk premiums.

Differences in rates of return within a table (e.g., one of Tables I–XII) were caused by four factors—differences in promised yields on bonds, differences in risk premiums, changes in interest rates, and changes in expected receipts. Thus, analyzing differences between stock and bond rates of return as well as differences within tables of returns for a given class of security should prove interesting.

---

[14]*For a period of time selected in advance, it may be possible to make the difference between promised and realized return extremely small. However, in a portfolio, this sort of "immunization" cannot be attained simultaneously for more than a single specific time period. See Fisher and Weil, op. cit.*

Part II
Rates of return on common stocks

Chapter 3
The Averaging Process

In finding rates of return on common stocks, we considered the investment performance of 2,655 different issues listed on the NYSE. Some of these issues became worthless; others increased in value several-hundred fold. The numbers that we report for any period reflect an averaging of the returns from hundreds of stocks. Moreover, the returns varied from year to year. Hence, the numbers presented for all but the one-year periods also reflect an averaging across years. Different methods of averaging produce different kinds of rates: (1) time-weighted rates of return, (2) internal rates of return, and (3) rates of change in prices.

In this chapter we describe, in general terms, the averaging processes that we have used both in rates of return of portfolios and in the processes inherent in finding rates of return from indexes.

Computations for Buy-and-Hold Portfolios

Measuring the Cash Flow

The process of finding the rate of return requires measuring the cash flow for the investor who owns the portfolio. As noted in the introduction, the cash flow has one negative element, the cost of the initial portfolio. If dividends are either reinvested or ignored, the cash flow has only one positive element, the value of the portfolio at the end of the period being considered. If dividends are withdrawn and spent on consumer goods, the cash flow has many positive elements. For simplicity, we assume that each dividend is received and either withdrawn or reinvested at the end of the month in which the stock first trades ex (without) that dividend. The cash flow for a portfolio is really simply an average of the cash flows for each of the individual common stocks that were in the portfolio at the beginning of the period. If we divide every element by the sum of the initial investments, the initial element of the cash flow is an outflow of one unit. Each positive element is an average of the ratios of each stock's element for that date to the initial investment in the stock. The average may be weighted. For the equally weighted portfolios, each stock's weight is one. For the value-weighted portfolios, each stock's weight is its total market value at the beginning of the period. The sum of the weights is proportional to the total initial investment.

In summary, the first step in finding a rate of return on the portfolio is to average the ratios of terminal value to initial value for all stocks. In addition, when it is assumed that dividends are consumed, one must find each month's average ratio of dividends to initial value.

Stating the Result as an Annual Rate of Return

Time-Weighted Rates of Return. The computations of rates of return with reinvestment of dividends are computations for true buy-and-hold portfolios, because the original investment in each stock is maintained even though the corporation may have distributed part of its wealth to its stockholders.

It might appear that the average ratio of terminal value to initial investment could easily be converted to a rate of return by subtracting one from the ratio. The result would be a simple "interest rate" but not an annual interest rate. Instead, it would be a rate per whatever the length of time between the initial purchase and the date of valuation. We could convert it to an annual rate by dividing by the number of years in the period (the technique used to convert monthly to annual rates under the Federal Truth in Lending Act). But we would obtain completely wrong answers—answers so wrong that they would be seriously misleading. For example, in Table I, we report a value for the period December 31, 1925 to December 31, 1975. From Table XXXI we see that the portfolio in question was worth about 61.57 times as much in 1975 as in 1925. Hence, the return was 6,057 percent in fifty years. "The simple annual interest rate" was therefore 6,057/50 = 121 percent per annum. This "rate of return" is precisely equivalent to a compound interest rate of 121 percent per annum, compounding *twice a century*. In Table I we also present the rate of return on the portfolio purchased on December 31, 1950 and held until December 31, 1975. That portfolio was worth about 11.53 times as much in 1975 as it was in 1950. The "rate of return" for the twenty-five year period was 1,053 percent. The "simple annual interest rate" was, therefore, 1,053/25 = 42 percent per annum. This figure is not comparable to the 121 percent per annum for the portfolio held for fifty years, because the compounding intervals are different. In fact, if a portfolio with the same return as that of the 1950–75 portfolio could have been obtained for two successive twenty-five year periods, the investor's wealth after fifty years would have been more than twice as great as for the 1925–75 portfolio (11.53² [or 133] vs. 62).

For interest rates (or rates of return) to be comparable, they must be stated as compound interest and the compounding periods must be the same. In our tables we have chosen to compound annually. For the two examples, the *annual* rates of return, *compounded annually*, were 8.6 percent for the fifty-year period and 10.3 percent for the twenty-five year period.

Since the actual rates of return vary from year to year, the process of converting the average ratio of terminal value to initial value is also an averaging process. The effect of the procedure we have used is to give the returns of all years equal weight in the averaging process. In earlier work, we have called a rate of return calculated in this manner a *time-weighted* rate of return to emphasize the fact that, when rates of return for several periods are averaged, only the length of a period affects its weight; the amount invested in each period has no effect.[1]

The actual averaging process depends on the compounding period used in stating the rates of return. For example, if rates of return are given as annual rates compounding continuously, the averaging process requires the taking of a time-weighted arithmetic mean. If rates of return are given as annual rates compounding at some finite interval, as in this volume, it is necessary to convert all of the periodic rates into their respective equivalent rates compounded continuously, find the average continuously compounded rate, and convert the average rate back to its periodically compounded equivalent.[2] The appropriate formulas are given in Appendix B. Because of the policy of reinvesting dividends, the final calculation is actually much simpler. The "time-weighted" rate of return for an overall period is

$$r = W^{1/(t_e - t_b)} - 1, \qquad (3.1)$$

where

   r = the annual rate of return compounding annually,

   W = the ratio of the value of the portfolio at the end of the period to its initial cost,

   t_e = the date the period ended (in years), and

   t_b = the date the period began.

Internal Rates of Return. If dividends and all other distributions are actually reinvested, the time-weighted rate of return calculated from Equation 3.1 is the only rate of return that can be relevant. If cash dividends or other distribu-

---

[1] *Bank Administration Institute*, Measuring the Investment Performance of Pension Funds for the Purpose of Interfund Comparisons *(Park Ridge, Illinois: Bank Administration Institute, 1968).*

[2] *Some writers call the rate just calculated a "geometric rate of return." We suppose they do because, under some circumstances, one step of the averaging process for periodically compounded rates of return is equivalent to the computation of a geometric mean. With such a procedure, however, the periods of time to which each of the rates applied must be equal in length and the geometric mean that is found is of quantities each of which is equal to 1.0 plus the rate of return, not the geometric mean of the rates of return themselves. We think that "geometric rate of return" is a needlessly confusing term. But cf. Haim Levy and Marshall Sarnat, Investment and Portfolio Analysis (New York: John Wiley & Sons, 1972), pp. 80–88.*

tions (e.g., rights) are actually withdrawn, the time-weighted rate of return may still be relevant. But two other rates may also be important. They are the well known "internal rate of return" and the "rate of price change." We may emphasize the difference between the time-weighted rate of return and the internal rate of return by calling the latter the "dollar-weighted rate of return."

The internal (or dollar-weighted) rate of return is defined by

$$V_0 = D_1/(1 + r')^{t_1} + D_2/(1 + r')^{t_2} + \ldots$$
$$+ (D_n + V_n)/(1 + r')^{t_n}$$

$$= \sum_{j=1}^{n} \frac{D_j}{(1 + r')^{t_j}} + V_n/(1 + r')^{t_n}, \qquad (3.2)$$

where

r' = the internal annual rate of return compounding annually,

V_0 = initial investment (at time t_b),

V_n = ending value of portfolio (at time t_e),

D_j = dividend (or other distribution that is withdrawn) at time t_j,

$t_0, t_1, t_2, \ldots, t_n$ are measured in years after t_0 (e.g., 0., 0.083, 0.167, ...)

The main purpose of the internal rate of return is to find the promised yield on a series of contractual payments, such as an annuity or the principal and interest of a bond. Implicitly, the value of r' is assumed to be constant. When the actual rate of return does vary during the period under consideration, the internal rate of return may be regarded as an average of the actual series of short-period rates. However, in the averaging process, subperiods of equal length receive unequal weights. In the problem under consideration here, successive subperiods, i.e., successive months, receive successively lower weights as the withdrawal of dividends progressively reduces the fraction of the initial investment remaining in the portfolio. Hence, the internal rate of return can be considered a "dollar-weighted" average of rates of return for short periods where the weights are approximately proportional to the net investment in the portfolio.[3]

We think that one should always examine the time-weighted rate of return on any portfolio for which it can be found at reasonable cost. For many portfolios the data needed to compute a time-weighted rate of return may not be available. Then, there may be good reason to examine internal rates of return.

Rates of Price Change. The question of how much of the total return, i.e., how much of the time-weighted rate of return, is due to dividends and how much to capital appreciation often arises. The answer may be found by defining

$$W_g = V_n/V_0 \qquad (3.3)$$

and substituting W_g for W in Equation 3.1 to obtain

$$r_g = W_g^{1/(t_e - t_b)} - 1, \qquad (3.4)$$

where r_g = the annual rate of price change (i.e., of capital gain).

Then the portion of the total rate of return that is due to dividends r_d is found from

$$r_d = (1 + r)/(1 + r_g) - 1. \qquad (3.5)$$

For example, if r = 9.0 percent per annum and r_g = 4.0 percent, Equation 3.5 shows that r_d is 4.8 percent per annum. Equation 3.5 may also be written

$$r_d = (r - r_g)/(1 + r_g); \qquad (3.6)$$

and Equation 3.6 is approximated by

$$r_d \approx r - r_g \qquad (3.7)$$

when r_g is "small."

Other Rates of Change

Rates of Change of Other Indexes. The CRSP Investment Performance Indexes take dividends into account. Since the indexes are constructed by adding 1.0 to each month's return to form a "wealth relative" and then taking the product of the wealth relatives for the period over which the index is calculated, we may define

$$W = X_e/X_b \qquad (3.8)$$

where X_e and X_b are values of the index at times t_e and t_b, respectively.

Then we find the time-weighted rate of return from Equation 3.1. The time-weighted rates of return for the indexes may differ from those for corresponding equally weighted or value-weighted portfolios because the rules followed for reallocating funds among individual securities differ, just as the rules for initial allocation make returns for the equally and value-weighted portfolios differ from one another. For the value-weighted index and portfolios the differences are small because they are due only to

---

[3]See Appendix 4 of Bank Administration Institute, op. cit., for a proof of this proposition.

changes in the list and to possible differences in dividend yields. For the equally weighted index and portfolios, the differences are sometimes large because weights in the portfolios are affected by past returns.[4]

Rates of change for other indexes are rates of change of prices. Hence, Equation 3.3 is directly applicable. Most of the differences among indexes will be due to differences in the weights given the returns of different stocks.

Real Portfolios. To find the rate of return for an actual portfolio that is comparable to the rate published in one of our tables of rates of return with reinvestment of dividends, one should follow the computational procedure reported in Appendix B. Comparability implies that dividends and other distributions be assumed to be received at the end of the ex-dividend month. Individual securities, however, should be given the weights they actually had in the portfolio being evaluated. Moreover, if taxes, commissions and other costs were paid from funds other than the portfolio itself, they should be counted as additional investments in the portfolio as they are paid.[5]

The actual management of a portfolio is too large a subject for us to deal with here. Under some widely held assumptions, a value-weighted portfolio of the type used for finding the results reported in this study is nearly ideal. If fewer securities must be held, then a compromise between our equally weighted and value-weighted portfolios may be desirable.

---

[4] *In "Some New Stock-Market Indexes,"* Journal of Business *39 (January 1966, Part 2): 191–225, one of us (Fisher) used an ad hoc method to make an equally weighted investment performance index behave more nearly like the equally weighted portfolios reported in "Rates (1964)" than the "arithmetic" index described here did. The ad hoc method was to combine each month's cross-sectional geometric mean with the usual link relative. The process caused the ad hoc "combination" index to rise less rapidly than the arithmetic index. For virtually all time periods beginning after 1940, however, the results reported in "Rates (1968)" agreed more closely with the arithmetic index than with the ad hoc index. Apparently, the portfolios bought before 1941 had become dominated by "low-beta stocks," which according to theory should have lower expected returns than the market as a whole. A similar surmise also applies to portfolios purchased during the past thirty years. Thus it now appears that the arithmetic investment performance index provides an unbiased although more volatile estimate of portfolio performance.*

Although it now appears that the ad hoc *index was a successful device only for the period for which it was originally computed, single-month differences in the returns of the* ad hoc *and arithmetic investment performance indexes are so small that the validity of research using the* ad hoc *index should not be questioned on that ground alone.*

[5] *For a fuller description but somewhat different recommendation see* Bank Administration Institute, op. cit.

Chapter 4

Rates of Return on Common Stocks: "Cash to Portfolio"

In the three chapters following this one, we present twenty-six tables showing rates of return on NYSE common stocks on a "cash-to-portfolio" basis. The cash-to-portfolio calculation is intended to provide estimates of the rate of return that would be found if an investor bought a portfolio and held it, reinvesting the dividends and other cash or property received. The rate of return could be found from the date the portfolio was purchased through any later date.

For a true buy-and-hold policy, no securities would be sold. Hence, no capital gains would be realized and no capital-gain taxes would be paid. In fact, however, some of the companies in the portfolios dissolved and distributed liquidating cash dividends; and the closed-end investment companies distributed capital gains to their stockholders. Hence, some capital gains and losses would, in fact, be realized. The computer program for "Rates (1964)" was written before we knew how small the effect of such realizations would prove to be. Since "Rates (1968)" used most parts of the original computer program, the realizations were again taken into account. The effects on the portfolio's rate of return of the capital-gain taxes on the intermediate realizations were very small and their direction varied.

Since the programs had to be rewritten in order to make use of a newer computer for this study, we decided to treat all cash distributions (other than in final liquidation) as ordinary cash dividends and to ignore taxes on intermediate sales transactions. This simplification had no significant effect on the accuracy of the computations, but it substantially reduced costs.

Brokerage commissions were charged on each purchase transaction either as an initial investment, as a reinvestment of dividends, or as the reinvestment of proceeds from the liquidation of a security, as described in Chapter 2.

Tables I–XII, in Chapter 5, show rates of return with dividends reinvested. These rates are time-weighted rates of return. Tables XIII–XXII, in Chapter 6, show rates of return with the assumption that dividends were consumed as they were received. These rates are internal rates of return. Tables XXIII–XXVI, in Chapter 7, show rates of price change. The tables in Chapter 7 differ from those of Chapter 5 and 6 by ignoring the stream of cash dividends used to compute the latter's rates of return. Returns in Chapter 7 are, therefore, always lower than those of Chapter 5 or 6.

The corresponding tables of Chapter 6 also differ from those of Chapter 5 because, within a holding period, returns for each month are weighted differently.

Order of the Tables

The tables for a particular type of computation (time-weighted rates of return, internal rates of return, rates of price change) are contained within a chapter. Within that chapter, the tables for equally weighted portfolios are presented before tables for value-weighted portfolios.

Within each group, a pair of tables for which it was assumed that the investor was exempt from federal income tax is first. The first pair may be followed by one or two pairs of tables for which it was assumed that the investor paid federal income taxes on cash dividends and similar distributions. If there are two such pairs, the first pair assumes the lower tax rate (the marginal rate on an income of $26,000 in 1976 and on equivalent incomes in earlier years); and the second pair assumes the higher tax rate (e.g., the marginal rate on an income of $131,000 in 1976).[1] If there is only one such pair, the higher tax rate is assumed. For the first of each pair of tables, actual current figures for prices and dividends are used in the computations. For the second

table of each pair, all money figures have been deflated by the Consumer Price Index (CPI). In the deflation process, each money figure was divided by the value of the CPI reported for the month in question and then multiplied by the value of the CPI for the month in which the portfolio was purchased.[2] If the CPI could be thought of as providing an exact measure of the rate of inflation, then it would be proper to assert that the deflated rates of return were in terms of constant (1967) dollars. As we pointed out in Chapter 2, however, the CPI tends to rise faster than an ideal index of the cost of maintaining a given standard of living. Hence, the constant-dollar assertion is not quite accurate.

---

[1]*See Appendix A.*

[2]*Data for a given month's CPI are collected over a period of time. Some data may be from one or two months prior to the month in question. Many of the other data are for a date nearer the beginning of the month than the end. However, in the month of the greatest percentage change in the CPI, July 1946, the changes did take place after June 30 when price controls from World War II expired. Therefore, use of the current month's CPI as the deflator seems to be appropriate for this study.*

Chapter 5

Time-Weighted Rates of Return on Common Stocks

(Dividends Reinvested, Cash to Portfolio)

In this chapter, we present time-weighted rates of return on investments in common stocks listed on the NYSE on a cash-to-portfolio basis with dividends reinvested. As we pointed out in Chapter 4, "cash to portfolio" means that brokerage commissions have been taken into account for the initial purchase of common stock, as each cash dividend is reinvested, and upon reinvestment of the proceeds from the liquidation of delisted stocks. Unless the investor is tax-exempt, cash to portfolio also implies that federal income taxes were paid out of each cash dividend or other taxable distribution. Except for occasional proceeds of liquidations and sales of subscription rights, no capital gains are actually realized because we assume that the portfolio is still owned on the date at which the rate of return is found. For our cash-to-portfolio calculations, we assume that no capital-gain taxes are paid at all.

Reinvestment of dividends for our purposes implies that all cash receipts (other than those used to pay taxes) are reinvested in the stock that paid them. For this study, we assume that the reinvestment takes place at the price quoted at the end of the ex-dividend month. Tables I, III, and V correspond to parts A, C, and E of

Table 1 of "Rates (1968)" but cover 1,326 overlapping periods instead of 820. Tables II, IV, and VI through XII are completely new. The three old tables provide rates of return for three categories of tax liability for portfolios that began with an equal number of dollars invested in each listed common stock, and with all returns found with prices stated in current dollars. The nine new tables provide for calculations on the bases of prices deflated by the Consumer Price Index (CPI) and of initial investment proportional to the total market value of each stock.

Equal Initial Weighting

Tables I–VI show rates of return for portfolios in which each stock receives the same initial investment. The relative values of the holdings do not remain equal, however, because some stocks are better performers than others. No reallocation is made.

Tax Exemption

Tables I and II show rates of return for tax-exempt investors.

Current Dollars. Table I shows time-weighted rates of return with calculations in

Held Until	Purchased 12/25	12/26	12/27	12/28	12/29	Purchased 12/30	12/31	12/32	12/33	12/34	Purchased 12/35	12/36	12/37	12/38	12/39	Purchased 12/40	12/41	12/42	12/43	12/44	Purchased 12/45	12/46	12/47	12/48	12/49
12/26	0.8																								
12/27	15.9	29.3																							
12/28	23.7	37.4	45.7																						
12/29	8.2	9.8	0.9	−29.4																					
12/30	−2.2	−3.7	−12.9	−31.7	−38.0																				
12/31	−11.3	−13.6	−21.6	−36.3	−41.2	−48.2																			
12/32	−10.8	−12.6	−18.7	−30.0	−32.1	−30.7	−9.8																		
12/33	−2.7	−3.3	−7.5	−15.5	−12.0	−1.4	37.1	106.0																	
12/34	−1.0	−1.5	−4.9	−11.1	−7.0	2.3	28.3	54.4	15.3																
12/35	2.4	2.1	−0.6	−5.6	−0.6	9.3	33.1	53.5	32.1	50.7															
12/36	4.7	4.7	2.4	−1.6	3.8	13.9	35.6	52.3	37.1	50.6	46.8														
12/37	0.7	0.2	−2.2	−6.2	−2.9	3.1	16.1	23.0	8.1	6.0	−11.7	−46.1													
12/38	2.9	2.6	0.6	−2.9	0.8	6.7	18.7	25.0	13.0	12.1	0.6	−16.2	30.7												
12/39	2.8	2.4	0.5	−2.6	0.8	5.8	15.6	20.3	10.3	8.8	0.0	−11.2	13.0	−3.1											
12/40	2.2	1.7	−0.1	−2.9	0.1	4.5	13.0	16.8	8.0	6.2	−1.3	−9.8	6.3	−4.9	−9.9										
12/41	1.5	1.0	−0.7	−3.2	−0.6	3.3	10.8	13.7	5.9	4.1	−2.2	−9.2	2.6	−5.5	−9.0	−9.9									
12/42	2.2	1.9	0.4	−1.9	0.8	4.6	11.5	14.1	7.2	5.9	0.6	−4.9	6.2	0.7	1.0	7.5	30.8								
12/43	3.6	3.5	2.2	0.1	3.0	7.0	13.7	16.3	10.2	9.5	5.2	0.8	12.3	9.4	12.1	22.2	46.8	57.0							
12/44	4.6	4.6	3.5	1.6	4.5	8.6	15.1	17.8	12.3	11.9	8.2	4.5	15.7	13.7	17.1	26.8	45.6	49.6	39.0						
12/45	6.3	6.4	5.5	3.8	6.9	11.1	17.6	20.4	15.4	15.4	12.3	9.3	20.4	19.4	23.7	33.7	51.5	55.7	50.5	60.7					
12/46	5.5	5.6	4.7	3.1	5.9	9.7	15.5	17.9	13.3	12.9	10.1	7.2	16.3	15.0	17.8	24.2	34.8	34.6	26.2	20.5	−9.5				
12/47	5.4	5.5	4.6	3.1	5.7	9.2	14.6	16.8	12.4	12.0	9.3	6.7	14.7	13.6	15.5	20.3	27.6	26.5	19.1	13.4	−4.2	0.0			
12/48	5.1	5.1	4.2	2.8	5.2	8.5	13.5	15.5	11.4	10.9	8.2	5.8	12.7	11.7	13.3	17.1	22.5	20.9	14.3	9.2	−3.4	−0.8	−3.1		
12/49	5.8	5.8	4.9	3.6	5.9	9.0	13.8	15.7	11.9	11.4	9.0	6.8	13.4	12.4	13.9	17.4	22.5	21.0	15.4	11.6	2.1	5.7	8.3	19.7	
12/50	6.5	6.6	5.9	4.6	6.9	10.2	15.0	16.7	13.0	12.8	10.5	8.5	14.8	14.1	15.7	19.1	23.7	22.7	18.1	15.2	7.9	12.6	16.7	27.3	35.9
12/51	6.9	7.1	6.3	5.1	7.4	10.5	15.1	16.7	13.2	13.0	10.9	9.0	14.9	14.2	15.7	18.7	22.8	21.8	17.9	15.4	9.5	13.5	16.5	23.4	25.3
12/52	7.1	7.2	6.5	5.3	7.5	10.4	14.9	16.4	13.1	12.9	10.9	9.1	14.6	13.8	15.2	18.0	21.8	20.7	17.0	14.7	9.6	13.0	15.3	19.9	19.9
12/53	6.7	6.8	6.1	4.9	7.0	9.7	13.9	15.4	12.2	12.1	10.0	8.4	13.4	12.5	13.8	16.2	19.5	18.3	14.9	12.7	8.0	10.6	12.1	15.2	13.7
12/54	8.0	8.2	7.5	6.4	8.6	11.4	15.6	17.1	14.1	14.1	12.1	10.6	15.6	14.9	16.3	18.8	22.1	21.3	18.4	16.6	12.7	15.7	17.9	21.5	21.7
12/55	8.4	8.6	8.0	6.9	9.1	11.9	16.0	17.5	14.5	14.6	12.7	11.2	16.0	15.3	16.7	19.0	22.0	21.4	18.8	17.1	13.6	16.3	18.3	21.5	21.9
12/56	8.5	8.7	8.1	7.1	9.2	11.8	15.8	17.2	14.4	14.5	12.6	11.2	15.7	15.2	16.3	18.4	21.1	20.5	18.1	16.6	13.4	15.8	17.3	20.0	20.1
12/57	7.8	7.9	7.3	6.3	8.3	10.7	14.4	15.6	13.0	12.9	11.1	9.8	14.0	13.4	14.3	16.1	18.5	17.7	15.3	13.8	10.7	12.5	13.6	15.5	14.9
12/58	8.9	9.0	8.4	7.5	9.5	12.0	15.7	16.9	14.4	14.4	12.7	11.5	15.6	15.1	16.2	18.0	20.5	19.7	17.5	16.2	13.5	15.5	16.8	19.0	18.9
12/59	9.0	9.2	8.6	7.7	9.7	12.1	15.7	16.9	14.5	14.5	12.9	11.7	15.7	15.2	16.1	17.9	20.2	19.4	17.3	16.1	13.5	15.5	16.8	18.8	18.8
12/60	8.8	9.0	8.4	7.5	9.4	11.7	15.1	16.2	14.0	14.0	12.4	11.2	14.9	14.3	15.2	16.8	19.0	18.2	16.1	14.9	12.5	14.3	15.4	17.1	16.8
12/61	9.4	9.6	9.0	8.1	10.0	12.3	15.6	16.7	14.5	14.6	13.0	11.9	15.5	15.0	15.9	17.5	19.6	18.8	16.8	15.7	13.4	15.2	16.2	17.8	17.5
12/62	8.7	8.8	8.3	7.3	9.1	11.3	14.4	15.4	13.3	13.3	11.8	10.7	14.1	13.6	14.4	15.8	17.6	16.8	14.9	13.8	11.5	13.0	13.9	15.1	14.7
12/63	9.0	9.1	8.5	7.6	9.4	11.6	14.7	15.7	13.6	13.6	12.1	11.1	14.4	13.9	14.6	16.0	17.7	16.9	15.1	14.1	12.0	13.5	14.2	15.4	15.1
12/64	9.2	9.2	8.8	7.9	9.6	11.7	14.6	15.6	13.6	13.6	12.3	11.3	14.5	14.0	14.7	16.0	17.6	17.0	15.2	14.3	12.3	13.7	14.4	15.5	15.2
12/65	9.4	9.5	9.0	8.2	10.0	12.0	15.0	16.0	14.0	14.0	12.6	11.6	14.7	14.3	15.0	16.3	17.8	17.2	15.6	14.7	12.8	14.4	15.1	16.2	16.0
12/66	8.9	9.0	8.6	7.8	9.4	11.4	14.2	15.1	13.2	13.2	11.9	10.9	13.8	13.4	14.1	15.2	16.7	16.0	14.4	13.5	11.7	13.1	13.8	14.7	14.5
12/67	9.6	9.7	9.2	8.5	10.1	12.1	14.8	15.7	14.0	14.0	12.7	11.8	14.7	14.3	15.0	16.1	17.5	17.0	15.4	14.6	12.9	14.2	14.9	15.9	15.8
12/68	9.8	9.9	9.5	8.8	10.4	12.3	15.0	15.9	14.1	14.1	12.9	12.0	14.8	14.5	15.2	16.3	17.7	17.1	15.6	14.8	13.2	14.5	15.2	16.2	16.0
12/69	9.3	9.4	8.9	8.2	9.7	11.4	13.9	14.8	13.1	13.1	11.9	11.0	13.7	13.4	13.9	14.9	16.1	15.5	14.1	13.3	11.7	12.8	13.4	14.3	14.0
12/70	9.1	9.2	8.7	8.0	9.4	11.1	13.5	14.3	12.7	12.6	11.5	10.7	13.3	13.0	13.4	14.3	15.5	14.9	13.4	12.7	11.2	12.2	12.7	13.5	13.2
12/71	9.2	9.3	8.9	8.2	9.7	11.3	13.6	14.4	12.8	12.7	11.7	10.9	13.4	13.1	13.5	14.4	15.5	15.0	13.6	12.9	11.4	12.5	13.0	13.8	13.5
12/72	9.3	9.4	9.0	8.4	9.9	11.4	13.6	14.4	12.9	12.8	11.7	10.9	13.4	13.0	13.4	14.3	15.4	14.8	13.5	12.8	11.5	12.5	12.9	13.7	13.5
12/73	8.8	8.8	8.4	7.8	9.1	10.5	12.7	13.3	11.8	11.7	10.7	9.9	12.2	11.8	12.2	13.0	13.9	13.4	12.1	11.5	10.2	11.0	11.4	12.0	11.8
12/74	8.1	8.1	7.7	7.1	8.3	9.6	11.6	12.2	10.8	10.7	9.7	8.9	11.1	10.9	11.0	11.8	12.6	12.0	10.8	10.2	8.9	9.6	9.8	10.4	10.1
12/75	8.6	8.6	8.3	7.7	9.0	10.3	12.3	13.0	11.5	11.4	10.5	9.7	11.9	11.8	11.9	12.6	13.5	13.0	11.8	11.1	9.9	10.6	10.9	11.5	11.2
12/76	9.0	9.0	8.7	8.1	9.4	10.7	12.8	13.4	12.0	11.9	11.0	10.2	12.4	12.2	12.4	13.1	14.0	13.5	12.3	11.7	10.5	11.3	11.6	12.2	12.0

Table I

Time-Weighted Rates of Return* on Common Stocks:
   Dividends Reinvested,
   Cash to Portfolio,
   Equal Initial Weighting,
   Tax-Exempt,
   Current Dollars

	____Purchased____					____Purchased____					____Purchased____					____Purchased____					____Purchased____					
	12/50	12/51	12/52	12/53	12/54	12/55	12/56	12/57	12/58	12/59	12/60	12/61	12/62	12/63	12/64	12/65	12/66	12/67	12/68	12/69	12/70	12/71	12/72	12/73	12/74	12/75
51	14.8																									
52	12.5	8.9																								
53	7.6	3.5	−3.2																							
54	18.0	18.6	22.9	55.2																						
55	18.6	19.2	22.3	37.4	19.1																					
56	17.1	17.1	18.8	27.0	13.5	6.6																				
57	12.1	11.3	11.3	14.7	3.6	−3.7	−13.8																			
58	16.7	16.7	17.8	22.2	14.7	13.1	16.8	58.1																		
59	16.8	16.8	17.8	21.5	15.3	14.1	17.2	36.1	14.5																	
60	15.1	15.0	15.6	18.1	12.8	11.3	12.9	22.0	6.5	−1.9																
61	16.2	16.2	16.8	19.3	14.9	14.1	16.0	23.8	13.7	13.0	27.6															
62	13.2	13.0	13.2	14.9	10.7	9.5	10.4	15.2	6.4	3.9	5.9	−13.4														
63	13.7	13.4	13.7	15.3	11.6	10.6	11.5	15.9	8.9	7.5	10.5	2.1	17.8													
64	13.9	13.7	14.0	15.6	12.2	11.4	12.3	16.3	10.5	9.7	12.8	7.7	18.6	16.5												
65	14.7	14.5	14.9	16.5	13.4	12.7	13.7	17.8	12.8	12.6	16.0	13.0	22.8	23.8	28.5											
66	13.1	12.9	13.2	14.6	11.5	10.7	11.4	14.9	10.2	9.7	12.1	9.0	14.9	13.0	10.1	−8.2										
67	14.5	14.4	14.8	16.3	13.6	13.0	13.8	17.4	13.4	13.4	16.2	14.3	20.8	21.4	22.5	17.9	51.5									
68	14.9	14.9	15.3	16.7	14.2	13.8	14.6	18.0	14.5	14.7	17.3	15.7	21.4	22.1	23.2	21.0	40.3	28.5								
69	12.9	12.8	13.0	14.1	11.7	11.1	11.6	14.2	10.9	10.6	12.2	10.3	14.1	13.5	12.9	9.3	16.1	1.7	−20.1							
70	12.2	12.0	12.2	13.2	10.9	10.3	10.7	12.9	9.8	9.4	10.7	8.7	11.7	10.7	9.6	6.4	10.8	0.4	−11.8	−4.4						
71	12.5	12.4	12.6	13.5	11.4	10.8	11.3	13.4	10.6	10.2	11.5	9.8	12.6	11.8	11.0	8.3	12.4	4.6	−2.5	6.8	17.0					
72	12.5	12.3	12.5	13.4	11.4	10.9	11.3	13.3	10.6	10.3	11.5	10.0	12.5	11.8	11.1	8.7	12.1	5.9	0.9	8.0	13.4	6.7				
73	10.8	10.5	10.6	11.4	9.4	8.7	8.9	10.5	8.0	7.7	8.5	7.0	8.9	7.9	6.6	4.1	6.0	0.5	−4.2	−0.5	−1.1	−9.9	−28.1			
74	9.0	8.7	8.7	9.4	7.4	6.7	6.8	8.0	5.6	5.2	5.7	4.2	5.6	4.4	3.0	0.4	1.6	−3.5	−7.9	−5.6	−7.4	−14.6	−26.0	−27.2		
75	10.3	10.1	10.1	10.8	9.0	8.4	8.6	9.9	7.7	7.3	8.1	6.7	8.3	7.4	6.4	4.3	5.9	1.7	−1.6	1.7	1.8	−2.0	−6.4	6.4	53.8	
76	11.0	10.9	10.9	11.6	9.9	9.4	9.6	11.0	8.9	8.7	9.6	8.4	10.0	9.3	8.4	6.7	8.4	4.8	2.2	6.0	7.1	5.0	3.4	16.9	48.3	40.1

Percent per annum, compounded annually.

Source: Lawrence Fisher and Myron Scholes (compilers), CRSP Monthly Master File for Common Stocks Listed on the New York Stock Exchange (magnetic tape). See Appendix A.

Held Until	Purchased					Purchased					Purchased					Purchased					Purchased				
	12/25	12/26	12/27	12/28	12/29	12/30	12/31	12/32	12/33	12/34	12/35	12/36	12/37	12/38	12/39	12/40	12/41	12/42	12/43	12/44	12/45	12/46	12/47	12/48	12/49
12/26	2.4																								
12/27	18.0	32.0																							
12/28	25.6	39.5	47.1																						
12/29	9.4	10.8	1.3	−29.6																					
12/30	−0.1	−1.5	−10.9	−29.6	−34.0																				
12/31	−8.2	−10.3	−18.1	−32.8	−36.2	−42.7																			
12/32	−6.7	−8.1	−14.0	−25.1	−25.6	−23.1	0.5																		
12/33	1.1	0.9	−3.1	−11.0	−5.9	5.5	44.4	105.0																	
12/34	2.2	1.9	−1.4	−7.4	−2.3	7.1	32.0	52.5	13.0																
12/35	5.1	4.9	2.2	−2.6	3.1	12.7	34.9	50.7	28.9	46.4															
12/36	7.1	7.2	4.9	0.9	6.9	16.7	36.8	49.8	34.3	47.5	45.0														
12/37	2.6	2.1	−0.5	−4.4	−0.8	4.7	16.4	20.6	5.6	3.5	−13.6	−47.7													
12/38	4.9	4.6	2.5	−0.9	3.1	8.6	19.3	23.6	11.5	10.9	0.1	−16.3	34.4												
12/39	4.6	4.2	2.3	−0.8	2.9	7.5	16.3	19.2	9.2	8.0	−0.2	−11.1	14.9	−2.6											
12/40	3.8	3.4	1.5	−1.3	2.0	5.9	13.4	15.7	6.9	5.4	−1.7	−10.0	7.1	−5.1	−10.8										
12/41	2.4	1.9	0.1	−2.4	0.3	3.7	10.2	11.6	3.8	2.0	−4.0	−11.0	0.8	−8.5	−13.5	−17.9									
12/42	2.6	2.2	0.6	−1.8	0.9	4.2	10.1	11.3	4.3	2.9	−2.2	−7.8	2.9	−3.9	−5.2	−1.8	19.7								
12/43	3.7	3.6	2.2	0.0	2.9	6.3	12.0	13.3	7.2	6.4	2.2	−2.3	8.8	4.7	6.0	13.8	38.2	52.2							
12/44	4.6	4.6	3.3	1.4	4.3	7.8	13.4	14.8	9.2	8.8	5.2	1.4	12.3	9.3	11.5	19.6	38.9	45.8	36.1						
12/45	6.2	6.3	5.2	3.5	6.5	10.2	15.7	17.4	12.3	12.2	9.3	6.1	16.9	15.0	18.4	27.1	45.4	51.9	47.3	57.1					
12/46	4.6	4.6	3.5	1.9	4.5	7.8	12.6	13.8	9.1	8.6	5.8	2.7	11.3	9.1	10.7	15.8	26.2	26.8	17.6	9.6	−23.4				
12/47	4.1	4.1	3.0	1.4	3.9	6.9	11.3	12.3	7.9	7.3	4.6	1.8	9.3	7.3	8.3	11.9	19.1	18.5	10.6	3.4	−15.6	−8.2			
12/48	3.8	3.7	2.6	1.0	3.3	6.1	10.2	11.2	7.0	6.3	3.7	1.1	7.6	5.9	6.6	9.5	15.0	14.0	7.2	1.3	−12.0	−6.3	−5.7		
12/49	4.6	4.5	3.4	2.0	4.2	6.9	10.8	11.7	7.8	7.3	4.9	2.6	8.8	7.2	8.1	10.8	16.1	15.4	9.7	5.4	−4.4	2.4	7.8	21.9	
12/50	5.1	5.1	4.2	2.8	5.0	7.8	11.8	12.6	8.8	8.5	6.2	4.1	10.1	8.8	9.7	12.5	17.3	16.8	12.2	8.8	1.3	8.4	14.2	24.9	28.5
12/51	5.4	5.4	4.5	3.1	5.3	7.9	11.7	12.5	8.9	8.6	6.5	4.5	10.0	8.7	9.7	12.1	16.4	15.9	11.9	9.1	2.9	8.8	13.0	19.5	18.4
12/52	5.5	5.5	4.7	3.3	5.5	7.9	11.6	12.3	8.9	8.7	6.6	4.7	10.0	8.7	9.6	11.9	15.8	15.3	11.6	9.0	3.7	9.0	12.3	16.8	15.1
12/53	5.2	5.2	4.3	3.0	5.1	7.3	10.8	11.5	8.3	8.0	6.1	4.3	9.0	7.8	8.6	10.6	14.1	13.4	10.0	7.6	2.9	7.1	9.6	12.7	10.1
12/54	6.5	6.6	5.8	4.6	6.7	9.0	12.6	13.3	10.3	10.2	8.3	6.7	11.5	10.4	11.4	13.5	17.1	16.7	13.9	11.9	7.9	12.6	15.7	19.4	18.7
12/55	7.0	7.0	6.3	5.2	7.3	9.6	13.1	13.9	10.9	10.9	9.0	7.4	12.0	11.0	12.0	14.0	17.3	17.1	14.6	12.8	9.3	13.5	16.3	19.7	19.3
12/56	7.0	7.1	6.4	5.3	7.3	9.5	12.9	13.6	10.8	10.8	8.9	7.5	11.8	11.0	11.7	13.5	16.5	16.3	14.0	12.4	9.2	13.0	15.2	18.0	17.5
12/57	6.2	6.3	5.6	4.5	6.4	8.4	11.5	12.1	9.4	9.3	7.5	6.2	10.2	9.2	9.9	11.4	14.1	13.7	11.4	9.7	6.7	9.7	11.4	13.4	12.3
12/58	7.3	7.4	6.7	5.7	7.6	9.7	12.8	13.4	10.8	10.8	9.1	7.8	11.9	11.0	11.8	13.4	16.1	15.8	13.6	12.2	9.5	12.7	14.6	16.8	16.2
12/59	7.4	7.5	6.8	5.8	7.8	9.8	12.9	13.5	11.0	11.0	9.4	8.1	12.0	11.2	11.9	13.4	16.0	15.6	13.6	12.3	9.7	12.8	14.7	16.7	16.2
12/60	7.3	7.3	6.6	5.7	7.5	9.4	12.3	12.9	10.6	10.6	9.0	7.7	11.3	10.5	11.1	12.5	14.9	14.5	12.5	11.3	8.8	11.6	13.3	15.0	14.3
12/61	7.9	7.9	7.2	6.3	8.1	10.0	12.8	13.4	11.2	11.3	9.7	8.5	12.1	11.3	12.0	13.4	15.7	15.3	13.3	12.2	9.9	12.6	14.2	15.8	15.2
12/62	7.2	7.2	6.5	5.5	7.3	9.1	11.7	12.2	10.1	10.1	8.6	7.5	10.8	10.0	10.6	11.8	13.9	13.4	11.5	10.4	8.2	10.6	11.9	13.2	12.5
12/63	7.4	7.4	6.8	5.9	7.6	9.4	12.0	12.5	10.4	10.4	9.0	7.9	11.1	10.3	10.9	12.1	14.1	13.6	11.8	10.8	8.8	11.1	12.3	13.5	12.9
12/64	7.6	7.6	7.0	6.1	7.7	9.5	12.0	12.5	10.5	10.5	9.2	8.1	11.2	10.5	11.1	12.2	14.1	13.7	12.1	11.1	9.1	11.3	12.5	13.6	13.1
12/65	7.8	7.8	7.3	6.4	8.1	9.9	12.4	12.9	10.9	10.9	9.5	8.5	11.5	10.9	11.4	12.5	14.3	14.0	12.5	11.5	9.7	12.0	13.1	14.3	13.9
12/66	7.3	7.4	6.8	5.9	7.5	9.2	11.6	12.0	10.1	10.1	8.8	7.8	10.6	10.0	10.5	11.5	13.2	12.8	11.3	10.4	8.6	10.7	11.7	12.7	12.3
12/67	8.0	8.0	7.4	6.6	8.2	9.8	12.2	12.6	10.8	10.8	9.6	8.6	11.5	10.9	11.4	12.4	14.0	13.7	12.3	11.4	9.7	11.8	12.8	13.8	13.5
12/68	8.1	8.1	7.6	6.8	8.3	10.0	12.2	12.7	10.9	10.9	9.7	8.8	11.6	11.0	11.5	12.5	14.1	13.8	12.4	11.5	9.9	11.9	12.9	13.9	13.6
12/69	7.5	7.5	6.9	6.1	7.5	9.0	11.1	11.5	9.9	9.8	8.7	7.8	10.3	9.8	10.2	11.1	12.5	12.2	10.7	9.9	8.4	10.1	10.9	11.8	11.4
12/70	7.2	7.2	6.6	5.9	7.2	8.6	10.6	11.0	9.4	9.3	8.2	7.3	9.8	9.4	9.6	10.4	11.8	11.4	10.0	9.3	7.7	9.3	10.1	10.9	10.5
12/71	7.2	7.3	6.7	6.1	7.4	8.8	10.7	11.1	9.5	9.4	8.4	7.5	10.0	9.5	9.7	10.5	11.8	11.5	10.2	9.4	8.0	9.6	10.4	11.1	10.7
12/72	7.4	7.4	6.9	6.2	7.6	8.8	10.7	11.1	9.5	9.4	8.4	7.6	9.9	9.4	9.7	10.4	11.7	11.3	10.1	9.4	8.0	9.6	10.3	11.0	10.6
12/73	6.7	6.6	6.1	5.5	6.7	7.8	9.6	9.9	8.3	8.2	7.3	6.4	8.6	8.1	8.3	9.0	10.1	9.7	8.5	7.9	6.6	7.9	8.5	9.1	8.7
12/74	5.8	5.7	5.2	4.6	5.7	6.7	8.4	8.6	7.1	7.0	6.1	5.2	7.3	6.9	7.0	7.6	8.6	8.2	7.0	6.3	5.0	6.2	6.6	7.1	6.7
12/75	6.2	6.1	5.7	5.1	6.2	7.3	9.0	9.2	7.8	7.6	6.7	5.9	8.0	7.7	7.7	8.3	9.3	9.0	7.8	7.1	5.8	7.0	7.5	8.1	7.6
12/76	6.5	6.4	6.0	5.4	6.6	7.7	9.4	9.6	8.1	8.0	7.2	6.3	8.4	8.1	8.1	8.7	9.8	9.4	8.3	7.7	6.4	7.6	8.1	8.7	8.3

Table II

Time-Weighted Rates of Return* on Common Stocks:
  Dividends Reinvested,
  Cash to Portfolio,
  Equal Initial Weighting,
  Tax-Exempt,
  Deflated by the Consumer Price Index

	Purchased				
	12/50	12/51	12/52	12/53	12/54
51	8.4				
52	8.8	8.0			
53	5.0	2.7	-3.8		
54	16.0	18.2	22.9	55.9	
55	16.9	18.8	22.1	37.5	18.6
56	15.2	16.1	17.8	25.8	11.7
57	10.0	9.9	9.9	13.1	1.4
58	14.6	15.2	16.2	20.4	12.5
59	14.7	15.3	16.2	19.7	13.2
60	13.1	13.5	14.0	16.4	10.7
61	14.2	14.8	15.3	17.7	13.0
62	11.4	11.6	11.7	13.3	8.9
63	11.8	12.0	12.2	13.7	9.8
64	12.1	12.3	12.5	14.0	10.5
65	12.8	13.0	13.4	14.9	11.6
66	11.2	11.3	11.5	12.8	9.6
67	12.5	12.7	13.0	14.4	11.5
68	12.7	12.9	13.3	14.6	11.9
69	10.5	10.6	10.8	11.7	9.2
70	9.6	9.6	9.7	10.6	8.2
71	9.9	9.9	10.0	10.9	8.6
72	9.8	9.8	9.9	10.7	8.6
73	7.8	7.8	7.8	8.4	6.3
74	5.8	5.6	5.5	6.0	3.9
75	6.8	6.7	6.7	7.2	5.3
76	7.5	7.4	7.4	8.0	6.1

	Purchased				
	12/55	12/56	12/57	12/58	12/59
56	3.6				
57	-6.4	-16.3			
58	10.3	14.1	55.3		
59	11.6	14.8	33.9	12.8	
60	9.0	10.7	20.1	4.9	-3.4
61	12.0	14.1	22.2	12.4	11.8
62	7.6	8.7	13.7	5.1	2.7
63	8.7	9.7	14.4	7.5	6.2
64	9.5	10.5	14.8	9.1	8.4
65	10.8	11.9	16.2	11.3	11.1
66	8.7	9.4	13.0	8.5	7.9
67	10.8	11.6	15.3	11.5	11.4
68	11.3	12.2	15.6	12.2	12.3
69	8.5	9.0	11.6	8.2	7.8
70	7.4	7.8	10.0	6.9	6.4
71	7.9	8.4	10.4	7.6	7.2
72	7.9	8.3	10.3	7.6	7.3
73	5.5	5.7	7.2	4.7	4.3
74	3.1	3.1	4.3	1.8	1.3
75	4.5	4.6	5.9	3.6	3.2
76	5.5	5.6	6.9	4.8	4.4

	Purchased				
	12/60	12/61	12/62	12/63	12/64
61	26.8				
62	5.0	-14.4			
63	9.2	0.6	15.9		
64	11.5	6.3	16.9	15.2	
65	14.5	11.3	20.9	21.9	26.1
66	10.2	7.0	12.6	10.6	7.2
67	14.1	12.0	18.2	18.6	19.2
68	14.8	13.0	18.2	18.7	19.3
69	9.3	7.2	10.6	9.8	8.7
70	7.5	5.3	8.0	6.8	5.3
71	8.3	6.4	8.9	7.9	6.7
72	8.2	6.6	8.8	7.9	6.9
73	4.9	3.2	4.8	3.6	2.1
74	1.6	-0.1	1.0	-0.4	-2.1
75	3.7	2.1	3.4	2.3	1.0
76	5.1	3.7	5.0	4.1	3.0

	Purchased				
	12/65	12/66	12/67	12/68	12/69
66	-11.1				
67	14.2	47.0			
68	16.7	35.1	22.7		
69	4.8	11.0	-3.6	-24.7	
70	1.8	5.7	-4.8	-16.6	-9.3
71	3.8	7.5	-0.3	-7.2	2.3
72	4.3	7.4	1.2	-3.6	3.7
73	-0.7	1.0	-4.5	-9.1	-5.5
74	-4.9	-4.0	-9.2	-13.5	-11.4
75	-1.3	-0.1	-4.4	-7.7	-4.7
76	1.0	2.4	-1.3	-3.9	-0.4

	Purchased					
	12/70	12/71	12/72	12/73	12/74	12/75
71	13.2					
72	9.7	3.2				
73	-6.0	-15.0	-33.9			
74	-13.3	-21.0	-33.0	-35.1		
75	-4.8	-9.1	-14.4	-2.9	43.8	
76	0.5	-2.1	-4.4	8.3	40.0	33.6

*Percent per annum, compounded annually.

Sources: Stock market data—Lawrence Fisher and Myron Scholes
(compilers), CRSP Monthly Master File for Common Stocks
Listed on the New York Stock Exchange (magnetic tape).
See Appendix A.
Consumer Price Index—U.S. Bureau of Labor Statistics.

Held Until	Purchased 12/25	12/26	12/27	12/28	12/29	12/30	12/31	12/32	12/33	12/34	12/35	12/36	12/37	12/38	12/39	12/40	12/41	12/42	12/43	12/44	12/45	12/46	12/47	12/48	12/49
12/26	0.8																								
12/27	15.9	29.3																							
12/28	23.7	37.4	45.7																						
12/29	8.2	9.8	0.9	−29.4																					
12/30	−2.2	−3.7	−12.9	−31.7	−38.0																				
12/31	−11.3	−13.6	−21.6	−36.3	−41.2	−48.2																			
12/32	−10.8	−12.6	−18.7	−30.0	−32.1	−30.7	−9.8																		
12/33	−2.7	−3.3	−7.5	−15.5	−12.0	−1.4	37.1	106.0																	
12/34	−1.0	−1.5	−4.9	−11.1	−7.0	2.3	28.3	54.4	15.3																
12/35	2.4	2.1	−0.6	−5.6	−0.6	9.3	33.1	53.5	32.1	50.7															
12/36	4.7	4.7	2.4	−1.6	3.8	13.9	35.6	52.3	37.1	50.6	46.8														
12/37	0.7	0.2	−2.2	−6.2	−2.9	3.1	16.1	23.0	8.1	6.0	−11.7	−46.1													
12/38	2.9	2.6	0.6	−2.9	0.8	6.7	18.7	25.0	13.0	12.1	0.6	−16.2	30.7												
12/39	2.8	2.4	0.5	−2.6	0.8	5.8	15.6	20.3	10.3	8.8	0.0	−11.2	13.0	−3.1											
12/40	2.1	1.7	−0.1	−2.9	0.1	4.4	12.9	16.8	8.0	6.2	−1.3	−9.8	6.2	−5.0	−10.1										
12/41	1.4	0.9	−0.7	−3.3	−0.7	3.3	10.7	13.6	5.8	3.9	−2.4	−9.4	2.3	−5.8	−9.4	−10.5									
12/42	2.1	1.8	0.3	−2.0	0.6	4.4	11.3	13.9	7.0	5.6	0.3	−5.2	5.8	0.2	0.4	6.7	29.7								
12/43	3.4	3.3	2.0	−0.1	2.7	6.7	13.4	16.0	9.9	9.1	4.8	0.4	11.7	8.7	11.2	21.2	45.5	55.4							
12/44	4.4	4.3	3.2	1.3	4.2	8.2	14.7	17.4	11.8	11.4	7.7	4.0	15.0	12.9	16.1	25.7	44.3	48.0	37.4						
12/45	6.0	6.1	5.2	3.5	6.5	10.7	17.1	19.9	14.9	14.8	11.7	8.6	19.6	18.6	22.7	32.6	50.3	54.2	49.1	59.3					
12/46	5.1	5.3	4.3	2.8	5.5	9.3	15.1	17.4	12.7	12.3	9.5	6.5	15.5	14.2	16.8	23.1	33.6	33.3	24.9	19.3	−10.4				
12/47	5.0	5.1	4.2	2.7	5.2	8.7	14.1	16.1	11.8	11.3	8.6	5.9	13.8	12.7	14.5	19.1	26.4	25.2	17.7	12.1	−5.4	−1.4			
12/48	4.7	4.7	3.8	2.3	4.6	7.9	12.9	14.8	10.7	10.1	7.5	4.9	11.8	10.8	12.2	15.9	21.3	19.6	13.0	8.0	−4.6	−2.1	−4.2		
12/49	5.3	5.3	4.4	3.1	5.3	8.4	13.2	14.9	11.1	10.7	8.2	6.0	12.4	11.4	12.8	16.1	21.2	19.7	14.0	10.3	0.8	4.4	7.0	18.3	
12/50	6.0	6.1	5.3	4.0	6.3	9.5	14.3	15.9	12.2	12.0	9.7	7.6	13.8	13.1	14.5	17.8	22.4	21.3	16.7	13.8	6.6	11.2	15.3	25.8	34.3
12/51	6.4	6.5	5.8	4.5	6.7	9.8	14.4	15.9	12.4	12.2	10.0	8.1	13.8	13.1	14.5	17.5	21.6	20.5	16.5	14.1	8.2	12.1	15.1	21.9	23.8
12/52	6.5	6.6	5.9	4.7	6.9	9.7	14.1	15.6	12.2	12.0	9.9	8.1	13.5	12.7	14.0	16.7	20.5	19.3	15.6	13.3	8.2	11.6	13.9	18.5	18.4
12/53	6.1	6.2	5.5	4.3	6.3	9.0	13.1	14.5	11.3	11.1	9.1	7.4	12.3	11.4	12.6	14.9	18.2	17.0	13.5	11.3	6.7	9.2	10.8	13.8	12.3
12/54	7.4	7.5	6.9	5.8	7.9	10.6	14.8	16.2	13.2	13.1	11.2	9.6	14.5	13.8	15.1	17.5	20.9	19.9	17.1	15.2	11.3	14.3	16.5	20.1	20.3
12/55	7.8	7.9	7.3	6.2	8.4	11.1	15.2	16.6	13.6	13.6	11.7	10.2	14.9	14.2	15.5	17.7	20.8	20.1	17.5	15.8	12.3	15.0	17.0	20.2	20.5
12/56	7.9	8.0	7.4	6.4	8.5	11.0	15.0	16.3	13.5	13.5	11.6	10.2	14.6	14.1	15.1	17.1	19.9	19.2	16.8	15.3	12.1	14.5	16.1	18.7	18.9
12/57	7.1	7.3	6.7	5.7	7.6	9.9	13.6	14.7	12.1	12.0	10.2	8.8	12.9	12.3	13.2	14.9	17.3	16.5	14.1	12.6	9.5	11.3	12.4	14.3	13.8
12/58	8.3	8.4	7.8	6.8	8.8	11.2	14.9	16.0	13.5	13.5	11.8	10.5	14.6	14.0	15.0	16.8	19.3	18.5	16.3	15.0	12.3	14.3	15.7	17.8	17.7
12/59	8.4	8.5	7.9	7.0	9.0	11.4	14.9	16.1	13.6	13.7	11.9	10.7	14.7	14.1	15.0	16.7	19.1	18.3	16.1	14.9	12.4	14.4	15.7	17.7	17.7
12/60	8.2	8.4	7.7	6.8	8.7	10.9	14.3	15.4	13.1	13.2	11.5	10.2	13.9	13.3	14.1	15.7	17.8	17.0	15.0	13.8	11.4	13.1	14.3	16.0	15.8
12/61	8.8	9.0	8.3	7.4	9.3	11.5	14.8	15.9	13.7	13.7	12.1	11.0	14.5	14.0	14.8	16.4	18.5	17.7	15.7	14.6	12.3	14.1	15.2	16.7	16.5
12/62	8.1	8.2	7.6	6.7	8.4	10.5	13.6	14.6	12.4	12.5	10.9	9.8	13.1	12.6	13.3	14.7	16.5	15.7	13.7	12.7	10.5	12.0	12.8	14.0	13.7
12/63	8.4	8.5	7.9	7.0	8.7	10.8	13.9	14.8	12.7	12.7	11.2	10.1	13.4	12.8	13.6	14.9	16.6	15.8	14.0	13.0	11.0	12.4	13.2	14.4	14.1
12/64	8.5	8.6	8.1	7.2	8.9	10.9	13.8	14.8	12.8	12.8	11.4	10.3	13.5	13.0	13.7	14.9	16.6	15.9	14.1	13.2	11.2	12.6	13.4	14.5	14.3
12/65	8.8	8.8	8.3	7.5	9.2	11.3	14.2	15.1	13.1	13.2	11.7	10.7	13.8	13.3	14.0	15.2	16.8	16.1	14.5	13.6	11.8	13.3	14.1	15.2	15.1
12/66	8.3	8.4	7.9	7.1	8.7	10.6	13.4	14.2	12.4	12.4	11.0	10.0	12.9	12.4	13.1	14.2	15.6	15.0	13.4	12.5	10.7	12.1	12.8	13.8	13.6
12/67	9.0	9.1	8.6	7.8	9.4	11.3	14.1	14.9	13.1	13.1	11.8	10.9	13.7	13.3	14.0	15.1	16.5	15.9	14.4	13.5	11.9	13.2	13.9	15.0	14.8
12/68	9.2	9.3	8.8	8.1	9.6	11.5	14.2	15.0	13.3	13.2	12.0	11.1	13.9	13.5	14.1	15.2	16.6	16.1	14.6	13.8	12.2	13.5	14.2	15.2	15.1
12/69	8.7	8.8	8.2	7.5	8.9	10.6	13.1	13.9	12.3	12.2	11.0	10.1	12.8	12.4	12.9	13.9	15.1	14.5	13.0	12.3	10.7	11.8	12.4	13.3	13.1
12/70	8.5	8.5	8.0	7.3	8.7	10.3	12.7	13.5	11.8	11.7	10.6	9.8	12.3	12.1	12.4	13.3	14.5	13.8	12.4	11.7	10.2	11.2	11.7	12.5	12.3
12/71	8.6	8.6	8.2	7.5	8.9	10.5	12.8	13.6	12.0	11.9	10.8	10.0	12.5	12.2	12.5	13.4	14.5	13.9	12.6	11.9	10.4	11.5	12.0	12.8	12.6
12/72	8.7	8.8	8.3	7.7	9.1	10.6	12.8	13.5	12.0	11.9	10.8	10.1	12.4	12.0	12.4	13.3	14.4	13.8	12.5	11.8	10.5	11.5	12.0	12.8	12.6
12/73	8.2	8.2	7.8	7.1	8.4	9.7	11.8	12.4	11.0	10.9	9.9	9.0	11.2	10.9	11.2	12.0	12.9	12.3	11.1	10.5	9.2	10.1	10.4	11.1	10.9
12/74	7.4	7.4	7.0	6.4	7.5	8.8	10.8	11.3	9.9	9.8	8.9	8.0	10.2	9.9	10.1	10.8	11.6	11.0	9.8	9.2	7.9	8.6	8.8	9.4	9.1
12/75	7.9	7.9	7.5	7.0	8.2	9.5	11.5	12.1	10.6	10.5	9.6	8.8	11.0	10.8	10.9	11.6	12.4	11.9	10.7	10.1	8.8	9.6	9.9	10.5	10.3
12/76	8.3	8.3	7.9	7.4	8.6	9.9	11.9	12.5	11.0	11.0	10.0	9.2	11.4	11.2	11.3	12.0	12.9	12.4	11.3	10.7	9.5	10.2	10.5	11.2	11.0

Table III

Time-Weighted Rates of Return* on Common Stocks:
  Dividends Reinvested,
  Cash to Portfolio,
  Equal Initial Weighting,
  Lower Tax Rate,
  Current Dollars

Purchased

	12/50	12/51	12/52	12/53	12/54	12/55	12/56	12/57	12/58	12/59	12/60	12/61	12/62	12/63	12/64	12/65	12/66	12/67	12/68	12/69	12/70	12/71	12/72	12/73	12/74	12/75
1	13.4																									
2	11.1	7.6																								
3	6.2	2.2	-4.4																							
4	16.6	17.3	21.6	53.8																						
5	17.3	18.0	21.2	36.4	18.3																					
6	15.9	16.0	17.8	26.0	12.7	5.8																				
7	11.0	10.2	10.4	13.9	2.8	-4.4	-14.4																			
8	15.6	15.7	16.8	21.3	14.0	12.3	16.1	57.1																		
9	15.7	15.8	16.9	20.7	14.6	13.4	16.4	35.4	13.9																	
0	14.1	14.1	14.7	17.4	12.0	10.6	12.2	21.3	5.9	-2.6																
1	15.2	15.3	16.0	18.6	14.2	13.4	15.3	23.1	13.1	12.3	27.0															
2	12.3	12.1	12.3	14.1	10.0	8.8	9.7	14.5	5.7	3.2	5.3	-14.0														
3	12.7	12.5	12.8	14.5	10.9	9.9	10.8	15.2	8.2	6.8	9.8	1.4	17.0													
4	13.0	12.8	13.2	14.8	11.5	10.6	11.5	15.6	9.8	9.0	12.1	7.0	17.8	15.8												
5	13.7	13.7	14.1	15.7	12.7	12.0	12.9	17.1	12.1	11.8	15.3	12.3	22.0	23.0	27.8											
6	12.3	12.1	12.4	13.8	10.8	10.0	10.6	14.2	9.5	9.0	11.3	8.3	14.2	12.3	9.3	-8.8										
7	13.6	13.6	14.0	15.5	12.8	12.2	13.0	16.7	12.7	12.7	15.4	13.6	20.1	20.7	21.8	17.1	50.6									
8	14.0	14.0	14.5	15.9	13.4	13.0	13.9	17.2	13.8	13.9	16.6	15.0	20.6	21.3	22.4	20.2	39.4	27.5								
9	12.0	11.9	12.2	13.4	10.9	10.4	10.9	13.5	10.1	9.8	11.4	9.5	13.4	12.8	12.1	8.6	15.3	0.9	-20.7							
0	11.3	11.2	11.4	12.4	10.2	9.5	9.9	12.1	9.0	8.6	9.9	7.9	10.9	9.9	8.8	5.6	10.0	-0.5	-12.5	-5.2						
1	11.6	11.5	11.7	12.8	10.6	10.1	10.5	12.6	9.8	9.5	10.7	9.1	11.8	11.0	10.2	7.5	11.6	3.8	-3.3	6.0	16.3					
2	11.6	11.5	11.7	12.6	10.6	10.1	10.5	12.5	9.8	9.6	10.7	9.2	11.8	11.1	10.3	7.9	11.3	5.1	0.1	7.1	12.6	6.0				
3	9.9	9.7	9.8	10.6	8.6	7.9	8.1	9.7	7.2	6.9	7.7	6.2	8.1	7.1	5.9	3.3	5.2	-0.3	-5.0	-1.4	-1.9	-10.6	-28.8			
4	8.1	7.9	7.9	8.6	6.6	5.9	6.0	7.2	4.8	4.4	4.9	3.4	4.8	3.6	2.1	-0.4	0.7	-4.4	-8.8	-6.5	-8.3	-15.5	-26.9	-28.2		
5	9.3	9.1	9.3	10.0	8.1	7.6	7.7	9.1	6.8	6.5	7.2	5.8	7.4	6.5	5.5	3.4	4.9	0.6	-2.6	0.6	0.8	-3.1	-7.7	4.9	51.8	
6	10.0	9.9	10.0	10.7	9.0	8.5	8.7	10.1	8.0	7.8	8.6	7.4	9.0	8.3	7.5	5.7	7.4	3.7	1.1	4.8	5.9	3.8	2.0	15.3	46.5	38.5

*Percent per annum, compounded annually.

Sources: Stock market data—Lawrence Fisher and Myron Scholes (compilers), CRSP Monthly Master File for Common Stocks Listed on the New York Stock Exchange (magnetic tape). See Appendix A.
Income tax rates—Income levels estimated from U.S. Bureau of the Census, Current Population Reports, Series P-60, Nos. 101 and 103 and Historical Statistics of the United States. Tax rates were found in U.S. Internal Revenue Service, Statistics of Income and Your Federal Income Tax.

Held Until	Purchased 12/25	12/26	12/27	12/28	12/29	Purchased 12/30	12/31	12/32	12/33	12/34	Purchased 12/35	12/36	12/37	12/38	12/39	Purchased 12/40	12/41	12/42	12/43	12/44	Purchased 12/45	12/46	12/47	12/48	12/49
12/26	2.4																								
12/27	18.0	32.0																							
12/28	25.6	39.5	47.1																						
12/29	9.4	10.8	1.3	−29.6																					
12/30	−0.1	−1.5	−10.9	−29.6	−34.0																				
12/31	−8.2	−10.3	−18.1	−32.8	−36.2	−42.7																			
12/32	−6.7	−8.1	−14.0	−25.1	−25.6	−23.1	0.5																		
12/33	1.1	0.9	−3.1	−11.0	−5.9	5.5	44.4	105.0																	
12/34	2.2	1.9	−1.4	−7.4	−2.3	7.1	32.0	52.5	13.0																
12/35	5.1	4.9	2.2	−2.6	3.1	12.7	34.9	50.7	28.9	46.4															
12/36	7.1	7.2	4.9	0.9	6.9	16.7	36.8	49.8	34.3	47.5	45.0														
12/37	2.6	2.1	−0.5	−4.4	−0.8	4.7	16.4	20.6	5.6	3.5	−13.6	−47.7													
12/38	4.9	4.6	2.5	−0.9	3.1	8.6	19.3	23.6	11.5	10.9	0.1	−16.3	34.4												
12/39	4.6	4.2	2.3	−0.8	2.9	7.5	16.3	19.2	9.2	8.0	−0.2	−11.1	14.9	−2.6											
12/40	3.8	3.3	1.5	−1.3	1.9	5.9	13.4	15.7	6.9	5.3	−1.7	−10.0	7.1	−5.2	−10.9										
12/41	2.4	1.8	0.1	−2.5	0.2	3.6	10.1	11.5	3.6	1.8	−4.2	−11.2	0.6	−8.8	−13.9	−18.4									
12/42	2.4	2.1	0.5	−2.0	0.8	4.0	9.9	11.0	4.0	2.6	−2.5	−8.1	2.5	−4.4	−5.8	−2.6	18.7								
12/43	3.6	3.4	2.0	−0.2	2.6	6.1	11.8	13.0	6.8	6.0	1.8	−2.7	8.3	4.1	5.2	12.9	37.0	50.7							
12/44	4.4	4.3	3.1	1.1	4.0	7.5	13.0	14.4	8.8	8.3	4.7	0.9	11.6	8.5	10.6	18.6	37.7	44.2	34.5						
12/45	5.9	6.0	4.9	3.1	6.2	9.8	15.3	16.9	11.8	11.7	8.7	5.5	16.2	14.2	17.4	26.0	44.3	50.5	45.9	55.8					
12/46	4.2	4.3	3.1	1.5	4.1	7.3	12.1	13.3	8.6	8.0	5.1	2.1	10.5	8.2	9.8	14.7	25.1	25.5	16.4	8.6	−24.2				
12/47	3.7	3.7	2.6	1.0	3.4	6.3	10.7	11.7	7.3	6.6	3.9	1.1	8.4	6.5	7.3	10.8	17.9	17.2	9.3	2.2	−16.6	−9.5			
12/48	3.4	3.2	2.1	0.6	2.8	5.5	9.6	10.5	6.3	5.6	3.0	0.3	6.7	4.9	5.6	8.4	13.9	12.7	5.9	0.1	−13.1	−7.5	−6.8		
12/49	4.1	4.0	3.0	1.5	3.7	6.3	10.2	11.0	7.1	6.6	4.1	1.8	7.8	6.2	7.0	9.6	15.0	14.1	8.4	4.2	−5.6	1.1	6.6	20.5	
12/50	4.6	4.6	3.6	2.2	4.4	7.2	11.1	11.9	8.0	7.7	5.4	3.2	9.1	7.7	8.6	11.3	16.1	15.5	10.9	7.5	0.0	7.1	12.8	23.4	27.0
12/51	4.8	4.8	3.9	2.5	4.7	7.3	11.0	11.7	8.1	7.8	5.6	3.6	9.0	7.7	8.5	10.9	15.2	14.6	10.6	7.8	1.6	7.5	11.7	18.1	17.0
12/52	5.0	4.9	4.1	2.7	4.8	7.2	10.8	11.5	8.1	7.8	5.8	3.8	8.9	7.6	8.4	10.7	14.6	14.0	10.3	7.7	2.5	7.7	11.0	15.4	13.7
12/53	4.6	4.6	3.7	2.4	4.4	6.6	10.0	10.6	7.4	7.2	5.1	3.3	8.0	6.7	7.4	9.4	12.9	12.2	8.7	6.3	1.6	5.8	8.3	11.3	8.8
12/54	5.9	6.0	5.2	4.0	6.0	8.3	11.8	12.5	9.4	9.3	7.4	5.7	10.4	9.3	10.2	12.3	15.9	15.4	12.6	10.6	6.6	11.2	14.3	18.0	17.3
12/55	6.4	6.4	5.7	4.5	6.5	8.8	12.3	13.0	10.0	9.9	8.1	6.4	11.0	9.9	10.8	12.8	16.1	15.9	13.3	11.6	8.0	12.2	15.0	18.4	18.0
12/56	6.4	6.4	5.7	4.6	6.6	8.8	12.1	12.7	9.9	9.8	8.0	6.5	10.8	9.9	10.6	12.3	15.3	15.1	12.8	11.2	8.0	11.7	14.0	16.7	16.3
12/57	5.6	5.7	4.9	3.8	5.7	7.6	10.7	11.2	8.5	8.4	6.6	5.2	9.2	8.2	8.8	10.3	12.9	12.5	10.2	8.6	5.5	8.5	10.3	12.2	11.2
12/58	6.7	6.7	6.0	5.0	6.9	8.9	12.0	12.5	9.9	9.9	8.2	6.9	10.9	10.0	10.7	12.2	15.0	14.6	12.4	11.1	8.4	11.5	13.5	15.7	15.1
12/59	6.8	6.9	6.1	5.1	7.1	9.1	12.1	12.6	10.1	10.1	8.5	7.2	11.0	10.2	10.8	12.3	14.9	14.5	12.4	11.1	8.6	11.7	13.6	15.6	15.2
12/60	6.7	6.7	6.0	5.0	6.8	8.7	11.5	12.0	9.7	9.7	8.1	6.8	10.3	9.5	10.1	11.5	13.8	13.4	11.4	10.2	7.8	10.5	12.2	14.0	13.4
12/61	7.3	7.3	6.6	5.6	7.4	9.3	12.1	12.6	10.4	10.4	8.8	7.6	11.1	10.3	10.9	12.3	14.6	14.2	12.2	11.1	8.9	11.6	13.2	14.8	14.2
12/62	6.6	6.6	5.9	4.9	6.5	8.4	10.9	11.4	9.2	9.2	7.7	6.6	9.8	9.0	9.5	10.8	12.8	12.3	10.5	9.4	7.2	9.6	10.9	12.2	11.5
12/63	6.8	6.8	6.2	5.2	6.9	8.7	11.2	11.7	9.5	9.5	8.1	7.0	10.1	9.3	9.9	11.1	13.0	12.5	10.8	9.8	7.7	10.0	11.3	12.5	11.9
12/64	7.0	7.0	6.4	5.4	7.0	8.8	11.2	11.7	9.7	9.6	8.3	7.2	10.3	9.5	10.1	11.2	13.0	12.7	11.0	10.1	8.1	10.3	11.5	12.7	12.2
12/65	7.2	7.2	6.6	5.7	7.4	9.1	11.6	12.1	10.0	10.1	8.7	7.6	10.6	9.9	10.4	11.5	13.3	13.0	11.4	10.5	8.7	11.0	12.2	13.3	12.9
12/66	6.7	6.7	6.1	5.3	6.8	8.4	10.8	11.2	9.3	9.3	7.9	6.9	9.7	9.0	9.5	10.5	12.2	11.8	10.3	9.4	7.6	9.7	10.8	11.8	11.4
12/67	7.4	7.4	6.7	5.9	7.5	9.1	11.4	11.8	10.0	10.0	8.7	7.7	10.5	9.9	10.4	11.4	13.0	12.7	11.3	10.4	8.7	10.8	11.8	12.9	12.6
12/68	7.5	7.5	6.9	6.1	7.6	9.2	11.4	11.9	10.1	10.0	8.8	7.9	10.6	10.1	10.5	11.5	13.1	12.8	11.4	10.5	8.9	10.9	12.0	13.0	12.7
12/69	6.9	6.9	6.2	5.4	6.8	8.2	10.3	10.7	9.0	8.9	7.8	6.9	9.4	8.9	9.2	10.1	11.5	11.2	9.7	8.9	7.4	9.1	10.0	10.9	10.5
12/70	6.6	6.5	5.9	5.2	6.5	7.8	9.8	10.2	8.5	8.4	7.4	6.5	8.9	8.5	8.6	9.5	10.8	10.4	9.0	8.3	6.8	8.4	9.2	10.0	9.6
12/71	6.6	6.6	6.1	5.4	6.7	8.0	9.9	10.3	8.7	8.5	7.5	6.6	9.1	8.6	8.8	9.6	10.8	10.5	9.2	8.5	7.0	8.6	9.4	10.2	9.8
12/72	6.7	6.7	6.2	5.5	6.8	8.1	9.9	10.2	8.7	8.6	7.5	6.7	9.0	8.4	8.7	9.4	10.7	10.3	9.1	8.4	7.1	8.6	9.4	10.1	9.7
12/73	6.0	6.0	5.5	4.8	5.9	7.1	8.8	9.0	7.5	7.4	6.4	5.6	7.7	7.1	7.3	8.0	9.1	8.7	7.5	6.9	5.6	7.0	7.6	8.3	7.8
12/74	5.1	5.1	4.5	3.9	4.9	5.9	7.6	7.7	6.3	6.1	5.2	4.4	6.4	6.0	6.0	6.6	7.6	7.2	6.0	5.3	4.0	5.2	5.7	6.2	5.8
12/75	5.5	5.4	5.0	4.3	5.4	6.5	8.2	8.4	6.9	6.8	5.9	5.0	7.1	6.8	6.7	7.3	8.3	7.9	6.8	6.1	4.9	6.1	6.6	7.1	6.7
12/76	5.8	5.7	5.3	4.7	5.8	6.9	8.5	8.7	7.3	7.2	6.3	5.4	7.5	7.1	7.1	7.7	8.7	8.4	7.3	6.7	5.4	6.6	7.1	7.7	7.3

Table IV

Time-Weighted Rates of Return* on Common Stocks:
    Dividends Reinvested,
    Cash to Portfolio,
    Equal Initial Weighting,
    Lower Tax Rate,
    Deflated by the Consumer Price Index

Purchased

	12/50	12/51	12/52	12/53	12/54	12/55	12/56	12/57	12/58	12/59	12/60	12/61	12/62	12/63	12/64	12/65	12/66	12/67	12/68	12/69	12/70	12/71	12/72	12/73	12/74	12/75
1	7.1																									
2	7.5	6.6																								
3	3.7	1.4	-5.0																							
4	14.7	16.9	21.5	54.6																						
5	15.7	17.6	21.0	36.5	17.9																					
6	14.0	15.0	16.8	24.9	11.0	2.9																				
7	9.0	8.9	9.0	12.3	0.7	-7.1	-16.9																			
8	13.5	14.2	15.3	19.6	11.7	9.5	13.3	54.4																		
9	13.7	14.4	15.3	18.9	12.4	10.8	14.0	33.2	12.2																	
10	12.1	12.6	13.2	15.6	10.0	8.3	10.0	19.4	4.3	-4.0																
11	13.3	13.9	14.5	16.9	12.3	11.3	13.4	21.5	11.7	11.1	26.1															
12	10.5	10.7	10.9	12.6	8.2	6.9	7.9	13.0	4.5	2.1	4.3	-15.1														
13	10.9	11.1	11.3	13.0	9.1	8.0	9.0	13.6	6.8	5.5	8.5	-0.1	15.1													
14	11.2	11.4	11.7	13.2	9.7	8.8	9.8	14.0	8.4	7.7	10.8	5.5	16.1	14.4												
15	11.9	12.2	12.6	14.1	10.9	10.1	11.1	15.4	10.6	10.3	13.8	10.6	20.1	21.1	25.3											
16	10.3	10.4	10.7	12.0	8.9	8.0	8.7	12.4	7.8	7.2	9.5	6.3	11.9	9.9	6.5	-11.8										
17	11.6	11.8	12.2	13.6	10.8	10.1	10.9	14.6	10.8	10.7	13.3	11.3	17.5	17.9	18.5	13.5	46.2									
18	11.8	12.1	12.5	13.8	11.2	10.6	11.5	14.9	11.5	11.6	14.0	12.2	17.5	18.0	18.5	15.9	34.2	21.8								
19	9.6	9.8	10.0	11.0	8.4	7.7	8.3	10.9	7.5	7.1	8.6	6.4	9.9	9.1	8.0	4.1	10.2	-4.3	-25.3							
20	8.7	8.8	8.9	9.8	7.5	6.7	7.1	9.3	6.2	5.7	6.8	4.6	7.2	6.0	4.5	1.0	4.9	-5.6	-17.3	-10.2						
21	9.0	9.1	9.2	10.1	7.9	7.2	7.6	9.7	6.9	6.5	7.6	5.7	8.1	7.1	6.0	3.0	6.8	-1.0	-7.9	1.5	12.5					
22	9.0	9.0	9.1	10.0	7.8	7.2	7.6	9.5	6.9	6.5	7.5	5.8	8.1	7.2	6.2	3.5	6.7	0.4	-4.3	2.9	9.0	2.5				
23	7.0	6.9	7.0	7.6	5.5	4.7	4.9	6.4	3.9	3.5	4.1	2.5	4.1	2.9	1.4	-1.4	0.2	-5.3	-9.9	-6.3	-6.7	-15.8	-34.6			
24	4.9	4.8	4.7	5.2	3.1	2.3	2.3	3.5	1.0	0.5	0.8	-0.9	0.2	-1.2	-2.9	-5.7	-4.9	-10.0	-14.3	-12.3	-14.2	-21.8	-33.8	-36.0		
25	5.9	5.8	5.8	6.4	4.4	3.7	3.8	5.1	2.8	2.3	2.8	1.2	2.5	1.4	0.1	-2.2	-1.0	-5.4	-8.6	-5.7	-5.8	-10.2	-15.5	-4.3	41.8	
26	6.5	6.5	6.5	7.1	5.2	4.6	4.7	6.1	3.9	3.5	4.2	2.8	4.1	3.2	2.1	0.1	1.5	-2.3	-4.9	-1.5	-0.6	-3.2	-5.7	6.8	38.3	32.1

*Percent per annum, compounded annually.

Sources: Stock market data—Lawrence Fisher and Myron Scholes
(compilers), CRSP Monthly Master File for Common Stocks
Listed on the New York Stock Exchange (magnetic tape).
See Appendix A.
Consumer Price Index—U.S. Bureau of Labor Statistics.
Income tax rates—Income levels estimated from U.S.
Bureau of the Census, Current Population Reports, Series
P-60, Nos. 101 and 103 and Historical Statistics of the
United States. Tax rates were found in U.S. Internal
Revenue Service, Statistics of Income and Your Federal
Income Tax.

Held Until	12/25	12/26	12/27	12/28	12/29	12/30	12/31	12/32	12/33	12/34	12/35	12/36	12/37	12/38	12/39	12/40	12/41	12/42	12/43	12/44	12/45	12/46	12/47	12/48	12/49
12/26	0.8																								
12/27	15.8	29.3																							
12/28	23.6	37.3	45.7																						
12/29	8.2	9.7	0.9	-29.4																					
12/30	-2.3	-3.8	-13.0	-31.8	-38.0																				
12/31	-11.3	-13.7	-21.6	-36.3	-41.2	-48.2																			
12/32	-10.8	-12.7	-18.7	-30.0	-32.1	-30.7	-9.9																		
12/33	-2.8	-3.3	-7.5	-15.6	-12.0	-1.5	37.0	106.0																	
12/34	-1.1	-1.6	-4.9	-11.2	-7.0	2.3	28.3	54.4	15.2																
12/35	2.3	2.0	-0.7	-5.6	-0.7	9.2	33.0	53.4	32.0	50.5															
12/36	4.6	4.6	2.3	-1.7	3.7	13.8	35.5	52.1	36.9	50.3	46.3														
12/37	0.6	0.0	-2.4	-6.4	-3.1	2.8	15.9	22.7	7.8	5.6	-12.1	-46.4													
12/38	2.8	2.4	0.4	-3.1	0.6	6.5	18.4	24.7	12.6	11.8	0.2	-16.6	30.3												
12/39	2.6	2.2	0.2	-2.8	0.5	5.5	15.3	20.0	9.9	8.4	-0.4	-11.6	12.6	-3.4											
12/40	1.9	1.4	-0.4	-3.2	-0.2	4.1	12.6	16.4	7.5	5.7	-1.8	-10.3	5.7	-5.5	-10.6										
12/41	1.1	0.5	-1.1	-3.7	-1.1	2.8	10.2	13.0	5.1	3.2	-3.1	-10.1	1.5	-6.7	-10.5	-12.0									
12/42	1.6	1.3	-0.2	-2.6	0.1	3.8	10.6	13.1	6.2	4.7	-0.6	-6.2	4.6	-1.0	-1.1	4.8	27.3								
12/43	2.9	2.7	1.4	-0.7	2.0	6.0	12.6	15.1	8.9	8.1	3.7	-0.8	10.4	7.3	9.6	19.2	43.2	52.8							
12/44	3.7	3.7	2.6	0.6	3.5	7.4	13.8	16.3	10.8	10.2	6.5	2.7	13.5	11.4	14.4	23.7	42.1	45.7	35.0						
12/45	5.3	5.4	4.4	2.8	5.7	9.8	16.2	18.8	13.8	13.7	10.5	7.3	18.1	17.0	21.0	30.7	48.3	52.1	46.9	57.2					
12/46	4.4	4.6	3.6	2.0	4.7	8.4	14.1	16.3	11.6	11.2	8.2	5.2	14.1	12.7	15.1	21.2	31.8	31.5	23.1	17.7	-11.7				
12/47	4.2	4.3	3.3	1.8	4.3	7.7	13.0	15.0	10.5	10.1	7.3	4.5	12.3	11.1	12.7	17.2	24.5	23.2	15.8	10.3	-7.0	-3.3			
12/48	3.9	3.8	2.9	1.4	3.7	6.8	11.7	13.5	9.4	8.8	6.1	3.5	10.2	9.2	10.4	14.0	19.5	17.7	11.1	6.2	-6.2	-3.9	-5.8		
12/49	4.5	4.4	3.5	2.1	4.3	7.3	12.0	13.7	9.8	9.3	6.8	4.5	10.8	9.7	11.0	14.3	19.5	17.9	12.2	8.5	-0.9	2.6	5.3	16.4	
12/50	5.2	5.2	4.4	3.0	5.3	8.4	13.0	14.6	10.8	10.6	8.2	6.1	12.2	11.4	12.7	16.0	20.6	19.5	14.8	12.0	4.8	9.3	13.4	23.8	32.1
12/51	5.5	5.6	4.8	3.5	5.6	8.6	13.1	14.5	11.0	10.7	8.5	6.5	12.1	11.4	12.7	15.6	19.7	18.6	14.6	12.2	6.3	10.1	13.2	19.9	21.7
12/52	5.5	5.6	4.9	3.6	5.7	8.5	12.7	14.1	10.8	10.6	8.4	6.5	11.8	11.0	12.2	14.8	18.7	17.4	13.7	11.5	6.4	9.7	12.0	16.4	16.3
12/53	5.1	5.2	4.4	3.2	5.2	7.7	11.7	13.0	9.9	9.6	7.5	5.8	10.5	9.6	10.7	13.0	16.4	15.1	11.6	9.4	4.8	7.2	8.8	11.7	10.2
12/54	6.4	6.5	5.8	4.6	6.7	9.3	13.4	14.7	11.6	11.6	9.6	7.9	12.7	12.0	13.2	15.6	19.0	18.0	15.1	13.3	9.3	12.3	14.4	18.0	18.1
12/55	6.7	6.8	6.2	5.1	7.2	9.8	13.8	15.0	12.1	12.1	10.1	8.5	13.1	12.4	13.6	15.8	18.9	18.1	15.5	13.9	10.3	13.0	15.0	18.1	18.5
12/56	6.8	6.9	6.3	5.2	7.2	9.7	13.5	14.8	11.9	11.9	10.0	8.5	12.9	12.3	13.3	15.2	18.0	17.2	14.8	13.4	10.2	12.5	14.1	16.7	16.8
12/57	6.1	6.2	5.5	4.5	6.3	8.6	12.2	13.2	10.6	10.5	8.6	7.2	11.2	10.5	11.3	13.0	15.5	14.6	12.2	10.7	7.6	9.4	10.5	12.4	11.8
12/58	7.2	7.3	6.6	5.6	7.5	9.9	13.4	14.5	11.9	12.0	10.2	8.8	12.8	12.3	13.2	14.9	17.4	16.6	14.4	13.1	10.4	12.4	13.8	15.9	15.8
12/59	7.3	7.4	6.7	5.8	7.7	10.0	13.5	14.5	12.1	12.1	10.3	9.1	12.9	12.4	13.2	14.8	17.2	16.4	14.2	13.1	10.5	12.5	13.8	15.8	15.8
12/60	7.2	7.3	6.5	5.6	7.4	9.6	12.9	13.9	11.6	11.6	9.9	8.6	12.2	11.6	12.3	13.8	16.0	15.2	13.1	12.0	9.6	11.3	12.5	14.2	14.0
12/61	7.8	7.8	7.1	6.2	8.0	10.2	13.4	14.4	12.1	12.2	10.5	9.3	12.8	12.3	13.0	14.5	16.6	15.8	13.8	12.8	10.5	12.2	13.4	14.9	14.7
12/62	7.0	7.1	6.4	5.4	7.1	9.2	12.2	13.1	10.9	10.9	9.4	8.2	11.4	10.9	11.5	12.9	14.7	13.9	11.9	10.9	8.7	10.2	11.1	12.3	11.9
12/63	7.3	7.3	6.7	5.8	7.5	9.5	12.5	13.3	11.2	11.2	9.7	8.5	11.7	11.1	11.8	13.1	14.8	14.0	12.2	11.3	9.2	10.7	11.5	12.6	12.4
12/64	7.4	7.5	6.9	6.0	7.6	9.6	12.4	13.3	11.3	11.3	9.9	8.8	11.8	11.3	12.0	13.2	14.8	14.1	12.4	11.5	9.5	10.9	11.7	12.8	12.6
12/65	7.7	7.7	7.2	6.3	8.0	10.0	12.9	13.7	11.6	11.7	10.2	9.1	12.1	11.6	12.3	13.5	15.1	14.4	12.8	11.9	10.1	11.7	12.4	13.5	13.4
12/66	7.3	7.3	6.7	5.9	7.4	9.3	12.1	12.8	10.9	10.9	9.5	8.5	11.3	10.8	11.4	12.5	14.0	13.3	11.7	10.9	9.1	10.5	11.2	12.2	12.0
12/67	8.0	8.0	7.4	6.6	8.2	10.0	12.7	13.5	11.7	11.7	10.3	9.3	12.1	11.7	12.3	13.4	14.8	14.2	12.7	11.9	10.2	11.6	12.3	13.4	13.3
12/68	8.1	8.2	7.7	6.9	8.4	10.2	12.8	13.6	11.8	11.8	10.5	9.6	12.3	11.9	12.5	13.6	15.0	14.4	12.9	12.1	10.6	11.9	12.6	13.6	13.6
12/69	7.6	7.7	7.1	6.3	7.7	9.3	11.7	12.5	10.8	10.8	9.6	8.7	11.2	10.9	11.3	12.3	13.5	12.9	11.4	10.7	9.1	10.3	10.9	11.8	11.6
12/70	7.4	7.4	6.9	6.2	7.5	9.0	11.3	12.0	10.4	10.3	9.2	8.3	10.8	10.6	10.8	11.7	12.9	12.2	10.8	10.1	8.6	9.6	10.2	11.0	10.8
12/71	7.5	7.6	7.0	6.4	7.7	9.2	11.5	12.1	10.5	10.5	9.4	8.5	11.0	10.7	10.9	11.8	12.9	12.3	11.0	10.3	8.9	10.0	10.5	11.3	11.1
12/72	7.7	7.7	7.2	6.6	7.9	9.3	11.5	12.1	10.6	10.5	9.4	8.6	10.9	10.5	10.9	11.7	12.8	12.2	10.9	10.3	9.0	10.0	10.5	11.3	11.1
12/73	7.1	7.1	6.6	6.0	7.1	8.4	10.5	11.1	9.6	9.5	8.5	7.6	9.7	9.4	9.7	10.4	11.4	10.8	9.6	9.0	7.7	8.6	9.0	9.7	9.5
12/74	6.3	6.3	5.9	5.2	6.3	7.5	9.5	9.9	8.5	8.4	7.5	6.6	8.7	8.5	8.6	9.3	10.1	9.5	8.2	7.7	6.4	7.1	7.4	8.0	7.8
12/75	6.8	6.8	6.4	5.8	6.9	8.2	10.2	10.7	9.3	9.1	8.2	7.4	9.5	9.4	9.4	10.1	10.9	10.4	9.1	8.6	7.4	8.1	8.4	9.1	8.9
12/76	7.2	7.2	6.7	6.2	7.3	8.6	10.6	11.1	9.6	9.6	8.6	7.8	9.9	9.8	9.8	10.5	11.4	10.9	9.7	9.2	8.0	8.7	9.0	9.7	9.5

Table V

Time-Weighted Rates of Return* on Common Stocks:
Dividends Reinvested,
Cash to Portfolio,
Equal Initial Weighting,
Higher Tax Rate,
Current Dollars

Sold	12/50	12/51	12/52	12/53	12/54	12/55	12/56	12/57	12/58	12/59	12/60	12/61	12/62	12/63	12/64	12/65	12/66	12/67	12/68	12/69	12/70	12/71	12/72	12/73	12/74	12/75
'51	11.4																									
'52	9.0	5.5																								
'53	4.1	0.1	−6.4																							
'54	14.4	15.1	19.4	51.4																						
'55	15.2	15.9	19.2	34.4	16.7																					
'56	13.9	14.0	15.8	24.2	11.1	4.2																				
'57	9.1	8.3	8.5	12.1	1.2	−6.0	−15.9																			
'58	13.7	13.8	15.0	19.5	12.3	10.6	14.2	54.9																		
'59	13.9	14.0	15.1	18.9	12.9	11.7	14.7	33.6	12.4																	
'60	12.3	12.3	13.0	15.7	10.5	9.0	10.6	19.7	4.5	−3.8																
'61	13.4	13.5	14.3	16.9	12.6	11.8	13.8	21.6	11.7	11.0	25.6															
'62	10.5	10.4	10.7	12.5	8.5	7.3	8.2	13.1	4.4	2.0	4.1	−15.0														
'63	11.0	10.8	11.2	13.0	9.4	8.4	9.3	13.8	6.9	5.5	8.6	0.2	15.7													
'64	11.3	11.2	11.6	13.3	10.0	9.2	10.1	14.2	8.5	7.8	10.9	5.8	16.6	14.7												
'65	12.1	12.1	12.6	14.3	11.2	10.6	11.5	15.8	10.8	10.6	14.1	11.1	20.9	21.9	26.6											
'66	10.7	10.5	10.9	12.4	9.4	8.7	9.3	12.9	8.3	7.8	10.2	7.2	13.1	11.2	8.3	−9.8										
'67	12.1	12.1	12.6	14.2	11.5	10.9	11.7	15.4	11.5	11.6	14.3	12.5	19.0	19.6	20.7	16.0	49.2									
'68	12.5	12.5	13.0	14.6	12.1	11.7	12.6	16.0	12.6	12.8	15.4	13.9	19.5	20.2	21.3	19.1	38.3	26.5								
'69	10.6	10.5	10.8	12.0	9.7	9.1	9.6	12.3	9.0	8.7	10.3	8.4	12.3	11.8	11.2	7.6	14.3	−0.0	−21.5							
'70	9.8	9.7	10.0	11.1	8.9	8.2	8.7	10.9	7.8	7.5	8.8	6.8	9.8	8.9	7.8	4.6	8.9	−1.5	−13.5	−6.4						
'71	10.2	10.1	10.4	11.4	9.4	8.8	9.3	11.4	8.6	8.4	9.6	8.0	10.8	10.0	9.2	6.5	10.6	2.8	−4.3	4.9	15.2					
'72	10.2	10.1	10.4	11.4	9.4	8.9	9.3	11.3	8.7	8.5	9.6	8.2	10.8	10.1	9.3	6.9	10.3	4.1	−0.9	6.1	11.7	5.1				
'73	8.5	8.3	8.5	9.4	7.4	6.7	7.0	8.6	6.1	5.8	6.6	5.2	7.1	6.1	4.9	2.3	4.2	−1.3	−6.0	−2.4	−2.8	−11.5	−29.7			
'74	6.7	6.5	6.6	7.3	5.4	4.7	4.8	6.0	3.6	3.2	3.8	2.3	3.7	2.5	1.1	−1.5	−0.4	−5.5	−9.8	−7.6	−9.3	−16.5	−28.0	−29.4		
'75	7.9	7.8	7.9	8.7	6.9	6.3	6.5	7.9	5.6	5.3	6.0	4.7	6.3	5.4	4.4	2.2	3.8	−0.5	−3.8	−0.7	−0.4	−4.4	−9.0	3.3	49.9	
'76	8.6	8.5	8.7	9.4	7.7	7.2	7.4	8.9	6.8	6.6	7.5	6.2	7.9	7.2	6.3	4.6	6.2	2.5	−0.1	3.5	4.6	2.4	0.6	13.7	44.8	36.9

*Percent per annum, compounded annually.

Sources: Stock market data—Lawrence Fisher and Myron Scholes (compilers), CRSP Monthly Master File for Common Stocks Listed on the New York Stock Exchange (magnetic tape). See Appendix A.
Income tax rates—Income levels estimated from U.S. Bureau of the Census, Current Population Reports, Series P-60, Nos. 101 and 103 and Historical Statistics of the United States. Tax rates were found in U.S. Internal Revenue Service, Statistics of Income and Your Federal Income Tax.

Held Until	Purchased 12/25	12/26	12/27	12/28	12/29	Purchased 12/30	12/31	12/32	12/33	12/34	Purchased 12/35	12/36	12/37	12/38	12/39	Purchased 12/40	12/41	12/42	12/43	12/44	Purchased 12/45	12/46	12/47	12/48	12/49
12/26	2.3																								
12/27	17.9	32.0																							
12/28	25.5	39.4	47.1																						
12/29	9.4	10.8	1.2	−29.6																					
12/30	−0.2	−1.6	−10.9	−29.7	−34.0																				
12/31	−8.2	−10.3	−18.2	−32.9	−36.2	−42.7																			
12/32	−6.7	−8.2	−14.0	−25.2	−25.7	−23.1	0.5																		
12/33	1.1	0.8	−3.2	−11.0	−6.0	5.5	44.3	105.0																	
12/34	2.2	1.9	−1.4	−7.5	−2.4	7.1	31.9	52.4	12.9																
12/35	5.0	4.9	2.1	−2.7	3.0	12.6	34.8	50.6	28.8	46.2															
12/36	7.0	7.1	4.8	0.8	6.8	16.5	36.6	49.6	34.1	47.2	44.5														
12/37	2.4	1.9	−0.6	−4.6	−1.0	4.5	16.1	20.3	5.3	3.1	−14.0	−48.0													
12/38	4.7	4.4	2.3	−1.1	2.9	8.3	19.1	23.3	11.2	10.6	−0.3	−16.7	34.0												
12/39	4.4	4.0	2.0	−1.0	2.6	7.2	16.0	18.9	8.8	7.6	−0.6	−11.6	14.5	−3.0											
12/40	3.5	3.1	1.2	−1.6	1.6	5.5	13.0	15.3	6.5	4.9	−2.2	−10.5	6.6	−5.7	−11.4										
12/41	2.0	1.4	−0.3	−2.9	−0.2	3.2	9.5	10.9	3.0	1.2	−4.9	−11.9	−0.3	−9.7	−14.9	−19.8									
12/42	2.0	1.6	−0.0	−2.5	0.2	3.4	9.2	10.2	3.2	1.7	−3.4	−9.1	1.3	−5.5	−7.2	−4.3	16.5								
12/43	3.0	2.8	1.4	−0.8	1.9	5.3	10.9	12.1	5.9	5.0	0.7	−3.8	7.0	2.8	3.7	11.0	34.8	48.1							
12/44	3.8	3.7	2.4	0.4	3.2	6.6	12.1	13.4	7.8	7.2	3.5	−0.4	10.2	7.1	8.9	16.7	35.6	41.9	32.2						
12/45	5.2	5.3	4.1	2.4	5.3	9.0	14.3	15.8	10.8	10.6	7.5	4.3	14.8	12.8	15.7	24.2	42.4	48.4	43.8	53.7					
12/46	3.5	3.5	2.4	0.7	3.3	6.4	11.1	12.2	7.5	6.9	3.9	0.8	9.1	6.8	8.2	13.0	23.4	23.8	14.8	7.1	−25.2				
12/47	3.0	2.9	1.8	0.1	2.5	5.4	9.7	10.6	6.1	5.4	2.6	−0.3	6.9	5.0	5.6	9.0	16.1	15.4	7.6	0.6	−18.1	−11.3			
12/48	2.6	2.4	1.3	−0.3	1.8	4.5	8.5	9.3	5.1	4.4	1.7	−1.1	5.2	3.4	3.9	6.6	12.2	11.0	4.2	−1.5	−14.6	−9.1	−8.2		
12/49	3.3	3.1	2.1	0.6	2.7	5.2	9.0	9.8	5.9	5.3	2.8	0.4	6.3	4.6	5.3	7.9	13.3	12.4	6.6	2.6	−7.2	−0.6	4.9	18.5	
12/50	3.8	3.7	2.7	1.3	3.4	6.0	9.9	10.6	6.7	6.3	4.0	1.8	7.5	6.1	6.9	9.5	14.4	13.7	9.1	5.8	−1.7	5.2	11.0	21.4	24.9
12/51	3.9	3.9	2.9	1.5	3.6	6.1	9.8	10.4	6.7	6.4	4.2	2.1	7.4	6.1	6.8	9.1	13.5	12.8	8.7	6.0	−0.1	5.6	9.8	16.1	15.0
12/52	4.0	4.0	3.1	1.7	3.7	6.0	9.5	10.1	6.7	6.4	4.3	2.3	7.3	6.0	6.7	8.9	12.9	12.2	8.4	5.9	0.7	5.8	9.1	13.4	11.7
12/53	3.6	3.5	2.7	1.3	3.2	5.3	8.7	9.2	6.0	5.7	3.6	1.8	6.3	5.0	5.7	7.5	11.1	10.3	6.9	4.5	−0.2	3.9	6.4	9.3	6.7
12/54	4.9	4.9	4.1	2.8	4.8	7.0	10.4	11.0	7.9	7.8	5.8	4.1	8.7	7.5	8.4	10.4	14.1	13.6	10.7	8.7	4.8	9.3	12.3	15.9	15.2
12/55	5.3	5.3	4.5	3.4	5.3	7.6	10.9	11.5	8.5	8.4	6.5	4.8	9.3	8.2	9.0	10.9	14.3	14.0	11.4	9.7	6.1	10.2	13.1	16.3	16.0
12/56	5.3	5.3	4.6	3.4	5.3	7.5	10.7	11.3	8.4	8.3	6.4	4.9	9.1	8.2	8.8	10.5	13.5	13.2	10.9	9.3	6.1	9.7	12.0	14.7	14.3
12/57	4.6	4.6	3.8	2.7	4.4	6.3	9.3	9.7	7.1	6.9	5.1	3.6	7.5	6.5	7.0	8.4	11.1	10.7	8.3	6.8	3.7	6.6	8.4	10.3	9.2
12/58	5.6	5.6	4.9	3.8	5.6	7.6	10.6	11.0	8.4	8.4	6.7	5.3	9.2	8.3	8.9	10.4	13.2	12.8	10.6	9.3	6.5	9.6	11.6	13.7	13.2
12/59	5.8	5.8	5.0	4.0	5.8	7.8	10.7	11.2	8.6	8.6	6.9	5.6	9.3	8.5	9.1	10.5	13.1	12.7	10.6	9.3	6.8	9.8	11.7	13.7	13.3
12/60	5.6	5.6	4.8	3.8	5.5	7.4	10.1	10.6	8.2	8.2	6.6	5.2	8.7	7.8	8.3	9.7	12.1	11.6	9.6	8.4	6.0	8.7	10.4	12.2	11.6
12/61	6.2	6.2	5.4	4.4	6.1	8.0	10.7	11.1	8.9	8.9	7.3	6.0	9.4	8.6	9.2	10.5	12.8	12.4	10.4	9.4	7.1	9.8	11.4	13.0	12.5
12/62	5.5	5.5	4.7	3.7	5.3	7.0	9.6	10.0	7.8	7.7	6.2	5.0	8.2	7.4	7.8	9.0	11.1	10.6	8.7	7.7	5.5	7.8	9.2	10.4	9.8
12/63	5.8	5.7	5.0	4.0	5.6	7.4	9.9	10.2	8.1	8.1	6.6	5.4	8.4	7.7	8.2	9.3	11.3	10.8	9.0	8.1	6.1	8.3	9.6	10.8	10.2
12/64	5.9	5.9	5.2	4.2	5.8	7.5	9.9	10.3	8.2	8.2	6.8	5.7	8.6	7.9	8.4	9.5	11.4	11.0	9.3	8.4	6.5	8.6	9.8	11.0	10.5
12/65	6.1	6.1	5.4	4.5	6.1	7.9	10.3	10.6	8.6	8.6	7.2	6.1	9.0	8.3	8.8	9.8	11.6	11.3	9.7	8.9	7.1	9.4	10.5	11.7	11.3
12/66	5.7	5.7	5.0	4.1	5.6	7.2	9.5	9.8	7.9	7.8	6.5	5.4	8.1	7.5	7.9	8.9	10.6	10.2	8.7	7.8	6.1	8.2	9.2	10.2	9.8
12/67	6.3	6.3	5.6	4.8	6.2	7.8	10.1	10.4	8.6	8.6	7.3	6.3	9.0	8.4	8.8	9.8	11.4	11.1	9.6	8.8	7.2	9.2	10.3	11.4	11.0
12/68	6.4	6.4	5.8	5.0	6.4	7.9	10.1	10.5	8.7	8.6	7.4	6.4	9.1	8.5	8.9	9.9	11.5	11.2	9.7	9.0	7.4	9.3	10.4	11.5	11.1
12/69	5.8	5.8	5.1	4.3	5.6	7.0	9.0	9.3	7.6	7.5	6.4	5.4	7.9	7.4	7.7	8.5	10.0	9.6	8.2	7.4	5.9	7.6	8.5	9.4	9.1
12/70	5.5	5.5	4.8	4.0	5.3	6.6	8.5	8.8	7.1	7.0	5.9	5.0	7.4	7.0	7.1	7.9	9.2	8.9	7.5	6.7	5.3	6.9	7.7	8.5	8.1
12/71	5.6	5.6	4.9	4.2	5.5	6.7	8.6	8.9	7.3	7.2	6.1	5.2	7.6	7.1	7.3	8.0	9.3	9.0	7.6	6.9	5.5	7.1	8.0	8.8	8.4
12/72	5.7	5.7	5.1	4.4	5.6	6.8	8.7	8.9	7.3	7.2	6.1	5.3	7.5	7.0	7.2	7.9	9.2	8.8	7.6	7.0	5.6	7.2	7.9	8.7	8.3
12/73	5.0	5.0	4.4	3.7	4.7	5.8	7.5	7.7	6.2	6.1	5.1	4.2	6.3	5.7	5.9	6.5	7.6	7.3	6.0	5.5	4.2	5.6	6.2	6.9	6.5
12/74	4.1	4.0	3.4	2.7	3.7	4.7	6.3	6.4	5.0	4.8	3.9	3.0	5.0	4.6	4.6	5.1	6.1	5.7	4.5	3.9	2.6	3.8	4.3	4.9	4.4
12/75	4.4	4.4	3.8	3.2	4.2	5.3	6.9	7.0	5.6	5.4	4.5	3.6	5.7	5.4	5.3	5.8	6.8	6.5	5.3	4.7	3.4	4.6	5.2	5.7	5.4
12/76	4.7	4.6	4.1	3.5	4.6	5.6	7.2	7.4	5.9	5.8	4.9	4.0	6.0	5.8	5.7	6.2	7.3	6.9	5.8	5.2	4.0	5.2	5.7	6.3	5.9

Table VI

Time-Weighted Rates of Return* on Common Stocks:
- Dividends Reinvested,
- Cash to Portfolio,
- Equal Initial Weighting,
- Higher Tax Rate,
- Deflated by the Consumer Price Index

Held until	12/50	12/51	12/52	12/53	12/54	12/55	12/56	12/57	12/58	12/59	12/60	12/61	12/62	12/63	12/64	12/65	12/66	12/67	12/68	12/69	12/70	12/71	12/72	12/73	12/74	12/75
/51	5.2																									
/52	5.5	4.6																								
/53	1.7	-0.6	-7.0																							
/54	12.5	14.7	19.3	52.2																						
/55	13.6	15.5	19.0	34.5	16.2																					
/56	12.0	13.0	14.9	23.1	9.3	1.3																				
/57	7.1	7.0	7.2	10.5	-0.8	-8.7	-18.4																			
/58	11.6	12.3	13.4	17.8	10.1	7.8	11.6	52.3																		
/59	11.8	12.5	13.5	17.2	10.8	9.2	12.4	31.4	10.8																	
/60	10.3	10.8	11.5	14.0	8.5	6.8	8.5	17.8	3.0	-5.2																
/61	11.5	12.1	12.8	15.3	10.7	9.8	11.9	20.0	10.3	9.8	24.8															
/62	8.8	9.0	9.3	11.0	6.7	5.4	6.5	11.6	3.2	0.8	3.1	-16.0														
/63	9.2	9.4	9.7	11.4	7.6	6.5	7.6	12.2	5.5	4.2	7.3	-1.2	13.8													
/64	9.5	9.8	10.1	11.7	8.3	7.3	8.4	12.7	7.1	6.5	9.6	4.4	14.9	13.3												
/65	10.3	10.6	11.0	12.7	9.5	8.7	9.8	14.1	9.3	9.2	12.6	9.5	19.0	20.0	24.2											
/66	8.8	8.9	9.3	10.7	7.5	6.7	7.4	11.1	6.6	6.1	8.4	5.3	10.9	8.9	5.5	-12.7										
/67	10.1	10.4	10.8	12.3	9.5	8.8	9.6	13.4	9.6	9.6	12.2	10.2	16.4	16.9	17.5	12.4	44.8									
/68	10.3	10.6	11.0	12.4	9.8	9.3	10.2	13.7	10.3	10.4	12.9	11.1	16.4	16.9	17.5	14.9	33.1	20.8								
/69	8.2	8.3	8.6	9.7	7.2	6.5	7.0	9.7	6.4	6.0	7.5	5.4	8.9	8.1	7.1	3.1	9.3	-5.2	-26.1							
/70	7.3	7.4	7.6	8.5	6.2	5.4	5.9	8.1	5.0	4.6	5.7	3.5	6.2	5.0	3.5	0.1	3.9	-6.6	-18.3	-11.2						
/71	7.6	7.7	7.9	8.8	6.6	5.9	6.4	8.6	5.7	5.4	6.5	4.6	7.1	6.1	5.0	2.1	5.8	-2.0	-8.9	0.4	11.5					
/72	7.6	7.7	7.8	8.7	6.6	6.0	6.4	8.4	5.8	5.5	6.4	4.8	7.1	6.2	5.2	2.6	5.7	-0.5	-5.2	1.9	8.1	1.6				
/73	5.6	5.6	5.7	6.4	4.3	3.6	3.8	5.3	2.9	2.5	3.1	1.4	3.1	1.9	0.4	-2.4	-0.7	-6.3	-10.8	-7.3	-7.6	-16.6	-35.4			
/74	3.5	3.4	3.4	4.0	1.9	1.1	1.1	2.4	-0.1	-0.6	-0.3	-2.0	-0.8	-2.2	-3.9	-6.7	-5.9	-11.0	-15.4	-13.3	-15.2	-22.8	-34.8	-37.1		
/75	4.5	4.5	4.6	5.2	3.2	2.5	2.6	3.9	1.6	1.2	1.7	0.2	1.5	0.4	-0.9	-3.3	-2.0	-6.5	-9.7	-6.9	-6.9	-11.3	-16.7	-5.7	40.1	
/76	5.1	5.1	5.2	5.8	4.0	3.3	3.5	4.9	2.7	2.4	3.1	1.6	3.0	2.1	1.0	-1.0	0.4	-3.5	-6.1	-2.7	-1.8	-4.4	-7.0	5.3	36.7	30.6

*Percent per annum, compounded annually.

Sources: Stock market data—Lawrence Fisher and Myron Scholes (compilers), CRSP Monthly Master File for Common Stocks Listed on the New York Stock Exchange (magnetic tape). See Appendix A.
Consumer Price Index—U.S. Bureau of Labor Statistics.
Income tax rates—Income levels estimated from U.S. Bureau of the Census, Current Population Reports, Series P-60, Nos. 101 and 103 and Historical Statistics of the United States. Tax rates were found in U.S. Internal Revenue Service, Statistics of Income and Your Federal Income Tax.

current dollars. The table shows a total of 1,326 annual rates of return for portfolios purchased at fifty-one dates and held from one to fifty-one years. These rates of return range from 106.2 percent per annum compounded annually (for December 1932–December 1933) to −48.3 percent per annum (for 1930–31). About ninety-three percent of the entries in the table are positive and most are greater than 10 percent per annum.

The variability is greatest among the figures that apply to relatively short periods. Longer periods tend to overlap each other. Hence, rates of return for longer periods are likely to include returns for some of the same short periods. Nevertheless, the annual rates of return for longer periods differ substantially from one another.

For the one-year periods (shown on the diagonal of the table), the range of rates of return is −48.2 percent to +106.0 percent. As the holding periods increase in length, the range of rates of return tends to decrease. The range for two-year holding periods is −41.2 percent per annum to +54.4 percent, for 1929–31 and 1932–34, respectively. The three-year range is −36.3 percent per annum (1928–31) to +55.7 percent (1942–45). The five-year range is −18.7 percent per annum (1927–32) to +35.6 percent (1931–36). For ten-year periods, the range of annual rates of return compounding annually is much narrower, −2.9 percent (1928–38) to +22.8 percent (1941–51). For twenty-year periods, it is +2.8 percent (1928–48) to +19.6 percent (1941–61). For periods of thirty years or longer, the range is 7.1 percent (1928–74) to 16.0 percent (1932–65).

The statistics in Table I are similar to those of the most frequently quoted tables in "Rates (1964)" and "Rates (1968)." The annual rate of return compounding annually for the longest period in Table I, December 31, 1925 to December 31, 1976, is 9.0 percent. This figure differs little from the rates of return for the longest periods of our earlier studies—8.8 percent per annum compounding annually for January 1926 to December 1960 and 9.3 percent for January 1926 to December 1965. Indeed, in Table I, the annual rates of return on the portfolio assumed to have been purchased at the end of December 1925 are in the range from 7.8 percent to 9.8 percent for all ending dates from December 1954 to December 1976.

In addition to the information that may be obtained directly from Table I, comparing Table I with a number of other tables should prove instructive. Table II shows rates of return calcu-

lated in the same way as Table I except that in Table II the initial investment and all valuations are deflated by the CPI. Table III shows returns calculated in the same way as Table I except that federal income tax is paid on all dividends at the "lower" tax rate. In Table V similar taxes are paid but at the "higher" tax rate.

In Table VII, all calculations are the same as in Table I except that the initial investment in each issue of common stock is proportional to the total market value of the issue. Hence, in Table VII, large companies receive much greater weight than in Table I.

Table XIII presents rates of return on the same portfolios as Table I, but in Table XIII dividends are assumed to be spent as they are received and internal rates of return are calculated. In Table XXIII dividends are ignored. In Table XXIX dividends are reinvested (as in Table I), but all brokerage commissions are ignored.

Table XXXI shows, as percentages, the ratios of ending value to initial investment that were used in calculating the annual rates of return shown in Table I. By comparing the two tables the reader can see the relationship between wealth ratios and rates of return for periods ranging from one year to fifty-one years.

Tables XXXIV, XL, and XLVI show rates of return on long-, intermediate-, and short-term U.S. Treasury securities that are comparable to the rates of return in Table I.

Values Deflated by the Consumer Price Index. Table II shows rates of return found after the ratios of ending value to initial investment were deflated by the ratio of the Consumer Price Index for the valuation month to the Consumer Price Index for the month of initial investment. As we pointed out in Chapter 2, they might be called "real rates of return," except that the manner in which the CPI is constructed makes it have an upward bias through time that may be one or two percent per annum, which is about half as large as its own reported rate of change for the entire period. Hence, the deflation is useful primarily for comparing returns for different periods.

The most striking thing about Table II is the lower rates of return for periods ending with valuation dates after 1968 compared with rates through 1960–68. For example, the rate of return after deflating is 7.3 percent per annum compounded annually for December 1925–December 1960 and 7.8 percent for 1925–65 but only 6.5 percent for December 1925–June 1976.

The ranges of the rates of return for various

holding periods are somewhat lower than in Table I. For one-year periods, the range is −47.7 percent (1936–37) to +105.0 percent (again 1932–33). For two-year periods the range is −36.2 percent (1929–31) to +52.5 percent (1932–34); for three-year periods, −32.8 percent (1928–31) to 51.9 percent (1942–45). The five-year range is −14.0 percent per annum (1927–32) to +36.8 percent (1931–36). The ten-year range is −2.1 percent (1964–74) to +16.4 percent (1941–51). For twenty-year periods the range is +1.0 percent per annum (1928–48) to +15.7 percent (1941–61). For periods of thirty years or longer the range is 4.6 percent (1928–74) to 12.9 percent (1932–65).

With caution Table II may be compared with Table I, which has calculations in current dollars. Table II may also be compared with Tables IV and VI, for which federal income taxes are assumed to be paid on cash dividends at the "lower" and "higher" tax rates, respectively; with Table VIII, in which initial investments are allocated on a value-weighted basis; with Table XIV, in which internal rates of return are presented; with Table XXIV, in which dividends are ignored; and with Tables XXXV, XLI, and XLVII, which present comparable rates of return for long-, intermediate-, and short-term Governments respectively.

Income Taxes at the "Lower" Rate

Tables III and IV show rates of return after paying federal income taxes on cash dividends and similar cash receipts at the "lower" tax rate. The lower tax rate ranges from zero for 1926–39 to 32 percent for 1975 and 1976.

Current Dollars. Table III shows time-weighted rates of return with calculations in current dollars. Since most of the extremely high and extremely low rates of return are for periods when the "lower" tax rate was zero, the extreme rates are like those of Table I. For periods that begin at the end of 1939 or later, however, taxes cause the rates of return to be roughly one percent per annum less than the corresponding rates in Table I. The differences are usually smaller for periods beginning earlier. For example, the rate of return for December 1925–76 was 8.3 percent per annum compounded annually.

Values Deflated by the Consumer Price Index. Table IV shows rates of return found after deflation of the after-tax ratios of valuation to initial investment.

Income Taxes at the "Higher" Rate

Tables V and VI show rates of return after paying federal income taxes on cash dividends and similar cash receipts at the "higher" tax rate. The higher tax rate ranges from zero in 1931 to 63.8 percent in 1969. Except for 1975 and 1976, the higher tax rate was always at least twice as great as the lower tax rate.[1]

Initial Weighting by Value

In producing Tables VII through XII, we proceeded in the same manner as for Tables I through VI, respectively, until it was time to average the results of the investments in each stock. In Tables I–VI, each issue was given equal weight. In Tables VII–XII, each issue was given a weight proportional to its total market value on the date the portfolio was purchased.

Equal weighting of all issues produces results similar to what would have been attained by selecting a large number of stocks for the portfolio by throwing darts at a page of stock quotations from the newspaper.[2] Initial weighting by value produces results similar to what would have been attained by putting all of the several billion shares outstanding into a large barrel and randomly selecting individual shares for purchase until all funds available for the portfolio had been allocated.

The returns for the individual stocks are the same in both cases, but they are weighted differently during the averaging process. Hence, some of the numbers in Table VII, for example, are higher than the corresponding numbers in Table I and some are lower.

During the fifty-one year period investigated here, the stocks of extremely large companies tended to be substantially less volatile than those of smaller companies—during general rises or falls in the stock market as a whole, prices of the stocks of large companies usually changed less, in percentage terms, than the stock prices of smaller companies.

Most periods of very high or very low rates of return for the equally weighted portfolios are also periods of similarly high or low rates of return for the value-weighted portfolios. But there are exceptions, such as 1967 and 1968.

Most of the rates of return in Tables VII–XII are lower than the corresponding rates in Tables I–VI.

---

[1]See Appendix A for a table showing all of the tax rates used.

[2]The second author was presented by one of his classes with such a page printed on cork.

Held Until	Purchased 12/25	12/26	12/27	12/28	12/29	Purchased 12/30	12/31	12/32	12/33	12/34	Purchased 12/35	12/36	12/37	12/38	12/39	Purchased 12/40	12/41	12/42	12/43	12/44	Purchased 12/45	12/46	12/47	12/48	12/49
12/26	10.1																								
12/27	21.2	32.9																							
12/28	26.6	35.7	38.8																						
12/29	15.8	17.9	11.3	-12.9																					
12/30	5.5	4.6	-3.3	-20.6	-28.2																				
12/31	-5.3	-7.9	-15.8	-29.6	-36.7	-44.6																			
12/32	-5.7	-7.9	-14.3	-24.7	-28.3	-28.5	-8.2																		
12/33	1.0	-0.1	-4.9	-12.3	-12.6	-7.2	19.7	56.0																	
12/34	1.4	0.4	-3.7	-9.8	-9.5	-4.4	14.2	27.2	3.2																
12/35	5.0	4.4	1.1	-3.8	-2.4	3.5	20.8	32.4	21.8	42.9															
12/36	7.1	6.8	4.1	-0.1	1.7	7.6	22.7	32.2	25.1	37.7	32.1														
12/37	2.9	2.3	-0.5	-4.5	-3.6	0.4	10.8	15.2	6.8	7.9	-6.6	-34.3													
12/38	4.7	4.2	1.8	-1.6	-0.5	3.4	12.9	17.0	10.5	12.2	3.3	-8.8	26.4												
12/39	4.5	4.1	1.9	-1.2	-0.1	3.5	11.8	15.0	9.2	10.2	3.1	-5.2	13.7	1.7											
12/40	3.8	3.3	1.2	-1.7	-0.8	2.3	9.5	11.9	6.6	7.0	0.9	-5.8	6.1	-3.1	-8.0										
12/41	2.7	2.3	0.3	-2.5	-1.7	1.0	7.2	9.1	4.3	4.4	-1.0	-6.7	1.8	-5.4	-9.0	-10.4									
12/42	3.5	3.1	1.3	-1.2	-0.3	2.3	8.1	9.9	5.7	5.9	1.4	-3.1	4.7	-0.3	-1.1	2.2	15.8								
12/43	4.6	4.3	2.7	0.4	1.4	4.1	9.6	11.4	7.7	8.1	4.4	0.9	8.3	4.8	5.5	10.2	21.8	27.7							
12/44	5.4	5.2	3.7	1.6	2.6	5.2	10.4	12.1	8.8	9.3	6.1	3.1	10.0	7.4	8.4	12.8	21.6	24.4	20.9						
12/45	6.7	6.5	5.1	3.3	4.3	6.9	12.0	13.8	10.9	11.5	8.8	6.5	13.1	11.3	12.9	17.5	25.6	28.9	29.3	38.1					
12/46	6.0	5.8	4.5	2.7	3.7	6.1	10.7	12.2	9.4	9.9	7.4	5.1	10.8	8.9	10.0	13.2	18.5	19.1	16.3	14.0	-6.4				
12/47	5.9	5.8	4.5	2.8	3.8	6.0	10.3	11.7	9.1	9.5	7.1	5.1	10.1	8.4	9.2	11.8	15.9	15.9	13.1	10.6	-1.4	3.1			
12/48	5.8	5.7	4.4	2.8	3.7	5.8	9.8	11.1	8.6	9.0	6.8	4.9	9.4	7.8	8.4	10.6	13.9	13.6	10.9	8.5	-0.2	2.7	1.3		
12/49	6.4	6.2	5.1	3.6	4.5	6.5	10.4	11.7	9.3	9.7	7.7	6.0	10.3	8.8	9.5	11.6	14.7	14.5	12.3	10.7	4.5	8.2	10.3	19.3	
12/50	7.2	7.1	6.0	4.6	5.6	7.6	11.3	12.6	10.5	10.9	9.1	7.6	11.8	10.6	11.4	13.5	16.5	16.5	14.9	14.0	9.5	13.6	17.0	25.1	29.6
12/51	7.6	7.6	6.6	5.3	6.2	8.1	11.8	13.0	11.0	11.5	9.8	8.4	12.4	11.3	12.1	14.1	16.9	17.0	15.6	14.9	11.3	15.0	17.9	23.7	25.3
12/52	7.9	7.9	7.0	5.7	6.6	8.5	12.0	13.1	11.2	11.7	10.1	8.8	12.5	11.5	12.3	14.1	16.6	16.7	15.5	14.8	11.7	14.8	17.1	21.1	21.3
12/53	7.6	7.6	6.7	5.5	6.3	8.1	11.4	12.4	10.6	11.0	9.5	8.2	11.7	10.7	11.3	12.9	15.1	15.0	13.8	13.0	10.1	12.5	13.9	16.5	15.5
12/54	9.0	9.0	8.1	7.0	7.8	9.7	12.9	14.0	12.4	12.8	11.5	10.4	13.8	13.0	13.8	15.5	17.7	17.9	17.0	16.6	14.3	17.0	19.0	22.0	22.2
12/55	9.6	9.6	8.8	7.7	8.6	10.3	13.5	14.6	13.0	13.5	12.2	11.2	14.5	13.8	14.6	16.3	18.4	18.6	17.8	17.5	15.5	18.1	19.9	22.6	22.8
12/56	9.5	9.5	8.7	7.7	8.5	10.2	13.3	14.3	12.8	13.2	12.0	11.0	14.2	13.5	14.2	15.8	17.7	17.8	17.1	16.7	14.9	17.1	18.6	20.8	20.7
12/57	8.7	8.7	8.0	6.9	7.7	9.3	12.2	13.1	11.6	12.0	10.7	9.8	12.7	11.9	12.5	13.8	15.5	15.5	14.7	14.2	12.3	14.1	15.1	16.6	16.2
12/58	9.7	9.7	9.0	8.0	8.8	10.4	13.2	14.2	12.8	13.2	12.0	11.2	14.0	13.4	14.1	15.4	17.1	17.1	16.5	16.1	14.5	16.4	17.6	19.2	19.1
12/59	9.7	9.7	9.1	8.1	8.9	10.5	13.2	14.1	12.7	13.1	12.0	11.2	13.9	13.3	14.0	15.2	16.8	16.8	16.2	15.8	14.3	16.1	17.1	18.6	18.3
12/60	9.3	9.3	8.7	7.8	8.5	10.0	12.6	13.5	12.1	12.5	11.4	10.6	13.1	12.5	13.0	14.2	15.6	15.6	14.9	14.5	13.0	14.6	15.5	16.6	16.3
12/61	9.8	9.8	9.3	8.4	9.2	10.6	13.2	14.0	12.7	13.1	12.0	11.3	13.8	13.2	13.7	14.9	16.2	16.2	15.6	15.3	13.9	15.5	16.3	17.5	17.3
12/62	9.4	9.4	8.8	8.0	8.7	10.0	12.5	13.2	12.0	12.3	11.3	10.5	12.8	12.3	12.7	13.7	15.0	14.9	14.3	13.9	12.5	13.8	14.5	15.5	15.1
12/63	9.8	9.8	9.2	8.4	9.1	10.4	12.8	13.6	12.4	12.7	11.7	11.0	13.2	12.7	13.2	14.2	15.4	15.3	14.7	14.4	13.1	14.4	15.1	16.0	15.7
12/64	10.1	10.1	9.5	8.7	9.4	10.7	13.0	13.7	12.6	12.9	12.0	11.3	13.5	13.0	13.4	14.4	15.6	15.5	15.0	14.7	13.4	14.7	15.3	16.2	15.9
12/65	10.1	10.1	9.6	8.8	9.4	10.7	12.9	13.7	12.6	12.9	12.0	11.3	13.4	12.9	13.4	14.3	15.4	15.4	14.9	14.6	13.4	14.6	15.2	16.0	15.7
12/66	9.4	9.4	8.8	8.1	8.7	9.9	12.0	12.7	11.6	11.9	11.0	10.3	12.3	11.8	12.2	13.1	14.1	14.0	13.4	13.1	12.0	13.0	13.5	14.2	13.8
12/67	9.7	9.7	9.2	8.5	9.1	10.3	12.4	13.1	12.0	12.3	11.4	10.8	12.7	12.3	12.7	13.5	14.5	14.4	13.9	13.6	12.6	13.6	14.1	14.8	14.5
12/68	9.8	9.8	9.3	8.6	9.2	10.4	12.4	13.1	12.1	12.3	11.5	10.9	12.8	12.3	12.7	13.5	14.5	14.4	13.9	13.6	12.6	13.6	14.1	14.7	14.4
12/69	9.3	9.3	8.8	8.1	8.6	9.8	11.7	12.3	11.3	11.6	10.7	10.1	11.9	11.5	11.8	12.5	13.4	13.3	12.8	12.5	11.5	12.4	12.8	13.3	13.0
12/70	9.3	9.3	8.8	8.1	8.6	9.7	11.6	12.2	11.2	11.4	10.6	10.0	11.8	11.3	11.6	12.3	13.2	13.1	12.6	12.3	11.3	12.1	12.5	13.0	12.6
12/71	9.4	9.3	8.9	8.2	8.7	9.8	11.6	12.2	11.3	11.5	10.7	10.1	11.8	11.4	11.7	12.4	13.2	13.1	12.6	12.3	11.4	12.2	12.6	13.0	12.7
12/72	9.5	9.5	9.0	8.4	8.9	10.0	11.8	12.3	11.4	11.6	10.9	10.3	12.0	11.6	11.9	12.5	13.3	13.2	12.8	12.5	11.6	12.4	12.8	13.2	12.9
12/73	9.0	9.0	8.5	7.8	8.4	9.3	11.1	11.6	10.7	10.9	10.2	9.6	11.2	10.8	11.1	11.7	12.4	12.3	11.8	11.6	10.6	11.4	11.6	12.0	11.7
12/74	8.2	8.1	7.7	7.0	7.5	8.4	10.1	10.6	9.7	9.9	9.2	8.6	10.1	9.6	9.9	10.4	11.1	10.9	10.4	10.1	9.2	9.8	10.0	10.4	10.0
12/75	8.7	8.7	8.3	7.6	8.1	9.1	10.7	11.2	10.4	10.6	9.8	9.3	10.8	10.4	10.6	11.2	11.9	11.7	11.3	11.0	10.1	10.8	11.0	11.3	11.0
12/76	9.1	9.1	8.7	8.0	8.5	9.5	11.1	11.6	10.8	11.0	10.3	9.7	11.2	10.8	11.0	11.6	12.3	12.2	11.7	11.5	10.7	11.3	11.5	11.9	11.6

Table VII

Time-Weighted Rates of Return* on Common Stocks:
  Dividends Reinvested,
  Cash to Portfolio,
  Initial Weighting by Value,
  Tax-Exempt,
  Current Dollars

Held until	12/50	12/51	12/52	12/53	12/54	12/55	12/56	12/57	12/58	12/59	12/60	12/61	12/62	12/63	12/64	12/65	12/66	12/67	12/68	12/69	12/70	12/71	12/72	12/73	12/74	12/75
/51	20.3																									
/52	16.9	12.7																								
/53	10.9	6.3	−0.3																							
/54	20.0	19.6	22.8	49.6																						
/55	21.2	21.2	23.8	37.0	24.5																					
/56	19.0	18.6	19.8	26.8	16.4	8.1																				
/57	14.2	13.1	12.9	16.2	6.7	−1.5	−11.2																			
/58	17.6	17.1	17.7	21.4	15.1	11.9	13.3	43.0																		
/59	17.0	16.5	16.9	19.8	14.4	11.9	13.1	27.2	12.2																	
/60	15.0	14.4	14.6	16.7	11.9	9.5	9.7	17.5	6.1	−0.2																
/61	16.1	15.6	15.9	18.0	14.0	12.3	13.1	19.9	12.8	12.7	26.2															
/62	13.9	13.3	13.3	14.8	11.0	9.1	9.2	13.7	7.1	5.1	7.2	−9.9														
/63	14.6	14.0	14.1	15.5	12.2	10.6	10.9	15.0	9.8	9.0	11.7	4.6	20.3													
/64	14.9	14.3	14.4	15.7	12.7	11.4	11.7	15.2	11.0	10.5	12.9	8.4	18.2	15.2												
/65	14.7	14.2	14.3	15.5	12.7	11.5	11.8	14.9	11.2	10.8	12.9	9.6	16.6	15.1	13.7											
/66	12.8	12.3	12.2	13.2	10.5	9.2	9.3	11.7	8.2	7.5	8.7	5.4	9.4	6.3	2.0	−9.5										
/67	13.5	13.0	13.0	13.9	11.5	10.4	10.5	12.9	9.9	9.5	10.8	8.5	12.4	11.2	9.7	7.1	26.1									
/68	13.5	13.1	13.0	13.9	11.6	10.6	10.8	13.0	10.3	10.0	11.2	9.2	12.6	11.5	10.6	9.3	19.7	12.7								
/69	12.1	11.6	11.4	12.1	9.9	8.9	8.9	10.8	8.1	7.7	8.5	6.5	9.0	7.7	6.2	4.1	8.9	0.7	−10.8							
/70	11.8	11.3	11.1	11.8	9.7	8.7	8.7	10.4	7.9	7.5	8.2	6.3	8.4	7.0	5.7	4.0	7.5	1.4	−4.5	0.9						
/71	11.9	11.4	11.3	11.9	9.9	9.0	9.0	10.6	8.3	8.0	8.7	7.0	9.0	8.0	6.8	5.6	8.8	4.5	1.6	7.9	14.2					
/72	12.1	11.7	11.6	12.2	10.3	9.5	9.6	11.1	9.0	8.7	9.4	8.0	9.9	9.1	8.2	7.3	10.3	7.0	5.5	11.1	16.2	16.7				
/73	10.9	10.4	10.3	10.8	9.0	8.1	8.1	9.4	7.3	7.0	7.4	6.0	7.5	6.5	5.4	4.3	6.3	3.1	1.1	3.9	4.4	−1.3	−18.0			
/74	9.2	8.7	8.5	8.8	7.1	6.2	6.0	7.1	5.1	4.6	4.8	3.3	4.4	3.1	1.9	0.6	1.9	−1.5	−3.9	−2.8	−4.2	−10.5	−22.5	−28.1		
/75	10.2	9.8	9.6	10.1	8.4	7.6	7.6	8.7	6.9	6.5	6.9	5.5	6.8	5.7	4.8	3.9	5.4	2.8	1.3	3.1	3.2	−0.1	−5.8	−0.0	36.7	
/76	10.8	10.4	10.3	10.7	9.2	8.5	8.5	9.6	7.9	7.6	8.0	6.8	8.1	7.1	6.5	5.8	7.4	5.3	4.2	6.2	6.8	4.8	1.4	8.1	31.4	23.9

Percent per annum, compounded annually.

Source: Lawrence Fisher and Myron Scholes (compilers), CRSP Monthly Master File for Common Stocks Listed on the New York Stock Exchange (magnetic tape). See Appendix A.

Purchased columns grouped: 12/25–12/29, 12/30–12/34, 12/35–12/39, 12/40–12/44, 12/45–12/49

Held Until	12/25	12/26	12/27	12/28	12/29	12/30	12/31	12/32	12/33	12/34	12/35	12/36	12/37	12/38	12/39	12/40	12/41	12/42	12/43	12/44	12/45	12/46	12/47	12/48	12/49
12/26	11.8																								
12/27	23.4	35.7																							
12/28	28.5	37.8	40.1																						
12/29	17.0	19.0	11.7	−13.0																					
12/30	7.8	7.0	−1.0	−18.1	−23.6																				
12/31	−1.9	−4.3	−12.2	−25.7	−31.4	−38.7																			
12/32	−1.4	−3.2	−9.4	−19.4	−21.6	−20.7	2.4																		
12/33	5.0	4.2	−0.4	−7.6	−6.6	−0.6	26.0	55.2																	
12/34	4.7	3.9	−0.2	−6.1	−4.9	0.0	17.4	25.6	1.1																
12/35	7.7	7.3	4.0	−0.8	1.1	6.8	22.5	30.0	18.8	38.7															
12/36	9.5	9.3	6.5	2.5	4.7	10.1	23.7	30.0	22.6	34.8	30.5														
12/37	4.8	4.2	1.4	−2.6	−1.5	2.1	11.0	13.0	4.4	5.4	−8.5	−36.3													
12/38	6.7	6.2	3.8	0.3	1.7	5.2	13.6	15.7	9.1	11.0	2.8	−8.9	30.0												
12/39	6.4	6.0	3.8	0.6	2.0	5.1	12.4	14.0	8.1	9.4	2.8	−5.2	15.6	2.2											
12/40	5.4	4.9	2.8	−0.1	1.0	3.7	9.9	10.9	5.6	6.2	0.5	−6.0	6.9	−3.3	−8.9										
12/41	3.7	3.2	1.1	−1.7	−0.8	1.4	6.6	7.1	2.2	2.3	−2.9	−8.6	0.1	−8.4	−13.5	−18.4									
12/42	3.8	3.4	1.5	−1.1	−0.2	1.9	6.7	7.1	2.8	2.9	−1.5	−6.1	1.4	−4.8	−7.2	−6.7	6.0								
12/43	4.8	4.4	2.7	0.3	1.3	3.5	8.0	8.6	4.7	5.1	1.4	−2.3	4.9	0.4	−0.2	2.6	14.7	23.8							
12/44	5.5	5.1	3.5	1.4	2.3	4.4	8.7	9.3	5.9	6.3	3.1	0.1	6.7	3.2	3.3	6.4	16.0	21.3	18.4						
12/45	6.6	6.3	4.8	2.9	4.0	6.1	10.3	10.9	7.9	8.5	5.9	3.4	9.9	7.2	8.0	11.6	20.6	25.7	26.5	35.0					
12/46	5.0	4.7	3.3	1.4	2.3	4.2	7.9	8.3	5.4	5.7	3.1	0.7	6.0	3.3	3.4	5.5	11.0	12.1	8.4	3.7	−20.8				
12/47	4.7	4.4	2.9	1.1	2.0	3.7	7.1	7.4	4.7	4.9	2.5	0.2	4.9	2.4	2.3	4.0	8.2	8.5	5.0	0.9	−13.1	−5.4			
12/48	4.5	4.2	2.8	1.1	1.9	3.5	6.7	7.0	4.4	4.6	2.3	0.2	4.4	2.1	2.1	3.5	7.0	7.1	4.0	0.6	−9.1	−3.0	−1.4		
12/49	5.1	4.9	3.6	2.0	2.8	4.4	7.5	7.8	5.4	5.7	3.6	1.8	5.8	3.8	3.9	5.4	8.7	9.1	6.7	4.6	−2.1	4.8	9.9	21.5	
12/50	5.8	5.5	4.3	2.8	3.7	5.2	8.2	8.6	6.4	6.7	4.9	3.2	7.1	5.4	5.6	7.2	10.4	10.9	9.2	7.7	2.7	9.4	14.5	22.7	22.5
12/51	6.0	5.8	4.7	3.3	4.1	5.6	8.5	8.9	6.8	7.1	5.4	3.9	7.6	6.0	6.3	7.8	10.7	11.3	9.7	8.6	4.6	10.3	14.4	19.8	18.4
12/52	6.4	6.2	5.1	3.8	4.6	6.0	8.8	9.2	7.2	7.5	5.9	4.5	8.0	6.5	6.8	8.2	11.0	11.5	10.1	9.2	5.8	10.7	14.1	18.0	16.4
12/53	6.1	5.9	4.9	3.6	4.3	5.7	8.3	8.6	6.7	7.0	5.5	4.1	7.4	6.0	6.2	7.5	9.9	10.2	8.9	7.9	4.8	9.0	11.4	13.9	11.9
12/54	7.5	7.3	6.4	5.2	6.0	7.4	10.0	10.4	8.6	9.0	7.6	6.5	9.8	8.6	9.0	10.4	12.9	13.5	12.5	11.9	9.5	13.9	16.7	19.9	19.2
12/55	8.1	8.0	7.1	6.0	6.7	8.1	10.7	11.1	9.4	9.8	8.5	7.4	10.6	9.6	10.0	11.4	13.8	14.4	13.6	13.2	11.1	15.2	17.9	20.7	20.3
12/56	8.0	7.9	7.0	5.9	6.6	8.0	10.4	10.8	9.2	9.6	8.4	7.3	10.3	9.3	9.8	11.0	13.2	13.7	13.0	12.5	10.6	14.2	16.4	18.7	18.1
12/57	7.1	7.0	6.2	5.1	5.8	7.0	9.3	9.6	8.1	8.4	7.1	6.1	8.9	7.9	8.2	9.2	11.2	11.5	10.7	10.1	8.2	11.2	12.9	14.5	13.5
12/58	8.1	8.0	7.2	6.1	6.9	8.1	10.4	10.8	9.3	9.6	8.5	7.6	10.3	9.4	9.8	10.9	12.8	13.3	12.6	12.2	10.5	13.6	15.3	17.0	16.4
12/59	8.1	8.0	7.3	6.3	7.0	8.2	10.4	10.7	9.3	9.6	8.5	7.7	10.3	9.4	9.8	10.8	12.7	13.1	12.4	12.0	10.5	13.3	14.9	16.4	15.8
12/60	7.7	7.6	6.9	5.9	6.6	7.8	9.9	10.2	8.8	9.1	8.0	7.1	9.6	8.7	9.0	10.0	11.7	12.0	11.3	10.9	9.4	12.0	13.3	14.6	13.9
12/61	8.3	8.2	7.5	6.6	7.3	8.4	10.5	10.8	9.5	9.8	8.8	7.9	10.3	9.5	9.8	10.8	12.5	12.8	12.2	11.8	10.4	12.9	14.3	15.5	15.0
12/62	7.9	7.8	7.1	6.2	6.8	7.9	9.8	10.1	8.8	9.1	8.1	7.3	9.5	8.7	9.0	9.8	11.3	11.6	11.0	10.6	9.2	11.4	12.6	13.6	12.9
12/63	8.2	8.2	7.5	6.6	7.2	8.3	10.2	10.5	9.2	9.5	8.5	7.8	10.0	9.2	9.5	10.3	11.8	12.1	11.5	11.1	9.8	12.0	13.1	14.1	13.5
12/64	8.5	8.4	7.8	6.9	7.5	8.6	10.4	10.7	9.5	9.8	8.9	8.1	10.3	9.5	9.8	10.6	12.1	12.3	11.8	11.5	10.3	12.3	13.4	14.3	13.7
12/65	8.5	8.5	7.8	7.0	7.6	8.6	10.4	10.6	9.5	9.8	8.9	8.2	10.2	9.6	9.8	10.6	12.0	12.3	11.8	11.4	10.3	12.2	13.2	14.1	13.6
12/66	7.8	7.7	7.1	6.2	6.8	7.7	9.5	9.7	8.6	8.8	7.9	7.2	9.2	8.5	8.7	9.4	10.7	10.9	10.3	10.0	8.9	10.7	11.5	12.2	11.6
12/67	8.1	8.0	7.4	6.6	7.1	8.1	9.8	10.0	8.9	9.2	8.4	7.7	9.6	8.9	9.1	9.8	11.1	11.3	10.8	10.5	9.4	11.2	12.0	12.7	12.2
12/68	8.1	8.0	7.4	6.6	7.2	8.1	9.7	10.0	8.9	9.2	8.4	7.7	9.6	8.9	9.1	9.8	11.0	11.2	10.7	10.4	9.4	11.1	11.9	12.5	12.0
12/69	7.5	7.4	6.8	6.0	6.5	7.4	9.0	9.2	8.1	8.3	7.5	6.9	8.6	8.0	8.1	8.7	9.8	10.0	9.5	9.2	8.1	9.7	10.4	10.9	10.4
12/70	7.4	7.3	6.7	6.0	6.4	7.3	8.8	9.0	7.9	8.1	7.3	6.7	8.4	7.8	7.9	8.5	9.5	9.7	9.2	8.9	7.8	9.3	9.9	10.4	9.9
12/71	7.4	7.3	6.8	6.0	6.5	7.3	8.8	9.0	8.0	8.2	7.4	6.8	8.4	7.8	8.0	8.6	9.6	9.7	9.2	8.9	7.9	9.4	10.0	10.4	9.9
12/72	7.5	7.4	6.9	6.2	6.7	7.5	8.9	9.1	8.1	8.3	7.6	7.0	8.6	8.0	8.1	8.7	9.7	9.8	9.4	9.1	8.1	9.5	10.1	10.6	10.1
12/73	6.9	6.8	6.2	5.5	5.9	6.7	8.1	8.2	7.3	7.5	6.8	6.2	7.7	7.1	7.2	7.7	8.6	8.7	8.2	7.9	7.0	8.2	8.7	9.2	8.6
12/74	5.8	5.7	5.2	4.5	4.9	5.6	6.9	7.0	6.1	6.3	5.5	4.9	6.3	5.7	5.8	6.3	7.1	7.1	6.6	6.3	5.3	6.4	6.9	7.2	6.6
12/75	6.3	6.2	5.7	5.0	5.4	6.1	7.4	7.6	6.6	6.8	6.1	5.5	6.9	6.3	6.4	6.9	7.7	7.8	7.3	7.0	6.1	7.2	7.6	7.9	7.4
12/76	6.6	6.5	6.0	5.3	5.7	6.5	7.7	7.9	7.0	7.1	6.5	5.9	7.3	6.7	6.8	7.3	8.1	8.2	7.7	7.4	6.6	7.6	8.1	8.4	7.9

Table VIII

Time-Weighted Rates of Return* on Common Stocks:
  Dividends Reinvested,
  Cash to Portfolio,
  Initial Weighting by Value,
  Tax-Exempt,
  Deflated by the Consumer Price Index

Held Until	12/50	12/51	12/52	12/53	12/54	12/55	12/56	12/57	12/58	12/59	12/60	12/61	12/62	12/63	12/64	12/65	12/66	12/67	12/68	12/69	12/70	12/71	12/72	12/73	12/74	12/75
12/51	13.6																									
12/52	13.1	11.7																								
12/53	8.3	5.5	-0.9																							
12/54	18.0	19.2	22.7	50.3																						
12/55	19.4	20.8	23.5	37.1	24.0																					
12/56	17.0	17.6	18.8	25.7	14.6	5.1																				
12/57	12.1	11.7	11.5	14.6	4.6	-4.4	-13.8																			
12/58	15.5	15.6	16.1	19.6	12.8	9.1	10.6	40.5																		
12/59	14.9	15.0	15.3	18.0	12.3	9.4	10.8	25.1	10.5																	
12/60	13.0	12.9	13.0	15.0	9.9	7.2	7.6	15.6	4.6	-1.6																
12/61	14.2	14.2	14.4	16.4	12.1	10.2	11.2	18.3	11.4	11.5	25.4															
12/62	12.1	11.9	11.8	13.2	9.3	7.2	7.5	12.2	5.8	4.0	6.2	-11.0														
12/63	12.7	12.6	12.6	13.9	10.4	8.7	9.2	13.4	8.4	7.6	10.4	3.1	18.3													
12/64	13.0	12.9	12.9	14.2	11.0	9.5	10.0	13.7	9.5	9.1	11.6	6.9	16.5	13.9												
12/65	12.9	12.7	12.7	13.9	10.9	9.6	10.0	13.3	9.6	9.4	11.4	8.0	14.8	13.3	11.5											
12/66	10.9	10.7	10.6	11.4	8.6	7.2	7.4	9.9	6.5	5.8	6.9	3.5	7.2	4.1	-0.7	-12.5										
12/67	11.5	11.3	11.2	12.0	9.4	8.2	8.5	11.0	8.0	7.6	8.8	6.3	10.0	8.6	6.8	3.7	22.4									
12/68	11.3	11.1	11.0	11.8	9.4	8.3	8.5	10.8	8.0	7.7	8.8	6.6	9.7	8.4	7.1	5.4	15.2	7.6								
12/69	9.7	9.4	9.2	9.8	7.5	6.3	6.4	8.2	5.6	5.1	5.7	3.5	5.7	4.2	2.3	-0.2	4.1	-4.5	-15.9							
12/70	9.2	8.9	8.7	9.2	7.0	5.9	5.9	7.6	5.1	4.6	5.1	3.0	4.8	3.2	1.5	-0.5	2.5	-3.8	-9.7	-4.4						
12/71	9.3	9.0	8.8	9.3	7.2	6.1	6.2	7.7	5.5	5.0	5.5	3.7	5.4	4.2	2.7	1.2	4.1	-0.4	-3.2	3.3	10.5					
12/72	9.5	9.2	9.0	9.5	7.5	6.6	6.6	8.1	6.0	5.7	6.2	4.6	6.2	5.3	4.1	2.9	5.7	2.3	0.9	6.7	12.4	12.8				
12/73	8.0	7.7	7.4	7.8	5.9	4.9	4.9	6.1	4.0	3.6	3.9	2.2	3.5	2.3	0.9	-0.5	1.3	-2.1	-4.1	-1.3	-0.7	-6.9	-24.6			
12/74	5.9	5.5	5.2	5.5	3.6	2.6	2.4	3.4	1.3	0.7	0.8	-0.9	-0.1	-1.6	-3.2	-4.7	-3.8	-7.3	-9.8	-8.8	-10.4	-17.2	-29.9	-36.0		
12/75	6.8	6.5	6.2	6.5	4.7	3.8	3.7	4.7	2.9	2.3	2.5	1.0	1.9	0.6	-0.5	-1.7	-0.5	-3.3	-5.0	-3.3	-3.5	-7.3	-13.9	-8.8	27.8	
12/76	7.3	7.0	6.8	7.1	5.4	4.6	4.5	5.5	3.8	3.4	3.6	2.2	3.2	2.0	1.1	0.2	1.4	-0.9	-2.0	-0.2	0.2	-2.3	-6.2	0.2	24.1	18.2

Percent per annum, compounded annually.

Sources: Stock market data—Lawrence Fisher and Myron Scholes (compilers), CRSP Monthly Master File for Common Stocks Listed on the New York Stock Exchange (magnetic tape). See Appendix A.
Consumer Price Index—U.S. Bureau of Labor Statistics.

Held Until	Purchased					Purchased					Purchased					Purchased					Purchased				
	12/25	12/26	12/27	12/28	12/29	12/30	12/31	12/32	12/33	12/34	12/35	12/36	12/37	12/38	12/39	12/40	12/41	12/42	12/43	12/44	12/45	12/46	12/47	12/48	12/49
12/26	10.1																								
12/27	21.2	32.9																							
12/28	26.6	35.7	38.8																						
12/29	15.8	17.9	11.3	-12.9																					
12/30	5.5	4.6	-3.3	-20.6	-28.2																				
12/31	-5.3	-7.9	-15.8	-29.6	-36.7	-44.6																			
12/32	-5.7	-7.9	-14.3	-24.7	-28.3	-28.5	-8.2																		
12/33	1.0	-0.1	-4.9	-12.3	-12.6	-7.2	19.7	56.0																	
12/34	1.4	0.4	-3.7	-9.8	-9.5	-4.4	14.2	27.2	3.2																
12/35	5.0	4.4	1.1	-3.8	-2.4	3.5	20.8	32.4	21.8	42.9															
12/36	7.1	6.8	4.1	-0.1	1.7	7.6	22.7	32.2	25.1	37.7	32.1														
12/37	2.9	2.3	-0.5	-4.5	-3.6	0.4	10.8	15.2	6.8	7.9	-6.6	-34.3													
12/38	4.7	4.2	1.8	-1.6	-0.5	3.4	12.9	17.0	10.5	12.2	3.3	-8.8	26.4												
12/39	4.5	4.1	1.9	-1.2	-0.1	3.5	11.8	15.0	9.2	10.2	3.1	-5.2	13.7	1.7											
12/40	3.7	3.2	1.2	-1.8	-0.8	2.3	9.4	11.9	6.6	7.0	0.8	-5.9	6.0	-3.2	-8.2										
12/41	2.7	2.2	0.2	-2.5	-1.7	1.0	7.1	9.0	4.2	4.2	-1.2	-6.9	1.6	-5.7	-9.4	-11.0									
12/42	3.4	3.0	1.2	-1.3	-0.5	2.2	7.9	9.7	5.5	5.7	1.1	-3.4	4.3	-0.7	-1.7	1.4	14.8								
12/43	4.5	4.2	2.5	0.3	1.2	3.8	9.3	11.1	7.4	7.8	4.0	0.4	7.7	4.2	4.7	9.2	20.6	26.3							
12/44	5.2	4.9	3.4	1.3	2.3	4.8	10.0	11.7	8.4	8.9	5.6	2.6	9.3	6.6	7.5	11.7	20.3	23.0	19.4						
12/45	6.4	6.2	4.8	2.9	4.0	6.6	11.6	13.3	10.4	11.0	8.3	5.8	12.3	10.4	11.9	16.3	24.2	27.4	27.8	36.7					
12/46	5.6	5.4	4.1	2.3	3.3	5.6	10.2	11.7	8.9	9.4	6.7	4.5	10.0	8.1	9.0	12.1	17.3	17.8	15.0	12.9	-7.4				
12/47	5.6	5.4	4.1	2.4	3.3	5.5	9.8	11.1	8.5	8.9	6.4	4.3	9.3	7.5	8.1	10.6	14.6	14.5	11.8	9.4	-2.6	1.8			
12/48	5.4	5.3	4.0	2.4	3.2	5.3	9.3	10.5	8.0	8.3	6.1	4.1	8.5	6.9	7.4	9.5	12.7	12.3	9.6	7.3	-1.3	1.4	0.2		
12/49	5.9	5.8	4.6	3.1	4.0	6.0	9.8	11.0	8.6	9.0	6.9	5.1	9.3	7.9	8.5	10.4	13.4	13.1	11.0	9.4	3.3	6.9	9.1	17.9	
12/50	6.7	6.6	5.5	4.1	5.0	7.0	10.7	11.9	9.7	10.2	8.3	6.7	10.8	9.5	10.3	12.3	15.1	15.2	13.6	12.7	8.2	12.2	15.6	23.6	28.0
12/51	7.1	7.0	6.0	4.7	5.6	7.5	11.1	12.2	10.2	10.7	8.9	7.5	11.4	10.2	11.0	12.9	15.5	15.6	14.3	13.6	10.0	13.6	16.5	22.2	23.8
12/52	7.4	7.4	6.4	5.1	6.0	7.8	11.2	12.3	10.4	10.8	9.2	7.8	11.5	10.4	11.1	12.9	15.3	15.3	14.1	13.5	10.4	13.4	15.7	19.7	19.8
12/53	7.0	7.0	6.1	4.8	5.6	7.4	10.6	11.6	9.8	10.1	8.6	7.3	10.6	9.6	10.2	11.7	13.8	13.6	12.4	11.7	8.8	11.1	12.6	15.1	14.1
12/54	8.4	8.3	7.5	6.3	7.2	8.9	12.1	13.2	11.5	11.9	10.5	9.4	12.7	11.9	12.6	14.2	16.4	16.5	15.6	15.2	13.0	15.6	17.6	20.5	20.8
12/55	9.0	9.0	8.2	7.1	7.9	9.6	12.7	13.8	12.2	12.6	11.3	10.2	13.5	12.7	13.4	15.0	17.1	17.2	16.5	16.2	14.2	16.7	18.6	21.2	21.5
12/56	8.9	8.9	8.1	7.0	7.8	9.5	12.5	13.5	11.9	12.4	11.1	10.1	13.1	12.4	13.1	14.5	16.4	16.5	15.8	15.5	13.6	15.8	17.3	19.5	19.5
12/57	8.1	8.1	7.3	6.3	7.0	8.6	11.4	12.3	10.8	11.1	9.8	8.8	11.7	10.9	11.4	12.7	14.3	14.2	13.5	13.0	11.2	12.9	14.0	15.5	15.1
12/58	9.0	9.0	8.3	7.3	8.1	9.7	12.5	13.4	12.0	12.3	11.1	10.2	13.0	12.4	13.0	14.2	15.9	15.9	15.3	15.0	13.4	15.2	16.4	18.1	18.0
12/59	9.1	9.1	8.4	7.5	8.2	9.7	12.4	13.3	11.9	12.3	11.1	10.3	12.9	12.3	12.9	14.1	15.6	15.7	15.0	14.7	13.2	15.0	16.0	17.5	17.3
12/60	8.7	8.7	8.0	7.1	7.8	9.3	11.9	12.7	11.3	11.6	10.5	9.7	12.2	11.5	12.0	13.1	14.5	14.4	13.8	13.4	12.0	13.5	14.4	15.6	15.4
12/61	9.2	9.2	8.6	7.7	8.5	9.9	12.4	13.2	11.9	12.2	11.2	10.4	12.8	12.2	12.7	13.8	15.1	15.1	14.5	14.2	12.9	14.4	15.3	16.5	16.3
12/62	8.8	8.8	8.2	7.3	8.0	9.3	11.7	12.4	11.2	11.4	10.4	9.6	11.9	11.3	11.7	12.7	13.9	13.8	13.2	12.9	11.5	12.8	13.5	14.5	14.2
12/63	9.2	9.2	8.6	7.7	8.4	9.7	12.0	12.8	11.5	11.8	10.8	10.1	12.3	11.7	12.1	13.1	14.3	14.2	13.7	13.4	12.1	13.4	14.1	15.0	14.7
12/64	9.4	9.4	8.9	8.0	8.7	10.0	12.2	12.9	11.8	12.0	11.1	10.4	12.5	12.0	12.4	13.3	14.5	14.4	13.9	13.6	12.4	13.6	14.3	15.2	14.9
12/65	9.5	9.5	8.9	8.1	8.7	10.0	12.2	12.9	11.7	12.0	11.1	10.4	12.5	12.0	12.4	13.2	14.3	14.3	13.8	13.5	12.4	13.6	14.2	15.0	14.8
12/66	8.7	8.7	8.2	7.4	8.0	9.2	11.3	11.9	10.8	11.1	10.1	9.4	11.4	10.9	11.2	12.0	13.0	12.9	12.4	12.1	11.0	12.1	12.6	13.2	12.9
12/67	9.1	9.1	8.6	7.8	8.4	9.6	11.6	12.3	11.2	11.5	10.6	9.9	11.8	11.3	11.7	12.5	13.4	13.4	12.9	12.6	11.6	12.7	13.2	13.8	13.5
12/68	9.1	9.1	8.6	7.9	8.5	9.6	11.6	12.3	11.2	11.5	10.6	10.0	11.8	11.4	11.7	12.5	13.4	13.4	12.9	12.6	11.6	12.7	13.1	13.8	13.5
12/69	8.6	8.6	8.1	7.4	7.9	9.0	10.9	11.5	10.5	10.7	9.9	9.3	11.0	10.5	10.8	11.5	12.4	12.3	11.8	11.5	10.5	11.5	11.9	12.4	12.1
12/70	8.6	8.6	8.1	7.4	7.9	9.0	10.8	11.4	10.4	10.6	9.8	9.2	10.8	10.4	10.6	11.3	12.1	12.0	11.5	11.3	10.3	11.2	11.5	12.0	11.7
12/71	8.7	8.6	8.2	7.5	8.0	9.0	10.9	11.4	10.4	10.6	9.8	9.3	10.9	10.4	10.7	11.3	12.2	12.1	11.6	11.3	10.4	11.3	11.6	12.1	11.8
12/72	8.8	8.8	8.3	7.7	8.2	9.2	11.0	11.5	10.6	10.8	10.0	9.5	11.1	10.6	10.9	11.5	12.3	12.2	11.8	11.5	10.6	11.5	11.8	12.3	12.0
12/73	8.3	8.3	7.8	7.1	7.6	8.6	10.3	10.8	9.9	10.1	9.3	8.7	10.3	9.8	10.1	10.6	11.4	11.3	10.8	10.6	9.6	10.4	10.7	11.1	10.8
12/74	7.4	7.4	6.9	6.3	6.7	7.7	9.3	9.8	8.8	9.0	8.3	7.7	9.1	8.7	8.8	9.4	10.0	9.9	9.4	9.1	8.2	8.9	9.1	9.4	9.0
12/75	8.0	8.0	7.5	6.9	7.4	8.3	9.9	10.4	9.5	9.6	8.9	8.3	9.8	9.4	9.6	10.1	10.8	10.7	10.2	9.9	9.1	9.7	10.0	10.3	10.0
12/76	8.3	8.3	7.9	7.2	7.7	8.6	10.2	10.7	9.8	10.0	9.3	8.7	10.2	9.7	10.0	10.5	11.2	11.1	10.6	10.4	9.6	10.2	10.5	10.8	10.5

Table IX

Time-Weighted Rates of Return* on Common Stocks:
  Dividends Reinvested,
  Cash to Portfolio,
  Initial Weighting by Value,
  Lower Tax Rate,
  Current Dollars

Held Until	Purchased 12/50	12/51	12/52	12/53	12/54	12/55	12/56	12/57	12/58	12/59	12/60	12/61	12/62	12/63	12/64	12/65	12/66	12/67	12/68	12/69	12/70	12/71	12/72	12/73	12/74	12/75
12/51	18.9																									
12/52	15.5	11.3																								
12/53	9.6	5.0	-1.5																							
12/54	18.7	18.3	21.5	48.3																						
12/55	19.9	20.0	22.6	36.0	23.7																					
12/56	17.9	17.5	18.8	25.9	15.7	7.5																				
12/57	13.1	12.1	12.1	15.4	6.1	-2.2	-11.8																			
12/58	16.6	16.2	16.8	20.6	14.4	11.2	12.5	42.2																		
12/59	16.0	15.6	16.0	19.0	13.7	11.2	12.4	26.5	11.6																	
12/60	14.1	13.5	13.7	16.0	11.2	8.8	9.0	16.8	5.5	-0.8																
12/61	15.2	14.8	15.1	17.3	13.3	11.6	12.4	19.2	12.2	12.1	25.6															
12/62	13.0	12.4	12.5	14.0	10.3	8.4	8.6	13.0	6.4	4.4	6.5	-10.6														
12/63	13.7	13.1	13.3	14.7	11.5	9.9	10.2	14.2	9.1	8.2	11.0	3.8	19.4													
12/64	14.0	13.5	13.6	15.0	12.0	10.7	11.0	14.5	10.2	9.7	12.1	7.6	17.4	14.5												
12/65	13.8	13.4	13.5	14.7	12.0	10.8	11.1	14.2	10.4	10.1	12.1	8.9	15.8	14.4	13.0											
12/66	12.0	11.5	11.4	12.4	9.8	8.5	8.6	11.0	7.5	6.8	7.9	4.7	8.7	5.6	1.3	-10.2										
12/67	12.7	12.2	12.2	13.2	10.7	9.7	9.8	12.2	9.2	8.8	10.1	7.7	11.7	10.5	9.0	6.3	25.3									
12/68	12.7	12.2	12.2	13.1	10.9	9.9	10.0	12.3	9.5	9.2	10.4	8.4	11.8	10.7	9.8	8.5	18.8	11.8								
12/69	11.2	10.7	10.6	11.4	9.2	8.2	8.2	10.0	7.4	6.9	7.7	5.7	8.2	6.9	5.5	3.3	8.0	-0.2	-11.5							
12/70	10.9	10.4	10.3	11.0	8.9	7.9	7.9	9.6	7.1	6.7	7.3	5.5	7.6	6.2	4.8	3.1	6.6	0.5	-5.3	-0.1						
12/71	11.0	10.5	10.4	11.1	9.1	8.2	8.2	9.8	7.5	7.2	7.8	6.2	8.2	7.2	6.0	4.7	7.9	3.6	0.7	7.0	13.4					
12/72	11.2	10.8	10.7	11.4	9.5	8.7	8.7	10.2	8.2	7.9	8.5	7.1	9.0	8.2	7.4	6.4	9.4	6.1	4.7	10.2	15.3	15.8				
12/73	10.0	9.6	9.4	10.0	8.2	7.3	7.3	8.5	6.5	6.1	6.6	5.1	6.7	5.7	4.5	3.4	5.4	2.2	0.2	3.0	3.6	-2.1	-18.7			
12/74	8.3	7.8	7.6	8.0	6.2	5.3	5.2	6.2	4.2	3.7	3.9	2.4	3.5	2.2	1.0	-0.3	0.9	-2.5	-4.9	-3.8	-5.2	-11.5	-23.4	-29.1		
12/75	9.3	8.8	8.7	9.1	7.5	6.7	6.6	7.7	5.9	5.5	5.9	4.6	5.8	4.7	3.8	2.9	4.4	1.8	0.2	2.0	2.0	-1.2	-7.0	-1.4	34.9	
12/76	9.8	9.4	9.3	9.8	8.2	7.5	7.5	8.6	6.9	6.6	7.0	5.8	7.0	6.1	5.4	4.7	6.2	4.1	3.0	5.0	5.5	3.5	0.1	6.7	29.6	22.3

*Percent per annum, compounded annually.

Sources: Stock market data—Lawrence Fisher and Myron Scholes (compilers), CRSP Monthly Master File for Common Stocks Listed on the New York Stock Exchange (magnetic tape). See Appendix A.
Income tax rates—Income levels estimated from U.S. Bureau of the Census, Current Population Reports, Series P-60, Nos. 101 and 103 and Historical Statistics of the United States. Tax rates were found in U.S. Internal Revenue Service, Statistics of Income and Your Federal Income Tax.

Held Until	12/25	12/26	12/27	12/28	12/29	12/30	12/31	12/32	12/33	12/34	12/35	12/36	12/37	12/38	12/39	12/40	12/41	12/42	12/43	12/44	12/45	12/46	12/47	12/48	12/49
12/26	11.8																								
12/27	23.4	35.7																							
12/28	28.5	37.8	40.1																						
12/29	17.0	19.0	11.7	-13.0																					
12/30	7.8	7.0	-1.0	-18.1	-23.6																				
12/31	-1.9	-4.3	-12.2	-25.7	-31.4	-38.7																			
12/32	-1.4	-3.2	-9.4	-19.4	-21.6	-20.7	2.4																		
12/33	5.0	4.2	-0.4	-7.6	-6.6	-0.6	26.0	55.2																	
12/34	4.7	3.9	-0.2	-6.1	-4.9	0.0	17.4	25.6	1.1																
12/35	7.7	7.3	4.0	-0.8	1.1	6.8	22.5	30.0	18.8	38.7															
12/36	9.5	9.3	6.5	2.5	4.7	10.1	23.7	30.0	22.6	34.8	30.5														
12/37	4.8	4.2	1.4	-2.6	-1.5	2.1	11.0	13.0	4.4	5.4	-8.5	-36.3													
12/38	6.7	6.2	3.8	0.3	1.7	5.2	13.6	15.7	9.1	11.0	2.8	-8.9	30.0												
12/39	6.4	6.0	3.8	0.6	2.0	5.1	12.4	14.0	8.1	9.4	2.8	-5.2	15.6	2.2											
12/40	5.4	4.9	2.8	-0.2	1.0	3.7	9.9	10.9	5.5	6.1	0.4	-6.1	6.8	-3.4	-9.1										
12/41	3.6	3.1	1.0	-1.8	-0.9	1.4	6.5	7.0	2.1	2.1	-3.0	-8.7	-0.2	-8.7	-13.9	-18.9									
12/42	3.7	3.3	1.3	-1.2	-0.3	1.8	6.5	7.0	2.6	2.7	-1.7	-6.4	1.1	-5.2	-7.8	-7.4	5.0								
12/43	4.6	4.2	2.5	0.1	1.1	3.2	7.7	8.3	4.4	4.7	1.0	-2.7	4.4	-0.2	-1.0	1.7	13.6	22.5							
12/44	5.3	4.9	3.2	1.1	2.1	4.1	8.4	8.9	5.4	5.8	2.7	-0.4	6.1	2.5	2.4	5.4	14.8	19.8	17.0						
12/45	6.3	6.0	4.5	2.6	3.6	5.7	9.8	10.5	7.4	8.0	5.3	2.8	9.1	6.4	7.0	10.5	19.3	24.3	25.1	33.7					
12/46	4.7	4.4	2.9	1.1	1.9	3.8	7.4	7.8	4.9	5.1	2.5	0.1	5.3	2.5	2.5	4.5	9.8	10.9	7.2	2.7	-21.6				
12/47	4.3	4.0	2.5	0.7	1.5	3.2	6.6	6.9	4.1	4.3	1.9	-0.5	4.1	1.5	1.4	2.9	7.0	7.3	3.8	-0.2	-14.1	-6.7			
12/48	4.1	3.8	2.4	0.7	1.4	3.0	6.1	6.4	3.7	3.9	1.6	-0.5	3.6	1.2	1.1	2.4	5.8	5.8	2.8	-0.5	-10.1	-4.2	-2.4		
12/49	4.7	4.4	3.1	1.5	2.3	3.8	6.9	7.2	4.7	5.0	2.9	1.0	4.9	2.9	2.9	4.3	7.5	7.8	5.5	3.4	-3.3	3.6	8.6	20.0	
12/50	5.3	5.0	3.8	2.3	3.1	4.6	7.6	7.9	5.7	6.0	4.1	2.4	6.2	4.4	4.6	6.0	9.2	9.6	7.9	6.5	1.5	8.1	13.1	21.2	21.0
12/51	5.5	5.3	4.2	2.7	3.5	5.0	7.8	8.2	6.0	6.3	4.6	3.0	6.6	5.0	5.2	6.6	9.5	10.0	8.5	7.3	3.4	9.0	13.0	18.4	17.0
12/52	5.8	5.7	4.6	3.2	3.9	5.4	8.1	8.4	6.4	6.7	5.0	3.6	7.0	5.5	5.7	7.0	9.7	10.1	8.8	7.9	4.5	9.4	12.7	16.6	15.0
12/53	5.5	5.3	4.3	3.0	3.7	5.0	7.6	7.9	5.9	6.2	4.6	3.2	6.4	4.9	5.1	6.3	8.6	9.0	7.6	6.7	3.6	7.6	10.0	12.5	10.5
12/54	6.9	6.7	5.8	4.5	5.3	6.7	9.2	9.6	7.8	8.2	6.7	5.5	8.7	7.5	7.8	9.1	11.6	12.1	11.2	10.6	8.2	12.5	15.4	18.5	17.8
12/55	7.5	7.4	6.5	5.3	6.0	7.4	9.9	10.3	8.6	9.0	7.6	6.5	9.6	8.5	8.9	10.2	12.5	13.1	12.3	11.9	9.8	13.9	16.6	19.4	19.0
12/56	7.4	7.3	6.4	5.2	6.0	7.2	9.6	10.0	8.4	8.7	7.5	6.4	9.3	8.3	8.6	9.8	12.0	12.5	11.8	11.3	9.4	13.0	15.2	17.5	16.9
12/57	6.5	6.4	5.6	4.4	5.1	6.3	8.6	8.9	7.3	7.5	6.3	5.2	7.9	6.8	7.1	8.1	10.0	10.3	9.6	9.0	7.1	10.1	11.8	13.4	12.4
12/58	7.5	7.4	6.6	5.5	6.2	7.4	9.6	10.0	8.5	8.8	7.6	6.7	9.3	8.4	8.7	9.8	11.7	12.1	11.4	11.1	9.4	12.4	14.2	15.9	15.3
12/59	7.5	7.4	6.6	5.6	6.3	7.5	9.6	10.0	8.5	8.8	7.7	6.8	9.3	8.4	8.7	9.8	11.6	11.9	11.3	10.9	9.4	12.2	13.9	15.4	14.8
12/60	7.1	7.0	6.3	5.3	5.9	7.1	9.1	9.4	8.0	8.2	7.2	6.3	8.7	7.8	8.0	8.9	10.6	10.9	10.2	9.8	8.3	10.9	12.3	13.6	12.9
12/61	7.7	7.6	6.9	5.9	6.6	7.7	9.7	10.0	8.7	8.9	7.9	7.1	9.4	8.6	8.8	9.8	11.4	11.7	11.1	10.8	9.4	11.9	13.3	14.5	14.0
12/62	7.2	7.1	6.4	5.5	6.1	7.2	9.1	9.3	8.0	8.2	7.2	6.4	8.6	7.7	8.0	8.8	10.3	10.5	9.9	9.6	8.2	10.4	11.6	12.6	12.0
12/63	7.6	7.5	6.8	5.9	6.5	7.6	9.4	9.7	8.4	8.6	7.7	6.9	9.0	8.2	8.5	9.3	10.7	11.0	10.5	10.1	8.8	11.0	12.1	13.1	12.5
12/64	7.9	7.8	7.1	6.3	6.8	7.8	9.7	9.9	8.7	8.9	8.0	7.2	9.3	8.6	8.8	9.6	11.0	11.3	10.8	10.5	9.3	11.3	12.4	13.3	12.8
12/65	7.9	7.8	7.2	6.3	6.9	7.9	9.6	9.9	8.7	8.9	8.0	7.3	9.3	8.6	8.8	9.6	11.0	11.2	10.7	10.4	9.3	11.3	12.3	13.1	12.6
12/66	7.1	7.0	6.4	5.5	6.1	7.0	8.7	8.9	7.8	8.0	7.1	6.4	8.3	7.5	7.7	8.4	9.7	9.9	9.3	9.0	7.9	9.7	10.6	11.3	10.7
12/67	7.5	7.3	6.8	5.9	6.5	7.4	9.0	9.3	8.2	8.4	7.5	6.8	8.7	8.0	8.2	8.9	10.1	10.3	9.8	9.5	8.5	10.2	11.1	11.8	11.3
12/68	7.4	7.3	6.7	5.9	6.5	7.4	9.0	9.2	8.1	8.3	7.5	6.9	8.6	8.0	8.2	8.8	10.0	10.2	9.7	9.4	8.4	10.1	10.9	11.6	11.1
12/69	6.8	6.7	6.1	5.3	5.8	6.7	8.2	8.4	7.3	7.5	6.7	6.0	7.7	7.0	7.2	7.8	8.8	9.0	8.5	8.2	7.2	8.8	9.5	10.0	9.5
12/70	6.7	6.6	6.0	5.3	5.7	6.5	8.0	8.2	7.1	7.3	6.5	5.8	7.5	6.8	6.9	7.5	8.5	8.7	8.2	7.9	6.9	8.3	9.0	9.5	9.0
12/71	6.7	6.6	6.1	5.3	5.8	6.6	8.0	8.2	7.2	7.3	6.6	5.9	7.5	6.9	7.0	7.6	8.6	8.7	8.2	7.9	7.0	8.4	9.0	9.5	9.0
12/72	6.8	6.7	6.2	5.5	5.9	6.7	8.1	8.3	7.3	7.5	6.7	6.1	7.7	7.1	7.2	7.7	8.7	8.8	8.4	8.1	7.2	8.6	9.2	9.7	9.2
12/73	6.2	6.1	5.5	4.8	5.2	6.0	7.3	7.4	6.5	6.6	5.9	5.3	6.8	6.1	6.2	6.7	7.6	7.7	7.2	7.0	6.1	7.3	7.8	8.2	7.7
12/74	5.1	5.0	4.5	3.7	4.1	4.8	6.1	6.2	5.3	5.4	4.7	4.0	5.4	4.8	4.8	5.3	6.1	6.1	5.6	5.3	4.4	5.5	5.9	6.2	5.7
12/75	5.6	5.5	4.9	4.2	4.6	5.3	6.6	6.7	5.8	5.9	5.2	4.6	6.0	5.4	5.4	5.9	6.7	6.7	6.3	6.0	5.1	6.2	6.6	7.0	6.4
12/76	5.9	5.7	5.2	4.5	4.9	5.6	6.9	7.0	6.1	6.2	5.5	4.9	6.3	5.7	5.8	6.2	7.0	7.1	6.6	6.4	5.5	6.6	7.0	7.4	6.9

Table X

Time-Weighted Rates of Return* on Common Stocks:
  Dividends Reinvested,
  Cash to Portfolio,
  Initial Weighting by Value,
  Lower Tax Rate,
  Deflated by the Consumer Price Index

Held until	Purchased 12/50	12/51	12/52	12/53	12/54	12/55	12/56	12/57	12/58	12/59	12/60	12/61	12/62	12/63	12/64	12/65	12/66	12/67	12/68	12/69	12/70	12/71	12/72	12/73	12/74	12/75
12/51	12.3																									
12/52	11.8	10.4																								
12/53	7.0	4.2	−2.1																							
12/54	16.7	17.9	21.4	49.0																						
12/55	18.2	19.6	22.4	36.1	23.3																					
12/56	15.9	16.5	17.8	24.8	13.9	4.5																				
12/57	11.1	10.8	10.6	13.8	3.9	−5.0	−14.4																			
12/58	14.5	14.7	15.3	18.8	12.1	8.4	9.9	39.7																		
12/59	14.0	14.1	14.5	17.3	11.6	8.7	10.1	24.4	10.0																	
12/60	12.1	12.0	12.2	14.3	9.2	6.5	6.9	15.0	4.0	−2.2																
12/61	13.3	13.3	13.6	15.7	11.5	9.5	10.6	17.6	10.8	10.9	24.7															
12/62	11.2	11.0	11.0	12.5	8.6	6.5	6.8	11.5	5.1	3.3	5.5	−11.6														
12/63	11.8	11.7	11.8	13.2	9.7	8.0	8.5	12.7	7.7	6.9	9.7	2.4	17.5													
12/64	12.2	12.0	12.1	13.4	10.3	8.8	9.3	13.0	8.8	8.4	10.8	6.2	15.8	13.1												
12/65	12.0	11.9	11.9	13.1	10.2	8.9	9.3	12.6	8.9	8.6	10.7	7.3	14.0	12.6	10.8	−13.1										
12/66	10.1	9.9	9.8	10.7	7.9	6.5	6.7	9.2	5.8	5.1	6.2	2.8	6.5	3.4	−1.3	−13.1										
12/67	10.7	10.5	10.4	11.3	8.7	7.5	7.8	10.2	7.3	6.9	8.1	5.6	9.2	7.9	6.1	3.0	21.6									
12/68	10.5	10.3	10.2	11.0	8.6	7.5	7.7	10.0	7.3	7.0	8.0	5.8	8.9	7.7	6.4	4.6	14.4	6.7								
12/69	8.8	8.6	8.4	9.0	6.7	5.6	5.6	7.5	4.8	4.3	5.0	2.8	4.9	3.4	1.6	−1.0	3.3	−5.3	−16.6							
12/70	8.3	8.1	7.9	8.4	6.2	5.2	5.2	6.8	4.3	3.8	4.3	2.2	4.0	2.5	0.7	−1.3	1.6	−4.7	−10.5	−5.3						
12/71	8.4	8.1	8.0	8.5	6.4	5.4	5.4	6.9	4.7	4.2	4.7	2.9	4.6	3.4	1.9	0.4	3.2	−1.3	−4.0	2.4	9.7					
12/72	8.6	8.3	8.2	8.7	6.7	5.8	5.9	7.3	5.2	4.9	5.4	3.8	5.4	4.5	3.3	2.1	4.8	1.5	0.1	5.9	11.5	12.0				
12/73	7.1	6.8	6.6	7.0	5.1	4.1	4.1	5.3	3.2	2.7	3.0	1.4	2.7	1.5	0.1	−1.3	0.5	−3.0	−5.0	−2.2	−1.5	−7.7	−25.3			
12/74	5.0	4.7	4.4	4.6	2.7	1.7	1.6	2.5	0.5	−0.2	−0.1	−1.8	−1.0	−2.5	−4.0	−5.6	−4.7	−8.2	−10.7	−9.8	−11.3	−18.1	−30.7	−36.8		
12/75	5.8	5.5	5.3	5.6	3.8	2.9	2.8	3.8	1.9	1.4	1.6	0.1	1.0	−0.3	−1.5	−2.7	−1.5	−4.3	−6.0	−4.4	−4.5	−8.4	−14.9	−10.0	26.0	
12/76	6.3	6.0	5.8	6.1	4.5	3.6	3.6	4.6	2.8	2.4	2.6	1.2	2.2	1.0	0.1	−0.9	0.3	−2.0	−3.2	−1.3	−1.0	−3.4	−7.4	−1.2	22.4	16.7

*Percent per annum, compounded annually.

Sources: *Stock market data—Lawrence Fisher and Myron Scholes (compilers),* CRSP Monthly Master File for Common Stocks Listed on the New York Stock Exchange *(magnetic tape).* See Appendix A.
Consumer Price Index—U.S. Bureau of Labor Statistics. Income tax rates—Income levels estimated from U.S. Bureau of the Census, Current Population Reports, *Series P-60, Nos. 101 and 103 and* Historical Statistics of the United States. *Tax rates were found in U.S. Internal Revenue Service,* Statistics of Income *and* Your Federal Income Tax.

Held Until	Purchased 12/25	12/26	12/27	12/28	12/29	Purchased 12/30	12/31	12/32	12/33	12/34	Purchased 12/35	12/36	12/37	12/38	12/39	Purchased 12/40	12/41	12/42	12/43	12/44	Purchased 12/45	12/46	12/47	12/48	12/49
12/26	10.0																								
12/27	21.1	32.8																							
12/28	26.5	35.7	38.7																						
12/29	15.7	17.9	11.3	-12.9																					
12/30	5.5	4.6	-3.3	-20.6	-28.3																				
12/31	-5.3	-7.9	-15.9	-29.6	-36.7	-44.6																			
12/32	-5.8	-8.0	-14.4	-24.7	-28.4	-28.6	-8.2																		
12/33	1.0	-0.2	-4.9	-12.4	-12.6	-7.2	19.6	55.9																	
12/34	1.4	0.4	-3.8	-9.9	-9.5	-4.5	14.2	27.2	3.2																
12/35	4.9	4.3	1.0	-3.9	-2.5	3.4	20.7	32.3	21.6	42.5															
12/36	7.0	6.7	3.9	-0.2	1.6	7.4	22.5	31.9	24.8	37.2	31.4														
12/37	2.8	2.1	-0.6	-4.6	-3.8	0.2	10.5	14.8	6.4	7.5	-7.1	-34.7													
12/38	4.5	4.0	1.6	-1.8	-0.7	3.2	12.6	16.7	10.1	11.7	2.8	-9.3	25.9												
12/39	4.3	3.9	1.7	-1.5	-0.3	3.2	11.4	14.6	8.8	9.7	2.6	-5.7	13.2	1.2											
12/40	3.5	3.0	0.9	-2.0	-1.1	2.0	9.0	11.5	6.1	6.5	0.3	-6.4	5.4	-3.7	-8.8										
12/41	2.4	1.8	-0.2	-2.9	-2.1	0.5	6.6	8.4	3.5	3.5	-1.9	-7.6	0.7	-6.6	-10.5	-12.6									
12/42	2.9	2.5	0.7	-1.8	-1.0	1.6	7.2	9.0	4.7	4.8	0.2	-4.3	3.2	-1.9	-3.1	-0.5	12.6								
12/43	3.9	3.6	2.0	-0.3	0.6	3.1	8.5	10.2	6.5	6.8	2.9	-0.7	6.5	2.8	3.1	7.2	18.3	24.0							
12/44	4.6	4.3	2.8	0.7	1.6	4.0	9.1	10.8	7.3	7.7	4.4	1.3	7.9	5.1	5.8	9.6	18.0	20.7	17.2						
12/45	5.7	5.5	4.1	2.2	3.2	5.7	10.6	12.3	9.3	9.8	7.0	4.5	10.9	8.8	10.1	14.2	22.0	25.2	25.7	34.7					
12/46	4.9	4.7	3.4	1.6	2.5	4.7	9.2	10.6	7.8	8.1	5.5	3.2	8.6	6.5	7.3	10.1	15.2	15.9	13.2	11.2	-8.7				
12/47	4.8	4.6	3.3	1.6	2.4	4.5	8.7	10.0	7.3	7.6	5.1	3.0	7.8	5.9	6.4	8.7	12.6	12.6	9.9	7.6	-4.1	-0.2			
12/48	4.6	4.4	3.2	1.5	2.3	4.3	8.2	9.4	6.8	7.0	4.7	2.7	7.0	5.3	5.7	7.6	10.8	10.4	7.9	5.6	-2.9	-0.3	-1.3		
12/49	5.1	4.9	3.7	2.2	3.0	4.9	8.7	9.8	7.4	7.7	5.5	3.7	7.8	6.2	6.7	8.6	11.5	11.3	9.2	7.7	1.6	5.1	7.4	16.0	
12/50	5.8	5.7	4.6	3.1	4.0	5.9	9.5	10.6	8.4	8.8	6.8	5.2	9.2	7.9	8.5	10.3	13.2	13.2	11.7	10.8	6.4	10.4	13.7	21.5	25.8
12/51	6.2	6.1	5.1	3.7	4.5	6.4	9.8	10.9	8.9	9.2	7.4	6.0	9.7	8.6	9.2	10.9	13.6	13.7	12.4	11.8	8.2	11.7	14.6	20.1	21.7
12/52	6.4	6.4	5.4	4.1	4.8	6.6	10.0	11.0	9.0	9.4	7.7	6.3	9.8	8.7	9.3	10.9	13.3	13.4	12.2	11.6	8.6	11.5	13.7	17.6	17.7
12/53	6.0	6.0	5.0	3.8	4.5	6.2	9.3	10.3	8.4	8.7	7.0	5.7	8.9	7.9	8.3	9.7	11.8	11.7	10.5	9.8	6.9	9.2	10.6	13.0	12.1
12/54	7.3	7.3	6.4	5.2	6.0	7.7	10.8	11.8	10.1	10.4	8.9	7.8	11.0	10.1	10.7	12.2	14.4	14.5	13.6	13.3	11.0	13.6	15.5	18.4	18.6
12/55	7.9	7.9	7.0	5.9	6.7	8.3	11.4	12.3	10.7	11.1	9.7	8.6	11.7	10.9	11.5	13.0	15.0	15.2	14.5	14.2	12.2	14.7	16.5	19.1	19.4
12/56	7.8	7.8	7.0	5.9	6.6	8.2	11.1	12.0	10.4	10.8	9.5	8.4	11.4	10.6	11.2	12.5	14.4	14.5	13.8	13.5	11.7	13.8	15.4	17.5	17.5
12/57	7.0	7.0	6.2	5.1	5.8	7.3	10.1	10.9	9.3	9.6	8.3	7.2	10.0	9.2	9.6	10.8	12.4	12.3	11.6	11.2	9.3	11.0	12.1	13.6	13.2
12/58	7.9	7.9	7.2	6.2	6.9	8.4	11.1	11.9	10.5	10.8	9.5	8.6	11.3	10.6	11.1	12.3	13.9	14.0	13.4	13.1	11.5	13.3	14.6	16.2	16.0
12/59	8.0	8.0	7.3	6.3	7.0	8.4	11.0	11.9	10.4	10.7	9.5	8.7	11.3	10.6	11.1	12.2	13.7	13.8	13.2	12.9	11.4	13.1	14.2	15.6	15.4
12/60	7.6	7.5	6.9	5.9	6.6	8.0	10.5	11.2	9.9	10.1	8.9	8.1	10.5	9.8	10.2	11.2	12.6	12.6	12.0	11.7	10.2	11.8	12.7	13.8	13.6
12/61	8.1	8.1	7.5	6.5	7.2	8.6	11.0	11.8	10.5	10.7	9.6	8.8	11.1	10.5	10.9	11.9	13.3	13.3	12.7	12.5	11.1	12.7	13.6	14.7	14.5
12/62	7.7	7.6	7.0	6.1	6.7	8.0	10.3	11.0	9.7	9.9	8.9	8.0	10.2	9.6	10.0	10.9	12.1	12.0	11.5	11.2	9.8	11.1	11.8	12.7	12.5
12/63	8.0	8.0	7.4	6.5	7.1	8.4	10.6	11.3	10.1	10.3	9.3	8.5	10.6	10.0	10.4	11.3	12.5	12.5	11.9	11.6	10.4	11.6	12.4	13.3	13.0
12/64	8.3	8.2	7.6	6.8	7.4	8.6	10.8	11.5	10.3	10.5	9.5	8.8	10.9	10.3	10.7	11.5	12.7	12.7	12.1	11.9	10.7	11.9	12.6	13.5	13.3
12/65	8.3	8.3	7.7	6.9	7.5	8.7	10.8	11.4	10.3	10.5	9.6	8.8	10.9	10.3	10.7	11.5	12.6	12.6	12.1	11.9	10.7	11.9	12.6	13.4	13.1
12/66	7.6	7.6	7.0	6.2	6.7	7.9	9.9	10.5	9.4	9.6	8.6	7.9	9.8	9.3	9.6	10.3	11.3	11.3	10.8	10.5	9.4	10.5	11.0	11.7	11.4
12/67	8.0	7.9	7.4	6.6	7.2	8.3	10.3	10.9	9.8	10.0	9.1	8.4	10.3	9.7	10.0	10.8	11.8	11.7	11.3	11.0	10.0	11.1	11.6	12.3	12.0
12/68	8.0	8.0	7.4	6.7	7.2	8.3	10.3	10.9	9.8	10.0	9.2	8.5	10.3	9.8	10.1	10.8	11.7	11.7	11.3	11.0	10.0	11.1	11.6	12.2	12.0
12/69	7.5	7.5	6.9	6.2	6.7	7.8	9.6	10.2	9.1	9.3	8.4	7.8	9.5	9.0	9.2	9.9	10.7	10.7	10.2	10.0	8.9	9.9	10.4	10.9	10.6
12/70	7.5	7.4	6.9	6.2	6.7	7.7	9.5	10.0	9.0	9.2	8.3	7.7	9.3	8.8	9.0	9.6	10.5	10.4	9.9	9.7	8.7	9.6	10.0	10.5	10.2
12/71	7.5	7.5	7.0	6.3	6.8	7.8	9.5	10.0	9.0	9.2	8.4	7.8	9.4	8.9	9.1	9.7	10.5	10.5	10.0	9.8	8.8	9.8	10.1	10.6	10.3
12/72	7.7	7.7	7.2	6.5	7.0	8.0	9.7	10.2	9.2	9.4	8.6	8.0	9.6	9.1	9.3	9.9	10.7	10.7	10.2	10.0	9.1	10.0	10.4	10.8	10.6
12/73	7.2	7.1	6.6	5.9	6.4	7.3	9.0	9.5	8.5	8.7	7.9	7.3	8.8	8.3	8.5	9.1	9.8	9.7	9.3	9.1	8.2	8.9	9.2	9.6	9.3
12/74	6.3	6.2	5.8	5.1	5.5	6.4	8.0	8.4	7.5	7.6	6.8	6.2	7.6	7.1	7.3	7.8	8.5	8.3	7.9	7.6	6.7	7.4	7.6	7.9	7.6
12/75	6.8	6.8	6.3	5.6	6.1	7.0	8.6	9.0	8.1	8.2	7.5	6.9	8.3	7.8	8.0	8.5	9.2	9.1	8.6	8.4	7.6	8.2	8.5	8.8	8.5
12/76	7.1	7.1	6.6	6.0	6.4	7.3	8.9	9.3	8.4	8.6	7.8	7.2	8.6	8.2	8.4	8.9	9.5	9.5	9.0	8.8	8.0	8.7	8.9	9.3	9.0

Table XI

Time-Weighted Rates of Return* on Common Stocks:
Dividends Reinvested,
Cash to Portfolio,
Initial Weighting by Value,
Higher Tax Rate,
Current Dollars

Held until	Purchased 12/50	12/51	12/52	12/53	12/54	Purchased 12/55	12/56	12/57	12/58	12/59	Purchased 12/60	12/61	12/62	12/63	12/64	Purchased 12/65	12/66	12/67	12/68	12/69	Purchased 12/70	12/71	12/72	12/73	12/74	12/75
12/51	16.9																									
12/52	13.5	9.3																								
12/53	7.6	3.0	−3.5																							
12/54	16.6	16.2	19.3	45.9																						
12/55	17.9	18.0	20.6	34.0	22.1																					
12/56	15.9	15.6	16.9	24.1	14.1	6.0																				
12/57	11.3	10.3	10.3	13.7	4.6	−3.6	−13.1																			
12/58	14.7	14.3	15.0	18.9	12.8	9.6	10.9	40.2																		
12/59	14.2	13.8	14.3	17.4	12.2	9.7	10.9	24.8	10.2																	
12/60	12.4	11.8	12.1	14.4	9.7	7.3	7.5	15.3	4.2	−2.0																
12/61	13.5	13.1	13.5	15.7	11.8	10.1	10.9	17.7	10.8	10.8	24.2															
12/62	11.3	10.8	10.9	12.5	8.9	7.0	7.1	11.6	5.1	3.2	5.3	−11.6														
12/63	12.0	11.5	11.7	13.2	10.0	8.5	8.8	12.8	7.8	7.0	9.7	2.7	18.1													
12/64	12.3	11.9	12.0	13.5	10.6	9.3	9.6	13.1	8.9	8.5	10.9	6.5	16.2	13.4												
12/65	12.2	11.8	12.0	13.3	10.6	9.4	9.7	12.8	9.2	8.9	10.9	7.7	14.7	13.3	11.9											
12/66	10.5	10.0	10.0	11.0	8.4	7.2	7.3	9.8	6.3	5.7	6.8	3.6	7.6	4.6	0.3	−11.2										
12/67	11.2	10.8	10.8	11.8	9.4	8.4	8.5	11.0	8.0	7.6	9.0	6.6	10.5	9.4	8.0	5.2	24.1									
12/68	11.2	10.8	10.8	11.7	9.5	8.6	8.7	11.0	8.3	8.1	9.3	7.3	10.7	9.7	8.8	7.3	17.7	10.7								
12/69	9.8	9.3	9.3	10.0	7.9	6.9	6.9	8.8	6.2	5.8	6.6	4.6	7.1	5.9	4.4	2.2	6.9	−1.2	−12.5							
12/70	9.4	9.0	8.9	9.6	7.6	6.6	6.7	8.3	5.9	5.5	6.2	4.3	6.4	5.1	3.7	2.0	5.4	−0.7	−6.5	−1.3						
12/71	9.6	9.1	9.1	9.7	7.8	6.9	7.0	8.5	6.3	6.0	6.6	5.1	7.0	6.1	4.9	3.6	6.7	2.4	−0.4	5.8	12.2					
12/72	9.8	9.4	9.4	10.1	8.2	7.4	7.5	9.0	7.0	6.7	7.4	6.0	7.9	7.2	6.3	5.3	8.3	5.0	3.6	9.1	14.2	14.8				
12/73	8.6	8.2	8.1	8.7	6.9	6.1	6.0	7.3	5.3	4.9	5.4	4.0	5.5	4.6	3.4	2.3	4.3	1.1	−0.9	1.9	2.5	−3.1	−19.6			
12/74	6.8	6.4	6.2	6.6	4.9	4.0	3.9	4.9	3.0	2.5	2.7	1.2	2.3	1.1	−0.2	−1.5	−0.3	−3.6	−6.0	−5.0	−6.3	−12.5	−24.4	−30.2		
12/75	7.8	7.4	7.3	7.8	6.2	5.4	5.3	6.4	4.6	4.3	4.6	3.3	4.5	3.5	2.6	1.6	3.1	0.5	−1.0	0.7	0.8	−2.4	−8.2	−2.8	33.2	
12/76	8.3	8.0	7.9	8.4	6.8	6.1	6.1	7.2	5.6	5.3	5.7	4.5	5.7	4.8	4.1	3.4	4.9	2.8	1.7	3.7	4.2	2.2	−1.2	5.2	28.0	20.8

*Percent per annum, compounded annually.

Sources: Stock market data—Lawrence Fisher and Myron Scholes (compilers), CRSP Monthly Master File for Common Stocks Listed on the New York Stock Exchange (magnetic tape). See Appendix A.
Income tax rates—Income levels estimated from U.S. Bureau of the Census, Current Population Reports, Series P-60, Nos. 101 and 103 and Historical Statistics of the United States. Tax rates were found in U.S. Internal Revenue Service, Statistics of Income and Your Federal Income Tax.

Held Until	12/25	12/26	12/27	12/28	12/29	12/30	12/31	12/32	12/33	12/34	12/35	12/36	12/37	12/38	12/39	12/40	12/41	12/42	12/43	12/44	12/45	12/46	12/47	12/48	12/49
12/26	11.7																								
12/27	23.3	35.7																							
12/28	28.4	37.8	40.1																						
12/29	17.0	19.0	11.7	-13.1																					
12/30	7.7	7.0	-1.0	-18.2	-23.6																				
12/31	-2.0	-4.3	-12.2	-25.7	-31.4	-38.7																			
12/32	-1.4	-3.3	-9.4	-19.5	-21.6	-20.7	2.3																		
12/33	5.0	4.1	-0.5	-7.6	-6.6	-0.7	26.0	55.1																	
12/34	4.7	3.9	-0.2	-6.1	-5.0	-0.0	17.4	25.6	1.1																
12/35	7.7	7.2	3.9	-0.9	1.1	6.7	22.3	29.9	18.7	38.4															
12/36	9.4	9.2	6.4	2.4	4.6	10.0	23.5	29.7	22.3	34.4	29.9														
12/37	4.6	4.0	1.2	-2.8	-1.7	1.8	10.7	12.6	4.0	4.9	-9.0	-36.7													
12/38	6.5	6.0	3.6	0.1	1.5	5.0	13.3	15.3	8.7	10.5	2.3	-9.4	29.5												
12/39	6.2	5.8	3.5	0.4	1.8	4.9	12.0	13.6	7.7	8.9	2.3	-5.6	15.0	1.7											
12/40	5.2	4.7	2.5	-0.4	0.7	3.4	9.5	10.4	5.1	5.6	-0.1	-6.6	6.3	-3.9	-9.7										
12/41	3.3	2.8	0.6	-2.2	-1.3	0.9	6.0	6.5	1.5	1.4	-3.7	-9.5	-1.0	-9.6	-14.9	-20.4									
12/42	3.3	2.8	0.9	-1.7	-0.9	1.2	5.8	6.2	1.8	1.8	-2.6	-7.3	-0.0	-6.4	-9.1	-9.1	3.0								
12/43	4.1	3.7	1.9	-0.5	0.5	2.5	7.0	7.4	3.5	3.7	-0.0	-3.8	3.1	-1.6	-2.5	-0.2	11.4	20.2							
12/44	4.7	4.3	2.6	0.4	1.3	3.3	7.5	8.0	4.4	4.7	1.5	-1.7	4.7	1.0	0.7	3.4	12.6	17.6	14.8						
12/45	5.6	5.3	3.8	1.8	2.8	4.8	8.9	9.5	6.4	6.8	4.1	1.5	7.7	4.8	5.3	8.5	17.1	22.2	23.0	31.7					
12/46	4.0	3.7	2.2	0.3	1.1	2.9	6.4	6.8	3.8	4.0	1.3	-1.2	3.8	1.0	0.8	2.6	7.9	9.1	5.5	1.2	-22.7				
12/47	3.6	3.2	1.8	-0.1	0.7	2.3	5.6	5.8	2.9	3.1	0.6	-1.8	2.7	-0.0	-0.3	1.1	5.1	5.5	2.1	-1.8	-15.5	-8.4			
12/48	3.3	3.0	1.6	-0.2	0.5	2.0	5.1	5.3	2.6	2.7	0.3	-1.8	2.2	-0.3	-0.5	0.6	4.0	4.1	1.1	-2.1	-11.5	-5.8	-3.9		
12/49	3.9	3.6	2.3	0.6	1.4	2.8	5.8	6.0	3.5	3.7	1.6	-0.4	3.5	1.3	1.2	2.5	5.7	6.1	3.8	1.8	-4.8	1.9	6.9	18.1	
12/50	4.4	4.2	2.9	1.4	2.1	3.6	6.4	6.7	4.4	4.6	2.7	1.0	4.7	2.8	2.9	4.2	7.3	7.8	6.1	4.7	-0.1	6.3	11.3	19.2	18.9
12/51	4.6	4.4	3.2	1.7	2.5	3.9	6.6	6.9	4.7	5.0	3.2	1.6	5.1	3.4	3.5	4.8	7.6	8.1	6.7	5.6	1.7	7.2	11.2	16.4	15.0
12/52	4.9	4.7	3.6	2.2	2.9	4.2	6.8	7.1	5.1	5.3	3.6	2.1	5.4	3.8	4.0	5.2	7.8	8.3	7.0	6.1	2.8	7.5	10.8	14.6	13.0
12/53	4.5	4.3	3.2	1.9	2.6	3.8	6.3	6.6	4.6	4.8	3.1	1.7	4.8	3.3	3.4	4.4	6.8	7.1	5.8	4.9	1.8	5.8	8.1	10.5	8.5
12/54	5.8	5.7	4.7	3.4	4.1	5.4	7.9	8.2	6.4	6.7	5.2	4.0	7.1	5.8	6.0	7.2	9.6	10.2	9.3	8.7	6.4	10.6	13.4	16.3	15.7
12/55	6.5	6.3	5.4	4.2	4.9	6.1	8.6	8.9	7.2	7.5	6.1	4.9	7.9	6.8	7.1	8.3	10.6	11.2	10.4	10.0	8.0	11.9	14.6	17.3	16.9
12/56	6.3	6.2	5.2	4.1	4.8	6.0	8.3	8.6	6.9	7.2	5.9	4.8	7.7	6.5	6.8	7.9	10.1	10.6	9.9	9.5	7.6	11.0	13.3	15.5	14.9
12/57	5.5	5.4	4.4	3.3	3.9	5.1	7.3	7.5	5.9	6.1	4.8	3.7	6.3	5.2	5.4	6.3	8.2	8.5	7.8	7.2	5.3	8.2	10.0	11.5	10.6
12/58	6.4	6.3	5.4	4.3	5.0	6.1	8.3	8.6	7.0	7.3	6.1	5.1	7.7	6.7	6.9	7.9	9.8	10.2	9.6	9.2	7.6	10.6	12.4	14.0	13.5
12/59	6.4	6.3	5.5	4.4	5.1	6.2	8.3	8.6	7.1	7.3	6.2	5.2	7.7	6.7	7.0	7.9	9.7	10.1	9.5	9.2	7.6	10.4	12.1	13.5	13.0
12/60	6.0	5.9	5.1	4.1	4.7	5.8	7.8	8.0	6.6	6.8	5.7	4.7	7.1	6.1	6.3	7.2	8.8	9.1	8.5	8.1	6.6	9.2	10.6	11.8	11.2
12/61	6.6	6.4	5.7	4.7	5.4	6.4	8.4	8.6	7.3	7.5	6.4	5.5	7.8	6.9	7.1	8.0	9.6	9.9	9.4	9.1	7.7	10.2	11.6	12.8	12.3
12/62	6.1	6.0	5.3	4.3	4.9	5.9	7.7	7.9	6.6	6.8	5.7	4.9	7.0	6.1	6.3	7.1	8.5	8.8	8.2	7.9	6.5	8.7	9.9	10.9	10.3
12/63	6.5	6.4	5.7	4.7	5.3	6.3	8.1	8.3	7.0	7.2	6.2	5.4	7.4	6.6	6.8	7.6	9.0	9.3	8.8	8.5	7.2	9.3	10.4	11.4	10.9
12/64	6.7	6.6	5.9	5.0	5.6	6.5	8.3	8.5	7.3	7.5	6.5	5.7	7.7	7.0	7.2	7.9	9.3	9.6	9.1	8.8	7.6	9.6	10.7	11.6	11.2
12/65	6.8	6.7	6.0	5.1	5.6	6.6	8.3	8.5	7.3	7.5	6.6	5.8	7.8	7.0	7.2	7.9	9.3	9.5	9.1	8.8	7.7	9.6	10.7	11.5	11.0
12/66	6.0	5.9	5.2	4.4	4.9	5.8	7.4	7.6	6.4	6.6	5.6	4.9	6.7	6.0	6.1	6.8	8.0	8.2	7.8	7.5	6.4	8.1	9.0	9.7	9.2
12/67	6.4	6.2	5.6	4.8	5.3	6.1	7.7	7.9	6.8	7.0	6.1	5.4	7.2	6.4	6.6	7.2	8.5	8.7	8.2	8.0	6.9	8.7	9.6	10.3	9.8
12/68	6.3	6.2	5.6	4.8	5.2	6.1	7.7	7.9	6.8	6.9	6.1	5.4	7.1	6.4	6.6	7.2	8.3	8.6	8.1	7.9	6.9	8.6	9.4	10.1	9.6
12/69	5.7	5.6	5.0	4.2	4.6	5.4	6.9	7.1	6.0	6.1	5.3	4.6	6.2	5.5	5.6	6.2	7.3	7.4	7.0	6.7	5.7	7.3	8.0	8.6	8.0
12/70	5.6	5.5	4.9	4.1	4.5	5.3	6.7	6.8	5.8	5.9	5.1	4.4	6.0	5.3	5.4	5.9	6.9	7.1	6.6	6.4	5.4	6.9	7.5	8.0	7.5
12/71	5.6	5.5	4.9	4.1	4.6	5.3	6.7	6.9	5.8	6.0	5.2	4.5	6.1	5.4	5.5	6.0	7.0	7.1	6.7	6.5	5.5	6.9	7.6	8.1	7.6
12/72	5.7	5.6	5.1	4.3	4.8	5.5	6.9	7.0	6.0	6.1	5.3	4.7	6.2	5.6	5.7	6.2	7.2	7.3	6.9	6.7	5.7	7.1	7.8	8.2	7.8
12/73	5.1	5.0	4.4	3.6	4.0	4.7	6.1	6.2	5.2	5.3	4.5	3.9	5.3	4.7	4.8	5.2	6.1	6.2	5.8	5.5	4.6	5.9	6.4	6.8	6.3
12/74	4.0	3.9	3.3	2.6	2.9	3.6	4.9	4.9	3.9	4.0	3.3	2.6	4.0	3.3	3.3	3.7	4.6	4.6	4.1	3.8	2.9	4.1	4.5	4.8	4.3
12/75	4.4	4.3	3.8	3.0	3.4	4.1	5.3	5.4	4.4	4.5	3.8	3.2	4.5	3.9	3.9	4.3	5.2	5.2	4.8	4.5	3.6	4.8	5.2	5.5	5.0
12/76	4.7	4.6	4.0	3.3	3.7	4.3	5.6	5.6	4.7	4.8	4.1	3.5	4.8	4.2	4.3	4.7	5.5	5.5	5.1	4.9	4.0	5.1	5.6	5.9	5.4

Table XII

Time-Weighted Rates of Return* on Common Stocks:
- Dividends Reinvested,
- Cash to Portfolio,
- Initial Weighting by Value,
- Higher Tax Rate,
- Deflated by the Consumer Price Index

Held until	\ Purchased \ 12/50	12/51	12/52	12/53	12/54	12/55	12/56	12/57	12/58	12/59	12/60	12/61	12/62	12/63	12/64	12/65	12/66	12/67	12/68	12/69	12/70	12/71	12/72	12/73	12/74	12/75
12/51	10.4																									
12/52	9.8	8.4																								
12/53	5.1	2.2	−4.1																							
12/54	14.6	15.8	19.2	46.7																						
12/55	16.2	17.6	20.4	34.1	21.6																					
12/56	14.0	14.6	16.0	23.0	12.3	3.0																				
12/57	9.3	9.0	8.9	12.1	2.4	−6.3	−15.7																			
12/58	12.6	12.9	13.5	17.1	10.5	6.9	8.3	37.8																		
12/59	12.2	12.3	12.8	15.6	10.1	7.2	8.6	22.8	8.6																	
12/60	10.4	10.4	10.6	12.7	7.8	5.1	5.5	13.5	2.7	−3.5																
12/61	11.6	11.7	12.0	14.1	10.0	8.1	9.1	16.2	9.5	9.6	23.3															
12/62	9.6	9.4	9.5	11.0	7.1	5.1	5.4	10.1	3.9	2.0	4.3	−12.6														
12/63	10.2	10.1	10.2	11.6	8.3	6.6	7.1	11.3	6.4	5.6	8.4	1.2	16.2													
12/64	10.5	10.5	10.6	11.9	8.8	7.4	7.9	11.6	7.5	7.1	9.6	5.0	14.5	12.1												
12/65	10.4	10.4	10.5	11.7	8.8	7.5	8.0	11.2	7.7	7.4	9.5	6.2	12.9	11.6	9.8											
12/66	8.6	8.4	8.4	9.3	6.6	5.2	5.4	8.0	4.6	4.0	5.1	1.7	5.4	2.4	−2.3	−14.1										
12/67	9.2	9.1	9.0	10.0	7.4	6.3	6.5	9.0	6.1	5.7	7.0	4.5	8.1	6.9	5.1	2.0	20.4									
12/68	9.0	8.9	8.8	9.7	7.3	6.3	6.5	8.8	6.1	5.8	6.9	4.7	7.8	6.6	5.3	3.5	13.3	5.7								
12/69	7.4	7.2	7.1	7.7	5.5	4.4	4.4	6.3	3.7	3.2	3.9	1.7	3.8	2.4	0.6	−2.0	2.2	−6.2	−17.5							
12/70	6.9	6.7	6.5	7.1	5.0	3.9	3.9	5.6	3.2	2.6	3.1	1.1	2.9	1.4	−0.4	−2.4	0.5	−5.8	−11.6	−6.4						
12/71	7.0	6.7	6.6	7.2	5.1	4.1	4.2	5.7	3.5	3.1	3.6	1.8	3.5	2.4	0.9	−0.7	2.1	−2.4	−5.1	1.3	8.6					
12/72	7.2	7.0	6.9	7.4	5.5	4.6	4.6	6.1	4.1	3.7	4.3	2.7	4.3	3.4	2.3	1.1	3.8	0.4	−1.0	4.8	10.5	11.0				
12/73	5.8	5.5	5.3	5.8	3.9	2.9	2.8	4.1	2.1	1.6	1.9	0.3	1.6	0.5	−1.0	−2.4	−0.6	−4.0	−6.0	−3.2	−2.5	−8.6	−26.1			
12/74	3.6	3.3	3.0	3.4	1.5	0.5	0.3	1.3	−0.7	−1.3	−1.3	−2.9	−2.1	−3.6	−5.1	−6.7	−5.8	−9.3	−11.8	−10.9	−12.3	−19.1	−31.6	−37.8		
12/75	4.4	4.2	3.9	4.3	2.5	1.6	1.5	2.5	0.7	0.2	0.4	−1.1	−0.2	−1.5	−2.6	−3.8	−2.7	−5.5	−7.1	−5.6	−5.7	−9.5	−16.0	−11.3	24.5	
12/76	4.9	4.6	4.4	4.8	3.1	2.3	2.2	3.3	1.5	1.1	1.3	−0.0	0.9	−0.2	−1.1	−2.1	−0.9	−3.2	−4.4	−2.6	−2.2	−4.7	−8.7	−2.6	20.8	15.2

*Percent per annum, compounded annually.

Sources: Stock market data—Lawrence Fisher and Myron Scholes (compilers), CRSP Monthly Master File for Common Stocks Listed on the New York Stock Exchange (magnetic tape). See Appendix A.
Consumer Price Index—U.S. Bureau of Labor Statistics.
Income tax rates—Income levels estimated from U.S. Bureau of the Census, Current Population Reports, Series P-60, Nos. 101 and 103 and Historical Statistics of the United States. Tax rates were found in U.S. Internal Revenue Service, Statistics of Income and Your Federal Income Tax.

Chapter 6

Internal Rates of Return on Common Stocks

(Dividends Consumed, Cash to Portfolio)

In this chapter, we present internal rates of return on investments in common stocks listed on the NYSE on a cash-to-portfolio basis with dividends consumed. The internal rates of return presented in this chapter would be the same as the time-weighted rates presented in Chapter 5, except that here we assume that dividends (net of federal income taxes) were consumed as they were received instead of being reinvested.

Time-weighted rates of return are similar to the rates of return implied by finding the "unit value" of a mutual fund or trust fund in which dividends have been used to purchase additional shares. Only two values are relevant for the final calculation of the time-weighted rate of return—the initial outlay and the accumulated value of the unit. See Equation 3.1 above.

Formally, internal rates of return are computed by the method used to find the promised yield (or yield to maturity) of a bond or mortgage. The computational process is iterative. One selects a trial rate of return (discount rate or yield) and finds the present value of each future payment of principal or interest. Then the present values are added together and their sum is compared with the purchase price. If the sum of present values and the price differ, other trial

rates of return are chosen until the error becomes negligible.[1] For our purposes, the relevant cash inflows are dividends each month and the value of the portfolio at the end of the period. "Price" is that of the portfolio—either the number of stocks listed at the portfolio's beginning date or the total market value of all common shares listed on the NYSE, depending on whether we are using equal initial weighting or initial weighting by value. The internal rate of return satisfies Equation 3.2.

The economic interpretation of the internal rate of return on investments in common stocks, however, differs from that of the promised yield on a bond or mortgage. The calculations for the bond or mortgage assume that the cash flow is completely specified in advance. Then a single—unchanging—rate of return is used for the entire period from the initial outlay until the last promised payment. For portfolios of common stocks, the cash flows are unknown until dividends are declared by boards of directors only a few weeks before each payment. The rate of return varies widely from subperiod to subpe-

---

[1] *Cf. Lawrence Fisher, "An Algorithm for Finding Exact Rates of Return,"* Journal of Business *39 (January 1966, Part II): 111–18.*

riod, e.g., from −48 percent to +106 percent for one-year periods and equally weighted portfolios. Moreover, high and low dividends and low and high rates of return appear to be due to many of the same causes.

The economic interpretation that we suggest is that realized rates of return for long periods are averages of the successive short-period rates during the period. If the subperiods vary in length, each subperiod's rate of return receives a weight that is proportional to the length of the subperiod. For time-weighted rates of return, that is all that the weight depends on. For internal rates of return, the weight is nearly proportional to the net investment in the portfolio as well as to the length of the period. For buy-and-hold portfolios of common stocks, consumption of dividends is equivalent to a gradual withdrawal of the initial investment. Hence, in contrast to time-weighted rates of return, computations of internal rates of return give higher weights to the early years that the portfolio is held.

Both rates are averages of rates for the same subperiods. Hence, there should be no tendency for one rate to be higher than the other. However, as sampling theory predicts, the equal weights given to subperiod rates in time-weighted rates of return make the long-term, time-weighted rates of return somewhat less variable than the corresponding internal rates.

Because of lower sampling variability, we think that for most purposes time-weighted rates of return are more useful than internal rates. There are many applications, however, in which it may be convenient to have tables like those presented in this chapter. When there have been intermediate additions to or withdrawals from a portfolio for consumption or other purposes, the time-weighted rate of return for that portfolio will not be available unless the market value of the portfolio as a whole has been recorded frequently (e.g., once a month).[2] Then it may be necessary to compare the internal rate of return for the portfolio with the internal rate reported here.

The internal rates of return that we have calculated are presented in Tables XIII through XXII. Tables XIII–XX are analogous to Tables I–VIII; Tables XXI and XXII to Tables XI and XII.

---

[2] *Cf. Bank Administration Institute,* op. cit.

Held Until	12/25	12/26	12/27	12/28	12/29	12/30	12/31	12/32	12/33	12/34	12/35	12/36	12/37	12/38	12/39	12/40	12/41	12/42	12/43	12/44	12/45	12/46	12/47	12/48	12/49
12/26	0.8																								
12/27	15.6	29.2																							
12/28	23.2	37.3	45.8																						
12/29	8.4	10.3	1.4	−29.3																					
12/30	−1.1	−2.4	−12.0	−31.5	−37.6																				
12/31	−9.0	−11.3	−19.9	−35.8	−40.8	−47.8																			
12/32	−8.9	−10.8	−17.7	−30.2	−32.4	−31.1	−10.3																		
12/33	−2.6	−3.1	−7.8	−16.9	−13.3	−2.5	36.4	106.4																	
12/34	−1.2	−1.7	−5.6	−12.8	−8.5	1.2	28.0	54.8	15.2																
12/35	1.7	1.5	−1.7	−7.4	−2.2	8.2	32.9	54.0	32.0	50.6															
12/36	3.9	4.0	1.3	−3.4	2.3	13.0	35.6	53.1	37.3	50.9	46.9														
12/37	0.5	0.1	−2.9	−7.6	−3.9	2.9	17.4	25.5	9.5	7.5	−10.6	−45.9													
12/38	2.2	1.9	−0.6	−4.7	−0.7	6.1	19.5	26.9	13.7	12.9	0.8	−16.9	30.5												
12/39	2.0	1.7	−0.6	−4.4	−0.7	5.2	16.6	22.4	10.9	9.5	−0.0	−12.1	12.9	−3.4											
12/40	1.6	1.2	−1.0	−4.6	−1.1	4.0	14.2	19.1	8.7	6.8	−1.4	−10.7	6.3	−5.2	−10.2										
12/41	1.2	0.8	−1.4	−4.7	−1.7	3.2	12.4	16.5	6.9	4.9	−2.3	−10.0	2.8	−5.6	−9.1	−9.7									
12/42	1.7	1.4	−0.6	−3.7	−0.6	4.1	12.8	16.6	7.8	6.2	0.1	−6.2	5.9	−0.0	0.3	7.0	30.6								
12/43	2.7	2.5	0.8	−2.0	1.2	6.0	14.4	18.2	10.3	9.4	4.3	−0.9	11.7	8.4	11.0	21.6	47.2	58.1							
12/44	3.4	3.4	1.9	−0.7	2.6	7.3	15.5	19.2	12.0	11.4	7.0	2.6	14.8	12.5	15.9	26.3	46.1	50.4	39.0						
12/45	4.7	4.9	3.5	1.2	4.7	9.5	17.4	21.1	14.6	14.5	10.7	7.1	19.1	17.8	22.2	32.9	51.9	56.2	50.4	60.6					
12/46	4.2	4.3	3.0	0.8	4.0	8.4	15.8	19.3	13.0	12.5	8.9	5.4	15.7	14.1	17.0	24.2	36.1	36.0	26.9	21.1	−9.4				
12/47	4.2	4.3	3.0	0.8	3.9	8.1	15.2	18.4	12.3	11.8	8.3	5.1	14.4	13.0	15.1	20.7	29.3	28.2	20.0	14.0	−4.4	−0.2			
12/48	4.1	4.1	2.7	0.7	3.6	7.6	14.4	17.5	11.5	10.9	7.5	4.4	12.9	11.5	13.4	18.0	24.8	23.2	15.6	10.1	−3.5	−0.8	−2.9		
12/49	4.5	4.5	3.2	1.3	4.1	8.0	14.6	17.6	11.8	11.3	8.1	5.2	13.3	12.0	13.8	18.1	24.6	23.1	16.3	12.0	1.4	5.2	7.9	19.3	
12/50	5.0	5.1	4.0	2.1	4.9	8.8	15.3	18.1	12.6	12.2	9.3	6.6	14.3	13.3	15.1	19.4	25.4	24.1	18.4	15.0	6.7	11.6	15.8	26.7	35.7
12/51	5.3	5.5	4.3	2.5	5.3	9.1	15.4	18.1	12.8	12.5	9.6	7.0	14.4	13.4	15.2	19.1	24.6	23.4	18.2	15.3	8.3	12.5	15.8	23.3	25.6
12/52	5.5	5.6	4.5	2.8	5.4	9.1	15.2	17.9	12.7	12.4	9.6	7.2	14.2	13.2	14.9	18.6	23.7	22.4	17.5	14.7	8.5	12.3	14.9	20.1	20.3
12/53	5.3	5.4	4.3	2.6	5.2	8.7	14.7	17.4	12.2	11.9	9.1	6.8	13.4	12.3	13.9	17.3	22.0	20.7	15.9	13.1	7.3	10.3	12.2	15.9	14.6
12/54	6.1	6.2	5.3	3.7	6.2	9.7	15.6	18.1	13.3	13.1	10.5	8.4	14.8	13.9	15.6	19.0	23.7	22.6	18.4	16.1	11.1	14.5	17.0	21.2	21.5
12/55	6.4	6.5	5.6	4.1	6.6	10.0	15.8	18.3	13.6	13.4	10.9	8.8	15.1	14.2	15.8	19.1	23.5	22.5	18.7	16.5	11.9	15.1	17.5	21.3	21.7
12/56	6.5	6.7	5.7	4.3	6.7	10.0	15.7	18.2	13.5	13.4	10.9	8.9	14.9	14.1	15.6	18.6	22.7	21.8	18.1	16.1	11.9	14.7	16.6	19.9	20.2
12/57	6.1	6.3	5.3	3.8	6.2	9.4	15.0	17.4	12.8	12.6	10.1	8.1	13.9	13.0	14.4	17.2	21.1	20.0	16.3	14.1	10.0	12.3	13.9	16.4	15.8
12/58	6.8	7.0	6.0	4.7	7.0	10.2	15.6	18.0	13.5	13.4	11.1	9.2	14.9	14.1	15.5	18.3	22.2	21.2	17.7	15.8	12.1	14.6	16.3	19.1	19.0
12/59	6.9	7.1	6.2	4.8	7.2	10.4	15.7	18.0	13.6	13.5	11.2	9.4	15.0	14.2	15.5	18.2	21.9	20.9	17.6	15.7	12.2	14.7	16.4	19.0	19.0
12/60	6.9	7.0	6.1	4.8	7.1	10.1	15.3	17.7	13.3	13.2	10.9	9.1	14.5	13.7	15.0	17.6	21.2	20.1	16.7	15.0	11.5	13.8	15.3	17.6	17.4
12/61	7.3	7.4	6.5	5.2	7.5	10.5	15.6	17.9	13.6	13.6	11.3	9.6	14.8	14.1	15.4	17.9	21.4	20.4	17.1	15.5	12.2	14.4	15.9	18.1	17.9
12/62	6.8	7.0	6.1	4.8	7.0	10.0	15.0	17.3	13.0	12.9	10.6	8.9	14.1	13.3	14.5	17.0	20.3	19.2	15.9	14.2	10.9	12.9	14.2	16.0	15.6
12/63	7.1	7.2	6.3	5.0	7.2	10.2	15.2	17.4	13.1	13.0	10.8	9.2	14.2	13.4	14.6	17.0	20.3	19.3	16.0	14.4	11.2	13.2	14.4	16.2	15.8
12/64	7.2	7.3	6.5	5.2	7.3	10.2	15.1	17.4	13.2	13.1	11.0	9.3	14.2	13.5	14.7	17.0	20.3	19.2	16.1	14.5	11.4	13.4	14.5	16.3	15.9
12/65	7.3	7.5	6.7	5.5	7.6	10.5	15.3	17.5	13.4	13.3	11.2	9.6	14.4	13.7	14.8	17.1	20.3	19.3	16.3	14.7	11.9	13.9	15.0	16.7	16.5
12/66	7.2	7.3	6.5	5.3	7.3	10.1	15.0	17.2	13.0	12.9	10.8	9.3	14.0	13.2	14.4	16.6	19.8	18.7	15.6	14.1	11.2	13.1	14.2	15.8	15.4
12/67	7.6	7.7	6.9	5.8	7.8	10.5	15.2	17.4	13.4	13.3	11.3	9.8	14.4	13.7	14.8	17.0	20.1	19.1	16.2	14.7	12.0	13.8	14.9	16.5	16.3
12/68	7.7	7.9	7.1	6.0	8.0	10.6	15.3	17.4	13.5	13.4	11.4	10.0	14.5	13.8	14.9	17.1	20.1	19.1	16.2	14.8	12.2	14.0	15.0	16.6	16.4
12/69	7.5	7.6	6.8	5.7	7.6	10.2	14.8	17.0	13.0	12.9	10.9	9.5	14.0	13.3	14.3	16.4	19.5	18.4	15.4	13.9	11.2	12.9	13.9	15.4	15.1
12/70	7.4	7.5	6.7	5.6	7.4	10.0	14.7	16.9	12.8	12.6	10.7	9.3	13.8	13.1	14.0	16.2	19.2	18.1	15.1	13.5	10.9	12.5	13.4	14.8	14.5
12/71	7.4	7.6	6.8	5.7	7.6	10.1	14.7	16.9	12.9	12.7	10.8	9.4	13.8	13.2	14.1	16.2	19.2	18.1	15.1	13.6	11.1	12.7	13.6	15.0	14.7
12/72	7.5	7.7	6.9	5.9	7.7	10.2	14.7	16.9	12.9	12.7	10.8	9.4	13.8	13.1	14.0	16.1	19.1	18.0	15.0	13.6	11.1	12.7	13.6	15.0	14.6
12/73	7.2	7.4	6.6	5.6	7.3	9.8	14.5	16.6	12.5	12.3	10.4	9.0	13.3	12.6	13.5	15.7	18.7	17.5	14.5	13.0	10.4	11.9	12.7	14.0	13.6
12/74	6.9	7.0	6.2	5.2	6.9	9.5	14.2	16.5	12.2	12.0	10.0	8.5	13.0	12.3	13.2	15.3	18.4	17.2	14.0	12.4	9.7	11.2	11.9	13.2	12.7
12/75	7.1	7.2	6.5	5.5	7.3	9.7	14.4	16.6	12.4	12.2	10.3	8.9	13.2	12.6	13.4	15.5	18.5	17.4	14.3	12.7	10.2	11.6	12.4	13.6	13.2
12/76	7.3	7.4	6.7	5.8	7.5	9.9	14.4	16.6	12.5	12.3	10.5	9.1	13.4	12.8	13.6	15.6	18.6	17.5	14.4	12.9	10.5	11.9	12.6	13.9	13.5

Table XIII

Internal Rates of Return* on Common Stocks:
  Dividends Consumed,
  Cash to Portfolio,
  Equal Initial Weighting,
  Tax-Exempt,
  Current Dollars

Held Until	12/50	12/51	12/52	12/53	12/54	12/55	12/56	12/57	12/58	12/59	12/60	12/61	12/62	12/63	12/64	12/65	12/66	12/67	12/68	12/69	12/70	12/71	12/72	12/73	12/74	12/75
12/51	14.9																									
12/52	12.5	8.8																								
12/53	7.9	3.6	-3.2																							
12/54	17.4	17.8	22.2	55.1																						
12/55	18.0	18.6	21.9	37.8	19.1																					
12/56	16.7	16.7	18.6	27.6	13.6	6.6																				
12/57	12.5	11.7	11.9	16.1	4.2	-3.3	-13.5																			
12/58	16.4	16.4	17.6	22.8	14.6	12.7	16.3	58.2																		
12/59	16.5	16.5	17.7	22.1	15.2	13.8	16.9	36.6	14.6																	
12/60	15.1	15.0	15.8	19.0	12.9	11.3	12.8	22.7	6.6	-2.0																
12/61	16.0	16.0	16.8	19.9	14.7	13.8	15.8	24.3	13.6	12.7	27.9															
12/62	13.6	13.3	13.6	16.0	10.9	9.6	10.5	16.1	6.5	3.9	6.2	-13.6														
12/63	13.9	13.6	14.0	16.3	11.7	10.5	11.5	16.6	8.9	7.3	10.6	1.8	17.9													
12/64	14.1	13.8	14.3	16.4	12.2	11.2	12.2	16.9	10.4	9.5	12.8	7.4	18.7	16.6												
12/65	14.7	14.5	15.0	17.2	13.3	12.4	13.5	18.2	12.6	12.2	15.9	12.6	22.9	23.8	28.6											
12/66	13.6	13.3	13.7	15.6	11.7	10.8	11.6	15.7	10.3	9.7	12.3	9.0	15.4	13.4	10.4	-8.2										
12/67	14.6	14.5	15.0	16.9	13.4	12.7	13.6	17.8	13.2	13.1	16.1	14.0	21.0	21.5	22.6	17.7	51.9									
12/68	14.8	14.8	15.3	17.2	13.9	13.3	14.3	18.2	14.1	14.2	17.1	15.2	21.3	22.0	23.0	20.7	40.6	28.4								
12/69	13.4	13.2	13.6	15.2	11.9	11.2	11.8	15.0	10.9	10.6	12.5	10.3	14.6	14.0	13.3	9.5	16.8	1.9	-20.1							
12/70	12.8	12.6	12.9	14.4	11.3	10.5	11.0	13.8	9.9	9.5	11.0	8.8	12.3	11.2	10.0	6.5	11.3	0.4	-12.2	-4.8						
12/71	13.1	12.9	13.1	14.6	11.6	10.9	11.5	14.2	10.6	10.3	11.8	9.8	13.1	12.2	11.2	8.3	12.8	4.5	-3.0	6.6	17.2					
12/72	13.0	12.8	13.1	14.5	11.7	11.0	11.5	14.1	10.7	10.4	11.8	10.0	13.0	12.2	11.3	8.7	12.5	5.7	0.4	7.8	13.5	6.8				
12/73	12.0	11.7	11.8	13.1	10.2	9.3	9.7	11.9	8.6	8.2	9.2	7.4	9.8	8.6	7.3	4.4	6.7	0.7	-4.4	-0.4	-0.8	-9.8	-28.2			
12/74	11.0	10.6	10.7	11.8	8.8	7.9	8.1	10.1	6.7	6.2	7.0	5.1	7.0	5.6	4.0	1.2	2.7	-3.0	-7.8	-5.2	-6.9	-14.4	-26.0	-27.0		
12/75	11.6	11.3	11.4	12.6	9.8	9.0	9.3	11.3	8.2	7.7	8.7	7.0	9.1	8.0	6.8	4.4	6.3	1.4	-2.2	1.3	1.6	-2.5	-7.2	5.9	54.9	
12/76	11.9	11.6	11.8	13.0	10.3	9.6	9.9	12.0	9.0	8.7	9.8	8.2	10.3	9.4	8.4	6.4	8.4	4.2	1.2	5.2	6.4	4.1	2.2	16.2	49.1	40.3

Purchase date column groups (as printed): 12/50–12/54; 12/55–12/59; 12/60–12/64; 12/65–12/69; 12/70–12/75.

Percent per annum, compounded annually.

Source: Lawrence Fisher and Myron Scholes (compilers), CRSP Monthly Master File for Common Stocks Listed on the New York Stock Exchange (magnetic tape). See Appendix A.

Held Until	Purchased 12/25	12/26	12/27	12/28	12/29	Purchased 12/30	12/31	12/32	12/33	12/34	Purchased 12/35	12/36	12/37	12/38	12/39	Purchased 12/40	12/41	12/42	12/43	12/44	Purchased 12/45	12/46	12/47	12/48	12/49
12/26	2.3																								
12/27	17.7	32.0																							
12/28	25.1	39.4	47.2																						
12/29	9.7	11.4	1.8	−29.5																					
12/30	0.9	−0.3	−10.0	−29.5	−33.6																				
12/31	−6.1	−8.1	−16.7	−32.4	−35.8	−42.3																			
12/32	−5.2	−6.7	−13.3	−25.6	−26.0	−23.5	0.1																		
12/33	1.0	0.9	−3.6	−12.4	−7.2	4.4	43.8	105.4																	
12/34	1.9	1.7	−2.2	−9.1	−3.8	6.1	31.7	52.9	12.9																
12/35	4.4	4.4	1.2	−4.4	1.6	11.8	34.9	51.2	28.8	46.3															
12/36	6.3	6.5	3.8	−0.9	5.5	15.8	36.9	50.6	34.5	47.8	45.2														
12/37	2.5	2.1	−0.9	−5.6	−1.5	4.8	17.9	23.1	7.0	4.9	−12.5	−47.5													
12/38	4.3	4.1	1.5	−2.6	1.8	8.1	20.3	25.3	12.1	11.5	0.2	−17.0	34.3												
12/39	4.0	3.8	1.3	−2.5	1.6	7.1	17.3	21.1	9.7	8.5	−0.3	−12.1	14.8	−2.9											
12/40	3.4	3.1	0.8	−2.8	0.9	5.7	14.8	17.9	7.5	5.9	−1.8	−10.9	7.2	−5.4	−11.0										
12/41	2.6	2.1	−0.1	−3.6	−0.3	4.1	12.2	14.5	4.9	2.9	−3.9	−11.7	1.3	−8.5	−13.5	−17.7									
12/42	2.6	2.3	0.1	−3.1	0.1	4.3	11.9	14.0	5.1	3.5	−2.4	−8.9	3.0	−4.4	−5.8	−2.3	19.5								
12/43	3.4	3.2	1.3	−1.7	1.6	6.0	13.4	15.5	7.5	6.5	1.5	−3.8	8.5	3.9	5.1	13.2	38.5	53.2							
12/44	4.1	4.0	2.2	−0.5	2.9	7.1	14.3	16.5	9.1	8.5	4.2	−0.3	11.6	8.2	10.4	18.9	39.3	46.5	36.1						
12/45	5.2	5.2	3.6	1.2	4.7	9.1	16.0	18.3	11.7	11.5	7.9	4.1	15.9	13.6	16.9	26.1	45.7	52.4	47.2	57.1					
12/46	4.1	4.1	2.5	0.1	3.3	7.3	13.8	15.8	9.2	8.6	5.0	1.2	11.1	8.4	10.2	15.8	27.5	28.4	18.6	10.4	−23.2				
12/47	3.9	3.8	2.2	−0.1	2.9	6.6	12.9	14.7	8.3	7.6	4.1	0.6	9.5	7.1	8.1	12.3	20.8	20.5	11.7	4.1	−15.8	−8.4			
12/48	3.7	3.6	2.0	−0.3	2.6	6.2	12.2	13.9	7.6	6.9	3.4	0.1	8.2	5.9	6.8	10.3	17.3	16.3	8.5	2.0	−12.3	−6.3	−5.5		
12/49	4.1	4.0	2.5	0.3	3.1	6.6	12.5	14.1	8.1	7.5	4.3	1.2	9.0	6.8	7.9	11.3	18.0	17.2	10.4	5.6	−5.4	1.7	7.3	21.5	
12/50	4.5	4.4	3.0	0.9	3.7	7.2	13.0	14.6	8.8	8.3	5.3	2.4	9.9	8.0	9.1	12.5	18.7	18.2	12.4	8.4	−0.2	7.3	13.4	24.5	28.4
12/51	4.7	4.6	3.2	1.2	3.9	7.4	12.9	14.5	8.8	8.4	5.5	2.8	9.8	8.0	9.1	12.2	17.9	17.4	12.2	8.7	1.5	7.9	12.5	19.6	18.7
12/52	4.7	4.7	3.4	1.4	4.1	7.4	12.8	14.3	8.9	8.4	5.6	3.1	9.8	8.1	9.1	12.1	17.5	16.8	11.9	8.7	2.3	8.2	12.0	17.1	15.4
12/53	4.6	4.5	3.2	1.3	3.9	7.0	12.4	13.9	8.5	8.0	5.3	2.8	9.2	7.4	8.4	11.1	16.1	15.4	10.7	7.7	1.8	6.7	9.7	13.4	10.8
12/54	5.3	5.4	4.1	2.3	4.9	8.0	13.2	14.7	9.6	9.3	6.8	4.5	10.7	9.2	10.3	13.1	18.1	17.6	13.5	11.0	6.0	11.2	14.7	19.1	18.3
12/55	5.6	5.6	4.5	2.7	5.3	8.4	13.5	14.9	10.0	9.8	7.3	5.1	11.1	9.7	10.8	13.4	18.1	17.8	14.1	11.7	7.2	12.1	15.4	19.3	18.9
12/56	5.6	5.7	4.5	2.9	5.3	8.3	13.4	14.8	10.0	9.7	7.3	5.2	11.0	9.7	10.6	13.1	17.4	17.1	13.6	11.4	7.2	11.7	14.5	17.9	17.3
12/57	5.3	5.3	4.1	2.4	4.8	7.7	12.7	14.1	9.2	8.9	6.5	4.4	10.0	8.6	9.5	11.8	15.9	15.4	11.8	9.6	5.5	9.3	11.6	14.3	13.0
12/58	5.9	5.9	4.8	3.2	5.6	8.5	13.3	14.6	10.0	9.8	7.5	5.6	11.1	9.8	10.7	13.0	17.1	16.7	13.3	11.4	7.7	11.6	14.1	16.9	16.2
12/59	6.0	6.0	4.9	3.4	5.7	8.6	13.4	14.7	10.1	10.0	7.7	5.8	11.2	9.9	10.8	13.0	16.9	16.5	13.3	11.4	8.0	11.7	14.2	16.8	16.2
12/60	5.9	6.0	4.8	3.3	5.6	8.4	13.1	14.4	9.9	9.7	7.5	5.6	10.8	9.5	10.3	12.4	16.3	15.8	12.6	10.8	7.4	10.9	13.2	15.5	14.7
12/61	6.3	6.3	5.2	3.7	6.0	8.8	13.3	14.6	10.2	10.1	7.9	6.2	11.2	10.0	10.8	12.9	16.6	16.2	13.1	11.4	8.3	11.7	13.8	16.0	15.3
12/62	5.9	5.9	4.8	3.3	5.5	8.2	12.8	14.1	9.7	9.5	7.3	5.5	10.4	9.2	10.0	12.0	15.6	15.1	11.9	10.2	7.0	10.2	12.1	14.0	13.2
12/63	6.1	6.1	5.0	3.6	5.8	8.4	12.9	14.2	9.8	9.6	7.5	5.8	10.6	9.4	10.2	12.2	15.6	15.1	12.1	10.5	7.5	10.6	12.4	14.2	13.4
12/64	6.2	6.2	5.2	3.7	5.9	8.5	12.9	14.2	9.9	9.7	7.7	6.0	10.7	9.5	10.3	12.2	15.6	15.2	12.2	10.7	7.8	10.8	12.5	14.3	13.6
12/65	6.3	6.4	5.3	4.0	6.1	8.7	13.1	14.3	10.1	10.0	7.9	6.3	10.9	9.8	10.6	12.4	15.7	15.3	12.5	11.0	8.3	11.3	13.0	14.8	14.2
12/66	6.1	6.1	5.1	3.8	5.8	8.4	12.8	14.0	9.7	9.6	7.6	6.0	10.5	9.3	10.1	11.9	15.1	14.7	11.8	10.3	7.6	10.5	12.1	13.7	13.1
12/67	6.5	6.5	5.5	4.2	6.2	8.7	13.0	14.2	10.1	10.0	8.1	6.5	10.9	9.9	10.6	12.4	15.5	15.1	12.4	10.9	8.4	11.2	12.8	14.4	13.8
12/68	6.5	6.6	5.6	4.4	6.3	8.8	13.0	14.2	10.2	10.0	8.1	6.7	10.9	9.9	10.7	12.4	15.5	15.1	12.4	11.0	8.5	11.2	12.8	14.4	13.8
12/69	6.3	6.3	5.3	4.0	5.9	8.3	12.6	13.8	9.7	9.4	7.6	6.1	10.4	9.3	10.0	11.7	14.8	14.3	11.5	10.1	7.5	10.1	11.6	13.1	12.4
12/70	6.1	6.1	5.1	3.8	5.8	8.2	12.4	13.6	9.4	9.2	7.3	5.9	10.1	9.2	9.7	11.4	14.4	13.9	11.1	9.6	7.1	9.6	11.0	12.5	11.7
12/71	6.2	6.2	5.2	4.0	5.9	8.2	12.4	13.6	9.5	9.3	7.4	6.0	10.2	9.2	9.7	11.4	14.4	13.9	11.2	9.7	7.3	9.8	11.2	12.6	11.9
12/72	6.2	6.2	5.3	4.1	5.9	8.3	12.4	13.6	9.5	9.3	7.5	6.0	10.1	9.1	9.7	11.3	14.3	13.8	11.1	9.7	7.4	9.8	11.1	12.5	11.8
12/73	5.9	5.9	4.9	3.7	5.5	7.9	12.1	13.4	9.1	8.8	7.0	5.5	9.6	8.5	9.1	10.8	13.8	13.3	10.4	9.0	6.6	8.9	10.2	11.5	10.7
12/74	5.6	5.5	4.6	3.3	5.1	7.5	11.9	13.2	8.8	8.5	6.5	5.0	9.3	8.2	8.7	10.3	13.5	12.9	9.9	8.3	5.8	8.1	9.3	10.6	9.7
12/75	5.7	5.7	4.7	3.5	5.3	7.7	12.0	13.3	8.9	8.6	6.8	5.2	9.4	8.4	8.9	10.5	13.6	13.0	10.1	8.6	6.1	8.4	9.6	10.9	10.1
12/76	5.8	5.8	4.9	3.7	5.5	7.8	12.0	13.3	9.0	8.7	6.9	5.4	9.5	8.6	9.0	10.6	13.6	13.1	10.2	8.8	6.4	8.6	9.8	11.1	10.3

Table XIV

Internal Rates of Return* on Common Stocks:
    Dividends Consumed,
    Cash to Portfolio,
    Equal Initial Weighting,
    Tax-Exempt,
    Deflated by the Consumer Price Index

Held Until	Purchased 12/50	12/51	12/52	12/53	12/54	Purchased 12/55	12/56	12/57	12/58	12/59	Purchased 12/60	12/61	12/62	12/63	12/64	Purchased 12/65	12/66	12/67	12/68	12/69	Purchased 12/70	12/71	12/72	12/73	12/74	12/75
12/51	8.5																									
12/52	8.8	7.9																								
12/53	5.2	2.8	−3.8																							
12/54	15.3	17.4	22.1	55.8																						
12/55	16.2	18.2	21.7	37.9	18.7																					
12/56	14.7	15.8	17.7	26.6	11.9	3.6																				
12/57	10.4	10.4	10.6	14.6	2.1	−6.1	−16.1																			
12/58	14.2	15.0	16.1	21.0	12.3	9.9	13.6	55.4																		
12/59	14.4	15.1	16.2	20.3	13.0	11.2	14.4	34.4	12.9																	
12/60	13.1	13.6	14.3	17.4	10.8	8.9	10.7	20.8	5.1	−3.5																
12/61	14.0	14.6	15.3	18.3	12.8	11.6	13.8	22.6	12.2	11.5	27.0															
12/62	11.6	11.9	12.2	14.4	9.1	7.6	8.7	14.5	5.3	2.7	5.2	−14.6														
12/63	12.0	12.2	12.6	14.7	9.9	8.5	9.7	15.0	7.5	6.0	9.3	0.4	16.0													
12/64	12.2	12.4	12.8	14.8	10.4	9.3	10.4	15.3	9.0	8.2	11.5	5.9	17.0	15.3												
12/65	12.8	13.1	13.5	15.6	11.5	10.5	11.7	16.6	11.0	10.7	14.4	11.0	21.0	21.9	26.2											
12/66	11.6	11.8	12.1	13.9	9.8	8.8	9.6	13.9	8.6	8.0	10.5	7.0	13.1	11.0	7.6	−11.1										
12/67	12.5	12.8	13.2	15.1	11.4	10.5	11.5	15.8	11.3	11.2	14.0	11.7	18.4	18.7	19.3	14.0	47.4									
12/68	12.6	12.9	13.4	15.2	11.7	11.0	12.0	15.9	11.9	11.9	14.6	12.6	18.3	18.7	19.2	16.4	35.4	22.6								
12/69	11.1	11.3	11.5	13.0	9.5	8.6	9.3	12.5	8.5	8.0	9.8	7.3	11.3	10.3	9.2	5.0	11.7	−3.3	−24.7							
12/70	10.4	10.5	10.7	12.1	8.7	7.8	8.3	11.1	7.3	6.7	8.1	5.6	8.7	7.3	5.7	2.0	6.2	−4.8	−17.0	−9.7						
12/71	10.6	10.7	10.9	12.3	9.1	8.2	8.7	11.4	7.9	7.4	8.8	6.6	9.5	8.3	7.0	3.8	7.9	−0.4	−7.6	2.0	13.4					
12/72	10.6	10.7	10.8	12.1	9.0	8.2	8.7	11.3	7.8	7.4	8.7	6.7	9.4	8.4	7.2	4.3	7.8	1.1	−4.0	3.5	9.8	3.2				
12/73	9.4	9.3	9.4	10.6	7.4	6.4	6.7	8.9	5.5	5.0	5.9	3.8	5.9	4.5	2.8	−0.3	1.7	−4.4	−9.3	−5.4	−5.6	−14.9	−34.0			
12/74	8.3	8.1	8.1	9.1	5.8	4.7	4.9	6.9	3.4	2.7	3.4	1.1	2.7	1.1	−0.9	−4.0	−2.8	−8.6	−13.4	−11.0	−12.7	−20.7	−33.0	−34.9		
12/75	8.7	8.6	8.7	9.7	6.6	5.6	5.8	7.8	4.6	4.0	4.8	2.7	4.5	3.1	1.6	−1.1	0.5	−4.5	−8.2	−4.9	−4.9	−9.5	−15.1	−3.4	44.7	
12/76	9.0	8.9	9.0	10.0	7.0	6.1	6.4	8.4	5.3	4.8	5.7	3.9	5.6	4.5	3.2	0.9	2.5	−1.8	−4.8	−1.1	−0.1	−2.9	−5.6	7.6	40.8	33.9

*Percent per annum, compounded annually.

Sources: Stock market data—Lawrence Fisher and Myron Scholes
    (compilers), CRSP Monthly Master File for Common Stocks
    Listed on the New York Stock Exchange (magnetic tape).
    See Appendix A.
    Consumer Price Index—U.S. Bureau of Labor Statistics.

Held Until	Purchased 12/25	12/26	12/27	12/28	12/29	12/30	12/31	12/32	12/33	12/34	12/35	12/36	12/37	12/38	12/39	12/40	12/41	12/42	12/43	12/44	12/45	12/46	12/47	12/48	12/49
12/26	0.8																								
12/27	15.6	29.2																							
12/28	23.2	37.3	45.8																						
12/29	8.4	10.3	1.4	−29.3																					
12/30	−1.1	−2.4	−12.0	−31.5	−37.6																				
12/31	−9.0	−11.3	−19.9	−35.8	−40.8	−47.8																			
12/32	−8.9	−10.8	−17.7	−30.2	−32.4	−31.1	−10.3																		
12/33	−2.6	−3.1	−7.8	−16.9	−13.3	−2.5	36.4	106.4																	
12/34	−1.2	−1.7	−5.6	−12.8	−8.5	1.2	28.0	54.8	15.2																
12/35	1.7	1.5	−1.7	−7.4	−2.2	8.2	32.9	54.0	32.0	50.6															
12/36	3.9	4.0	1.3	−3.4	2.3	13.0	35.6	53.1	37.3	50.9	46.9														
12/37	0.5	0.1	−2.9	−7.6	−3.9	2.9	17.4	25.5	9.5	7.5	−10.6	−45.9													
12/38	2.2	1.9	−0.6	−4.7	−0.7	6.1	19.5	26.9	13.7	12.9	0.8	−16.9	30.5												
12/39	2.0	1.7	−0.6	−4.4	−0.7	5.2	16.6	22.4	10.9	9.5	−0.0	−12.1	12.9	−3.4											
12/40	1.6	1.2	−1.0	−4.6	−1.1	4.0	14.2	19.1	8.7	6.8	−1.5	−10.7	6.2	−5.3	−10.3										
12/41	1.2	0.7	−1.4	−4.7	−1.7	3.1	12.3	16.4	6.8	4.8	−2.4	−10.2	2.6	−5.9	−9.5	−10.3									
12/42	1.6	1.3	−0.7	−3.8	−0.7	3.9	12.6	16.4	7.6	6.0	−0.1	−6.4	5.6	−0.4	−0.2	6.3	29.6								
12/43	2.6	2.4	0.7	−2.1	1.1	5.8	14.2	17.9	10.0	9.1	4.0	−1.2	11.2	7.9	10.4	20.8	45.9	56.2							
12/44	3.3	3.3	1.7	−0.8	2.4	7.1	15.2	18.9	11.7	11.1	6.7	2.3	14.3	12.0	15.2	25.3	44.8	48.7	37.4						
12/45	4.6	4.7	3.3	1.1	4.5	9.3	17.1	20.8	14.3	14.2	10.4	6.7	18.6	17.3	21.6	32.0	50.7	54.7	49.0	59.2					
12/46	4.0	4.1	2.8	0.6	3.7	8.1	15.5	18.9	12.6	12.1	8.5	5.0	15.0	13.4	16.2	23.1	34.6	34.4	25.4	19.8	−10.3				
12/47	4.0	4.0	2.7	0.6	3.6	7.7	14.7	17.9	11.8	11.3	7.8	4.5	13.6	12.3	14.2	19.5	27.7	26.5	18.4	12.6	−5.5	−1.5			
12/48	3.8	3.8	2.5	0.4	3.2	7.2	13.9	16.9	11.0	10.3	6.9	3.8	12.0	10.6	12.3	16.6	23.1	21.3	14.0	8.6	−4.7	−2.1	−4.1		
12/49	4.2	4.2	2.9	1.0	3.7	7.6	14.1	17.0	11.3	10.7	7.5	4.6	12.4	11.1	12.7	16.8	22.9	21.3	14.8	10.6	0.3	4.0	6.7	18.0	
12/50	4.8	4.8	3.7	1.8	4.6	8.4	14.8	17.5	12.0	11.7	8.7	6.0	13.5	12.4	14.1	18.1	23.8	22.4	17.0	13.7	5.6	10.4	14.6	25.3	34.2
12/51	5.1	5.2	4.1	2.3	4.9	8.7	14.9	17.5	12.2	11.9	9.0	6.5	13.5	12.5	14.1	17.8	23.0	21.7	16.8	13.9	7.2	11.3	14.6	21.8	24.0
12/52	5.2	5.3	4.2	2.5	5.1	8.6	14.7	17.2	12.1	11.8	9.0	6.6	13.3	12.2	13.8	17.2	22.1	20.7	16.0	13.4	7.4	11.0	13.6	18.6	18.8
12/53	4.9	5.0	4.0	2.3	4.8	8.2	14.1	16.6	11.5	11.2	8.4	6.1	12.5	11.3	12.8	15.9	20.2	18.8	14.4	11.7	6.1	9.0	10.9	14.4	13.0
12/54	5.8	6.0	5.0	3.4	5.9	9.3	15.0	17.5	12.7	12.5	9.9	7.8	14.0	13.0	14.6	17.7	22.1	20.9	17.0	14.8	10.1	13.4	15.8	19.9	20.1
12/55	6.1	6.3	5.3	3.8	6.3	9.6	15.3	17.7	13.0	12.9	10.4	8.3	14.2	13.3	14.8	17.8	21.9	20.9	17.3	15.3	11.0	14.1	16.3	20.0	20.4
12/56	6.2	6.4	5.5	4.0	6.4	9.6	15.1	17.5	12.9	12.8	10.3	8.3	14.1	13.3	14.6	17.3	21.1	20.2	16.8	14.9	10.9	13.7	15.5	18.7	18.9
12/57	5.8	6.0	5.0	3.5	5.8	9.0	14.4	16.7	12.1	11.9	9.4	7.5	13.0	12.1	13.3	15.8	19.4	18.3	14.8	12.9	9.0	11.2	12.6	15.1	14.5
12/58	6.5	6.7	5.8	4.4	6.7	9.8	15.1	17.3	12.9	12.8	10.5	8.7	14.1	13.3	14.6	17.1	20.6	19.6	16.4	14.7	11.2	13.6	15.3	17.9	17.8
12/59	6.7	6.8	5.9	4.6	6.9	10.0	15.1	17.3	13.0	12.9	10.7	8.9	14.1	13.4	14.6	17.0	20.4	19.4	16.3	14.6	11.3	13.7	15.3	17.8	17.8
12/60	6.6	6.8	5.8	4.5	6.7	9.7	14.7	16.9	12.7	12.6	10.4	8.6	13.6	12.8	13.9	16.3	19.5	18.5	15.4	13.8	10.6	12.8	14.3	16.5	16.2
12/61	7.0	7.2	6.2	5.0	7.2	10.1	15.0	17.1	13.0	13.0	10.8	9.1	14.0	13.3	14.4	16.7	19.8	18.8	15.9	14.4	11.4	13.5	14.9	17.0	16.8
12/62	6.6	6.7	5.8	4.5	6.6	9.5	14.4	16.5	12.3	12.2	10.0	8.4	13.2	12.4	13.4	15.6	18.6	17.5	14.5	13.0	10.0	11.9	13.1	14.8	14.4
12/63	6.8	6.9	6.0	4.7	6.9	9.7	14.5	16.6	12.5	12.4	10.2	8.6	13.3	12.5	13.6	15.7	18.6	17.6	14.7	13.2	10.3	12.2	13.4	15.0	14.7
12/64	6.9	7.0	6.2	4.9	7.0	9.8	14.5	16.6	12.5	12.4	10.4	8.8	13.4	12.6	13.6	15.7	18.6	17.6	14.8	13.3	10.6	12.4	13.5	15.1	14.8
12/65	7.1	7.2	6.4	5.2	7.3	10.1	14.7	16.7	12.8	12.7	10.6	9.1	13.6	12.8	13.9	15.9	18.6	17.7	15.0	13.6	11.0	13.0	14.1	15.6	15.4
12/66	6.9	7.0	6.2	5.0	7.0	9.7	14.3	16.3	12.4	12.2	10.2	8.7	13.1	12.3	13.3	15.3	18.0	17.0	14.3	12.9	10.3	12.1	13.1	14.6	14.3
12/67	7.4	7.5	6.7	5.5	7.5	10.1	14.6	16.6	12.8	12.7	10.8	9.3	13.6	12.9	13.9	15.8	18.4	17.5	14.9	13.6	11.1	12.9	13.9	15.4	15.3
12/68	7.5	7.6	6.8	5.7	7.6	10.2	14.6	16.6	12.9	12.7	10.9	9.5	13.6	13.0	14.0	15.9	18.5	17.5	15.0	13.7	11.4	13.1	14.1	15.6	15.4
12/69	7.2	7.3	6.5	5.4	7.2	9.7	14.1	16.2	12.3	12.2	10.3	8.9	13.0	12.4	13.2	15.1	17.7	16.7	14.0	12.8	10.4	11.9	12.9	14.2	14.0
12/70	7.1	7.2	6.3	5.3	7.1	9.6	14.0	16.0	12.1	11.9	10.1	8.7	12.8	12.2	12.9	14.8	17.3	16.3	13.6	12.4	10.0	11.5	12.3	13.6	13.3
12/71	7.1	7.3	6.5	5.4	7.2	9.7	14.0	16.0	12.2	12.0	10.2	8.8	12.9	12.3	13.0	14.8	17.3	16.3	13.7	12.5	10.2	11.7	12.5	13.8	13.5
12/72	7.3	7.4	6.6	5.6	7.4	9.7	14.0	16.0	12.2	12.0	10.2	8.9	12.8	12.1	12.9	14.7	17.2	16.2	13.6	12.5	10.2	11.7	12.5	13.8	13.5
12/73	6.9	7.0	6.3	5.2	6.9	9.3	13.7	15.7	11.7	11.5	9.7	8.3	12.3	11.6	12.3	14.1	16.6	15.6	12.9	11.7	9.4	10.8	11.5	12.7	12.4
12/74	6.5	6.6	5.8	4.8	6.5	8.9	13.4	15.4	11.4	11.1	9.3	7.8	11.9	11.2	11.9	13.7	16.2	15.1	12.3	11.0	8.6	9.9	10.6	11.7	11.3
12/75	6.8	6.9	6.1	5.2	6.8	9.2	13.5	15.6	11.6	11.4	9.6	8.2	12.2	11.6	12.2	13.9	16.4	15.3	12.7	11.4	9.2	10.4	11.1	12.2	11.9
12/76	7.0	7.1	6.4	5.4	7.1	9.4	13.6	15.6	11.7	11.5	9.8	8.5	12.3	11.8	12.4	14.1	16.5	15.5	12.9	11.7	9.5	10.8	11.4	12.5	12.2

Table XV

Internal Rates of Return* on Common Stocks:
  Dividends Consumed,
  Cash to Portfolio,
  Equal Initial Weighting,
  Lower Tax Rate,
  Current Dollars

Held until	12/50	12/51	12/52	12/53	12/54	12/55	12/56	12/57	12/58	12/59	12/60	12/61	12/62	12/63	12/64	12/65	12/66	12/67	12/68	12/69	12/70	12/71	12/72	12/73	12/74	12/75
12/51	13.5																									
12/52	11.2	7.5																								
12/53	6.5	2.3	-4.4																							
12/54	16.1	16.7	21.0	53.8																						
12/55	16.9	17.5	20.8	36.7	18.4																					
12/56	15.6	15.7	17.6	26.6	12.9	5.9																				
12/57	11.4	10.6	10.9	15.0	3.4	-4.1	-14.2																			
12/58	15.4	15.4	16.7	21.8	13.8	12.0	15.6	57.2																		
12/59	15.5	15.6	16.8	21.2	14.5	13.1	16.2	35.8	14.0																	
12/60	14.1	14.1	14.9	18.1	12.1	10.6	12.1	21.9	6.0	-2.7																
12/61	15.0	15.1	16.0	19.1	14.0	13.1	15.1	23.5	13.0	12.1	27.1															
12/62	12.6	12.3	12.7	15.0	10.2	8.9	9.8	15.2	5.9	3.2	5.5	-14.2														
12/63	12.9	12.7	13.1	15.3	10.9	9.8	10.8	15.8	8.2	6.7	9.9	1.1	17.1													
12/64	13.1	12.9	13.4	15.5	11.5	10.5	11.5	16.0	9.7	8.8	12.1	6.7	17.9	15.9												
12/65	13.7	13.6	14.2	16.3	12.6	11.8	12.8	17.4	11.9	11.6	15.2	12.0	22.1	23.0	27.8											
12/66	12.6	12.4	12.8	14.7	11.0	10.1	10.8	14.8	9.6	9.0	11.6	8.3	14.6	12.6	9.6	-8.8										
12/67	13.7	13.6	14.1	16.1	12.8	12.1	12.9	17.0	12.6	12.5	15.4	13.3	20.2	20.8	21.8	17.0	50.9									
12/68	13.9	13.9	14.5	16.3	13.2	12.7	13.6	17.5	13.5	13.6	16.4	14.6	20.6	21.3	22.3	20.0	39.6	27.5								
12/69	12.4	12.3	12.7	14.3	11.2	10.5	11.1	14.2	10.2	9.9	11.7	9.5	13.8	13.1	12.5	8.7	15.9	1.1	-20.8							
12/70	11.8	11.6	11.9	13.4	10.5	9.7	10.2	12.9	9.2	8.7	10.2	8.0	11.3	10.3	9.1	5.7	10.4	-0.5	-12.8	-5.5						
12/71	12.1	11.9	12.2	13.7	10.9	10.2	10.7	13.3	9.9	9.5	11.0	9.1	12.2	11.3	10.4	7.5	11.9	3.7	-3.6	5.8	16.4					
12/72	12.1	11.9	12.2	13.6	10.9	10.2	10.7	13.2	9.9	9.6	11.0	9.2	12.2	11.4	10.5	7.9	11.6	5.0	-0.2	7.0	12.8	6.0				
12/73	10.9	10.6	10.8	12.0	9.3	8.5	8.8	10.9	7.7	7.3	8.3	6.5	8.8	7.7	6.4	3.6	5.8	-0.2	-5.1	-1.3	-1.7	-10.6	-28.9			
12/74	9.7	9.4	9.5	10.6	7.8	6.9	7.1	8.9	5.7	5.2	5.9	4.1	5.9	4.5	3.0	0.2	1.6	-4.0	-8.7	-6.2	-7.9	-15.3	-26.9	-28.1		
12/75	10.4	10.1	10.3	11.4	8.8	8.1	8.3	10.2	7.2	6.8	7.7	6.1	8.0	7.0	5.8	3.5	5.3	0.5	-3.0	0.4	0.6	-3.5	-8.2	4.6	52.5	
12/76	10.8	10.6	10.8	11.9	9.4	8.8	9.0	10.9	8.2	7.9	8.9	7.4	9.3	8.5	7.5	5.5	7.5	3.3	0.4	4.3	5.5	3.1	1.2	14.9	47.0	38.6

*Percent per annum, compounded annually.

Sources: Stock market data—Lawrence Fisher and Myron Scholes (compilers), CRSP Monthly Master File for Common Stocks Listed on the New York Stock Exchange (magnetic tape). See Appendix A.
Income tax rates—Income levels estimated from U.S. Bureau of the Census, Current Population Reports, Series P-60, Nos. 101 and 103 and Historical Statistics of the United States. Tax rates were found in U.S. Internal Revenue Service, Statistics of Income and Your Federal Income Tax.

Held Until	12/25	12/26	12/27	12/28	12/29	12/30	12/31	12/32	12/33	12/34	12/35	12/36	12/37	12/38	12/39	12/40	12/41	12/42	12/43	12/44	12/45	12/46	12/47	12/48	12/49
12/26	2.3																								
12/27	17.7	32.0																							
12/28	25.1	39.4	47.2																						
12/29	9.7	11.4	1.8	−29.5																					
12/30	0.9	−0.3	−10.0	−29.5	−33.6																				
12/31	−6.1	−8.1	−16.7	−32.4	−35.8	−42.3																			
12/32	−5.2	−6.7	−13.3	−25.6	−26.0	−23.5	0.1																		
12/33	1.0	0.9	−3.6	−12.4	−7.2	4.4	43.8	105.4																	
12/34	1.9	1.7	−2.2	−9.1	−3.8	6.1	31.7	52.9	12.9																
12/35	4.4	4.4	1.2	−4.4	1.6	11.8	34.9	51.2	28.8	46.3															
12/36	6.3	6.5	3.8	−0.9	5.5	15.8	36.9	50.6	34.5	47.8	45.2														
12/37	2.5	2.1	−0.9	−5.6	−1.5	4.8	17.9	23.1	7.0	4.9	−12.5	−47.5													
12/38	4.3	4.1	1.5	−2.6	1.8	8.1	20.3	25.3	12.1	11.5	0.2	−17.0	34.3												
12/39	4.0	3.8	1.3	−2.5	1.6	7.1	17.3	21.1	9.7	8.5	−0.3	−12.1	14.8	−2.9											
12/40	3.4	3.1	0.7	−2.8	0.9	5.7	14.8	17.9	7.5	5.8	−1.9	−10.9	7.1	−5.5	−11.2										
12/41	2.5	2.1	−0.2	−3.6	−0.4	4.0	12.1	14.4	4.7	2.8	−4.1	−11.8	1.1	−8.8	−13.9	−18.3									
12/42	2.5	2.2	0.0	−3.2	0.0	4.2	11.8	13.8	4.9	3.3	−2.7	−9.1	2.6	−4.7	−6.3	−3.0	18.5								
12/43	3.3	3.1	1.2	−1.8	1.5	5.8	13.2	15.2	7.2	6.2	1.2	−4.1	8.1	3.4	4.5	12.4	37.3	51.4							
12/44	3.9	3.8	2.1	−0.7	2.7	6.9	14.1	16.2	8.8	8.2	3.9	−0.6	11.1	7.7	9.7	18.0	38.0	44.8	34.5						
12/45	5.0	5.1	3.5	1.1	4.6	8.9	15.8	18.0	11.4	11.2	7.6	3.7	15.4	13.1	16.3	25.3	44.5	50.9	45.8	55.7					
12/46	3.9	3.9	2.3	−0.1	3.1	7.0	13.4	15.4	8.8	8.1	4.5	0.8	10.5	7.8	9.4	14.8	26.2	26.8	17.2	9.2	−24.1				
12/47	3.7	3.6	2.0	−0.4	2.6	6.3	12.4	14.2	7.8	7.0	3.6	0.1	8.7	6.3	7.2	11.2	19.3	18.7	10.2	2.8	−16.8	−9.6			
12/48	3.4	3.3	1.7	−0.7	2.2	5.7	11.7	13.3	7.0	6.2	2.8	−0.6	7.3	5.0	5.8	9.1	15.6	14.5	6.9	0.7	−13.3	−7.5	−6.7		
12/49	3.8	3.7	2.2	−0.0	2.7	6.2	11.9	13.5	7.6	6.9	3.7	0.6	8.1	6.0	6.9	10.0	16.4	15.5	9.0	4.3	−6.3	0.6	6.1	20.1	
12/50	4.2	4.1	2.7	0.6	3.4	6.8	12.4	14.0	8.2	7.7	4.7	1.8	9.0	7.2	8.2	11.4	17.2	16.6	11.0	7.2	−1.1	6.2	12.2	23.1	26.9
12/51	4.4	4.3	2.9	0.9	3.6	6.9	12.4	13.8	8.2	7.8	4.9	2.2	9.0	7.2	8.1	11.1	16.4	15.7	10.8	7.5	0.5	6.8	11.3	18.2	17.2
12/52	4.4	4.4	3.0	1.1	3.7	6.9	12.2	13.7	8.2	7.8	5.0	2.5	8.9	7.2	8.1	10.9	15.9	15.2	10.5	7.5	1.4	7.0	10.7	15.7	14.0
12/53	4.2	4.2	2.9	0.9	3.4	6.5	11.8	13.1	7.8	7.4	4.6	2.1	8.3	6.5	7.4	9.9	14.5	13.7	9.3	6.4	0.8	5.5	8.4	11.9	9.3
12/54	5.0	5.1	3.8	2.0	4.5	7.6	12.7	14.1	9.1	8.8	6.2	4.0	9.9	8.4	9.4	12.0	16.6	16.1	12.3	9.9	5.1	10.2	13.6	17.8	17.0
12/55	5.3	5.3	4.2	2.5	4.9	8.0	12.9	14.3	9.5	9.2	6.7	4.6	10.3	8.9	9.9	12.4	16.7	16.3	12.9	10.7	6.4	11.1	14.3	18.1	17.7
12/56	5.3	5.4	4.2	2.6	5.0	7.9	12.8	14.1	9.4	9.2	6.7	4.7	10.2	8.9	9.8	12.0	16.0	15.7	12.4	10.4	6.4	10.7	13.4	16.6	16.2
12/57	5.0	5.0	3.8	2.1	4.4	7.3	12.1	13.3	8.6	8.3	5.9	3.8	9.1	7.7	8.5	10.6	14.4	13.8	10.5	8.5	4.6	8.2	10.5	13.0	11.8
12/58	5.6	5.6	4.5	2.9	5.2	8.0	12.7	14.0	9.5	9.3	7.0	5.1	10.3	9.1	9.9	12.0	15.7	15.3	12.2	10.4	6.9	10.6	13.1	15.7	15.1
12/59	5.7	5.7	4.6	3.1	5.4	8.2	12.8	14.0	9.6	9.4	7.2	5.4	10.4	9.2	10.0	12.0	15.6	15.1	12.2	10.5	7.2	10.8	13.2	15.7	15.2
12/60	5.7	5.7	4.5	3.0	5.3	7.9	12.5	13.7	9.3	9.1	6.9	5.1	9.9	8.7	9.5	11.4	14.8	14.4	11.4	9.8	6.6	10.0	12.1	14.4	13.7
12/61	6.0	6.1	4.9	3.5	5.7	8.3	12.7	13.9	9.7	9.6	7.4	5.7	10.4	9.3	10.0	11.9	15.3	14.8	12.0	10.5	7.5	10.8	12.8	15.0	14.3
12/62	5.6	5.6	4.5	3.0	5.2	7.8	12.2	13.4	9.0	8.9	6.7	5.0	9.6	8.4	9.1	10.9	14.1	13.6	10.7	9.2	6.3	9.3	11.1	12.9	12.1
12/63	5.8	5.8	4.7	3.3	5.4	8.0	12.3	13.5	9.2	9.1	7.0	5.3	9.8	8.6	9.4	11.1	14.2	13.7	10.9	9.5	6.7	9.6	11.4	13.1	12.4
12/64	5.9	5.9	4.9	3.5	5.5	8.1	12.3	13.4	9.3	9.1	7.2	5.6	9.9	8.8	9.5	11.2	14.2	13.7	11.1	9.7	7.1	9.9	11.5	13.2	12.5
12/65	6.0	6.1	5.1	3.7	5.8	8.3	12.5	13.6	9.6	9.4	7.4	5.9	10.1	9.1	9.8	11.4	14.3	13.9	11.4	10.1	7.6	10.4	12.1	13.7	13.2
12/66	5.8	5.8	4.8	3.5	5.5	7.9	12.1	13.2	9.1	9.0	7.0	5.5	9.6	8.6	9.2	10.8	13.7	13.2	10.7	9.3	6.8	9.5	11.1	12.6	12.0
12/67	6.2	6.3	5.2	4.0	5.9	8.3	12.4	13.4	9.6	9.4	7.6	6.1	10.1	9.1	9.8	11.4	14.1	13.7	11.3	10.0	7.7	10.3	11.8	13.4	12.9
12/68	6.3	6.3	5.3	4.1	6.0	8.4	12.3	13.4	9.6	9.4	7.6	6.2	10.2	9.2	9.9	11.4	14.2	13.7	11.3	10.1	7.8	10.4	11.9	13.4	12.9
12/69	6.0	6.0	4.9	3.7	5.5	7.8	11.9	13.0	9.0	8.8	7.0	5.6	9.5	8.6	9.1	10.6	13.3	12.8	10.3	9.1	6.8	9.2	10.5	11.9	11.3
12/70	5.8	5.8	4.8	3.5	5.3	7.6	11.7	12.8	8.8	8.5	6.7	5.3	9.2	8.4	8.7	10.2	12.8	12.3	9.9	8.6	6.3	8.6	9.9	11.2	10.6
12/71	5.8	5.8	4.9	3.7	5.5	7.7	11.7	12.8	8.8	8.6	6.9	5.5	9.3	8.4	8.8	10.2	12.8	12.3	9.9	8.7	6.5	8.8	10.1	11.4	10.8
12/72	5.9	5.9	4.9	3.8	5.6	7.7	11.7	12.8	8.8	8.6	6.9	5.5	9.3	8.3	8.8	10.2	12.7	12.2	9.9	8.7	6.6	8.8	10.1	11.3	10.7
12/73	5.5	5.5	4.6	3.4	5.1	7.3	11.3	12.4	8.3	8.1	6.3	4.9	8.6	7.6	8.1	9.5	12.1	11.5	9.1	7.8	5.7	7.8	8.9	10.1	9.5
12/74	5.1	5.1	4.1	2.9	4.6	6.9	11.0	12.2	7.9	7.6	5.8	4.3	8.1	7.2	7.5	8.9	11.6	10.9	8.4	7.0	4.7	6.8	7.9	9.0	8.2
12/75	5.3	5.3	4.3	3.1	4.8	7.1	11.1	12.3	8.1	7.8	6.0	4.6	8.4	7.5	7.8	9.2	11.7	11.2	8.6	7.4	5.2	7.2	8.3	9.4	8.7
12/76	5.4	5.4	4.5	3.3	5.0	7.2	11.2	12.3	8.2	7.9	6.2	4.8	8.5	7.7	7.9	9.3	11.8	11.3	8.8	7.6	5.5	7.5	8.5	9.6	9.0

Purchased-year header groups: 12/25–12/29; 12/30–12/34; 12/35–12/39; 12/40–12/44; 12/45–12/49

Table XVI

Internal Rates of Return* on Common Stocks:
  Dividends Consumed,
  Cash to Portfolio,
  Equal Initial Weighting,
  Lower Tax Rate,
  Deflated by the Consumer Price Index

	__ Purchased __					__ Purchased __					__ Purchased __					__ Purchased __					__ Purchased __					
	12/50	12/51	12/52	12/53	12/54	12/55	12/56	12/57	12/58	12/59	12/60	12/61	12/62	12/63	12/64	12/65	12/66	12/67	12/68	12/69	12/70	12/71	12/72	12/73	12/74	12/75
51	7.2																									
52	7.5	6.6																								
53	3.8	1.5	−5.0																							
54	14.1	16.3	20.9	54.5																						
55	15.1	17.1	20.6	36.8	17.9																					
56	13.7	14.8	16.7	25.5	11.1	2.9																				
57	9.3	9.3	9.6	13.5	1.3	−6.8	−16.8																			
58	13.2	14.0	15.2	20.1	11.6	9.2	12.9	54.5																		
59	13.4	14.2	15.3	19.4	12.3	10.6	13.8	33.6	12.3																	
60	12.1	12.7	13.4	16.4	10.1	8.2	10.0	20.0	4.4	−4.1																
61	13.1	13.7	14.5	17.5	12.2	11.0	13.2	21.9	11.6	10.9	26.3															
62	10.7	11.0	11.3	13.5	8.4	6.9	8.0	13.7	4.6	2.0	4.5	−15.2														
63	11.0	11.3	11.7	13.8	9.2	7.9	9.0	14.2	6.8	5.3	8.6	−0.3	15.2													
64	11.2	11.5	11.9	13.9	9.7	8.6	9.7	14.5	8.3	7.5	10.8	5.3	16.2	14.5												
65	11.9	12.2	12.7	14.7	10.8	9.8	11.0	15.8	10.4	10.1	13.7	10.3	20.2	21.2	25.4											
66	10.7	10.8	11.2	13.0	9.1	8.1	8.9	13.0	7.9	7.3	9.8	6.3	12.3	10.2	6.8	−11.8										
67	11.6	12.0	12.4	14.2	10.7	9.9	10.8	15.0	10.6	10.5	13.3	11.1	17.6	18.0	18.5	13.3	46.5									
68	11.8	12.1	12.6	14.3	11.0	10.3	11.3	15.2	11.2	11.3	13.9	11.9	17.5	18.0	18.5	15.7	34.4	21.7								
69	10.1	10.3	10.6	12.1	8.8	7.9	8.5	11.6	7.7	7.3	8.9	6.6	10.4	9.5	8.4	4.3	10.8	−4.1	−25.3							
70	9.4	9.5	9.7	11.1	7.9	7.0	7.5	10.2	6.5	5.9	7.2	4.8	7.8	6.5	4.9	1.2	5.3	−5.6	−17.6	−10.4						
71	9.6	9.7	10.0	11.3	8.2	7.4	7.9	10.5	7.1	6.6	7.9	5.8	8.6	7.5	6.2	3.1	7.1	−1.1	−8.2	1.3	12.6					
72	9.6	9.7	9.9	11.1	8.2	7.4	7.9	10.4	7.1	6.7	7.9	5.9	8.6	7.6	6.4	3.6	7.0	0.3	−4.6	2.8	9.1	2.5				
73	8.2	8.2	8.3	9.4	6.4	5.5	5.7	7.8	4.6	4.1	4.9	2.9	4.9	3.6	1.9	−1.1	0.8	−5.2	−10.0	−6.2	−6.4	−15.6	−34.6			
74	6.9	6.8	6.8	7.8	4.7	3.7	3.8	5.6	2.3	1.6	2.2	0.1	1.5	−0.1	−1.9	−5.0	−3.9	−9.6	−14.2	−11.9	−13.7	−21.6	−33.8	−35.9		
75	7.4	7.4	7.4	8.4	5.5	4.6	4.8	6.6	3.6	3.0	3.7	1.8	3.4	2.1	0.6	−2.0	−0.5	−5.4	−8.9	−5.8	−5.8	−10.4	−16.0	−4.6	42.5	
76	7.8	7.8	7.8	8.8	6.0	5.2	5.4	7.3	4.4	3.9	4.7	3.0	4.6	3.5	2.2	0.0	1.6	−2.7	−5.5	−1.9	−1.0	−3.8	−6.5	6.3	38.8	32.3

*Percent per annum, compounded annually.

Sources: Stock market data—Lawrence Fisher and Myron Scholes (compilers), CRSP Monthly Master File for Common Stocks Listed on the New York Stock Exchange (magnetic tape). See Appendix A.
Consumer Price Index—U.S. Bureau of Labor Statistics.
Income tax rates—Income levels estimated from U.S. Bureau of the Census, Current Population Reports, Series P-60, Nos. 101 and 103 and Historical Statistics of the United States. Tax rates were found in U.S. Internal Revenue Service, Statistics of Income and Your Federal Income Tax.

Held Until	Purchased 12/25	12/26	12/27	12/28	12/29	12/30	12/31	12/32	12/33	12/34	12/35	12/36	12/37	12/38	12/39	12/40	12/41	12/42	12/43	12/44	12/45	12/46	12/47	12/48	12/49
12/26	0.7																								
12/27	15.6	29.2																							
12/28	23.2	37.2	45.7																						
12/29	8.4	10.3	1.4	−29.4																					
12/30	−1.2	−2.5	−12.0	−31.5	−37.6																				
12/31	−9.0	−11.4	−20.0	−35.8	−40.8	−47.8																			
12/32	−8.9	−10.9	−17.7	−30.3	−32.4	−31.1	−10.3																		
12/33	−2.6	−3.1	−7.8	−16.9	−13.3	−2.5	36.4	106.3																	
12/34	−1.3	−1.7	−5.7	−12.8	−8.5	1.2	28.0	54.8	15.2																
12/35	1.7	1.5	−1.7	−7.5	−2.2	8.2	32.9	53.9	31.9	50.5															
12/36	3.8	3.9	1.2	−3.5	2.2	12.9	35.5	52.9	37.1	50.6	46.4														
12/37	0.4	−0.1	−3.0	−7.7	−4.1	2.7	17.1	25.0	9.1	7.0	−11.2	−46.2													
12/38	2.1	1.8	−0.7	−4.9	−0.8	5.8	19.1	26.5	13.3	12.4	0.3	−17.2	30.1												
12/39	1.9	1.6	−0.8	−4.6	−0.9	4.9	16.2	21.9	10.5	9.0	−0.5	−12.4	12.5	−3.7											
12/40	1.4	1.0	−1.2	−4.8	−1.4	3.7	13.7	18.5	8.2	6.3	−1.9	−11.1	5.7	−5.8	−10.8										
12/41	0.9	0.4	−1.7	−5.0	−2.1	2.7	11.7	15.6	6.1	4.0	−3.1	−10.8	1.8	−6.8	−10.6	−11.9									
12/42	1.3	0.9	−1.0	−4.2	−1.1	3.4	11.9	15.5	6.8	5.2	−0.9	−7.1	4.5	−1.5	−1.5	4.5	27.2								
12/43	2.2	2.1	0.3	−2.5	0.6	5.3	13.5	17.0	9.2	8.2	3.2	−1.9	10.2	6.8	9.1	18.9	43.4	53.3							
12/44	2.9	2.9	1.3	−1.2	2.0	6.6	14.5	18.0	10.9	10.2	5.9	1.5	13.2	10.8	13.8	23.5	42.4	46.0	35.0						
12/45	4.2	4.4	3.0	0.7	4.1	8.8	16.4	20.0	13.6	13.4	9.7	6.0	17.6	16.3	20.3	30.4	48.6	52.4	46.9	57.2					
12/46	3.6	3.7	2.3	0.1	3.2	7.5	14.6	17.8	11.7	11.2	7.6	4.1	13.8	12.2	14.8	21.3	32.4	32.0	23.4	18.0	−11.6				
12/47	3.5	3.5	2.2	0.1	3.0	7.0	13.8	16.7	10.8	10.2	6.8	3.6	12.2	10.9	12.6	17.4	25.2	23.9	16.2	10.5	−7.1	−3.4			
12/48	3.3	3.2	1.9	−0.2	2.5	6.4	12.8	15.6	9.8	9.1	5.8	2.7	10.4	9.1	10.5	14.5	20.5	18.7	11.7	6.6	−6.3	−3.8	−5.6		
12/49	3.7	3.7	2.4	0.4	3.1	6.7	12.9	15.6	10.1	9.5	6.4	3.6	10.9	9.6	11.0	14.7	20.4	18.7	12.6	8.7	−1.2	2.3	5.1	16.2	
12/50	4.3	4.3	3.1	1.3	3.9	7.7	13.7	16.2	10.9	10.5	7.6	5.0	12.1	11.0	12.5	16.1	21.4	20.0	14.9	11.8	4.2	8.7	12.9	23.5	32.0
12/51	4.6	4.7	3.5	1.7	4.3	7.9	13.8	16.1	11.0	10.7	7.9	5.5	12.0	11.1	12.5	15.8	20.5	19.2	14.7	12.1	5.7	9.6	12.9	19.8	21.8
12/52	4.6	4.7	3.6	1.9	4.4	7.8	13.5	15.8	10.9	10.6	7.9	5.6	11.8	10.8	12.1	15.2	19.6	18.2	13.9	11.5	5.8	9.3	11.8	16.5	16.6
12/53	4.3	4.4	3.3	1.7	4.0	7.3	12.8	15.0	10.2	9.9	7.2	5.0	10.8	9.7	10.9	13.6	17.6	16.2	12.1	9.7	4.5	7.1	8.9	12.1	10.7
12/54	5.3	5.4	4.4	2.9	5.2	8.5	13.9	16.0	11.5	11.3	8.9	6.8	12.5	11.6	12.9	15.7	19.7	18.5	15.0	13.0	8.6	11.7	14.0	17.9	18.1
12/55	5.6	5.7	4.8	3.3	5.7	8.9	14.1	16.3	11.9	11.7	9.3	7.3	12.8	11.9	13.2	15.9	19.6	18.6	15.4	13.5	9.5	12.4	14.6	18.1	18.4
12/56	5.7	5.8	4.9	3.5	5.7	8.8	14.0	16.0	11.8	11.6	9.3	7.4	12.6	11.9	13.0	15.3	18.7	17.8	14.8	13.1	9.5	12.0	13.8	16.7	16.9
12/57	5.2	5.3	4.4	2.9	5.1	8.0	13.0	15.0	10.8	10.5	8.2	6.3	11.3	10.5	11.5	13.6	16.7	15.6	12.6	10.9	7.3	9.3	10.7	12.8	12.3
12/58	6.0	6.2	5.2	3.9	6.1	9.0	13.9	15.8	11.8	11.7	9.5	7.7	12.6	11.9	12.9	15.1	18.2	17.2	14.4	12.9	9.8	11.9	13.5	15.9	15.9
12/59	6.2	6.3	5.3	4.1	6.3	9.2	13.9	15.8	11.9	11.8	9.6	7.9	12.7	12.0	13.0	15.0	18.0	17.0	14.3	12.9	9.9	12.1	13.6	15.9	15.9
12/60	6.1	6.2	5.2	4.0	6.1	8.9	13.5	15.3	11.5	11.4	9.3	7.6	12.1	11.3	12.2	14.2	17.0	16.0	13.4	12.0	9.1	11.1	12.5	14.5	14.2
12/61	6.6	6.7	5.7	4.5	6.6	9.3	13.8	15.6	11.9	11.8	9.8	8.2	12.5	11.9	12.8	14.7	17.4	16.4	13.9	12.6	10.0	11.9	13.2	15.1	14.9
12/62	6.0	6.1	5.2	3.9	5.9	8.6	13.0	14.8	11.0	10.9	8.9	7.3	11.5	10.8	11.6	13.4	15.9	14.9	12.4	11.1	8.4	10.1	11.2	12.7	12.4
12/63	6.2	6.3	5.4	4.2	6.2	8.9	13.2	14.9	11.2	11.1	9.1	7.6	11.7	11.0	11.8	13.6	16.0	15.0	12.6	11.4	8.9	10.5	11.6	13.0	12.7
12/64	6.4	6.5	5.6	4.4	6.3	8.9	13.2	14.9	11.3	11.2	9.3	7.8	11.8	11.1	11.9	13.6	15.9	15.0	12.7	11.6	9.1	10.8	11.7	13.1	12.9
12/65	6.6	6.7	5.9	4.7	6.7	9.3	13.5	15.1	11.6	11.5	9.6	8.2	12.0	11.4	12.2	13.8	16.1	15.2	13.0	11.9	9.7	11.4	12.4	13.8	13.6
12/66	6.3	6.4	5.6	4.4	6.3	8.8	12.9	14.6	11.1	11.0	9.1	7.7	11.5	10.8	11.6	13.1	15.3	14.4	12.2	11.1	8.9	10.5	11.4	12.6	12.4
12/67	6.9	7.0	6.1	5.1	6.9	9.3	13.3	14.9	11.6	11.5	9.7	8.4	12.1	11.5	12.3	13.8	15.9	15.1	13.0	11.9	9.8	11.4	12.3	13.6	13.5
12/68	7.0	7.1	6.3	5.3	7.1	9.4	13.4	15.0	11.7	11.6	9.9	8.6	12.2	11.7	12.4	13.9	16.0	15.2	13.1	12.1	10.1	11.6	12.5	13.8	13.7
12/69	6.7	6.8	5.9	4.9	6.6	8.8	12.7	14.3	11.0	10.9	9.2	7.9	11.4	10.9	11.5	12.9	14.9	14.1	12.0	11.0	9.0	10.3	11.1	12.3	12.1
12/70	6.5	6.6	5.8	4.7	6.4	8.6	12.5	14.1	10.7	10.5	8.9	7.7	11.1	10.7	11.1	12.5	14.4	13.6	11.5	10.5	8.5	9.8	10.5	11.6	11.4
12/71	6.6	6.7	5.9	4.9	6.6	8.7	12.5	14.1	10.8	10.6	9.1	7.8	11.2	10.8	11.2	12.6	14.4	13.6	11.6	10.6	8.7	10.1	10.8	11.9	11.6
12/72	6.7	6.8	6.0	5.1	6.7	8.8	12.5	14.1	10.8	10.7	9.1	7.9	11.2	10.6	11.2	12.5	14.3	13.5	11.5	10.7	8.8	10.1	10.8	11.9	11.6
12/73	6.3	6.4	5.6	4.7	6.2	8.2	12.0	13.6	10.2	10.0	8.4	7.2	10.4	9.9	10.4	11.7	13.5	12.6	10.6	9.7	7.9	9.0	9.6	10.6	10.3
12/74	5.8	5.8	5.1	4.1	5.6	7.7	11.5	13.1	9.7	9.4	7.8	6.5	9.8	9.4	9.7	11.0	12.7	11.8	9.7	8.7	6.9	7.9	8.4	9.3	8.9
12/75	6.1	6.2	5.5	4.5	6.0	8.1	11.8	13.4	10.0	9.8	8.3	7.1	10.3	10.0	10.2	11.4	13.1	12.3	10.3	9.3	7.5	8.6	9.1	10.0	9.7
12/76	6.4	6.4	5.7	4.9	6.3	8.3	12.0	13.5	10.2	10.0	8.5	7.4	10.5	10.2	10.5	11.7	13.3	12.5	10.6	9.7	8.0	9.0	9.5	10.4	10.2

Table XVII

Internal Rates of Return* on Common Stocks:
  Dividends Consumed,
  Cash to Portfolio,
  Equal Initial Weighting,
  Higher Tax Rate,
  Current Dollars

	Purchased					Purchased					Purchased					Purchased					Purchased					
	12/50	12/51	12/52	12/53	12/54	12/55	12/56	12/57	12/58	12/59	12/60	12/61	12/62	12/63	12/64	12/65	12/66	12/67	12/68	12/69	12/70	12/71	12/72	12/73	12/74	12/75
51	11.4																									
52	9.1	5.5																								
53	4.3	0.2	−6.4																							
54	14.2	14.7	19.1	51.4																						
55	15.0	15.7	19.0	34.6	16.7																					
56	13.7	13.8	15.8	24.5	11.2	4.2																				
57	9.3	8.6	8.9	12.8	1.5	−5.8	−15.8																			
58	13.5	13.6	14.9	19.8	12.2	10.4	14.0	55.0																		
59	13.7	13.9	15.1	19.2	12.9	11.6	14.6	33.8	12.5																	
60	12.3	12.3	13.1	16.2	10.5	9.0	10.6	20.0	4.6	−3.9																
61	13.3	13.4	14.3	17.2	12.5	11.7	13.6	21.8	11.6	10.9	25.7															
62	10.7	10.5	10.9	13.0	8.6	7.3	8.3	13.5	4.5	2.0	4.2	−15.1														
63	11.1	10.9	11.4	13.4	9.4	8.3	9.3	14.1	6.9	5.5	8.6	0.1	15.8													
64	11.4	11.2	11.7	13.7	10.0	9.1	10.1	14.5	8.4	7.7	10.9	5.7	16.6	14.7												
65	12.1	12.1	12.6	14.6	11.2	10.4	11.5	16.0	10.7	10.5	14.1	11.0	20.9	21.9	26.7											
66	10.9	10.7	11.2	12.9	9.5	8.7	9.4	13.3	8.4	7.9	10.4	7.2	13.3	11.4	8.5	−9.8										
67	12.1	12.1	12.6	14.5	11.4	10.8	11.7	15.6	11.4	11.5	14.3	12.3	19.1	19.7	20.7	15.9	49.4									
68	12.4	12.5	13.0	14.8	12.0	11.5	12.4	16.1	12.4	12.6	15.3	13.7	19.5	20.2	21.3	19.0	38.4	26.4								
69	10.8	10.7	11.1	12.5	9.8	9.2	9.7	12.7	9.0	8.7	10.5	8.5	12.6	12.0	11.3	7.7	14.6	0.1	−21.6							
70	10.1	10.0	10.3	11.6	9.0	8.4	8.8	11.3	7.9	7.6	8.9	6.9	10.1	9.1	8.0	4.7	9.2	−1.5	−13.7	−6.5						
71	10.4	10.3	10.7	11.9	9.5	8.9	9.4	11.8	8.7	8.4	9.8	8.0	11.0	10.2	9.3	6.5	10.8	2.7	−4.5	4.8	15.3					
72	10.4	10.3	10.7	11.9	9.5	8.9	9.4	11.7	8.8	8.5	9.8	8.2	11.0	10.3	9.5	7.0	10.5	4.0	−1.0	6.0	11.8	5.1				
73	9.0	8.8	9.1	10.1	7.8	7.0	7.3	9.2	6.4	6.1	7.0	5.4	7.5	6.5	5.2	2.5	4.5	−1.2	−6.0	−2.3	−2.7	−11.5	−29.7			
74	7.6	7.4	7.5	8.4	6.0	5.3	5.4	7.0	4.2	3.7	4.4	2.7	4.3	3.1	1.6	−1.1	0.1	−5.2	−9.8	−7.4	−9.1	−16.4	−28.0	−29.4		
75	8.5	8.3	8.5	9.5	7.3	6.6	6.8	8.5	5.9	5.5	6.4	4.8	6.7	5.7	4.6	2.3	4.0	−0.6	−4.0	−0.7	−0.5	−4.5	−9.2	3.1	50.3	
76	9.0	8.9	9.1	10.1	8.0	7.4	7.6	9.4	6.9	6.7	7.6	6.2	8.1	7.3	6.4	4.5	6.3	2.3	−0.5	3.3	4.4	2.1	0.2	13.5	45.1	37.0

*Percent per annum, compounded annually.

Sources: Stock market data—Lawrence Fisher and Myron Scholes (compilers), CRSP Monthly Master File for Common Stocks Listed on the New York Stock Exchange (magnetic tape). See Appendix A.
Income tax rates—Income levels estimated from U.S. Bureau of the Census, Current Population Reports, Series P-60, Nos. 101 and 103 and Historical Statistics of the United States. Tax rates were found in U.S. Internal Revenue Service, Statistics of Income and Your Federal Income Tax.

Held Until	12/25	12/26	12/27	12/28	12/29	12/30	12/31	12/32	12/33	12/34	12/35	12/36	12/37	12/38	12/39	12/40	12/41	12/42	12/43	12/44	12/45	12/46	12/47	12/48	12/49
12/26	2.3																								
12/27	17.7	31.9																							
12/28	25.1	39.4	47.2																						
12/29	9.6	11.4	1.8	−29.5																					
12/30	0.8	−0.3	−10.0	−29.5	−33.7																				
12/31	−6.2	−8.2	−16.7	−32.4	−35.8	−42.3																			
12/32	−5.2	−6.7	−13.3	−25.6	−26.1	−23.5	0.0																		
12/33	1.0	0.9	−3.7	−12.5	−7.3	4.4	43.8	105.3																	
12/34	1.9	1.6	−2.2	−9.2	−3.8	6.1	31.7	52.9	12.9																
12/35	4.3	4.3	1.1	−4.5	1.5	11.7	34.8	51.2	28.7	46.1															
12/36	6.2	6.4	3.7	−0.9	5.4	15.7	36.8	50.4	34.3	47.5	44.7														
12/37	2.4	2.0	−1.1	−5.8	−1.7	4.6	17.5	22.6	6.6	4.4	−13.0	−47.9													
12/38	4.1	3.9	1.3	−2.8	1.6	7.9	20.0	24.9	11.8	11.1	−0.2	−17.3	33.9												
12/39	3.9	3.6	1.1	−2.6	1.4	6.9	17.0	20.6	9.3	8.1	−0.7	−12.4	14.4	−3.2											
12/40	3.2	2.9	0.5	−3.0	0.7	5.4	14.3	17.3	7.1	5.3	−2.3	−11.3	6.6	−6.0	−11.6										
12/41	2.2	1.7	−0.5	−3.9	−0.8	3.5	11.5	13.6	4.1	2.0	−4.7	−12.5	0.2	−9.6	−14.9	−19.7									
12/42	2.2	1.8	−0.4	−3.6	−0.5	3.6	11.0	12.9	4.1	2.4	−3.5	−9.8	1.6	−5.8	−7.5	−4.6	16.4								
12/43	2.9	2.7	0.7	−2.2	1.0	5.2	12.4	14.3	6.4	5.3	0.4	−4.8	7.0	2.4	3.2	10.7	35.0	48.5							
12/44	3.5	3.4	1.6	−1.1	2.2	6.3	13.3	15.2	8.0	7.3	3.1	−1.4	10.0	6.6	8.4	16.4	35.8	42.2	32.2						
12/45	4.6	4.7	3.1	0.7	4.1	8.3	15.1	17.2	10.7	10.4	6.8	3.1	14.4	12.1	15.1	23.8	42.6	48.6	43.7	53.7					
12/46	3.4	3.4	1.8	−0.6	2.5	6.3	12.5	14.2	7.8	7.1	3.6	−0.1	9.2	6.6	8.0	13.0	24.0	24.4	15.1	7.4	−25.2				
12/47	3.1	3.0	1.4	−1.0	1.9	5.4	11.3	12.9	6.7	5.9	2.5	−1.0	7.2	4.9	5.6	9.2	16.9	16.2	8.0	0.9	−18.1	−11.4			
12/48	2.8	2.6	1.0	−1.3	1.4	4.8	10.4	11.8	5.8	5.0	1.6	−1.7	5.7	3.5	4.1	7.0	13.2	12.0	4.7	−1.2	−14.7	−9.1	−8.2		
12/49	3.2	3.1	1.5	−0.6	2.0	5.3	10.7	12.1	6.4	5.6	2.5	−0.4	6.6	4.5	5.3	8.1	14.1	13.1	6.9	2.6	−7.6	−1.0	4.6	18.3	
12/50	3.6	3.5	2.1	0.0	2.7	6.0	11.3	12.6	7.0	6.5	3.6	0.9	7.6	5.9	6.7	9.6	15.0	14.3	9.1	5.6	−2.4	4.7	10.6	21.2	24.9
12/51	3.8	3.7	2.3	0.3	2.9	6.0	11.2	12.4	7.1	6.6	3.8	1.2	7.5	5.8	6.6	9.2	14.1	13.4	8.8	5.8	−0.8	5.1	9.5	16.2	15.1
12/52	3.8	3.8	2.4	0.5	2.9	6.0	11.0	12.2	7.0	6.6	3.9	1.4	7.4	5.8	6.5	9.0	13.7	12.8	8.5	5.8	0.0	5.4	8.9	13.6	11.9
12/53	3.6	3.5	2.2	0.3	2.6	5.5	10.4	11.5	6.5	6.0	3.4	1.0	6.6	4.9	5.7	7.9	12.1	11.2	7.2	4.6	−0.7	3.7	6.4	9.7	7.1
12/54	4.5	4.4	3.2	1.5	3.8	6.7	11.5	12.6	7.9	7.6	5.2	3.0	8.5	7.1	8.0	10.3	14.5	13.9	10.5	8.3	3.8	8.6	11.9	15.8	15.1
12/55	4.8	4.8	3.6	1.9	4.3	7.1	11.8	12.9	8.4	8.1	5.8	3.7	9.0	7.6	8.5	10.7	14.7	14.2	11.1	9.1	5.1	9.6	12.6	16.2	15.8
12/56	4.8	4.8	3.7	2.0	4.3	7.1	11.6	12.7	8.3	8.1	5.7	3.7	8.8	7.6	8.3	10.3	13.9	13.5	10.6	8.8	5.2	9.1	11.7	14.7	14.2
12/57	4.3	4.3	3.1	1.4	3.6	6.3	10.7	11.7	7.3	7.0	4.7	2.8	7.6	6.3	6.9	8.7	12.0	11.4	8.5	6.7	3.2	6.5	8.5	10.8	9.6
12/58	5.0	5.0	3.9	2.4	4.5	7.2	11.5	12.5	8.3	8.2	6.0	4.2	8.9	7.8	8.5	10.3	13.6	13.1	10.4	8.9	5.7	9.1	11.4	13.8	13.2
12/59	5.1	5.1	4.0	2.5	4.7	7.3	11.5	12.5	8.5	8.3	6.2	4.5	9.0	7.9	8.6	10.3	13.5	13.0	10.4	8.9	6.0	9.3	11.5	13.8	13.3
12/60	5.1	5.1	3.9	2.4	4.5	7.0	11.1	12.1	8.2	8.0	5.9	4.2	8.5	7.4	8.0	9.6	12.6	12.1	9.6	8.2	5.4	8.4	10.4	12.4	11.8
12/61	5.5	5.5	4.3	2.9	5.0	7.5	11.5	12.4	8.6	8.5	6.5	4.9	9.1	8.0	8.7	10.3	13.2	12.7	10.2	9.0	6.3	9.3	11.2	13.1	12.5
12/62	5.0	4.9	3.9	2.4	4.4	6.8	10.8	11.7	7.8	7.6	5.6	4.1	8.1	7.1	7.6	9.1	11.8	11.3	8.8	7.5	4.9	7.6	9.3	10.8	10.1
12/63	5.2	5.2	4.1	2.7	4.7	7.1	11.0	11.8	8.0	7.9	5.9	4.4	8.3	7.3	7.9	9.3	11.9	11.4	9.1	7.9	5.5	8.1	9.6	11.1	10.5
12/64	5.3	5.3	4.3	2.9	4.9	7.1	10.9	11.8	8.1	8.0	6.2	4.7	8.5	7.5	8.1	9.5	12.0	11.5	9.3	8.2	5.8	8.4	9.8	11.3	10.7
12/65	5.5	5.5	4.5	3.2	5.1	7.5	11.2	12.0	8.4	8.3	6.5	5.0	8.8	7.8	8.4	9.7	12.2	11.8	9.7	8.6	6.4	9.0	10.5	11.9	11.5
12/66	5.2	5.2	4.2	2.9	4.7	7.0	10.7	11.5	7.9	7.8	6.0	4.5	8.2	7.2	7.7	9.0	11.4	10.9	8.9	7.8	5.6	8.0	9.4	10.7	10.2
12/67	5.7	5.7	4.7	3.4	5.3	7.5	11.0	11.9	8.5	8.3	6.6	5.3	8.8	7.9	8.5	9.7	12.0	11.6	9.6	8.6	6.6	8.9	10.3	11.6	11.2
12/68	5.7	5.7	4.8	3.6	5.4	7.5	11.0	11.9	8.5	8.4	6.7	5.4	8.9	8.1	8.6	9.8	12.1	11.6	9.7	8.7	6.7	9.0	10.3	11.7	11.3
12/69	5.4	5.4	4.3	3.1	4.8	6.9	10.3	11.2	7.8	7.6	6.0	4.7	8.0	7.2	7.6	8.8	10.9	10.5	8.5	7.5	5.5	7.6	8.8	10.0	9.5
12/70	5.1	5.1	4.1	2.9	4.6	6.6	10.1	10.9	7.4	7.2	5.6	4.3	7.7	7.0	7.2	8.3	10.4	9.9	7.9	6.9	5.0	7.0	8.1	9.2	8.7
12/71	5.2	5.2	4.2	3.1	4.7	6.7	10.1	10.9	7.5	7.3	5.8	4.5	7.8	7.1	7.3	8.4	10.4	9.9	8.0	7.1	5.2	7.2	8.3	9.4	8.9
12/72	5.3	5.3	4.3	3.2	4.8	6.7	10.1	10.9	7.5	7.3	5.8	4.6	7.7	6.9	7.2	8.3	10.3	9.8	8.0	7.1	5.3	7.3	8.3	9.4	8.9
12/73	4.8	4.8	3.8	2.7	4.2	6.1	9.5	10.3	6.9	6.6	5.1	3.8	6.9	6.1	6.3	7.4	9.3	8.8	6.9	6.0	4.3	6.1	7.0	7.9	7.4
12/74	4.2	4.2	3.2	2.0	3.6	5.5	9.0	9.9	6.2	5.9	4.3	3.0	6.2	5.4	5.5	6.5	8.4	7.9	5.9	4.9	3.1	4.8	5.6	6.5	5.8
12/75	4.5	4.4	3.5	2.4	3.9	5.8	9.2	10.0	6.5	6.2	4.7	3.4	6.6	5.9	6.0	6.9	8.8	8.3	6.4	5.4	3.6	5.3	6.1	7.0	6.5
12/76	4.6	4.6	3.7	2.6	4.1	6.0	9.3	10.1	6.7	6.4	4.9	3.7	6.7	6.1	6.2	7.2	9.0	8.5	6.6	5.7	4.0	5.7	6.5	7.4	6.8

Table XVIII

Internal Rates of Return* on Common Stocks:
  Dividends Consumed,
  Cash to Portfolio,
  Equal Initial Weighting,
  Higher Tax Rate,
  Deflated by the Consumer Price Index

Held til	12/50	12/51	12/52	12/53	12/54	12/55	12/56	12/57	12/58	12/59	12/60	12/61	12/62	12/63	12/64	12/65	12/66	12/67	12/68	12/69	12/70	12/71	12/72	12/73	12/74	12/75
/51	5.2																									
/52	5.5	4.6																								
/53	1.8	-0.6	-7.0																							
/54	12.2	14.4	19.0	52.1																						
/55	13.3	15.3	18.8	34.7	16.3																					
/56	11.8	12.9	14.8	23.4	9.4	1.3																				
/57	7.3	7.3	7.5	11.3	-0.5	-8.5	-18.3																			
/58	11.5	12.2	13.4	18.1	10.0	7.6	11.3	52.3																		
/59	11.7	12.4	13.6	17.5	10.8	9.1	12.2	31.7	10.8																	
/60	10.3	10.9	11.6	14.5	8.5	6.7	8.4	18.2	3.0	-5.3																
/61	11.4	12.0	12.8	15.6	10.7	9.6	11.7	20.2	10.3	9.7	24.9															
/62	8.9	9.2	9.5	11.5	6.8	5.4	6.5	12.0	3.3	0.8	3.2	-16.1														
/63	9.3	9.5	9.9	11.9	7.7	6.4	7.6	12.5	5.5	4.2	7.4	-1.3	13.9													
/64	9.6	9.8	10.3	12.1	8.3	7.2	8.4	12.9	7.1	6.4	9.6	4.3	15.0	13.4												
/65	10.3	10.6	11.1	13.0	9.4	8.6	9.7	14.3	9.2	9.0	12.6	9.4	19.0	20.1	24.3											
/66	9.0	9.2	9.6	11.2	7.7	6.7	7.5	11.5	6.7	6.1	8.6	5.3	11.1	9.1	5.7	-12.7										
/67	10.1	10.4	10.9	12.6	9.4	8.7	9.6	13.6	9.5	9.5	12.2	10.1	16.5	16.9	17.5	12.3	45.0									
/68	10.3	10.6	11.1	12.7	9.8	9.1	10.1	13.8	10.2	10.3	12.9	11.0	16.4	16.9	17.5	14.8	33.2	20.7								
/69	8.5	8.7	9.0	10.3	7.4	6.6	7.2	10.1	6.5	6.1	7.7	5.5	9.2	8.4	7.3	3.2	9.6	-5.1	-26.1							
/70	7.7	7.8	8.0	9.2	6.4	5.6	6.1	8.6	5.2	4.7	5.9	3.7	6.5	5.3	3.8	0.1	4.1	-6.6	-18.4	-11.4						
/71	7.9	8.1	8.3	9.5	6.8	6.1	6.6	9.0	5.9	5.5	6.7	4.7	7.4	6.4	5.2	2.1	5.9	-2.1	-9.0	0.3	11.5					
/72	7.9	8.0	8.3	9.3	6.8	6.1	6.6	8.9	5.9	5.6	6.7	4.9	7.4	6.5	5.4	2.6	5.9	-0.6	-5.4	1.9	8.1	1.6				
/73	6.3	6.3	6.5	7.4	4.8	4.0	4.2	6.1	3.2	2.8	3.5	1.7	3.6	2.3	0.8	-2.2	-0.4	-6.2	-10.8	-7.2	-7.5	-16.5	-35.4			
/74	4.7	4.6	4.6	5.4	2.8	1.9	2.0	3.5	0.7	0.1	0.5	-1.4	-0.1	-1.6	-3.3	-6.3	-5.3	-10.8	-15.3	-13.1	-14.9	-22.7	-34.8	-37.1		
/75	5.4	5.4	5.5	6.3	3.8	3.0	3.2	4.8	2.1	1.6	2.2	0.5	2.0	0.8	-0.6	-3.1	-1.8	-6.5	-9.9	-6.9	-6.9	-11.4	-17.0	-5.9	40.4	
/76	5.8	5.8	5.9	6.8	4.4	3.7	3.9	5.5	3.0	2.6	3.4	1.8	3.3	2.3	1.1	-1.0	0.4	-3.6	-6.4	-2.9	-2.0	-4.7	-7.4	5.1	37.0	30.7

*Percent per annum, compounded annually.

Sources: Stock market data—Lawrence Fisher and Myron Scholes (compilers), CRSP Monthly Master File for Common Stocks Listed on the New York Stock Exchange (magnetic tape). See Appendix A.
Consumer Price Index—U.S. Bureau of Labor Statistics.
Income tax rates—Income levels estimated from U.S. Bureau of the Census, Current Population Reports, Series P-60, Nos. 101 and 103 and Historical Statistics of the United States. Tax rates were found in U.S. Internal Revenue Service, Statistics of Income and Your Federal Income Tax.

Held Until	12/25	12/26	12/27	12/28	12/29	12/30	12/31	12/32	12/33	12/34	12/35	12/36	12/37	12/38	12/39	12/40	12/41	12/42	12/43	12/44	12/45	12/46	12/47	12/48	12/49
12/26	9.6																								
12/27	20.7	32.8																							
12/28	26.0	35.6	38.7																						
12/29	16.1	18.7	11.9	−12.5																					
12/30	6.9	6.3	−2.0	−20.0	−27.8																				
12/31	−2.2	−4.8	−13.6	−28.5	−35.9	−44.0																			
12/32	−3.0	−5.3	−12.7	−24.3	−28.4	−28.9	−8.9																		
12/33	1.9	0.7	−4.9	−13.3	−13.9	−8.6	18.6	56.2																	
12/34	2.2	1.0	−3.9	−11.0	−10.9	−5.8	13.6	27.8	3.2																
12/35	4.9	4.3	0.3	−5.4	−4.2	1.8	20.0	32.6	21.3	42.6															
12/36	6.7	6.4	3.0	−1.8	−0.1	6.0	22.1	32.6	24.9	37.8	32.2														
12/37	3.5	2.8	−0.7	−5.5	−4.6	−0.2	11.5	17.0	7.8	9.5	−5.5	−34.0													
12/38	4.7	4.2	1.1	−3.1	−1.9	2.4	13.2	18.3	10.9	13.0	3.4	−9.5	26.1												
12/39	4.5	4.0	1.1	−2.8	−1.6	2.4	12.0	16.3	9.5	10.8	3.0	−6.0	13.5	1.4											
12/40	3.9	3.3	0.6	−3.1	−2.1	1.5	10.1	13.6	7.2	7.9	1.0	−6.5	6.2	−3.3	−8.3										
12/41	3.3	2.7	−0.0	−3.5	−2.6	0.6	8.5	11.4	5.3	5.6	−0.7	−7.1	2.4	−5.3	−9.0	−10.2									
12/42	3.7	3.2	0.7	−2.6	−1.6	1.5	8.9	11.7	6.3	6.7	1.3	−4.0	4.7	−0.8	−1.8	1.6	15.3								
12/43	4.5	4.0	1.7	−1.3	−0.2	2.9	10.0	12.7	7.8	8.4	3.8	−0.5	7.8	3.9	4.4	9.4	21.5	28.2							
12/44	5.0	4.6	2.4	−0.3	0.7	3.7	10.5	13.1	8.6	9.3	5.2	1.6	9.3	6.2	7.2	11.9	21.3	24.7	20.9						
12/45	5.8	5.5	3.6	1.0	2.2	5.2	11.7	14.3	10.2	11.0	7.5	4.5	12.0	9.7	11.3	16.3	25.1	28.8	29.0	38.0					
12/46	5.4	5.1	3.1	0.7	1.8	4.6	10.8	13.2	9.2	9.8	6.4	3.6	10.2	7.9	9.0	12.7	18.8	19.7	16.7	14.5	−6.3				
12/47	5.4	5.1	3.2	0.9	1.9	4.6	10.6	12.8	9.0	9.5	6.3	3.7	9.7	7.6	8.5	11.6	16.5	16.7	13.6	11.1	−1.5	3.0			
12/48	5.4	5.1	3.2	1.0	2.0	4.6	10.3	12.4	8.7	9.2	6.1	3.6	9.2	7.2	7.9	10.6	14.7	14.6	11.6	9.1	−0.3	2.6	1.4		
12/49	5.7	5.4	3.7	1.5	2.5	5.1	10.6	12.7	9.1	9.7	6.8	4.5	9.8	8.0	8.8	11.4	15.2	15.2	12.6	10.8	3.9	7.7	9.9	18.9	
12/50	6.2	6.0	4.3	2.3	3.3	5.8	11.2	13.2	9.9	10.5	7.8	5.7	10.9	9.3	10.2	12.8	16.6	16.7	14.7	13.6	8.4	12.7	16.1	24.5	29.4
12/51	6.5	6.3	4.8	2.9	3.9	6.3	11.5	13.4	10.3	10.9	8.4	6.4	11.4	10.0	10.9	13.4	16.9	17.1	15.4	14.5	10.2	14.1	17.2	23.4	25.4
12/52	6.7	6.6	5.0	3.2	4.2	6.6	11.6	13.5	10.4	11.0	8.6	6.8	11.6	10.2	11.1	13.4	16.7	16.8	15.2	14.4	10.6	14.0	16.5	21.1	21.5
12/53	6.5	6.4	4.9	3.1	4.1	6.4	11.2	13.1	10.1	10.6	8.3	6.5	11.0	9.7	10.5	12.6	15.6	15.6	14.0	13.0	9.4	12.2	14.0	17.0	16.2
12/54	7.3	7.2	5.9	4.2	5.1	7.4	12.1	14.0	11.2	11.8	9.6	8.0	12.5	11.3	12.2	14.4	17.4	17.6	16.3	15.7	12.8	15.9	18.1	21.6	21.9
12/55	7.7	7.6	6.3	4.7	5.7	7.9	12.5	14.3	11.6	12.2	10.2	8.7	13.0	11.9	12.8	15.0	17.8	18.1	16.9	16.5	13.8	16.8	18.9	22.1	22.5
12/56	7.7	7.6	6.4	4.8	5.8	7.9	12.4	14.1	11.5	12.1	10.1	8.7	12.8	11.8	12.6	14.6	17.4	17.5	16.4	15.9	13.5	16.1	17.9	20.6	20.7
12/57	7.3	7.2	6.0	4.4	5.3	7.4	11.8	13.5	10.9	11.4	9.4	8.0	12.0	10.9	11.6	13.5	16.0	16.1	14.9	14.2	11.7	14.0	15.4	17.4	17.0
12/58	7.9	7.8	6.6	5.1	6.1	8.1	12.4	14.1	11.6	12.1	10.3	8.9	12.8	11.8	12.6	14.5	17.0	17.1	16.1	15.6	13.4	15.7	17.2	19.4	19.3
12/59	7.9	7.9	6.7	5.3	6.2	8.2	12.4	14.0	11.6	12.1	10.3	9.0	12.8	11.8	12.6	14.4	16.8	16.9	15.9	15.4	13.3	15.5	16.9	18.9	18.7
12/60	7.7	7.7	6.5	5.1	6.0	8.0	12.1	13.7	11.3	11.8	10.0	8.7	12.3	11.4	12.1	13.8	16.1	16.2	15.1	14.5	12.4	14.5	15.7	17.5	17.1
12/61	8.0	8.0	6.9	5.5	6.4	8.4	12.4	14.0	11.6	12.1	10.4	9.2	12.7	11.8	12.5	14.2	16.5	16.6	15.5	15.1	13.1	15.1	16.3	18.0	17.8
12/62	7.8	7.7	6.7	5.3	6.1	8.0	12.0	13.6	11.2	11.7	9.9	8.7	12.2	11.3	11.9	13.6	15.7	15.7	14.7	14.1	12.1	14.0	15.0	16.5	16.1
12/63	8.0	8.0	6.9	5.6	6.4	8.3	12.2	13.7	11.4	11.9	10.2	9.0	12.4	11.5	12.2	13.8	15.9	15.9	14.9	14.4	12.5	14.3	15.3	16.8	16.4
12/64	8.2	8.1	7.1	5.8	6.7	8.5	12.3	13.8	11.5	12.0	10.4	9.2	12.6	11.7	12.4	13.9	16.0	16.0	15.1	14.6	12.7	14.5	15.5	16.8	16.5
12/65	8.2	8.2	7.2	6.0	6.8	8.5	12.3	13.8	11.5	12.0	10.4	9.3	12.6	11.7	12.4	13.9	15.9	15.9	15.0	14.5	12.8	14.5	15.4	16.7	16.4
12/66	7.9	7.9	6.9	5.6	6.4	8.1	11.9	13.4	11.1	11.6	9.9	8.8	12.0	11.2	11.8	13.3	15.2	15.2	14.2	13.7	11.9	13.5	14.4	15.5	15.1
12/67	8.2	8.1	7.1	5.9	6.7	8.4	12.1	13.6	11.3	11.8	10.2	9.2	12.3	11.4	12.1	13.5	15.4	15.4	14.5	14.0	12.3	13.9	14.8	15.9	15.5
12/68	8.2	8.1	7.2	6.0	6.8	8.5	12.1	13.5	11.3	11.8	10.3	9.2	12.3	11.5	12.1	13.5	15.4	15.4	14.4	14.0	12.3	13.9	14.7	15.8	15.4
12/69	8.0	7.9	7.0	5.8	6.5	8.2	11.8	13.3	11.0	11.5	9.9	8.8	11.9	11.1	11.6	13.0	14.9	14.9	13.9	13.4	11.7	13.2	13.9	15.0	14.5
12/70	8.0	7.9	7.0	5.8	6.5	8.2	11.7	13.2	11.0	11.4	9.9	8.8	11.8	11.0	11.5	12.9	14.8	14.7	13.7	13.2	11.5	13.0	13.7	14.7	14.2
12/71	8.0	8.0	7.0	5.9	6.6	8.2	11.8	13.2	11.0	11.4	9.9	8.9	11.8	11.0	11.6	12.9	14.8	14.7	13.7	13.3	11.6	13.0	13.7	14.7	14.3
12/72	8.1	8.1	7.2	6.0	6.8	8.4	11.8	13.3	11.1	11.5	10.0	9.0	11.9	11.1	11.7	13.0	14.8	14.8	13.8	13.4	11.7	13.1	13.8	14.8	14.4
12/73	7.9	7.9	6.9	5.8	6.5	8.1	11.6	13.0	10.8	11.2	9.7	8.7	11.6	10.8	11.3	12.7	14.5	14.4	13.4	12.9	11.2	12.6	13.2	14.1	13.7
12/74	7.6	7.5	6.6	5.4	6.1	7.7	11.3	12.8	10.5	10.9	9.3	8.2	11.2	10.3	10.8	12.2	14.0	13.9	12.8	12.2	10.5	11.8	12.4	13.3	12.8
12/75	7.8	7.7	6.8	5.7	6.4	8.0	11.5	12.9	10.7	11.1	9.5	8.5	11.4	10.6	11.1	12.4	14.2	14.1	13.1	12.5	10.9	12.2	12.8	13.7	13.1
12/76	7.9	7.9	6.9	5.8	6.5	8.1	11.5	12.9	10.8	11.2	9.7	8.7	11.5	10.7	11.2	12.5	14.3	14.2	13.2	12.7	11.1	12.3	12.9	13.8	13.3

Table XIX

Internal Rates of Return* on Common Stocks:
  Dividends Consumed,
  Cash to Portfolio,
  Initial Weighting by Value,
  Tax-Exempt,
  Current Dollars

	Purchased 12/50	12/51	12/52	12/53	12/54	Purchased 12/55	12/56	12/57	12/58	12/59	Purchased 12/60	12/61	12/62	12/63	12/64	Purchased 12/65	12/66	12/67	12/68	12/69	Purchased 12/70	12/71	12/72	12/73	12/74	12/75
'51	20.4																									
'52	16.9	12.5																								
'53	11.3	6.3	-0.4																							
'54	19.5	18.9	22.0	49.4																						
'55	20.6	20.5	23.2	37.2	24.5																					
'56	18.8	18.3	19.7	27.4	16.6	8.2																				
'57	14.8	13.5	13.5	17.5	7.4	-1.2	-11.0																			
'58	17.6	17.0	17.7	22.0	15.0	11.5	12.8	42.9																		
'59	17.1	16.5	17.0	20.5	14.5	11.7	12.8	27.5	12.2																	
'60	15.5	14.7	14.9	17.7	12.1	9.4	9.6	17.9	6.2	-0.3																
'61	16.3	15.7	16.1	18.6	14.0	11.9	12.8	20.1	12.6	12.5	26.3															
'62	14.5	13.7	13.8	15.8	11.3	9.1	9.2	14.2	7.1	5.0	7.4	-10.1														
'63	15.0	14.3	14.4	16.3	12.2	10.4	10.7	15.3	9.6	8.7	11.7	4.2	20.3													
'64	15.1	14.5	14.6	16.4	12.7	11.1	11.5	15.5	10.7	10.2	12.8	8.0	18.3	15.3												
'65	15.0	14.4	14.5	16.2	12.7	11.2	11.6	15.2	11.0	10.6	12.9	9.3	16.8	15.2	13.7											
'66	13.7	13.0	13.0	14.4	10.9	9.4	9.5	12.5	8.4	7.7	9.0	5.5	9.9	6.7	2.2	-9.6										
'67	14.2	13.6	13.6	14.9	11.7	10.4	10.6	13.5	9.9	9.5	11.0	8.4	12.7	11.3	9.8	6.9	26.3									
'68	14.1	13.5	13.5	14.8	11.8	10.5	10.7	13.4	10.2	9.9	11.3	9.0	12.8	11.5	10.5	9.0	19.8	12.6								
'69	13.2	12.5	12.4	13.6	10.6	9.3	9.3	11.7	8.5	8.0	9.0	6.7	9.6	8.1	6.5	4.2	9.4	0.9	-10.7							
'70	12.9	12.2	12.1	13.2	10.3	9.0	9.0	11.2	8.2	7.7	8.5	6.4	8.9	7.3	5.8	3.9	7.7	1.3	-4.8	0.5						
'71	13.0	12.3	12.2	13.2	10.4	9.2	9.3	11.4	8.5	8.1	9.0	7.0	9.4	8.2	6.9	5.5	9.0	4.3	1.3	7.6	14.3					
'72	13.1	12.5	12.4	13.4	10.7	9.6	9.7	11.7	9.1	8.7	9.6	7.9	10.2	9.2	8.2	7.1	10.4	6.8	5.2	10.9	16.2	16.7				
'73	12.4	11.6	11.5	12.5	9.8	8.6	8.6	10.4	7.8	7.3	7.9	6.2	8.1	6.9	5.6	4.4	6.7	3.1	0.9	3.9	4.7	-1.1	-18.0			
'74	11.4	10.6	10.4	11.2	8.5	7.2	7.1	8.7	6.0	5.5	5.9	4.0	5.5	3.9	2.5	1.1	2.6	-1.1	-3.7	-2.4	-3.7	-10.2	-22.6	-28.2		
'75	11.8	11.1	10.9	11.8	9.2	8.1	8.1	9.7	7.2	6.8	7.3	5.6	7.2	5.9	4.8	3.8	5.6	2.6	0.9	2.9	3.0	-0.4	-6.5	-0.6	37.3	
'76	12.1	11.4	11.3	12.1	9.6	8.6	8.6	10.2	7.9	7.5	8.1	6.5	8.2	7.0	6.1	5.3	7.1	4.6	3.4	5.6	6.2	4.0	0.4	7.3	31.7	24.0

Percent per annum, compounded annually.

Source: *Lawrence Fisher and Myron Scholes (compilers),* CRSP Monthly Master File for Common Stocks Listed on the New York Stock Exchange *(magnetic tape). See Appendix A.*

Held Until	Purchased 12/25	12/26	12/27	12/28	12/29	Purchased 12/30	12/31	12/32	12/33	12/34	Purchased 12/35	12/36	12/37	12/38	12/39	Purchased 12/40	12/41	12/42	12/43	12/44	Purchased 12/45	12/46	12/47	12/48	12/49
12/26	11.3																								
12/27	22.9	35.7																							
12/28	27.9	37.7	40.1																						
12/29	17.5	19.9	12.4	-12.7																					
12/30	9.1	8.6	0.2	-17.6	-23.1																				
12/31	0.8	-1.4	-10.1	-24.7	-30.5	-38.1																			
12/32	0.9	-1.0	-8.1	-19.3	-21.7	-21.1	1.7																		
12/33	5.7	4.8	-0.6	-8.7	-7.9	-2.0	25.1	55.6																	
12/34	5.4	4.5	-0.4	-7.3	-6.2	-1.2	17.1	26.3	1.1																
12/35	7.7	7.2	3.2	-2.4	-0.5	5.3	22.0	30.3	18.3	38.4															
12/36	9.3	9.0	5.6	0.9	3.1	8.8	23.4	30.4	22.3	34.9	30.6														
12/37	5.6	4.9	1.4	-3.4	-2.1	1.8	12.1	14.8	5.4	6.8	-7.5	-36.0													
12/38	6.9	6.4	3.2	-1.0	0.6	4.4	14.1	16.9	9.4	11.6	2.9	-9.7	29.8												
12/39	6.6	6.1	3.1	-0.7	0.7	4.3	12.9	15.1	8.3	9.8	2.7	-6.0	15.5	1.9											
12/40	5.9	5.3	2.4	-1.3	-0.0	3.2	10.8	12.4	6.0	6.9	0.5	-6.7	7.1	-3.5	-9.2										
12/41	4.8	4.2	1.3	-2.3	-1.2	1.6	8.4	9.5	3.3	3.7	-2.3	-8.8	0.9	-8.2	-13.4	-18.2									
12/42	4.8	4.2	1.5	-1.9	-0.8	1.8	8.2	9.3	3.6	3.9	-1.3	-6.7	1.8	-5.1	-7.7	-7.2	5.4								
12/43	5.4	4.8	2.3	-0.9	0.3	2.9	9.1	10.1	5.0	5.5	1.0	-3.4	4.8	-0.4	-1.2	1.8	14.3	24.2							
12/44	5.8	5.3	2.9	-0.1	1.1	3.7	9.5	10.6	5.9	6.4	2.5	-1.3	6.3	2.2	2.1	5.4	15.6	21.4	18.4						
12/45	6.4	6.0	3.8	1.1	2.3	4.9	10.6	11.7	7.4	8.2	4.8	1.6	9.0	5.8	6.4	10.3	19.9	25.7	26.3	35.0					
12/46	5.6	5.1	2.8	0.2	1.2	3.6	9.0	9.9	5.6	6.1	2.7	-0.4	5.9	2.6	2.7	5.1	11.3	13.0	9.1	4.4	-20.6				
12/47	5.4	4.9	2.7	0.0	1.1	3.3	8.5	9.3	5.1	5.5	2.3	-0.7	5.1	1.9	1.9	3.8	8.9	9.6	5.8	1.5	-13.2	-5.5			
12/48	5.3	4.8	2.6	0.1	1.0	3.2	8.2	9.0	4.9	5.3	2.1	-0.7	4.7	1.8	1.7	3.4	7.8	8.2	4.7	1.1	-9.4	-3.1	-1.3		
12/49	5.6	5.1	3.0	0.6	1.7	3.8	8.6	9.4	5.5	5.9	3.0	0.5	5.7	3.1	3.2	5.0	9.1	9.7	7.0	4.5	-3.0	4.2	9.4	21.0	
12/50	5.9	5.5	3.5	1.2	2.3	4.4	9.0	9.8	6.2	6.6	3.9	1.6	6.7	4.3	4.5	6.4	10.4	11.1	8.9	7.2	1.5	8.5	13.7	22.4	22.4
12/51	6.0	5.7	3.8	1.6	2.6	4.6	9.2	9.9	6.4	6.9	4.4	2.2	7.0	4.8	5.1	6.9	10.7	11.4	9.5	8.0	3.3	9.5	13.9	19.8	18.5
12/52	6.2	5.9	4.0	1.9	2.9	4.9	9.3	10.0	6.7	7.1	4.7	2.7	7.3	5.3	5.5	7.3	10.8	11.5	9.7	8.5	4.4	9.9	13.6	18.1	16.6
12/53	6.0	5.7	3.9	1.8	2.8	4.8	9.0	9.7	6.5	6.9	4.5	2.6	7.0	5.0	5.2	6.8	10.1	10.6	8.9	7.6	3.8	8.5	11.4	14.5	12.3
12/54	6.7	6.5	4.8	2.9	3.8	5.8	9.9	10.6	7.6	8.1	6.0	4.2	8.5	6.8	7.2	8.9	12.1	12.9	11.5	10.7	7.6	12.5	15.8	19.4	18.7
12/55	7.1	6.8	5.2	3.4	4.4	6.3	10.3	11.0	8.1	8.6	6.6	5.0	9.1	7.5	8.0	9.7	12.8	13.6	12.4	11.7	9.0	13.7	16.8	20.1	19.7
12/56	7.0	6.8	5.2	3.5	4.4	6.2	10.2	10.9	8.0	8.5	6.6	5.0	9.0	7.4	7.9	9.4	12.4	13.1	12.0	11.3	8.8	13.0	15.7	18.5	17.9
12/57	6.7	6.4	4.8	3.0	4.0	5.7	9.6	10.3	7.4	7.9	5.9	4.3	8.2	6.6	6.9	8.4	11.2	11.7	10.5	9.7	7.2	10.9	13.1	15.3	14.2
12/58	7.1	6.9	5.4	3.7	4.6	6.4	10.1	10.8	8.1	8.6	6.8	5.3	9.1	7.6	8.0	9.5	12.2	12.9	11.8	11.2	8.9	12.7	15.0	17.2	16.5
12/59	7.2	6.9	5.5	3.9	4.8	6.5	10.2	10.8	8.2	8.6	6.9	5.5	9.1	7.7	8.1	9.5	12.2	12.8	11.8	11.1	9.0	12.6	14.7	16.7	16.0
12/60	7.0	6.7	5.3	3.7	4.6	6.3	9.9	10.6	7.9	8.3	6.6	5.2	8.7	7.3	7.7	9.0	11.6	12.1	11.0	10.4	8.3	11.7	13.6	15.4	14.5
12/61	7.2	7.0	5.7	4.1	5.0	6.6	10.2	10.8	8.3	8.7	7.1	5.8	9.2	7.9	8.3	9.6	12.1	12.6	11.6	11.1	9.1	12.4	14.2	16.0	15.3
12/62	7.0	6.8	5.4	3.9	4.7	6.3	9.9	10.5	7.9	8.3	6.6	5.3	8.7	7.4	7.7	9.0	11.4	11.8	10.8	10.2	8.2	11.2	12.9	14.5	13.7
12/63	7.2	7.0	5.7	4.2	5.0	6.6	10.0	10.6	8.2	8.6	6.9	5.7	9.0	7.7	8.1	9.3	11.8	12.2	11.2	10.6	8.7	11.6	13.3	14.8	14.0
12/64	7.3	7.1	5.9	4.4	5.2	6.8	10.1	10.7	8.3	8.7	7.2	6.0	9.2	7.9	8.3	9.5	11.8	12.3	11.4	10.8	9.0	11.9	13.4	14.9	14.2
12/65	7.4	7.2	5.9	4.5	5.3	6.8	10.1	10.7	8.4	8.8	7.2	6.1	9.2	8.0	8.4	9.5	11.8	12.2	11.3	10.8	9.1	11.8	13.4	14.7	14.0
12/66	7.1	6.9	5.6	4.1	4.9	6.4	9.7	10.3	7.9	8.3	6.7	5.6	8.6	7.4	7.7	8.9	11.1	11.5	10.5	10.0	8.3	10.9	12.3	13.5	12.7
12/67	7.2	7.0	5.8	4.4	5.2	6.7	9.9	10.5	8.2	8.5	7.0	5.9	8.9	7.7	8.0	9.2	11.3	11.7	10.8	10.3	8.7	11.2	12.6	13.9	13.1
12/68	7.2	7.0	5.8	4.4	5.2	6.7	9.9	10.4	8.1	8.5	7.0	5.9	8.9	7.7	8.0	9.1	11.2	11.6	10.7	10.2	8.6	11.1	12.5	13.6	12.9
12/69	7.0	6.8	5.5	4.1	4.9	6.4	9.6	10.2	7.8	8.2	6.6	5.5	8.4	7.3	7.5	8.6	10.7	11.0	10.1	9.6	7.9	10.4	11.6	12.7	11.9
12/70	7.0	6.7	5.5	4.1	4.8	6.3	9.5	10.1	7.7	8.0	6.5	5.4	8.3	7.1	7.4	8.5	10.5	10.8	9.9	9.4	7.7	10.1	11.3	12.4	11.5
12/71	7.0	6.8	5.5	4.2	4.9	6.3	9.5	10.1	7.7	8.1	6.6	5.5	8.3	7.2	7.5	8.5	10.5	10.8	9.9	9.4	7.8	10.1	11.3	12.3	11.5
12/72	7.1	6.9	5.6	4.3	5.0	6.4	9.5	10.1	7.8	8.2	6.7	5.6	8.4	7.3	7.6	8.6	10.6	10.9	10.0	9.5	7.9	10.2	11.4	12.4	11.6
12/73	6.8	6.6	5.4	4.0	4.7	6.1	9.3	9.8	7.5	7.8	6.3	5.2	8.0	6.9	7.1	8.1	10.1	10.4	9.5	8.9	7.3	9.5	10.7	11.6	10.8
12/74	6.5	6.3	5.0	3.6	4.3	5.7	9.0	9.6	7.1	7.4	5.8	4.7	7.6	6.3	6.6	7.6	9.6	9.9	8.8	8.2	6.5	8.7	9.8	10.8	9.8
12/75	6.6	6.4	5.1	3.8	4.5	5.9	9.1	9.6	7.2	7.6	6.0	4.9	7.7	6.5	6.8	7.8	9.7	10.0	9.0	8.4	6.8	9.0	10.1	11.0	10.1
12/76	6.7	6.5	5.2	3.9	4.6	6.0	9.1	9.7	7.3	7.6	6.1	5.0	7.8	6.7	6.9	7.9	9.8	10.1	9.1	8.6	7.0	9.1	10.2	11.1	10.2

Table XX

Internal Rates of Return* on Common Stocks:
  Dividends Consumed,
  Cash to Portfolio,
  Initial Weighting by Value,
  Tax-Exempt,
  Deflated by the Consumer Price Index

Held until	Purchased 12/50	12/51	12/52	12/53	12/54	Purchased 12/55	12/56	12/57	12/58	12/59	Purchased 12/60	12/61	12/62	12/63	12/64	Purchased 12/65	12/66	12/67	12/68	12/69	Purchased 12/70	12/71	12/72	12/73	12/74	12/75
12/51	13.7																									
12/52	13.0	11.6																								
12/53	8.5	5.5	−1.0																							
12/54	17.4	18.5	21.9	50.2																						
12/55	18.8	20.1	23.0	37.3	24.1																					
12/56	16.7	17.3	18.7	26.3	14.8	5.2																				
12/57	12.6	12.2	12.2	15.9	5.2	−4.0	−13.6																			
12/58	15.4	15.6	16.2	20.3	12.8	8.7	10.1	40.4																		
12/59	14.9	15.0	15.5	18.8	12.3	9.1	10.5	25.4	10.6																	
12/60	13.4	13.3	13.4	16.0	10.1	7.1	7.5	16.1	4.6	−1.8																
12/61	14.3	14.3	14.6	17.1	12.1	9.8	10.9	18.5	11.3	11.3	25.5															
12/62	12.6	12.3	12.4	14.2	9.5	7.1	7.4	12.6	5.8	3.9	6.4	−11.2														
12/63	13.0	12.8	12.9	14.7	10.4	8.5	9.0	13.7	8.2	7.4	10.4	2.8	18.4													
12/64	13.2	13.1	13.2	14.8	10.9	9.2	9.7	13.9	9.3	8.8	11.5	6.6	16.6	13.9												
12/65	13.1	13.0	13.0	14.6	10.9	9.3	9.8	13.6	9.5	9.1	11.4	7.7	14.9	13.4	11.6											
12/66	11.7	11.5	11.4	12.7	9.0	7.4	7.6	10.7	6.7	6.0	7.3	3.6	7.8	4.5	−0.4	−12.5										
12/67	12.2	11.9	11.9	13.1	9.7	8.3	8.5	11.6	8.1	7.6	9.1	6.2	10.3	8.8	6.8	3.6	22.6									
12/68	12.0	11.7	11.7	12.8	9.6	8.2	8.5	11.3	8.0	7.7	8.9	6.4	9.9	8.5	7.1	5.1	15.4	7.5								
12/69	10.9	10.6	10.4	11.4	8.2	6.7	6.8	9.3	6.1	5.5	6.3	3.8	6.4	4.7	2.7	−0.0	4.6	−4.3	−15.8							
12/70	10.5	10.1	10.0	10.9	7.8	6.3	6.4	8.6	5.6	4.9	5.6	3.2	5.4	3.6	1.7	−0.5	2.8	−3.9	−10.0	−4.8						
12/71	10.5	10.2	10.0	10.9	7.9	6.5	6.6	8.7	5.8	5.3	6.0	3.9	5.9	4.5	2.8	1.1	4.3	−0.6	−3.5	3.1	10.6					
12/72	10.7	10.3	10.1	11.0	8.1	6.9	7.0	9.0	6.3	5.9	6.6	4.6	6.6	5.5	4.1	2.8	5.8	2.1	0.5	6.5	12.4	12.8				
12/73	9.8	9.4	9.1	9.9	7.0	5.6	5.6	7.4	4.7	4.2	4.6	2.6	4.3	2.8	1.2	−0.3	1.7	−2.1	−4.2	−1.2	−0.4	−6.8	−24.7			
12/74	8.7	8.2	7.8	8.6	5.5	4.1	3.9	5.6	2.7	2.0	2.3	0.1	1.3	−0.5	−2.3	−4.1	−2.9	−6.8	−9.5	−8.3	−9.7	−16.8	−29.9	−36.0		
12/75	9.0	8.6	8.3	9.0	6.1	4.7	4.7	6.3	3.7	3.1	3.4	1.4	2.7	1.1	−0.3	−1.6	−0.2	−3.4	−5.3	−3.4	−3.5	−7.6	−14.5	−9.4	28.3	
12/76	9.2	8.7	8.5	9.2	6.4	5.1	5.1	6.7	4.2	3.7	4.1	2.3	3.6	2.1	1.0	−0.2	1.3	−1.4	−2.8	−0.7	−0.3	−3.0	−7.3	−0.7	24.4	18.3

*Percent per annum, compounded annually.

Sources: Stock market data—Lawrence Fisher and Myron Scholes
(compilers), CRSP Monthly Master File for Common Stocks
Listed on the New York Stock Exchange (magnetic tape).
See Appendix A.
Consumer Price Index—U.S. Bureau of Labor Statistics.

Held Until	12/25	12/26	12/27	12/28	12/29	12/30	12/31	12/32	12/33	12/34	12/35	12/36	12/37	12/38	12/39	12/40	12/41	12/42	12/43	12/44	12/45	12/46	12/47	12/48	12/49
12/26	9.6																								
12/27	20.6	32.8																							
12/28	25.9	35.6	38.6																						
12/29	16.1	18.6	11.9	−12.6																					
12/30	6.8	6.2	−2.1	−20.0	−27.8																				
12/31	−2.3	−4.9	−13.6	−28.5	−35.9	−44.0																			
12/32	−3.0	−5.4	−12.8	−24.4	−28.4	−29.0	−8.9																		
12/33	1.9	0.7	−4.9	−13.4	−13.9	−8.6	18.5	56.2																	
12/34	2.1	1.0	−4.0	−11.1	−10.9	−5.9	13.6	27.8	3.1																
12/35	4.9	4.2	0.3	−5.5	−4.2	1.8	19.9	32.5	21.2	42.3															
12/36	6.7	6.3	2.9	−1.9	−0.2	5.8	21.9	32.3	24.6	37.3	31.5														
12/37	3.4	2.6	−0.8	−5.6	−4.7	−0.4	11.2	16.6	7.4	8.8	−6.1	−34.4													
12/38	4.6	4.0	1.0	−3.2	−2.1	2.1	12.9	17.9	10.5	12.4	2.9	−9.9	25.6												
12/39	4.4	3.8	0.9	−2.9	−1.8	2.1	11.7	15.8	9.1	10.3	2.5	−6.4	13.0	1.0											
12/40	3.7	3.1	0.3	−3.3	−2.3	1.2	9.7	13.0	6.7	7.2	0.4	−7.0	5.6	−3.9	−9.1										
12/41	3.0	2.4	−0.4	−3.9	−3.0	0.1	7.8	10.6	4.5	4.7	−1.6	−7.9	1.2	−6.5	−10.5	−12.5									
12/42	3.3	2.8	0.2	−3.0	−2.1	0.9	8.2	10.7	5.3	5.6	0.2	−5.0	3.3	−2.2	−3.6	−0.8	12.3								
12/43	4.0	3.5	1.2	−1.8	−0.8	2.2	9.1	11.6	6.7	7.2	2.6	−1.6	6.3	2.2	2.4	6.7	18.1	24.2							
12/44	4.5	4.1	1.9	−0.9	0.1	3.0	9.5	11.9	7.5	7.9	3.9	0.3	7.6	4.4	5.1	9.2	17.9	20.8	17.2						
12/45	5.3	5.0	3.0	0.5	1.5	4.4	10.7	13.1	9.1	9.7	6.3	3.3	10.4	8.0	9.3	13.7	21.8	25.2	25.6	34.6					
12/46	4.8	4.4	2.5	0.0	1.0	3.7	9.6	11.8	7.9	8.3	5.0	2.2	8.3	6.0	6.7	9.9	15.3	16.1	13.3	11.4	−8.6				
12/47	4.7	4.4	2.5	0.1	1.1	3.6	9.2	11.2	7.5	7.9	4.7	2.1	7.6	5.4	6.0	8.6	12.9	12.9	10.1	7.8	−4.2	−0.2			
12/48	4.6	4.3	2.4	0.2	1.0	3.5	8.8	10.7	7.1	7.4	4.4	2.0	7.0	4.9	5.4	7.6	11.1	10.8	8.1	5.9	−2.9	−0.3	−1.2		
12/49	4.9	4.6	2.8	0.7	1.6	4.0	9.2	11.0	7.5	7.9	5.1	2.9	7.7	5.8	6.4	8.4	11.7	11.6	9.3	7.8	1.4	4.9	7.2	15.7	
12/50	5.4	5.2	3.5	1.5	2.5	4.8	9.8	11.6	8.3	8.8	6.2	4.2	8.9	7.2	7.9	10.0	13.2	13.2	11.6	10.6	5.9	9.9	13.3	21.2	25.7
12/51	5.7	5.5	4.0	2.1	3.0	5.3	10.0	11.8	8.7	9.2	6.8	4.9	9.4	7.9	8.6	10.6	13.5	13.6	12.2	11.5	7.6	11.2	14.3	20.0	21.7
12/52	5.9	5.7	4.2	2.4	3.3	5.5	10.1	11.8	8.8	9.3	7.0	5.2	9.4	8.1	8.7	10.6	13.3	13.4	12.0	11.4	8.0	11.1	13.5	17.5	17.8
12/53	5.6	5.5	4.0	2.2	3.1	5.2	9.7	11.2	8.4	8.7	6.5	4.8	8.8	7.4	7.9	9.6	12.0	12.0	10.6	9.8	6.6	9.1	10.7	13.3	12.4
12/54	6.5	6.4	5.0	3.4	4.3	6.4	10.7	12.3	9.6	10.1	8.1	6.5	10.4	9.3	9.9	11.7	14.2	14.3	13.3	12.8	10.3	13.1	15.1	18.2	18.5
12/55	6.9	6.9	5.6	4.0	4.9	6.9	11.1	12.7	10.1	10.6	8.7	7.3	11.0	10.0	10.7	12.4	14.7	14.9	14.0	13.7	11.4	14.1	16.1	18.9	19.3
12/56	6.9	6.8	5.6	4.1	4.9	6.9	11.0	12.5	10.0	10.4	8.6	7.2	10.8	9.8	10.4	12.0	14.2	14.3	13.5	13.1	11.0	13.4	15.0	17.4	17.5
12/57	6.4	6.3	5.1	3.5	4.4	6.3	10.2	11.7	9.2	9.5	7.7	6.3	9.7	8.7	9.2	10.6	12.6	12.6	11.7	11.2	9.1	11.0	12.3	14.0	13.6
12/58	7.0	7.0	5.8	4.4	5.2	7.1	10.9	12.4	10.0	10.4	8.7	7.5	10.8	9.9	10.4	11.9	13.8	13.9	13.2	12.8	11.0	13.0	14.4	16.2	16.2
12/59	7.1	7.0	5.9	4.5	5.4	7.2	10.9	12.3	10.0	10.4	8.8	7.6	10.8	9.9	10.4	11.8	13.7	13.8	13.0	12.7	10.9	12.9	14.1	15.8	15.6
12/60	6.8	6.7	5.6	4.3	5.1	6.9	10.5	11.9	9.6	10.0	8.3	7.1	10.2	9.3	9.8	11.1	12.8	12.9	12.1	11.7	9.9	11.7	12.8	14.2	14.0
12/61	7.2	7.1	6.1	4.8	5.6	7.3	10.9	12.2	10.1	10.4	8.8	7.7	10.7	9.9	10.4	11.6	13.3	13.4	12.7	12.3	10.7	12.5	13.6	15.0	14.8
12/62	6.9	6.8	5.8	4.4	5.2	6.9	10.4	11.7	9.5	9.8	8.3	7.1	10.0	9.2	9.6	10.8	12.4	12.4	11.6	11.2	9.6	11.1	12.0	13.2	12.9
12/63	7.1	7.1	6.1	4.8	5.5	7.2	10.6	11.9	9.8	10.1	8.6	7.5	10.3	9.5	10.0	11.1	12.7	12.7	12.0	11.6	10.1	11.6	12.5	13.6	13.3
12/64	7.3	7.3	6.3	5.1	5.8	7.4	10.7	12.0	9.9	10.3	8.8	7.8	10.5	9.7	10.2	11.3	12.8	12.8	12.2	11.9	10.4	11.8	12.7	13.8	13.5
12/65	7.4	7.3	6.4	5.2	5.9	7.5	10.7	11.9	9.9	10.3	8.9	7.9	10.5	9.8	10.2	11.3	12.8	12.8	12.1	11.8	10.4	11.8	12.6	13.7	13.4
12/66	7.0	6.9	5.9	4.7	5.4	7.0	10.2	11.4	9.3	9.6	8.2	7.2	9.8	9.0	9.4	10.4	11.8	11.8	11.1	10.8	9.4	10.7	11.4	12.3	11.9
12/67	7.3	7.2	6.2	5.1	5.8	7.3	10.4	11.6	9.7	10.0	8.6	7.6	10.1	9.4	9.8	10.8	12.2	12.2	11.5	11.2	9.9	11.2	11.9	12.8	12.5
12/68	7.3	7.2	6.3	5.2	5.8	7.4	10.4	11.6	9.7	10.0	8.6	7.7	10.1	9.4	9.8	10.8	12.1	12.1	11.5	11.2	9.9	11.2	11.9	12.7	12.4
12/69	7.0	6.9	6.0	4.8	5.5	7.0	10.0	11.1	9.2	9.5	8.1	7.2	9.6	8.8	9.2	10.1	11.4	11.3	10.7	10.4	9.1	10.3	10.9	11.6	11.3
12/70	6.9	6.8	5.9	4.8	5.5	6.9	9.9	11.0	9.1	9.4	8.0	7.1	9.4	8.7	9.0	10.0	11.2	11.1	10.5	10.2	8.9	10.0	10.6	11.3	10.9
12/71	7.0	6.9	6.0	5.0	5.6	7.0	9.9	11.0	9.1	9.4	8.1	7.2	9.5	8.8	9.1	10.0	11.2	11.2	10.5	10.2	9.0	10.1	10.7	11.4	11.0
12/72	7.1	7.1	6.2	5.1	5.8	7.1	10.1	11.1	9.3	9.5	8.3	7.4	9.7	9.0	9.3	10.2	11.4	11.3	10.7	10.4	9.2	10.3	10.9	11.5	11.2
12/73	6.8	6.7	5.9	4.8	5.4	6.7	9.6	10.7	8.8	9.1	7.8	6.9	9.1	8.4	8.7	9.6	10.7	10.6	10.0	9.7	8.5	9.5	10.0	10.6	10.2
12/74	6.3	6.2	5.3	4.2	4.8	6.1	9.1	10.1	8.2	8.4	7.1	6.2	8.4	7.6	7.9	8.7	9.9	9.7	9.0	8.6	7.4	8.3	8.8	9.3	8.9
12/75	6.6	6.5	5.6	4.6	5.2	6.5	9.4	10.4	8.5	8.8	7.5	6.6	8.8	8.0	8.3	9.2	10.3	10.2	9.5	9.2	8.0	8.9	9.3	9.9	9.5
12/76	6.8	6.7	5.8	4.8	5.4	6.7	9.5	10.5	8.7	8.9	7.7	6.8	9.0	8.3	8.6	9.4	10.5	10.4	9.7	9.4	8.3	9.2	9.6	10.2	9.8

Table XXI

Internal Rates of Return* on Common Stocks:
  Dividends Consumed,
  Cash to Portfolio,
  Initial Weighting by Value,
  Higher Tax Rate,
  Current Dollars

Yield until	12/50	12/51	12/52	12/53	12/54	12/55	12/56	12/57	12/58	12/59	12/60	12/61	12/62	12/63	12/64	12/65	12/66	12/67	12/68	12/69	12/70	12/71	12/72	12/73	12/74	12/75
12/51	16.9																									
12/52	13.5	9.3																								
12/53	7.8	3.0	-3.5																							
12/54	16.4	15.9	19.0	45.9																						
12/55	17.6	17.7	20.4	34.1	22.1																					
12/56	15.8	15.5	16.9	24.4	14.2	6.0																				
12/57	11.6	10.5	10.6	14.4	4.9	-3.4	-13.0																			
12/58	14.7	14.3	15.0	19.1	12.7	9.4	10.7	40.2																		
12/59	14.3	13.8	14.4	17.7	12.2	9.6	10.7	25.0	10.3																	
12/60	12.6	12.0	12.3	14.8	9.8	7.3	7.5	15.5	4.2	-2.1																
12/61	13.6	13.1	13.5	16.0	11.8	10.0	10.8	17.8	10.7	10.6	24.2															
12/62	11.6	11.0	11.1	13.0	9.0	7.0	7.1	11.8	5.1	3.1	5.4	-11.7														
12/63	12.2	11.6	11.8	13.6	10.0	8.4	8.7	12.9	7.7	6.8	9.7	2.5	18.1													
12/64	12.4	11.9	12.1	13.8	10.5	9.1	9.5	13.2	8.8	8.3	10.9	6.3	16.2	13.4												
12/65	12.4	11.9	12.1	13.6	10.6	9.3	9.6	13.0	9.1	8.8	10.9	7.6	14.7	13.4	12.0											
12/66	10.9	10.3	10.3	11.6	8.7	7.3	7.4	10.1	6.4	5.7	7.0	3.7	7.8	4.8	0.4	-11.2										
12/67	11.5	11.0	11.1	12.3	9.6	8.4	8.6	11.2	8.0	7.7	9.1	6.6	10.7	9.5	8.0	5.2	24.1									
12/68	11.4	11.0	11.0	12.1	9.6	8.5	8.7	11.2	8.3	8.0	9.3	7.2	10.7	9.7	8.7	7.2	17.7	10.7								
12/69	10.3	9.7	9.7	10.7	8.2	7.1	7.1	9.2	6.4	5.9	6.8	4.7	7.4	6.1	4.6	2.3	7.2	-1.1	-12.4							
12/70	9.9	9.4	9.3	10.2	7.9	6.8	6.8	8.7	6.1	5.6	6.3	4.4	6.6	5.2	3.8	2.0	5.5	-0.7	-6.6	-1.5						
12/71	10.1	9.5	9.5	10.3	8.1	7.1	7.1	8.9	6.4	6.1	6.8	5.1	7.2	6.2	4.9	3.6	6.8	2.4	-0.5	5.7	12.3					
12/72	10.3	9.8	9.8	10.6	8.5	7.5	7.6	9.3	7.1	6.8	7.5	6.0	8.1	7.3	6.3	5.3	8.3	5.0	3.4	9.0	14.2	14.8				
12/73	9.3	8.8	8.7	9.4	7.3	6.3	6.3	7.8	5.5	5.1	5.7	4.1	5.8	4.8	3.6	2.4	4.5	1.1	-0.9	1.9	2.6	-3.0	-19.6			
12/74	7.9	7.3	7.1	7.7	5.6	4.6	4.4	5.7	3.4	2.9	3.2	1.6	2.8	1.5	0.1	-1.3	0.0	-3.5	-5.9	-4.8	-6.1	-12.4	-24.4	-30.2		
12/75	8.6	8.1	7.9	8.6	6.6	5.7	5.6	6.9	4.9	4.4	4.9	3.4	4.8	3.6	2.6	1.6	3.2	0.5	-1.1	0.7	0.8	-2.6	-8.5	-3.0	33.4	
12/76	8.9	8.4	8.4	9.0	7.1	6.3	6.2	7.5	5.6	5.3	5.7	4.4	5.8	4.8	4.0	3.2	4.8	2.6	1.4	3.4	4.0	1.9	-1.6	4.9	28.1	20.8

*Percent per annum, compounded annually.

Sources: Stock market data—Lawrence Fisher and Myron Scholes (compilers), CRSP Monthly Master File for Common Stocks Listed on the New York Stock Exchange (magnetic tape). See Appendix A.
Income tax rates—Income levels estimated from U.S. Bureau of the Census, Current Population Reports, Series P-60, Nos. 101 and 103 and Historical Statistics of the United States. Tax rates were found in U.S. Internal Revenue Service, Statistics of Income and Your Federal Income Tax.

Held Until	Purchased 12/25	12/26	12/27	12/28	12/29	12/30	12/31	12/32	12/33	12/34	12/35	12/36	12/37	12/38	12/39	12/40	12/41	12/42	12/43	12/44	12/45	12/46	12/47	12/48	12/49
12/26	11.3																								
12/27	22.8	35.6																							
12/28	27.9	37.7	40.0																						
12/29	17.4	19.8	12.4	-12.7																					
12/30	9.0	8.6	0.1	-17.7	-23.2																				
12/31	0.8	-1.5	-10.1	-24.7	-30.6	-38.1																			
12/32	0.9	-1.0	-8.1	-19.3	-21.7	-21.1	1.6																		
12/33	5.6	4.7	-0.6	-8.7	-7.9	-2.0	25.1	55.5																	
12/34	5.3	4.4	-0.5	-7.3	-6.2	-1.2	17.0	26.2	1.0																
12/35	7.7	7.2	3.2	-2.4	-0.5	5.3	21.9	30.2	18.2	38.1															
12/36	9.2	8.9	5.5	0.8	3.0	8.7	23.2	30.2	22.0	34.5	30.0														
12/37	5.5	4.8	1.2	-3.6	-2.3	1.5	11.8	14.4	4.9	6.2	-8.1	-36.4													
12/38	6.7	6.2	3.1	-1.1	0.4	4.2	13.8	16.5	9.0	11.0	2.3	-10.1	29.3												
12/39	6.4	5.9	3.0	-0.9	0.5	4.0	12.5	14.6	7.9	9.3	2.2	-6.4	15.0	1.5											
12/40	5.6	5.1	2.2	-1.5	-0.3	2.9	10.3	11.9	5.5	6.3	-0.1	-7.2	6.5	-4.1	-9.9										
12/41	4.5	3.8	0.9	-2.7	-1.7	1.0	7.7	8.7	2.5	2.7	-3.2	-9.6	-0.2	-9.4	-14.8	-20.2									
12/42	4.4	3.8	1.0	-2.4	-1.4	1.2	7.4	8.3	2.7	2.8	-2.4	-7.7	0.4	-6.5	-9.4	-9.4	2.7								
12/43	4.9	4.3	1.7	-1.4	-0.3	2.2	8.1	9.0	4.0	4.3	-0.1	-4.5	3.2	-2.0	-3.1	-0.6	11.2	20.4							
12/44	5.2	4.7	2.3	-0.7	0.4	2.9	8.5	9.4	4.7	5.1	1.2	-2.5	4.6	0.4	0.1	2.9	12.4	17.7	14.8						
12/45	5.9	5.4	3.2	0.5	1.7	4.1	9.6	10.5	6.3	6.9	3.5	0.4	7.4	4.1	4.5	7.9	16.8	22.2	22.9	31.7					
12/46	4.8	4.3	2.0	-0.6	0.4	2.6	7.7	8.4	4.2	4.5	1.1	-1.9	4.0	0.6	0.4	2.4	8.0	9.4	5.8	1.5	-22.6				
12/47	4.5	4.0	1.8	-0.9	0.1	2.2	7.0	7.6	3.5	3.7	0.6	-2.3	2.9	-0.2	-0.5	1.0	5.4	5.9	2.4	-1.6	-15.6	-8.4			
12/48	4.4	3.9	1.6	-0.9	-0.0	2.0	6.6	7.2	3.2	3.4	0.3	-2.3	2.5	-0.4	-0.7	0.6	4.3	4.5	1.4	-1.9	-11.7	-5.8	-3.9		
12/49	4.7	4.2	2.1	-0.3	0.6	2.6	7.0	7.6	3.9	4.1	1.3	-1.1	3.5	1.0	0.9	2.3	5.8	6.3	3.9	1.7	-5.2	1.5	6.7	17.8	
12/50	5.0	4.6	2.6	0.3	1.3	3.2	7.5	8.1	4.6	4.9	2.3	0.1	4.6	2.3	2.3	3.8	7.2	7.8	5.9	4.4	-0.8	5.7	10.9	19.0	18.9
12/51	5.1	4.7	2.8	0.7	1.6	3.5	7.6	8.2	4.9	5.2	2.7	0.7	4.9	2.8	2.9	4.3	7.5	8.1	6.5	5.3	1.0	6.7	10.9	16.4	15.0
12/52	5.2	4.9	3.1	1.0	1.9	3.7	7.7	8.3	5.1	5.4	3.1	1.2	5.2	3.2	3.3	4.7	7.7	8.2	6.8	5.7	2.1	7.1	10.6	14.6	13.1
12/53	5.0	4.7	2.9	0.9	1.7	3.5	7.3	7.8	4.7	5.0	2.8	0.9	4.7	2.8	2.9	4.1	6.8	7.2	5.8	4.7	1.3	5.5	8.2	10.8	8.8
12/54	5.8	5.6	3.9	2.0	2.9	4.7	8.4	9.0	6.1	6.4	4.4	2.8	6.6	4.9	5.1	6.5	9.3	9.9	8.8	8.1	5.5	9.9	12.9	16.2	15.5
12/55	6.2	6.0	4.4	2.6	3.5	5.2	8.9	9.4	6.7	7.1	5.2	3.6	7.3	5.8	6.1	7.4	10.1	10.7	9.8	9.3	7.0	11.2	14.1	17.0	16.7
12/56	6.1	5.9	4.4	2.6	3.5	5.1	8.7	9.2	6.6	6.9	5.1	3.6	7.1	5.6	5.9	7.2	9.7	10.2	9.4	8.9	6.7	10.5	12.9	15.4	14.8
12/57	5.7	5.4	3.8	2.1	2.9	4.5	8.0	8.4	5.8	6.1	4.2	2.8	6.1	4.6	4.8	5.9	8.1	8.6	7.7	7.0	4.9	8.1	10.1	11.9	10.9
12/58	6.2	6.0	4.5	2.9	3.7	5.3	8.6	9.1	6.7	7.0	5.3	3.9	7.2	5.8	6.1	7.2	9.5	10.0	9.2	8.8	6.9	10.1	12.2	14.1	13.5
12/59	6.3	6.0	4.6	3.0	3.8	5.4	8.6	9.1	6.7	7.0	5.4	4.1	7.2	6.0	6.2	7.3	9.5	9.9	9.2	8.7	6.9	10.1	12.0	13.7	13.1
12/60	6.0	5.7	4.4	2.8	3.6	5.1	8.3	8.8	6.4	6.6	5.0	3.8	6.7	5.5	5.7	6.7	8.7	9.1	8.4	7.9	6.1	9.1	10.7	12.2	11.5
12/61	6.3	6.1	4.8	3.3	4.1	5.6	8.7	9.1	6.9	7.1	5.6	4.4	7.3	6.1	6.4	7.4	9.4	9.8	9.1	8.7	7.1	9.9	11.6	13.0	12.4
12/62	6.0	5.8	4.5	3.0	3.7	5.2	8.2	8.6	6.4	6.6	5.1	3.9	6.7	5.5	5.7	6.7	8.5	8.9	8.1	7.7	6.1	8.6	10.1	11.3	10.6
12/63	6.3	6.0	4.8	3.3	4.0	5.4	8.4	8.9	6.7	6.9	5.5	4.3	7.0	5.9	6.1	7.1	8.9	9.2	8.6	8.2	6.7	9.1	10.5	11.7	11.1
12/64	6.4	6.2	5.0	3.6	4.3	5.7	8.6	9.0	6.9	7.1	5.7	4.7	7.3	6.2	6.4	7.4	9.1	9.5	8.8	8.5	7.0	9.4	10.8	11.9	11.3
12/65	6.4	6.2	5.0	3.7	4.4	5.7	8.6	9.0	6.9	7.2	5.8	4.8	7.3	6.3	6.5	7.4	9.1	9.5	8.8	8.5	7.1	9.4	10.7	11.8	11.2
12/66	6.0	5.8	4.6	3.2	3.9	5.2	8.0	8.4	6.3	6.5	5.2	4.1	6.6	5.5	5.7	6.5	8.2	8.5	7.8	7.4	6.1	8.3	9.4	10.3	9.7
12/67	6.3	6.0	4.8	3.5	4.2	5.5	8.2	8.6	6.6	6.9	5.5	4.5	6.9	5.9	6.1	6.9	8.5	8.8	8.2	7.9	6.6	8.7	9.9	10.8	10.2
12/68	6.2	6.0	4.8	3.5	4.2	5.5	8.2	8.6	6.6	6.8	5.5	4.5	6.9	5.9	6.1	6.9	8.4	8.7	8.1	7.8	6.5	8.6	9.7	10.6	10.0
12/69	5.9	5.6	4.5	3.1	3.8	5.0	7.7	8.1	6.1	6.3	5.0	4.0	6.3	5.3	5.4	6.2	7.6	7.9	7.3	6.9	5.6	7.6	8.6	9.4	8.7
12/70	5.8	5.5	4.4	3.1	3.7	4.9	7.6	7.9	5.9	6.1	4.8	3.8	6.1	5.1	5.2	5.9	7.4	7.6	7.0	6.6	5.4	7.2	8.2	8.9	8.3
12/71	5.8	5.6	4.4	3.2	3.8	5.0	7.6	7.9	5.9	6.1	4.9	3.9	6.1	5.2	5.3	6.0	7.4	7.7	7.0	6.7	5.5	7.3	8.2	8.9	8.3
12/72	5.9	5.7	4.6	3.3	3.9	5.1	7.7	8.0	6.1	6.3	5.0	4.1	6.3	5.3	5.5	6.2	7.6	7.8	7.2	6.9	5.7	7.5	8.4	9.0	8.5
12/73	5.6	5.3	4.1	2.9	3.5	4.6	7.2	7.5	5.5	5.7	4.5	3.5	5.7	4.7	4.8	5.5	6.8	7.0	6.4	6.0	4.8	6.5	7.3	8.0	7.3
12/74	5.0	4.7	3.5	2.2	2.8	4.0	6.6	6.9	4.8	5.0	3.7	2.6	4.8	3.8	3.9	4.5	5.8	5.9	5.3	4.8	3.6	5.2	5.9	6.5	5.8
12/75	5.2	4.9	3.7	2.5	3.1	4.2	6.8	7.1	5.1	5.2	4.0	3.0	5.1	4.1	4.2	4.9	6.1	6.3	5.6	5.3	4.1	5.6	6.4	6.9	6.3
12/76	5.3	5.0	3.9	2.6	3.2	4.3	6.9	7.2	5.2	5.4	4.1	3.2	5.3	4.3	4.4	5.0	6.3	6.5	5.8	5.5	4.3	5.8	6.6	7.1	6.5

Table XXII

Internal Rates of Return* on Common Stocks:
Dividends Consumed,
Cash to Portfolio,
Initial Weighting by Value,
Higher Tax Rate,
Deflated by the Consumer Price Index

Held until	Purchased 12/50	12/51	12/52	12/53	12/54	12/55	12/56	12/57	12/58	12/59	12/60	12/61	12/62	12/63	12/64	12/65	12/66	12/67	12/68	12/69	12/70	12/71	12/72	12/73	12/74	12/75
/51	10.4																									
/52	9.8	8.3																								
/53	5.2	2.2	-4.1																							
/54	14.4	15.5	18.9	46.6																						
/55	15.9	17.3	20.2	34.2	21.6																					
/56	13.9	14.5	15.9	23.3	12.4	3.0																				
/57	9.5	9.3	9.3	12.8	2.8	-6.2	-15.6																			
/58	12.6	12.9	13.5	17.4	10.5	6.7	8.1	37.7																		
/59	12.2	12.4	12.9	16.0	10.1	7.1	8.5	23.0	8.6																	
/60	10.6	10.6	10.8	13.2	7.9	5.0	5.4	13.7	2.7	-3.5																
/61	11.7	11.7	12.1	14.4	10.0	7.9	8.9	16.3	9.4	9.5	23.4															
/62	9.8	9.6	9.7	11.4	7.2	5.1	5.4	10.3	3.9	2.0	4.4	-12.7														
/63	10.3	10.2	10.4	12.0	8.3	6.5	7.0	11.4	6.3	5.5	8.4	1.1	16.2													
/64	10.6	10.5	10.7	12.2	8.8	7.3	7.8	11.7	7.4	7.0	9.6	4.9	14.6	12.1												
/65	10.6	10.5	10.6	12.0	8.8	7.4	7.9	11.4	7.6	7.3	9.5	6.0	13.0	11.6	9.8											
/66	9.0	8.8	8.7	9.9	6.8	5.3	5.5	8.3	4.7	4.1	5.2	1.8	5.7	2.6	-2.2	-14.1										
/67	9.5	9.3	9.4	10.5	7.6	6.3	6.6	9.3	6.2	5.8	7.1	4.5	8.3	7.0	5.1	1.9	20.5									
/68	9.3	9.1	9.1	10.1	7.5	6.3	6.5	9.0	6.1	5.8	7.0	4.7	7.9	6.7	5.3	3.4	13.3	5.7								
/69	8.0	7.7	7.6	8.5	5.8	4.6	4.6	6.8	3.9	3.4	4.1	1.9	4.2	2.7	0.7	-1.9	2.4	-6.2	-17.5							
/70	7.5	7.2	7.1	7.9	5.3	4.1	4.2	6.0	3.4	2.8	3.4	1.2	3.1	1.6	-0.3	-2.4	0.6	-5.8	-11.7	-6.6						
/71	7.6	7.3	7.2	7.9	5.5	4.3	4.4	6.2	3.7	3.2	3.8	1.9	3.7	2.5	0.9	-0.7	2.2	-2.4	-5.2	1.2	8.6					
/72	7.8	7.5	7.4	8.1	5.8	4.7	4.8	6.5	4.2	3.8	4.5	2.8	4.5	3.6	2.3	1.0	3.8	0.3	-1.1	4.7	10.5	11.0				
/73	6.6	6.3	6.1	6.7	4.4	3.3	3.2	4.7	2.4	1.9	2.3	0.5	1.9	0.7	-0.8	-2.3	-0.4	-4.0	-6.0	-3.2	-2.4	-8.6	-26.1			
/74	4.9	4.6	4.3	4.8	2.4	1.2	1.1	2.3	-0.0	-0.7	-0.6	-2.5	-1.5	-3.1	-4.8	-6.4	-5.4	-9.1	-11.6	-10.6	-12.1	-18.9	-31.6	-37.8		
/75	5.5	5.1	4.9	5.4	3.2	2.1	2.0	3.3	1.1	0.6	0.8	-0.9	0.2	-1.2	-2.5	-3.8	-2.6	-5.5	-7.2	-5.6	-5.7	-9.6	-16.3	-11.5	24.6	
/76	5.8	5.4	5.2	5.7	3.6	2.6	2.6	3.8	1.8	1.3	1.6	0.1	1.1	-0.1	-1.2	-2.2	-0.9	-3.4	-4.6	-2.8	-2.4	-4.9	-9.1	-2.9	21.0	15.3

*Percent per annum, compounded annually.

Sources: Stock market data—Lawrence Fisher and Myron Scholes (compilers), CRSP Monthly Master File for Common Stocks Listed on the New York Stock Exchange (magnetic tape). See Appendix A.
Consumer Price Index—U.S. Bureau of Labor Statistics.
Income tax rates—Income levels estimated from U.S. Bureau of the Census, Current Population Reports, Series P-60, Nos. 101 and 103 and Historical Statistics of the United States. Tax rates were found in U.S. Internal Revenue Service, Statistics of Income and Your Federal Income Tax.

Chapter 7

Rates of Price Change of Common Stocks

(Cash to Portfolio)

For some investors, there is a distinction among the various parts of the total return on investment. Hence, the frequently asked questions, "How much of the overall rate of return was due to capital gains?" and "How much was due to dividends?" The first question may be especially relevant for the remainderman of an estate, for example.

Tables XXIII through XXVI present our answer to the first question. The annual rates of change reported in these tables are found by assuming that dividends were taxed at the rate of 100 percent or were not available to the investor for some other reason. Thus, they are lower than the corresponding rates of return reported in all of the previous tables. The rates of price change were found from Equation 3.4.

The second question may be answered by comparing an entry in any of Tables I–XII with the corresponding entry in Tables XXIII–XXVI. For example, Tables I, III, and V may be used with Table XXIII. The calculation is made by applying Equation 3.6 to obtain precise results or by subtracting the rate of price change from the time-weighted rate of return (cf. Approximation 3.7). These comparisons are valid because all of the cash-to-portfolio calculations assume that no capital-gain taxes have been paid.

Held Until	12/25	12/26	12/27	12/28	12/29	12/30	12/31	12/32	12/33	12/34	12/35	12/36	12/37	12/38	12/39	12/40	12/41	12/42	12/43	12/44	12/45	12/46	12/47	12/48	12/49
12/26	−3.2																								
12/27	11.5	24.5																							
12/28	19.3	33.0	41.8																						
12/29	4.1	5.9	−2.4	−32.0																					
12/30	−6.3	−7.5	−16.3	−34.7	−40.9																				
12/31	−15.3	−17.3	−24.9	−39.4	−44.1	−50.5																			
12/32	−15.0	−16.6	−22.3	−33.7	−35.6	−33.8	−13.4																		
12/33	−7.3	−7.5	−11.4	−19.6	−15.9	−5.0	33.4	102.4																	
12/34	−5.6	−5.8	−9.0	−15.4	−11.1	−1.3	25.0	51.3	12.6																
12/35	−2.2	−2.2	−4.8	−9.8	−4.6	5.8	30.0	50.5	29.2	47.4															
12/36	0.3	0.5	−1.7	−5.8	−0.1	10.4	32.5	49.2	34.0	47.2	42.5														
12/37	−3.9	−4.3	−6.6	−10.7	−7.3	−0.9	12.5	19.4	4.6	2.5	−15.2	−48.8													
12/38	−1.8	−2.0	−4.0	−7.5	−3.7	2.7	15.0	21.4	9.3	8.5	−3.1	−19.7	26.6												
12/39	−2.0	−2.3	−4.1	−7.3	−3.8	1.7	11.8	16.5	6.4	5.1	−3.8	−15.1	9.0	−6.7											
12/40	−2.7	−3.0	−4.7	−7.7	−4.5	0.1	8.9	12.6	3.8	2.0	−5.5	−14.0	1.9	−9.2	−14.3										
12/41	−3.4	−3.8	−5.4	−8.1	−5.5	−1.3	6.4	9.1	1.3	−0.6	−6.9	−14.0	−2.5	−10.5	−14.3	−15.7									
12/42	−2.9	−3.1	−4.6	−7.1	−4.4	−0.3	6.7	9.1	2.2	0.8	−4.5	−10.1	0.4	−5.0	−5.2	0.6	22.6								
12/43	−1.5	−1.6	−2.8	−5.0	−2.2	2.0	8.9	11.3	5.2	4.5	0.1	−4.5	6.7	3.8	5.9	15.6	39.6	49.8							
12/44	−0.4	−0.4	−1.5	−3.5	−0.5	3.7	10.3	12.9	7.3	6.9	3.1	−0.7	10.1	8.2	11.0	20.5	39.1	43.1	32.6						
12/45	1.3	1.5	0.6	−1.2	2.0	6.3	12.9	15.6	10.5	10.5	7.4	4.1	15.0	14.0	18.0	27.9	45.8	49.9	44.7	55.1					
12/46	0.6	0.8	−0.2	−1.8	1.0	4.9	10.8	13.1	8.4	8.1	5.2	2.1	11.0	9.8	12.2	18.6	29.5	29.4	21.2	15.9	−13.2				
12/47	0.5	0.6	−0.3	−1.9	0.7	4.3	9.8	11.8	7.4	7.1	4.3	1.5	9.3	8.4	9.9	14.6	22.2	21.1	13.8	8.3	−9.0	−5.7			
12/48	0.1	0.2	−0.8	−2.3	0.1	3.4	8.5	10.3	6.2	5.7	3.0	0.4	7.2	6.3	7.5	11.3	17.0	15.3	8.7	3.7	−8.8	−6.9	−9.4		
12/49	0.6	0.7	−0.2	−1.6	0.7	3.8	8.6	10.3	6.5	6.1	3.6	1.2	7.6	6.7	8.0	11.4	16.8	15.3	9.4	5.7	−3.9	−0.9	1.2	11.9	
12/50	1.4	1.5	0.7	−0.7	1.7	4.9	9.7	11.3	7.5	7.3	5.0	2.8	8.9	8.2	9.5	12.9	17.8	16.6	11.8	8.8	1.5	5.5	9.1	19.1	27.2
12/51	1.8	1.9	1.2	−0.2	2.1	5.2	9.8	11.2	7.6	7.5	5.3	3.2	8.9	8.2	9.5	12.5	16.9	15.7	11.5	9.1	3.0	6.4	9.2	15.7	17.7
12/52	1.9	2.0	1.3	0.0	2.2	5.1	9.5	10.8	7.5	7.4	5.3	3.3	8.6	7.9	9.1	11.9	15.9	14.6	10.7	8.4	3.2	6.2	8.2	12.7	12.9
12/53	1.5	1.7	0.9	−0.3	1.7	4.4	8.5	9.8	6.6	6.5	4.4	2.6	7.4	6.6	7.7	10.1	13.7	12.3	8.7	6.5	1.7	4.0	5.4	8.4	7.1
12/54	2.8	3.0	2.3	1.2	3.2	6.0	10.1	11.4	8.4	8.4	6.5	4.8	9.5	8.9	10.1	12.6	16.3	15.2	12.1	10.3	6.2	9.0	11.0	14.6	14.9
12/55	3.2	3.4	2.8	1.7	3.8	6.5	10.6	11.8	8.9	9.0	7.0	5.4	10.0	9.4	10.6	12.9	16.2	15.3	12.5	10.9	7.3	9.8	11.6	14.9	15.4
12/56	3.3	3.6	3.0	1.9	3.9	6.5	10.4	11.6	8.8	8.9	7.0	5.4	9.8	9.4	10.3	12.3	15.2	14.5	11.9	10.4	7.2	9.4	10.8	13.5	13.9
12/57	2.7	2.9	2.2	1.2	3.0	5.4	9.1	10.1	7.5	7.5	5.6	4.2	8.1	7.6	8.4	10.2	12.8	11.9	9.4	7.9	4.8	6.4	7.5	9.4	9.0
12/58	3.8	4.0	3.4	2.4	4.3	6.8	10.4	11.4	8.9	9.0	7.2	5.9	9.8	9.4	10.3	12.1	14.8	14.0	11.6	10.3	7.6	9.4	10.7	12.9	13.0
12/59	4.0	4.2	3.5	2.6	4.5	7.0	10.5	11.5	9.0	9.1	7.4	6.1	10.0	9.6	10.4	12.1	14.6	13.8	11.5	10.3	7.8	9.6	10.9	13.0	13.2
12/60	4.0	4.1	3.4	2.5	4.3	6.6	9.9	10.9	8.6	8.7	7.0	5.7	9.3	8.8	9.5	11.1	13.4	12.6	10.5	9.4	6.9	8.6	9.7	11.5	11.5
12/61	4.6	4.7	4.0	3.1	4.9	7.2	10.5	11.4	9.2	9.3	7.7	6.5	9.9	9.5	10.3	11.9	14.1	13.3	11.2	10.2	7.9	9.5	10.7	12.3	12.3
12/62	3.9	4.0	3.4	2.4	4.1	6.3	9.4	10.2	8.0	8.1	6.6	5.4	8.6	8.2	8.9	10.3	12.2	11.4	9.4	8.4	6.2	7.6	8.4	9.7	9.5
12/63	4.2	4.3	3.7	2.7	4.5	6.6	9.7	10.5	8.4	8.5	6.9	5.8	8.9	8.5	9.2	10.6	12.4	11.6	9.7	8.8	6.7	8.1	8.9	10.2	10.0
12/64	4.4	4.5	3.9	3.0	4.7	6.8	9.7	10.5	8.5	8.6	7.2	6.1	9.1	8.7	9.4	10.7	12.4	11.7	9.9	9.1	7.1	8.4	9.2	10.4	10.3
12/65	4.7	4.8	4.2	3.4	5.1	7.2	10.2	11.0	8.9	9.0	7.6	6.5	9.5	9.1	9.8	11.0	12.7	12.1	10.4	9.6	7.7	9.2	10.0	11.2	11.2
12/66	4.4	4.5	3.9	3.0	4.6	6.6	9.5	10.2	8.2	8.3	6.9	5.9	8.7	8.3	8.9	10.1	11.7	11.0	9.4	8.6	6.8	8.2	8.9	10.0	9.9
12/67	5.1	5.2	4.6	3.8	5.4	7.3	10.1	10.8	9.0	9.1	7.8	6.8	9.6	9.3	9.9	11.1	12.6	12.0	10.4	9.6	8.0	9.3	10.0	11.2	11.2
12/68	5.3	5.4	4.9	4.1	5.6	7.5	10.2	11.0	9.2	9.3	8.0	7.1	9.8	9.5	10.1	11.3	12.8	12.2	10.7	9.9	8.3	9.6	10.3	11.4	11.5
12/69	4.9	5.0	4.3	3.6	5.0	6.7	9.2	10.0	8.3	8.3	7.2	6.2	8.8	8.6	9.0	10.0	11.4	10.8	9.2	8.5	7.0	8.1	8.7	9.7	9.7
12/70	4.7	4.7	4.1	3.4	4.7	6.4	8.8	9.5	7.9	7.9	6.8	5.9	8.4	8.4	8.5	9.5	10.7	10.1	8.6	8.0	6.5	7.5	8.0	8.9	8.9
12/71	4.8	4.9	4.3	3.6	5.0	6.7	9.0	9.7	8.1	8.1	7.0	6.1	8.6	8.5	8.7	9.6	10.8	10.2	8.8	8.2	6.8	7.9	8.4	9.3	9.2
12/72	5.0	5.1	4.5	3.9	5.2	6.8	9.1	9.7	8.1	8.1	7.1	6.2	8.6	8.3	8.6	9.6	10.7	10.1	8.8	8.3	6.9	8.0	8.5	9.4	9.3
12/73	4.5	4.5	4.0	3.3	4.5	5.9	8.1	8.6	7.2	7.2	6.2	5.3	7.5	7.3	7.5	8.3	9.4	8.8	7.5	7.0	5.8	6.7	7.0	7.8	7.7
12/74	3.7	3.7	3.2	2.6	3.6	5.0	7.1	7.6	6.2	6.2	5.3	4.4	6.5	6.5	6.5	7.2	8.1	7.5	6.2	5.7	4.4	5.2	5.5	6.1	6.0
12/75	4.2	4.3	3.8	3.2	4.3	5.7	7.8	8.3	6.9	6.9	6.0	5.2	7.3	7.4	7.3	8.1	8.9	8.4	7.1	6.6	5.4	6.2	6.5	7.2	7.1
12/76	4.6	4.6	4.2	3.6	4.7	6.1	8.2	8.7	7.3	7.3	6.4	5.6	7.7	7.8	7.8	8.5	9.4	8.9	7.7	7.2	6.0	6.8	7.1	7.8	7.7

Table XXIII

Rates of Change* in Prices of Common Stocks: Cash to Portfolio, Equal Initial Weighting, Tax-Exempt, Current Dollars

Purchased	12/50	12/51	12/52	12/53	12/54	12/55	12/56	12/57	12/58	12/59	12/60	12/61	12/62	12/63	12/64	12/65	12/66	12/67	12/68	12/69	12/70	12/71	12/72	12/73	12/74	12/75
'51	8.2																									
'52	6.1	2.9																								
'53	1.5	−2.3	−8.6																							
'54	11.6	12.3	16.6	47.9																						
'55	12.4	13.2	16.5	31.5	14.2																					
'56	11.2	11.4	13.3	21.5	8.8	2.0																				
'57	6.5	5.9	6.2	9.7	−0.9	−8.0	−17.8																			
'58	11.1	11.3	12.6	17.1	10.0	8.3	11.9	52.1																		
'59	11.4	11.6	12.8	16.6	10.8	9.6	12.6	31.4	10.8																	
'60	10.0	10.1	10.9	13.6	8.4	7.1	8.6	17.8	2.9	−5.4																
'61	11.1	11.3	12.2	14.8	10.6	9.9	11.8	19.7	10.0	9.4	24.0															
'62	8.3	8.2	8.6	10.5	6.5	5.4	6.4	11.4	2.9	0.5	2.6	−16.3														
'63	8.8	8.8	9.2	11.0	7.5	6.5	7.5	12.1	5.3	4.0	7.1	−1.2	14.2													
'64	9.2	9.1	9.6	11.3	8.1	7.3	8.3	12.5	6.9	6.2	9.3	4.3	15.0	13.1												
'65	10.0	10.1	10.6	12.4	9.4	8.8	9.8	14.1	9.3	9.1	12.6	9.7	19.3	20.3	25.0											
'66	8.7	8.6	9.1	10.6	7.7	7.0	7.7	11.4	6.8	6.4	8.8	5.8	11.7	9.8	6.9	−11.1										
'67	10.1	10.2	10.7	12.4	9.8	9.2	10.1	13.9	10.0	10.1	12.8	11.0	17.5	18.2	19.2	14.5	47.4									
'68	10.5	10.7	11.2	12.8	10.4	10.0	10.9	14.4	11.1	11.3	14.0	12.4	18.0	18.8	19.9	17.7	36.7	25.1								
'69	8.7	8.7	9.1	10.4	8.0	7.5	8.1	10.8	7.5	7.3	9.0	7.1	11.0	10.5	9.9	6.4	13.1	−1.1	−22.3							
'70	8.0	7.9	8.3	9.4	7.2	6.7	7.1	9.4	6.4	6.1	7.4	5.4	8.5	7.5	6.5	3.3	7.7	−2.7	−14.6	−7.7						
'71	8.4	8.4	8.7	9.8	7.8	7.3	7.8	10.0	7.2	7.0	8.3	6.7	9.5	8.7	7.9	5.3	9.4	1.6	−5.5	3.6	14.0					
'72	8.4	8.4	8.8	9.8	7.9	7.4	7.8	10.0	7.3	7.2	8.3	6.9	9.5	8.9	8.2	5.8	9.2	2.9	−2.0	4.9	10.6	4.0				
'73	6.8	6.7	7.0	7.8	5.9	5.3	5.5	7.2	4.8	4.5	5.3	3.9	5.9	4.9	3.7	1.1	3.1	−2.5	−7.1	−3.6	−3.9	−12.6	−30.6			
'74	5.0	4.9	5.0	5.8	3.9	3.2	3.3	4.6	2.3	1.9	2.4	0.9	2.4	1.3	−0.1	−2.7	−1.6	−6.7	−11.0	−8.9	−10.5	−17.8	−29.2	−30.8		
'75	6.2	6.1	6.3	7.1	5.3	4.8	5.0	6.5	4.2	4.0	4.7	3.3	5.0	4.1	3.1	1.0	2.5	−1.8	−5.1	−2.1	−1.8	−5.8	−10.5	1.4	47.5	
'76	6.9	6.8	7.1	7.9	6.2	5.7	5.9	7.5	5.4	5.2	6.1	4.8	6.5	5.9	5.0	3.2	4.9	1.1	−1.5	2.0	3.2	0.9	−1.0	11.9	42.7	35.1

**Percent per annum, compounded annually.*

Source: Lawrence Fisher and Myron Scholes (compilers), CRSP Monthly Master File for Common Stocks Listed on the New York Stock Exchange *(magnetic tape). See Appendix A.*

Held Until	12/25	12/26	12/27	12/28	12/29	12/30	12/31	12/32	12/33	12/34	12/35	12/36	12/37	12/38	12/39	12/40	12/41	12/42	12/43	12/44	12/45	12/46	12/47	12/48	12/49
12/26	-1.7																								
12/27	13.5	27.2																							
12/28	21.2	35.1	43.1																						
12/29	5.2	7.0	-2.0	-32.2																					
12/30	-4.3	-5.3	-14.3	-32.8	-37.1																				
12/31	-12.4	-14.1	-21.6	-36.1	-39.4	-45.2																			
12/32	-11.1	-12.3	-17.9	-29.1	-29.5	-26.5	-3.4																		
12/33	-3.6	-3.5	-7.2	-15.3	-10.1	1.7	40.5	101.4																	
12/34	-2.5	-2.6	-5.7	-11.9	-6.6	3.3	28.5	49.4	10.4																
12/35	0.4	0.5	-2.1	-7.0	-1.1	9.1	31.8	47.8	26.0	43.2															
12/36	2.5	2.8	0.7	-3.4	2.9	13.1	33.6	46.8	31.3	44.1	40.8														
12/37	-2.2	-2.5	-4.9	-9.0	-5.3	0.7	12.7	17.1	2.2	0.0	-17.0	-50.3													
12/38	0.1	-0.1	-2.1	-5.6	-1.5	4.5	15.7	20.0	7.9	7.3	-3.6	-19.8	30.2												
12/39	-0.3	-0.5	-2.4	-5.6	-1.8	3.3	12.4	15.4	5.4	4.2	-4.1	-15.0	10.8	-6.3											
12/40	-1.1	-1.4	-3.2	-6.2	-2.8	1.5	9.3	11.6	2.8	1.2	-5.9	-14.2	2.7	-9.4	-15.1										
12/41	-2.5	-3.0	-4.7	-7.4	-4.6	-0.9	5.7	7.1	-0.8	-2.6	-8.6	-15.7	-4.2	-13.3	-18.6	-23.2									
12/42	-2.5	-2.9	-4.4	-7.0	-4.2	-0.7	5.2	6.4	-0.6	-2.1	-7.2	-12.9	-2.7	-9.4	-11.0	-8.1	12.2								
12/43	-1.3	-1.5	-2.8	-5.1	-2.3	1.4	7.3	8.5	2.3	1.5	-2.8	-7.4	3.4	-0.6	0.2	7.7	31.5	45.2							
12/44	-0.4	-0.4	-1.6	-3.7	-0.7	2.9	8.6	10.0	4.4	3.9	0.3	-3.7	6.8	4.0	5.8	13.7	32.7	39.4	29.9						
12/45	1.2	1.4	0.3	-1.5	1.6	5.5	11.1	12.7	7.6	7.5	4.5	1.1	11.7	9.9	12.9	21.5	40.0	46.2	41.6	51.7					
12/46	-0.3	-0.2	-1.3	-3.1	-0.3	3.0	8.0	9.2	4.4	4.0	1.0	-2.2	6.2	4.1	5.5	10.5	21.2	21.9	13.0	5.5	-26.5				
12/47	-0.7	-0.7	-1.8	-3.5	-1.0	2.0	6.5	7.6	3.1	2.6	-0.2	-3.2	4.1	2.4	3.0	6.6	14.0	13.4	5.6	-1.2	-19.8	-13.4			
12/48	-1.1	-1.2	-2.3	-4.0	-1.7	1.1	5.3	6.2	2.0	1.4	-1.3	-4.1	2.3	0.7	1.2	4.0	9.8	8.7	1.9	-3.8	-16.9	-12.0	-11.8		
12/49	-0.5	-0.6	-1.6	-3.1	-0.9	1.7	5.8	6.6	2.6	2.2	-0.3	-2.8	3.2	1.7	2.4	5.1	10.8	9.9	4.0	-0.2	-10.0	-4.0	0.8	14.0	
12/50	0.1	0.0	-0.9	-2.4	-0.1	2.6	6.6	7.3	3.5	3.2	0.9	-1.4	4.4	3.1	3.9	6.6	11.7	11.0	6.2	2.8	-4.8	1.6	6.8	16.8	20.3
12/51	0.3	0.3	-0.6	-2.1	0.1	2.7	6.6	7.2	3.5	3.3	1.1	-1.1	4.2	3.0	3.8	6.2	10.8	10.1	5.8	3.0	-3.2	2.1	5.9	12.1	11.2
12/52	0.4	0.4	-0.4	-1.8	0.2	2.7	6.4	7.0	3.5	3.4	1.3	-0.8	4.2	3.0	3.8	6.1	10.3	9.5	5.6	3.0	-2.3	2.4	5.4	9.8	8.4
12/53	0.0	0.1	-0.7	-2.1	-0.2	2.1	5.5	6.1	2.9	2.7	0.6	-1.3	3.3	2.1	2.8	4.8	8.5	7.7	4.1	1.7	-3.1	0.7	3.0	6.0	3.7
12/54	1.4	1.5	0.7	-0.6	1.4	3.8	7.3	7.9	4.8	4.8	2.8	1.1	5.6	4.6	5.5	7.6	11.5	10.9	7.8	5.9	1.8	6.0	8.9	12.6	12.1
12/55	1.9	2.0	1.2	0.0	2.0	4.4	7.8	8.4	5.4	5.4	3.5	1.8	6.2	5.3	6.1	8.1	11.7	11.3	8.6	6.8	3.2	7.1	9.8	13.1	12.9
12/56	1.9	2.0	1.3	0.2	2.0	4.3	7.6	8.2	5.3	5.4	3.5	1.9	6.1	5.3	5.9	7.7	10.9	10.5	8.1	6.5	3.2	6.7	8.8	11.6	11.4
12/57	1.2	1.3	0.5	-0.6	1.2	3.2	6.3	6.7	4.1	4.0	2.2	0.7	4.5	3.7	4.2	5.7	8.6	8.1	5.6	4.1	1.0	3.7	5.4	7.4	6.5
12/58	2.3	2.4	1.7	0.6	2.4	4.5	7.6	8.1	5.5	5.5	3.8	2.4	6.3	5.5	6.1	7.7	10.6	10.2	7.9	6.6	3.8	6.7	8.6	10.9	10.5
12/59	2.5	2.6	1.8	0.8	2.7	4.8	7.8	8.2	5.7	5.8	4.1	2.8	6.5	5.8	6.3	7.8	10.6	10.1	7.9	6.7	4.1	7.0	8.9	11.0	10.7
12/60	2.5	2.5	1.7	0.7	2.4	4.4	7.2	7.7	5.3	5.4	3.8	2.4	5.9	5.1	5.7	7.1	9.6	9.1	7.0	5.9	3.4	6.1	7.7	9.6	9.1
12/61	3.1	3.1	2.3	1.3	3.1	5.1	7.9	8.3	6.0	6.1	4.5	3.2	6.6	6.0	6.5	7.9	10.3	9.9	7.9	6.8	4.6	7.1	8.7	10.4	10.0
12/62	2.4	2.4	1.7	0.7	2.3	4.2	6.8	7.2	5.0	5.0	3.5	2.3	5.4	4.8	5.2	6.5	8.7	8.2	6.2	5.2	3.0	5.3	6.6	7.9	7.5
12/63	2.7	2.8	2.0	1.0	2.7	4.6	7.2	7.5	5.3	5.4	3.9	2.7	5.8	5.1	5.6	6.8	8.9	8.5	6.6	5.7	3.7	5.9	7.1	8.4	8.0
12/64	2.9	3.0	2.3	1.3	2.9	4.7	7.2	7.6	5.5	5.5	4.2	3.1	6.0	5.4	5.9	7.0	9.0	8.7	6.9	6.0	4.1	6.2	7.4	8.6	8.3
12/65	3.2	3.2	2.6	1.7	3.3	5.2	7.7	8.0	5.9	6.0	4.6	3.5	6.4	5.8	6.3	7.4	9.4	9.0	7.4	6.6	4.8	7.0	8.2	9.4	9.2
12/66	2.8	2.9	2.2	1.3	2.8	4.5	6.9	7.2	5.3	5.3	4.0	2.9	5.7	5.1	5.5	6.6	8.4	8.0	6.4	5.6	3.8	5.9	7.0	8.1	7.8
12/67	3.5	3.6	2.9	2.0	3.5	5.2	7.6	7.9	6.0	6.1	4.8	3.8	6.5	6.0	6.5	7.5	9.2	8.9	7.4	6.6	5.0	6.9	8.0	9.2	9.0
12/68	3.6	3.7	3.0	2.2	3.7	5.3	7.6	7.9	6.1	6.2	5.0	4.0	6.7	6.2	6.6	7.7	9.4	9.0	7.5	6.8	5.2	7.1	8.2	9.3	9.1
12/69	3.2	3.2	2.4	1.6	2.9	4.4	6.5	6.9	5.2	5.2	4.0	3.1	5.6	5.2	5.4	6.3	7.9	7.5	6.0	5.3	3.8	5.5	6.4	7.4	7.1
12/70	2.8	2.8	2.1	1.4	2.6	4.0	6.1	6.4	4.7	4.7	3.6	2.7	5.1	4.9	4.9	5.8	7.2	6.8	5.4	4.7	3.2	4.8	5.6	6.5	6.2
12/71	2.9	3.0	2.3	1.6	2.8	4.2	6.2	6.5	4.9	4.9	3.8	2.9	5.3	5.0	5.1	5.9	7.3	6.9	5.5	4.9	3.5	5.1	5.9	6.8	6.5
12/72	3.1	3.1	2.4	1.7	3.0	4.4	6.3	6.5	4.9	4.9	3.9	3.0	5.3	4.8	5.0	5.8	7.2	6.8	5.5	5.0	3.6	5.2	6.0	6.8	6.5
12/73	2.4	2.4	1.8	1.1	2.2	3.4	5.2	5.4	3.9	3.9	2.9	2.0	4.1	3.7	3.8	4.5	5.7	5.3	4.1	3.6	2.3	3.7	4.3	5.0	4.8
12/74	1.5	1.4	0.8	0.1	1.1	2.2	3.9	4.1	2.7	2.6	1.8	0.8	2.9	2.7	2.6	3.2	4.2	3.8	2.6	2.0	0.7	1.9	2.4	3.0	2.7
12/75	1.9	1.9	1.3	0.6	1.7	2.9	4.6	4.7	3.3	3.3	2.4	1.5	3.6	3.5	3.3	3.9	4.9	4.6	3.3	2.8	1.5	2.7	3.2	3.9	3.6
12/76	2.2	2.2	1.6	1.0	2.0	3.2	4.9	5.1	3.7	3.6	2.8	1.9	4.0	3.9	3.7	4.3	5.3	5.0	3.8	3.3	2.1	3.3	3.8	4.4	4.2

Table XXIV

Rates of Change* in Prices of Common Stocks:
 Cash to Portfolio,
 Equal Initial Weighting,
 Tax-Exempt,
 Deflated by the Consumer Price Index

Held until	Purchased 12/50	12/51	12/52	12/53	12/54
/51	2.2				
/52	2.7	2.0			
/53	−0.9	−3.0	−9.2		
/54	9.7	11.9	16.5	48.6	
/55	10.8	12.9	16.3	31.5	13.8
/56	9.3	10.5	12.3	20.4	7.0
/57	4.6	4.6	4.8	8.2	−2.9
/58	9.1	9.9	11.1	15.4	7.8
/59	9.4	10.2	11.3	14.9	8.7
/60	8.0	8.6	9.4	11.9	6.5
/61	9.3	9.9	10.7	13.2	8.8
/62	6.6	6.9	7.2	9.0	4.8
/63	7.1	7.4	7.8	9.5	5.8
/64	7.4	7.7	8.2	9.8	6.5
/65	8.3	8.6	9.1	10.8	7.7
/66	6.9	7.1	7.5	8.9	5.8
/67	8.1	8.5	9.0	10.5	7.8
/68	8.4	8.8	9.2	10.7	8.2
/69	6.4	6.6	6.9	8.1	5.6
/70	5.5	5.6	5.9	6.9	4.6
/71	5.8	6.0	6.3	7.3	5.1
/72	5.8	6.0	6.3	7.2	5.1
/73	4.0	4.0	4.2	4.9	2.9
/74	1.9	1.8	1.9	2.5	0.5
/75	2.9	2.9	3.0	3.7	1.7
/76	3.5	3.5	3.6	4.3	2.5

Held until	Purchased 12/55	12/56	12/57	12/58	12/59
/56	−0.8				
/57	−10.6	−20.2			
/58	5.6	9.3	49.5		
/59	7.2	10.3	29.3	9.1	
/60	4.8	6.5	16.0	1.4	−6.7
/61	7.9	10.0	18.1	8.7	8.2
/62	3.6	4.7	9.9	1.6	−0.7
/63	4.7	5.8	10.6	4.0	2.7
/64	5.6	6.7	11.0	5.6	4.9
/65	7.0	8.1	12.5	7.8	7.6
/66	5.0	5.8	9.6	5.1	4.7
/67	7.1	8.0	11.9	8.1	8.1
/68	7.7	8.6	12.2	8.8	9.0
/69	4.9	5.5	8.3	5.0	4.7
/70	3.9	4.4	6.6	3.6	3.2
/71	4.4	4.9	7.1	4.4	4.0
/72	4.5	5.0	7.1	4.4	4.2
/73	2.1	2.4	4.0	1.6	1.2
/74	−0.3	−0.3	1.0	−1.4	−1.9
/75	1.1	1.2	2.6	0.3	−0.1
/76	1.9	2.0	3.5	1.4	1.1

Held until	Purchased 12/60	12/61	12/62	12/63	12/64
/61	23.1				
/62	1.7	−17.3			
/63	5.8	−2.6	12.4		
/64	8.1	2.9	13.4	11.8	
/65	11.1	8.0	17.5	18.5	22.6
/66	7.0	3.9	9.4	7.5	4.1
/67	10.8	8.8	15.0	15.4	16.0
/68	11.5	9.7	15.0	15.5	16.1
/69	6.2	4.1	7.6	6.9	5.9
/70	4.3	2.2	4.9	3.7	2.3
/71	5.2	3.4	5.9	4.9	3.8
/72	5.2	3.6	5.9	5.1	4.1
/73	1.8	0.2	1.9	0.8	−0.7
/74	−1.5	−3.2	−2.1	−3.4	−5.1
/75	0.4	−1.1	0.2	−0.8	−2.1
/76	1.7	0.3	1.7	0.8	−0.3

Held until	Purchased 12/65	12/66	12/67	12/68	12/69
/66	−14.0				
/67	11.0	43.1			
/68	13.5	31.6	19.5		
/69	2.0	8.1	−6.2	−26.8	
/70	−1.1	2.7	−7.7	−19.3	−12.5
/71	0.9	4.6	−3.1	−9.9	−0.8
/72	1.5	4.6	−1.6	−6.3	0.8
/73	−3.5	−1.8	−7.4	−11.8	−8.4
/74	−7.8	−7.0	−12.2	−16.5	−14.5
/75	−4.5	−3.3	−7.7	−11.0	−8.2
/76	−2.3	−0.9	−4.8	−7.4	−4.1

Held until	Purchased 12/70	12/71	12/72	12/73	12/74	12/75
/71	10.3					
/72	7.0	0.6				
/73	−8.6	−17.6	−36.2			
/74	−16.3	−23.9	−35.9	−38.4		
/75	−8.1	−12.6	−18.1	−7.4	37.8	
/76	−3.1	−5.9	−8.5	3.6	34.7	28.9

*Percent per annum, compounded annually.

Sources: Stock market data—Lawrence Fisher and Myron Scholes
 (compilers), CRSP Monthly Master File for Common Stocks
 Listed on the New York Stock Exchange (magnetic tape).
 See Appendix A.
 Consumer Price Index—U.S. Bureau of Labor Statistics.

Held Until	Purchased 12/25	12/26	12/27	12/28	12/29	Purchased 12/30	12/31	12/32	12/33	12/34	Purchased 12/35	12/36	12/37	12/38	12/39	Purchased 12/40	12/41	12/42	12/43	12/44	Purchased 12/45	12/46	12/47	12/48	12/49
12/26	4.1																								
12/27	15.1	26.8																							
12/28	20.8	30.0	33.5																						
12/29	10.7	13.1	7.0	−16.1																					
12/30	0.8	0.2	−7.3	−23.9	−31.5																				
12/31	−9.7	−12.1	−19.7	−32.9	−40.0	−47.7																			
12/32	−10.3	−12.4	−18.6	−28.6	−32.4	−33.0	−14.4																		
12/33	−4.0	−5.0	−9.6	−16.8	−17.3	−12.3	13.2	49.6																	
12/34	−3.5	−4.4	−8.4	−14.4	−14.2	−9.5	8.4	22.0	−1.0																
12/35	−0.0	−0.5	−3.6	−8.4	−7.2	−1.5	15.2	27.1	17.0	37.3															
12/36	2.1	1.9	−0.7	−4.7	−3.0	2.6	17.3	27.0	20.3	32.2	26.6														
12/37	−2.0	−2.5	−5.1	−9.0	−8.3	−4.4	5.6	10.2	2.2	3.1	−11.0	−37.8													
12/38	−0.3	−0.6	−2.9	−6.3	−5.3	−1.5	7.7	12.0	5.7	7.2	−1.5	−13.2	21.2												
12/39	−0.5	−0.8	−3.0	−6.0	−5.0	−1.6	6.4	9.9	4.3	5.2	−1.8	−9.8	8.6	−3.0											
12/40	−1.3	−1.7	−3.8	−6.6	−5.7	−2.8	4.1	6.7	1.6	1.9	−4.1	−10.6	0.9	−8.0	−13.2										
12/41	−2.3	−2.7	−4.7	−7.3	−6.6	−4.1	1.9	3.9	−0.8	−0.9	−6.2	−11.7	−3.5	−10.7	−14.5	−16.4									
12/42	−1.8	−2.1	−3.8	−6.3	−5.5	−3.0	2.5	4.4	0.3	0.4	−4.1	−8.5	−1.1	−6.1	−7.3	−4.6	8.3								
12/43	−0.6	−0.9	−2.5	−4.7	−3.8	−1.3	4.0	5.8	2.2	2.5	−1.2	−4.7	2.4	−1.1	−0.8	3.5	14.8	21.4							
12/44	0.2	−0.0	−1.5	−3.5	−2.7	−0.3	4.8	6.6	3.3	3.7	0.5	−2.4	4.0	1.4	2.2	6.3	14.9	18.3	15.0						
12/45	1.4	1.3	−0.0	−1.9	−0.9	1.5	6.4	8.3	5.4	5.9	3.2	0.9	7.2	5.3	6.7	11.1	19.1	22.9	23.6	32.6					
12/46	0.8	0.7	−0.6	−2.3	−1.5	0.8	5.2	6.8	4.1	4.5	1.9	−0.2	5.2	3.3	4.2	7.3	12.7	13.8	11.3	9.4	−10.2				
12/47	0.8	0.7	−0.6	−2.2	−1.4	0.7	4.9	6.3	3.7	4.1	1.7	−0.3	4.5	2.8	3.4	6.0	10.2	10.5	7.9	5.7	−6.0	−2.4			
12/48	0.6	0.5	−0.7	−2.2	−1.5	0.5	4.4	5.7	3.3	3.5	1.3	−0.6	3.8	2.1	2.6	4.7	8.1	8.0	5.5	3.2	−5.3	−3.2	−4.8		
12/49	1.1	1.0	−0.2	−1.6	−0.8	1.1	4.8	6.1	3.8	4.1	2.0	0.3	4.4	3.0	3.6	5.5	8.6	8.6	6.5	4.9	−1.3	1.7	3.4	11.4	
12/50	1.8	1.7	0.7	−0.7	0.1	2.0	5.6	6.9	4.8	5.1	3.3	1.7	5.7	4.5	5.1	7.1	10.1	10.2	8.7	7.7	3.1	6.5	9.3	16.6	20.9
12/51	2.2	2.2	1.2	−0.1	0.7	2.6	6.1	7.3	5.3	5.7	3.9	2.5	6.3	5.2	5.9	7.7	10.5	10.7	9.4	8.6	4.9	8.0	10.6	15.9	17.6
12/52	2.5	2.5	1.6	0.3	1.1	2.9	6.2	7.4	5.5	5.8	4.2	2.9	6.4	5.4	6.0	7.8	10.2	10.4	9.2	8.5	5.4	8.0	9.9	13.7	14.2
12/53	2.2	2.2	1.3	0.1	0.8	2.5	5.7	6.7	4.9	5.2	3.6	2.4	5.6	4.6	5.2	6.7	8.8	8.8	7.6	6.8	3.9	5.9	7.2	9.6	8.9
12/54	3.5	3.5	2.7	1.6	2.3	4.0	7.2	8.3	6.6	7.0	5.5	4.4	7.7	6.9	7.5	9.1	11.3	11.5	10.7	10.2	7.9	10.3	12.0	14.9	15.4
12/55	4.1	4.1	3.3	2.3	3.0	4.7	7.8	8.8	7.2	7.6	6.3	5.3	8.4	7.7	8.3	9.9	12.0	12.3	11.5	11.2	9.1	11.4	13.1	15.7	16.3
12/56	4.0	4.1	3.4	2.3	3.1	4.7	7.6	8.6	7.1	7.5	6.2	5.2	8.2	7.4	8.1	9.5	11.4	11.6	10.9	10.6	8.7	10.7	12.1	14.3	14.5
12/57	3.4	3.4	2.7	1.7	2.4	3.9	6.6	7.6	6.1	6.4	5.1	4.1	6.9	6.1	6.6	7.9	9.5	9.6	8.9	8.4	6.5	8.1	9.1	10.6	10.4
12/58	4.3	4.4	3.7	2.7	3.4	4.9	7.7	8.6	7.2	7.5	6.4	5.5	8.2	7.6	8.1	9.4	11.1	11.2	10.6	10.3	8.7	10.4	11.6	13.2	13.3
12/59	4.4	4.5	3.8	2.9	3.6	5.1	7.7	8.6	7.3	7.6	6.5	5.6	8.3	7.6	8.2	9.4	11.0	11.1	10.5	10.2	8.7	10.3	11.3	12.8	12.9
12/60	4.1	4.1	3.5	2.6	3.3	4.7	7.2	8.1	6.8	7.0	5.9	5.1	7.6	7.0	7.4	8.5	10.0	10.1	9.4	9.1	7.6	9.1	10.0	11.2	11.1
12/61	4.6	4.7	4.1	3.2	3.9	5.3	7.8	8.6	7.4	7.7	6.6	5.9	8.3	7.7	8.2	9.3	10.7	10.8	10.2	9.9	8.6	10.1	10.9	12.2	12.1
12/62	4.2	4.2	3.7	2.8	3.5	4.8	7.1	7.9	6.7	6.9	5.9	5.2	7.4	6.8	7.2	8.2	9.5	9.6	9.0	8.7	7.3	8.6	9.2	10.2	10.1
12/63	4.6	4.6	4.1	3.3	3.9	5.2	7.5	8.3	7.1	7.3	6.4	5.7	7.8	7.3	7.7	8.7	10.0	10.0	9.5	9.2	7.9	9.2	9.8	10.8	10.7
12/64	4.9	4.9	4.4	3.6	4.2	5.5	7.7	8.5	7.3	7.6	6.7	6.0	8.1	7.6	8.0	9.0	10.2	10.3	9.8	9.5	8.3	9.5	10.1	11.1	11.0
12/65	5.0	5.0	4.5	3.7	4.3	5.6	7.7	8.5	7.4	7.6	6.7	6.1	8.1	7.6	8.1	9.0	10.1	10.2	9.7	9.5	8.4	9.5	10.1	11.0	10.9
12/66	4.4	4.4	3.9	3.1	3.7	4.9	7.0	7.7	6.6	6.8	5.9	5.3	7.2	6.7	7.1	7.9	9.0	9.0	8.5	8.2	7.1	8.2	8.7	9.4	9.3
12/67	4.8	4.8	4.4	3.6	4.2	5.4	7.4	8.1	7.1	7.3	6.5	5.8	7.7	7.2	7.6	8.4	9.5	9.5	9.1	8.8	7.8	8.9	9.4	10.1	10.0
12/68	4.9	4.9	4.4	3.7	4.3	5.4	7.4	8.1	7.1	7.3	6.5	5.9	7.7	7.3	7.6	8.4	9.4	9.5	9.0	8.8	7.8	8.9	9.4	10.1	9.9
12/69	4.5	4.5	4.0	3.3	3.8	4.9	6.8	7.5	6.5	6.7	5.9	5.3	7.0	6.5	6.9	7.6	8.5	8.5	8.1	7.8	6.8	7.8	8.3	8.9	8.7
12/70	4.4	4.4	4.0	3.3	3.8	4.8	6.7	7.3	6.4	6.6	5.8	5.2	6.9	6.4	6.7	7.4	8.3	8.3	7.8	7.6	6.6	7.5	7.9	8.5	8.3
12/71	4.6	4.6	4.1	3.4	4.0	5.0	6.8	7.4	6.5	6.7	5.9	5.3	7.0	6.5	6.8	7.5	8.4	8.4	7.9	7.7	6.8	7.7	8.1	8.6	8.4
12/72	4.8	4.8	4.4	3.7	4.2	5.2	7.0	7.6	6.7	6.9	6.2	5.6	7.2	6.8	7.1	7.7	8.6	8.6	8.2	8.0	7.1	8.0	8.4	8.9	8.7
12/73	4.3	4.3	3.9	3.2	3.7	4.7	6.4	6.9	6.1	6.2	5.5	4.9	6.5	6.1	6.3	6.9	7.7	7.7	7.3	7.1	6.2	7.0	7.3	7.7	7.5
12/74	3.5	3.4	3.0	2.4	2.8	3.7	5.4	5.9	5.0	5.2	4.4	3.9	5.3	4.9	5.1	5.6	6.4	6.3	5.9	5.6	4.7	5.4	5.7	6.0	5.8
12/75	4.0	4.0	3.6	2.9	3.4	4.3	5.9	6.5	5.6	5.8	5.1	4.5	6.0	5.6	5.8	6.4	7.1	7.1	6.6	6.4	5.6	6.3	6.5	6.9	6.7
12/76	4.3	4.3	3.9	3.3	3.7	4.6	6.2	6.7	5.9	6.1	5.4	4.9	6.3	5.9	6.1	6.7	7.4	7.4	7.0	6.8	6.0	6.7	6.9	7.3	7.1

Table XXV

Rates of Change* in Prices of Common Stocks:
Cash to Portfolio,
Initial Weighting by Value,
Tax-Exempt,
Current Dollars

Held Until	12/50	12/51	12/52	12/53	12/54	12/55	12/56	12/57	12/58	12/59	12/60	12/61	12/62	12/63	12/64	12/65	12/66	12/67	12/68	12/69	12/70	12/71	12/72	12/73	12/74	12/75
12/51	13.7																									
12/52	10.6	6.8																								
12/53	5.0	0.6	−5.6																							
12/54	13.7	13.5	16.6	42.5																						
12/55	15.1	15.3	17.9	31.0	19.6																					
12/56	13.3	13.1	14.4	21.5	11.9	4.0																				
12/57	8.9	8.0	8.0	11.4	2.5	−5.4	−14.9																			
12/58	12.2	12.0	12.7	16.5	10.6	7.5	8.8	37.7																		
12/59	11.9	11.6	12.1	15.2	10.2	7.8	8.9	22.8	8.7																	
12/60	10.1	9.7	10.0	12.3	7.8	5.5	5.7	13.5	2.6	−3.5																
12/61	11.3	11.0	11.4	13.6	9.9	8.2	9.1	15.9	9.2	9.1	22.5															
12/62	9.2	8.7	8.9	10.5	7.0	5.2	5.4	9.8	3.5	1.6	3.8	−12.9														
12/63	9.9	9.5	9.7	11.2	8.2	6.7	7.1	11.1	6.2	5.4	8.1	1.2	16.5													
12/64	10.2	9.9	10.1	11.5	8.7	7.5	7.9	11.4	7.3	6.9	9.3	4.9	14.6	11.8												
12/65	10.2	9.9	10.0	11.4	8.8	7.7	8.0	11.1	7.6	7.3	9.4	6.2	13.1	11.8	10.4											
12/66	8.5	8.1	8.2	9.2	6.7	5.6	5.6	8.2	4.8	4.2	5.3	2.2	6.1	3.2	−1.1	−12.5										
12/67	9.3	8.9	9.0	10.0	7.7	6.7	6.9	9.4	6.5	6.1	7.5	5.2	9.1	8.0	6.5	3.8	22.4									
12/68	9.3	8.9	9.0	10.0	7.8	6.9	7.1	9.4	6.8	6.5	7.8	5.8	9.2	8.2	7.3	5.9	16.1	9.4								
12/69	8.0	7.6	7.6	8.4	6.3	5.4	5.4	7.3	4.8	4.4	5.2	3.3	5.7	4.6	3.1	0.9	5.7	−2.3	−13.4							
12/70	7.6	7.2	7.2	7.9	6.0	5.0	5.1	6.8	4.4	4.0	4.7	2.9	4.9	3.7	2.3	0.6	4.0	−2.0	−7.7	−2.8						
12/71	7.8	7.4	7.4	8.1	6.2	5.4	5.4	7.0	4.9	4.5	5.2	3.7	5.6	4.7	3.5	2.2	5.4	1.2	−1.6	4.4	10.9					
12/72	8.1	7.8	7.7	8.4	6.7	5.9	6.0	7.5	5.5	5.3	6.0	4.6	6.5	5.9	5.0	4.0	7.0	3.8	2.3	7.7	12.9	13.5				
12/73	6.9	6.5	6.5	7.1	5.3	4.5	4.5	5.8	3.9	3.5	4.0	2.6	4.2	3.3	2.1	1.0	3.0	−0.2	−2.1	0.6	1.3	−4.2	−20.6			
12/74	5.1	4.7	4.6	5.0	3.3	2.5	2.4	3.4	1.5	1.0	1.3	−0.2	0.9	−0.3	−1.6	−2.8	−1.7	−5.0	−7.3	−6.3	−7.6	−13.8	−25.6	−31.4		
12/75	6.1	5.7	5.6	6.1	4.6	3.8	3.8	4.9	3.1	2.8	3.1	1.9	3.1	2.0	1.1	0.2	1.7	−0.9	−2.4	−0.7	−0.7	−3.9	−9.7	−4.4	31.0	
12/76	6.6	6.2	6.2	6.7	5.2	4.5	4.5	5.6	4.0	3.7	4.1	3.0	4.2	3.3	2.6	1.9	3.4	1.3	0.2	2.1	2.6	0.6	−2.8	3.4	26.0	19.0

*Percent per annum, compounded annually.

Source: Lawrence Fisher and Myron Scholes (compilers), CRSP Monthly Master File for Common Stocks Listed on the New York Stock Exchange (magnetic tape). See Appendix A.

Held Until	Purchased 12/25	12/26	12/27	12/28	12/29	Purchased 12/30	12/31	12/32	12/33	12/34	Purchased 12/35	12/36	12/37	12/38	12/39	Purchased 12/40	12/41	12/42	12/43	12/44	Purchased 12/45	12/46	12/47	12/48	12/49
12/26	5.6																								
12/27	17.2	29.5																							
12/28	22.6	32.0	34.8																						
12/29	11.9	14.2	7.4	−16.3																					
12/30	3.0	2.5	−5.1	−21.6	−27.1																				
12/31	−6.5	−8.6	−16.2	−29.2	−34.9	−42.2																			
12/32	−6.2	−7.9	−13.9	−23.6	−26.0	−25.6	−4.6																		
12/33	−0.2	−0.9	−5.4	−12.3	−11.6	−6.1	19.2	48.9																	
12/34	−0.4	−1.1	−5.1	−10.8	−9.9	−5.2	11.5	20.4	−3.0																
12/35	2.6	2.3	−0.9	−5.6	−3.8	1.5	16.8	24.8	14.1	33.3															
12/36	4.5	4.3	1.7	−2.2	−0.1	5.0	18.3	24.9	17.8	29.5	25.1														
12/37	−0.2	−0.7	−3.4	−7.3	−6.2	−2.9	5.8	8.1	−0.2	0.6	−12.9	−39.7													
12/38	1.6	1.3	−1.1	−4.4	−3.1	0.2	8.3	10.8	4.4	6.1	−1.9	−13.3	24.7												
12/39	1.3	1.0	−1.2	−4.2	−3.0	−0.0	7.0	8.9	3.3	4.3	−2.0	−9.7	10.4	−2.5											
12/40	0.3	−0.1	−2.2	−5.1	−4.0	−1.5	4.5	5.8	0.6	1.1	−4.5	−10.8	1.7	−8.3	−14.0										
12/41	−1.4	−1.9	−3.9	−6.6	−5.8	−3.7	1.3	2.0	−2.8	−2.8	−7.9	−13.4	−5.2	−13.6	−18.8	−23.8									
12/42	−1.4	−1.8	−3.7	−6.2	−5.4	−3.4	1.2	1.8	−2.5	−2.5	−6.8	−11.3	−4.2	−10.4	−13.0	−12.8	−0.9								
12/43	−0.5	−0.8	−2.5	−4.8	−3.9	−1.9	2.4	3.1	−0.6	−0.4	−4.0	−7.6	−0.8	−5.3	−6.2	−3.6	8.1	17.7							
12/44	0.2	−0.1	−1.7	−3.8	−2.9	−1.0	3.2	3.9	0.5	0.8	−2.3	−5.3	1.0	−2.6	−2.7	0.2	9.6	15.2	12.7						
12/45	1.3	1.1	−0.3	−2.2	−1.3	0.7	4.8	5.5	2.6	3.1	0.4	−2.0	4.2	1.5	2.1	5.5	14.4	19.9	20.9	29.7					
12/46	−0.1	−0.3	−1.7	−3.6	−2.8	−1.0	2.6	3.1	0.2	0.5	−2.1	−4.4	0.6	−2.1	−2.1	−0.0	5.5	7.1	3.7	−0.4	−24.0				
12/47	−0.4	−0.7	−2.1	−3.8	−3.1	−1.5	1.8	2.3	−0.5	−0.3	−2.7	−4.9	−0.4	−2.9	−3.1	−1.5	2.8	3.5	0.2	−3.6	−17.2	−10.5			
12/48	−0.6	−0.9	−2.2	−3.9	−3.2	−1.7	1.4	1.8	−0.8	−0.7	−2.9	−5.0	−1.0	−3.3	−3.4	−2.0	1.5	1.8	−1.1	−4.3	−13.8	−8.5	−7.3		
12/49	−0.1	−0.3	−1.6	−3.1	−2.4	−0.9	2.0	2.5	0.1	0.2	−1.8	−3.6	0.2	−1.8	−1.8	−0.4	3.0	3.5	1.2	−0.9	−7.5	−1.5	2.9	13.4	
12/50	0.4	0.3	−0.9	−2.4	−1.6	−0.2	2.7	3.1	0.9	1.1	−0.7	−2.4	1.3	−0.5	−0.3	1.1	4.3	5.0	3.2	1.7	−3.2	2.6	7.0	14.4	14.3
12/51	0.7	0.6	−0.5	−1.9	−1.2	0.2	2.9	3.4	1.3	1.5	−0.2	−1.7	1.8	0.2	0.4	1.7	4.7	5.3	3.8	2.6	−1.4	3.6	7.2	12.2	11.2
12/52	1.0	0.9	−0.2	−1.5	−0.8	0.5	3.2	3.6	1.6	1.9	0.2	−1.2	2.2	0.7	0.9	2.2	4.9	5.4	4.1	3.1	−0.3	4.1	7.1	10.8	9.6
12/53	0.7	0.6	−0.4	−1.7	−1.0	0.3	2.8	3.1	1.2	1.4	−0.1	−1.5	1.6	0.2	0.4	1.5	3.9	4.3	3.1	2.1	−1.1	2.6	4.8	7.2	5.5
12/54	2.0	2.0	1.0	−0.2	0.5	1.9	4.4	4.8	3.0	3.3	1.9	0.7	3.9	2.6	2.9	4.2	6.7	7.4	6.4	5.8	3.4	7.3	9.9	12.9	12.6
12/55	2.7	2.6	1.7	0.6	1.3	2.6	5.1	5.5	3.8	4.1	2.8	1.7	4.7	3.6	4.0	5.3	7.7	8.3	7.6	7.1	5.0	8.7	11.2	13.9	13.8
12/56	2.6	2.6	1.7	0.6	1.3	2.5	4.9	5.3	3.7	4.0	2.7	1.7	4.5	3.5	3.8	5.0	7.2	7.8	7.1	6.6	4.7	8.0	10.1	12.3	12.0
12/57	1.9	1.8	1.0	−0.1	0.5	1.7	3.9	4.3	2.7	2.9	1.7	0.7	3.3	2.2	2.5	3.5	5.4	5.9	5.1	4.6	2.6	5.4	7.0	8.6	7.9
12/58	2.8	2.8	2.0	0.9	1.6	2.8	5.0	5.4	3.9	4.2	3.0	2.1	4.7	3.7	4.1	5.1	7.1	7.6	7.0	6.6	4.9	7.7	9.4	11.1	10.8
12/59	2.9	2.9	2.1	1.1	1.8	2.9	5.0	5.4	4.0	4.3	3.2	2.3	4.8	3.9	4.2	5.2	7.1	7.6	7.0	6.6	5.0	7.7	9.3	10.8	10.4
12/60	2.6	2.5	1.8	0.8	1.5	2.6	4.6	4.9	3.6	3.8	2.7	1.9	4.2	3.3	3.6	4.5	6.2	6.6	6.0	5.6	4.1	6.6	8.0	9.3	8.8
12/61	3.1	3.1	2.4	1.5	2.1	3.2	5.2	5.6	4.3	4.5	3.5	2.7	5.0	4.2	4.5	5.4	7.1	7.5	6.9	6.6	5.2	7.7	9.0	10.3	9.9
12/62	2.7	2.7	2.0	1.1	1.7	2.7	4.6	4.9	3.7	3.9	2.9	2.1	4.2	3.4	3.7	4.5	6.1	6.4	5.8	5.5	4.1	6.2	7.4	8.4	8.0
12/63	3.1	3.1	2.4	1.5	2.1	3.1	5.0	5.3	4.1	4.3	3.4	2.6	4.7	4.0	4.2	5.0	6.5	6.9	6.4	6.1	4.8	6.9	8.0	9.0	8.6
12/64	3.4	3.3	2.7	1.9	2.4	3.4	5.3	5.6	4.4	4.6	3.7	3.0	5.1	4.3	4.6	5.4	6.9	7.2	6.8	6.5	5.2	7.2	8.3	9.3	8.9
12/65	3.5	3.4	2.8	2.0	2.5	3.5	5.3	5.6	4.5	4.7	3.8	3.1	5.1	4.4	4.7	5.5	6.9	7.2	6.8	6.5	5.4	7.3	8.3	9.2	8.9
12/66	2.8	2.8	2.2	1.4	1.9	2.8	4.5	4.8	3.7	3.9	3.0	2.3	4.2	3.5	3.7	4.4	5.7	6.0	5.5	5.3	4.2	5.9	6.8	7.5	7.2
12/67	3.2	3.2	2.6	1.8	2.3	3.3	4.9	5.2	4.1	4.3	3.5	2.8	4.7	4.0	4.2	4.9	6.2	6.5	6.1	5.8	4.8	6.5	7.4	8.2	7.8
12/68	3.2	3.2	2.6	1.8	2.3	3.3	4.9	5.1	4.1	4.3	3.5	2.9	4.6	4.0	4.2	4.9	6.1	6.4	6.0	5.7	4.7	6.4	7.2	7.9	7.6
12/69	2.7	2.7	2.1	1.3	1.8	2.7	4.2	4.4	3.4	3.6	2.8	2.2	3.9	3.2	3.4	4.0	5.1	5.3	4.9	4.7	3.6	5.2	5.9	6.6	6.2
12/70	2.6	2.5	2.0	1.2	1.7	2.5	4.0	4.2	3.2	3.4	2.6	2.0	3.6	3.0	3.1	3.7	4.8	5.0	4.6	4.3	3.3	4.8	5.5	6.0	5.6
12/71	2.7	2.6	2.1	1.4	1.8	2.6	4.1	4.3	3.3	3.5	2.7	2.1	3.7	3.1	3.3	3.9	4.9	5.1	4.7	4.5	3.5	4.9	5.6	6.1	5.7
12/72	2.9	2.8	2.3	1.6	2.0	2.8	4.3	4.5	3.5	3.7	3.0	2.4	4.0	3.4	3.5	4.1	5.1	5.3	4.9	4.7	3.8	5.2	5.8	6.3	6.0
12/73	2.3	2.2	1.7	1.0	1.4	2.1	3.5	3.7	2.8	2.9	2.2	1.6	3.1	2.5	2.6	3.1	4.1	4.3	3.8	3.6	2.7	4.0	4.5	5.0	4.6
12/74	1.2	1.2	0.6	−0.1	0.3	1.0	2.3	2.5	1.6	1.7	1.0	0.3	1.7	1.1	1.2	1.7	2.5	2.6	2.2	1.9	1.0	2.2	2.6	3.0	2.5
12/75	1.7	1.6	1.1	0.4	0.8	1.5	2.8	2.9	2.1	2.2	1.5	0.9	2.3	1.7	1.8	2.3	3.1	3.3	2.8	2.6	1.7	2.8	3.3	3.7	3.2
12/76	1.9	1.8	1.3	0.7	1.1	1.8	3.0	3.2	2.3	2.5	1.8	1.2	2.6	2.0	2.1	2.6	3.4	3.6	3.2	2.9	2.1	3.2	3.6	4.0	3.6

Table XXVI

Rates of Change* in Prices of Common Stocks:
　　Cash to Portfolio,
　　Initial Weighting by Value,
　　Tax-Exempt,
　　Deflated by the Consumer Price Index

Held until	12/50	12/51	12/52	12/53	12/54	12/55	12/56	12/57	12/58	12/59	12/60	12/61	12/62	12/63	12/64	12/65	12/66	12/67	12/68	12/69	12/70	12/71	12/72	12/73	12/74	12/75
12/51	7.4																									
12/52	7.0	5.8																								
12/53	2.5	-0.1	-6.2																							
12/54	11.9	13.1	16.5	43.2																						
12/55	13.5	14.9	17.7	31.1	19.1																					
12/56	11.4	12.1	13.5	20.4	10.1	1.1																				
12/57	6.9	6.7	6.7	9.9	0.4	-8.1	-17.3																			
12/58	10.2	10.5	11.2	14.8	8.4	4.8	6.2	35.3																		
12/59	9.9	10.1	10.6	13.5	8.1	5.4	6.7	20.9	7.1																	
12/60	8.2	8.3	8.5	10.6	5.9	3.3	3.7	11.7	1.1	-4.9																
12/61	9.5	9.6	10.0	12.1	8.1	6.3	7.3	14.4	7.9	8.0	21.7															
12/62	7.4	7.4	7.5	9.0	5.3	3.4	3.7	8.4	2.3	0.5	2.8	-14.0														
12/63	8.1	8.1	8.3	9.7	6.4	4.9	5.4	9.6	4.8	4.1	6.9	-0.2	14.6													
12/64	8.5	8.5	8.6	10.0	7.0	5.7	6.2	9.9	6.0	5.6	8.0	3.5	13.0	10.5												
12/65	8.4	8.4	8.6	9.8	7.1	5.8	6.3	9.6	6.1	5.9	7.9	4.7	11.3	10.1	8.3											
12/66	6.7	6.6	6.6	7.5	4.9	3.6	3.8	6.4	3.1	2.5	3.6	0.3	4.0	1.0	-3.7	-15.3										
12/67	7.3	7.3	7.3	8.2	5.8	4.7	4.9	7.5	4.6	4.3	5.5	3.1	6.7	5.5	3.7	0.6	18.8									
12/68	7.1	7.1	7.1	7.9	5.7	4.6	4.9	7.2	4.6	4.3	5.4	3.3	6.4	5.2	3.9	2.1	11.8	4.4								
12/69	5.7	5.5	5.4	6.1	3.9	2.8	2.9	4.8	2.3	1.8	2.5	0.4	2.5	1.2	-0.7	-3.2	1.0	-7.3	-18.4							
12/70	5.1	4.9	4.8	5.4	3.4	2.3	2.4	4.1	1.7	1.2	1.7	-0.3	1.5	0.0	-1.7	-3.8	-0.8	-7.0	-12.8	-7.8						
12/71	5.3	5.1	5.0	5.5	3.6	2.6	2.7	4.3	2.1	1.6	2.2	0.4	2.1	1.1	-0.4	-2.0	0.8	-3.6	-6.3	-0.0	7.3					
12/72	5.5	5.3	5.3	5.8	4.0	3.1	3.2	4.7	2.7	2.3	2.9	1.4	3.0	2.2	1.0	-0.2	2.5	-0.8	-2.2	3.5	9.2	9.8				
12/73	4.1	3.9	3.7	4.2	2.4	1.4	1.4	2.6	0.7	0.2	0.6	-1.0	0.3	-0.8	-2.2	-3.6	-1.9	-5.2	-7.2	-4.4	-3.7	-9.7	-27.0			
12/74	2.0	1.7	1.4	1.8	-0.0	-1.0	-1.2	-0.2	-2.1	-2.7	-2.6	-4.3	-3.5	-4.9	-6.4	-8.0	-7.1	-10.6	-13.0	-12.1	-13.5	-20.2	-32.6	-38.8		
12/75	2.8	2.5	2.3	2.7	1.0	0.1	0.0	1.0	-0.7	-1.2	-1.1	-2.5	-1.6	-2.8	-4.0	-5.2	-4.1	-6.8	-8.5	-6.9	-7.1	-10.9	-17.4	-12.8	22.4	
12/76	3.2	2.9	2.8	3.1	1.5	0.7	0.7	1.7	0.0	-0.4	-0.1	-1.5	-0.5	-1.6	-2.6	-3.5	-2.3	-4.6	-5.8	-4.0	-3.7	-6.1	-10.1	-4.2	19.0	13.6

Percent per annum, compounded annually.

Sources: Stock market data—Lawrence Fisher and Myron Scholes (compilers), CRSP Monthly Master File for Common Stocks Listed on the New York Stock Exchange (magnetic tape). See Appendix A.
Consumer Price Index—U.S. Bureau of Labor Statistics.

Chapter 8

Time-Weighted Rates of Return on Common Stocks: "Cash to Cash"

The rates of return and rates of price change on a cash-to-portfolio basis that were given in Tables I–XXVI show how well the portfolio performed from its initial purchase date to the date in question, but the computation process assumes that the portfolio continues to be held. Time-weighted rates of return on a cash-to-cash basis, which are presented in this chapter, assume that the portfolio is liquidated on the date in question. The differences between the rates of return on the two bases are due to the effects of brokerage commissions and capital-gain taxes on the net sale proceeds.

Our original plan was to present only Tables XXVII and XXVIII in this chapter. They are for the higher tax rate and are calculated in current dollars. However, after we had seen the effects of deflating the rates of return for holding periods ending in recent years, we added Table 8–1. Table 8–1 shows rates of return similar to those in Tables XXVII and XXVIII for holding periods that ended December 31, 1976, except that values have been deflated by the Consumer Price Index. The effects for other taxable cases may be estimated by applying differences between Tables V and XXVII or Tables XI and XXVIII to the figures in other tables. The effects of sales commissions alone may be estimated with the aid of the tables presented in Chapter 9.

The reader may note that some figures in the tables in this chapter are higher than the corresponding figures on a cash-to-portfolio basis. This is due to an assumption implicit in the computation process that a portion of net capital losses realized on the date in question may be used to offset ordinary income. At some dates it might have taken several years before the total offset could take place.

Purchased	Equally Weighted Portfolios	Value-Weighted Portfolios
12/25	4.3	4.3
12/26	4.2	4.1
12/27	3.7	3.6
12/28	3.1	2.9
12/29	4.1	3.3
12/30	5.1	3.9
12/31	6.6	5.1
12/32	6.8	5.1
12/33	5.3	4.2
12/34	5.2	4.3
12/35	4.3	3.6
12/36	3.4	3.0
12/37	5.4	4.3
12/38	5.1	3.6
12/39	4.9	3.7
12/40	5.5	4.0
12/41	6.4	4.8
12/42	6.1	4.9
12/43	5.0	4.5
12/44	4.4	4.2
12/45	3.2	3.4
12/46	4.4	4.4
12/47	4.8	4.8
12/48	5.4	5.1
12/49	5.0	4.6
12/50	4.2	4.1
12/51	4.2	3.8
12/52	4.2	3.6
12/53	4.8	3.9
12/54	3.0	2.4
12/55	2.4	1.6
12/56	2.5	1.5
12/57	3.7	2.4
12/58	1.8	0.8
12/59	1.4	0.4
12/60	2.0	0.6
12/61	0.7	−0.7
12/62	1.8	0.1
12/63	0.9	−0.9
12/64	−0.1	−1.8
12/65	−1.8	−2.6
12/66	−0.8	−1.7
12/67	−3.9	−3.7
12/68	−6.0	−4.6
12/69	−3.4	−3.2
12/70	−2.8	−3.0
12/71	−5.0	−5.1
12/72	−7.2	−8.4
12/73	2.1	−3.8
12/74	26.5	14.5
12/75	19.8	9.3

Table 8-1

Time-Weighted Rates of Return* on Common Stocks for Holding Periods Ending December 31, 1976:
    Dividends Reinvested,
    Cash to Cash,
    Higher Tax Rate,
    Deflated by the Consumer Price Index

*Percent per annum, compounded annually.

Sources: Stock market data—Lawrence Fisher and Myron Scholes (compilers), CRSP Monthly Master File for Common Stocks Listed on the New York Stock Exchange (magnetic tape). See Appendix A.
    Consumer Price Index—U.S. Bureau of Labor Statistics.
    Income tax rates—Income levels estimated from U.S. Bureau of the Census, Current Population Reports, Series P-60, Nos. 101 and 103 and Historical Statistics of the United States. Tax rates were found in U.S. Internal Revenue Service, Statistics of Income and Your Federal Income Tax.

Held Until	Purchased 12/25	12/26	12/27	12/28	12/29	Purchased 12/30	12/31	12/32	12/33	12/34	Purchased 12/35	12/36	12/37	12/38	12/39	Purchased 12/40	12/41	12/42	12/43	12/44	Purchased 12/45	12/46	12/47	12/48	12/49
12/26	0.5																								
12/27	14.9	27.1																							
12/28	22.5	35.3	42.5																						
12/29	7.8	9.2	0.8	-27.9																					
12/30	-1.9	-3.4	-12.0	-29.4	-36.1																				
12/31	-10.3	-12.5	-19.9	-33.4	-38.7	-46.9																			
12/32	-8.9	-10.6	-15.8	-25.2	-27.9	-28.0	-14.8																		
12/33	-2.1	-2.6	-6.3	-13.3	-10.5	-1.5	33.3	93.6																	
12/34	-0.6	-1.1	-4.1	-9.5	-6.1	2.1	26.0	49.7	12.8																
12/35	2.5	2.2	-0.3	-4.7	-0.4	8.7	31.1	50.0	29.2	44.8															
12/36	4.6	4.6	2.5	-1.2	3.8	13.3	34.0	49.9	34.9	47.2	42.4														
12/37	0.8	0.3	-1.9	-5.5	-2.6	2.8	15.2	21.6	7.3	5.2	-11.5	-43.7													
12/38	2.8	2.5	0.6	-2.6	0.7	6.3	17.8	23.8	12.0	11.0	-0.1	-16.1	26.6												
12/39	2.7	2.3	0.4	-2.4	0.7	5.4	14.8	19.3	9.5	8.0	-0.4	-11.1	11.6	-4.1											
12/40	2.1	1.6	-0.1	-2.6	0.1	4.1	12.0	15.7	7.2	5.4	-1.7	-9.4	5.0	-5.7	-12.0										
12/41	1.5	1.0	-0.4	-2.6	-0.5	2.9	9.6	12.2	5.0	3.3	-2.2	-8.0	1.6	-5.4	-8.7	-10.6									
12/42	2.1	1.8	0.6	-1.2	0.7	3.8	9.7	11.9	5.7	4.5	0.3	-3.8	4.3	-0.1	-0.1	4.1	20.4								
12/43	3.0	2.8	1.7	0.0	2.2	5.3	11.1	13.4	7.8	7.0	3.2	-0.3	8.5	5.6	6.5	7.4	25.3	26.0							
12/44	3.6	3.6	2.6	1.0	3.3	6.6	12.4	14.7	9.5	8.9	5.6	2.5	11.5	9.5	11.9	19.4	34.1	35.9	26.3						
12/45	4.9	5.0	4.1	2.6	5.1	8.7	14.5	16.9	12.1	11.9	9.0	6.2	15.5	14.4	17.6	25.7	40.5	42.6	36.9	43.0					
12/46	4.2	4.3	3.4	2.0	4.3	7.5	12.7	14.7	10.3	9.8	7.1	4.5	12.1	10.7	12.7	17.9	26.7	25.9	18.5	13.9	-8.5				
12/47	4.0	4.0	3.2	1.9	3.9	6.9	11.7	13.5	9.3	8.8	6.3	3.9	10.6	9.5	10.7	14.5	20.6	19.2	12.8	8.1	-5.1	-2.7			
12/48	3.8	3.7	2.9	1.6	3.5	6.3	10.9	12.6	8.6	8.0	5.5	3.2	9.2	8.1	9.2	12.3	17.1	15.4	9.5	5.4	-4.6	-2.8	-4.6		
12/49	4.3	4.2	3.4	2.2	4.1	6.8	11.1	12.7	9.0	8.5	6.1	4.1	9.7	8.7	9.8	12.7	17.2	15.7	10.6	7.4	-0.3	2.4	4.6	12.9	
12/50	4.9	4.9	4.1	2.9	4.9	7.7	12.1	13.6	9.9	9.6	7.4	5.5	11.0	10.2	11.3	14.2	18.4	17.2	12.9	10.3	4.3	7.9	11.3	19.4	25.2
12/51	5.1	5.1	4.4	3.3	5.2	7.8	12.0	13.4	9.9	9.7	7.6	5.8	10.8	10.0	11.1	13.7	17.4	16.2	12.5	10.4	5.4	8.5	10.9	16.1	17.1
12/52	5.1	5.2	4.5	3.4	5.2	7.7	11.7	13.0	9.7	9.5	7.5	5.8	10.5	9.7	10.7	13.0	16.4	15.2	11.8	9.7	5.4	8.1	9.9	13.4	13.1
12/53	4.8	4.8	4.1	3.1	4.8	7.1	10.8	12.0	9.0	8.7	6.8	5.2	9.4	8.6	9.5	11.5	14.4	13.2	10.0	8.1	4.2	6.2	7.5	9.8	8.4
12/54	5.9	6.0	5.3	4.3	6.1	8.5	12.3	13.6	10.6	10.5	8.6	7.0	11.4	10.6	11.7	13.9	16.9	15.9	13.1	11.4	7.9	10.4	12.2	15.1	14.9
12/55	6.2	6.3	5.7	4.7	6.5	8.9	12.7	13.9	11.0	10.9	9.1	7.5	11.8	11.1	12.1	14.1	16.9	16.1	13.6	12.0	8.8	11.1	12.8	15.4	15.4
12/56	6.3	6.4	5.8	4.8	6.6	8.9	12.5	13.7	10.9	10.9	9.0	7.6	11.6	11.0	11.9	13.6	16.2	15.4	13.1	11.7	8.8	10.8	12.1	14.2	14.2
12/57	5.7	5.7	5.1	4.2	5.8	7.9	11.3	12.3	9.7	9.6	7.8	6.5	10.2	9.5	10.2	11.7	14.0	13.1	10.8	9.4	6.7	8.2	9.1	10.7	10.1
12/58	6.6	6.7	6.1	5.2	6.9	9.1	12.5	13.5	10.9	10.9	9.2	7.9	11.7	11.1	11.9	13.5	15.8	14.9	12.8	11.5	9.0	10.7	11.9	13.7	13.5
12/59	6.8	6.8	6.2	5.3	7.1	9.3	12.5	13.5	11.1	11.1	9.4	8.1	11.8	11.2	11.9	13.4	15.6	14.8	12.7	11.5	9.2	10.9	12.1	13.7	13.6
12/60	6.6	6.7	6.0	5.2	6.8	8.8	12.0	12.9	10.7	10.6	9.0	7.8	11.1	10.5	11.2	12.6	14.5	13.7	11.7	10.6	8.4	9.9	10.9	12.4	12.1
12/61	7.2	7.2	6.6	5.7	7.4	9.4	12.5	13.4	11.2	11.2	9.6	8.4	11.7	11.1	11.8	13.2	15.1	14.3	12.4	11.4	9.2	10.8	11.8	13.1	12.8
12/62	6.5	6.5	5.9	5.0	6.6	8.5	11.4	12.2	10.1	10.1	8.5	7.4	10.5	9.9	10.5	11.7	13.4	12.6	10.7	9.7	7.7	9.0	9.7	10.8	10.4
12/63	6.8	6.8	6.2	5.3	6.9	8.8	11.7	12.5	10.4	10.3	8.8	7.7	10.7	10.2	10.8	12.0	13.6	12.8	11.0	10.1	8.1	9.4	10.1	11.1	10.8
12/64	6.9	6.9	6.4	5.6	7.0	8.9	11.6	12.5	10.4	10.4	9.0	7.9	10.8	10.3	10.9	12.0	13.5	12.8	11.2	10.3	8.4	9.7	10.3	11.3	11.1
12/65	7.1	7.2	6.6	5.9	7.4	9.2	12.0	12.8	10.8	10.8	9.3	8.3	11.1	10.6	11.2	12.3	13.8	13.1	11.6	10.7	9.0	10.4	11.1	12.0	11.9
12/66	6.8	6.8	6.2	5.5	6.9	8.7	11.3	12.0	10.1	10.1	8.7	7.7	10.4	9.9	10.4	11.4	12.8	12.1	10.6	9.8	8.1	9.3	10.0	10.8	10.6
12/67	7.4	7.4	6.9	6.2	7.6	9.3	11.9	12.6	10.8	10.8	9.5	8.5	11.2	10.7	11.3	12.3	13.6	13.0	11.5	10.7	9.1	10.4	11.0	12.0	11.8
12/68	7.5	7.6	7.1	6.4	7.7	9.4	11.9	12.7	10.9	10.8	9.6	8.7	11.3	10.9	11.4	12.4	13.7	13.1	11.7	10.9	9.3	10.5	11.2	12.1	12.0
12/69	7.1	7.1	6.5	5.8	7.1	8.6	10.9	11.7	10.0	9.9	8.7	7.9	10.3	9.9	10.3	11.2	12.3	11.7	10.3	9.6	8.1	9.1	9.7	10.5	10.3
12/70	6.9	6.9	6.4	5.7	6.9	8.4	10.6	11.3	9.6	9.5	8.4	7.6	9.9	9.7	9.9	10.7	11.8	11.2	9.8	9.1	7.7	8.6	9.1	9.8	9.6
12/71	7.0	7.0	6.5	5.9	7.1	8.6	10.7	11.4	9.8	9.7	8.6	7.8	10.1	9.8	10.1	10.9	11.9	11.3	10.0	9.3	8.0	8.9	9.4	10.2	10.0
12/72	7.2	7.2	6.7	6.1	7.3	8.7	10.8	11.4	9.9	9.7	8.7	7.9	10.1	9.7	10.0	10.8	11.8	11.2	9.9	9.4	8.1	9.0	9.5	10.2	10.0
12/73	6.7	6.7	6.2	5.6	6.6	7.9	9.9	10.4	9.0	8.8	7.8	7.0	9.0	8.7	8.9	9.6	10.5	9.9	8.7	8.2	7.0	7.8	8.1	8.8	8.5
12/74	6.0	6.0	5.5	4.9	5.9	7.1	9.0	9.5	8.0	7.9	7.0	6.1	8.1	7.9	8.0	8.6	9.4	8.8	7.6	7.1	5.8	6.5	6.8	7.3	7.0
12/75	6.4	6.4	6.0	5.4	6.5	7.7	9.6	10.1	8.7	8.5	7.6	6.8	8.8	8.7	8.7	9.3	10.1	9.6	8.4	7.8	6.6	7.4	7.6	8.2	8.0
12/76	6.7	6.7	6.3	5.8	6.8	8.0	9.9	10.4	9.0	8.9	8.0	7.2	9.2	9.1	9.1	9.7	10.5	10.0	8.9	8.3	7.2	7.9	8.2	8.8	8.6

Table XXVII

Time-Weighted Rates of Return* on Common Stocks:
Dividends Reinvested,
Cash to Cash,
Equal Initial Weighting,
Higher Tax Rate,
Current Dollars

Held Until	12/50	12/51	12/52	12/53	12/54	12/55	12/56	12/57	12/58	12/59	12/60	12/61	12/62	12/63	12/64	12/65	12/66	12/67	12/68	12/69	12/70	12/71	12/72	12/73	12/74	12/75
12/51	8.5																									
12/52	7.1	4.0																								
12/53	3.5	0.3	−5.0																							
12/54	11.7	11.9	14.9	38.1																						
12/55	12.4	12.8	15.1	26.7	12.1																					
12/56	11.5	11.4	12.7	19.3	8.6	2.9																				
12/57	7.6	7.0	7.1	9.9	1.3	−4.2	−12.1																			
12/58	11.5	11.5	12.3	16.0	9.8	8.3	10.8	40.3																		
12/59	11.8	11.8	12.6	15.7	10.4	9.3	11.5	25.9	8.8																	
12/60	10.5	10.4	10.9	13.1	8.5	7.3	8.4	15.5	3.3	−3.4																
12/61	11.5	11.5	12.1	14.3	10.4	9.6	11.1	17.3	9.0	8.2	18.5															
12/62	9.1	8.8	9.1	10.6	7.0	6.0	6.7	10.6	3.5	1.5	3.0	−11.7														
12/63	9.5	9.3	9.6	11.1	7.8	6.9	7.6	11.3	5.5	4.3	6.6	0.0	11.1													
12/64	9.8	9.6	9.9	11.4	8.4	7.6	8.3	11.7	6.8	6.2	8.5	4.4	12.5	10.4												
12/65	10.6	10.5	10.8	12.3	9.5	8.8	9.6	13.2	8.8	8.5	11.3	8.7	16.3	16.6	19.3											
12/66	9.4	9.2	9.5	10.7	8.0	7.3	7.8	10.8	6.8	6.3	8.2	5.7	10.3	8.6	6.1	−8.0										
12/67	10.6	10.6	11.0	12.3	9.8	9.2	9.9	13.1	9.6	9.5	11.7	10.1	15.4	15.6	16.2	12.0	36.1									
12/68	10.9	10.9	11.3	12.6	10.3	9.8	10.6	13.5	10.4	10.5	12.6	11.1	15.7	16.1	16.7	14.5	28.8	18.7								
12/69	9.2	9.1	9.4	10.4	8.2	7.6	8.1	10.3	7.4	7.1	8.4	6.7	9.9	9.3	8.7	5.7	10.8	−0.1	−16.1							
12/70	8.6	8.5	8.7	9.7	7.6	7.0	7.3	9.3	6.5	6.2	7.2	5.5	7.9	7.1	6.1	3.5	6.8	−1.2	−10.1	−5.7						
12/71	9.0	8.9	9.1	10.1	8.1	7.5	7.9	9.8	7.3	7.0	8.0	6.5	8.9	8.1	7.3	5.1	8.3	2.1	−3.3	3.3	10.1					
12/72	9.0	8.9	9.1	10.0	8.1	7.6	8.0	9.8	7.3	7.1	8.1	6.7	8.9	8.2	7.5	5.5	8.2	3.1	−0.7	4.5	8.4	2.7				
12/73	7.6	7.4	7.5	8.3	6.4	5.8	6.0	7.4	5.2	4.9	5.6	4.3	5.9	5.0	4.0	1.9	3.4	−0.9	−4.3	−1.8	−2.3	−8.9	−23.2			
12/74	6.1	5.8	5.9	6.5	4.8	4.1	4.2	5.3	3.2	2.9	3.3	2.1	3.2	2.2	1.1	−0.8	−0.0	−3.7	−6.8	−5.4	−6.7	−11.9	−20.4	−23.2		
12/75	7.1	6.9	7.0	7.7	6.0	5.5	5.6	6.8	4.8	4.5	5.1	3.9	5.3	4.5	3.6	1.9	3.1	−0.3	−2.6	−0.4	−0.3	−3.3	−6.7	1.9	35.0	
12/76	7.7	7.5	7.7	8.4	6.7	6.3	6.4	7.7	5.8	5.6	6.3	5.2	6.6	6.0	5.2	3.7	5.1	2.0	0.0	2.8	3.6	1.8	0.4	10.3	33.9	25.6

*Percent per annum, compounded annually.

Sources: Stock market data—Lawrence Fisher and Myron Scholes (compilers), CRSP Monthly Master File for Common Stocks Listed on the New York Stock Exchange (magnetic tape). See Appendix A.
Income tax rates—Income levels estimated from U.S. Bureau of the Census, Current Population Reports, Series P-60, Nos. 101 and 103 and Historical Statistics of the United States. Tax rates were found in U.S. Internal Revenue Service, Statistics of Income and Your Federal Income Tax.

Held Until	12/25	12/26	12/27	12/28	12/29	12/30	12/31	12/32	12/33	12/34	12/35	12/36	12/37	12/38	12/39	12/40	12/41	12/42	12/43	12/44	12/45	12/46	12/47	12/48	12/49
12/26	9.4																								
12/27	20.1	30.9																							
12/28	25.3	33.9	36.4																						
12/29	15.1	17.1	10.7	−12.1																					
12/30	5.4	4.6	−2.9	−19.0	−26.5																				
12/31	−4.6	−7.1	−14.5	−27.2	−34.3	−42.4																			
12/32	−4.4	−6.4	−12.0	−20.9	−24.4	−25.3	−7.5																		
12/33	1.4	0.3	−4.0	−10.6	−10.9	−6.3	18.1	50.6																	
12/34	1.7	0.8	−3.0	−8.4	−8.2	−3.8	13.3	25.1	2.8																
12/35	4.9	4.3	1.3	−3.3	−2.1	3.4	19.6	30.4	20.1	38.9															
12/36	6.8	6.5	3.9	0.0	1.6	7.1	21.6	30.5	23.5	35.1	29.2														
12/37	2.9	2.3	−0.3	−4.0	−3.3	0.4	10.2	14.3	6.2	7.2	−6.5	−32.5													
12/38	4.5	4.0	1.7	−1.6	−0.5	3.1	12.3	16.2	9.8	11.3	2.7	−8.8	24.2												
12/39	4.3	3.9	1.8	−1.2	−0.2	3.2	11.1	14.2	8.5	9.4	2.5	−5.4	12.5	0.9											
12/40	3.6	3.1	1.1	−1.6	−0.7	2.1	8.8	11.1	6.0	6.3	0.5	−5.7	5.2	−3.3	−8.2										
12/41	2.7	2.2	0.5	−1.9	−1.2	1.0	6.5	8.2	3.7	3.7	−1.0	−5.8	1.2	−5.0	−8.4	−10.5									
12/42	3.3	3.0	1.5	−0.5	0.1	2.1	6.9	8.4	4.7	4.8	1.2	−2.3	3.5	−0.5	−1.4	0.5	10.2								
12/43	4.0	3.7	2.3	0.4	1.1	3.2	7.9	9.4	6.0	6.3	3.1	0.2	5.8	2.9	3.0	6.1	14.6	18.3							
12/44	4.5	4.2	2.9	1.1	1.8	3.9	8.3	9.8	6.7	7.0	4.1	1.7	6.9	4.6	5.1	8.1	14.6	16.3	13.2						
12/45	5.3	5.1	3.9	2.2	3.0	5.2	9.6	11.0	8.2	8.7	6.2	4.0	9.3	7.5	8.5	11.8	18.0	20.3	20.1	26.2					
12/46	4.7	4.5	3.3	1.8	2.5	4.4	8.4	9.6	7.0	7.3	4.9	3.0	7.4	5.7	6.2	8.5	12.6	12.9	10.6	8.9	−6.2				
12/47	4.6	4.4	3.2	1.7	2.4	4.2	7.9	9.1	6.6	6.8	4.6	2.8	6.8	5.1	5.5	7.4	10.5	10.4	8.1	6.1	−2.9	−0.1			
12/48	4.5	4.3	3.1	1.7	2.3	4.1	7.6	8.7	6.3	6.5	4.4	2.6	6.4	4.8	5.1	6.7	9.4	9.0	6.8	4.9	−1.9	0.1	−0.8		
12/49	4.9	4.7	3.6	2.2	2.9	4.6	8.1	9.1	6.8	7.1	5.1	3.5	7.1	5.6	6.0	7.6	10.1	9.9	8.0	6.7	1.7	4.5	6.4	12.9	
12/50	5.5	5.3	4.3	3.0	3.7	5.4	8.8	9.8	7.7	8.0	6.2	4.8	8.3	7.0	7.5	9.2	11.7	11.6	10.2	9.4	5.6	8.9	11.6	17.8	20.6
12/51	5.7	5.6	4.7	3.4	4.1	5.8	9.0	10.0	8.0	8.3	6.6	5.3	8.6	7.5	8.0	9.5	11.8	11.8	10.6	10.0	7.0	9.8	12.1	16.4	17.2
12/52	5.9	5.9	4.9	3.7	4.4	6.0	9.1	10.0	8.1	8.4	6.8	5.6	8.7	7.6	8.1	9.5	11.6	11.5	10.4	9.9	7.2	9.6	11.4	14.4	14.2
12/53	5.6	5.5	4.6	3.5	4.1	5.6	8.5	9.4	7.6	7.8	6.3	5.1	8.0	6.9	7.3	8.5	10.3	10.2	9.1	8.4	5.9	7.8	9.0	10.8	9.9
12/54	6.7	6.7	5.8	4.7	5.4	7.0	9.9	10.8	9.1	9.4	8.0	6.9	9.8	9.0	9.5	10.8	12.7	12.7	11.9	11.4	9.4	11.6	13.2	15.5	15.4
12/55	7.3	7.2	6.4	5.3	6.0	7.5	10.4	11.3	9.7	10.0	8.7	7.6	10.5	9.7	10.2	11.5	13.4	13.5	12.7	12.4	10.5	12.6	14.1	16.3	16.3
12/56	7.2	7.1	6.3	5.3	6.0	7.5	10.2	11.1	9.5	9.8	8.5	7.5	10.3	9.5	10.0	11.2	12.9	12.9	12.2	11.8	10.1	12.0	13.2	15.0	14.8
12/57	6.5	6.5	5.7	4.7	5.3	6.7	9.3	10.1	8.5	8.7	7.5	6.5	9.0	8.2	8.6	9.6	11.1	11.0	10.3	9.8	8.1	9.6	10.5	11.7	11.3
12/58	7.3	7.3	6.6	5.6	6.2	7.6	10.2	11.0	9.6	9.8	8.6	7.7	10.2	9.5	10.0	11.1	12.5	12.5	11.9	11.6	10.1	11.7	12.7	14.0	13.8
12/59	7.4	7.3	6.6	5.7	6.4	7.7	10.2	11.0	9.6	9.8	8.6	7.8	10.2	9.5	9.9	11.0	12.4	12.4	11.7	11.4	10.0	11.5	12.4	13.6	13.4
12/60	7.0	7.0	6.3	5.4	6.0	7.3	9.7	10.4	9.1	9.3	8.1	7.3	9.5	8.9	9.2	10.2	11.4	11.4	10.7	10.4	9.0	10.4	11.1	12.1	11.8
12/61	7.5	7.5	6.8	6.0	6.6	7.9	10.2	10.9	9.6	9.8	8.7	7.9	10.2	9.5	9.9	10.8	12.1	12.0	11.4	11.1	9.8	11.2	12.0	13.0	12.7
12/62	7.1	7.1	6.4	5.6	6.1	7.4	9.6	10.2	9.0	9.1	8.1	7.3	9.3	8.7	9.0	9.9	11.0	10.9	10.3	10.0	8.7	9.8	10.5	11.3	10.9
12/63	7.5	7.4	6.8	5.9	6.5	7.7	9.9	10.5	9.3	9.5	8.5	7.7	9.7	9.1	9.4	10.3	11.4	11.3	10.7	10.5	9.2	10.4	11.0	11.8	11.4
12/64	7.7	7.6	7.1	6.2	6.8	8.0	10.1	10.7	9.5	9.7	8.7	8.0	10.0	9.4	9.7	10.5	11.6	11.6	11.0	10.7	9.6	10.7	11.3	12.0	11.7
12/65	7.7	7.7	7.1	6.3	6.9	8.0	10.1	10.7	9.5	9.7	8.8	8.1	10.0	9.4	9.7	10.5	11.5	11.5	11.0	10.7	9.6	10.7	11.2	11.9	11.7
12/66	7.1	7.0	6.5	5.7	6.2	7.3	9.3	9.8	8.7	8.9	7.9	7.2	9.1	8.5	8.8	9.5	10.4	10.3	9.8	9.5	8.4	9.4	9.9	10.4	10.1
12/67	7.5	7.4	6.9	6.1	6.6	7.7	9.6	10.2	9.1	9.3	8.4	7.7	9.5	8.9	9.2	9.9	10.8	10.8	10.3	10.0	9.0	10.0	10.5	11.1	10.8
12/68	7.4	7.4	6.9	6.1	6.6	7.7	9.6	10.1	9.1	9.3	8.4	7.7	9.4	8.9	9.2	9.8	10.7	10.7	10.2	10.0	9.0	9.9	10.4	10.9	10.6
12/69	7.0	6.9	6.4	5.7	6.1	7.1	9.0	9.5	8.4	8.6	7.7	7.1	8.7	8.2	8.4	9.0	9.8	9.7	9.2	9.0	8.0	8.9	9.3	9.7	9.4
12/70	7.0	6.9	6.4	5.7	6.2	7.1	8.9	9.4	8.4	8.5	7.7	7.0	8.6	8.1	8.3	8.9	9.7	9.6	9.1	8.8	7.9	8.7	9.0	9.5	9.2
12/71	7.1	7.0	6.5	5.8	6.3	7.2	8.9	9.4	8.4	8.6	7.8	7.2	8.7	8.2	8.4	9.0	9.7	9.7	9.2	9.0	8.0	8.8	9.2	9.6	9.3
12/72	7.2	7.2	6.7	6.0	6.5	7.4	9.1	9.6	8.6	8.7	8.0	7.4	8.9	8.4	8.6	9.2	9.9	9.8	9.4	9.2	8.3	9.1	9.4	9.8	9.5
12/73	6.8	6.7	6.2	5.5	6.0	6.8	8.5	8.9	8.0	8.1	7.3	6.7	8.2	7.7	7.9	8.4	9.1	9.0	8.5	8.3	7.4	8.1	8.4	8.8	8.5
12/74	6.0	5.9	5.4	4.7	5.2	6.0	7.6	8.0	7.0	7.2	6.4	5.8	7.1	6.6	6.8	7.3	7.9	7.8	7.3	7.0	6.2	6.8	7.0	7.3	6.9
12/75	6.4	6.4	5.9	5.3	5.7	6.5	8.1	8.5	7.6	7.7	6.9	6.4	7.7	7.3	7.4	7.9	8.5	8.4	8.0	7.7	6.9	7.5	7.8	8.1	7.8
12/76	6.7	6.7	6.2	5.6	6.0	6.8	8.3	8.7	7.9	8.0	7.3	6.7	8.0	7.6	7.8	8.2	8.9	8.8	8.3	8.1	7.3	7.9	8.2	8.5	8.2

Table XXVIII

Time-Weighted Rates of Return* on Common Stocks:
> Dividends Reinvested,
> Cash to Cash,
> Initial Weighting by Value,
> Higher Tax Rate,
> Current Dollars

Purchased

Held until	12/50	12/51	12/52	12/53	12/54	12/55	12/56	12/57	12/58	12/59	12/60	12/61	12/62	12/63	12/64	12/65	12/66	12/67	12/68	12/69	12/70	12/71	12/72	12/73	12/74	12/75
/51	12.9																									
/52	10.6	7.0																								
/53	6.2	2.5	-2.6																							
/54	13.5	12.9	15.0	34.5																						
/55	14.7	14.6	16.4	26.6	16.5																					
/56	13.2	12.8	13.7	19.3	11.0	4.4																				
/57	9.5	8.6	8.5	11.2	3.8	-2.4	-9.9																			
/58	12.5	12.0	12.4	15.5	10.3	7.6	8.4	29.9																		
/59	12.1	11.6	12.0	14.5	9.9	7.8	8.6	19.2	7.4																	
/60	10.6	10.0	10.2	12.1	8.0	5.9	6.0	12.0	3.2	-1.8																
/61	11.7	11.2	11.4	13.3	9.8	8.2	8.8	14.2	8.4	8.2	17.8															
/62	9.8	9.3	9.3	10.6	7.4	5.8	5.8	9.4	4.1	2.6	4.1	-8.9														
/63	10.5	9.9	10.0	11.3	8.4	7.0	7.2	10.5	6.2	5.5	7.6	2.0	13.3													
/64	10.8	10.3	10.4	11.6	8.9	7.7	8.0	10.8	7.2	6.8	8.6	5.0	12.4	9.8												
/65	10.8	10.3	10.4	11.5	9.0	7.9	8.1	10.7	7.5	7.2	8.8	6.1	11.5	10.2	8.7											
/66	9.2	8.7	8.7	9.6	7.2	6.1	6.1	8.2	5.2	4.7	5.5	3.0	6.0	3.6	0.3	-8.6										
/67	9.9	9.5	9.4	10.3	8.1	7.1	7.2	9.3	6.6	6.3	7.3	5.4	8.5	7.5	6.2	4.0	17.7									
/68	9.8	9.4	9.4	10.2	8.1	7.2	7.3	9.2	6.8	6.6	7.5	5.8	8.5	7.6	6.8	5.6	13.2	7.5								
/69	8.6	8.1	8.0	8.7	6.7	5.8	5.8	7.4	5.2	4.8	5.4	3.8	5.7	4.7	3.5	1.8	5.3	-0.8	-9.3							
/70	8.4	7.9	7.8	8.4	6.6	5.7	5.7	7.1	5.0	4.6	5.1	3.6	5.2	4.1	3.0	1.6	4.2	-0.5	-4.9	-1.6						
/71	8.5	8.1	8.0	8.6	6.8	6.0	6.0	7.3	5.4	5.0	5.6	4.2	5.8	5.0	4.0	2.9	5.3	1.9	-0.3	4.2	8.5					
/72	8.8	8.4	8.3	8.9	7.2	6.4	6.5	7.8	5.9	5.7	6.2	5.0	6.6	5.9	5.1	4.3	6.6	4.0	2.8	6.9	10.6	10.4				
/73	7.7	7.3	7.2	7.7	6.0	5.3	5.2	6.3	4.5	4.2	4.6	3.4	4.6	3.8	2.9	2.0	3.5	0.9	-0.6	1.5	1.9	-2.5	-15.3			
/74	6.2	5.8	5.6	6.0	4.4	3.6	3.5	4.4	2.7	2.3	2.5	1.3	2.2	1.1	0.1	-0.8	0.1	-2.4	-4.1	-3.5	-4.5	-9.0	-17.8	-23.2		
/75	7.1	6.7	6.5	6.9	5.4	4.7	4.7	5.6	4.0	3.7	4.0	2.9	3.9	3.0	2.2	1.5	2.6	0.6	-0.6	0.7	0.7	-1.8	-6.1	-2.3	23.8	
/76	7.5	7.2	7.0	7.5	6.0	5.4	5.3	6.3	4.8	4.5	4.8	3.8	4.8	4.0	3.4	2.8	4.0	2.3	1.4	3.0	3.3	1.7	-0.9	3.9	21.2	14.6

Percent per annum, compounded annually.

Sources: Stock market data—Lawrence Fisher and Myron Scholes (compilers), CRSP Monthly Master File for Common Stocks Listed on the New York Stock Exchange (magnetic tape). See Appendix A.
Consumer Price Index—U.S. Bureau of Labor Statistics.
Income tax rates—Income levels estimated from U.S. Bureau of the Census, Current Population Reports, Series P-60, Nos. 101 and 103 and Historical Statistics of the United States. Tax rates were found in U.S. Internal Revenue Service, Statistics of Income and Your Federal Income Tax.

Chapter 9

Time-Weighted Rates of Return on Common Stocks
(Dividends Reinvested, no Commissions or Taxes)

Most studies of rates of return are based on indexes, for which the effects of taxes and commissions are hard to take into account. In this chapter we present Tables XXIX and XXX, which differ from Tables I and VII only by ignoring all commissions on purchases—both at the time the portfolio is acquired and as dividends are reinvested. The major differences are for one-year periods. They tend to be greatest for the equally weighted portfolios, especially when prices were low (e.g., December 1932 to December 1933) and in the period since 1971.

Held Until	Purchased					Purchased					Purchased					Purchased					Purchased				
	12/25	12/26	12/27	12/28	12/29	12/30	12/31	12/32	12/33	12/34	12/35	12/36	12/37	12/38	12/39	12/40	12/41	12/42	12/43	12/44	12/45	12/46	12/47	12/48	12/49
12/26	1.4																								
12/27	16.2	30.1																							
12/28	23.9	37.8	46.7																						
12/29	8.4	10.0	1.2	−29.1																					
12/30	−2.1	−3.6	−12.7	−31.6	−37.5																				
12/31	−11.2	−13.5	−21.4	−36.2	−41.0	−47.5																			
12/32	−10.7	−12.5	−18.5	−29.9	−31.9	−30.2	−7.9																		
12/33	−2.7	−3.2	−7.3	−15.4	−11.8	−0.9	38.7	111.0																	
12/34	−0.9	−1.4	−4.8	−11.0	−6.8	2.7	29.4	56.3	17.0																
12/35	2.5	2.2	−0.5	−5.5	−0.4	9.6	33.9	54.8	33.1	52.8															
12/36	4.8	4.8	2.6	−1.5	4.0	14.3	36.3	53.4	37.9	51.8	48.4														
12/37	0.8	0.3	−2.1	−6.1	−2.8	3.3	16.6	23.6	8.5	6.5	−11.3	−45.7													
12/38	3.0	2.7	0.7	−2.8	0.9	6.9	19.1	25.5	13.3	12.5	0.9	−15.9	32.3												
12/39	2.8	2.5	0.6	−2.5	0.9	6.0	16.0	20.7	10.6	9.2	0.3	−11.0	13.8	−2.0											
12/40	2.2	1.8	−0.0	−2.8	0.3	4.6	13.3	17.2	8.2	6.5	−1.1	−9.6	6.8	−4.4	−8.9										
12/41	1.5	1.0	−0.6	−3.1	−0.5	3.5	11.1	14.0	6.1	4.3	−2.0	−9.1	2.9	−5.1	−8.5	−8.7									
12/42	2.3	2.0	0.5	−1.8	0.9	4.8	11.8	14.4	7.4	6.1	0.8	−4.7	6.5	1.0	1.5	8.3	33.0								
12/43	3.6	3.6	2.3	0.2	3.1	7.1	14.0	16.6	10.4	9.7	5.4	1.0	12.6	9.7	12.5	22.9	48.2	59.2							
12/44	4.7	4.7	3.6	1.7	4.6	8.7	15.4	18.1	12.5	12.1	8.4	4.7	16.0	14.0	17.4	27.4	46.6	50.8	40.1						
12/45	6.3	6.5	5.6	3.9	7.0	11.3	17.8	20.7	15.6	15.6	12.5	9.4	20.6	19.7	24.0	34.3	52.4	56.6	51.2	61.4					
12/46	5.5	5.7	4.8	3.2	6.0	9.9	15.8	18.2	13.5	13.1	10.2	7.3	16.6	15.3	18.1	24.6	35.4	35.2	26.5	20.8	−9.3				
12/47	5.4	5.6	4.7	3.2	5.8	9.4	14.8	17.0	12.6	12.2	9.4	6.8	14.9	13.9	15.8	20.6	28.1	26.9	19.3	13.5	−4.0	0.4			
12/48	5.2	5.2	4.3	2.8	5.2	8.6	13.7	15.7	11.5	11.0	8.3	5.9	12.9	11.9	13.5	17.3	22.9	21.2	14.5	9.4	−3.3	−0.6	−2.1		
12/49	5.8	5.8	5.0	3.6	6.0	9.2	14.0	15.9	12.0	11.6	9.1	6.9	13.5	12.6	14.1	17.6	22.8	21.3	15.6	11.7	2.2	5.9	8.9	21.2	
12/50	6.6	6.7	5.9	4.6	7.0	10.3	15.2	16.9	13.1	12.9	10.6	8.6	15.0	14.3	15.9	19.3	24.0	23.0	18.3	15.3	8.0	12.8	17.2	28.1	37.6
12/51	7.0	7.1	6.4	5.1	7.5	10.6	15.3	16.9	13.3	13.2	11.0	9.1	15.0	14.3	15.8	19.0	23.1	22.1	18.0	15.6	9.6	13.6	16.9	23.9	26.1
12/52	7.1	7.3	6.6	5.3	7.6	10.6	15.0	16.6	13.2	13.1	11.0	9.2	14.7	14.0	15.4	18.2	22.0	20.9	17.2	14.8	9.7	13.2	15.6	20.3	20.4
12/53	6.7	6.9	6.2	5.0	7.1	9.8	14.1	15.5	12.4	12.2	10.2	8.5	13.5	12.7	13.9	16.4	19.7	18.6	15.1	12.8	8.1	10.7	12.4	15.5	14.1
12/54	8.1	8.2	7.6	6.5	8.7	11.5	15.8	17.3	14.2	14.2	12.2	10.7	15.7	15.1	16.5	19.0	22.4	21.5	18.6	16.7	12.7	15.8	18.1	21.8	22.0
12/55	8.5	8.6	8.0	7.0	9.2	12.0	16.2	17.7	14.7	14.7	12.8	11.3	16.1	15.5	16.8	19.2	22.3	21.6	18.9	17.2	13.7	16.5	18.5	21.8	22.2
12/56	8.5	8.7	8.2	7.1	9.3	11.9	16.0	17.4	14.5	14.6	12.7	11.3	15.9	15.3	16.5	18.5	21.3	20.6	18.3	16.7	13.5	15.9	17.5	20.2	20.4
12/57	7.8	8.0	7.4	6.4	8.4	10.8	14.6	15.8	13.1	13.1	11.2	9.9	14.1	13.5	14.5	16.3	18.7	17.9	15.4	13.9	10.8	12.6	13.8	15.7	15.1
12/58	8.9	9.1	8.5	7.6	9.6	12.1	15.8	17.1	14.5	14.5	12.8	11.5	15.8	15.2	16.3	18.2	20.7	19.9	17.6	16.3	13.6	15.6	17.0	19.2	19.1
12/59	9.0	9.2	8.6	7.7	9.8	12.2	15.9	17.1	14.6	14.7	13.0	11.7	15.8	15.3	16.3	18.0	20.4	19.6	17.4	16.2	13.6	15.6	17.0	19.0	19.0
12/60	8.9	9.1	8.4	7.6	9.5	11.8	15.2	16.4	14.1	14.2	12.5	11.3	15.0	14.5	15.4	17.0	19.1	18.3	16.2	15.0	12.6	14.3	15.6	17.2	17.0
12/61	9.5	9.6	9.0	8.2	10.1	12.4	15.7	16.9	14.6	14.7	13.1	12.0	15.7	15.2	16.1	17.7	19.7	19.0	16.9	15.8	13.5	15.2	16.4	18.0	17.7
12/62	8.7	8.9	8.3	7.4	9.2	11.4	14.5	15.6	13.4	13.4	11.9	10.8	14.2	13.7	14.5	16.0	17.8	16.9	15.0	13.8	11.6	13.1	14.0	15.2	14.8
12/63	9.0	9.1	8.6	7.7	9.5	11.7	14.8	15.8	13.7	13.7	12.2	11.1	14.5	14.0	14.8	16.1	17.9	17.1	15.2	14.2	12.1	13.5	14.4	15.5	15.2
12/64	9.2	9.3	8.8	7.9	9.7	11.8	14.7	15.8	13.7	13.8	12.4	11.4	14.6	14.1	14.9	16.1	17.8	17.1	15.3	14.4	12.4	13.7	14.5	15.7	15.4
12/65	9.4	9.5	9.1	8.3	10.0	12.1	15.1	16.1	14.1	14.1	12.7	11.7	14.8	14.4	15.1	16.4	18.0	17.3	15.7	14.8	12.9	14.4	15.2	16.3	16.1
12/66	9.0	9.1	8.6	7.8	9.5	11.4	14.3	15.2	13.3	13.3	11.9	11.0	13.9	13.5	14.2	15.4	16.8	16.2	14.5	13.6	11.8	13.2	13.9	14.8	14.6
12/67	9.7	9.8	9.3	8.6	10.2	12.2	15.0	15.9	14.1	14.1	12.8	11.9	14.8	14.4	15.1	16.3	17.7	17.1	15.5	14.7	12.9	14.3	15.0	16.1	15.9
12/68	9.9	10.0	9.6	8.8	10.4	12.4	15.1	16.0	14.2	14.2	13.0	12.1	15.0	14.6	15.3	16.4	17.8	17.2	15.7	14.9	13.2	14.6	15.3	16.3	16.2
12/69	9.3	9.4	8.9	8.2	9.7	11.5	14.0	14.9	13.2	13.2	12.0	11.1	13.8	13.5	14.0	15.0	16.3	15.7	14.2	13.4	11.8	12.9	13.5	14.4	14.2
12/70	9.1	9.2	8.8	8.1	9.5	11.2	13.6	14.4	12.8	12.7	11.6	10.8	13.4	13.1	13.5	14.4	15.6	15.0	13.5	12.8	11.2	12.3	12.8	13.6	13.4
12/71	9.3	9.3	8.9	8.3	9.7	11.4	13.7	14.5	12.9	12.8	11.8	11.0	13.5	13.3	13.6	14.5	15.7	15.1	13.7	12.9	11.5	12.5	13.1	13.9	13.6
12/72	9.4	9.5	9.1	8.5	9.9	11.5	13.8	14.5	13.0	12.9	11.8	11.0	13.5	13.1	13.5	14.4	15.5	14.9	13.6	12.9	11.5	12.6	13.1	13.8	13.6
12/73	8.8	8.9	8.5	7.9	9.2	10.6	12.8	13.4	11.9	11.8	10.8	10.0	12.3	11.9	12.3	13.1	14.1	13.5	12.2	11.6	10.2	11.1	11.5	12.2	11.9
12/74	8.1	8.2	7.8	7.2	8.4	9.6	11.7	12.3	10.9	10.8	9.8	9.0	11.2	11.0	11.1	11.9	12.7	12.1	10.9	10.2	8.9	9.7	9.9	10.5	10.2
12/75	8.6	8.7	8.3	7.8	9.0	10.4	12.5	13.1	11.6	11.5	10.6	9.8	12.0	11.9	12.0	12.7	13.6	13.1	11.8	11.2	9.9	10.7	11.0	11.6	11.4
12/76	9.0	9.1	8.7	8.2	9.5	10.8	12.9	13.5	12.1	12.0	11.1	10.3	12.5	12.3	12.5	13.2	14.1	13.6	12.4	11.8	10.6	11.4	11.7	12.3	12.1

Table XXIX

Time-Weighted Rates of Return* on Common Stocks:
  Dividends Reinvested,
  No Commissions or Taxes,
  Equal Initial Weighting,
  Current Dollars

Purchased

Sold	12/50	12/51	12/52	12/53	12/54	12/55	12/56	12/57	12/58	12/59	12/60	12/61	12/62	12/63	12/64	12/65	12/66	12/67	12/68	12/69	12/70	12/71	12/72	12/73	12/74	12/75
1	16.0																									
2	13.1	10.1																								
3	8.0	4.1	-2.2																							
4	18.3	19.1	23.6	57.2																						
5	18.9	19.6	22.8	38.3	20.4																					
6	17.3	17.4	19.1	27.5	14.1	7.7																				
7	12.3	11.5	11.6	15.1	4.0	-3.2	-12.8																			
8	16.9	16.9	18.0	22.6	15.1	13.6	17.6	60.1																		
9	17.0	17.0	18.0	21.8	15.6	14.5	17.7	37.0	15.9																	
0	15.2	15.2	15.8	18.4	13.0	11.6	13.2	22.6	7.1	-0.8																
1	16.3	16.4	17.0	19.6	15.1	14.4	16.3	24.3	14.2	13.7	29.3															
2	13.4	13.1	13.3	15.1	10.9	9.8	10.7	15.6	6.8	4.3	6.7	-12.4														
3	13.8	13.6	13.8	15.5	11.8	10.8	11.7	16.2	9.2	7.9	11.1	2.7	19.4													
4	14.0	13.8	14.2	15.8	12.4	11.5	12.5	16.6	10.8	10.1	13.2	8.2	19.4	18.0												
5	14.8	14.7	15.1	16.7	13.6	12.9	13.9	18.1	13.0	12.8	16.4	13.4	23.4	24.6	30.2											
6	13.3	13.0	13.3	14.7	11.7	10.9	11.5	15.1	10.4	10.0	12.4	9.3	15.4	13.5	10.8	-7.1										
7	14.6	14.6	15.0	16.5	13.7	13.1	13.9	17.6	13.7	13.7	16.5	14.6	21.3	21.9	23.1	18.6	53.6									
8	15.1	15.1	15.4	16.9	14.4	13.9	14.8	18.2	14.7	14.9	17.6	16.0	21.7	22.5	23.6	21.5	41.3	30.0								
9	13.0	12.9	13.2	14.3	11.8	11.3	11.8	14.4	11.0	10.8	12.4	10.5	14.4	13.8	13.2	9.7	16.7	2.3	-19.3							
0	12.3	12.1	12.3	13.3	11.1	10.4	10.8	13.0	9.9	9.6	10.9	8.9	11.9	11.0	9.9	6.7	11.2	0.8	-11.3	-3.1						
1	12.6	12.5	12.7	13.7	11.5	11.0	11.4	13.6	10.7	10.4	11.7	10.0	12.8	12.0	11.2	8.6	12.7	5.0	-2.2	7.6	19.3					
2	12.6	12.5	12.6	13.6	11.5	11.0	11.4	13.4	10.7	10.5	11.7	10.2	12.8	12.0	11.3	8.9	12.4	6.1	1.2	8.5	14.5	8.7				
3	10.9	10.6	10.7	11.5	9.5	8.8	9.0	10.6	8.2	7.9	8.7	7.2	9.1	8.1	6.9	4.3	6.3	0.8	-3.9	-0.2	-0.4	-9.0	-26.8			
4	9.1	8.8	8.9	9.5	7.5	6.8	6.9	8.2	5.7	5.3	5.9	4.4	5.8	4.6	3.2	0.6	1.8	-3.2	-7.7	-5.3	-6.9	-14.0	-25.2	-25.2		
5	10.4	10.2	10.3	10.9	9.1	8.5	8.7	10.1	7.8	7.5	8.3	6.9	8.5	7.6	6.6	4.5	6.1	1.9	-1.4	2.0	2.3	-1.4	-5.7	7.9	59.0	
6	11.1	11.0	11.1	11.8	10.0	9.6	9.7	11.2	9.1	8.9	9.8	8.5	10.2	9.5	8.6	6.9	8.7	5.0	2.4	6.3	7.5	5.5	4.0	18.1	50.9	44.0

*Percent per annum, compounded annually.

Source: Lawrence Fisher and Myron Scholes (compilers), CRSP Monthly Master File for Common Stocks Listed on the New York Stock Exchange (magnetic tape). See Appendix A.

Held Until	12/25	12/26	12/27	12/28	12/29	12/30	12/31	12/32	12/33	12/34	12/35	12/36	12/37	12/38	12/39	12/40	12/41	12/42	12/43	12/44	12/45	12/46	12/47	12/48	12/49
12/26	10.4																								
12/27	21.3	33.3																							
12/28	26.7	36.0	39.2																						
12/29	15.9	18.0	11.4	-12.7																					
12/30	5.6	4.7	-3.2	-20.5	-28.0																				
12/31	-5.2	-7.8	-15.8	-29.5	-36.6	-44.3																			
12/32	-5.7	-7.9	-14.3	-24.6	-28.3	-28.4	-7.6																		
12/33	1.1	-0.1	-4.8	-12.3	-12.5	-7.0	20.1	57.1																	
12/34	1.5	0.4	-3.7	-9.8	-9.4	-4.3	14.5	27.7	3.7																
12/35	5.0	4.4	1.2	-3.8	-2.4	3.6	21.1	32.8	22.1	43.7															
12/36	7.1	6.8	4.1	-0.0	1.8	7.7	22.9	32.4	25.4	38.0	32.6														
12/37	2.9	2.3	-0.4	-4.4	-3.5	0.5	11.0	15.4	6.9	8.1	-6.4	-34.1													
12/38	4.7	4.2	1.9	-1.6	-0.5	3.5	13.1	17.2	10.6	12.3	3.4	-8.7	27.1												
12/39	4.6	4.1	2.0	-1.2	-0.0	3.5	11.9	15.1	9.3	10.3	3.2	-5.1	14.0	2.2											
12/40	3.8	3.3	1.2	-1.7	-0.7	2.4	9.6	12.1	6.7	7.1	1.0	-5.7	6.3	-2.8	-7.6										
12/41	2.8	2.3	0.3	-2.4	-1.6	1.1	7.3	9.3	4.4	4.4	-1.0	-6.7	2.0	-5.3	-8.7	-10.0									
12/42	3.5	3.1	1.3	-1.2	-0.3	2.4	8.2	10.0	5.8	6.0	1.5	-3.0	4.8	-0.1	-0.9	2.5	16.5								
12/43	4.7	4.4	2.7	0.5	1.5	4.1	9.7	11.5	7.8	8.2	4.5	0.9	8.4	5.0	5.6	10.4	22.2	28.2							
12/44	5.5	5.2	3.7	1.6	2.6	5.2	10.5	12.2	8.9	9.4	6.2	3.2	10.1	7.5	8.6	13.0	21.9	24.7	21.3						
12/45	6.7	6.5	5.2	3.3	4.4	7.0	12.1	13.9	10.9	11.6	8.9	6.5	13.2	11.4	13.0	17.7	25.8	29.1	29.5	38.4					
12/46	6.0	5.8	4.5	2.7	3.7	6.1	10.8	12.3	9.5	10.0	7.4	5.2	10.9	9.0	10.1	13.4	18.7	19.2	16.4	14.2	-6.2				
12/47	6.0	5.8	4.5	2.9	3.8	6.0	10.4	11.8	9.1	9.6	7.2	5.1	10.2	8.5	9.3	11.9	16.1	16.0	13.2	10.7	-1.3	3.4			
12/48	5.9	5.7	4.5	2.9	3.7	5.8	9.9	11.2	8.7	9.1	6.8	4.9	9.5	7.9	8.5	10.8	14.1	13.7	11.0	8.6	-0.1	2.8	2.0		
12/49	6.4	6.3	5.1	3.6	4.5	6.6	10.5	11.7	9.4	9.8	7.7	6.0	10.3	8.9	9.6	11.7	14.8	14.5	12.4	10.8	4.6	8.3	10.8	20.2	
12/50	7.2	7.1	6.1	4.7	5.6	7.6	11.4	12.7	10.5	11.0	9.2	7.6	11.8	10.7	11.5	13.6	16.6	16.6	15.0	14.1	9.6	13.8	17.3	25.6	30.6
12/51	7.6	7.6	6.6	5.3	6.2	8.2	11.8	13.1	11.0	11.5	9.8	8.4	12.4	11.4	12.2	14.2	17.0	17.0	15.7	15.0	11.4	15.1	18.2	24.0	25.8
12/52	8.0	8.0	7.0	5.8	6.6	8.5	12.0	13.2	11.3	11.8	10.1	8.8	12.6	11.6	12.4	14.2	16.7	16.8	15.5	14.9	11.8	14.9	17.3	21.4	21.6
12/53	7.6	7.6	6.7	5.5	6.3	8.1	11.4	12.5	10.7	11.1	9.5	8.3	11.7	10.8	11.4	13.0	15.2	15.1	13.8	13.1	10.2	12.6	14.1	16.7	15.8
12/54	9.0	9.0	8.2	7.0	7.9	9.7	13.0	14.1	12.4	12.9	11.5	10.4	13.9	13.1	13.9	15.6	17.8	18.0	17.0	16.6	14.4	17.1	19.1	22.2	22.4
12/55	9.6	9.6	8.9	7.8	8.6	10.4	13.6	14.7	13.1	13.6	12.3	11.2	14.6	13.9	14.7	16.4	18.5	18.6	17.9	17.5	15.5	18.1	20.0	22.8	23.0
12/56	9.5	9.5	8.8	7.7	8.6	10.3	13.3	14.4	12.8	13.3	12.0	11.1	14.3	13.6	14.3	15.8	17.8	17.9	17.1	16.8	14.9	17.2	18.7	20.9	20.9
12/57	8.7	8.7	8.0	7.0	7.8	9.4	12.2	13.2	11.7	12.0	10.8	9.8	12.7	12.0	12.6	13.9	15.6	15.5	14.7	14.2	12.4	14.1	15.2	16.8	16.3
12/58	9.7	9.7	9.0	8.1	8.9	10.5	13.3	14.3	12.8	13.2	12.1	11.2	14.1	13.5	14.1	15.5	17.2	17.2	16.5	16.2	14.6	16.5	17.7	19.4	19.2
12/59	9.8	9.8	9.1	8.2	9.0	10.5	13.2	14.2	12.8	13.2	12.1	11.2	14.0	13.4	14.0	15.3	16.9	16.9	16.2	15.9	14.4	16.1	17.2	18.7	18.5
12/60	9.3	9.3	8.7	7.8	8.6	10.0	12.7	13.5	12.2	12.5	11.4	10.6	13.2	12.6	13.1	14.3	15.7	15.6	14.9	14.6	13.1	14.7	15.6	16.8	16.4
12/61	9.9	9.9	9.3	8.4	9.2	10.7	13.2	14.1	12.8	13.1	12.1	11.3	13.8	13.3	13.8	14.9	16.3	16.3	15.7	15.4	14.0	15.5	16.4	17.6	17.4
12/62	9.4	9.4	8.9	8.0	8.7	10.1	12.5	13.3	12.0	12.3	11.3	10.6	12.9	12.3	12.8	13.8	15.1	15.0	14.3	14.0	12.6	13.9	14.6	15.6	15.2
12/63	9.8	9.8	9.3	8.4	9.1	10.5	12.9	13.6	12.4	12.7	11.7	11.0	13.3	12.8	13.2	14.2	15.4	15.4	14.8	14.5	13.2	14.4	15.2	16.1	15.7
12/64	10.1	10.1	9.6	8.8	9.4	10.7	13.1	13.8	12.6	12.9	12.0	11.3	13.5	13.0	13.5	14.4	15.6	15.6	15.0	14.7	13.5	14.7	15.4	16.3	16.0
12/65	10.2	10.2	9.6	8.8	9.5	10.8	13.0	13.7	12.6	12.9	12.0	11.3	13.5	13.0	13.4	14.4	15.5	15.5	14.9	14.6	13.5	14.6	15.3	16.1	15.8
12/66	9.4	9.4	8.9	8.1	8.7	9.9	12.1	12.8	11.7	11.9	11.0	10.4	12.4	11.9	12.3	13.1	14.1	14.0	13.5	13.2	12.0	13.1	13.6	14.3	13.9
12/67	9.8	9.8	9.3	8.5	9.1	10.3	12.4	13.1	12.1	12.4	11.5	10.9	12.8	12.3	12.7	13.5	14.6	14.5	14.0	13.7	12.6	13.7	14.2	14.9	14.5
12/68	9.8	9.8	9.3	8.6	9.2	10.4	12.5	13.1	12.1	12.4	11.6	10.9	12.8	12.4	12.8	13.6	14.5	14.5	14.0	13.7	12.7	13.7	14.2	14.8	14.5
12/69	9.3	9.3	8.8	8.1	8.7	9.8	11.8	12.4	11.4	11.6	10.8	10.2	12.0	11.5	11.8	12.6	13.5	13.4	12.8	12.5	11.5	12.5	12.9	13.4	13.0
12/70	9.3	9.3	8.8	8.1	8.7	9.8	11.7	12.3	11.3	11.5	10.7	10.1	11.8	11.4	11.7	12.4	13.2	13.1	12.6	12.3	11.3	12.2	12.6	13.1	12.7
12/71	9.4	9.4	8.9	8.2	8.8	9.8	11.7	12.3	11.3	11.5	10.8	10.2	11.9	11.4	11.7	12.4	13.3	13.2	12.7	12.4	11.4	12.3	12.6	13.1	12.8
12/72	9.5	9.5	9.1	8.4	9.0	10.0	11.8	12.4	11.5	11.7	10.9	10.4	12.1	11.6	11.9	12.6	13.4	13.3	12.8	12.6	11.6	12.5	12.8	13.3	13.0
12/73	9.0	9.0	8.6	7.9	8.4	9.4	11.2	11.7	10.8	11.0	10.3	9.7	11.3	10.8	11.1	11.7	12.5	12.4	11.9	11.6	10.7	11.4	11.7	12.1	11.8
12/74	8.2	8.2	7.7	7.0	7.5	8.5	10.2	10.7	9.8	10.0	9.2	8.6	10.2	9.7	9.9	10.5	11.2	11.0	10.5	10.2	9.3	9.9	10.1	10.5	10.1
12/75	8.8	8.8	8.3	7.7	8.2	9.1	10.8	11.3	10.4	10.6	9.9	9.3	10.9	10.4	10.7	11.2	11.9	11.8	11.3	11.0	10.2	10.8	11.1	11.4	11.1
12/76	9.1	9.1	8.7	8.1	8.6	9.5	11.2	11.6	10.8	11.0	10.3	9.8	11.3	10.9	11.1	11.7	12.4	12.2	11.8	11.5	10.7	11.3	11.6	12.0	11.6

Table XXX

Time-Weighted Rates of Return* on Common Stocks:
  Dividends Reinvested,
  No Commissions or Taxes,
  Initial Weighting by Value,
  Current Dollars

Purchased

	12/50	12/51	12/52	12/53	12/54	12/55	12/56	12/57	12/58	12/59	12/60	12/61	12/62	12/63	12/64	12/65	12/66	12/67	12/68	12/69	12/70	12/71	12/72	12/73	12/74	12/75
	21.1																									
	17.3	13.4																								
	11.2	6.6	0.4																							
	20.3	19.9	23.2	50.8																						
	21.4	21.4	24.1	37.6	25.3																					
	19.2	18.8	20.0	27.2	16.8	8.9																				
	14.3	13.2	13.1	16.5	7.0	-1.2	-10.5																			
	17.7	17.3	17.9	21.6	15.3	12.2	13.7	44.2																		
	17.1	16.6	17.0	20.0	14.6	12.1	13.4	27.7	13.0																	
	15.1	14.5	14.7	16.9	12.1	9.6	9.9	17.8	6.5	0.6																
	16.2	15.8	16.0	18.2	14.1	12.4	13.3	20.2	13.1	13.2	27.3															
	14.0	13.4	13.4	14.9	11.1	9.3	9.4	13.9	7.3	5.4	7.7	-9.2														
	14.7	14.1	14.2	15.6	12.3	10.8	11.1	15.1	10.0	9.2	12.1	5.0	21.3													
	14.9	14.4	14.5	15.9	12.8	11.5	11.9	15.4	11.1	10.7	13.2	8.7	18.7	16.1												
	14.8	14.3	14.4	15.6	12.8	11.6	11.9	15.0	11.3	11.0	13.1	9.9	17.0	15.5	14.6											
	12.9	12.4	12.3	13.3	10.6	9.3	9.4	11.9	8.3	7.7	8.8	5.6	9.7	6.6	2.4	-8.8										
	13.6	13.1	13.1	14.0	11.5	10.5	10.6	13.1	10.0	9.7	11.0	8.6	12.6	11.4	10.1	7.5	27.2									
	13.6	13.2	13.1	14.0	11.7	10.7	10.9	13.1	10.4	10.1	11.4	9.3	12.8	11.7	10.9	9.6	20.3	13.6								
	12.2	11.6	11.5	12.2	10.0	9.0	9.0	10.9	8.3	7.8	8.6	6.6	9.1	7.8	6.4	4.3	9.2	1.1	-10.0							
	11.8	11.3	11.2	11.9	9.8	8.8	8.8	10.5	8.1	7.6	8.3	6.4	8.6	7.2	5.9	4.2	7.7	1.7	-4.0	1.8						
	12.0	11.5	11.3	12.0	10.0	9.1	9.1	10.7	8.4	8.1	8.8	7.1	9.1	8.1	7.0	5.8	9.0	4.7	1.9	8.4	15.7					
	12.2	11.7	11.6	12.3	10.4	9.6	9.6	11.2	9.1	8.8	9.5	8.1	10.0	9.2	8.3	7.4	10.5	7.2	5.8	11.5	16.9	18.1				
	11.0	10.5	10.4	10.9	9.1	8.2	8.2	9.5	7.4	7.1	7.5	6.1	7.6	6.6	5.5	4.4	6.5	3.2	1.3	4.1	4.9	-0.7	-17.0			
	9.3	8.7	8.5	8.9	7.1	6.3	6.1	7.2	5.2	4.7	4.9	3.4	4.6	3.2	2.0	0.8	2.0	-1.3	-3.7	-2.6	-3.9	-10.1	-22.0	-27.0		
	10.3	9.9	9.7	10.1	8.5	7.7	7.7	8.8	7.0	6.6	7.0	5.6	6.9	5.8	4.9	4.1	5.6	3.0	1.5	3.3	3.5	0.3	-5.4	0.8	39.4	
	10.9	10.5	10.4	10.8	9.3	8.6	8.6	9.7	8.0	7.7	8.1	7.0	8.2	7.3	6.6	6.0	7.5	5.4	4.4	6.4	7.1	5.1	1.8	8.8	32.8	26.0

*Percent per annum, compounded annually.

Source: Lawrence Fisher and Myron Scholes (compilers), CRSP Monthly Master File for Common Stocks Listed on the New York Stock Exchange (magnetic tape). See Appendix A.

Chapter 10

Indexes of Portfolio Value for Common Stocks

(Purchase Date = 100, Dividends Reinvested,
Cash to Portfolio)

The final step in computing each of the 45,084 time-weighted rates of return and 5,304 rates of price change presented in this volume was to apply Equation 3.1 or Equation 3.3 to cash flows with two elements—the initial investment and the value of the portfolio on the ending date in question. The series of ratios of ending values to initial investment for each portfolio may therefore be stated as a series of index numbers. Tables XXXI and XXXII present two groups of these series. They were used to calculate Tables I and VII, respectively. Each column of indexes in Tables XXXI and XXXII was found by multiplying the wealth ratio, W, used in Equation 3.1 by 100.

The indexes may be of interest in themselves. They may also be of interest in examining the behavior of portfolios containing only a few different stocks. As we noted in Chapter 2, an index provides an unbiased estimate of the expected value of one hundred dollars' worth of a randomly selected portfolio. However, the annual rate of return compounded annually for such an index will tend to be higher than the average rate of return on randomly selected portfolios of only a few stocks for periods longer than one year.

Having rates of return makes it easy to compare time periods of unequal length with each other. However, the rates should be converted to indexes before examining the performance of "small" portfolios. In Tables XXXI and XXXII we have, in effect, made that conversion for annual rates of return on NYSE common stocks that were computed on a cash-to-portfolio basis, assuming tax exemption, calculation in current dollars, and both equal initial weighting or initial weighting by value.

Time-weighted rates of return and the rates of price change from other tables may be converted to similar indexes[1] with the aid of the tables in Appendix C or by applying the standard formula for the "amount of one"

$$\text{Index} = 100 \, (1 + r)^{(t_e - t_b)} \qquad (10.1)$$

where r, t_e, and t_b are as defined at Equation 3.1.

[1]The indexes may also be obtained from the Center for Research in Security Prices (CRSP) in a form and at a price that had not yet been determined at press time. For information contact CRSP, Graduate School of Business, University of Chicago, 5836 South Greenwood Avenue, Chicago, Illinois 60637.

Purchased

Held Until	12/25	12/26	12/27	12/28	12/29	12/30	12/31	12/32	12/33	12/34	12/35	12/36	12/37	12/38	12/39	12/40	12/41	12/42	12/43	12/44	12/45	12/46	12/47	12/48	12/49
12/25	100																								
12/26	101	100																							
12/27	134	129	100																						
12/28	189	189	146	100																					
12/29	137	132	102	71	100																				
12/30	89	86	66	47	62	100																			
12/31	49	48	38	26	35	52	100																		
12/32	45	45	36	24	31	48	90	100																	
12/33	80	79	63	43	60	96	188	206	100																
12/34	91	88	70	49	70	110	211	238	115	100															
12/35	127	121	95	67	96	156	314	361	174	151	100														
12/36	166	159	124	88	130	219	459	539	258	227	147	100													
12/37	109	102	80	56	79	123	245	281	136	119	78	54	100												
12/38	146	136	106	75	107	168	332	382	184	158	102	70	131	100											
12/39	147	136	106	75	108	166	319	364	180	153	100	70	128	97	100										
12/40	138	127	99	70	102	155	299	346	171	144	94	66	120	90	90	100									
12/41	127	115	91	66	93	144	279	318	158	132	87	62	111	84	83	90	100								
12/42	145	135	107	76	111	172	333	375	187	158	104	74	135	103	103	116	131	100							
12/43	188	179	143	102	151	240	468	528	264	226	150	106	201	157	158	182	215	157	100						
12/44	235	225	180	129	194	316	623	714	357	307	203	143	277	216	220	259	309	224	139	100					
12/45	337	327	261	190	291	485	963	1,114	558	482	319	222	441	346	358	428	526	377	227	161	100				
12/46	306	300	239	175	267	442	873	1,006	507	431	288	201	390	307	315	368	445	328	201	145	91	100			
12/47	316	307	245	178	272	448	890	1,024	515	436	291	204	394	316	318	365	433	324	201	146	92	100	100		
12/48	315	300	238	172	260	431	863	998	502	423	279	196	374	304	307	353	415	312	195	142	90	98	97	100	
12/49	384	365	288	209	314	517	1,032	1,190	601	507	334	236	450	361	368	422	506	381	236	173	109	118	117	120	100
12/50	488	464	370	267	408	696	1,418	1,620	795	686	448	314	605	489	496	574	678	513	321	233	147	161	159	162	136
12/51	573	552	437	312	479	815	1,673	1,891	931	803	522	364	696	561	574	661	781	592	373	273	172	188	184	188	157
12/52	633	610	482	343	530	888	1,836	2,088	1,031	894	577	401	769	613	630	729	871	655	411	300	190	209	204	207	172
12/53	613	591	468	332	512	845	1,750	2,011	1,007	870	560	392	744	588	610	706	845	637	402	293	185	203	199	203	167
12/54	935	902	711	503	785	1,321	2,809	3,217	1,590	1,388	882	613	1,174	924	966	1,118	1,346	1,014	643	464	292	322	316	322	267
12/55	1,129	1,085	858	609	969	1,650	3,543	4,062	1,983	1,743	1,087	748	1,439	1,130	1,178	1,356	1,627	1,240	792	569	357	391	384	392	327
12/56	1,242	1,208	957	676	1,074	1,829	3,952	4,526	2,215	1,949	1,202	831	1,606	1,278	1,308	1,483	1,764	1,355	874	631	399	434	421	430	361
12/57	1,090	1,066	833	593	934	1,551	3,326	3,757	1,875	1,646	1,019	713	1,373	1,082	1,112	1,268	1,513	1,154	737	536	339	366	359	366	304
12/58	1,651	1,595	1,235	882	1,401	2,380	5,111	5,785	2,864	2,541	1,561	1,088	2,118	1,670	1,720	1,969	2,366	1,784	1,127	819	517	563	554	568	474
12/59	1,865	1,804	1,383	988	1,612	2,778	5,979	6,820	3,371	2,984	1,825	1,263	2,476	1,942	1,996	2,275	2,745	2,050	1,290	936	592	654	647	667	559
12/60	1,936	1,873	1,423	1,016	1,629	2,749	5,879	6,772	3,426	3,042	1,856	1,275	2,442	1,904	1,961	2,249	2,705	2,025	1,268	926	584	646	643	662	551
12/61	2,563	2,450	1,861	1,308	2,104	3,611	7,709	8,867	4,467	3,982	2,417	1,663	3,198	2,510	2,587	2,983	3,571	2,641	1,638	1,194	751	831	823	840	696
12/62	2,184	2,084	1,610	1,108	1,785	3,049	6,466	7,430	3,740	3,331	2,046	1,416	2,722	2,135	2,198	2,531	3,013	2,234	1,390	1,018	641	710	702	713	593
12/63	2,637	2,493	1,911	1,319	2,154	3,717	8,007	9,163	4,554	4,047	2,468	1,700	3,274	2,568	2,656	3,035	3,603	2,670	1,663	1,223	770	856	841	854	713
12/64	3,047	2,878	2,228	1,537	2,474	4,250	8,987	10,463	5,265	4,643	2,897	1,990	3,828	3,006	3,110	3,526	4,180	3,141	1,962	1,441	904	1,001	982	1,004	839
12/65	3,614	3,428	2,649	1,847	3,049	5,333	11,620	13,263	6,595	5,859	3,531	2,427	4,693	3,671	3,807	4,318	5,116	3,857	2,424	1,773	1,119	1,279	1,253	1,278	1,074
12/66	3,350	3,198	2,457	1,713	2,775	4,802	10,400	11,825	5,986	5,319	3,222	2,221	4,284	3,376	3,500	3,989	4,712	3,543	2,227	1,630	1,027	1,171	1,159	1,182	997
12/67	4,719	4,467	3,401	2,404	3,909	6,777	14,612	16,682	8,526	7,536	4,589	3,157	6,095	4,826	4,994	5,679	6,648	5,028	3,138	2,284	1,435	1,628	1,607	1,655	1,392
12/68	5,609	5,341	4,128	2,907	4,687	8,101	17,349	20,097	10,191	8,891	5,473	3,761	7,306	5,803	5,998	6,834	8,096	6,076	3,778	2,746	1,723	1,957	1,940	2,008	1,687
12/69	4,973	4,727	3,562	2,515	4,017	6,715	13,986	16,432	8,474	7,346	4,608	3,172	6,087	4,879	4,926	5,608	6,587	4,939	3,069	2,255	1,421	1,596	1,581	1,643	1,381
12/70	5,019	4,718	3,611	2,569	4,044	6,688	13,902	16,153	8,274	7,189	4,547	3,146	6,101	5,019	4,891	5,548	6,490	4,864	3,016	2,230	1,407	1,578	1,553	1,609	1,358
12/71	5,734	5,434	4,190	3,020	4,837	7,948	16,416	19,067	9,801	8,441	5,362	3,718	7,245	5,887	5,772	6,502	7,610	5,698	3,541	2,625	1,658	1,884	1,867	1,939	1,628
12/72	6,666	6,296	4,863	3,516	5,691	9,202	18,966	21,563	11,174	9,588	6,045	4,211	8,070	6,360	6,372	7,206	8,424	6,271	3,940	2,944	1,875	2,127	2,094	2,175	1,822
12/73	5,711	5,356	4,153	2,996	4,621	7,266	14,899	16,667	8,689	7,544	4,801	3,308	6,236	4,962	4,955	5,585	6,485	4,870	3,088	2,346	1,508	1,691	1,639	1,713	1,449
12/74	4,482	4,213	3,300	2,383	3,594	5,556	11,234	12,616	6,621	5,745	3,749	2,574	4,898	4,087	3,906	4,402	5,038	3,792	2,403	1,820	1,170	1,294	1,246	1,298	1,098
12/75	6,157	5,784	4,540	3,300	5,162	8,190	16,720	19,031	9,739	8,444	5,455	3,714	7,229	6,103	5,707	6,411	7,388	5,573	3,502	2,637	1,679	1,861	1,807	1,883	1,594
12/76	8,002	7,426	5,913	4,278	6,772	10,876	22,337	25,411	12,841	11,163	7,151	4,848	9,458	7,919	7,484	8,378	9,781	7,392	4,660	3,489	2,220	2,469	2,381	2,488	2,110

Table XXXI

Indexes of Portfolio Value (Purchase Date = 100):
Dividends Reinvested,
Cash to Portfolio,
Equal Initial Weighting,
Tax-Exempt,
Current Dollars

ld til	12/50	12/51	12/52	12/53	12/54	12/55	12/56	12/57	12/58	12/59	12/60	12/61	12/62	12/63	12/64	12/65	12/66	12/67	12/68	12/69	12/70	12/71	12/72	12/73	12/74	12/75
'50	100																									
'51	115	100																								
'52	126	109	100																							
'53	124	107	97	100																						
'54	194	167	151	155	100																					
'55	234	202	183	189	119	100																				
'56	258	220	199	205	129	107	100																			
'57	222	190	171	173	111	93	86	100																		
'58	344	295	267	272	173	145	137	158	100																	
'59	403	347	314	321	204	170	161	185	115	100	100															
'60	407	352	318	321	206	171	162	182	113	98	100															
'61	520	449	405	411	264	221	210	235	147	128	128	100														
'62	444	382	345	349	226	189	181	203	128	112	112	87	100													
'63	528	453	409	416	268	224	214	243	153	134	135	104	118	100												
'64	618	531	482	491	316	263	252	288	182	159	162	125	141	117	100	100										
'65	778	669	609	626	399	331	317	371	232	203	210	163	185	153	129	100										
'66	722	618	567	585	370	307	293	349	218	191	198	154	174	144	121	92	100									
'67	1,001	866	795	828	523	432	413	496	311	274	286	223	258	218	184	139	152	100								
'68	1,222	1,063	975	1,015	642	535	515	616	388	343	359	278	319	271	230	177	197	128	100							
'69	1,006	872	802	828	525	437	418	493	311	273	282	218	252	214	183	143	156	103	80	100	100					
'70	998	864	791	821	525	435	415	482	306	268	275	212	242	204	173	136	151	101	78	96	100					
'71	1,192	1,034	946	981	626	519	497	581	368	322	332	256	291	244	207	161	179	120	93	114	117	100				
'72	1,331	1,152	1,057	1,094	698	577	552	647	409	359	368	285	326	273	231	179	198	133	104	126	129	107	100			
'73	1,049	903	833	863	548	450	427	494	317	283	289	226	256	214	178	138	150	103	81	98	97	81	72	100		
'74	796	686	632	656	418	344	326	372	239	213	218	171	192	160	134	104	113	78	61	75	74	62	55	73	100	
'75	1,153	999	921	956	609	503	476	551	351	311	321	248	281	235	197	152	167	114	89	110	109	92	82	113	154	100
'76	1,518	1,316	1,210	1,259	799	662	625	732	467	414	433	333	378	317	264	205	225	152	119	150	151	128	114	160	220	140

Source: Lawrence Fisher and Myron Scholes (compilers), CRSP Monthly Master File for Common Stocks Listed on the New York Stock Exchange *(magnetic tape). See Appendix A.*

Held Until	Purchased					Purchased					Purchased					Purchased					Purchased				
	12/25	12/26	12/27	12/28	12/29	12/30	12/31	12/32	12/33	12/34	12/35	12/36	12/37	12/38	12/39	12/40	12/41	12/42	12/43	12/44	12/45	12/46	12/47	12/48	12/49
12/25	100																								
12/26	110	100																							
12/27	147	133	100																						
12/28	203	184	139	100																					
12/29	180	164	124	87	100																				
12/30	131	120	91	63	72	100																			
12/31	72	66	50	35	40	55	100																		
12/32	66	61	46	32	37	51	92	100																	
12/33	109	99	74	52	58	80	143	156	100																
12/34	114	103	77	54	61	83	149	162	103	100	100														
12/35	162	147	109	76	86	119	213	232	148	143	100														
12/36	212	193	143	100	113	155	278	305	196	189	132	100													
12/37	141	128	95	66	75	103	185	203	130	126	87	66	100												
12/38	181	164	122	85	96	131	234	257	165	158	110	83	126	100											
12/39	186	168	126	87	99	136	243	266	170	163	113	85	129	102	100	100									
12/40	174	157	117	81	92	126	226	246	157	150	104	79	119	94	92	100									
12/41	154	140	104	72	82	112	201	220	140	135	94	71	107	85	83	90	100								
12/42	179	163	121	85	96	132	236	257	164	158	110	83	126	99	97	104	116	100							
12/43	226	206	153	107	122	168	301	329	210	202	141	106	161	127	124	134	148	128	100						
12/44	274	248	185	129	147	202	362	396	253	244	170	128	195	153	150	162	180	155	121	100	100				
12/45	363	330	246	173	197	273	490	536	345	333	233	176	268	211	207	224	249	214	167	138	100				
12/46	337	308	229	162	185	256	460	503	323	312	219	165	252	198	194	211	234	201	157	130	94	100			
12/47	356	325	242	170	194	268	480	526	337	326	229	172	262	206	202	219	243	209	164	135	97	103	100		
12/48	368	336	249	175	200	275	494	543	347	335	235	177	269	212	207	225	249	215	168	139	99	105	101	100	
12/49	439	400	297	209	240	331	594	651	416	402	282	212	323	254	249	269	299	257	201	166	119	127	122	119	100
12/50	565	516	384	271	311	430	770	847	543	527	370	278	425	334	328	355	395	340	265	219	157	167	160	156	130
12/51	674	621	462	325	372	515	923	1,017	653	634	444	334	511	402	394	427	475	409	320	265	191	201	193	189	157
12/52	787	726	540	380	433	598	1,070	1,177	755	732	512	384	586	461	452	489	543	468	365	302	217	229	220	215	178
12/53	779	718	536	378	432	597	1,069	1,171	752	727	509	382	583	459	450	487	540	465	363	300	216	228	219	214	178
12/54	1,203	1,103	824	579	661	913	1,636	1,797	1,156	1,121	784	590	902	711	697	755	836	720	561	463	333	352	337	329	272
12/55	1,560	1,427	1,065	748	851	1,169	2,093	2,299	1,479	1,430	999	750	1,148	905	888	962	1,063	915	714	588	421	445	427	416	344
12/56	1,656	1,522	1,137	797	913	1,256	2,249	2,474	1,591	1,544	1,078	810	1,243	980	962	1,041	1,151	991	775	639	459	484	463	452	374
12/57	1,443	1,330	997	701	803	1,104	1,980	2,174	1,396	1,347	939	708	1,085	854	838	907	1,003	865	679	560	403	425	408	400	331
12/58	2,100	1,922	1,441	1,010	1,162	1,601	2,868	3,151	2,026	1,956	1,365	1,031	1,579	1,243	1,221	1,322	1,462	1,258	984	813	583	619	593	580	480
12/59	2,341	2,134	1,608	1,127	1,301	1,789	3,202	3,518	2,260	2,177	1,521	1,149	1,760	1,386	1,362	1,476	1,634	1,407	1,098	907	650	694	666	651	538
12/60	2,235	2,043	1,556	1,092	1,265	1,744	3,127	3,429	2,201	2,119	1,477	1,115	1,702	1,338	1,312	1,421	1,574	1,354	1,058	875	626	674	648	634	528
12/61	2,936	2,675	2,052	1,437	1,656	2,286	4,093	4,484	2,874	2,767	1,923	1,452	2,208	1,734	1,697	1,836	2,030	1,746	1,363	1,127	803	866	832	814	676
12/62	2,786	2,545	1,933	1,352	1,545	2,132	3,808	4,166	2,668	2,564	1,784	1,344	2,042	1,604	1,570	1,700	1,879	1,617	1,264	1,047	745	797	765	749	624
12/63	3,499	3,191	2,415	1,687	1,917	2,638	4,709	5,146	3,300	3,173	2,209	1,661	2,525	1,985	1,942	2,100	2,322	1,999	1,562	1,293	920	983	944	922	766
12/64	4,228	3,852	2,908	2,035	2,308	3,165	5,643	6,162	3,947	3,804	2,646	1,989	3,023	2,376	2,325	2,514	2,778	2,395	1,873	1,550	1,099	1,174	1,126	1,100	912
12/65	4,722	4,292	3,246	2,266	2,569	3,519	6,276	6,864	4,405	4,254	2,961	2,227	3,391	2,667	2,614	2,826	3,125	2,694	2,106	1,744	1,240	1,330	1,276	1,245	1,030
12/66	3,930	3,580	2,724	1,901	2,170	2,981	5,321	5,823	3,753	3,636	2,533	1,903	2,911	2,289	2,246	2,429	2,690	2,319	1,819	1,507	1,079	1,160	1,113	1,088	904
12/67	4,959	4,486	3,424	2,394	2,726	3,753	6,703	7,347	4,737	4,596	3,206	2,405	3,659	2,872	2,813	3,040	3,368	2,906	2,280	1,890	1,352	1,464	1,405	1,371	1,137
12/68	5,554	5,042	3,832	2,689	3,076	4,255	7,599	8,333	5,379	5,211	3,640	2,740	4,166	3,269	3,201	3,464	3,836	3,305	2,594	2,150	1,537	1,664	1,598	1,561	1,292
12/69	4,964	4,507	3,431	2,403	2,738	3,765	6,719	7,370	4,754	4,598	3,206	2,423	3,682	2,886	2,820	3,047	3,376	2,911	2,278	1,897	1,350	1,476	1,415	1,383	1,144
12/70	5,440	4,952	3,770	2,640	2,988	4,083	7,281	7,958	5,118	4,938	3,441	2,593	3,945	3,092	3,020	3,262	3,614	3,116	2,441	2,033	1,442	1,564	1,500	1,467	1,215
12/71	6,110	5,554	4,218	2,955	3,372	4,601	8,206	8,936	5,762	5,576	3,894	2,943	4,481	3,512	3,434	3,712	4,117	3,550	2,775	2,315	1,637	1,789	1,715	1,678	1,389
12/72	7,096	6,473	4,928	3,444	3,952	5,398	9,627	10,470	6,769	6,559	4,577	3,463	5,278	4,129	4,039	4,362	4,838	4,173	3,261	2,724	1,929	2,101	2,010	1,967	1,629
12/73	6,230	5,655	4,286	2,980	3,415	4,667	8,332	9,077	5,883	5,747	4,012	3,021	4,611	3,609	3,532	3,813	4,240	3,653	2,851	2,383	1,693	1,828	1,746	1,714	1,421
12/74	4,656	4,254	3,235	2,251	2,589	3,545	6,329	6,893	4,467	4,376	3,058	2,293	3,509	2,744	2,685	2,900	3,226	2,777	2,168	1,812	1,292	1,386	1,325	1,302	1,079
12/75	6,594	6,029	4,578	3,190	3,666	5,004	8,921	9,715	6,305	6,131	4,272	3,203	4,913	3,847	3,771	4,073	4,524	3,899	3,039	2,534	1,807	1,938	1,855	1,818	1,505
12/76	8,479	7,750	5,860	4,080	4,691	6,421	11,443	12,430	8,069	7,873	5,483	4,108	6,290	4,922	4,820	5,203	5,773	4,972	3,884	3,233	2,311	2,467	2,361	2,315	1,914

Table XXXII

Indexes of Portfolio Value (Purchase Date = 100):
  Dividends Reinvested,
  Cash to Portfolio,
  Initial Weighting by Value,
  Tax-Exempt,
  Current Dollars

Held Until	12/50	12/51	12/52	12/53	12/54	12/55	12/56	12/57	12/58	12/59	12/60	12/61	12/62	12/63	12/64	12/65	12/66	12/67	12/68	12/69	12/70	12/71	12/72	12/73	12/74	12/75
12/50	100																									
12/51	120	100																								
12/52	137	113	100																							
12/53	137	113	100	100																						
12/54	208	171	151	150	100																					
12/55	261	216	190	188	125	100																				
12/56	284	235	206	204	136	108	100																			
12/57	253	209	184	182	122	97	89	100																		
12/58	366	302	266	264	175	140	128	143	100																	
12/59	410	339	298	296	196	157	145	162	112	100																
12/60	405	335	297	295	197	157	145	162	113	100	100															
12/61	518	428	378	376	250	200	185	207	144	127	126	100														
12/62	478	394	348	346	231	184	170	190	132	116	115	90	100													
12/63	585	482	425	423	281	224	207	231	160	141	139	109	120	100												
12/64	695	571	503	499	331	264	243	270	187	165	163	127	140	115	100											
12/65	784	644	567	563	372	297	273	304	210	185	183	144	159	132	114	100										
12/66	691	570	503	501	331	264	243	272	188	166	165	130	143	120	104	90	100									
12/67	864	709	624	620	409	327	301	337	233	207	205	163	179	153	132	115	126	100								
12/68	983	807	710	704	466	372	342	384	266	236	234	185	204	172	150	130	143	113	100							
12/69	872	716	631	626	415	331	304	342	237	210	209	165	183	156	135	117	129	101	89	100						
12/70	925	759	669	664	440	351	323	362	250	222	219	173	191	161	139	122	133	104	91	101	100					
12/71	1,056	865	761	755	498	397	366	410	283	251	249	197	217	185	159	139	152	119	105	116	114	100				
12/72	1,239	1,015	893	888	585	466	431	482	333	296	293	232	256	218	188	163	180	140	124	137	135	117	100			
12/73	1,082	889	782	778	513	409	375	418	290	257	254	201	222	188	160	140	154	120	105	116	114	97	82	100		
12/74	823	677	596	593	392	312	288	320	222	196	194	153	169	140	120	106	116	90	79	87	84	72	60	72	100	
12/75	1,146	941	829	823	546	435	401	447	309	274	271	213	234	194	168	147	161	125	110	120	117	100	84	100	137	100
12/76	1,455	1,195	1,052	1,044	693	553	510	569	394	348	344	270	297	245	213	186	204	159	139	153	148	126	106	126	173	124

Source: Lawrence Fisher and Myron Scholes (compilers), CRSP Monthly Master File for Common Stocks Listed on the New York Stock Exchange (magnetic tape). See Appendix A.

Chapter 11

CRSP Investment-Performance and Price Indexes for Common Stocks

In this chapter, we present the year-end levels and annual returns from December 31, 1925 through December 31, 1976 for four indexes computed from the *CRSP Monthly Master File for Common Stocks Listed on the New York Stock Exchange*. The first two indexes show average total return (investment performance); the other two show average relative price change. In one of each pair of indexes, each stock included for a month is given equal weight; in the other, each stock is given a weight equal to its total market value at the end of the previous month. The indexes and their annual percentage changes are shown in Table XXXIII. In addition, Table XXXIII shows the number of issues with "good" price quotations at the end of each year and the aggregate market value of those issues in billions of dollars.

The rates of return implied by the indexes differ from those for the buy-and-hold portfolios because the funds invested in a portfolio that behaved like one of the indexes (an "index portfolio") would have to be reallocated monthly. There are four causes of reallocation:

1. Differences of performance within a month. Reallocation from this cause is automatic for value-weighted portfolios.

Hence, there is a differential effect only for equally weighted portfolios.

2. Additions to the NYSE list. This cause has only a small effect on value-weighted portfolios because new firms have usually been much smaller than average.

3. Changes in the number of shares of already-listed securities. It is not clear which index portfolio would differ more from the corresponding buy-and-hold portfolio from this cause. Changes due to stock dividends and splits are taken care of automatically in all. Changes due to the issuance of additional shares in mergers of other NYSE stocks are automatic in the value-weighted portfolios but cause the weight of the successor to rise in the equally weighted buy-and-hold portfolios. Conversions and new floatations cause reallocation for the value-weighted portfolios but may be ignored for equal weighting.

4. Differences in dividend yields. This cause appears to be minor.

The annual returns for the investment performance indexes would be almost exactly the same as the rates of return along the diagonals

Table XXXIII

Year-End Values and Annual Returns of Four Indexes Computed from the
CRSP Monthly Master File for Common Stocks Listed on the New York Stock Exchange

			Investment-Performance Indexes				Price Indexes			
			Equal Weights		Value Weights		Equal Weights		Value Weights	
Year	Number of Stocks at Year-End	Aggregate Market Value (Billions of Dollars)	Index	Return for Year	Index	Return for Year	Index	Return for Year	Index	Return for Year
(1)	(2)	(3)	(4)	(5)	(6)	(7)	(8)	(9)	(10)	(11)
1925	501	$ 27.4	100	—	100	—	100	—	100	—
1926	545	31.3	100	0.2%	109	9.5%	96	−3.8%	104	3.6%
1927	592	41.2	131	31.1	146	33.0	121	26.1	131	26.7
1928	631	57.2	188	42.8	202	38.9	168	38.6	175	33.5
1929	723	54.0	126	−32.7	172	−14.7	109	−35.0	144	−17.9
1930	739	40.1	79	−37.7	124	−28.4	65	−40.4	98	−31.6
1931	723	20.9	43	−44.8	68	−44.6	34	−47.1	51	−47.8
1932	709	17.9	49	12.5	62	−9.0	37	8.2	44	−15.1
1933	710	27.2	117	139.7	99	58.3	88	135.0	66	51.7
1934	710	27.7	140	19.3	102	3.6	102	16.8	66	−0.6
1935	721	38.8	225	60.6	148	44.6	160	56.7	91	38.8
1936	745	50.4	344	53.2	196	33.0	238	48.3	116	27.3
1937	778	31.6	186	−45.8	129	−34.3	123	−48.3	72	−37.8
1938	777	39.0	256	37.5	164	27.4	164	33.2	88	22.1
1939	782	38.2	266	3.9	168	2.2	164	0.2	86	−2.6
1940	792	33.6	248	−6.9	155	−7.6	146	−11.2	75	−12.8
1941	800	28.5	228	−7.9	140	−9.8	126	−13.7	63	−15.9
1942	804	31.1	308	35.1	163	16.5	159	26.3	69	8.9
1943	815	38.6	500	61.9	209	28.1	244	53.9	84	21.7
1944	831	44.9	703	40.7	253	21.3	328	34.1	96	15.4
1945	856	60.3	1,142	62.5	351	38.5	513	56.6	128	33.0
1946	906	59.5	1,029	−9.9	328	−6.4	445	−13.3	155	−10.2
1947	942	60.0	1,026	−0.3	339	3.3	419	−5.8	113	−2.3
1948	965	58.4	1,004	−2.2	346	2.1	383	−8.4	108	−4.1
1949	991	67.4	1,219	21.4	416	20.2	435	13.5	121	12.2
1950	1,012	85.0	1,670	37.0	543	30.5	558	28.3	147	21.7
1951	1,031	101.1	1,937	16.0	658	21.2	610	9.3	169	14.5
1952	1,045	111.5	2,128	9.9	746	13.4	633	3.8	181	7.4
1953	1,046	108.6	2,067	−2.9	749	0.4	581	−8.2	172	−5.1
1954	1,053	162.0	3,247	57.1	1,133	51.3	869	49.6	248	44.2
1955	1,056	200.2	3,908	20.4	1,425	25.7	1,003	15.4	299	20.6
1956	1,057	217.0	4,177	6.9	1,549	8.7	1,026	2.3	313	4.5
1957	1,077	193.7	3,579	−14.3	1,381	−10.8	838	−18.4	267	−14.5
1958	1,066	276.0	5,721	59.8	1,992	44.2	1,286	53.6	371	38.8
1959	1,087	308.8	6,607	15.5	2,256	13.2	1,437	11.7	407	9.6
1960	1,118	307.3	6,506	−1.5	2,273	0.7	1,365	−5.0	396	−2.7
1961	1,141	387.4	8,424	29.5	2,887	27.0	1,716	25.8	488	23.3
1962	1,166	346.6	7,352	−12.7	2,617	−9.4	1,449	−15.6	427	−12.4
1963	1,190	418.8	8,727	18.7	3,173	21.3	1,668	15.1	502	17.5
1964	1,226	476.3	10,312	18.2	3,690	16.3	1,912	14.7	567	12.9
1965	1,250	534.3	13,266	28.6	4,225	14.5	2,388	24.9	630	11.1
1966	1,266	476.9	12,324	−7.1	3,844	−9.0	2,146	−10.1	554	−12.0
1967	1,254	597.2	18,505	50.2	4,891	27.2	3,127	45.7	683	23.4
1968	1,252	678.2	24,102	30.2	5,551	13.5	3,965	26.8	752	10.1
1969	1,291	607.2	19,180	−20.4	4,999	−9.9	3,066	−22.7	657	−12.7
1970	1,332	621.4	18,620	−2.9	5,073	1.5	2,877	−6.2	642	−2.2
1971	1,401	722.3	22,244	19.5	5,861	15.5	3,444	16.2	720	12.1
1972	1,480	856.9	24,124	8.5	6,915	18.0	3,531	5.6	826	14.7
1973	1,538	694.8	17,050	−29.3	5,720	−17.3	2,408	−31.8	662	−19.9
1974	1,545	487.2	12,526	−26.5	4,171	−27.1	1,679	−30.3	461	−30.4
1975	1,532	668.3	20,279	61.9	5,805	39.2	2,601	54.9	614	33.3
1976	1,545	832.7	29,502	45.5	7,333	26.3	3,643	40.1	745	21.3

of Tables XXIX and XXX if differences in reallocation had no effect. Since the principal causes of reallocation cause about the same reallocations in both value-weighted portfolios, the indexes describe the behavior of the value-weighted buy-and-hold portfolios rather well.

The methods of constructing these indexes are like those described for the "arithmetic" index in Lawrence Fisher, "Some New Stock-Market Indexes," *Journal of Business* 39 (January 1966, Part II): 191–225. The computation of the monthly returns used in the indexes employs an improved algorithm developed by Myron Scholes.[1] The annual returns shown are found from successive year-end values of the index. The Center also computes total returns for daily indexes for a broader base of stocks since July 1962.

The CRSP indexes differ from other indexes in a number of ways. Some of the ways are of obvious importance. The indexes produced by the NYSE itself cover all NYSE common stocks. However, the NYSE indexes ignore bid and ask quotations that are for a later date than the most recent sale price. Such nonsimultaneity of quotations reduces the usefulness of an index by introducing an element of positive serial corre-

lation into its returns or changes.[2] Moreover, the NYSE indexes have been found with consistent methods only since 1964.

For the CRSP indexes, the same method of computation is applied over the entire period of the index. Any changes in its statistical characteristics are attributable to changes in the characteristics of NYSE stocks rather than to our choice about what to include. However, the actual values of the indexes are subject to revision because the underlying *CRSP Master File* is corrected as errors are found.

The indexes in Table XXXIII are presented on a base of December 31, 1925 = 100. To examine the indexes on some other base, do the following: (1) define a factor that is equal to the ratio of the desired new base value to the original level of the index on the new base date and (2) multiply the original levels of the index by the factor.

---

[1] *Myron Scholes, "Returns to Investing in Common Stocks Listed on the New York Stock Exchange,"* Proceedings: Seminar on the Analysis of Security Prices *20 (May 1975): 127–30.*

[2] *Lawrence Fisher, "Some New Stock-Market Indexes,"* op. cit. Cf. *Myron Scholes, "Predicting Betas and Variances Using Daily Data,"* Proceedings: Seminar on the Analysis of Security Prices *21 (May 1976): 205–34.*

Part III
Rates of return on
U.S. Treasury Securities

Chapter 12

"Strategies" Used for Investments in Governments

In Chapters 13, 14, and 15, we will present eighteen tables that show rates of return on Governments. The tables show the results of following three alternative naïve investment policies:

Hold a long-term bond (Chapter 13),

Hold an intermediate-term bond or note (Chapter 14), and

Hold a short-term security (Chapter 15).

The instrument in question is held for only a year (long- and intermediate-term) or six months (short-term) before it may be exchanged for a similar instrument.

The alternative strategies are intended to show the opportunity cost of having invested in common stocks rather than in Governments.

The rates of return on common stocks in Tables I through XII are with reinvestment of dividends. For comparability, the tables for Governments assume reinvestment of interest. The tables for stocks are consistent with a diffuse time horizon for the investor. The presentation in this part also assumes a diffuse horizon.

Factors Affecting Rates of Return

It can be shown that the rates of return that result from the naïve investment policy for Governments depend directly on four variables:

1. The promised yield (yield to maturity) at the time the initial investment is made
2. Changes in interest rates while the investment is held
3. The income tax rates actually applied to the interest
4. When figures are deflated by the Consumer Price Index, by the rate of inflation during the holding period.[1]

Other things being equal, the higher the promised yield, the higher the rate of return; the higher the income-tax rate, the lower the return; the greater the rate of inflation, the lower the "real" return. However, the effect of changes in the interest rate depends on the relationship between the remaining length of the holding period at the time a change takes place and the *duration* of the security held at that time.

The duration of a bond (or any other fixed-income security or portfolio) was defined by Frederic R. Macaulay as the weighted *average time to payment* of the bond, where the weight given each time of payment is equal to the present value of the payment (interest or principal) due at that time.[2] For example, a Treasury

---

[1] *We do not assert that these variables are independent of one another. A large part of economic and financial literature is concerned with their determination.*

[2] Some Theoretical Problems Suggested by the Movement of Interest Rates, Bond Yields and Stock Prices in the United States since 1856 *(New York: National Bureau of Economic Research, 1938), pp. 44–51.*

bill that is due in 12 months has a duration of one year; a 6 percent, ten-year bond yielding 6 percent has a duration of 7.7 years; an annuity paying a dollar a year forever and yielding 10 percent per annum compounded annually has a duration of 11 years.

Duration is important because the proportional change in the price of any instrument with respect to a change in its yield (compounded continuously) is equal to its duration (but opposite in sign).[3] Hence, if duration is equal to the remaining holding period, a change in the interest rate affects by the same amount both the price of the security and the present value of the end-of-period wealth that was implied by the promised yield. Thus, the realized rate of return will not be affected in this case.[4] If the duration is less than the remaining holding period, an increase in the interest rate will raise the realized rate of return because receipts can be reinvested at the new, higher interest rate. If the duration is greater than the remainder of the holding period, the loss of principal will more than offset any increase in interest income.

Redington called portfolios in which the duration of the assets is equal to the duration of the liabilities "immunized portfolios." For the case of tax exemption and calculations in current dollars, we could have found the yield on 1,326 immunized portfolios and, perhaps, could have eliminated the effects of changes in interest rates on realized returns. As shown by Fisher and Weil,[5] the risk of the portfolios of Governments would have been reduced. However, all the other effects would remain. Since common stocks carry no promises to pay at specified times, portfolios containing substantial amounts of common stock cannot be immunized. Therefore, we forgo the use of immunization of the portfolios of Governments for this study. We merely ask the question: "What happened to investment in long- (or intermediate- or short-) term Governments?"

It seems reasonable to suppose that rates of return on common stocks are affected by all of the factors that affect rates of return on bonds and by additional factors as well. Certainly, rates of return on stocks have been more variable than rates of return on bonds.

A theoretical model to illustrate these effects may be built along the following lines:

Common stock has value because its holders will ultimately receive the difference between two cash flows—the gross receipts of the issuing corporation and the payments to be made to everyone other than the common stockholders.

The value of the common stock is equal to the difference between the present values of the two cash flows. The present value of a cash flow is determined by its expected payments, their times, and the interest rate to be applied. Changes in this interest rate are caused by changes in the interest rate on Governments and, perhaps, by changes in the riskiness of the cash flow. In addition, changes in the expected payments will also affect the value of the cash flow.[6]

Carrying Out the Investment Policy

If all Governments were issued with the same terms except for maturity dates, carrying out the hypothetical policy of holding Governments of a particular maturity class would have been easy. However, both by contractual terms and by provisions of the income-tax laws, Governments have had a variety of special features. These special features make it hard to choose U.S. Treasury securities whose realized rates of return are commensurable with those of common stocks or even each other.

The special features of some Governments that may make their realized returns poor measures of the opportunity cost of giving up an alternative in order to invest in common stock are the following:

1. Exemption of interest from income taxes
2. Prices that are substantially below par
3. Acceptability at par for the payment of estate taxes ("flower bonds")
4. Lack of "bank eligibility"

[3] Lawrence Fisher, "An Algorithm for Finding Exact Rates of Return," Journal of Business 39 (January 1966, Part II): 111–18. The statement applies to infinitesimal changes.

[4] Cf. F. M. Redington, "Review of the Principles of Life-office Valuations," Journal of the Institute of the Society of Actuaries (England) 78 (1952): 286–340, including the accompanying discussion. See Fisher and Weil, op. cit., for a proof of the proposition put forth by Redington and an empirical test.

[5] Ibid.

[6] In addition, the two cash flows may have their present values change as if they were generated by random-walk processes. Then, unless the two random walks are perfectly correlated, the value of the stock will also be generated by a random-walk process. However, if the present values approach each other, the value of the stock will fall. If the variances of the changes in present value for the two cash flows do not change, the variance of the relative price changes of the stock will increase. Moreover, the changes in the underlying cash flows for various companies can be taken as correlated in this model. Hence, the same factors that change variance of return for a stock relative to the market as a whole also produce changes in systematic risk (β) in the same direction. And these changes in systematic risk will act as if they, too, were generated by a random-walk process.

5. Partial tax exemption of interest when dividends are fully taxable (and vice versa)

6. Membership in a class of security for which a worthwhile exchange offer could be expected several months before maturity.

Tax exemption makes an issue most attractive to those who are in the highest tax bracket. Even our higher tax rate is substantially below the maximum tax rate in all but the last five or ten years.

Selling at a discount from par converts part of the promised yield from ordinary income to capital gains, which have been taxed at lower rates than interest or dividends since 1936 for the income levels we have assumed.

"Flower bonds" are issues that may be tendered at par value in the payment of federal estate taxes. Recently, flower bonds due in the 1990s were selling at about 75 percent of par value, i.e., at a yield to maturity of about 5.5 percent per annum. However, the rate of return on such bonds if acquired by a person who was on his deathbed was substantially higher.[7]

Many of the 2¼s and 2½s issued during World War II were not fully negotiable because commercial banks were not allowed to buy them on the open market for the first several years that they were outstanding. During the period of the restriction, fully negotiable bonds were referred to as being "bank eligible." At the end of 1945, bank eligibility appeared to be worth up to four points (four percent of par value). All of the bonds that were not bank eligible were also flower bonds.

Many Treasury bonds are callable at the option of the Secretary of the Treasury for several years before the final maturity date. Hence, such bonds sell at lower prices (and higher yields) than noncallable bonds with the same coupon rate that are due at any single time between the first call date and the final maturity date.

The Secretary of the Treasury usually offers to exchange issues other than Treasury bills that are to mature within a period of a few months for one or more new issues. Through 1940, the securities offered in exchange were normally worth between 100¾ and 101. As a consequence, the "promised yields" on securities with up to two or three years to maturity were often negative.

Selection Procedures

Because of the many special features, each portfolio (long-, intermediate-, or short-term) held only one security at a time. We set up procedures so that the issue we selected would be the one that would come closest to having a yield that reflected appropriately taxed interest and a known cash flow to the holder.

The selection criteria were applied serially as follows:

1. Appropriate time to maturity (or to first call if callable)

2. Appropriate tax status (partially tax-exempt through 1935, fully taxable thereafter)

3. Avoid flower bonds. If flower bonds cannot be avoided, choose the highest priced flower bond that is bank eligible.

4. Avoid callable bonds and callable notes. If a callable issue cannot be avoided, choose one with a price close to par and as long a maturity date as feasible, preferring a short period between first call and maturity to a long period.

5. Choose a Treasury bill if one is available and has both bid and ask quotations present.

6. Choose an issue that
   a. has a small spread between bid and ask,
   b. is relatively long-term, and
   c. has a price close to par.

---

[7]*How much higher is a complicated matter because the twenty-five point gain is subject to income and estate taxes.*

Chapter 13

Time-Weighted Rates of Return on Long-Term Governments

In this chapter, we present Tables XXXIV through XXXIX, which show annual rates of return on a "portfolio" that contains one Government bond at a time. Like the tables of time-weighted rates of return on investments in common stocks (I-XII), these tables apply to tax-exempt investors and to investors who were subject to taxation at either the lower or higher tax rate.

Sixteen different bonds appeared in the portfolio, although two issues were used for two time periods and two others were used for three periods. As noted in Chapter 2, the complete set of criteria for selection was met only for the issues held after 1971. Through 1957, the selection criteria resulted in selecting callable bonds. During 1958–71, the only bonds that had ten or more years to maturity were flower bonds.

The flower bonds most likely to have their prices affected by estate-tax privilege are those with the lowest prices. Fortunately, except for 1971, the flower bonds used for the portfolio sold for several points more than the lowest-priced flower bond. For 1971, there were two partially offsetting effects. The bond held became one of the flower bonds *par excellence* during the year; hence, there was a tendency for the ostensible yield to be lower than what investors truly expected to realize. Offsetting this effect was the fact that nearly seven percent of the amount of the issue in the hands of the public was redeemed, with the estates of the owners receiving high returns.

Results

Tables XXXIV through XXXIX tell several different stories.

The tables in current dollars suggest that returns on bonds were almost always positive, although lower than the average rates of return on stocks. For portfolios with almost all purchase dates, the rate of return through December 1976 was at least 3 percent per annum, compounded annually. The more recently purchased portfolios show the highest rates of return among all holding periods that are at least several years in length.

However, when price quotations are deflated by the Consumer Price Index, one can see that since the beginning of World War II gross rates of returns on long-term Governments have been about equal to the rate of change of the Consumer Price Index. After taxes, the deflated rates of return have been rather consistently negative since December 1940.

Held Until	| Purchased 12/25	12/26	12/27	12/28	12/29	| Purchased 12/30	12/31	12/32	12/33	12/34	| Purchased 12/35	12/36	12/37	12/38	12/39	| Purchased 12/40	12/41	12/42	12/43	12/44	| Purchased 12/45	12/46	12/47	12/48	12/49
12/26	7.2																								
12/27	7.7	8.2																							
12/28	4.7	3.5	−0.9																						
12/29	4.7	3.8	1.7	4.4																					
12/30	5.0	4.4	3.2	5.3	6.2																				
12/31	2.8	1.9	0.4	0.8	−0.9	−7.6																			
12/32	4.0	3.4	2.5	3.4	3.1	1.5	11.5																		
12/33	3.4	2.9	2.0	2.6	2.2	0.8	5.3	−0.5																	
12/34	4.0	3.6	3.0	3.7	3.5	2.8	6.6	4.2	9.0																
12/35	4.1	3.8	3.2	3.9	3.8	3.3	6.2	4.5	7.1	5.1															
12/36	4.4	4.2	3.7	4.3	4.3	4.0	6.5	5.2	7.2	6.3	7.5														
12/37	4.1	3.8	3.4	3.9	3.8	3.5	5.5	4.3	5.6	4.4	4.1	0.7													
12/38	4.2	4.0	3.6	4.1	4.0	3.8	5.5	4.5	5.6	4.7	4.6	3.2	5.6												
12/39	4.4	4.2	3.8	4.3	4.3	4.1	5.6	4.8	5.7	5.1	5.1	4.2	6.0	6.5											
12/40	4.5	4.3	4.0	4.4	4.4	4.2	5.6	4.9	5.7	5.1	5.1	4.6	5.9	6.0	5.5										
12/41	4.2	4.1	3.8	4.1	4.1	3.9	5.1	4.5	5.1	4.5	4.4	3.8	4.6	4.3	3.3	1.1									
12/42	4.2	4.0	3.7	4.1	4.0	3.9	5.0	4.3	4.9	4.4	4.3	3.7	4.4	4.0	3.2	2.1	3.2								
12/43	4.1	3.9	3.6	3.9	3.9	3.7	4.7	4.1	4.6	4.1	4.0	3.5	4.0	3.6	2.9	2.1	2.6	2.1							
12/44	4.0	3.8	3.6	3.9	3.8	3.7	4.6	4.0	4.4	4.0	3.9	3.4	3.8	3.5	2.9	2.3	2.7	2.4	2.8						
12/45	4.3	4.2	4.0	4.3	4.2	4.1	5.0	4.5	4.9	4.6	4.5	4.2	4.6	4.5	4.2	3.9	4.7	5.1	6.7	10.7					
12/46	4.1	4.0	3.7	4.0	4.0	3.8	4.7	4.2	4.6	4.2	4.1	3.8	4.1	3.9	3.6	3.2	3.7	3.8	4.4	5.2	−0.1				
12/47	3.8	3.6	3.4	3.6	3.6	3.5	4.2	3.7	4.0	3.6	3.5	3.2	3.4	3.2	2.8	2.4	2.6	2.5	2.6	2.5	−1.4	−2.6			
12/48	3.8	3.6	3.4	3.6	3.6	3.5	4.1	3.7	4.0	3.6	3.5	3.2	3.4	3.2	2.8	2.5	2.7	2.6	2.7	2.7	0.2	0.3	3.4		
12/49	3.9	3.7	3.5	3.8	3.7	3.6	4.3	3.9	4.1	3.8	3.7	3.4	3.7	3.5	3.2	2.9	3.2	3.2	3.4	3.5	1.7	2.3	4.9	6.4	
12/50	3.7	3.6	3.4	3.6	3.6	3.4	4.0	8.6	3.9	3.6	3.5	3.2	3.4	3.2	2.9	2.6	2.8	2.8	2.9	2.9	1.4	1.8	3.3	3.2	0.1
12/51	3.4	3.3	3.1	3.3	3.2	3.1	3.6	3.2	3.4	3.1	3.0	2.7	2.8	2.6	2.3	2.0	2.1	2.0	2.0	1.9	0.5	0.6	1.4	0.8	−2.0
12/52	3.3	3.2	3.0	3.2	3.1	3.0	3.5	3.1	3.3	3.0	2.9	2.6	2.7	2.5	2.2	2.0	2.0	1.9	1.9	1.8	0.6	0.7	1.4	0.9	−0.9
12/53	3.4	3.2	3.0	3.2	3.1	3.0	3.5	3.1	3.3	3.0	2.9	2.7	2.8	2.6	2.3	2.1	2.2	2.1	2.1	2.0	1.0	1.1	1.7	1.4	0.2
12/54	3.4	3.3	3.1	3.3	3.2	3.1	3.6	3.2	3.4	3.1	3.0	2.8	2.9	2.7	2.5	2.3	2.4	2.3	2.3	2.3	1.4	1.6	2.2	2.0	1.1
12/55	3.2	3.1	2.9	3.1	3.0	2.9	3.4	3.0	3.2	2.9	2.8	2.6	2.7	2.5	2.2	2.0	2.1	2.0	2.0	1.9	1.1	1.2	1.7	1.5	0.7
12/56	3.0	2.8	2.6	2.8	2.7	2.6	3.0	2.7	2.8	2.5	2.4	2.2	2.2	2.1	1.8	1.6	1.6	1.5	1.4	1.3	0.5	0.6	0.9	0.6	−0.2
12/57	3.2	3.0	2.9	3.0	2.9	2.8	3.2	2.9	3.1	2.8	2.7	2.5	2.6	2.4	2.2	2.0	2.1	2.0	2.0	1.9	1.2	1.4	1.8	1.6	1.0
12/58	2.9	2.8	2.6	2.8	2.7	2.6	3.0	2.7	2.8	2.5	2.4	2.2	2.3	2.1	1.9	1.7	1.7	1.6	1.6	1.5	0.8	0.9	1.3	1.0	0.5
12/59	2.7	2.6	2.4	2.6	2.5	2.4	2.7	2.4	2.5	2.3	2.2	1.9	2.0	1.8	1.6	1.4	1.4	1.3	1.3	1.2	0.5	0.6	0.8	0.6	0.0
12/60	3.0	2.9	2.8	2.9	2.8	2.7	3.1	2.8	2.9	2.7	2.6	2.4	2.5	2.3	2.2	2.0	2.0	2.0	2.0	1.9	1.4	1.5	1.8	1.6	1.2
12/61	3.0	2.8	2.7	2.8	2.7	2.6	3.0	2.7	2.8	2.6	2.5	2.3	2.4	2.2	2.1	1.9	1.9	1.9	1.9	1.8	1.3	1.4	1.7	1.5	1.1
12/62	3.0	2.9	2.8	2.9	2.8	2.7	3.1	2.8	2.9	2.7	2.6	2.4	2.5	2.4	2.2	2.1	2.1	2.0	2.0	2.0	1.5	1.6	1.9	1.8	1.4
12/63	3.0	2.9	2.7	2.8	2.8	2.7	3.0	2.8	2.9	2.7	2.6	2.4	2.5	2.3	2.2	2.0	2.1	2.0	2.0	2.0	1.5	1.6	1.9	1.8	1.4
12/64	3.0	2.9	2.7	2.9	2.8	2.7	3.0	2.8	2.9	2.7	2.6	2.4	2.5	2.4	2.2	2.1	2.1	2.1	2.1	2.0	1.6	1.7	2.0	1.9	1.6
12/65	2.9	2.8	2.7	2.8	2.7	2.6	3.0	2.7	2.8	2.6	2.5	2.4	2.4	2.3	2.2	2.0	2.1	2.0	2.0	2.0	1.5	1.6	1.9	1.8	1.5
12/66	3.0	2.9	2.7	2.8	2.8	2.7	3.0	2.8	2.9	2.7	2.6	2.4	2.5	2.4	2.2	2.1	2.1	2.1	2.1	2.1	1.7	1.8	2.0	1.9	1.7
12/67	2.8	2.7	2.5	2.6	2.6	2.5	2.8	2.5	2.6	2.4	2.3	2.2	2.2	2.1	2.0	1.8	1.9	1.8	1.8	1.7	1.4	1.4	1.6	1.5	1.3
12/68	2.7	2.6	2.5	2.6	2.6	2.5	2.7	2.5	2.6	2.4	2.3	2.2	2.2	2.1	2.0	1.8	1.9	1.8	1.8	1.8	1.4	1.5	1.7	1.6	1.3
12/69	2.5	2.4	2.2	2.3	2.3	2.2	2.4	2.2	2.3	2.1	2.0	1.8	1.9	1.8	1.6	1.5	1.5	1.4	1.4	1.3	1.0	1.0	1.2	1.1	0.8
12/70	2.9	2.8	2.6	2.7	2.7	2.6	2.9	2.6	2.7	2.6	2.5	2.3	2.4	2.3	2.2	2.1	2.1	2.1	2.0	2.0	1.7	1.8	2.0	1.9	1.7
12/71	3.1	3.0	2.9	3.0	3.0	2.9	3.2	3.0	3.0	2.9	2.8	2.7	2.8	2.7	2.5	2.5	2.5	2.5	2.5	2.5	2.2	2.3	2.5	2.4	2.3
12/72	3.2	3.1	3.0	3.0	3.0	2.9	3.2	3.0	3.1	3.0	2.9	2.8	2.8	2.7	2.6	2.5	2.6	2.6	2.6	2.6	2.3	2.4	2.6	2.6	2.4
12/73	3.1	3.0	2.9	3.0	3.0	2.9	3.1	2.9	3.0	2.9	2.8	2.7	2.8	2.7	2.6	2.5	2.5	2.5	2.5	2.5	2.2	2.3	2.5	2.5	2.3
12/74	3.1	3.0	2.9	3.0	3.0	2.9	3.2	3.0	3.1	2.9	2.9	2.7	2.8	2.7	2.6	2.5	2.6	2.6	2.6	2.6	2.3	2.4	2.6	2.5	2.4
12/75	3.2	3.1	3.0	3.1	3.0	3.0	3.2	3.0	3.1	3.0	2.9	2.8	2.9	2.8	2.7	2.6	2.7	2.7	2.7	2.7	2.4	2.5	2.7	2.7	2.5
12/76	3.4	3.4	3.3	3.4	3.3	3.3	3.5	3.4	3.5	3.3	3.3	3.2	3.2	3.2	3.1	3.0	3.1	3.1	3.1	3.1	2.9	3.0	3.2	3.2	3.1

Table XXXIV

Time-Weighted Rates of Return* on Long-Term U.S. Treasury Bonds:
  Interest Reinvested,
  Tax-Exempt,
  Current Dollars

Purchased

	12/50	12/51	12/52	12/53	12/54	12/55	12/56	12/57	12/58	12/59	12/60	12/61	12/62	12/63	12/64	12/65	12/66	12/67	12/68	12/69	12/70	12/71	12/72	12/73	12/74	12/75
51	−3.9																									
52	−1.4	1.2																								
53	0.2	2.4	3.6																							
54	1.4	3.2	4.2	4.9																						
55	0.8	2.0	2.3	1.6	−1.5																					
56	−0.2	0.6	0.4	−0.6	−3.2	−4.9																				
57	1.1	2.0	2.2	1.8	0.8	2.0	9.4																			
58	0.5	1.2	1.2	0.7	−0.4	0.0	2.6	−3.7																		
59	0.0	0.6	0.5	−0.0	−1.0	−0.9	0.5	−3.6	−3.5																	
60	1.3	1.9	2.0	1.8	1.3	1.9	3.7	1.9	4.8	13.8																
61	1.2	1.7	1.8	1.6	1.1	1.6	2.9	1.4	3.1	6.6	−0.0															
62	1.6	2.1	2.2	2.0	1.6	2.1	3.3	2.2	3.7	6.2	2.6	5.4														
63	1.5	2.0	2.1	1.9	1.6	2.0	3.0	2.0	3.2	5.0	2.2	3.3	1.3													
64	1.7	2.1	2.2	2.1	1.8	2.2	3.1	2.3	3.3	4.7	2.6	3.5	2.5	3.7												
65	1.6	2.0	2.1	1.9	1.7	2.0	2.8	2.0	2.9	4.0	2.1	2.7	1.8	2.0	0.3											
66	1.8	2.2	2.2	2.1	1.9	2.2	3.0	2.3	3.1	4.0	2.5	3.0	2.4	2.8	2.3	4.3										
67	1.3	1.7	1.7	1.6	1.3	1.6	2.2	1.5	2.1	2.8	1.3	1.6	0.8	0.7	−0.3	−0.6	−5.3									
68	1.4	1.7	1.8	1.6	1.4	1.6	2.2	1.6	2.1	2.8	1.5	1.7	1.1	1.0	0.4	0.4	−1.5	2.4								
69	0.9	1.1	1.1	1.0	0.7	0.9	1.3	0.7	1.1	1.6	0.3	0.4	−0.3	−0.6	−1.4	−1.9	−3.9	−3.2	−8.4							
70	1.8	2.1	2.1	2.0	1.9	2.1	2.6	2.1	2.6	3.2	2.2	2.4	2.1	2.2	1.9	2.2	1.7	4.2	5.1	20.5						
71	2.4	2.7	2.8	2.7	2.6	2.9	3.4	3.0	3.5	4.1	3.3	3.6	3.5	3.7	3.7	4.3	4.3	6.8	8.4	17.8	15.2					
72	2.5	2.8	2.9	2.9	2.8	3.0	3.5	3.2	3.7	4.2	3.5	3.8	3.6	3.9	3.9	4.5	4.5	6.5	7.6	13.5	10.2	5.4				
73	2.4	2.7	2.8	2.7	2.6	2.9	3.3	3.0	3.4	3.9	3.2	3.5	3.3	3.5	3.5	3.9	3.9	5.5	6.1	10.0	6.8	2.8	0.2			
74	2.5	2.8	2.8	2.8	2.7	2.9	3.4	3.0	3.5	4.0	3.3	3.6	3.4	3.6	3.6	4.0	3.9	5.3	5.8	8.9	6.2	3.3	2.3	4.4		
75	2.6	2.9	3.0	2.9	2.9	3.1	3.5	3.2	3.6	4.1	3.5	3.7	3.6	3.8	3.8	4.2	4.1	5.4	5.8	8.4	6.1	4.0	3.5	5.2	6.0	
76	3.2	3.5	3.6	3.6	3.5	3.7	4.2	3.9	4.4	4.9	4.3	4.6	4.6	4.8	4.9	5.3	5.4	6.7	7.3	9.7	8.0	6.6	6.9	9.3	11.8	17.9

*Percent per annum, compounded annually.

Source: Lawrence Fisher (compiler), CRSP Monthly Return File for
  U.S. Treasury Securities (magnetic tape). See Appendix A.

Held Until	Purchased 12/25	12/26	12/27	12/28	12/29	Purchased 12/30	12/31	12/32	12/33	12/34	Purchased 12/35	12/36	12/37	12/38	12/39	Purchased 12/40	12/41	12/42	12/43	12/44	Purchased 12/45	12/46	12/47	12/48	12/49
12/26	8.8																								
12/27	9.7	10.5																							
12/28	6.3	5.1	0.0																						
12/29	5.8	4.8	2.1	4.2																					
12/30	7.2	6.8	5.6	8.5	13.0																				
12/31	6.4	5.9	4.7	6.4	7.5	2.1																			
12/32	8.7	8.7	8.4	10.6	12.8	12.7	24.3																		
12/33	7.5	7.3	6.8	8.2	9.2	7.9	10.9	−1.0																	
12/34	7.4	7.2	6.8	8.0	8.7	7.7	9.6	2.9	6.9																
12/35	6.9	6.7	6.2	7.1	7.6	6.5	7.6	2.6	4.4	2.1															
12/36	6.8	6.6	6.2	7.0	7.4	6.5	7.4	3.5	5.0	4.1	6.2														
12/37	6.0	5.8	5.3	5.9	6.1	5.2	5.7	2.3	3.2	1.9	1.9	−2.3													
12/38	6.2	6.0	5.6	6.2	6.4	5.6	6.1	3.3	4.2	3.6	4.1	3.0	8.6												
12/39	6.3	6.1	5.7	6.3	6.5	5.8	6.2	3.9	4.7	4.2	4.8	4.3	7.8	7.0											
12/40	6.2	6.0	5.6	6.1	6.3	5.6	6.0	3.9	4.7	4.3	4.7	4.4	6.7	5.7	4.5										
12/41	5.2	5.0	4.6	5.0	5.0	4.3	4.5	2.5	3.0	2.5	2.5	1.8	2.8	1.0	−1.9	−7.9									
12/42	4.5	4.3	3.9	4.2	4.2	3.5	3.6	1.7	2.0	1.4	1.3	0.5	1.1	−0.7	−3.1	−6.7	−5.6								
12/43	4.2	4.0	3.6	3.8	3.8	3.1	3.2	1.5	1.7	1.1	1.0	0.3	0.7	−0.8	−2.6	−4.9	−3.3	−1.0							
12/44	4.0	3.8	3.4	3.6	3.6	2.9	3.0	1.4	1.6	1.1	1.0	0.4	0.7	−0.5	−2.0	−3.5	−2.0	−0.2	0.7						
12/45	4.3	4.0	3.7	3.9	3.9	3.3	3.4	1.9	2.1	1.7	1.7	1.2	1.6	0.7	−0.3	−1.3	0.5	2.6	4.4	8.3					
12/46	3.2	2.9	2.6	2.7	2.6	2.0	2.0	0.6	0.7	0.2	0.0	−0.6	−0.4	−1.5	−2.6	−3.8	−2.9	−2.3	−2.7	−4.3	−15.5				
12/47	2.5	2.2	1.9	2.0	1.8	1.2	1.1	−0.2	−0.2	−0.7	−0.9	−1.6	−1.5	−2.6	−3.7	−4.8	−4.3	−4.0	−4.7	−6.5	−13.1	−10.7			
12/48	2.5	2.2	1.8	1.9	1.8	1.2	1.1	−0.2	−0.1	−0.6	−0.8	−1.4	−1.3	−2.2	−3.2	−4.1	−3.6	−3.2	−3.7	−4.7	−8.7	−5.2	0.7		
12/49	2.7	2.4	2.1	2.2	2.1	1.5	1.5	0.3	0.4	−0.0	−0.2	−0.7	−0.5	−1.3	−2.1	−2.8	−2.2	−1.7	−1.8	−2.2	−4.7	−0.8	4.5	8.4	
12/50	2.4	2.1	1.8	1.8	1.7	1.2	1.1	−0.0	0.0	−0.4	−0.5	−1.0	−0.9	−1.7	−2.4	−3.1	−2.5	−2.1	−2.3	−2.8	−4.9	−2.0	1.1	1.3	−5.4
12/51	1.9	1.6	1.3	1.3	1.2	0.7	0.6	−0.5	−0.5	−0.9	−1.1	−1.6	−1.5	−2.3	−3.0	−3.7	−3.2	−3.0	−3.2	−3.7	−5.6	−3.5	−1.6	−2.4	−7.4
12/52	1.8	1.6	1.2	1.3	1.1	0.6	0.6	−0.5	−0.5	−0.9	−1.0	−1.5	−1.4	−2.1	−2.8	−3.3	−2.9	−2.6	−2.8	−3.2	−4.8	−2.9	−1.2	−1.7	−4.9
12/53	1.9	1.6	1.3	1.3	1.2	0.7	0.7	−0.3	−0.3	−0.7	−0.8	−1.2	−1.1	−1.8	−2.4	−2.9	−2.4	−2.1	−2.3	−2.6	−3.9	−2.1	−0.6	−0.8	−3.0
12/54	2.0	1.8	1.4	1.5	1.4	0.9	0.9	−0.1	−0.0	−0.4	−0.5	−0.9	−0.8	−1.3	−1.9	−2.3	−1.9	−1.5	−1.6	−1.8	−2.9	−1.2	0.3	0.2	−1.4
12/55	1.9	1.6	1.3	1.4	1.3	0.8	0.8	−0.2	−0.1	−0.4	−0.6	−0.9	−0.8	−1.4	−1.9	−2.3	−1.9	−1.6	−1.6	−1.8	−2.8	−1.2	−0.0	−0.1	−1.4
12/56	1.5	1.3	1.0	1.0	0.9	0.5	0.4	−0.5	−0.5	−0.8	−0.9	−1.3	−1.2	−1.7	−2.2	−2.6	−2.2	−2.0	−2.1	−2.3	−3.2	−1.9	−0.9	−1.1	−2.3
12/57	1.7	1.5	1.2	1.2	1.1	0.7	0.6	−0.2	−0.2	−0.5	−0.6	−0.9	−0.8	−1.3	−1.8	−2.1	−1.7	−1.5	−1.5	−1.7	−2.5	−1.2	−0.2	−0.3	−1.3
12/58	1.5	1.2	0.9	1.0	0.9	0.5	0.4	−0.4	−0.4	−0.7	−0.8	−1.1	−1.1	−1.5	−2.0	−2.3	−2.0	−1.7	−1.8	−1.9	−2.7	−1.5	−0.7	−0.8	−1.8
12/59	1.3	1.0	0.8	0.8	0.7	0.3	0.2	−0.6	−0.6	−0.9	−1.0	−1.3	−1.2	−1.7	−2.1	−2.4	−2.1	−1.9	−2.0	−2.2	−2.9	−1.8	−1.0	−1.2	−2.1
12/60	1.6	1.4	1.1	1.1	1.0	0.6	0.6	−0.2	−0.1	−0.4	−0.5	−0.8	−0.7	−1.1	−1.5	−1.8	−1.4	−1.2	−1.2	−1.3	−1.9	−0.9	−0.1	−0.1	−0.9
12/61	1.5	1.3	1.0	1.1	1.0	0.6	0.5	−0.2	−0.2	−0.4	−0.5	−0.8	−0.7	−1.1	−1.4	−1.7	−1.4	−1.2	−1.2	−1.3	−1.8	−0.9	−0.1	−0.2	−0.9
12/62	1.6	1.4	1.1	1.2	1.1	0.7	0.7	−0.0	−0.0	−0.2	−0.3	−0.6	−0.5	−0.9	−1.2	−1.5	−1.1	−0.9	−0.9	−1.0	−1.5	−0.6	0.1	0.1	−0.5
12/63	1.5	1.3	1.1	1.1	1.0	0.7	0.6	−0.1	−0.0	−0.3	−0.3	−0.6	−0.5	−0.9	−1.2	−1.4	−1.1	−0.9	−0.9	−1.0	−1.4	−0.6	0.1	0.1	−0.5
12/64	1.5	1.4	1.1	1.1	1.1	0.7	0.7	0.0	0.1	−0.2	−0.2	−0.5	−0.4	−0.7	−1.0	−1.2	−0.9	−0.7	−0.7	−0.8	−1.2	−0.4	0.3	0.2	−0.3
12/65	1.5	1.3	1.0	1.1	1.0	0.7	0.6	−0.0	0.0	−0.2	−0.3	−0.5	−0.4	−0.8	−1.0	−1.3	−1.0	−0.8	−0.8	−0.8	−1.3	−0.4	0.2	0.1	−0.4
12/66	1.4	1.3	1.0	1.1	1.0	0.7	0.6	0.0	0.0	−0.2	−0.2	−0.5	−0.4	−0.7	−1.0	−1.2	−0.9	−0.7	−0.7	−0.7	−1.2	−0.4	0.2	0.2	−0.3
12/67	1.2	1.0	0.8	0.8	0.7	0.4	0.4	−0.2	−0.2	−0.4	−0.5	−0.7	−0.7	−1.0	−1.2	−1.4	−1.2	−1.0	−1.0	−1.1	−1.5	−0.8	−0.2	−0.3	−0.7
12/68	1.1	1.0	0.7	0.7	0.7	0.4	0.3	−0.3	−0.3	−0.5	−0.5	−0.8	−0.7	−1.0	−1.3	−1.5	−1.2	−1.0	−1.0	−1.1	−1.5	−0.8	−0.3	−0.4	−0.8
12/69	0.8	0.6	0.4	0.4	0.3	−0.0	−0.1	−0.7	−0.7	−0.9	−1.0	−1.2	−1.1	−1.4	−1.7	−1.9	−1.7	−1.5	−1.6	−1.7	−2.0	−1.4	−1.0	−1.1	−1.5
12/70	1.0	0.9	0.7	0.7	0.6	0.3	0.3	−0.3	−0.3	−0.5	−0.6	−0.8	−0.7	−1.0	−1.2	−1.4	−1.2	−1.0	−1.0	−1.1	−1.4	−0.8	−0.4	−0.4	−0.8
12/71	1.3	1.1	0.9	0.9	0.8	0.6	0.5	−0.0	−0.0	−0.2	−0.2	−0.4	−0.4	−0.6	−0.9	−1.0	−0.8	−0.6	−0.6	−0.6	−1.0	−0.3	0.1	0.1	−0.3
12/72	1.3	1.1	0.9	0.9	0.9	0.6	0.6	0.0	0.0	−0.1	−0.2	−0.4	−0.3	−0.6	−0.8	−0.9	−0.7	−0.5	−0.5	−0.6	−0.9	−0.3	0.2	0.2	−0.2
12/73	1.1	0.9	0.7	0.7	0.7	0.4	0.3	−0.2	−0.2	−0.3	−0.4	−0.6	−0.5	−0.8	−1.0	−1.1	−0.9	−0.8	−0.8	−0.8	−1.1	−0.6	−0.1	−0.2	−0.5
12/74	0.9	0.7	0.5	0.6	0.5	0.2	0.2	−0.3	−0.3	−0.5	−0.6	−0.7	−0.7	−0.9	−1.2	−1.3	−1.1	−1.0	−1.0	−1.0	−1.3	−0.8	−0.4	−0.4	−0.8
12/75	0.9	0.7	0.5	0.5	0.4	0.2	0.1	−0.4	−0.3	−0.5	−0.6	−0.7	−0.7	−0.9	−1.2	−1.3	−1.1	−1.0	−1.0	−1.0	−1.3	−0.8	−0.4	−0.5	−0.8
12/76	1.1	0.9	0.7	0.8	0.7	0.4	0.4	−0.1	−0.1	−0.2	−0.3	−0.4	−0.4	−0.6	−0.8	−1.0	−0.8	−0.6	−0.6	−0.6	−0.9	−0.4	−0.0	−0.0	−0.3

Table XXXV

Time-Weighted Rates of Return* on Long-Term U.S. Treasury Bonds:
  Interest Reinvested,
  Tax-Exempt,
  Deflated by the Consumer Price Index

Yield until	12/50	12/51	12/52	12/53	12/54	12/55	12/56	12/57	12/58	12/59	12/60	12/61	12/62	12/63	12/64	12/65	12/66	12/67	12/68	12/69	12/70	12/71	12/72	12/73	12/74	12/75
12/51	−9.3																									
12/52	−4.6	0.3																								
12/53	−2.1	1.6	3.0																							
12/54	−0.3	2.9	4.2	5.4																						
12/55	−0.6	1.6	2.1	1.7	−1.9																					
12/56	−1.8	−0.3	−0.4	−1.5	−4.8	−7.6																				
12/57	−0.7	0.8	0.9	0.4	−1.3	−0.9	6.2																			
12/58	−1.3	−0.1	−0.2	−0.8	−2.3	−2.4	0.2	−5.4																		
12/59	−1.7	−0.7	−0.9	−1.5	−2.8	−3.1	−1.5	−5.2	−5.0																	
12/60	−0.4	0.6	0.7	0.3	−0.5	−0.2	1.7	0.3	3.2	12.1																
12/61	−0.5	0.5	0.5	0.2	−0.5	−0.3	1.2	0.0	1.9	5.5	−0.7															
12/62	−0.1	0.8	0.9	0.6	0.0	0.3	1.7	0.8	2.4	5.0	1.7	4.1														
12/63	−0.1	0.7	0.7	0.5	0.0	0.2	1.4	0.6	1.9	3.7	1.0	1.9	−0.3													
12/64	0.1	0.8	0.9	0.7	0.2	0.5	1.5	0.9	2.0	3.4	1.4	2.1	1.1	2.5												
12/65	−0.0	0.7	0.7	0.5	0.1	0.3	1.2	0.6	1.5	2.6	0.8	1.2	0.2	0.5	−1.6											
12/66	0.0	0.7	0.7	0.5	0.2	0.3	1.2	0.6	1.4	2.4	0.8	1.1	0.4	0.6	−0.3	0.9										
12/67	−0.5	0.1	0.1	−0.1	−0.5	−0.4	0.3	−0.3	0.3	1.0	−0.5	−0.5	−1.4	−1.6	−3.0	−3.7	−8.1									
12/68	−0.6	−0.0	−0.0	−0.2	−0.6	−0.5	0.1	−0.5	0.0	0.6	−0.7	−0.7	−1.5	−1.8	−2.8	−3.2	−5.2	−2.3								
12/69	−1.3	−0.8	−0.9	−1.1	−1.6	−1.5	−1.0	−1.6	−1.3	−0.9	−2.3	−2.4	−3.3	−3.8	−5.1	−5.9	−8.1	−8.1	−13.6							
12/70	−0.6	−0.1	−0.1	−0.3	−0.6	−0.6	−0.0	−0.5	−0.1	0.4	−0.7	−0.7	−1.3	−1.4	−2.1	−2.2	−3.0	−1.2	−0.7	14.2						
12/71	−0.0	0.5	0.5	0.3	0.0	0.2	0.7	0.3	0.8	1.3	0.3	0.4	0.0	0.1	−0.3	−0.0	−0.2	1.8	3.2	12.8	11.5					
12/72	0.1	0.5	0.5	0.4	0.1	0.3	0.8	0.4	0.9	1.3	0.5	0.6	0.2	0.3	0.0	0.2	0.1	1.8	2.9	9.1	6.6	1.9				
12/73	−0.3	0.1	0.1	−0.0	−0.3	−0.2	0.2	−0.1	0.2	0.6	−0.2	−0.2	−0.5	−0.6	−0.9	−0.8	−1.1	0.1	0.6	4.6	1.5	−3.1	−7.9			
12/74	−0.6	−0.2	−0.2	−0.4	−0.6	−0.6	−0.2	−0.5	−0.2	0.1	−0.7	−0.7	−1.1	−1.2	−1.5	−1.5	−1.8	−0.9	−0.7	2.1	−0.7	−4.4	−7.4	−7.0		
12/75	−0.6	−0.2	−0.2	−0.4	−0.7	−0.6	−0.2	−0.6	−0.3	0.0	−0.7	−0.7	−1.1	−1.1	−1.5	−1.5	−1.7	−0.9	−0.7	1.6	−0.7	−3.6	−5.3	−4.0	−0.9	
12/76	−0.1	0.3	0.3	0.1	−0.1	−0.0	0.4	0.1	0.4	0.7	0.1	0.1	−0.2	−0.2	−0.4	−0.3	−0.4	0.5	0.8	3.1	1.4	−0.5	−1.2	1.2	5.6	12.5

Purchased column groups span 12/50–12/54, 12/55–12/59, 12/60–12/64, 12/65–12/69, and 12/70–12/75.

*Percent per annum, compounded annually.

Sources: Bond market data—Lawrence Fisher (compiler), CRSP
  Monthly Return File for U.S. Treasury Securities (mag-
  netic tape). See Appendix A.
  Consumer Price Index—U.S. Bureau of Labor Statistics.

Held Until	Purchased 12/25	12/26	12/27	12/28	12/29	Purchased 12/30	12/31	12/32	12/33	12/34	Purchased 12/35	12/36	12/37	12/38	12/39	Purchased 12/40	12/41	12/42	12/43	12/44	Purchased 12/45	12/46	12/47	12/48	12/49
12/26	7.2																								
12/27	7.7	8.2																							
12/28	4.7	3.5	−0.9																						
12/29	4.7	3.8	1.7	4.4																					
12/30	5.0	4.4	3.2	5.3	6.2																				
12/31	2.8	1.9	0.4	0.8	−0.9	−7.6																			
12/32	4.0	3.4	2.5	3.4	3.1	1.5	11.5																		
12/33	3.4	2.9	2.0	2.6	2.2	0.8	5.3	−0.5																	
12/34	4.0	3.6	3.0	3.7	3.5	2.8	6.6	4.2	9.0																
12/35	4.1	3.8	3.2	3.9	3.8	3.3	6.2	4.5	7.1	5.1															
12/36	4.4	4.2	3.7	4.3	4.3	4.0	6.5	5.2	7.2	6.3	7.5														
12/37	4.1	3.8	3.4	3.9	3.8	3.5	5.5	4.3	5.6	4.4	4.1	0.7													
12/38	4.2	4.0	3.6	4.1	4.0	3.8	5.5	4.5	5.6	4.7	4.6	3.2	5.6												
12/39	4.4	4.2	3.8	4.3	4.3	4.1	5.6	4.8	5.7	5.1	5.1	4.2	6.0	6.5											
12/40	4.5	4.3	4.0	4.4	4.4	4.2	5.6	4.9	5.7	5.1	5.1	4.5	5.8	6.0	5.5										
12/41	4.2	4.0	3.7	4.1	4.1	3.9	5.1	4.4	5.1	4.5	4.4	3.8	4.6	4.2	3.2	0.9									
12/42	4.2	4.0	3.7	4.0	4.0	3.8	4.9	4.3	4.8	4.3	4.2	3.7	4.2	3.9	3.1	1.9	2.9								
12/43	4.0	3.8	3.6	3.9	3.8	3.6	4.6	4.0	4.5	4.0	3.9	3.4	3.8	3.4	2.7	1.8	2.2	1.5							
12/44	3.9	3.7	3.5	3.8	3.7	3.5	4.4	3.9	4.3	3.8	3.7	3.2	3.6	3.2	2.6	1.9	2.2	1.9	2.2						
12/45	4.2	4.1	3.8	4.1	4.1	4.0	4.8	4.3	4.8	4.4	4.3	4.0	4.4	4.2	3.8	3.5	4.1	4.5	6.1	10.1					
12/46	4.0	3.8	3.6	3.9	3.8	3.7	4.5	4.0	4.3	4.0	3.9	3.5	3.8	3.6	3.2	2.8	3.2	3.3	3.9	4.7	−0.4				
12/47	3.7	3.5	3.3	3.5	3.4	3.3	4.0	3.5	3.8	3.4	3.3	2.9	3.1	2.8	2.4	2.0	2.2	2.0	2.1	2.1	−1.7	−2.9			
12/48	3.6	3.5	3.3	3.5	3.4	3.3	3.9	3.5	3.8	3.4	3.3	2.9	3.1	2.9	2.5	2.1	2.3	2.2	2.3	2.3	−0.2	−0.0	3.0		
12/49	3.7	3.6	3.4	3.6	3.5	3.4	4.1	3.6	3.9	3.6	3.5	3.1	3.3	3.1	2.8	2.5	2.7	2.7	2.9	3.1	1.4	2.0	4.5	6.0	
12/50	3.6	3.4	3.2	3.4	3.4	3.2	3.8	3.4	3.6	3.3	3.2	2.9	3.1	2.8	2.5	2.2	2.4	2.3	2.4	2.5	1.0	1.4	2.9	2.8	−0.3
12/51	3.2	3.1	2.9	3.1	3.0	2.8	3.4	3.0	3.2	2.8	2.7	2.4	2.5	2.3	1.9	1.6	1.7	1.6	1.6	1.5	0.1	0.2	1.0	0.3	−2.4
12/52	3.1	3.0	2.8	2.9	2.9	2.7	3.3	2.9	3.0	2.7	2.6	2.3	2.4	2.1	1.8	1.5	1.6	1.5	1.4	1.4	0.2	0.3	0.9	0.4	−1.4
12/53	3.1	3.0	2.8	3.0	2.9	2.7	3.2	2.9	3.0	2.7	2.6	2.3	2.4	2.2	1.9	1.6	1.7	1.6	1.6	1.5	0.5	0.6	1.2	0.9	−0.3
12/54	3.2	3.0	2.9	3.0	2.9	2.8	3.3	2.9	3.1	2.8	2.7	2.4	2.5	2.3	2.1	1.8	1.9	1.8	1.8	1.8	0.9	1.1	1.7	1.5	0.6
12/55	3.0	2.9	2.7	2.8	2.7	2.6	3.1	2.7	2.9	2.6	2.4	2.2	2.3	2.1	1.8	1.6	1.6	1.5	1.5	1.5	0.6	0.7	1.2	1.0	0.1
12/56	2.7	2.6	2.4	2.5	2.4	2.3	2.7	2.4	2.5	2.2	2.1	1.8	1.8	1.6	1.4	1.1	1.1	1.0	1.0	0.9	0.1	0.1	0.4	0.1	−0.7
12/57	2.9	2.8	2.6	2.7	2.6	2.5	2.9	2.6	2.7	2.5	2.3	2.1	2.2	2.0	1.8	1.5	1.6	1.5	1.5	1.4	0.7	0.8	1.2	1.0	0.4
12/58	2.7	2.5	2.4	2.5	2.4	2.3	2.6	2.3	2.4	2.2	2.0	1.8	1.9	1.7	1.4	1.2	1.2	1.1	1.1	1.0	0.3	0.4	0.7	0.5	−0.1
12/59	2.5	2.3	2.1	2.2	2.2	2.0	2.4	2.1	2.2	1.9	1.8	1.5	1.6	1.4	1.1	0.9	0.9	0.8	0.7	0.6	−0.0	0.0	0.3	0.0	−0.5
12/60	2.7	2.6	2.4	2.6	2.5	2.4	2.7	2.4	2.5	2.3	2.2	2.0	2.0	1.9	1.6	1.5	1.5	1.4	1.4	1.4	0.8	0.9	1.2	1.0	0.6
12/61	2.6	2.5	2.3	2.4	2.4	2.3	2.6	2.3	2.4	2.2	2.1	1.8	1.9	1.7	1.5	1.3	1.4	1.3	1.3	1.2	0.7	0.8	1.0	0.9	0.5
12/62	2.7	2.6	2.4	2.5	2.4	2.3	2.7	2.4	2.5	2.2	2.1	1.9	2.0	1.8	1.6	1.5	1.5	1.4	1.4	1.4	0.9	1.0	1.2	1.1	0.8
12/63	2.6	2.5	2.3	2.4	2.4	2.3	2.6	2.3	2.4	2.2	2.1	1.9	1.9	1.8	1.6	1.4	1.4	1.4	1.4	1.3	0.9	0.9	1.2	1.1	0.7
12/64	2.6	2.5	2.3	2.4	2.4	2.3	2.6	2.3	2.4	2.2	2.1	1.9	2.0	1.8	1.6	1.5	1.5	1.4	1.4	1.4	1.0	1.0	1.3	1.2	0.9
12/65	2.5	2.4	2.3	2.4	2.3	2.2	2.5	2.2	2.3	2.1	2.0	1.8	1.9	1.7	1.5	1.4	1.4	1.4	1.3	1.3	0.9	0.9	1.2	1.1	0.8
12/66	2.6	2.4	2.3	2.4	2.3	2.2	2.5	2.3	2.3	2.1	2.0	1.9	1.9	1.8	1.6	1.5	1.5	1.4	1.4	1.4	1.0	1.1	1.3	1.2	0.9
12/67	2.3	2.2	2.1	2.1	2.1	2.0	2.3	2.0	2.1	1.9	1.8	1.6	1.6	1.5	1.3	1.2	1.2	1.1	1.1	1.0	0.6	0.7	0.9	0.8	0.5
12/68	2.3	2.2	2.0	2.1	2.1	1.9	2.2	2.0	2.0	1.8	1.7	1.6	1.6	1.5	1.3	1.2	1.2	1.1	1.1	1.0	0.7	0.7	0.9	0.8	0.5
12/69	2.0	1.9	1.7	1.8	1.7	1.6	1.9	1.6	1.7	1.5	1.4	1.2	1.2	1.1	0.9	0.7	0.7	0.7	0.6	0.6	0.2	0.2	0.4	0.2	−0.0
12/70	2.3	2.2	2.1	2.2	2.1	2.0	2.3	2.0	2.1	1.9	1.8	1.7	1.7	1.6	1.4	1.3	1.3	1.2	1.2	1.2	0.9	0.9	1.1	1.0	0.8
12/71	2.6	2.5	2.3	2.4	2.4	2.3	2.5	2.3	2.4	2.2	2.1	2.0	2.0	1.9	1.8	1.7	1.7	1.6	1.7	1.6	1.3	1.4	1.6	1.5	1.3
12/72	2.6	2.5	2.4	2.4	2.4	2.3	2.6	2.4	2.4	2.3	2.2	2.0	2.1	2.0	1.8	1.7	1.8	1.7	1.7	1.7	1.4	1.5	1.7	1.6	1.4
12/73	2.5	2.4	2.3	2.4	2.3	2.2	2.5	2.3	2.3	2.2	2.1	1.9	2.0	1.9	1.7	1.6	1.6	1.6	1.6	1.6	1.3	1.4	1.5	1.5	1.3
12/74	2.5	2.4	2.3	2.3	2.3	2.2	2.5	2.2	2.3	2.2	2.1	1.9	2.0	1.9	1.7	1.6	1.7	1.6	1.6	1.6	1.3	1.4	1.5	1.5	1.3
12/75	2.5	2.4	2.3	2.4	2.3	2.2	2.5	2.3	2.3	2.2	2.1	2.0	2.0	1.9	1.8	1.7	1.7	1.7	1.7	1.7	1.4	1.5	1.6	1.6	1.4
12/76	2.7	2.7	2.5	2.6	2.6	2.5	2.7	2.6	2.6	2.5	2.4	2.3	2.3	2.2	2.1	2.0	2.1	2.0	2.1	2.1	1.8	1.9	2.1	2.0	1.9

Table XXXVI

Time-Weighted Rates of Return* on Long-Term U.S. Treasury Bonds:
Interest Reinvested,
Lower Tax Rate,
Current Dollars

Held until	12/50	12/51	12/52	12/53	12/54	12/55	12/56	12/57	12/58	12/59	12/60	12/61	12/62	12/63	12/64	12/65	12/66	12/67	12/68	12/69	12/70	12/71	12/72	12/73	12/74	12/75
/51	-4.4																									
/52	-2.0	0.6																								
/53	-0.3	1.8	3.0																							
/54	0.8	2.6	3.6	4.3																						
/55	0.2	1.4	1.7	1.1	-2.1																					
/56	-0.8	-0.0	-0.1	-1.2	-3.8	-5.5																				
/57	0.5	1.4	1.6	1.2	0.2	1.3	8.6																			
/58	-0.1	0.5	0.5	0.1	-1.0	-0.6	1.9	-4.4																		
/59	-0.6	-0.1	-0.2	-0.7	-1.7	-1.6	-0.2	-4.3	-4.3																	
/60	0.7	1.3	1.4	1.1	0.6	1.2	2.9	1.0	3.9	12.8																
/61	0.5	1.0	1.1	0.9	0.4	0.8	2.1	0.5	2.2	5.7	-1.0															
/62	0.8	1.3	1.4	1.2	0.9	1.3	2.5	1.3	2.7	5.2	1.6	4.3														
/63	0.8	1.2	1.3	1.1	0.8	1.2	2.1	1.1	2.2	3.9	1.2	2.3	0.3													
/64	0.9	1.4	1.4	1.3	1.0	1.3	2.2	1.3	2.3	3.7	1.5	2.4	1.5	2.7												
/65	0.8	1.2	1.3	1.1	0.8	1.1	1.9	1.1	1.9	3.0	1.1	1.7	0.8	1.1	-0.6											
/66	1.0	1.4	1.4	1.3	1.0	1.3	2.0	1.3	2.1	3.0	1.5	2.0	1.4	1.8	1.3	3.3										
/67	0.5	0.9	0.9	0.7	0.5	0.7	1.3	0.5	1.1	1.8	0.3	0.6	-0.2	-0.3	-1.3	-1.6	-6.3									
/68	0.6	0.9	0.9	0.7	0.5	0.7	1.2	0.6	1.1	1.7	0.4	0.6	-0.0	-0.1	-0.8	-0.8	-2.8	0.9								
/69	-0.0	0.2	0.2	0.0	-0.2	-0.1	0.3	-0.4	0.0	0.5	-0.8	-0.8	-1.5	-1.8	-2.7	-3.2	-5.2	-4.7	-10.0							
/70	0.8	1.1	1.1	1.0	0.8	1.0	1.5	1.0	1.4	2.0	0.9	1.2	0.8	0.9	0.5	0.8	0.2	2.4	3.2	18.3						
/71	1.4	1.7	1.8	1.7	1.5	1.8	2.3	1.8	2.3	2.9	2.0	2.3	2.1	2.4	2.3	2.8	2.7	5.1	6.5	15.9	13.5					
/72	1.5	1.8	1.8	1.8	1.6	1.9	2.3	1.9	2.4	2.9	2.2	2.5	2.3	2.5	2.5	2.9	2.9	4.8	5.8	11.7	8.5	3.6				
/73	1.4	1.6	1.7	1.6	1.5	1.7	2.1	1.7	2.1	2.6	1.9	2.1	1.9	2.1	2.0	2.3	2.2	3.7	4.3	8.2	5.0	1.0	-1.6			
/74	1.4	1.6	1.7	1.6	1.5	1.7	2.1	1.7	2.1	2.6	1.9	2.1	1.9	2.1	2.0	2.3	2.2	3.5	3.9	6.9	4.3	1.3	0.2	2.1		
/75	1.5	1.7	1.8	1.7	1.6	1.8	2.2	1.8	2.2	2.6	2.0	2.2	2.0	2.2	2.1	2.4	2.3	3.5	3.8	6.3	4.1	1.9	1.3	2.8	3.4	
/76	2.0	2.2	2.3	2.3	2.2	2.4	2.8	2.5	2.9	3.3	2.8	3.0	2.9	3.1	3.2	3.5	3.5	4.7	5.2	7.6	5.9	4.4	4.6	6.7	9.1	15.1

*Percent per annum, compounded annually

Sources: Bond market data—Lawrence Fisher (compiler), CRSP Monthly Return File for U.S. Treasury Securities (magnetic tape). See Appendix A.
Income tax rates—Income levels estimated from U.S. Bureau of the Census, Current Population Reports, Series P-60, Nos. 101 and 103 and Historical Statistics of the United States. Tax rates were found in U.S. Internal Revenue Service, Statistics of Income and Your Federal Income Tax.

Held Until	\-\-\- Purchased \-\-\-					Purchased					Purchased					Purchased					Purchased				
	12/25	12/26	12/27	12/28	12/29	12/30	12/31	12/32	12/33	12/34	12/35	12/36	12/37	12/38	12/39	12/40	12/41	12/42	12/43	12/44	12/45	12/46	12/47	12/48	12/49
12/26	8.8																								
12/27	9.7	10.5																							
12/28	6.3	5.1	0.0																						
12/29	5.8	4.8	2.1	4.2																					
12/30	7.2	6.8	5.6	8.5	13.0																				
12/31	6.4	5.9	4.7	6.4	7.5	2.1																			
12/32	8.7	8.7	8.4	10.6	12.8	12.7	24.3																		
12/33	7.5	7.3	6.8	8.2	9.2	7.9	10.9	-1.0																	
12/34	7.4	7.2	6.8	8.0	8.7	7.7	9.6	2.9	6.9																
12/35	6.9	6.7	6.2	7.1	7.6	6.5	7.6	2.6	4.4	2.1															
12/36	6.8	6.6	6.2	7.0	7.4	6.5	7.4	3.5	5.0	4.1	6.2														
12/37	6.0	5.8	5.3	5.9	6.1	5.2	5.7	2.3	3.2	1.9	1.9	-2.3													
12/38	6.2	6.0	5.6	6.2	6.4	5.6	6.1	3.3	4.2	3.6	4.1	3.0	8.6												
12/39	6.3	6.1	5.7	6.3	6.5	5.8	6.2	3.9	4.7	4.2	4.8	4.3	7.8	7.0											
12/40	6.2	6.0	5.6	6.1	6.3	5.6	6.0	3.9	4.6	4.3	4.7	4.4	6.7	5.7	4.5										
12/41	5.2	5.0	4.6	4.9	5.0	4.3	4.5	2.5	3.0	2.4	2.5	1.8	2.8	0.9	-2.0	-8.0									
12/42	4.5	4.3	3.9	4.1	4.1	3.4	3.5	1.7	2.0	1.4	1.3	0.4	1.0	-0.8	-3.3	-6.9	-5.9								
12/43	4.2	3.9	3.5	3.7	3.7	3.0	3.1	1.4	1.6	1.0	0.9	0.2	0.6	-1.0	-2.9	-5.2	-3.7	-1.6							
12/44	4.0	3.7	3.3	3.5	3.5	2.8	2.9	1.3	1.5	0.9	0.8	0.1	0.5	-0.8	-2.3	-3.9	-2.5	-0.8	0.1						
12/45	4.1	3.9	3.5	3.7	3.7	3.1	3.2	1.7	2.0	1.5	1.5	1.0	1.4	0.4	-0.7	-1.7	-0.0	2.0	3.8	7.7					
12/46	3.1	2.8	2.4	2.6	2.5	1.8	1.8	0.4	0.5	-0.0	-0.2	-0.8	-0.7	-1.8	-3.0	-4.2	-3.4	-2.8	-3.2	-4.7	-15.7				
12/47	2.4	2.1	1.7	1.8	1.7	1.0	1.0	-0.4	-0.4	-0.9	-1.2	-1.8	-1.8	-2.9	-4.0	-5.2	-4.7	-4.5	-5.2	-6.9	-13.4	-11.0			
12/48	2.3	2.0	1.6	1.7	1.6	1.0	0.9	-0.4	-0.3	-0.8	-1.1	-1.6	-1.6	-2.6	-3.6	-4.5	-4.0	-3.7	-4.1	-5.1	-9.0	-5.5	0.3		
12/49	2.5	2.3	1.9	2.0	1.9	1.3	1.3	0.1	0.2	-0.3	-0.4	-0.9	-0.8	-1.6	-2.5	-3.2	-2.6	-2.1	-2.2	-2.6	-5.1	-1.2	4.1	8.0	
12/50	2.2	1.9	1.6	1.6	1.5	1.0	0.9	-0.2	-0.2	-0.6	-0.8	-1.3	-1.2	-2.0	-2.8	-3.5	-2.9	-2.6	-2.7	-3.2	-5.2	-2.4	0.7	0.9	-5.8
12/51	1.7	1.4	1.1	1.1	1.0	0.4	0.4	-0.8	-0.8	-1.2	-1.4	-1.9	-1.8	-2.6	-3.4	-4.0	-3.6	-3.4	-3.6	-4.1	-6.0	-3.9	-2.0	-2.8	-7.8
12/52	1.6	1.4	1.0	1.1	0.9	0.4	0.3	-0.7	-0.7	-1.1	-1.3	-1.8	-1.7	-2.4	-3.1	-3.7	-3.3	-3.1	-3.3	-3.7	-5.2	-3.3	-1.7	-2.2	-5.3
12/53	1.7	1.4	1.1	1.1	1.0	0.5	0.4	-0.6	-0.6	-1.0	-1.1	-1.5	-1.5	-2.1	-2.8	-3.3	-2.9	-2.6	-2.7	-3.0	-4.3	-2.5	-1.0	-1.3	-3.5
12/54	1.8	1.5	1.2	1.3	1.1	0.7	0.6	-0.4	-0.3	-0.7	-0.8	-1.2	-1.1	-1.7	-2.3	-2.7	-2.3	-2.0	-2.0	-2.3	-3.3	-1.6	-0.2	-0.3	-1.9
12/55	1.6	1.4	1.1	1.1	1.0	0.5	0.5	-0.4	-0.4	-0.8	-0.9	-1.3	-1.2	-1.8	-2.3	-2.7	-2.3	-2.0	-2.1	-2.3	-3.2	-1.7	-0.5	-0.6	-2.0
12/56	1.3	1.1	0.7	0.8	0.6	0.2	0.1	-0.8	-0.8	-1.1	-1.3	-1.6	-1.6	-2.1	-2.6	-3.1	-2.7	-2.5	-2.6	-2.8	-3.7	-2.4	-1.4	-1.6	-2.9
12/57	1.4	1.2	0.9	0.9	0.8	0.4	0.3	-0.5	-0.5	-0.8	-1.0	-1.3	-1.2	-1.7	-2.2	-2.6	-2.2	-2.0	-2.0	-2.2	-2.9	-1.7	-0.7	-0.8	-1.9
12/58	1.2	1.0	0.7	0.7	0.6	0.1	0.1	-0.8	-0.7	-1.1	-1.2	-1.5	-1.5	-2.0	-2.4	-2.8	-2.5	-2.2	-2.3	-2.4	-3.2	-2.1	-1.2	-1.4	-2.3
12/59	1.0	0.7	0.5	0.5	0.4	-0.1	-0.1	-0.9	-0.9	-1.2	-1.4	-1.7	-1.7	-2.1	-2.6	-2.9	-2.6	-2.4	-2.5	-2.7	-3.4	-2.3	-1.6	-1.8	-2.7
12/60	1.3	1.0	0.8	0.8	0.7	0.3	0.2	-0.5	-0.5	-0.8	-0.9	-1.2	-1.1	-1.6	-2.0	-2.3	-2.0	-1.7	-1.7	-1.9	-2.5	-1.4	-0.7	-0.7	-1.5
12/61	1.2	1.0	0.7	0.7	0.6	0.2	0.2	-0.6	-0.6	-0.8	-0.9	-1.2	-1.2	-1.6	-1.9	-2.2	-1.9	-1.7	-1.7	-1.8	-2.4	-1.5	-0.7	-0.8	-1.5
12/62	1.2	1.0	0.8	0.8	0.7	0.3	0.3	-0.5	-0.4	-0.7	-0.8	-1.1	-1.0	-1.4	-1.7	-2.0	-1.7	-1.5	-1.5	-1.6	-2.1	-1.2	-0.5	-0.5	-1.2
12/63	1.2	1.0	0.7	0.7	0.6	0.3	0.2	-0.5	-0.5	-0.7	-0.8	-1.1	-1.0	-1.4	-1.7	-2.0	-1.7	-1.5	-1.5	-1.6	-2.1	-1.2	-0.5	-0.6	-1.2
12/64	1.2	1.0	0.7	0.7	0.6	0.3	0.2	-0.4	-0.4	-0.6	-0.7	-1.0	-0.9	-1.3	-1.6	-1.8	-1.6	-1.4	-1.3	-1.4	-1.9	-1.0	-0.4	-0.5	-1.0
12/65	1.1	0.9	0.6	0.7	0.6	0.2	0.2	-0.5	-0.5	-0.7	-0.8	-1.0	-1.0	-1.3	-1.6	-1.9	-1.6	-1.4	-1.4	-1.5	-1.9	-1.1	-0.5	-0.6	-1.1
12/66	1.0	0.9	0.6	0.6	0.5	0.2	0.2	-0.5	-0.5	-0.7	-0.8	-1.0	-0.9	-1.3	-1.6	-1.8	-1.5	-1.4	-1.3	-1.4	-1.8	-1.1	-0.5	-0.6	-1.0
12/67	0.8	0.6	0.4	0.4	0.3	-0.0	-0.1	-0.7	-0.7	-0.9	-1.0	-1.3	-1.2	-1.6	-1.8	-2.1	-1.8	-1.7	-1.7	-1.8	-2.2	-1.5	-1.0	-1.0	-1.5
12/68	0.7	0.5	0.3	0.3	0.2	-0.1	-0.2	-0.8	-0.8	-1.0	-1.1	-1.3	-1.3	-1.6	-1.9	-2.1	-1.9	-1.8	-1.8	-1.8	-2.2	-1.6	-1.1	-1.2	-1.6
12/69	0.3	0.1	-0.1	-0.1	-0.2	-0.6	-0.6	-1.2	-1.2	-1.5	-1.6	-1.8	-1.8	-2.1	-2.4	-2.6	-2.4	-2.3	-2.3	-2.4	-2.8	-2.2	-1.8	-1.9	-2.3
12/70	0.5	0.4	0.1	0.1	0.0	-0.3	-0.3	-0.9	-0.9	-1.1	-1.2	-1.4	-1.4	-1.7	-1.9	-2.2	-1.9	-1.8	-1.8	-1.9	-2.2	-1.6	-1.2	-1.3	-1.7
12/71	0.7	0.6	0.3	0.4	0.3	-0.0	-0.1	-0.6	-0.6	-0.8	-0.9	-1.1	-1.1	-1.3	-1.6	-1.8	-1.6	-1.4	-1.4	-1.5	-1.8	-1.2	-0.8	-0.8	-1.2
12/72	0.7	0.6	0.3	0.4	0.3	-0.0	-0.1	-0.6	-0.6	-0.8	-0.9	-1.1	-1.0	-1.3	-1.5	-1.7	-1.5	-1.4	-1.4	-1.4	-1.7	-1.1	-0.7	-0.8	-1.1
12/73	0.5	0.3	0.1	0.1	0.0	-0.3	-0.3	-0.8	-0.8	-1.0	-1.1	-1.3	-1.3	-1.5	-1.8	-2.0	-1.8	-1.6	-1.6	-1.7	-2.0	-1.5	-1.1	-1.1	-1.5
12/74	0.3	0.1	-0.1	-0.1	-0.2	-0.5	-0.5	-1.1	-1.1	-1.2	-1.3	-1.5	-1.5	-1.8	-2.0	-2.2	-2.0	-1.9	-1.9	-2.0	-2.3	-1.8	-1.4	-1.5	-1.8
12/75	0.2	0.1	-0.2	-0.2	-0.3	-0.5	-0.6	-1.1	-1.1	-1.3	-1.4	-1.6	-1.5	-1.8	-2.0	-2.2	-2.0	-1.9	-1.9	-2.0	-2.3	-1.8	-1.5	-1.5	-1.9
12/76	0.4	0.2	0.0	0.0	-0.0	-0.3	-0.4	-0.9	-0.9	-1.0	-1.1	-1.3	-1.3	-1.5	-1.7	-1.9	-1.7	-1.6	-1.6	-1.7	-1.9	-1.4	-1.1	-1.1	-1.5

Table XXXVII

Time-Weighted Rates of Return* on Long-Term U.S. Treasury Bonds:
Interest Reinvested,
Lower Tax Rate,
Deflated by the Consumer Price Index

Yield Until	Purchased 12/50	12/51	12/52	12/53	12/54	Purchased 12/55	12/56	12/57	12/58	12/59	Purchased 12/60	12/61	12/62	12/63	12/64	Purchased 12/65	12/66	12/67	12/68	12/69	Purchased 12/70	12/71	12/72	12/73	12/74	12/75
12/51	-9.7																									
12/52	-5.1	-0.3																								
12/53	-2.7	1.0	2.3																							
12/54	-0.9	2.3	3.6	4.9																						
12/55	-1.2	1.1	1.5	1.1	-2.4																					
12/56	-2.4	-0.8	-1.0	-2.0	-5.3	-8.1																				
12/57	-1.3	0.2	0.3	-0.2	-1.9	-1.6	5.5																			
12/58	-1.9	-0.7	-0.8	-1.4	-2.9	-3.1	-0.4	-6.0																		
12/59	-2.3	-1.4	-1.5	-2.1	-3.5	-3.7	-2.2	-5.9	-5.7																	
12/60	-1.1	-0.1	-0.0	-0.4	-1.2	-0.9	0.9	-0.5	2.3	11.1																
12/61	-1.1	-0.2	-0.2	-0.5	-1.3	-1.1	0.4	-0.8	1.0	4.5	-1.7															
12/62	-0.8	0.1	0.1	-0.1	-0.7	-0.5	0.8	-0.1	1.5	4.0	0.6	3.0														
12/63	-0.8	-0.0	-0.0	-0.3	-0.8	-0.6	0.5	-0.3	0.9	2.7	-0.0	0.8	-1.3													
12/64	-0.7	0.1	0.1	-0.1	-0.6	-0.4	0.7	-0.0	1.0	2.4	0.4	1.1	0.1	1.5												
12/65	-0.8	-0.1	-0.1	-0.3	-0.7	-0.6	0.3	-0.3	0.5	1.6	-0.2	0.2	-0.8	-0.5	-2.5											
12/66	-0.7	-0.1	-0.1	-0.3	-0.7	-0.5	0.3	-0.3	0.4	1.4	-0.2	0.1	-0.6	-0.4	-1.3	-0.1										
12/67	-1.2	-0.7	-0.7	-0.9	-1.4	-1.3	-0.6	-1.2	-0.7	-0.0	-1.5	-1.5	-2.4	-2.6	-3.9	-4.7	-9.0									
12/68	-1.4	-0.9	-0.9	-1.1	-1.5	-1.5	-0.9	-1.4	-1.0	-0.4	-1.8	-1.8	-2.6	-2.8	-3.9	-4.4	-6.4	-3.7								
12/69	-2.2	-1.7	-1.8	-2.1	-2.5	-2.5	-2.1	-2.7	-2.4	-2.0	-3.4	-3.6	-4.5	-5.0	-6.3	-7.2	-9.4	-9.6	-15.2							
12/70	-1.5	-1.0	-1.1	-1.3	-1.6	-1.6	-1.1	-1.6	-1.2	-0.8	-1.9	-1.9	-2.5	-2.7	-3.4	-3.6	-4.5	-2.9	-2.5	12.2						
12/71	-1.0	-0.5	-0.5	-0.7	-1.0	-0.9	-0.4	-0.8	-0.4	0.0	-0.9	-0.8	-1.2	-1.2	-1.6	-1.5	-1.7	0.2	1.5	11.0	9.9					
12/72	-0.9	-0.5	-0.5	-0.6	-0.9	-0.8	-0.4	-0.8	-0.4	0.1	-0.8	-0.7	-1.1	-1.1	-1.4	-1.2	-1.4	0.2	1.2	7.3	4.9	0.2				
12/73	-1.3	-0.9	-0.9	-1.1	-1.4	-1.4	-0.9	-1.3	-1.0	-0.7	-1.5	-1.5	-1.9	-2.0	-2.3	-2.3	-2.6	-1.5	-1.1	2.8	-0.2	-4.8	-9.6			
12/74	-1.7	-1.3	-1.3	-1.5	-1.8	-1.8	-1.4	-1.8	-1.5	-1.2	-2.1	-2.1	-2.5	-2.6	-3.0	-3.1	-3.5	-2.6	-2.4	0.3	-2.4	-6.2	-9.3	-9.0		
12/75	-1.7	-1.4	-1.4	-1.6	-1.9	-1.9	-1.5	-1.9	-1.6	-1.4	-2.2	-2.2	-2.6	-2.7	-3.1	-3.1	-3.4	-2.7	-2.6	-0.3	-2.6	-5.5	-7.4	-6.2	-3.4	
12/76	-1.3	-0.9	-1.0	-1.1	-1.4	-1.3	-1.0	-1.3	-1.0	-0.7	-1.4	-1.4	-1.7	-1.8	-2.0	-2.0	-2.2	-1.4	-1.1	1.1	-0.6	-2.6	-3.3	-1.1	3.0	9.9

*Percent per annum, compounded annually.

Sources: Bond market data—Lawrence Fisher (compiler), CRSP Monthly Return File for U.S. Treasury Securities (magnetic tape). See Appendix A.
Consumer Price Index—U.S. Bureau of Labor Statistics.
Income tax rates—Income levels estimated from U.S. Bureau of the Census, Current Population Reports, Series P-60, Nos. 101 and 103 and Historical Statistics of the United States. Tax rates were found in U.S. Internal Revenue Service, Statistics of Income and Your Federal Income Tax.

Held Until	12/25	12/26	12/27	12/28	12/29	12/30	12/31	12/32	12/33	12/34	12/35	12/36	12/37	12/38	12/39	12/40	12/41	12/42	12/43	12/44	12/45	12/46	12/47	12/48	12/49
12/26	7.1																								
12/27	7.7	8.2																							
12/28	4.7	3.5	−1.0																						
12/29	4.6	3.8	1.7	4.4																					
12/30	4.9	4.4	3.2	5.3	6.2																				
12/31	2.7	1.9	0.4	0.8	−0.9	−7.6																			
12/32	3.9	3.4	2.5	3.4	3.0	1.5	11.5																		
12/33	3.4	2.8	2.0	2.6	2.1	0.8	5.3	−0.5																	
12/34	4.0	3.6	3.0	3.6	3.5	2.8	6.5	4.1	9.0																
12/35	4.1	3.7	3.2	3.8	3.7	3.2	6.1	4.4	7.0	4.9															
12/36	4.4	4.1	3.6	4.2	4.2	3.9	6.4	5.1	7.1	6.1	7.3														
12/37	4.0	3.8	3.3	3.8	3.8	3.4	5.4	4.2	5.4	4.2	3.9	0.5													
12/38	4.1	3.9	3.5	4.0	3.9	3.7	5.4	4.4	5.4	4.5	4.4	3.0	5.5												
12/39	4.3	4.1	3.8	4.2	4.2	4.0	5.5	4.7	5.6	4.9	4.9	4.1	5.9	6.3											
12/40	4.4	4.2	3.9	4.3	4.3	4.1	5.5	4.7	5.5	4.9	4.9	4.4	5.7	5.7	5.2										
12/41	4.1	3.9	3.6	4.0	3.9	3.7	5.0	4.3	4.9	4.3	4.2	3.6	4.3	4.0	2.8	0.5									
12/42	4.0	3.8	3.5	3.8	3.8	3.6	4.7	4.0	4.6	4.0	3.9	3.3	3.9	3.5	2.6	1.3	2.2								
12/43	3.8	3.6	3.3	3.6	3.6	3.4	4.4	3.7	4.2	3.6	3.5	2.9	3.4	2.9	2.1	1.1	1.4	0.6							
12/44	3.7	3.5	3.2	3.5	3.4	3.2	4.1	3.5	3.9	3.4	3.2	2.7	3.0	2.7	1.9	1.1	1.4	1.0	1.3						
12/45	3.9	3.8	3.5	3.8	3.8	3.6	4.5	3.9	4.3	3.9	3.8	3.4	3.8	3.6	3.1	2.7	3.3	3.6	5.2	9.2					
12/46	3.7	3.5	3.3	3.5	3.5	3.3	4.1	3.6	3.9	3.5	3.3	2.9	3.2	2.9	2.5	2.0	2.3	2.4	3.0	3.8	−1.3				
12/47	3.3	3.2	2.9	3.1	3.0	2.9	3.6	3.1	3.3	2.9	2.7	2.3	2.5	2.2	1.7	1.2	1.3	1.1	1.2	1.2	−2.6	−3.9			
12/48	3.3	3.1	2.9	3.1	3.0	2.8	3.5	3.0	3.2	2.8	2.7	2.3	2.5	2.2	1.7	1.3	1.4	1.3	1.4	1.5	−1.0	−0.8	2.4		
12/49	3.4	3.2	3.0	3.2	3.1	3.0	3.6	3.2	3.4	3.0	2.9	2.6	2.7	2.5	2.1	1.8	1.9	1.9	2.1	2.3	0.6	1.3	3.9	5.5	
12/50	3.2	3.0	2.8	3.0	2.9	2.8	3.4	2.9	3.1	2.8	2.6	2.3	2.4	2.2	1.8	1.5	1.6	1.5	1.7	1.7	0.3	0.7	2.3	2.3	−0.9
12/51	2.9	2.7	2.5	2.6	2.6	2.4	2.9	2.5	2.7	2.3	2.1	1.8	1.9	1.6	1.2	0.9	0.9	0.8	0.8	0.7	−0.6	−0.5	0.4	−0.3	−3.0
12/52	2.8	2.6	2.4	2.5	2.4	2.3	2.8	2.3	2.5	2.1	2.0	1.7	1.7	1.5	1.1	0.8	0.8	0.7	0.7	0.6	−0.6	−0.4	0.2	−0.3	−2.1
12/53	2.7	2.6	2.4	2.5	2.4	2.2	2.7	2.3	2.5	2.1	2.0	1.7	1.7	1.5	1.2	0.9	0.9	0.8	0.8	0.7	−0.3	−0.1	0.5	0.1	−1.1
12/54	2.7	2.6	2.4	2.5	2.5	2.3	2.8	2.4	2.5	2.2	2.1	1.8	1.8	1.6	1.3	1.0	1.1	1.0	1.0	1.0	0.1	0.3	0.9	0.7	−0.2
12/55	2.6	2.4	2.2	2.3	2.2	2.1	2.5	2.1	2.3	1.9	1.8	1.5	1.6	1.3	1.0	0.8	0.8	0.7	0.7	0.6	−0.2	−0.0	0.4	0.2	−0.7
12/56	2.2	2.1	1.9	2.0	1.9	1.7	2.1	1.8	1.9	1.5	1.4	1.1	1.1	0.9	0.6	0.3	0.3	0.2	0.1	0.0	−0.8	−0.7	−0.4	−0.7	−1.6
12/57	2.4	2.3	2.1	2.2	2.1	1.9	2.3	2.0	2.1	1.8	1.6	1.4	1.4	1.2	0.9	0.7	0.7	0.6	0.6	0.6	−0.1	−0.0	0.4	0.2	−0.5
12/58	2.2	2.0	1.8	1.9	1.8	1.7	2.0	1.7	1.8	1.5	1.3	1.1	1.1	0.9	0.6	0.3	0.3	0.2	0.2	0.1	−0.6	−0.5	−0.2	−0.4	−1.1
12/59	1.9	1.7	1.6	1.6	1.5	1.4	1.7	1.4	1.5	1.2	1.0	0.7	0.8	0.5	0.3	0.0	−0.0	−0.1	−0.2	−0.3	−0.9	−0.9	−0.7	−0.9	−1.6
12/60	2.2	2.0	1.8	1.9	1.8	1.7	2.0	1.7	1.8	1.5	1.4	1.2	1.2	1.0	0.8	0.5	0.5	0.4	0.4	0.4	−0.2	−0.1	0.2	0.0	−0.5
12/61	2.0	1.9	1.7	1.8	1.7	1.6	1.9	1.6	1.7	1.4	1.3	1.0	1.0	0.9	0.6	0.4	0.4	0.3	0.3	0.2	−0.3	−0.2	0.0	−0.2	−0.6
12/62	2.1	1.9	1.7	1.8	1.7	1.6	1.9	1.6	1.7	1.4	1.3	1.1	1.1	0.9	0.7	0.5	0.5	0.4	0.4	0.4	−0.1	−0.0	0.2	0.1	−0.3
12/63	2.0	1.8	1.7	1.7	1.7	1.5	1.8	1.5	1.6	1.4	1.2	1.0	1.0	0.9	0.6	0.4	0.4	0.4	0.3	0.3	−0.2	−0.1	0.1	−0.0	−0.4
12/64	2.0	1.8	1.7	1.7	1.7	1.5	1.8	1.5	1.6	1.4	1.2	1.0	1.0	0.9	0.7	0.5	0.5	0.4	0.4	0.3	−0.1	−0.0	0.2	0.1	−0.3
12/65	1.9	1.7	1.6	1.6	1.6	1.4	1.7	1.4	1.5	1.2	1.1	0.9	0.9	0.8	0.6	0.4	0.4	0.3	0.3	0.2	−0.2	−0.1	0.1	−0.1	−0.4
12/66	1.9	1.7	1.6	1.6	1.6	1.4	1.7	1.4	1.5	1.3	1.1	0.9	1.0	0.8	0.6	0.4	0.4	0.4	0.3	0.3	−0.1	−0.0	0.2	0.0	−0.3
12/67	1.6	1.5	1.3	1.4	1.3	1.2	1.4	1.2	1.2	1.0	0.9	0.7	0.7	0.5	0.3	0.1	0.1	0.0	−0.0	−0.1	−0.5	−0.4	−0.2	−0.4	−0.7
12/68	1.6	1.4	1.3	1.3	1.2	1.1	1.4	1.1	1.1	0.9	0.8	0.6	0.6	0.4	0.3	0.1	0.1	−0.0	−0.0	−0.1	−0.5	−0.4	−0.3	−0.4	−0.7
12/69	1.2	1.1	0.9	1.0	0.9	0.8	1.0	0.7	0.7	0.5	0.4	0.2	0.2	0.0	−0.2	−0.4	−0.4	−0.5	−0.5	−0.6	−1.0	−1.0	−0.9	−1.0	−1.3
12/70	1.5	1.4	1.2	1.3	1.2	1.1	1.3	1.1	1.1	0.9	0.8	0.6	0.6	0.5	0.3	0.1	0.1	0.0	0.0	−0.0	−0.4	−0.3	−0.2	−0.3	−0.6
12/71	1.7	1.6	1.5	1.5	1.4	1.3	1.6	1.3	1.4	1.2	1.1	0.9	0.9	0.8	0.6	0.5	0.5	0.4	0.4	0.4	0.0	0.1	0.3	0.2	−0.1
12/72	1.7	1.6	1.5	1.5	1.5	1.3	1.6	1.3	1.4	1.2	1.1	0.9	0.9	0.8	0.6	0.5	0.5	0.4	0.4	0.4	0.1	0.2	0.3	0.2	0.0
12/73	1.6	1.5	1.3	1.4	1.3	1.2	1.4	1.2	1.2	1.1	1.0	0.8	0.8	0.7	0.5	0.4	0.4	0.3	0.3	0.3	−0.0	0.0	0.2	0.1	−0.2
12/74	1.6	1.4	1.3	1.4	1.3	1.2	1.4	1.2	1.2	1.0	0.9	0.8	0.8	0.6	0.5	0.3	0.3	0.3	0.3	0.2	−0.1	−0.0	0.1	0.0	−0.2
12/75	1.5	1.4	1.3	1.3	1.3	1.2	1.4	1.2	1.2	1.0	0.9	0.8	0.8	0.6	0.5	0.4	0.4	0.3	0.3	0.3	−0.0	0.0	0.2	0.1	−0.1
12/76	1.7	1.6	1.5	1.6	1.5	1.4	1.6	1.4	1.5	1.3	1.2	1.0	1.1	0.9	0.8	0.7	0.7	0.6	0.6	0.6	0.4	0.4	0.6	0.5	0.3

Table XXXVIII

Time-Weighted Rates of Return* on Long-Term U.S. Treasury Bonds:
  Interest Reinvested,
  Higher Tax Rate,
  Current Dollars

ld til	12/50	12/51	12/52	12/53	12/54	12/55	12/56	12/57	12/58	12/59	12/60	12/61	12/62	12/63	12/64	12/65	12/66	12/67	12/68	12/69	12/70	12/71	12/72	12/73	12/74	12/75
12/51	−5.1																									
12/52	−2.8	−0.3																								
12/53	−1.2	0.8	1.9																							
12/54	−0.1	1.7	2.7	3.5																						
12/55	−0.7	0.5	0.8	0.2	−3.0																					
12/56	−1.7	−1.0	−1.1	−2.1	−4.8	−6.5																				
12/57	−0.4	0.4	0.5	0.2	−0.9	0.1	7.3																			
12/58	−1.1	−0.5	−0.5	−1.0	−2.1	−1.8	0.7	−5.6																		
12/59	−1.6	−1.2	−1.3	−1.8	−2.9	−2.8	−1.6	−5.7	−5.9																	
12/60	−0.4	0.1	0.2	−0.1	−0.7	−0.2	1.5	−0.4	2.3	11.1																
12/61	−0.6	−0.1	−0.1	−0.4	−0.9	−0.5	0.7	−0.9	0.7	4.2	−2.3															
12/62	−0.3	0.1	0.2	0.0	−0.4	−0.0	1.1	−0.1	1.3	3.8	0.3	2.9														
12/63	−0.4	0.0	0.1	−0.1	−0.5	−0.2	0.8	−0.3	0.8	2.5	−0.2	0.9	−1.1													
12/64	−0.2	0.1	0.2	0.0	−0.3	−0.0	0.8	−0.1	0.9	2.3	0.2	1.0	0.1	1.4												
12/65	−0.4	−0.0	0.0	−0.1	−0.5	−0.2	0.5	−0.3	0.5	1.6	−0.2	0.3	−0.6	−0.3	−1.9											
12/66	−0.2	0.1	0.1	0.0	−0.3	−0.0	0.6	−0.1	0.6	1.6	0.1	0.6	−0.0	0.4	−0.1	1.7										
12/67	−0.7	−0.4	−0.4	−0.6	−0.9	−0.7	−0.2	−0.9	−0.3	0.4	−1.1	−0.9	−1.6	−1.7	−2.7	−3.2	−7.8									
12/68	−0.7	−0.4	−0.4	−0.6	−0.9	−0.7	−0.2	−0.9	−0.4	0.2	−1.1	−0.9	−1.5	−1.6	−2.3	−2.4	−4.4	−0.9								
12/69	−1.3	−1.1	−1.2	−1.4	−1.7	−1.6	−1.2	−1.9	−1.5	−1.1	−2.3	−2.4	−3.1	−3.4	−4.3	−4.9	−7.1	−6.7	−12.1							
12/70	−0.6	−0.3	−0.3	−0.4	−0.7	−0.5	−0.1	−0.6	−0.2	0.3	−0.7	−0.5	−0.9	−0.9	−1.3	−1.2	−1.9	0.2	0.8	15.5						
12/71	−0.0	0.2	0.3	0.2	−0.0	0.2	0.6	0.2	0.6	1.2	0.3	0.6	0.3	0.5	0.4	0.8	0.6	2.9	4.2	13.4	11.3					
12/72	0.0	0.3	0.3	0.3	0.1	0.3	0.7	0.3	0.7	1.2	0.4	0.7	0.5	0.7	0.6	0.9	0.8	2.6	3.5	9.3	6.3	1.6				
12/73	−0.1	0.1	0.1	0.0	−0.1	0.0	0.4	0.0	0.4	0.9	0.1	0.3	0.1	0.2	0.1	0.3	0.1	1.5	2.0	5.9	2.8	−1.1	−3.8			
12/74	−0.1	0.1	0.1	0.0	−0.1	0.0	0.4	−0.0	0.3	0.8	0.1	0.2	0.0	0.1	0.0	0.2	0.0	1.2	1.6	4.6	2.0	−0.9	−2.2	−0.5		
12/75	−0.1	0.1	0.1	0.1	−0.1	0.1	0.4	0.0	0.4	0.8	0.1	0.3	0.1	0.2	0.1	0.3	0.2	1.2	1.5	4.0	1.8	−0.4	−1.1	0.3	1.1	
12/76	0.4	0.6	0.6	0.6	0.4	0.6	1.0	0.7	1.0	1.4	0.9	1.1	0.9	1.1	1.1	1.4	1.3	2.4	2.8	5.2	3.5	2.0	2.1	4.2	6.6	12.5

*Percent per annum, compounded annually

Sources: Bond market data—Lawrence Fisher (compiler), CRSP Monthly Return File for U.S. Treasury Securities (magnetic tape). See Appendix A.
Income tax rates—Income levels estimated from U.S. Bureau of the Census, Current Population Reports, Series P-60, Nos. 101 and 103 and Historical Statistics of the United States. Tax rates were found in U.S. Internal Revenue Service, Statistics of Income and Your Federal Income Tax.

Held Until	Purchased 12/25	12/26	12/27	12/28	12/29	Purchased 12/30	12/31	12/32	12/33	12/34	Purchased 12/35	12/36	12/37	12/38	12/39	Purchased 12/40	12/41	12/42	12/43	12/44	Purchased 12/45	12/46	12/47	12/48	12/49
12/26	8.8																								
12/27	9.6	10.5																							
12/28	6.3	5.1	0.0																						
12/29	5.8	4.8	2.1	4.2																					
12/30	7.2	6.8	5.6	8.5	13.0																				
12/31	6.3	5.8	4.7	6.3	7.4	2.1																			
12/32	8.7	8.7	8.4	10.6	12.8	12.7	24.2																		
12/33	7.5	7.3	6.7	8.1	9.2	7.9	10.9	−1.0																	
12/34	7.4	7.2	6.8	7.9	8.7	7.6	9.5	2.8	6.8																
12/35	6.8	6.6	6.1	7.0	7.5	6.5	7.6	2.5	4.3	1.9															
12/36	6.7	6.5	6.1	6.9	7.3	6.4	7.3	3.4	4.9	3.9	6.0														
12/37	5.9	5.7	5.2	5.8	6.0	5.1	5.6	2.2	3.0	1.7	1.7	−2.5													
12/38	6.1	5.9	5.5	6.1	6.3	5.5	6.0	3.2	4.1	3.4	3.9	2.8	8.5												
12/39	6.2	6.0	5.6	6.1	6.3	5.6	6.1	3.7	4.5	4.1	4.6	4.1	7.6	6.8											
12/40	6.1	5.9	5.5	6.0	6.2	5.5	5.9	3.8	4.5	4.1	4.5	4.2	6.5	5.5	4.2										
12/41	5.1	4.8	4.5	4.8	4.9	4.1	4.3	2.3	2.8	2.2	2.3	1.5	2.5	0.6	−2.3	−8.4									
12/42	4.4	4.1	3.7	4.0	3.9	3.2	3.3	1.4	1.7	1.1	1.0	0.1	0.7	−1.2	−3.7	−7.5	−6.5								
12/43	4.0	3.7	3.3	3.5	3.5	2.8	2.8	1.1	1.3	0.7	0.5	−0.2	0.1	−1.4	−3.4	−5.8	−4.5	−2.4							
12/44	3.7	3.4	3.0	3.2	3.2	2.5	2.5	0.9	1.1	0.5	0.4	−0.3	0.0	−1.3	−2.9	−4.6	−3.3	−1.6	−0.8						
12/45	3.9	3.6	3.2	3.4	3.4	2.8	2.8	1.3	1.5	1.1	1.0	0.5	0.8	−0.2	−1.3	−2.4	−0.9	1.1	2.9	6.8					
12/46	2.8	2.5	2.1	2.2	2.1	1.5	1.4	−0.0	0.0	−0.5	−0.7	−1.4	−1.3	−2.4	−3.7	−4.9	−4.2	−3.6	−4.0	−5.6	−16.5				
12/47	2.1	1.8	1.4	1.4	1.3	0.6	0.5	−0.9	−0.9	−1.4	−1.7	−2.4	−2.4	−3.5	−4.7	−5.9	−5.5	−5.3	−6.0	−7.7	−14.2	−11.8			
12/48	2.0	1.7	1.3	1.3	1.2	0.6	0.5	−0.8	−0.8	−1.4	−1.6	−2.2	−2.2	−3.2	−4.2	−5.2	−4.8	−4.5	−4.9	−5.9	−9.8	−6.2	−0.3		
12/49	2.2	1.9	1.5	1.6	1.5	0.9	0.9	−0.4	−0.3	−0.8	−1.0	−1.5	−1.4	−2.3	−3.1	−3.9	−3.3	−2.9	−3.0	−3.4	−5.8	−1.9	3.5	7.4	
12/50	1.8	1.6	1.2	1.2	1.1	0.6	0.5	−0.7	−0.7	−1.1	−1.3	−1.8	−1.8	−2.6	−3.4	−4.2	−3.7	−3.3	−3.4	−3.9	−5.9	−3.0	0.1	0.3	−6.3
12/51	1.3	1.1	0.7	0.7	0.6	0.0	−0.1	−1.2	−1.3	−1.7	−1.9	−2.4	−2.4	−3.2	−4.0	−4.7	−4.4	−4.1	−4.3	−4.8	−6.6	−4.5	−2.6	−3.4	−8.4
12/52	1.2	1.0	0.6	0.6	0.5	−0.1	−0.2	−1.2	−1.3	−1.7	−1.9	−2.4	−2.4	−3.1	−3.8	−4.5	−4.1	−3.8	−4.0	−4.4	−5.9	−4.0	−2.3	−2.8	−6.0
12/53	1.2	1.0	0.6	0.7	0.5	0.0	−0.1	−1.1	−1.1	−1.5	−1.7	−2.2	−2.1	−2.8	−3.5	−4.0	−3.6	−3.4	−3.5	−3.8	−5.0	−3.3	−1.8	−2.0	−4.3
12/54	1.3	1.1	0.8	0.8	0.7	0.2	0.1	−0.9	−0.9	−1.3	−1.4	−1.8	−1.8	−2.4	−3.0	−3.5	−3.1	−2.8	−2.8	−3.0	−4.1	−2.4	−1.0	−1.1	−2.7
12/55	1.2	0.9	0.6	0.6	0.5	0.0	−0.1	−1.0	−1.0	−1.4	−1.5	−1.9	−1.9	−2.5	−3.0	−3.5	−3.1	−2.8	−2.9	−3.0	−4.0	−2.5	−1.3	−1.4	−2.8
12/56	0.8	0.6	0.3	0.3	0.1	−0.3	−0.4	−1.4	−1.4	−1.7	−1.9	−2.3	−2.3	−2.8	−3.4	−3.8	−3.5	−3.3	−3.4	−3.6	−4.5	−3.2	−2.2	−2.4	−3.7
12/57	0.9	0.7	0.4	0.4	0.3	−0.2	−0.3	−1.1	−1.1	−1.5	−1.6	−2.0	−2.0	−2.5	−3.0	−3.4	−3.1	−2.8	−2.8	−3.0	−3.8	−2.5	−1.5	−1.7	−2.8
12/58	0.7	0.4	0.1	0.1	−0.0	−0.4	−0.5	−1.4	−1.4	−1.7	−1.9	−2.2	−2.2	−2.7	−3.2	−3.6	−3.3	−3.1	−3.1	−3.3	−4.0	−2.9	−2.1	−2.2	−3.3
12/59	0.4	0.2	−0.1	−0.1	−0.3	−0.7	−0.8	−1.6	−1.6	−2.0	−2.1	−2.5	−2.4	−2.9	−3.4	−3.8	−3.5	−3.3	−3.4	−3.6	−4.3	−3.3	−2.5	−2.7	−3.7
12/60	0.7	0.5	0.2	0.2	0.0	−0.4	−0.4	−1.2	−1.2	−1.5	−1.7	−2.0	−2.0	−2.4	−2.8	−3.2	−2.9	−2.7	−2.7	−2.8	−3.4	−2.4	−1.6	−1.8	−2.5
12/61	0.6	0.4	0.1	0.1	−0.0	−0.4	−0.5	−1.3	−1.3	−1.6	−1.7	−2.0	−2.0	−2.4	−2.8	−3.2	−2.9	−2.7	−2.7	−2.8	−3.4	−2.4	−1.7	−1.8	−2.6
12/62	0.6	0.4	0.1	0.1	0.0	−0.4	−0.5	−1.2	−1.2	−1.5	−1.6	−1.9	−1.9	−2.3	−2.6	−2.9	−2.7	−2.5	−2.5	−2.6	−3.1	−2.2	−1.5	−1.6	−2.3
12/63	0.5	0.3	0.0	0.0	−0.1	−0.5	−0.5	−1.2	−1.2	−1.5	−1.6	−1.9	−1.9	−2.3	−2.6	−2.9	−2.7	−2.5	−2.5	−2.6	−3.1	−2.2	−1.6	−1.7	−2.3
12/64	0.5	0.3	0.0	0.0	−0.1	−0.4	−0.5	−1.2	−1.2	−1.5	−1.6	−1.8	−1.8	−2.2	−2.5	−2.8	−2.6	−2.4	−2.4	−2.4	−2.9	−2.1	−1.5	−1.6	−2.1
12/65	0.4	0.2	−0.1	−0.1	−0.2	−0.5	−0.6	−1.3	−1.3	−1.5	−1.6	−1.9	−1.9	−2.2	−2.6	−2.8	−2.6	−2.4	−2.4	−2.5	−2.9	−2.2	−1.6	−1.7	−2.2
12/66	0.4	0.2	−0.1	−0.1	−0.2	−0.6	−0.6	−1.3	−1.3	−1.5	−1.6	−1.9	−1.9	−2.2	−2.5	−2.8	−2.6	−2.4	−2.4	−2.5	−2.9	−2.1	−1.6	−1.7	−2.2
12/67	0.1	−0.1	−0.4	−0.4	−0.5	−0.8	−0.9	−1.6	−1.6	−1.8	−1.9	−2.2	−2.2	−2.5	−2.8	−3.1	−2.9	−2.7	−2.7	−2.8	−3.2	−2.6	−2.1	−2.2	−2.7
12/68	−0.1	−0.3	−0.5	−0.5	−0.6	−1.0	−1.0	−1.7	−1.7	−1.9	−2.0	−2.3	−2.3	−2.6	−2.9	−3.2	−3.0	−2.8	−2.9	−2.9	−3.3	−2.7	−2.2	−2.3	−2.7
12/69	−0.5	−0.7	−0.9	−1.0	−1.1	−1.4	−1.5	−2.1	−2.2	−2.4	−2.5	−2.8	−2.8	−3.1	−3.4	−3.7	−3.5	−3.4	−3.4	−3.5	−4.0	−3.4	−3.0	−3.1	−3.6
12/70	−0.3	−0.5	−0.7	−0.7	−0.8	−1.2	−1.2	−1.8	−1.9	−2.1	−2.2	−2.4	−2.4	−2.8	−3.0	−3.3	−3.1	−3.0	−3.0	−3.1	−3.5	−2.9	−2.5	−2.6	−3.0
12/71	−0.1	−0.3	−0.5	−0.5	−0.6	−1.0	−1.0	−1.6	−1.6	−1.8	−1.9	−2.2	−2.1	−2.5	−2.7	−2.9	−2.8	−2.6	−2.6	−2.7	−3.0	−2.5	−2.1	−2.1	−2.5
12/72	−0.1	−0.3	−0.5	−0.6	−0.7	−1.0	−1.0	−1.6	−1.6	−1.8	−1.9	−2.1	−2.1	−2.4	−2.7	−2.9	−2.7	−2.6	−2.6	−2.7	−3.0	−2.4	−2.0	−2.1	−2.5
12/73	−0.4	−0.6	−0.8	−0.8	−0.9	−1.2	−1.3	−1.9	−1.9	−2.1	−2.2	−2.4	−2.4	−2.7	−3.0	−3.2	−3.0	−2.9	−2.9	−3.0	−3.3	−2.8	−2.4	−2.5	−2.9
12/74	−0.6	−0.8	−1.0	−1.1	−1.2	−1.5	−1.6	−2.1	−2.1	−2.3	−2.4	−2.7	−2.7	−3.0	−3.2	−3.4	−3.3	−3.2	−3.2	−3.3	−3.6	−3.1	−2.8	−2.9	−3.3
12/75	−0.7	−0.9	−1.1	−1.2	−1.3	−1.6	−1.6	−2.2	−2.2	−2.4	−2.5	−2.7	−2.7	−3.0	−3.3	−3.5	−3.3	−3.2	−3.3	−3.4	−3.7	−3.2	−2.9	−3.0	−3.3
12/76	−0.6	−0.8	−1.0	−1.0	−1.1	−1.4	−1.5	−2.0	−2.0	−2.2	−2.3	−2.5	−2.5	−2.8	−3.0	−3.2	−3.1	−3.0	−3.0	−3.0	−3.3	−2.9	−2.5	−2.6	−3.0

Table XXXIX

Time-Weighted Rates of Return* on Long-Term U.S. Treasury Bonds:
  Interest Reinvested,
  Higher Tax Rate,
  Deflated by the Consumer Price Index

Held until	Purchased				
	12/50	12/51	12/52	12/53	12/54
12/51	−10.4				
12/52	−5.9	−1.2			
12/53	−3.6	0.0	1.2		
12/54	−1.7	1.3	2.6	4.0	
12/55	−2.1	0.1	0.6	0.3	−3.3
12/56	−3.3	−1.8	−1.9	−3.0	−6.3
12/57	−2.3	−0.8	−0.7	−1.2	−2.9
12/58	−2.9	−1.8	−1.8	−2.5	−4.0
12/59	−3.4	−2.5	−2.6	−3.3	−4.7
12/60	−2.2	−1.2	−1.2	−1.5	−2.4
12/61	−2.2	−1.4	−1.4	−1.7	−2.5
12/62	−1.9	−1.1	−1.1	−1.3	−2.0
12/63	−2.0	−1.2	−1.2	−1.5	−2.1
12/64	−1.8	−1.1	−1.1	−1.3	−1.9
12/65	−2.0	−1.3	−1.3	−1.5	−2.0
12/66	−1.9	−1.3	−1.3	−1.5	−2.0
12/67	−2.5	−1.9	−2.0	−2.2	−2.7
12/68	−2.6	−2.1	−2.2	−2.4	−2.9
12/69	−3.4	−3.0	−3.2	−3.4	−3.9
12/70	−2.8	−2.4	−2.5	−2.7	−3.1
12/71	−2.4	−1.9	−2.0	−2.2	−2.5
12/72	−2.3	−1.9	−2.0	−2.1	−2.5
12/73	−2.8	−2.4	−2.5	−2.6	−3.0
12/74	−3.1	−2.8	−2.9	−3.1	−3.4
12/75	−3.2	−2.9	−3.0	−3.2	−3.5
12/76	−2.8	−2.5	−2.6	−2.7	−3.0

Held until	Purchased				
	12/55	12/56	12/57	12/58	12/59
12/56	−9.1				
12/57	−2.7	4.2			
12/58	−4.2	−1.7	−7.2		
12/59	−5.0	−3.6	−7.2	−7.3	
12/60	−2.3	−0.5	−2.0	0.8	9.5
12/61	−2.4	−1.0	−2.2	−0.5	3.1
12/62	−1.8	−0.5	−1.4	0.1	2.6
12/63	−1.9	−0.8	−1.7	−0.5	1.3
12/64	−1.7	−0.7	−1.4	−0.4	1.0
12/65	−1.9	−1.1	−1.7	−0.9	0.2
12/66	−1.9	−1.1	−1.7	−1.0	−0.0
12/67	−2.6	−2.0	−2.6	−2.1	−1.4
12/68	−2.8	−2.3	−2.9	−2.4	−1.9
12/69	−3.9	−3.5	−4.1	−3.9	−3.5
12/70	−3.1	−2.7	−3.2	−2.8	−2.4
12/71	−2.5	−2.0	−2.4	−2.0	−1.6
12/72	−2.4	−2.0	−2.4	−2.0	−1.6
12/73	−2.9	−2.6	−3.0	−2.7	−2.4
12/74	−3.4	−3.1	−3.5	−3.3	−3.0
12/75	−3.5	−3.2	−3.6	−3.4	−3.1
12/76	−3.0	−2.7	−3.1	−2.8	−2.6

Held until	Purchased				
	12/60	12/61	12/62	12/63	12/64
12/61	−2.9				
12/62	−0.6	1.7			
12/63	−1.3	−0.5	−2.7		
12/64	−1.0	−0.3	−1.3	0.2	
12/65	−1.5	−1.2	−2.1	−1.8	−3.7
12/66	−1.5	−1.3	−2.0	−1.7	−2.7
12/67	−2.9	−2.9	−3.8	−4.0	−5.4
12/68	−3.2	−3.2	−4.0	−4.3	−5.4
12/69	−4.9	−5.1	−6.0	−6.6	−7.9
12/70	−3.5	−3.6	−4.2	−4.4	−5.2
12/71	−2.5	−2.5	−3.0	−3.0	−3.4
12/72	−2.5	−2.4	−2.8	−2.9	−3.2
12/73	−3.2	−3.2	−3.7	−3.8	−4.2
12/74	−3.8	−3.9	−4.3	−4.5	−4.9
12/75	−3.9	−4.0	−4.4	−4.6	−5.0
12/76	−3.3	−3.3	−3.6	−3.7	−4.0

Held until	Purchased				
	12/65	12/66	12/67	12/68	12/69
12/66	−1.6				
12/67	−6.2	−10.5			
12/68	−5.9	−8.0	−5.4		
12/69	−8.9	−11.2	−11.5	−17.2	
12/70	−5.5	−6.4	−5.0	−4.8	9.5
12/71	−3.4	−3.7	−2.0	−0.8	8.6
12/72	−3.2	−3.4	−1.9	−1.0	5.0
12/73	−4.2	−4.6	−3.6	−3.2	0.6
12/74	−5.1	−5.5	−4.7	−4.6	−1.9
12/75	−5.1	−5.5	−4.8	−4.8	−2.5
12/76	−4.0	−4.3	−3.6	−3.3	−1.2

Held until	Purchased					
	12/70	12/71	12/72	12/73	12/74	12/75
12/71	7.7					
12/72	2.9	−1.7				
12/73	−2.2	−6.8	−11.6			
12/74	−4.6	−8.3	−11.5	−11.3		
12/75	−4.8	−7.6	−9.5	−8.5	−5.5	
12/76	−2.8	−4.8	−5.6	−3.5	0.7	7.3

Percent per annum, compounded annually.

Sources: Bond market data—Lawrence Fisher (compiler), CRSP Monthly Return File for U.S. Treasury Securities (magnetic tape). See Appendix A.
Consumer Price Index—U.S. Bureau of Labor Statistics.
Income tax rates—Income levels estimated from U.S. Bureau of the Census, Current Population Reports, Series P-60, Nos. 101 and 103 and Historical Statistics of the United States. Tax rates were found in U.S. Internal Revenue Service, Statistics of Income and Your Federal Income Tax.

Chapter 14

Time-Weighted Rates of Return on Intermediate-Term Governments

Tables XL through XLV show rates of return on intermediate-term Governments. The criteria for selecting securities for the intermediate portfolio were the same as for the long-term portfolio, except that the term to maturity (or to first call if callable) was supposed to be between five and ten years. No appropriate issue was available in either December 1928 or December 1929. An issue first callable in March 1940 was used instead. Flower bonds were avoided except for 1926 through 1928, and those flower bonds were priced at a premium. Occasionally, it was necessary to use callable bonds; but the issue selected was usually priced near par.

The rates of return in Tables XL through XLV are nearly the same as the rates in the corresponding tables for long-term bonds. The main differences are that the highest and lowest rates of return are closer to the average rate, as would be expected from the fact that intermediate-term securities have shorter durations than long-term securities and, therefore, their prices are less sensitive to yield changes.

Held Until	Purchased 12/25	12/26	12/27	12/28	12/29	Purchased 12/30	12/31	12/32	12/33	12/34	Purchased 12/35	12/36	12/37	12/38	12/39	Purchased 12/40	12/41	12/42	12/43	12/44	Purchased 12/45	12/46	12/47	12/48	12/49
12/26	5.5																								
12/27	5.1	4.6																							
12/28	3.6	2.6	0.6																						
12/29	3.7	3.2	2.4	4.3																					
12/30	4.2	3.9	3.7	5.2	6.2																				
12/31	2.5	1.9	1.2	1.4	−0.0	−5.8																			
12/32	4.0	3.8	3.6	4.3	4.4	3.5	13.7																		
12/33	3.6	3.3	3.1	3.6	3.4	2.5	6.9	0.6																	
12/34	4.2	4.0	3.9	4.5	4.5	4.1	7.6	4.7	9.0																
12/35	4.4	4.3	4.3	4.8	4.9	4.7	7.5	5.5	8.0	7.0															
12/36	4.3	4.2	4.2	4.6	4.6	4.4	6.6	4.9	6.3	5.0	3.1														
12/37	4.0	3.8	3.7	4.1	4.1	3.8	5.4	3.9	4.7	3.3	1.5	0.0													
12/38	4.1	4.0	4.0	4.3	4.3	4.1	5.6	4.3	5.0	4.0	3.1	3.1	6.2												
12/39	4.1	4.0	4.0	4.3	4.3	4.1	5.4	4.3	4.9	4.1	3.4	3.5	5.2	4.3											
12/40	4.2	4.1	4.0	4.3	4.3	4.1	5.3	4.3	4.8	4.1	3.6	3.7	5.0	4.3	4.4										
12/41	3.9	3.7	3.7	3.9	3.9	3.7	4.7	3.7	4.1	3.5	2.9	2.8	3.6	2.7	1.9	−0.6									
12/42	3.7	3.6	3.5	3.7	3.7	3.5	4.4	3.5	3.8	3.2	2.7	2.6	3.1	2.4	1.8	0.5	1.5								
12/43	3.7	3.6	3.5	3.7	3.6	3.5	4.3	3.4	3.7	3.2	2.7	2.6	3.1	2.5	2.0	1.2	2.2	2.8							
12/44	3.6	3.5	3.4	3.6	3.6	3.4	4.1	3.4	3.6	3.1	2.7	2.6	3.0	2.5	2.1	1.6	2.3	2.7	2.6						
12/45	3.7	3.6	3.6	3.7	3.7	3.6	4.3	3.6	3.8	3.4	3.0	3.0	3.4	3.0	2.8	2.4	3.2	3.7	4.2	5.9					
12/46	3.6	3.5	3.4	3.6	3.5	3.4	4.0	3.4	3.6	3.1	2.8	2.8	3.1	2.7	2.5	2.1	2.7	3.0	3.0	3.3	0.7				
12/47	3.4	3.3	3.3	3.4	3.4	3.2	3.8	3.2	3.3	2.9	2.6	2.5	2.8	2.4	2.2	1.9	2.3	2.5	2.4	2.3	0.6	0.4			
12/48	3.4	3.3	3.3	3.4	3.4	3.2	3.8	3.2	3.4	3.0	2.7	2.6	2.9	2.5	2.3	2.1	2.5	2.6	2.6	2.6	1.5	2.0	3.5		
12/49	3.5	3.4	3.3	3.5	3.4	3.3	3.8	3.3	3.4	3.1	2.8	2.8	3.0	2.7	2.6	2.4	2.7	2.9	2.9	3.0	2.3	2.8	4.1	4.6	
12/50	3.3	3.2	3.2	3.3	3.3	3.1	3.6	3.1	3.2	2.9	2.6	2.6	2.8	2.5	2.3	2.1	2.4	2.5	2.5	2.5	1.8	2.1	2.6	2.2	−0.2
12/51	3.2	3.1	3.1	3.2	3.1	3.0	3.4	2.9	3.1	2.7	2.5	2.4	2.6	2.3	2.2	2.0	2.2	2.3	2.2	2.2	1.6	1.7	2.1	1.6	0.1
12/52	3.2	3.1	3.1	3.2	3.1	3.0	3.4	2.9	3.1	2.7	2.5	2.5	2.6	2.4	2.2	2.1	2.3	2.4	2.3	2.3	1.8	2.0	2.3	2.0	1.1
12/53	3.2	3.1	3.1	3.2	3.1	3.0	3.4	3.0	3.1	2.8	2.5	2.5	2.7	2.4	2.3	2.1	2.4	2.4	2.4	2.4	2.0	2.1	2.4	2.2	1.6
12/54	3.2	3.1	3.0	3.1	3.1	3.0	3.4	2.9	3.0	2.7	2.5	2.5	2.6	2.4	2.3	2.1	2.4	2.4	2.4	2.4	2.0	2.1	2.4	2.2	1.7
12/55	3.1	3.0	2.9	3.0	2.9	2.8	3.2	2.8	2.9	2.6	2.4	2.3	2.5	2.2	2.1	2.0	2.1	2.2	2.1	2.1	1.7	1.8	2.0	1.8	1.3
12/56	2.9	2.9	2.8	2.9	2.8	2.7	3.0	2.6	2.7	2.4	2.2	2.2	2.3	2.1	2.0	1.8	2.0	2.0	1.9	1.9	1.5	1.6	1.7	1.5	1.1
12/57	3.1	3.0	3.0	3.0	3.0	2.9	3.2	2.8	2.9	2.7	2.5	2.4	2.6	2.4	2.3	2.2	2.3	2.4	2.3	2.3	2.0	2.2	2.3	2.2	1.9
12/58	3.0	2.9	2.8	2.9	2.8	2.7	3.1	2.7	2.8	2.5	2.3	2.3	2.4	2.2	2.1	2.0	2.1	2.1	2.1	2.1	1.8	1.9	2.0	1.9	1.5
12/59	2.9	2.8	2.7	2.8	2.7	2.6	2.9	2.6	2.6	2.4	2.2	2.2	2.3	2.1	2.0	1.8	2.0	2.0	1.9	1.9	1.6	1.7	1.8	1.6	1.4
12/60	3.1	3.0	3.0	3.1	3.0	2.9	3.2	2.9	3.0	2.7	2.6	2.5	2.7	2.5	2.4	2.3	2.5	2.5	2.5	2.5	2.3	2.4	2.5	2.5	2.3
12/61	3.1	3.0	3.0	3.0	3.0	2.9	3.2	2.9	2.9	2.7	2.6	2.5	2.6	2.5	2.4	2.3	2.5	2.5	2.5	2.5	2.3	2.4	2.5	2.4	2.3
12/62	3.1	3.1	3.0	3.1	3.1	3.0	3.3	2.9	3.0	2.8	2.7	2.7	2.8	2.6	2.5	2.5	2.6	2.7	2.7	2.7	2.5	2.6	2.7	2.7	2.5
12/63	3.1	3.0	3.0	3.1	3.0	2.9	3.2	2.9	3.0	2.8	2.6	2.6	2.7	2.6	2.5	2.4	2.6	2.6	2.6	2.6	2.4	2.5	2.7	2.6	2.5
12/64	3.1	3.1	3.0	3.1	3.0	3.0	3.2	2.9	3.0	2.8	2.7	2.6	2.7	2.6	2.5	2.5	2.6	2.7	2.6	2.6	2.5	2.6	2.7	2.7	2.5
12/65	3.1	3.0	3.0	3.0	3.0	2.9	3.2	2.9	2.9	2.8	2.6	2.6	2.7	2.6	2.5	2.4	2.5	2.6	2.6	2.6	2.4	2.5	2.6	2.6	2.4
12/66	3.1	3.0	3.0	3.1	3.0	3.0	3.2	2.9	3.0	2.8	2.7	2.7	2.8	2.6	2.6	2.5	2.6	2.7	2.7	2.7	2.5	2.6	2.7	2.7	2.6
12/67	3.1	3.0	3.0	3.0	3.0	2.9	3.2	2.9	2.9	2.8	2.6	2.6	2.7	2.6	2.5	2.5	2.6	2.6	2.6	2.6	2.5	2.5	2.6	2.6	2.5
12/68	3.0	3.0	2.9	3.0	3.0	2.9	3.1	2.9	2.9	2.7	2.6	2.6	2.7	2.6	2.5	2.5	2.6	2.6	2.6	2.6	2.5	2.5	2.6	2.6	2.5
12/69	3.0	2.9	2.9	2.9	2.9	2.8	3.0	2.8	2.8	2.6	2.5	2.5	2.6	2.5	2.4	2.3	2.4	2.5	2.5	2.5	2.3	2.4	2.5	2.4	2.3
12/70	3.2	3.1	3.1	3.2	3.1	3.1	3.3	3.0	3.1	2.9	2.8	2.8	2.9	2.8	2.8	2.7	2.8	2.9	2.9	2.9	2.8	2.8	3.0	2.9	2.8
12/71	3.3	3.3	3.2	3.3	3.3	3.2	3.4	3.2	3.2	3.1	3.0	3.0	3.1	3.0	2.9	2.9	3.0	3.1	3.1	3.1	3.0	3.1	3.2	3.2	3.1
12/72	3.3	3.3	3.2	3.3	3.3	3.2	3.4	3.2	3.3	3.1	3.0	3.0	3.1	3.0	3.0	2.9	3.0	3.1	3.1	3.1	3.0	3.1	3.2	3.2	3.1
12/73	3.3	3.3	3.3	3.3	3.3	3.2	3.5	3.2	3.3	3.1	3.0	3.0	3.1	3.0	3.0	3.0	3.1	3.1	3.1	3.2	3.1	3.2	3.3	3.2	3.2
12/74	3.4	3.3	3.3	3.4	3.3	3.3	3.5	3.3	3.3	3.2	3.1	3.1	3.2	3.1	3.1	3.0	3.1	3.2	3.2	3.2	3.1	3.2	3.3	3.3	3.3
12/75	3.4	3.4	3.4	3.4	3.4	3.3	3.6	3.3	3.4	3.3	3.2	3.2	3.3	3.2	3.2	3.1	3.2	3.3	3.3	3.3	3.2	3.3	3.4	3.4	3.4
12/76	3.6	3.6	3.6	3.6	3.6	3.5	3.8	3.6	3.6	3.5	3.4	3.4	3.5	3.4	3.4	3.4	3.5	3.6	3.6	3.6	3.5	3.6	3.8	3.8	3.7

Table XL

Time-Weighted Rates of Return* on Intermediate-Term U.S. Treasury Bonds and Notes:
  Interest Reinvested,
  Tax-Exempt,
  Current Dollars

Sold	12/50	12/51	12/52	12/53	12/54	12/55	12/56	12/57	12/58	12/59	12/60	12/61	12/62	12/63	12/64	12/65	12/66	12/67	12/68	12/69	12/70	12/71	12/72	12/73	12/74	12/75
12/51	0.4																									
12/52	1.7	3.2																								
12/53	2.2	3.2	3.2																							
12/54	2.2	2.9	2.7	2.2																						
12/55	1.7	2.0	1.6	0.8	-0.6																					
12/56	1.3	1.5	1.1	0.4	-0.5	-0.4																				
12/57	2.2	2.5	2.4	2.2	2.2	3.6	7.8																			
12/58	1.8	2.0	1.8	1.5	1.3	2.0	3.2	-1.3																		
12/59	1.5	1.7	1.5	1.2	1.0	1.4	2.0	-0.8	-0.4																	
12/60	2.5	2.8	2.7	2.6	2.7	3.4	4.4	3.3	5.6	12.0																
12/61	2.5	2.7	2.7	2.6	2.7	3.2	3.9	3.0	4.5	7.0	2.2															
12/62	2.8	3.0	3.0	2.9	3.0	3.6	4.2	3.5	4.8	6.5	3.9	5.6														
12/63	2.7	2.9	2.8	2.8	2.9	3.3	3.9	3.2	4.1	5.3	3.2	3.6	1.7													
12/64	2.7	2.9	2.9	2.9	2.9	3.3	3.8	3.2	4.0	4.9	3.2	3.6	2.6	3.4												
12/65	2.6	2.8	2.8	2.7	2.8	3.1	3.5	3.0	3.6	4.3	2.8	3.0	2.1	2.3	1.2											
12/66	2.8	2.9	2.9	2.9	2.9	3.3	3.6	3.2	3.8	4.4	3.1	3.3	2.7	3.1	2.9	4.7										
12/67	2.7	2.8	2.8	2.7	2.8	3.1	3.4	3.0	3.4	3.9	2.8	2.9	2.4	2.6	2.3	2.8	1.0									
12/68	2.6	2.8	2.8	2.7	2.8	3.0	3.3	2.9	3.4	3.8	2.8	2.9	2.4	2.6	2.4	2.7	1.8	2.5								
12/69	2.5	2.6	2.5	2.5	2.5	2.7	3.0	2.6	3.0	3.3	2.4	2.4	1.9	2.0	1.7	1.8	0.9	0.8	-1.0							
12/70	3.0	3.1	3.1	3.1	3.2	3.5	3.7	3.4	3.8	4.2	3.5	3.6	3.4	3.6	3.6	4.1	4.0	5.0	6.2	14.0						
12/71	3.3	3.4	3.4	3.4	3.5	3.8	4.1	3.8	4.2	4.6	3.9	4.1	3.9	4.2	4.3	4.9	4.9	5.9	7.1	11.3	8.7					
12/72	3.3	3.4	3.4	3.5	3.5	3.8	4.0	3.8	4.2	4.5	3.9	4.1	3.9	4.2	4.3	4.7	4.7	5.5	6.3	8.8	6.3	3.9				
12/73	3.3	3.5	3.5	3.5	3.6	3.8	4.1	3.8	4.2	4.5	4.0	4.1	4.0	4.2	4.3	4.7	4.7	5.3	5.9	7.7	5.6	4.1	4.4			
12/74	3.4	3.5	3.6	3.6	3.6	3.9	4.1	3.9	4.2	4.5	4.0	4.2	4.1	4.3	4.4	4.7	4.7	5.3	5.7	7.1	5.5	4.4	4.6	4.9		
12/75	3.5	3.7	3.7	3.7	3.8	4.0	4.3	4.1	4.4	4.7	4.2	4.4	4.3	4.5	4.6	4.9	4.9	5.4	5.9	7.1	5.7	5.0	5.3	5.8	6.8	
12/76	3.9	4.0	4.1	4.1	4.2	4.4	4.7	4.5	4.8	5.2	4.7	4.9	4.9	5.1	5.3	5.6	5.7	6.3	6.7	7.9	6.9	6.5	7.2	8.2	9.8	13.0

Percent per annum, compounded annually.

Source: Lawrence Fisher (compiler), CRSP Monthly Return File for U.S. Treasury Securities (magnetic tape). See Appendix A.

123

Held Until	Purchased 12/25	12/26	12/27	12/28	12/29	Purchased 12/30	12/31	12/32	12/33	12/34	Purchased 12/35	12/36	12/37	12/38	12/39	Purchased 12/40	12/41	12/42	12/43	12/44	Purchased 12/45	12/46	12/47	12/48	12/49
12/26	7.1																								
12/27	7.0	6.8																							
12/28	5.1	4.2	1.6																						
12/29	4.9	4.1	2.8	4.1																					
12/30	6.5	6.3	6.1	8.4	13.0																				
12/31	6.1	5.8	5.6	7.0	8.4	4.1																			
12/32	8.8	9.1	9.5	11.6	14.2	14.8	26.7																		
12/33	7.7	7.7	7.9	9.2	10.5	9.7	12.6	0.1																	
12/34	7.6	7.6	7.7	8.8	9.8	9.0	10.7	3.4	6.8																
12/35	7.2	7.2	7.3	8.1	8.8	7.9	8.9	3.6	5.4	3.9															
12/36	6.7	6.7	6.6	7.3	7.7	6.9	7.5	3.1	4.2	2.9	1.8														
12/37	5.9	5.7	5.6	6.1	6.3	5.4	5.6	1.9	2.3	0.9	-0.6	-3.0													
12/38	6.1	6.0	6.0	6.4	6.7	5.9	6.2	3.1	3.7	2.9	2.6	3.0	9.3												
12/39	6.0	5.9	5.9	6.3	6.5	5.8	6.0	3.3	3.9	3.3	3.1	3.6	7.0	4.8											
12/40	5.8	5.8	5.7	6.0	6.2	5.5	5.7	3.3	3.8	3.3	3.2	3.5	5.8	4.1	3.4										
12/41	4.8	4.7	4.5	4.7	4.8	4.1	4.1	1.8	2.1	1.4	1.0	0.8	1.8	-0.6	-3.2	-9.4									
12/42	4.1	3.9	3.7	3.8	3.8	3.1	3.0	0.9	1.0	0.3	-0.2	-0.6	-0.1	-2.3	-4.5	-8.2	-7.1								
12/43	3.8	3.6	3.4	3.6	3.5	2.8	2.7	0.8	0.9	0.2	-0.2	-0.5	-0.1	-1.9	-3.5	-5.7	-3.8	-0.3							
12/44	3.6	3.5	3.3	3.4	3.3	2.7	2.6	0.8	0.8	0.2	-0.2	-0.4	-0.0	-1.5	-2.7	-4.2	-2.4	0.1	0.5						
12/45	3.6	3.5	3.3	3.4	3.3	2.7	2.6	1.0	1.0	0.5	0.2	0.0	0.4	-0.8	-1.7	-2.7	-0.9	1.2	2.0	3.5					
12/46	2.7	2.5	2.2	2.3	2.2	1.5	1.4	-0.2	-0.3	-0.8	-1.3	-1.6	-1.4	-2.7	-3.7	-4.8	-3.9	-3.0	-3.9	-6.1	-14.8				
12/47	2.2	1.9	1.7	1.7	1.6	1.0	0.8	-0.8	-0.8	-1.4	-1.8	-2.2	-2.1	-3.3	-4.2	-5.3	-4.5	-4.0	-4.9	-6.7	-11.4	-7.9			
12/48	2.1	1.9	1.7	1.7	1.5	0.9	0.8	-0.7	-0.7	-1.2	-1.6	-1.9	-1.8	-2.9	-3.7	-4.5	-3.8	-3.2	-3.8	-4.9	-7.5	-3.6	0.8		
12/49	2.3	2.1	1.9	1.9	1.8	1.2	1.1	-0.3	-0.3	-0.7	-1.1	-1.3	-1.1	-2.0	-2.7	-3.3	-2.6	-1.9	-2.2	-2.7	-4.2	-0.4	3.6	6.6	
12/50	2.0	1.8	1.5	1.5	1.4	0.9	0.7	-0.6	-0.6	-1.1	-1.4	-1.6	-1.5	-2.3	-3.0	-3.6	-2.9	-2.4	-2.7	-3.2	-4.5	-1.7	0.4	0.3	-5.7
12/51	1.7	1.5	1.3	1.2	1.1	0.6	0.4	-0.8	-0.9	-1.3	-1.6	-1.8	-1.8	-2.6	-3.2	-3.7	-3.1	-2.7	-3.0	-3.5	-4.6	-2.4	-1.0	-1.6	-5.4
12/52	1.7	1.5	1.3	1.3	1.2	0.7	0.5	-0.7	-0.7	-1.1	-1.4	-1.6	-1.5	-2.2	-2.7	-3.2	-2.7	-2.2	-2.4	-2.8	-3.6	-1.7	-0.4	-0.7	-2.9
12/53	1.7	1.5	1.3	1.3	1.2	0.7	0.6	-0.5	-0.5	-0.9	-1.2	-1.4	-1.3	-1.9	-2.4	-2.8	-2.2	-1.8	-1.9	-2.2	-2.9	-1.1	0.1	-0.0	-1.6
12/54	1.8	1.6	1.4	1.4	1.3	0.8	0.7	-0.4	-0.4	-0.7	-1.0	-1.1	-1.0	-1.6	-2.0	-2.4	-1.9	-1.4	-1.5	-1.7	-2.3	-0.6	0.5	0.4	-0.7
12/55	1.7	1.5	1.3	1.3	1.2	0.7	0.6	-0.4	-0.4	-0.8	-1.0	-1.1	-1.0	-1.6	-2.0	-2.3	-1.8	-1.4	-1.5	-1.6	-2.2	-0.6	0.3	0.2	-0.8
12/56	1.5	1.3	1.1	1.1	1.0	0.6	0.5	-0.5	-0.5	-0.9	-1.1	-1.2	-1.1	-1.7	-2.1	-2.4	-1.9	-1.5	-1.6	-1.8	-2.2	-0.9	-0.1	-0.2	-1.1
12/57	1.6	1.4	1.3	1.3	1.2	0.7	0.6	-0.3	-0.3	-0.6	-0.8	-1.0	-0.9	-1.4	-1.7	-2.0	-1.5	-1.1	-1.2	-1.3	-1.7	-0.4	0.4	0.3	-0.4
12/58	1.5	1.3	1.1	1.1	1.0	0.6	0.5	-0.4	-0.4	-0.7	-0.9	-1.1	-1.0	-1.4	-1.8	-2.0	-1.6	-1.2	-1.3	-1.4	-1.8	-0.6	0.1	-0.0	-0.7
12/59	1.4	1.2	1.0	1.0	0.9	0.5	0.4	-0.5	-0.5	-0.8	-1.0	-1.1	-1.0	-1.5	-1.8	-2.0	-1.6	-1.3	-1.3	-1.4	-1.8	-0.7	-0.1	-0.2	-0.8
12/60	1.6	1.5	1.3	1.3	1.2	0.8	0.7	-0.1	-0.1	-0.4	-0.5	-0.6	-0.5	-1.0	-1.2	-1.4	-1.0	-0.7	-0.7	-0.8	-1.0	0.0	0.7	0.7	0.1
12/61	1.6	1.5	1.3	1.3	1.2	0.9	0.7	-0.0	-0.1	-0.3	-0.5	-0.5	-0.4	-0.8	-1.1	-1.3	-0.9	-0.5	-0.6	-0.6	-0.9	0.1	0.7	0.7	0.3
12/62	1.7	1.5	1.4	1.4	1.3	1.0	0.9	0.1	0.1	-0.1	-0.3	-0.4	-0.3	-0.6	-0.9	-1.1	-0.6	-0.3	-0.3	-0.3	-0.6	0.4	1.0	1.0	0.6
12/63	1.6	1.5	1.4	1.3	1.3	0.9	0.8	0.1	0.1	-0.1	-0.3	-0.3	-0.2	-0.6	-0.8	-1.0	-0.6	-0.3	-0.3	-0.3	-0.5	0.4	0.9	0.9	0.5
12/64	1.7	1.5	1.4	1.4	1.3	1.0	0.9	0.2	0.2	-0.1	-0.2	-0.3	-0.2	-0.5	-0.7	-0.9	-0.5	-0.2	-0.2	-0.2	-0.4	0.5	1.0	1.0	0.6
12/65	1.6	1.5	1.3	1.3	1.2	0.9	0.8	0.1	0.1	-0.1	-0.2	-0.3	-0.2	-0.5	-0.7	-0.9	-0.5	-0.2	-0.2	-0.2	-0.4	0.4	0.9	0.9	0.6
12/66	1.6	1.5	1.3	1.3	1.2	0.9	0.8	0.2	0.2	-0.0	-0.2	-0.2	-0.1	-0.4	-0.6	-0.8	-0.4	-0.1	-0.1	-0.2	-0.3	0.5	0.9	0.9	0.6
12/67	1.5	1.4	1.2	1.2	1.2	0.9	0.8	0.1	0.1	-0.1	-0.2	-0.3	-0.2	-0.5	-0.7	-0.9	-0.5	-0.2	-0.2	-0.2	-0.4	0.3	0.8	0.8	0.5
12/68	1.4	1.3	1.2	1.1	1.1	0.8	0.7	0.0	0.0	-0.1	-0.3	-0.3	-0.2	-0.6	-0.7	-0.9	-0.5	-0.2	-0.3	-0.3	-0.5	0.2	0.6	0.6	0.3
12/69	1.2	1.1	1.0	0.9	0.9	0.6	0.5	-0.1	-0.1	-0.3	-0.5	-0.5	-0.5	-0.8	-0.9	-1.1	-0.8	-0.5	-0.5	-0.6	-0.7	-0.1	0.3	0.3	-0.0
12/70	1.4	1.2	1.1	1.1	1.0	0.8	0.7	0.1	0.1	-0.1	-0.2	-0.3	-0.2	-0.5	-0.7	-0.8	-0.5	-0.2	-0.2	-0.3	-0.4	0.2	0.6	0.6	0.3
12/71	1.5	1.3	1.2	1.2	1.1	0.9	0.8	0.2	0.2	0.0	-0.1	-0.1	-0.1	-0.3	-0.5	-0.6	-0.3	-0.1	-0.0	-0.1	-0.2	0.4	0.8	0.8	0.5
12/72	1.4	1.3	1.2	1.2	1.1	0.9	0.8	0.2	0.2	0.0	-0.1	-0.1	-0.0	-0.3	-0.4	-0.6	-0.3	-0.1	-0.0	-0.0	-0.2	0.4	0.8	0.8	0.5
12/73	1.3	1.2	1.1	1.1	1.0	0.7	0.7	0.1	0.1	-0.1	-0.2	-0.2	-0.2	-0.4	-0.6	-0.7	-0.4	-0.2	-0.2	-0.2	-0.3	0.3	0.6	0.6	0.3
12/74	1.1	1.0	0.9	0.9	0.8	0.6	0.5	-0.1	-0.1	-0.2	-0.3	-0.4	-0.3	-0.6	-0.7	-0.9	-0.6	-0.4	-0.4	-0.4	-0.5	0.0	0.3	0.3	0.1
12/75	1.1	1.0	0.9	0.9	0.8	0.5	0.5	-0.1	-0.1	-0.2	-0.3	-0.4	-0.3	-0.6	-0.7	-0.8	-0.6	-0.4	-0.4	-0.4	-0.5	0.0	0.3	0.3	0.1
12/76	1.2	1.1	1.0	1.0	0.9	0.7	0.6	0.1	0.1	-0.1	-0.2	-0.2	-0.1	-0.4	-0.5	-0.6	-0.3	-0.1	-0.1	-0.1	-0.3	0.3	0.6	0.5	0.3

Table XLI

Time-Weighted Rates of Return* on Intermediate-Term U.S. Treasury Bonds and Notes:
  Interest Reinvested,
  Tax-Exempt,
  Deflated by the Consumer Price Index

	Purchased 12/50	12/51	12/52	12/53	12/54	Purchased 12/55	12/56	12/57	12/58	12/59	Purchased 12/60	12/61	12/62	12/63	12/64	Purchased 12/65	12/66	12/67	12/68	12/69	Purchased 12/70	12/71	12/72	12/73	12/74	12/75
1	−5.2																									
2	−1.5	2.3																								
3	−0.2	2.4	2.6																							
4	0.5	2.5	2.7	2.7																						
5	0.2	1.6	1.4	0.8	−1.0																					
6	−0.4	0.6	0.2	−0.5	−2.1	−3.2																				
7	0.3	1.3	1.1	0.8	0.1	0.7	4.7																			
8	−0.1	0.7	0.4	−0.0	−0.7	−0.6	0.8	−3.0																		
9	−0.3	0.4	0.1	−0.3	−0.9	−0.9	−0.1	−2.4	−1.9																	
0	0.7	1.4	1.3	1.1	0.9	1.3	2.4	1.7	4.1	10.3																
1	0.8	1.4	1.3	1.2	1.0	1.3	2.2	1.6	3.2	5.9	1.5															
2	1.1	1.7	1.6	1.5	1.4	1.7	2.6	2.2	3.5	5.4	2.9	4.4														
3	1.0	1.6	1.5	1.4	1.2	1.5	2.2	1.8	2.8	4.0	2.0	2.2	0.0													
4	1.1	1.6	1.6	1.5	1.3	1.6	2.2	1.9	2.7	3.6	2.0	2.2	1.1	2.2												
5	1.0	1.4	1.4	1.3	1.2	1.4	1.9	1.5	2.2	2.9	1.5	1.5	0.5	0.8	−0.7											
6	1.0	1.4	1.4	1.3	1.2	1.4	1.8	1.5	2.1	2.7	1.4	1.4	0.7	0.9	0.3	1.3										
7	0.8	1.2	1.1	1.0	0.9	1.1	1.5	1.2	1.6	2.1	1.0	0.9	0.2	0.2	−0.5	−0.4	−2.0									
8	0.7	1.0	0.9	0.8	0.7	0.8	1.2	0.9	1.3	1.6	0.6	0.4	−0.2	−0.3	−0.9	−0.9	−2.0	−2.1								
9	0.3	0.6	0.5	0.3	0.2	0.3	0.5	0.2	0.5	0.8	−0.3	−0.5	−1.2	−1.4	−2.1	−2.4	−3.6	−4.4	−6.7							
0	0.6	1.0	0.9	0.8	0.7	0.8	1.1	0.8	1.1	1.4	0.5	0.4	−0.1	−0.1	−0.4	−0.4	−0.8	−0.4	0.4	8.0						
1	0.9	1.2	1.1	1.0	0.9	1.0	1.3	1.1	1.4	1.7	1.0	0.9	0.5	0.6	0.3	0.5	0.4	1.0	2.0	6.6	5.2					
2	0.8	1.1	1.1	1.0	0.9	1.0	1.3	1.1	1.4	1.6	0.9	0.9	0.5	0.6	0.4	0.5	0.4	0.9	1.6	4.5	2.8	0.5				
3	0.6	0.9	0.8	0.7	0.6	0.7	1.0	0.7	1.0	1.2	0.5	0.4	0.1	0.1	−0.1	−0.1	−0.3	0.0	0.4	2.3	0.4	−1.8	−4.1			
4	0.3	0.6	0.5	0.4	0.3	0.3	0.5	0.3	0.5	0.7	0.0	−0.1	−0.5	−0.5	−0.8	−0.8	−1.1	−0.9	−0.8	0.5	−1.3	−3.4	−5.3	−6.5		
5	0.3	0.5	0.4	0.4	0.2	0.3	0.5	0.3	0.5	0.6	−0.0	−0.1	−0.5	−0.5	−0.7	−0.8	−1.0	−0.9	−0.7	0.4	−1.1	−2.6	−3.6	−3.4	−0.2	
6	0.6	0.8	0.7	0.7	0.6	0.6	0.8	0.6	0.9	1.0	0.5	0.4	0.1	0.1	−0.1	−0.0	−0.1	0.1	0.3	1.4	0.3	−0.6	−0.9	0.2	3.7	7.8

Percent per annum, compounded annually.

Sources: Bond market data—Lawrence Fisher (compiler), CRSP
  Monthly Return File for U.S. Treasury Securities (mag-
  netic tape). See Appendix A.
  Consumer Price Index—U.S. Bureau of Labor Statistics.

Held Until	Purchased 12/25	12/26	12/27	12/28	12/29	Purchased 12/30	12/31	12/32	12/33	12/34	Purchased 12/35	12/36	12/37	12/38	12/39	Purchased 12/40	12/41	12/42	12/43	12/44	Purchased 12/45	12/46	12/47	12/48	12/49
12/26	5.5																								
12/27	5.1	4.6																							
12/28	3.6	2.6	0.6																						
12/29	3.7	3.2	2.4	4.3																					
12/30	4.2	3.9	3.7	5.2	6.2																				
12/31	2.5	1.9	1.2	1.4	−0.0	−5.8																			
12/32	4.0	3.8	3.6	4.3	4.4	3.5	13.7																		
12/33	3.6	3.3	3.1	3.6	3.4	2.5	6.9	0.6																	
12/34	4.2	4.0	3.9	4.5	4.5	4.1	7.6	4.7	9.0																
12/35	4.4	4.3	4.3	4.8	4.9	4.7	7.5	5.5	8.0	7.0															
12/36	4.3	4.2	4.2	4.6	4.6	4.4	6.6	4.9	6.3	5.0	3.1														
12/37	4.0	3.8	3.7	4.1	4.1	3.8	5.4	3.9	4.7	3.3	1.5	0.0													
12/38	4.1	4.0	4.0	4.3	4.3	4.1	5.6	4.3	5.0	4.0	3.1	3.1	6.2												
12/39	4.1	4.0	4.0	4.3	4.3	4.1	5.4	4.3	4.9	4.1	3.4	3.5	5.2	4.3											
12/40	4.2	4.1	4.0	4.3	4.3	4.1	5.3	4.3	4.8	4.1	3.6	3.7	5.0	4.3	4.4										
12/41	3.8	3.7	3.7	3.9	3.9	3.7	4.7	3.7	4.1	3.4	2.9	2.8	3.5	2.6	1.8	−0.7									
12/42	3.7	3.6	3.5	3.7	3.7	3.5	4.4	3.5	3.8	3.2	2.6	2.6	3.1	2.3	1.7	0.3	1.3								
12/43	3.6	3.5	3.4	3.6	3.6	3.4	4.2	3.4	3.7	3.1	2.6	2.5	3.0	2.3	1.9	1.0	1.9	2.5							
12/44	3.5	3.4	3.4	3.5	3.5	3.3	4.0	3.3	3.5	3.0	2.6	2.5	2.8	2.3	1.9	1.3	2.0	2.3	2.1						
12/45	3.6	3.5	3.5	3.7	3.6	3.4	4.1	3.4	3.7	3.2	2.8	2.8	3.2	2.7	2.5	2.1	2.8	3.3	3.8	5.4					
12/46	3.5	3.4	3.3	3.5	3.4	3.3	3.9	3.2	3.4	3.0	2.6	2.6	2.9	2.5	2.2	1.8	2.4	2.6	2.7	3.0	0.5				
12/47	3.3	3.2	3.2	3.3	3.2	3.1	3.7	3.0	3.2	2.8	2.4	2.4	2.6	2.2	2.0	1.6	2.0	2.1	2.1	2.0	0.4	0.2			
12/48	3.3	3.2	3.2	3.3	3.2	3.1	3.6	3.0	3.2	2.8	2.5	2.4	2.7	2.3	2.1	1.8	2.2	2.3	2.3	2.3	1.3	1.7	3.2		
12/49	3.4	3.3	3.2	3.3	3.3	3.1	3.7	3.1	3.3	2.9	2.6	2.6	2.8	2.5	2.3	2.1	2.4	2.6	2.6	2.7	2.0	2.6	3.7	4.3	
12/50	3.2	3.1	3.1	3.2	3.1	3.0	3.4	2.9	3.0	2.7	2.4	2.4	2.5	2.2	2.1	1.8	2.1	2.2	2.2	2.2	1.5	1.8	2.3	1.9	−0.5
12/51	3.1	3.0	2.9	3.0	3.0	2.8	3.3	2.7	2.9	2.5	2.2	2.2	2.3	2.1	1.9	1.6	1.9	1.9	1.9	1.9	1.3	1.4	1.7	1.2	−0.3
12/52	3.1	3.0	2.9	3.0	3.0	2.8	3.2	2.7	2.9	2.5	2.3	2.2	2.4	2.1	1.9	1.7	1.9	2.0	2.0	1.9	1.5	1.6	1.9	1.6	0.7
12/53	3.1	3.0	2.9	3.0	2.9	2.8	3.2	2.7	2.8	2.5	2.3	2.2	2.4	2.1	2.0	1.8	2.0	2.1	2.0	2.0	1.6	1.8	2.0	1.8	1.2
12/54	3.0	2.9	2.9	2.9	2.9	2.8	3.1	2.7	2.8	2.5	2.3	2.2	2.3	2.1	2.0	1.8	2.0	2.0	2.0	2.0	1.6	1.8	2.0	1.8	1.3
12/55	2.9	2.8	2.7	2.8	2.7	2.6	3.0	2.5	2.6	2.3	2.1	2.0	2.1	1.9	1.8	1.6	1.8	1.8	1.7	1.7	1.3	1.4	1.6	1.4	0.9
12/56	2.7	2.6	2.6	2.7	2.6	2.5	2.8	2.4	2.4	2.2	1.9	1.9	2.0	1.7	1.6	1.4	1.6	1.6	1.5	1.5	1.1	1.2	1.3	1.1	0.6
12/57	2.9	2.8	2.7	2.8	2.7	2.6	3.0	2.6	2.6	2.4	2.2	2.1	2.2	2.0	1.9	1.8	1.9	1.9	1.9	1.9	1.6	1.7	1.9	1.7	1.4
12/58	2.7	2.6	2.6	2.6	2.6	2.5	2.8	2.4	2.5	2.2	2.0	1.9	2.0	1.8	1.7	1.5	1.7	1.7	1.7	1.6	1.3	1.4	1.5	1.3	1.0
12/59	2.6	2.5	2.5	2.5	2.5	2.3	2.6	2.2	2.3	2.1	1.8	1.8	1.9	1.7	1.5	1.4	1.5	1.5	1.5	1.4	1.1	1.2	1.3	1.1	0.8
12/60	2.8	2.8	2.7	2.8	2.7	2.6	2.9	2.5	2.6	2.4	2.2	2.2	2.3	2.1	2.0	1.9	2.0	2.0	2.0	2.0	1.8	1.9	2.0	1.9	1.7
12/61	2.8	2.7	2.7	2.7	2.7	2.6	2.9	2.5	2.6	2.3	2.2	2.1	2.2	2.0	1.9	1.8	2.0	2.0	2.0	2.0	1.7	1.8	1.9	1.8	1.6
12/62	2.8	2.8	2.7	2.8	2.7	2.6	2.9	2.6	2.6	2.4	2.3	2.2	2.3	2.2	2.1	2.0	2.1	2.1	2.1	2.1	1.9	2.0	2.1	2.0	1.9
12/63	2.8	2.7	2.7	2.7	2.7	2.6	2.8	2.5	2.6	2.4	2.2	2.2	2.2	2.1	2.0	1.9	2.0	2.1	2.0	2.0	1.8	1.9	2.0	2.0	1.8
12/64	2.8	2.7	2.7	2.7	2.7	2.6	2.8	2.5	2.6	2.4	2.2	2.2	2.3	2.1	2.0	1.9	2.0	2.1	2.1	2.0	1.9	1.9	2.1	2.0	1.8
12/65	2.7	2.6	2.6	2.6	2.6	2.5	2.8	2.4	2.5	2.3	2.1	2.1	2.2	2.0	2.0	1.9	2.0	2.0	2.0	2.0	1.8	1.9	2.0	1.9	1.7
12/66	2.7	2.7	2.6	2.7	2.6	2.5	2.8	2.5	2.5	2.3	2.2	2.2	2.2	2.1	2.0	1.9	2.0	2.1	2.0	2.0	1.9	1.9	2.0	2.0	1.8
12/67	2.7	2.6	2.5	2.6	2.6	2.5	2.7	2.4	2.5	2.3	2.1	2.1	2.2	2.0	1.9	1.8	1.9	2.0	1.9	1.9	1.8	1.8	1.9	1.9	1.7
12/68	2.6	2.6	2.5	2.6	2.5	2.4	2.6	2.4	2.4	2.2	2.1	2.0	2.1	2.0	1.9	1.8	1.9	1.9	1.9	1.9	1.8	1.8	1.9	1.8	1.7
12/69	2.5	2.4	2.4	2.4	2.4	2.3	2.5	2.2	2.3	2.1	1.9	1.9	2.0	1.8	1.7	1.7	1.7	1.8	1.7	1.7	1.6	1.6	1.7	1.6	1.5
12/70	2.7	2.6	2.6	2.6	2.6	2.5	2.7	2.5	2.5	2.3	2.2	2.2	2.2	2.1	2.1	2.0	2.1	2.1	2.1	2.1	2.0	2.0	2.1	2.0	1.9
12/71	2.8	2.7	2.7	2.7	2.7	2.6	2.8	2.6	2.6	2.5	2.3	2.3	2.4	2.3	2.2	2.1	2.2	2.3	2.3	2.3	2.2	2.2	2.3	2.3	2.2
12/72	2.8	2.7	2.7	2.7	2.7	2.6	2.8	2.6	2.6	2.5	2.3	2.3	2.4	2.3	2.2	2.1	2.2	2.3	2.3	2.3	2.2	2.2	2.3	2.3	2.2
12/73	2.8	2.7	2.7	2.7	2.7	2.6	2.8	2.6	2.6	2.5	2.3	2.3	2.4	2.3	2.2	2.2	2.2	2.3	2.3	2.3	2.2	2.2	2.3	2.3	2.2
12/74	2.8	2.7	2.7	2.7	2.7	2.6	2.8	2.6	2.6	2.5	2.3	2.3	2.4	2.3	2.2	2.2	2.3	2.3	2.3	2.3	2.2	2.2	2.3	2.3	2.2
12/75	2.8	2.7	2.7	2.8	2.7	2.6	2.8	2.6	2.7	2.5	2.4	2.4	2.4	2.3	2.3	2.2	2.3	2.3	2.3	2.4	2.2	2.3	2.4	2.4	2.3
12/76	2.9	2.9	2.9	2.9	2.9	2.8	3.0	2.8	2.8	2.7	2.6	2.6	2.6	2.5	2.5	2.4	2.5	2.6	2.6	2.6	2.5	2.6	2.7	2.6	2.6

Table XLII

Time-Weighted Rates of Return* on Intermediate-Term U.S. Treasury Bonds and Notes:
Interest Reinvested,
Lower Tax Rate,
Current Dollars

Held until	Purchased 12/50	12/51	12/52	12/53	12/54	12/55	12/56	12/57	12/58	12/59	12/60	12/61	12/62	12/63	12/64	12/65	12/66	12/67	12/68	12/69	12/70	12/71	12/72	12/73	12/74	12/75
'51	−0.0																									
'52	1.3	2.6																								
'53	1.7	2.6	2.6																							
'54	1.7	2.3	2.2	1.8																						
'55	1.1	1.4	1.1	0.3	−1.2																					
'56	0.8	0.9	0.5	−0.2	−1.1	−1.0																				
'57	1.7	1.9	1.8	1.6	1.6	2.9	7.1																			
'58	1.2	1.4	1.2	0.9	0.7	1.3	2.5	−1.9																		
'59	0.9	1.1	0.8	0.5	0.3	0.7	1.2	−1.6	−1.2																	
'60	1.9	2.1	2.1	2.0	2.0	2.7	3.6	2.5	4.7	11.0																
'61	1.8	2.0	2.0	1.9	1.9	2.4	3.1	2.2	3.5	6.0	1.2															
'62	2.1	2.3	2.2	2.2	2.2	2.7	3.4	2.7	3.8	5.6	2.9	4.6														
'63	2.0	2.1	2.1	2.0	2.1	2.5	3.0	2.3	3.2	4.3	2.2	2.6	0.7													
'64	2.0	2.2	2.1	2.1	2.1	2.5	2.9	2.3	3.1	3.9	2.2	2.6	1.5	2.5												
'65	1.9	2.0	2.0	1.9	1.9	2.3	2.6	2.1	2.7	3.3	1.8	2.0	1.1	1.4	0.3											
'66	2.0	2.1	2.1	2.0	2.1	2.4	2.7	2.2	2.8	3.3	2.1	2.3	1.7	2.1	1.9	3.5										
'67	1.9	2.0	1.9	1.9	1.9	2.2	2.5	2.0	2.4	2.9	1.8	1.9	1.4	1.5	1.2	1.7	−0.1									
'68	1.8	1.9	1.9	1.8	1.8	2.1	2.3	1.9	2.3	2.7	1.7	1.8	1.3	1.4	1.2	1.5	0.5	1.0								
'69	1.6	1.7	1.6	1.5	1.5	1.7	1.9	1.5	1.8	2.1	1.2	1.2	0.7	0.7	0.4	0.4	−0.6	−0.9	−2.8							
'70	2.1	2.2	2.1	2.1	2.1	2.4	2.6	2.3	2.6	3.0	2.2	2.3	2.0	2.2	2.2	2.6	2.4	3.2	4.3	11.9						
'71	2.3	2.4	2.4	2.4	2.4	2.7	2.9	2.6	3.0	3.3	2.7	2.8	2.6	2.9	2.9	3.4	3.3	4.2	5.3	9.5	7.2					
'72	2.3	2.4	2.4	2.4	2.4	2.6	2.9	2.6	2.9	3.2	2.6	2.7	2.6	2.8	2.8	3.2	3.1	3.8	4.5	7.0	4.7	2.2				
'73	2.3	2.4	2.4	2.4	2.4	2.6	2.8	2.6	2.9	3.2	2.6	2.7	2.6	2.7	2.8	3.1	3.0	3.5	4.1	5.9	3.9	2.3	2.4			
'74	2.3	2.4	2.4	2.4	2.4	2.6	2.8	2.6	2.9	3.2	2.6	2.7	2.6	2.7	2.8	3.0	3.0	3.4	3.8	5.2	3.6	2.4	2.6	2.7		
'75	2.4	2.5	2.5	2.5	2.5	2.7	2.9	2.7	3.0	3.2	2.7	2.8	2.7	2.9	2.9	3.2	3.1	3.5	3.9	5.1	3.7	2.9	3.1	3.5	4.2	
'76	2.7	2.8	2.8	2.8	2.9	3.1	3.3	3.1	3.4	3.6	3.2	3.3	3.2	3.4	3.5	3.8	3.8	4.3	4.7	5.8	4.8	4.4	4.9	5.7	7.3	10.5

Percent per annum, compounded annually

Sources: Bond market data—Lawrence Fisher (compiler), CRSP Monthly Return File for U.S. Treasury Securities (magnetic tape). See Appendix A.
Income tax rates—Income levels estimated from U.S. Bureau of the Census, Current Population Reports, Series P-60, Nos. 101 and 103 and Historical Statistics of the United States. Tax rates were found in U.S. Internal Revenue Service, Statistics of Income and Your Federal Income Tax.

Held Until	Purchased					Purchased					Purchased					Purchased					Purchased				
	12/25	12/26	12/27	12/28	12/29	12/30	12/31	12/32	12/33	12/34	12/35	12/36	12/37	12/38	12/39	12/40	12/41	12/42	12/43	12/44	12/45	12/46	12/47	12/48	12/49
12/26	7.1																								
12/27	7.0	6.8																							
12/28	5.1	4.2	1.6																						
12/29	4.9	4.1	2.8	4.1																					
12/30	6.5	6.3	6.1	8.4	13.0																				
12/31	6.1	5.8	5.6	7.0	8.4	4.1																			
12/32	8.8	9.1	9.5	11.6	14.2	14.8	26.7																		
12/33	7.7	7.7	7.9	9.2	10.5	9.7	12.6	0.1																	
12/34	7.6	7.6	7.7	8.8	9.8	9.0	10.7	3.4	6.8																
12/35	7.2	7.2	7.3	8.1	8.8	7.9	8.9	3.6	5.4	3.9															
12/36	6.7	6.7	6.6	7.3	7.7	6.9	7.5	3.1	4.2	2.9	1.8														
12/37	5.9	5.7	5.6	6.1	6.3	5.4	5.6	1.9	2.3	0.9	-0.6	-3.0													
12/38	6.1	6.0	6.0	6.4	6.7	5.9	6.2	3.1	3.7	2.9	2.6	3.0	9.3												
12/39	6.0	5.9	5.9	6.3	6.5	5.8	6.0	3.3	3.9	3.3	3.1	3.6	7.0	4.8											
12/40	5.8	5.7	5.7	6.0	6.2	5.5	5.7	3.3	3.8	3.3	3.2	3.5	5.8	4.1	3.4										
12/41	4.8	4.7	4.5	4.7	4.8	4.1	4.1	1.8	2.0	1.4	1.0	0.8	1.7	-0.6	-3.2	-9.5									
12/42	4.1	3.9	3.7	3.8	3.8	3.1	3.0	0.9	1.0	0.2	-0.3	-0.6	-0.1	-2.4	-4.6	-8.4	-7.3								
12/43	3.8	3.6	3.4	3.5	3.5	2.8	2.7	0.7	0.8	0.1	-0.3	-0.6	-0.2	-2.0	-3.6	-5.9	-4.0	-0.7							
12/44	3.6	3.4	3.2	3.3	3.2	2.6	2.5	0.7	0.7	0.1	-0.3	-0.5	-0.2	-1.7	-2.9	-4.5	-2.7	-0.3	-0.0						
12/45	3.6	3.4	3.2	3.3	3.2	2.6	2.5	0.9	0.9	0.4	0.1	-0.1	0.2	-1.0	-1.9	-3.0	-1.3	0.8	1.6	3.1					
12/46	2.6	2.4	2.1	2.2	2.1	1.4	1.2	-0.4	-0.4	-1.0	-1.4	-1.7	-1.6	-2.9	-3.9	-5.1	-4.2	-3.4	-4.3	-6.3	-14.9				
12/47	2.1	1.9	1.6	1.6	1.5	0.8	0.6	-0.9	-1.0	-1.5	-2.0	-2.3	-2.3	-3.5	-4.4	-5.5	-4.8	-4.3	-5.2	-6.9	-11.6	-8.1			
12/48	2.0	1.8	1.6	1.6	1.4	0.8	0.6	-0.8	-0.9	-1.4	-1.8	-2.1	-2.0	-3.1	-3.9	-4.8	-4.1	-3.6	-4.1	-5.1	-7.7	-3.9	0.4		
12/49	2.2	2.0	1.8	1.8	1.7	1.1	0.9	-0.4	-0.4	-0.9	-1.2	-1.5	-1.4	-2.3	-2.9	-3.6	-2.9	-2.2	-2.5	-3.0	-4.4	-0.6	3.3	6.3	
12/50	1.8	1.6	1.4	1.4	1.3	0.7	0.6	-0.7	-0.8	-1.2	-1.6	-1.8	-1.7	-2.6	-3.2	-3.9	-3.2	-2.7	-3.0	-3.5	-4.7	-2.0	0.1	-0.0	-5.9
12/51	1.6	1.3	1.1	1.1	1.0	0.4	0.2	-1.0	-1.1	-1.5	-1.8	-2.1	-2.0	-2.8	-3.4	-4.0	-3.5	-3.0	-3.3	-3.8	-4.9	-2.7	-1.3	-1.9	-5.8
12/52	1.6	1.3	1.1	1.1	1.0	0.5	0.3	-0.9	-0.9	-1.3	-1.6	-1.8	-1.8	-2.5	-3.0	-3.6	-3.0	-2.6	-2.8	-3.1	-4.0	-2.0	-0.7	-1.0	-3.3
12/53	1.6	1.4	1.2	1.2	1.0	0.5	0.4	-0.7	-0.8	-1.1	-1.4	-1.6	-1.5	-2.2	-2.7	-3.1	-2.6	-2.1	-2.3	-2.5	-3.2	-1.4	-0.3	-0.4	-2.0
12/54	1.6	1.4	1.2	1.2	1.1	0.6	0.5	-0.6	-0.6	-1.0	-1.2	-1.4	-1.3	-1.9	-2.4	-2.8	-2.2	-1.8	-1.9	-2.1	-2.6	-1.0	0.1	0.0	-1.2
12/55	1.5	1.3	1.1	1.1	1.0	0.5	0.4	-0.6	-0.7	-1.0	-1.2	-1.4	-1.3	-1.9	-2.3	-2.7	-2.2	-1.8	-1.9	-2.0	-2.5	-1.0	-0.1	-0.2	-1.2
12/56	1.3	1.1	0.9	0.9	0.8	0.4	0.2	-0.8	-0.8	-1.1	-1.4	-1.5	-1.4	-2.0	-2.4	-2.7	-2.3	-1.9	-2.0	-2.2	-2.6	-1.3	-0.5	-0.7	-1.6
12/57	1.4	1.2	1.0	1.0	0.9	0.5	0.4	-0.6	-0.6	-0.9	-1.1	-1.3	-1.2	-1.7	-2.1	-2.4	-1.9	-1.5	-1.6	-1.7	-2.1	-0.9	-0.1	-0.2	-0.9
12/58	1.2	1.1	0.9	0.9	0.8	0.3	0.2	-0.7	-0.7	-1.0	-1.2	-1.4	-1.3	-1.8	-2.1	-2.4	-2.0	-1.7	-1.7	-1.8	-2.2	-1.1	-0.4	-0.5	-1.2
12/59	1.1	0.9	0.8	0.7	0.6	0.2	0.1	-0.8	-0.8	-1.1	-1.3	-1.4	-1.4	-1.8	-2.2	-2.4	-2.0	-1.7	-1.8	-1.9	-2.3	-1.2	-0.6	-0.7	-1.4
12/60	1.4	1.2	1.0	1.0	0.9	0.5	0.4	-0.4	-0.4	-0.7	-0.9	-1.0	-0.9	-1.4	-1.6	-1.9	-1.5	-1.1	-1.2	-1.2	-1.5	-0.5	0.1	0.1	-0.4
12/61	1.3	1.2	1.0	1.0	0.9	0.5	0.4	-0.4	-0.4	-0.7	-0.8	-0.9	-0.9	-1.3	-1.5	-1.8	-1.4	-1.0	-1.1	-1.1	-1.4	-0.4	0.2	0.1	-0.4
12/62	1.4	1.2	1.1	1.1	1.0	0.6	0.5	-0.3	-0.3	-0.5	-0.7	-0.8	-0.7	-1.1	-1.3	-1.5	-1.1	-0.8	-0.8	-0.9	-1.1	-0.2	0.4	0.4	-0.1
12/63	1.3	1.2	1.0	1.0	0.9	0.6	0.5	-0.3	-0.3	-0.5	-0.7	-0.8	-0.7	-1.1	-1.3	-1.5	-1.1	-0.8	-0.8	-0.9	-1.1	-0.2	0.3	0.3	-0.1
12/64	1.3	1.2	1.0	1.0	0.9	0.6	0.5	-0.2	-0.3	-0.5	-0.6	-0.7	-0.6	-1.0	-1.2	-1.4	-1.0	-0.7	-0.7	-0.8	-1.0	-0.1	0.3	0.3	-0.1
12/65	1.2	1.1	1.0	0.9	0.9	0.5	0.4	-0.3	-0.3	-0.5	-0.7	-0.7	-0.7	-1.0	-1.2	-1.4	-1.1	-0.8	-0.8	-0.8	-1.0	-0.2	0.2	0.2	-0.1
12/66	1.2	1.1	0.9	0.9	0.8	0.5	0.4	-0.3	-0.3	-0.5	-0.6	-0.7	-0.6	-1.0	-1.2	-1.4	-1.0	-0.7	-0.7	-0.8	-1.0	-0.2	0.2	0.2	-0.1
12/67	1.1	1.0	0.8	0.8	0.7	0.4	0.3	-0.4	-0.4	-0.6	-0.7	-0.8	-0.7	-1.0	-1.2	-1.4	-1.1	-0.8	-0.8	-0.9	-1.1	-0.3	0.1	0.0	-0.3
12/68	1.0	0.9	0.7	0.7	0.6	0.3	0.2	-0.4	-0.5	-0.7	-0.8	-0.9	-0.8	-1.1	-1.3	-1.5	-1.2	-0.9	-1.0	-1.0	-1.2	-0.5	-0.1	-0.1	-0.5
12/69	0.8	0.6	0.5	0.5	0.4	0.1	-0.0	-0.7	-0.7	-0.9	-1.0	-1.1	-1.1	-1.4	-1.6	-1.7	-1.4	-1.2	-1.2	-1.3	-1.5	-0.8	-0.5	-0.5	-0.9
12/70	0.9	0.8	0.6	0.6	0.5	0.2	0.1	-0.5	-0.5	-0.7	-0.8	-0.9	-0.8	-1.1	-1.3	-1.5	-1.2	-1.0	-1.0	-1.0	-1.2	-0.6	-0.2	-0.3	-0.6
12/71	1.0	0.8	0.7	0.7	0.6	0.3	0.2	-0.4	-0.4	-0.6	-0.7	-0.8	-0.7	-1.0	-1.2	-1.3	-1.0	-0.8	-0.8	-0.9	-1.0	-0.4	-0.1	-0.1	-0.4
12/72	0.9	0.8	0.7	0.6	0.5	0.3	0.2	-0.4	-0.4	-0.6	-0.7	-0.8	-0.7	-1.0	-1.2	-1.3	-1.0	-0.8	-0.8	-0.9	-1.0	-0.4	-0.1	-0.1	-0.4
12/73	0.8	0.6	0.5	0.5	0.4	0.1	0.0	-0.5	-0.6	-0.7	-0.9	-0.9	-0.9	-1.2	-1.3	-1.5	-1.2	-1.0	-1.0	-1.0	-1.2	-0.6	-0.3	-0.4	-0.6
12/74	0.6	0.4	0.3	0.3	0.2	-0.1	-0.2	-0.7	-0.8	-0.9	-1.1	-1.1	-1.1	-1.4	-1.5	-1.7	-1.4	-1.2	-1.3	-1.3	-1.4	-0.9	-0.7	-0.7	-1.0
12/75	0.5	0.4	0.2	0.2	0.1	-0.1	-0.2	-0.8	-0.8	-1.0	-1.1	-1.2	-1.1	-1.4	-1.6	-1.7	-1.5	-1.3	-1.3	-1.3	-1.5	-1.0	-0.7	-0.8	-1.0
12/76	0.6	0.5	0.3	0.3	0.2	-0.0	-0.1	-0.6	-0.7	-0.8	-0.9	-1.0	-1.0	-1.2	-1.4	-1.5	-1.3	-1.1	-1.1	-1.1	-1.3	-0.8	-0.5	-0.6	-0.8

Table XLIII

Time-Weighted Rates of Return* on Intermediate-Term U.S. Treasury Bonds and Notes:
   Interest Reinvested,
   Lower Tax Rate,
   Deflated by the Consumer Price Index

	12/50	12/51	12/52	12/53	12/54	12/55	12/56	12/57	12/58	12/59	12/60	12/61	12/62	12/63	12/64	12/65	12/66	12/67	12/68	12/69	12/70	12/71	12/72	12/73	12/74	12/75
51	−5.6																									
52	−2.0	1.7																								
53	−0.7	1.9	2.0																							
54	0.0	2.0	2.1	2.3																						
55	−0.3	1.1	0.9	0.4	−1.5																					
56	−0.9	0.1	−0.3	−1.0	−2.7	−3.8																				
57	−0.2	0.7	0.5	0.2	−0.5	0.0	3.9																			
58	−0.6	0.1	−0.2	−0.6	−1.3	−1.2	0.1	−3.6																		
59	−0.9	−0.2	−0.5	−0.9	−1.6	−1.6	−0.8	−3.1	−2.7																	
60	0.1	0.8	0.7	0.5	0.2	0.5	1.6	0.9	3.2	9.4																
61	0.2	0.8	0.7	0.5	0.2	0.5	1.4	0.8	2.3	4.9	0.6															
62	0.4	1.0	0.9	0.8	0.6	0.9	1.7	1.3	2.6	4.4	1.9	3.3														
63	0.3	0.8	0.7	0.6	0.4	0.7	1.3	0.9	1.8	3.0	1.0	1.2	−1.0													
64	0.4	0.9	0.8	0.7	0.5	0.8	1.3	1.0	1.7	2.7	1.0	1.2	0.1	1.2												
65	0.3	0.7	0.6	0.5	0.3	0.5	1.0	0.6	1.3	1.9	0.5	0.5	−0.4	−0.2	−1.6											
66	0.2	0.6	0.6	0.5	0.3	0.5	0.9	0.6	1.1	1.7	0.4	0.4	−0.3	−0.1	−0.7	0.2										
67	0.1	0.4	0.3	0.2	0.1	0.2	0.6	0.2	0.7	1.1	−0.1	−0.2	−0.8	−0.8	−1.5	−1.4	−3.0									
68	−0.2	0.2	0.1	−0.0	−0.2	−0.1	0.2	−0.1	0.2	0.6	−0.5	−0.7	−1.3	−1.4	−2.0	−2.2	−3.3	−3.6								
69	−0.6	−0.3	−0.4	−0.6	−0.8	−0.7	−0.5	−0.8	−0.6	−0.4	−1.4	−1.7	−2.3	−2.6	−3.3	−3.7	−5.0	−6.0	−8.4							
70	−0.3	0.0	−0.1	−0.2	−0.4	−0.3	−0.0	−0.3	−0.0	0.2	−0.7	−0.8	−1.3	−1.4	−1.8	−1.9	−2.4	−2.1	−1.4	6.1						
71	−0.1	0.2	0.1	0.0	−0.1	−0.0	0.2	−0.0	0.2	0.5	−0.3	−0.4	−0.8	−0.8	−1.0	−0.9	−1.2	−0.7	0.3	4.9	3.7					
72	−0.1	0.1	0.0	−0.1	−0.2	−0.1	0.1	−0.1	0.1	0.4	−0.4	−0.5	−0.8	−0.8	−1.1	−1.0	−1.2	−0.8	−0.1	2.8	1.2	−1.2				
73	−0.4	−0.2	−0.2	−0.4	−0.5	−0.4	−0.2	−0.5	−0.3	−0.1	−0.8	−0.9	−1.3	−1.3	−1.6	−1.6	−1.9	−1.7	−1.3	0.6	−1.2	−3.6	−5.9			
74	−0.7	−0.5	−0.6	−0.8	−0.9	−0.9	−0.7	−1.0	−0.8	−0.7	−1.4	−1.5	−1.9	−2.0	−2.3	−2.4	−2.7	−2.7	−2.5	−1.3	−3.1	−5.2	−7.2	−8.5		
75	−0.8	−0.6	−0.7	−0.8	−1.0	−1.0	−0.8	−1.1	−0.9	−0.8	−1.5	−1.6	−2.0	−2.0	−2.3	−2.4	−2.7	−2.7	−2.5	−1.5	−3.0	−4.6	−5.7	−5.6	−2.6	
76	−0.6	−0.4	−0.5	−0.6	−0.7	−0.7	−0.5	−0.7	−0.6	−0.4	−1.0	−1.1	−1.5	−1.5	−1.7	−1.7	−1.9	−1.8	−1.6	−0.6	−1.6	−2.7	−3.0	−2.1	1.3	5.4

*Percent per annum, compounded annually.

Sources: Bond market data—Lawrence Fisher (compiler), CRSP Monthly Return File for U.S. Treasury Securities (magnetic tape). See Appendix A.
Consumer Price Index—U.S. Bureau of Labor Statistics.
Income tax rates—Income levels estimated from U.S. Bureau of the Census, Current Population Reports, Series P-60, Nos. 101 and 103 and Historical Statistics of the United States. Tax rates were found in U.S. Internal Revenue Service, Statistics of Income and Your Federal Income Tax.

129

Held Until	Purchased					Purchased					Purchased					Purchased					Purchased				
	12/25	12/26	12/27	12/28	12/29	12/30	12/31	12/32	12/33	12/34	12/35	12/36	12/37	12/38	12/39	12/40	12/41	12/42	12/43	12/44	12/45	12/46	12/47	12/48	12/49
12/26	5.5																								
12/27	5.0	4.6																							
12/28	3.5	2.6	0.6																						
12/29	3.7	3.1	2.4	4.3																					
12/30	4.2	3.9	3.6	5.2	6.1																				
12/31	2.4	1.8	1.2	1.4	−0.0	−5.8																			
12/32	4.0	3.7	3.6	4.3	4.3	3.4	13.6																		
12/33	3.5	3.3	3.1	3.6	3.4	2.5	6.9	0.6																	
12/34	4.1	4.0	3.9	4.4	4.5	4.1	7.6	4.7	9.0																
12/35	4.4	4.3	4.2	4.8	4.9	4.6	7.4	5.4	7.9	6.9	2.9														
12/36	4.3	4.1	4.1	4.6	4.6	4.3	6.5	4.8	6.2	4.9	2.9														
12/37	3.9	3.7	3.7	4.0	4.0	3.7	5.4	3.8	4.6	3.2	1.4	−0.2													
12/38	4.1	3.9	3.9	4.2	4.2	4.0	5.5	4.2	4.9	3.9	2.9	2.9	6.1												
12/39	4.1	4.0	3.9	4.2	4.2	4.0	5.3	4.2	4.8	4.0	3.2	3.3	5.1	4.2											
12/40	4.1	4.0	3.9	4.2	4.2	4.0	5.2	4.2	4.7	4.0	3.4	3.6	4.8	4.2	4.3	−1.0									
12/41	3.8	3.6	3.6	3.8	3.8	3.6	4.6	3.6	4.0	3.3	2.7	2.6	3.4	2.5	1.6	−1.0									
12/42	3.6	3.5	3.4	3.6	3.5	3.3	4.2	3.3	3.6	3.0	2.4	2.3	2.8	2.0	1.3	−0.1	0.8								
12/43	3.5	3.4	3.3	3.5	3.4	3.2	4.0	3.2	3.4	2.8	2.4	2.3	2.7	2.0	1.5	0.6	1.3	1.9							
12/44	3.4	3.3	3.2	3.3	3.3	3.1	3.8	3.0	3.3	2.7	2.2	2.2	2.5	1.9	1.5	0.8	1.4	1.6	1.4						
12/45	3.4	3.3	3.3	3.4	3.4	3.2	3.9	3.2	3.4	2.9	2.5	2.5	2.8	2.3	2.0	1.6	2.2	2.7	3.1	4.8					
12/46	3.3	3.2	3.1	3.2	3.2	3.0	3.6	2.9	3.1	2.6	2.3	2.2	2.5	2.0	1.7	1.3	1.8	2.0	2.0	2.4	−0.0				
12/47	3.1	3.0	2.9	3.0	3.0	2.8	3.4	2.7	2.9	2.4	2.0	2.0	2.2	1.7	1.4	1.1	1.4	1.5	1.4	1.4	−0.2	−0.4			
12/48	3.1	3.0	2.9	3.0	3.0	2.8	3.3	2.7	2.8	2.4	2.1	2.0	2.2	1.8	1.6	1.3	1.6	1.7	1.7	1.7	0.7	1.1	2.7		
12/49	3.1	3.0	3.0	3.1	3.0	2.8	3.3	2.8	2.9	2.5	2.2	2.2	2.4	2.0	1.8	1.5	1.9	2.0	2.0	2.2	1.5	2.0	3.3	3.9	
12/50	3.0	2.9	2.8	2.9	2.8	2.7	3.1	2.6	2.7	2.3	2.0	1.9	2.1	1.8	1.6	1.3	1.6	1.6	1.6	1.7	1.0	1.3	1.9	1.5	−0.9
12/51	2.8	2.7	2.6	2.7	2.7	2.5	2.9	2.4	2.5	2.1	1.8	1.8	1.9	1.6	1.4	1.1	1.3	1.4	1.3	1.3	0.7	0.9	1.2	0.8	−0.8
12/52	2.8	2.7	2.6	2.7	2.6	2.5	2.9	2.4	2.5	2.1	1.8	1.8	1.9	1.6	1.4	1.2	1.4	1.4	1.4	1.4	0.9	1.0	1.3	1.0	0.1
12/53	2.7	2.6	2.6	2.6	2.6	2.4	2.8	2.3	2.4	2.1	1.8	1.8	1.9	1.6	1.4	1.2	1.4	1.4	1.4	1.4	1.0	1.1	1.4	1.1	0.5
12/54	2.7	2.6	2.5	2.6	2.5	2.4	2.7	2.3	2.4	2.0	1.8	1.7	1.8	1.6	1.4	1.2	1.4	1.4	1.4	1.4	1.0	1.1	1.3	1.1	0.6
12/55	2.5	2.4	2.3	2.4	2.3	2.2	2.5	2.1	2.1	1.8	1.6	1.5	1.6	1.4	1.2	1.0	1.1	1.1	1.1	1.1	0.7	0.8	0.9	0.7	0.1
12/56	2.4	2.3	2.2	2.2	2.2	2.0	2.3	1.9	2.0	1.6	1.4	1.3	1.4	1.2	1.0	0.8	0.9	0.9	0.8	0.8	0.4	0.5	0.6	0.3	−0.2
12/57	2.5	2.4	2.3	2.4	2.3	2.2	2.5	2.0	2.1	1.8	1.6	1.5	1.6	1.4	1.2	1.1	1.2	1.2	1.2	1.2	0.9	0.9	1.1	0.9	0.5
12/58	2.3	2.2	2.1	2.2	2.1	2.0	2.3	1.9	1.9	1.6	1.4	1.3	1.4	1.2	1.0	0.8	0.9	1.0	0.9	0.9	0.6	0.6	0.7	0.5	0.1
12/59	2.1	2.0	2.0	2.0	1.9	1.8	2.1	1.7	1.7	1.4	1.2	1.1	1.2	1.0	0.8	0.6	0.7	0.7	0.7	0.6	0.3	0.3	0.4	0.2	−0.2
12/60	2.3	2.3	2.2	2.2	2.2	2.0	2.3	1.9	2.0	1.7	1.5	1.5	1.5	1.3	1.2	1.1	1.2	1.2	1.1	1.1	0.9	1.0	1.1	0.9	0.7
12/61	2.3	2.2	2.1	2.2	2.1	2.0	2.2	1.9	1.9	1.7	1.5	1.4	1.5	1.3	1.2	1.0	1.1	1.1	1.1	1.1	0.8	0.9	1.0	0.9	0.6
12/62	2.3	2.2	2.2	2.2	2.1	2.0	2.3	1.9	2.0	1.7	1.5	1.5	1.6	1.4	1.3	1.1	1.2	1.2	1.2	1.2	1.0	1.0	1.1	1.0	0.8
12/63	2.2	2.1	2.1	2.1	2.1	1.9	2.2	1.8	1.9	1.6	1.5	1.4	1.5	1.3	1.2	1.0	1.1	1.1	1.1	1.1	0.9	0.9	1.0	0.9	0.7
12/64	2.2	2.1	2.0	2.1	2.0	1.9	2.2	1.8	1.9	1.6	1.4	1.4	1.5	1.3	1.2	1.0	1.1	1.1	1.1	1.1	0.9	0.9	1.0	0.9	0.7
12/65	2.1	2.0	2.0	2.0	1.9	1.8	2.1	1.7	1.8	1.5	1.4	1.3	1.4	1.2	1.1	1.0	1.0	1.0	1.0	1.0	0.8	0.8	0.9	0.8	0.6
12/66	2.1	2.0	2.0	2.0	1.9	1.8	2.1	1.7	1.8	1.5	1.4	1.3	1.4	1.2	1.1	1.0	1.1	1.1	1.0	1.0	0.9	0.9	1.0	0.9	0.7
12/67	2.0	1.9	1.9	1.9	1.8	1.7	1.9	1.6	1.7	1.4	1.3	1.2	1.3	1.1	1.0	0.9	1.0	1.0	0.9	0.9	0.7	0.8	0.8	0.7	0.6
12/68	1.9	1.9	1.8	1.8	1.8	1.7	1.9	1.6	1.6	1.4	1.2	1.2	1.2	1.0	0.9	0.8	0.9	0.9	0.9	0.8	0.7	0.7	0.8	0.7	0.5
12/69	1.8	1.7	1.6	1.7	1.6	1.5	1.7	1.4	1.4	1.2	1.0	1.0	1.0	0.8	0.7	0.6	0.7	0.7	0.6	0.6	0.4	0.4	0.5	0.4	0.2
12/70	1.9	1.9	1.8	1.8	1.8	1.7	1.9	1.6	1.6	1.4	1.3	1.2	1.2	1.1	1.0	0.9	1.0	1.0	0.9	0.9	0.8	0.8	0.8	0.8	0.6
12/71	2.0	1.9	1.9	1.9	1.9	1.7	1.9	1.7	1.7	1.5	1.4	1.3	1.4	1.2	1.1	1.0	1.1	1.1	1.1	1.1	0.9	1.0	1.0	0.9	0.8
12/72	2.0	1.9	1.8	1.9	1.8	1.7	1.9	1.6	1.7	1.5	1.3	1.3	1.3	1.2	1.1	1.0	1.1	1.1	1.0	1.0	0.9	0.9	1.0	0.9	0.8
12/73	1.9	1.9	1.8	1.8	1.8	1.7	1.9	1.6	1.6	1.4	1.3	1.3	1.3	1.2	1.1	1.0	1.0	1.0	1.0	1.0	0.9	0.9	1.0	0.9	0.8
12/74	1.9	1.8	1.8	1.8	1.7	1.6	1.8	1.6	1.6	1.4	1.3	1.2	1.3	1.1	1.0	0.9	1.0	1.0	1.0	1.0	0.8	0.9	0.9	0.9	0.7
12/75	1.9	1.8	1.8	1.8	1.7	1.6	1.8	1.6	1.6	1.4	1.3	1.2	1.3	1.1	1.1	1.0	1.0	1.0	1.0	1.0	0.9	0.9	1.0	0.9	0.8
12/76	2.0	1.9	1.9	1.9	1.9	1.8	2.0	1.7	1.7	1.6	1.4	1.4	1.4	1.3	1.2	1.2	1.2	1.2	1.2	1.2	1.1	1.1	1.2	1.1	1.0

Table XLIV

Time-Weighted Rates of Return* on Intermediate-Term U.S. Treasury Bonds and Notes:
    Interest Reinvested,
    Higher Tax Rate,
    Current Dollars

Columns below are grouped under **Purchased** (purchase date). Rows are labelled by **Yield until** date.

Yield until	12/50	12/51	12/52	12/53	12/54	12/55	12/56	12/57	12/58	12/59	12/60	12/61	12/62	12/63	12/64	12/65	12/66	12/67	12/68	12/69	12/70	12/71	12/72	12/73	12/74	12/75
12/51	−0.7																									
12/52	0.5	1.7																								
12/53	0.9	1.7	1.7																							
12/54	0.9	1.5	1.3	1.0																						
12/55	0.3	0.6	0.2	−0.5	−2.0																					
12/56	−0.1	0.0	−0.4	−1.1	−2.1	−2.1																				
12/57	0.7	1.0	0.8	0.6	0.4	1.7	5.7																			
12/58	0.3	0.4	0.2	−0.1	−0.4	0.1	1.3	−2.9																		
12/59	−0.1	−0.0	−0.3	−0.6	−0.9	−0.6	−0.1	−2.9	−2.9																	
12/60	0.8	1.0	0.9	0.8	0.8	1.3	2.2	1.1	3.1	9.5																
12/61	0.7	0.9	0.8	0.7	0.6	1.1	1.8	0.8	2.1	4.6	−0.0															
12/62	1.0	1.1	1.0	1.0	1.0	1.4	2.0	1.3	2.4	4.2	1.6	3.3														
12/63	0.8	1.0	0.9	0.8	0.8	1.1	1.6	0.9	1.7	2.9	0.8	1.3	−0.8													
12/64	0.8	1.0	0.9	0.8	0.8	1.1	1.6	1.0	1.6	2.6	0.9	1.2	0.2	1.1												
12/65	0.7	0.8	0.8	0.7	0.6	0.9	1.3	0.7	1.3	2.0	0.5	0.7	−0.2	0.1	−1.0											
12/66	0.8	0.9	0.8	0.8	0.7	1.0	1.3	0.8	1.3	1.9	0.7	0.9	0.3	0.6	0.4	1.9										
12/67	0.6	0.7	0.7	0.6	0.6	0.8	1.0	0.6	1.0	1.5	0.4	0.5	−0.1	0.1	−0.3	0.1	−1.7									
12/68	0.6	0.6	0.6	0.5	0.5	0.7	0.9	0.5	0.8	1.2	0.2	0.3	−0.2	−0.1	−0.4	−0.2	−1.3	−0.8								
12/69	0.3	0.3	0.2	0.1	0.1	0.2	0.4	−0.0	0.2	0.6	−0.4	−0.4	−0.9	−1.0	−1.4	−1.5	−2.6	−3.0	−5.1							
12/70	0.7	0.8	0.7	0.6	0.6	0.8	1.0	0.7	1.0	1.3	0.5	0.6	0.3	0.4	0.3	0.6	0.3	0.9	1.8	9.3						
12/71	0.9	1.0	0.9	0.9	0.9	1.1	1.3	1.0	1.3	1.6	1.0	1.0	0.8	1.0	1.0	1.3	1.2	1.9	2.9	7.1	5.1					
12/72	0.9	0.9	0.9	0.9	0.8	1.0	1.2	0.9	1.2	1.5	0.9	1.0	0.7	0.9	0.9	1.2	1.0	1.6	2.2	4.8	2.6	0.3				
12/73	0.8	0.9	0.9	0.8	0.8	1.0	1.2	0.9	1.1	1.4	0.8	0.9	0.7	0.8	0.8	1.0	0.9	1.4	1.8	3.6	1.8	0.2	0.2			
12/74	0.8	0.9	0.8	0.8	0.8	0.9	1.1	0.8	1.1	1.3	0.8	0.8	0.6	0.8	0.7	0.9	0.8	1.2	1.5	2.9	1.4	0.2	0.1	0.1		
12/75	0.8	0.9	0.9	0.8	0.8	1.0	1.1	0.9	1.1	1.4	0.9	0.9	0.7	0.9	0.8	1.0	0.9	1.3	1.6	2.7	1.5	0.6	0.7	1.0	1.9	
12/76	1.1	1.2	1.2	1.1	1.1	1.3	1.5	1.3	1.5	1.8	1.3	1.4	1.2	1.4	1.4	1.6	1.6	2.0	2.4	3.5	2.6	2.1	2.5	3.3	4.9	8.0

Percent per annum, compounded annually

Sources: Bond market data—*Lawrence Fisher (compiler)*, CRSP Monthly Return File for U.S. Treasury Securities *(magnetic tape)*. See Appendix A.
Income tax rates—Income levels estimated from *U.S. Bureau of the Census*, Current Population Reports, *Series P-60, Nos. 101 and 103 and* Historical Statistics of the United States. *Tax rates were found in U.S. Internal Revenue Service*, Statistics of Income *and* Your Federal Income Tax.

Held Until	12/25	12/26	12/27	12/28	12/29	12/30	12/31	12/32	12/33	12/34	12/35	12/36	12/37	12/38	12/39	12/40	12/41	12/42	12/43	12/44	12/45	12/46	12/47	12/48	12/49
12/26	7.1																								
12/27	6.9	6.8																							
12/28	5.1	4.1	1.6																						
12/29	4.8	4.1	2.8	4.1																					
12/30	6.4	6.2	6.1	8.4	12.9																				
12/31	6.0	5.8	5.6	7.0	8.4	4.1																			
12/32	8.8	9.0	9.5	11.6	14.2	14.8	26.7																		
12/33	7.6	7.7	7.9	9.2	10.5	9.7	12.6	0.1																	
12/34	7.5	7.6	7.7	8.8	9.7	9.0	10.6	3.4	6.8																
12/35	7.2	7.2	7.2	8.0	8.7	7.9	8.9	3.5	5.3	3.8															
12/36	6.6	6.6	6.6	7.2	7.7	6.8	7.4	3.1	4.1	2.7	1.7														
12/37	5.8	5.7	5.6	6.0	6.3	5.4	5.6	1.8	2.2	0.7	-0.8	-3.2													
12/38	6.0	6.0	5.9	6.3	6.6	5.8	6.1	3.0	3.6	2.8	2.4	2.8	9.1												
12/39	5.9	5.9	5.8	6.2	6.4	5.7	5.9	3.2	3.7	3.1	3.0	3.4	6.9	4.7											
12/40	5.8	5.7	5.6	5.9	6.1	5.4	5.6	3.2	3.7	3.2	3.0	3.4	5.7	4.0	3.3										
12/41	4.7	4.6	4.4	4.6	4.7	4.0	3.9	1.7	1.9	1.2	0.8	0.6	1.6	-0.8	-3.4	-9.7									
12/42	3.9	3.8	3.6	3.7	3.7	2.9	2.8	0.7	0.8	0.0	-0.5	-0.8	-0.4	-2.6	-4.9	-8.8	-7.8								
12/43	3.6	3.5	3.2	3.4	3.3	2.6	2.5	0.5	0.6	-0.1	-0.6	-0.9	-0.5	-2.3	-4.0	-6.3	-4.6	-1.2							
12/44	3.4	3.2	3.0	3.1	3.0	2.4	2.2	0.4	0.5	-0.2	-0.6	-0.9	-0.5	-2.1	-3.4	-4.9	-3.3	-1.0	-0.7						
12/45	3.4	3.2	3.0	3.1	3.0	2.4	2.3	0.6	0.6	0.1	-0.3	-0.5	-0.2	-1.4	-2.4	-3.5	-1.9	0.2	0.9	2.5					
12/46	2.4	2.2	1.9	1.9	1.8	1.2	1.0	-0.7	-0.7	-1.3	-1.8	-2.1	-2.0	-3.3	-4.4	-5.6	-4.7	-4.0	-4.9	-6.9	-15.4				
12/47	1.9	1.6	1.4	1.4	1.2	0.6	0.3	-1.2	-1.3	-1.9	-2.4	-2.7	-2.7	-3.9	-4.9	-6.0	-5.4	-4.9	-5.8	-7.5	-12.1	-8.6			
12/48	1.8	1.5	1.3	1.3	1.1	0.5	0.3	-1.1	-1.2	-1.8	-2.2	-2.5	-2.4	-3.5	-4.4	-5.3	-4.7	-4.1	-4.7	-5.7	-8.2	-4.4	-0.0		
12/49	1.9	1.7	1.5	1.5	1.4	0.8	0.6	-0.7	-0.8	-1.3	-1.6	-1.9	-1.8	-2.7	-3.4	-4.1	-3.4	-2.8	-3.0	-3.5	-4.9	-1.1	2.9	5.8	
12/50	1.6	1.4	1.1	1.1	1.0	0.4	0.2	-1.1	-1.1	-1.6	-1.9	-2.2	-2.1	-3.0	-3.7	-4.3	-3.7	-3.2	-3.5	-4.0	-5.2	-2.5	-0.3	-0.4	-6.3
12/51	1.3	1.1	0.8	0.8	0.7	0.1	-0.1	-1.3	-1.4	-1.9	-2.2	-2.5	-2.4	-3.3	-3.9	-4.5	-4.0	-3.5	-3.8	-4.3	-5.4	-3.2	-1.8	-2.4	-6.2
12/52	1.3	1.1	0.8	0.8	0.7	0.1	-0.0	-1.2	-1.3	-1.7	-2.0	-2.3	-2.2	-3.0	-3.5	-4.1	-3.5	-3.1	-3.3	-3.6	-4.5	-2.5	-1.3	-1.6	-3.9
12/53	1.3	1.1	0.8	0.8	0.7	0.2	0.0	-1.1	-1.2	-1.6	-1.9	-2.1	-2.0	-2.7	-3.2	-3.7	-3.2	-2.7	-2.9	-3.1	-3.8	-2.0	-0.9	-1.1	-2.7
12/54	1.3	1.1	0.9	0.8	0.7	0.2	0.1	-1.0	-1.0	-1.4	-1.7	-1.9	-1.8	-2.4	-2.9	-3.3	-2.8	-2.4	-2.5	-2.7	-3.2	-1.6	-0.6	-0.6	-1.9
12/55	1.1	0.9	0.7	0.7	0.6	0.1	-0.0	-1.1	-1.1	-1.5	-1.7	-1.9	-1.8	-2.4	-2.9	-3.3	-2.8	-2.4	-2.5	-2.7	-3.2	-1.7	-0.8	-0.9	-2.0
12/56	0.9	0.7	0.5	0.5	0.4	-0.1	-0.2	-1.2	-1.3	-1.6	-1.9	-2.1	-2.0	-2.6	-3.0	-3.4	-2.9	-2.6	-2.7	-2.8	-3.3	-2.0	-1.2	-1.4	-2.4
12/57	1.0	0.8	0.6	0.6	0.5	0.0	-0.1	-1.1	-1.1	-1.4	-1.7	-1.8	-1.8	-2.3	-2.7	-3.0	-2.6	-2.2	-2.3	-2.4	-2.8	-1.6	-0.9	-1.0	-1.8
12/58	0.8	0.6	0.4	0.4	0.3	-0.1	-0.3	-1.2	-1.3	-1.6	-1.8	-2.0	-1.9	-2.4	-2.8	-3.1	-2.7	-2.4	-2.5	-2.6	-3.0	-1.9	-1.2	-1.3	-2.1
12/59	0.7	0.5	0.3	0.3	0.1	-0.3	-0.4	-1.3	-1.4	-1.7	-1.9	-2.1	-2.0	-2.5	-2.9	-3.2	-2.8	-2.5	-2.6	-2.7	-3.1	-2.0	-1.5	-1.6	-2.3
12/60	0.9	0.7	0.5	0.5	0.4	-0.0	-0.2	-1.0	-1.1	-1.3	-1.5	-1.7	-1.6	-2.1	-2.4	-2.7	-2.3	-2.0	-2.0	-2.1	-2.4	-1.4	-0.8	-0.8	-1.4
12/61	0.8	0.7	0.5	0.4	0.3	-0.0	-0.2	-1.0	-1.0	-1.3	-1.5	-1.6	-1.6	-2.0	-2.3	-2.6	-2.2	-1.9	-1.9	-2.0	-2.3	-1.3	-0.8	-0.8	-1.4
12/62	0.9	0.7	0.5	0.5	0.4	0.0	-0.1	-0.9	-0.9	-1.2	-1.4	-1.5	-1.4	-1.8	-2.1	-2.4	-2.0	-1.7	-1.7	-1.8	-2.0	-1.1	-0.6	-0.6	-1.1
12/63	0.8	0.6	0.4	0.4	0.3	-0.1	-0.2	-0.9	-1.0	-1.2	-1.4	-1.5	-1.5	-1.9	-2.1	-2.4	-2.0	-1.7	-1.7	-1.8	-2.0	-1.2	-0.7	-0.7	-1.2
12/64	0.8	0.6	0.4	0.4	0.3	-0.1	-0.2	-0.9	-1.0	-1.2	-1.4	-1.5	-1.4	-1.8	-2.0	-2.3	-1.9	-1.6	-1.7	-1.7	-1.9	-1.1	-0.7	-0.7	-1.1
12/65	0.7	0.5	0.3	0.3	0.2	-0.1	-0.3	-1.0	-1.0	-1.3	-1.4	-1.5	-1.5	-1.8	-2.1	-2.3	-2.0	-1.7	-1.7	-1.8	-2.0	-1.2	-0.8	-0.8	-1.2
12/66	0.6	0.5	0.3	0.3	0.2	-0.2	-0.3	-1.0	-1.0	-1.3	-1.4	-1.5	-1.5	-1.8	-2.1	-2.3	-1.9	-1.7	-1.7	-1.8	-2.0	-1.2	-0.8	-0.9	-1.2
12/67	0.5	0.3	0.2	0.1	0.0	-0.3	-0.4	-1.1	-1.1	-1.4	-1.5	-1.6	-1.6	-1.9	-2.1	-2.3	-2.0	-1.8	-1.8	-1.9	-2.1	-1.4	-1.0	-1.1	-1.4
12/68	0.3	0.2	0.0	-0.0	-0.1	-0.4	-0.6	-1.2	-1.3	-1.5	-1.6	-1.7	-1.7	-2.0	-2.3	-2.4	-2.2	-1.9	-2.0	-2.0	-2.2	-1.6	-1.2	-1.3	-1.6
12/69	0.1	-0.1	-0.2	-0.3	-0.4	-0.7	-0.8	-1.5	-1.5	-1.8	-1.9	-2.0	-2.0	-2.3	-2.5	-2.7	-2.5	-2.3	-2.3	-2.4	-2.6	-2.0	-1.7	-1.7	-2.1
12/70	0.2	0.0	-0.2	-0.2	-0.3	-0.6	-0.7	-1.4	-1.4	-1.6	-1.8	-1.9	-1.8	-2.1	-2.4	-2.5	-2.3	-2.1	-2.1	-2.2	-2.3	-1.8	-1.4	-1.5	-1.9
12/71	0.2	0.0	-0.1	-0.1	-0.2	-0.5	-0.7	-1.3	-1.3	-1.5	-1.7	-1.8	-1.7	-2.0	-2.2	-2.4	-2.2	-2.0	-2.0	-2.0	-2.2	-1.6	-1.3	-1.4	-1.7
12/72	0.1	-0.0	-0.2	-0.2	-0.3	-0.6	-0.7	-1.3	-1.4	-1.6	-1.7	-1.8	-1.8	-2.1	-2.3	-2.4	-2.2	-2.0	-2.0	-2.1	-2.2	-1.7	-1.4	-1.4	-1.8
12/73	-0.1	-0.2	-0.4	-0.4	-0.5	-0.8	-0.9	-1.5	-1.5	-1.7	-1.9	-2.0	-1.9	-2.2	-2.4	-2.6	-2.4	-2.2	-2.2	-2.3	-2.4	-1.9	-1.7	-1.7	-2.0
12/74	-0.3	-0.4	-0.6	-0.6	-0.7	-1.0	-1.1	-1.7	-1.8	-2.0	-2.1	-2.2	-2.2	-2.5	-2.7	-2.8	-2.6	-2.5	-2.5	-2.6	-2.7	-2.3	-2.0	-2.1	-2.4
12/75	-0.4	-0.5	-0.7	-0.7	-0.8	-1.1	-1.2	-1.8	-1.8	-2.0	-2.2	-2.3	-2.3	-2.5	-2.7	-2.9	-2.7	-2.5	-2.6	-2.6	-2.8	-2.3	-2.1	-2.2	-2.5
12/76	-0.3	-0.5	-0.6	-0.6	-0.7	-1.0	-1.1	-1.7	-1.7	-1.9	-2.1	-2.1	-2.1	-2.4	-2.6	-2.7	-2.5	-2.4	-2.4	-2.5	-2.6	-2.2	-1.9	-2.0	-2.3

Table XLV

Time-Weighted Rates of Return* on Intermediate-Term U.S. Treasury Bonds and Notes:
Interest Reinvested,
Higher Tax Rate,
Deflated by the Consumer Price Index

Held	12/50	12/51	12/52	12/53	12/54	12/55	12/56	12/57	12/58	12/59	12/60	12/61	12/62	12/63	12/64	12/65	12/66	12/67	12/68	12/69	12/70	12/71	12/72	12/73	12/74	12/75
'51	-6.2																									
'52	-2.7	0.8																								
'53	-1.5	0.9	1.0																							
'54	-0.7	1.1	1.3	1.5																						
'55	-1.1	0.2	0.0	-0.5	-2.4																					
'56	-1.7	-0.8	-1.2	-1.9	-3.6	-4.9																				
'57	-1.1	-0.2	-0.5	-0.8	-1.6	-1.2	2.6																			
'58	-1.6	-0.9	-1.2	-1.6	-2.4	-2.3	-1.1	-4.6																		
'59	-1.9	-1.3	-1.6	-2.1	-2.8	-2.8	-2.2	-4.5	-4.3																	
'60	-0.9	-0.3	-0.5	-0.7	-1.1	-0.8	0.3	-0.5	1.6	7.9																
'61	-0.9	-0.4	-0.5	-0.7	-1.0	-0.8	0.1	-0.6	0.8	3.5	-0.7															
'62	-0.7	-0.1	-0.2	-0.4	-0.6	-0.4	0.4	-0.0	1.1	3.0	0.7	2.1														
'63	-0.8	-0.3	-0.4	-0.6	-0.8	-0.6	0.0	-0.4	0.4	1.7	-0.3	-0.2	-2.4													
'64	-0.7	-0.3	-0.4	-0.5	-0.7	-0.6	-0.0	-0.4	0.3	1.3	-0.3	-0.1	-1.2	-0.1												
'65	-0.9	-0.5	-0.6	-0.7	-0.9	-0.8	-0.3	-0.7	-0.1	0.6	-0.8	-0.8	-1.8	-1.5	-2.9											
'66	-0.9	-0.6	-0.7	-0.8	-1.0	-0.9	-0.4	-0.8	-0.3	0.3	-0.9	-1.0	-1.7	-1.5	-2.2	-1.5										
'67	-1.1	-0.8	-0.9	-1.1	-1.3	-1.2	-0.8	-1.2	-0.8	-0.3	-1.4	-1.6	-2.3	-2.3	-3.0	-3.0	-4.6									
'68	-1.4	-1.1	-1.2	-1.4	-1.6	-1.5	-1.2	-1.5	-1.2	-0.9	-1.9	-2.1	-2.8	-2.9	-3.6	-3.8	-5.0	-5.3								
'69	-1.9	-1.6	-1.8	-2.0	-2.2	-2.2	-2.0	-2.3	-2.1	-1.9	-2.9	-3.2	-4.0	-4.2	-5.0	-5.5	-6.9	-8.0	-10.6							
'70	-1.6	-1.4	-1.5	-1.6	-1.8	-1.8	-1.6	-1.9	-1.7	-1.4	-2.3	-2.5	-3.0	-3.1	-3.6	-3.8	-4.4	-4.3	-3.8	3.6						
'71	-1.5	-1.2	-1.3	-1.5	-1.6	-1.6	-1.4	-1.6	-1.4	-1.2	-2.0	-2.1	-2.5	-2.5	-2.9	-2.9	-3.2	-2.8	-2.0	2.6	1.7					
'72	-1.5	-1.3	-1.4	-1.5	-1.7	-1.7	-1.5	-1.7	-1.5	-1.3	-2.0	-2.2	-2.6	-2.6	-2.9	-2.9	-3.2	-2.9	-2.3	0.7	-0.7	-3.0				
'73	-1.8	-1.6	-1.7	-1.9	-2.1	-2.0	-1.9	-2.1	-2.0	-1.8	-2.5	-2.7	-3.1	-3.2	-3.5	-3.6	-3.9	-3.7	-3.4	-1.5	-3.2	-5.5	-7.9			
'74	-2.2	-2.0	-2.2	-2.3	-2.5	-2.5	-2.4	-2.7	-2.5	-2.4	-3.1	-3.3	-3.7	-3.9	-4.2	-4.4	-4.8	-4.8	-4.7	-3.5	-5.1	-7.3	-9.4	-10.8		
'75	-2.3	-2.2	-2.3	-2.4	-2.6	-2.6	-2.5	-2.8	-2.7	-2.6	-3.2	-3.4	-3.8	-3.9	-4.3	-4.4	-4.8	-4.8	-4.7	-3.7	-5.1	-6.7	-7.9	-7.8	-4.7	
'76	-2.1	-2.0	-2.1	-2.2	-2.4	-2.4	-2.2	-2.5	-2.4	-2.3	-2.9	-3.0	-3.3	-3.4	-3.7	-3.8	-4.0	-3.9	-3.8	-2.7	-3.8	-4.8	-5.2	-4.3	-0.9	3.1

*Percent per annum, compounded annually.

Sources: Bond market data—Lawrence Fisher (compiler), CRSP Monthly Return File for U.S. Treasury Securities (magnetic tape). See Appendix A.
Consumer Price Index—U.S. Bureau of Labor Statistics.
Income tax rates—Income levels estimated from U.S. Bureau of the Census, Current Population Reports, Series P-60, Nos. 101 and 103 and Historical Statistics of the United States. Tax rates were found in U.S. Internal Revenue Service, Statistics of Income and Your Federal Income Tax.

Chapter 15

Time-Weighted Rates of Return on Short-Term Governments

Tables XLVI through LI show rates of return on short-term Governments. The only problem in meeting the selection criteria is that the issues held from July 1930 through June 1942 were tax-exempt. Not surprisingly, the short-term securities had lower pre-tax rates of return than longer-term securities through the end of 1942. After that date, the rates of return were, on average, the same for short-term and for intermediate-term securities—a fact that may be surprising to many.

For the short-term portfolio, we chose to acquire a Treasury bill, certificate of indebtedness, or note with about one year to maturity and to hold it for six months. Many researchers prefer holding successive thirty- or ninety-one-day Treasury bills to maturity. We do not think such a policy establishes the opportunity cost of an alternative investment for stockholders because of the liquidity premium that attaches to very short-term Governments but not to stocks. By exchanging one security for another a few months before maturity, we avoid reporting rates of return that have been reduced by the liquidity premium.

In addition, data on Treasury bills either could not be found or were not optimum for our purposes before the end of the Treasury-Federal Reserve accord in 1951. Before 1929, there were no U.S. Treasury bills. From 1929 to the mid-1930s, quotations usually were either hard to find or were only bid quotations. Because of the Treasury-Federal accord, Treasury bills were like demand obligations of the Federal Reserve System from early in World War II until 1951. Their yields could be kept extremely low because, with prices pegged, owners of bills had the option of holding or redeeming them and therefore enjoyed both a guaranteed return and liquidity.

The rates of return shown in Tables XXXIV through LI were calculated from a single index for each table. The deflated indexes—at all tax rates—have their peak values in December 1940 for long- and intermediate-term Governments. The deflated indexes for short-term securities have their peaks in December 1934. Thus long- and intermediate-term rates have, on average, been less than the rate of change in the Consumer Price Index (CPI) since December 1940—for thirty-six years—and rates of return on short-term issues have been less than the rate of change in the CPI for the past forty-two years.

Held Until	12/25	12/26	12/27	12/28	12/29	12/30	12/31	12/32	12/33	12/34	12/35	12/36	12/37	12/38	12/39	12/40	12/41	12/42	12/43	12/44	12/45	12/46	12/47	12/48	12/49
12/26	3.9																								
12/27	3.5	3.2																							
12/28	3.5	3.2	3.3																						
12/29	3.9	3.9	4.2	5.1																					
12/30	3.8	3.8	4.0	4.3	3.5																				
12/31	3.4	3.3	3.3	3.3	2.5	1.5																			
12/32	3.4	3.3	3.4	3.4	2.8	2.5	3.5																		
12/33	3.0	2.9	2.9	2.8	2.2	1.8	1.9	0.4																	
12/34	3.0	2.9	2.8	2.7	2.3	2.0	2.1	1.5	2.6																
12/35	2.8	2.6	2.6	2.5	2.0	1.7	1.8	1.2	1.7	0.7															
12/36	2.6	2.4	2.4	2.2	1.8	1.6	1.6	1.1	1.3	0.7	0.7														
12/37	2.4	2.2	2.1	2.0	1.6	1.4	1.4	0.9	1.1	0.6	0.5	0.3													
12/38	2.2	2.1	2.0	1.9	1.5	1.3	1.2	0.9	1.0	0.5	0.5	0.4	0.5												
12/39	2.1	2.0	1.9	1.8	1.5	1.2	1.2	0.9	1.0	0.6	0.6	0.6	0.7	0.9											
12/40	2.0	1.9	1.8	1.7	1.4	1.1	1.1	0.8	0.9	0.6	0.6	0.5	0.6	0.7	0.4										
12/41	1.9	1.7	1.6	1.5	1.2	1.0	1.0	0.7	0.7	0.5	0.4	0.4	0.4	0.3	0.0	-0.4									
12/42	1.8	1.7	1.6	1.4	1.2	1.0	0.9	0.7	0.7	0.5	0.4	0.4	0.4	0.4	0.2	0.0	0.4								
12/43	1.7	1.6	1.5	1.4	1.1	1.0	0.9	0.7	0.7	0.5	0.5	0.4	0.5	0.5	0.4	0.3	0.7	0.9							
12/44	1.7	1.6	1.5	1.4	1.1	0.9	0.9	0.7	0.7	0.5	0.5	0.5	0.5	0.5	0.4	0.4	0.7	0.9	0.8						
12/45	1.6	1.5	1.4	1.3	1.1	0.9	0.9	0.7	0.7	0.6	0.6	0.5	0.6	0.6	0.5	0.5	0.8	0.9	0.8	0.9					
12/46	1.6	1.5	1.4	1.3	1.1	0.9	0.9	0.7	0.7	0.6	0.6	0.6	0.6	0.6	0.6	0.6	0.8	0.9	0.8	0.9	0.8				
12/47	1.6	1.5	1.4	1.3	1.1	0.9	0.9	0.7	0.7	0.6	0.6	0.6	0.6	0.6	0.6	0.6	0.8	0.8	0.8	0.8	0.8	0.8			
12/48	1.5	1.4	1.4	1.3	1.1	0.9	0.9	0.7	0.8	0.6	0.6	0.6	0.7	0.7	0.6	0.7	0.8	0.9	0.9	0.9	0.9	0.9	1.0		
12/49	1.5	1.4	1.4	1.3	1.1	1.0	0.9	0.8	0.8	0.7	0.7	0.7	0.7	0.7	0.7	0.7	0.9	0.9	0.9	1.0	1.0	1.0	1.2	1.3	
12/50	1.5	1.4	1.3	1.3	1.1	1.0	0.9	0.8	0.8	0.7	0.7	0.7	0.7	0.8	0.7	0.8	0.9	0.9	1.0	1.0	1.0	1.0	1.1	1.2	1.0
12/51	1.5	1.4	1.4	1.3	1.1	1.0	1.0	0.8	0.9	0.8	0.8	0.8	0.8	0.8	0.8	0.8	1.0	1.0	1.0	1.1	1.1	1.2	1.2	1.3	1.3
12/52	1.5	1.4	1.4	1.3	1.1	1.0	1.0	0.9	0.9	0.8	0.8	0.8	0.9	0.9	0.9	0.9	1.0	1.1	1.1	1.2	1.2	1.3	1.4	1.4	1.5
12/53	1.6	1.5	1.4	1.4	1.2	1.1	1.1	1.0	1.0	0.9	0.9	0.9	1.0	1.0	1.0	1.1	1.2	1.3	1.3	1.3	1.4	1.5	1.6	1.7	1.8
12/54	1.6	1.5	1.4	1.4	1.2	1.1	1.1	1.0	1.0	0.9	1.0	1.0	1.0	1.0	1.1	1.1	1.2	1.3	1.3	1.4	1.4	1.5	1.6	1.7	1.8
12/55	1.6	1.5	1.4	1.3	1.2	1.1	1.1	1.0	1.0	1.0	1.0	1.0	1.0	1.0	1.1	1.1	1.2	1.3	1.3	1.3	1.4	1.4	1.5	1.6	1.6
12/56	1.6	1.5	1.5	1.4	1.3	1.2	1.2	1.1	1.1	1.0	1.0	1.1	1.1	1.1	1.1	1.2	1.3	1.4	1.4	1.4	1.5	1.5	1.6	1.7	1.8
12/57	1.7	1.6	1.5	1.5	1.3	1.3	1.3	1.2	1.2	1.1	1.2	1.2	1.2	1.3	1.3	1.3	1.4	1.5	1.5	1.6	1.7	1.7	1.8	1.9	2.0
12/58	1.7	1.6	1.5	1.5	1.4	1.3	1.3	1.2	1.2	1.2	1.2	1.2	1.3	1.3	1.3	1.4	1.5	1.5	1.6	1.6	1.7	1.8	1.9	1.9	2.0
12/59	1.7	1.6	1.6	1.5	1.4	1.4	1.3	1.3	1.3	1.3	1.3	1.3	1.3	1.4	1.4	1.5	1.6	1.6	1.7	1.7	1.8	1.9	2.0	2.0	2.1
12/60	1.8	1.7	1.7	1.7	1.5	1.5	1.5	1.4	1.4	1.4	1.4	1.5	1.5	1.6	1.6	1.6	1.8	1.8	1.9	1.9	2.0	2.1	2.2	2.3	2.4
12/61	1.8	1.8	1.7	1.7	1.6	1.5	1.5	1.5	1.5	1.5	1.5	1.5	1.6	1.6	1.6	1.7	1.8	1.9	1.9	2.0	2.1	2.1	2.2	2.3	2.4
12/62	1.9	1.8	1.8	1.7	1.6	1.6	1.6	1.5	1.6	1.5	1.5	1.6	1.6	1.7	1.7	1.8	1.9	1.9	2.0	2.1	2.1	2.2	2.3	2.4	2.5
12/63	1.9	1.8	1.8	1.8	1.7	1.6	1.6	1.6	1.6	1.6	1.6	1.6	1.7	1.7	1.8	1.8	1.9	2.0	2.0	2.1	2.2	2.3	2.4	2.4	2.5
12/64	2.0	1.9	1.9	1.9	1.7	1.7	1.7	1.6	1.7	1.6	1.7	1.7	1.8	1.8	1.8	1.9	2.0	2.1	2.1	2.2	2.3	2.4	2.4	2.5	2.6
12/65	2.0	1.9	1.9	1.9	1.8	1.7	1.8	1.7	1.7	1.7	1.7	1.8	1.8	1.9	1.9	2.0	2.1	2.2	2.2	2.3	2.3	2.4	2.5	2.6	2.7
12/66	2.1	2.0	2.0	2.0	1.9	1.8	1.8	1.8	1.8	1.8	1.9	1.9	2.0	2.0	2.0	2.1	2.2	2.3	2.3	2.4	2.5	2.6	2.7	2.8	2.8
12/67	2.1	2.1	2.1	2.0	2.0	1.9	1.9	1.9	1.9	1.9	2.0	2.0	2.1	2.1	2.2	2.2	2.3	2.4	2.5	2.5	2.6	2.7	2.8	2.9	3.0
12/68	2.2	2.2	2.2	2.1	2.1	2.0	2.1	2.0	2.1	2.0	2.1	2.1	2.2	2.2	2.3	2.4	2.5	2.5	2.6	2.7	2.8	2.8	2.9	3.0	3.1
12/69	2.3	2.3	2.3	2.3	2.2	2.2	2.2	2.1	2.2	2.2	2.2	2.3	2.3	2.4	2.4	2.5	2.6	2.7	2.8	2.8	2.9	3.0	3.1	3.2	3.3
12/70	2.5	2.5	2.5	2.4	2.4	2.3	2.4	2.3	2.4	2.4	2.4	2.5	2.6	2.6	2.7	2.8	2.9	2.9	3.0	3.1	3.2	3.3	3.4	3.5	3.6
12/71	2.6	2.6	2.6	2.5	2.5	2.4	2.5	2.4	2.5	2.5	2.5	2.6	2.7	2.7	2.8	2.9	3.0	3.1	3.1	3.2	3.3	3.4	3.5	3.6	3.8
12/72	2.6	2.6	2.6	2.6	2.5	2.5	2.5	2.5	2.6	2.6	2.6	2.7	2.7	2.8	2.8	2.9	3.0	3.1	3.2	3.3	3.4	3.5	3.6	3.7	3.8
12/73	2.7	2.7	2.7	2.7	2.6	2.6	2.6	2.6	2.6	2.6	2.7	2.7	2.8	2.9	2.9	3.0	3.1	3.2	3.3	3.4	3.5	3.6	3.7	3.8	3.9
12/74	2.8	2.8	2.8	2.8	2.7	2.7	2.7	2.7	2.8	2.8	2.8	2.9	3.0	3.0	3.1	3.2	3.3	3.4	3.5	3.6	3.7	3.8	3.9	4.0	4.1
12/75	2.9	2.9	2.9	2.9	2.8	2.8	2.9	2.9	2.9	2.9	3.0	3.0	3.1	3.2	3.2	3.3	3.4	3.5	3.6	3.7	3.8	3.9	4.0	4.1	4.2
12/76	3.0	3.0	3.0	3.0	2.9	2.9	3.0	3.0	3.0	3.0	3.1	3.1	3.2	3.3	3.4	3.4	3.5	3.6	3.7	3.8	3.9	4.0	4.1	4.2	4.3

Table XLVI

Time-Weighted Rates of Return* on Short-Term U.S. Treasury Securities:
Interest Reinvested,
Tax-Exempt,
Current Dollars

Held Until	12/50	12/51	12/52	12/53	12/54	12/55	12/56	12/57	12/58	12/59	12/60	12/61	12/62	12/63	12/64	12/65	12/66	12/67	12/68	12/69	12/70	12/71	12/72	12/73	12/74	12/75
12/51	1.6																									
12/52	1.7	1.9																								
12/53	2.1	2.3	2.7																							
12/54	1.9	2.1	2.2	1.6																						
12/55	1.8	1.8	1.8	1.3	1.0																					
12/56	1.9	2.0	2.0	1.7	1.8	2.5																				
12/57	2.1	2.2	2.3	2.2	2.4	3.1	3.7																			
12/58	2.1	2.2	2.3	2.2	2.3	2.8	2.9	2.1																		
12/59	2.2	2.3	2.4	2.3	2.5	2.8	2.9	2.5	3.0																	
12/60	2.5	2.6	2.7	2.7	2.9	3.3	3.5	3.4	4.1	5.2																
12/61	2.6	2.6	2.7	2.7	2.9	3.2	3.3	3.3	3.7	4.0	2.8															
12/62	2.6	2.7	2.8	2.8	2.9	3.2	3.3	3.3	3.5	3.7	3.0	3.2														
12/63	2.6	2.7	2.8	2.8	3.0	3.2	3.3	3.2	3.4	3.6	3.0	3.1	3.0													
12/64	2.7	2.8	2.9	2.9	3.1	3.3	3.4	3.3	3.5	3.6	3.2	3.4	3.5	3.9												
12/65	2.8	2.9	3.0	3.0	3.1	3.3	3.4	3.4	3.6	3.7	3.4	3.5	3.6	3.9	3.8											
12/66	3.0	3.0	3.1	3.2	3.3	3.5	3.6	3.6	3.8	3.9	3.7	3.9	4.0	4.3	4.5	5.3										
12/67	3.1	3.2	3.3	3.3	3.4	3.6	3.7	3.8	3.9	4.1	3.9	4.1	4.3	4.6	4.8	5.3	5.2									
12/68	3.3	3.4	3.4	3.5	3.6	3.8	3.9	4.0	4.2	4.3	4.2	4.4	4.6	4.9	5.1	5.5	5.7	6.1								
12/69	3.4	3.6	3.7	3.7	3.9	4.1	4.2	4.2	4.4	4.6	4.5	4.7	4.9	5.2	5.5	5.9	6.1	6.6	7.0							
12/70	3.8	3.9	4.0	4.1	4.2	4.4	4.6	4.6	4.9	5.0	5.0	5.3	5.5	5.9	6.2	6.7	7.0	7.6	8.4	9.9						
12/71	3.9	4.0	4.1	4.2	4.4	4.6	4.7	4.8	5.0	5.1	5.1	5.4	5.6	6.0	6.2	6.7	6.9	7.4	7.8	8.2	6.5					
12/72	3.9	4.0	4.1	4.2	4.4	4.6	4.7	4.8	4.9	5.1	5.1	5.3	5.5	5.8	6.0	6.3	6.5	6.8	7.0	6.9	5.5	4.5				
12/73	4.0	4.1	4.2	4.3	4.5	4.7	4.8	4.8	5.0	5.2	5.2	5.4	5.6	5.8	6.0	6.3	6.5	6.7	6.8	6.8	5.8	5.4	6.2			
12/74	4.2	4.3	4.4	4.5	4.7	4.9	5.0	5.1	5.3	5.4	5.4	5.6	5.8	6.1	6.3	6.6	6.8	7.0	7.1	7.2	6.5	6.5	7.5	8.8		
12/75	4.4	4.5	4.6	4.7	4.8	5.0	5.2	5.2	5.4	5.6	5.6	5.8	6.0	6.3	6.5	6.7	6.9	7.1	7.3	7.3	6.8	6.9	7.7	8.4	8.0	
12/76	4.5	4.6	4.7	4.8	4.9	5.1	5.3	5.4	5.5	5.7	5.7	5.9	6.1	6.3	6.6	6.8	7.0	7.2	7.3	7.3	6.9	7.0	7.6	8.1	7.7	7.4

Percent per annum, compounded annually.

Source: Lawrence Fisher (compiler), CRSP Monthly Return File for U.S. Treasury Securities (magnetic tape). See Appendix A.

Held Until	12/25	12/26	12/27	12/28	12/29	12/30	12/31	12/32	12/33	12/34	12/35	12/36	12/37	12/38	12/39	12/40	12/41	12/42	12/43	12/44	12/45	12/46	12/47	12/48	12/49
12/26	5.4																								
12/27	5.4	5.4																							
12/28	5.0	4.8	4.3																						
12/29	5.0	4.9	4.6	4.9																					
12/30	6.0	6.2	6.4	7.5	10.2																				
12/31	7.0	7.3	7.8	9.0	11.1	12.1																			
12/32	8.2	8.6	9.3	10.6	12.5	13.7	15.4																		
12/33	7.1	7.3	7.7	8.3	9.2	8.9	7.3	-0.1																	
12/34	6.3	6.5	6.6	7.0	7.4	6.8	5.0	0.2	0.6																
12/35	5.5	5.5	5.5	5.6	5.8	4.9	3.2	-0.6	-0.8	-2.2															
12/36	4.9	4.9	4.8	4.9	4.9	4.0	2.4	-0.6	-0.7	-1.3	-0.5														
12/37	4.2	4.1	4.0	4.0	3.9	3.0	1.6	-1.0	-1.2	-1.8	-1.6	-2.7													
12/38	4.2	4.1	4.0	3.9	3.8	3.0	1.8	-0.3	-0.3	-0.5	0.0	0.3	3.3												
12/39	4.0	3.9	3.7	3.7	3.6	2.9	1.8	-0.0	-0.0	-0.2	0.4	0.6	2.4	1.4											
12/40	3.7	3.5	3.4	3.3	3.2	2.5	1.5	-0.1	-0.1	-0.2	0.2	0.4	1.4	0.5	-0.5										
12/41	2.8	2.6	2.5	2.3	2.1	1.4	0.4	-1.2	-1.3	-1.6	-1.4	-1.6	-1.4	-2.9	-5.0	-9.2									
12/42	2.1	1.9	1.7	1.5	1.3	0.6	-0.4	-1.9	-2.1	-2.4	-2.4	-2.7	-2.7	-4.2	-6.0	-8.6	-8.1								
12/43	1.9	1.7	1.5	1.3	1.0	0.4	-0.6	-1.9	-2.1	-2.4	-2.4	-2.7	-2.6	-3.8	-5.1	-6.5	-5.2	-2.2							
12/44	1.7	1.5	1.3	1.1	0.9	0.2	-0.6	-1.9	-2.0	-2.3	-2.3	-2.5	-2.5	-3.4	-4.3	-5.2	-3.9	-1.7	-1.3						
12/45	1.6	1.4	1.2	1.0	0.7	0.1	-0.7	-1.8	-2.0	-2.2	-2.2	-2.4	-2.3	-3.1	-3.8	-4.5	-3.3	-1.6	-1.3	-1.4					
12/46	0.7	0.5	0.3	0.0	-0.2	-0.9	-1.7	-2.8	-3.0	-3.3	-3.4	-3.7	-3.8	-4.6	-5.5	-6.3	-5.7	-5.0	-6.0	-8.2	-14.7				
12/47	0.3	0.1	-0.2	-0.4	-0.7	-1.3	-2.1	-3.1	-3.3	-3.6	-3.7	-4.0	-4.2	-5.0	-5.7	-6.4	-6.0	-5.5	-6.4	-8.0	-11.2	-7.5			
12/48	0.3	0.0	-0.2	-0.4	-0.7	-1.3	-2.0	-3.0	-3.2	-3.5	-3.6	-3.8	-3.9	-4.6	-5.3	-5.9	-5.4	-4.9	-5.4	-6.4	-8.1	-4.6	-1.6		
12/49	0.4	0.2	-0.1	-0.3	-0.5	-1.1	-1.7	-2.7	-2.8	-3.0	-3.1	-3.3	-3.4	-3.9	-4.5	-4.9	-4.3	-3.8	-4.1	-4.6	-5.4	-2.1	0.7	3.1	
12/50	0.2	-0.0	-0.3	-0.5	-0.7	-1.2	-1.9	-2.8	-2.9	-3.1	-3.2	-3.4	-3.4	-4.0	-4.5	-4.9	-4.4	-3.9	-4.1	-4.6	-5.2	-2.7	-1.0	-0.8	-4.5
12/51	0.0	-0.2	-0.4	-0.6	-0.9	-1.4	-2.0	-2.8	-3.0	-3.2	-3.3	-3.4	-3.5	-4.0	-4.4	-4.8	-4.3	-3.9	-4.1	-4.5	-5.0	-3.0	-1.8	-1.9	-4.3
12/52	0.0	-0.2	-0.4	-0.6	-0.8	-1.3	-1.9	-2.7	-2.8	-3.0	-3.0	-3.2	-3.2	-3.6	-4.0	-4.3	-3.9	-3.4	-3.6	-3.8	-4.2	-2.3	-1.3	-1.2	-2.6
12/53	0.1	-0.1	-0.3	-0.5	-0.7	-1.1	-1.7	-2.4	-2.5	-2.7	-2.7	-2.9	-2.9	-3.3	-3.6	-3.8	-3.4	-2.9	-3.0	-3.2	-3.4	-1.7	-0.7	-0.5	-1.4
12/54	0.2	0.0	-0.2	-0.4	-0.6	-1.0	-1.5	-2.2	-2.3	-2.5	-2.5	-2.6	-2.6	-2.9	-3.2	-3.4	-3.0	-2.5	-2.6	-2.7	-2.8	-1.2	-0.3	-0.1	-0.7
12/55	0.2	0.0	-0.2	-0.3	-0.5	-0.9	-1.4	-2.1	-2.2	-2.3	-2.3	-2.4	-2.4	-2.7	-3.0	-3.2	-2.7	-2.3	-2.3	-2.4	-2.5	-1.0	-0.2	0.0	-0.5
12/56	0.2	0.0	-0.2	-0.3	-0.5	-0.9	-1.4	-2.0	-2.1	-2.2	-2.2	-2.3	-2.3	-2.6	-2.8	-3.0	-2.6	-2.1	-2.1	-2.2	-2.3	-1.0	-0.2	-0.0	-0.5
12/57	0.2	0.0	-0.1	-0.3	-0.5	-0.8	-1.3	-1.9	-2.0	-2.1	-2.1	-2.2	-2.2	-2.4	-2.6	-2.8	-2.4	-2.0	-1.9	-2.0	-2.0	-0.8	-0.1	0.1	-0.3
12/58	0.2	0.0	-0.1	-0.3	-0.4	-0.8	-1.3	-1.8	-1.9	-2.0	-2.0	-2.1	-2.0	-2.3	-2.5	-2.6	-2.2	-1.8	-1.8	-1.8	-1.9	-0.7	-0.1	0.1	-0.3
12/59	0.2	0.1	-0.1	-0.2	-0.4	-0.7	-1.2	-1.7	-1.8	-1.9	-1.9	-1.9	-1.9	-2.1	-2.3	-2.4	-2.0	-1.6	-1.6	-1.6	-1.6	-0.6	0.1	0.2	-0.1
12/60	0.3	0.2	0.0	-0.1	-0.3	-0.6	-1.0	-1.5	-1.6	-1.7	-1.6	-1.7	-1.6	-1.9	-2.0	-2.1	-1.7	-1.3	-1.3	-1.3	-1.3	-0.3	0.3	0.5	0.3
12/61	0.4	0.2	0.1	-0.0	-0.2	-0.5	-0.9	-1.4	-1.5	-1.5	-1.5	-1.5	-1.5	-1.7	-1.8	-1.9	-1.5	-1.2	-1.1	-1.1	-1.1	-0.1	0.5	0.6	0.4
12/62	0.4	0.3	0.1	0.0	-0.1	-0.4	-0.8	-1.3	-1.3	-1.4	-1.4	-1.4	-1.4	-1.5	-1.7	-1.7	-1.4	-1.0	-0.9	-0.9	-0.9	0.0	0.6	0.7	0.5
12/63	0.5	0.3	0.2	0.1	-0.1	-0.4	-0.7	-1.2	-1.2	-1.3	-1.3	-1.3	-1.3	-1.4	-1.6	-1.6	-1.2	-0.9	-0.8	-0.8	-0.8	0.1	0.6	0.8	0.6
12/64	0.5	0.4	0.3	0.1	0.0	-0.3	-0.6	-1.1	-1.1	-1.2	-1.1	-1.2	-1.1	-1.3	-1.4	-1.4	-1.1	-0.7	-0.7	-0.6	-0.6	0.2	0.7	0.9	0.7
12/65	0.5	0.4	0.3	0.2	0.1	-0.2	-0.6	-1.0	-1.0	-1.1	-1.0	-1.1	-1.0	-1.2	-1.3	-1.3	-0.9	-0.6	-0.6	-0.5	-0.5	0.3	0.8	0.9	0.8
12/66	0.6	0.5	0.3	0.2	0.1	-0.2	-0.5	-0.9	-0.9	-1.0	-1.0	-1.0	-0.9	-1.1	-1.1	-1.2	-0.8	-0.5	-0.4	-0.4	-0.4	0.4	0.8	1.0	0.9
12/67	0.6	0.5	0.4	0.3	0.2	-0.1	-0.4	-0.8	-0.9	-0.9	-0.9	-0.9	-0.8	-0.9	-1.0	-1.1	-0.7	-0.4	-0.3	-0.3	-0.3	0.5	0.9	1.0	0.9
12/68	0.6	0.5	0.4	0.3	0.2	-0.1	-0.4	-0.8	-0.8	-0.8	-0.8	-0.8	-0.7	-0.9	-1.0	-1.0	-0.6	-0.4	-0.3	-0.2	-0.2	0.5	0.9	1.1	0.9
12/69	0.6	0.5	0.4	0.3	0.2	-0.0	-0.3	-0.7	-0.7	-0.8	-0.7	-0.8	-0.7	-0.8	-0.9	-0.9	-0.6	-0.3	-0.2	-0.2	-0.1	0.5	0.9	1.0	0.9
12/70	0.7	0.6	0.5	0.4	0.3	0.1	-0.2	-0.6	-0.6	-0.7	-0.6	-0.6	-0.5	-0.7	-0.7	-0.7	-0.4	-0.2	-0.1	-0.0	0.0	0.7	1.1	1.2	1.1
12/71	0.8	0.7	0.6	0.5	0.4	0.1	-0.1	-0.5	-0.5	-0.6	-0.5	-0.5	-0.4	-0.6	-0.6	-0.6	-0.3	-0.0	0.0	0.1	0.1	0.8	1.1	1.3	1.2
12/72	0.8	0.7	0.6	0.5	0.4	0.2	-0.1	-0.5	-0.5	-0.5	-0.5	-0.5	-0.4	-0.5	-0.6	-0.6	-0.3	-0.0	0.1	0.1	0.2	0.8	1.1	1.3	1.2
12/73	0.7	0.6	0.5	0.4	0.3	0.1	-0.2	-0.5	-0.5	-0.6	-0.5	-0.5	-0.5	-0.6	-0.6	-0.6	-0.3	-0.1	-0.0	0.0	0.1	0.7	1.0	1.1	1.0
12/74	0.6	0.5	0.4	0.3	0.2	0.0	-0.2	-0.6	-0.6	-0.6	-0.6	-0.6	-0.5	-0.6	-0.7	-0.7	-0.4	-0.2	-0.1	-0.1	-0.0	0.5	0.9	0.9	0.9
12/75	0.6	0.5	0.4	0.4	0.3	0.0	-0.2	-0.5	-0.6	-0.6	-0.5	-0.5	-0.5	-0.6	-0.6	-0.6	-0.4	-0.1	-0.1	-0.0	0.0	0.6	0.9	0.9	0.9
12/76	0.7	0.6	0.5	0.4	0.3	0.1	-0.2	-0.5	-0.5	-0.5	-0.5	-0.5	-0.4	-0.5	-0.6	-0.6	-0.3	-0.1	-0.0	0.0	0.1	0.6	0.9	1.0	0.9

Table XLVII

Time-Weighted Rates of Return* on Short-Term U.S. Treasury Securities:
  Interest Reinvested,
  Tax-Exempt,
  Deflated by the Consumer Price Index

Sold until	12/50	12/51	12/52	12/53	12/54	12/55	12/56	12/57	12/58	12/59	12/60	12/61	12/62	12/63	12/64	12/65	12/66	12/67	12/68	12/69	12/70	12/71	12/72	12/73	12/74	12/75
'51	−4.0																									
'52	−1.6	1.0																								
'53	−0.4	1.5	2.1																							
'54	0.2	1.7	2.1	2.1																						
'55	0.3	1.5	1.6	1.4	0.7																					
'56	0.2	1.1	1.1	0.8	0.2	−0.3																				
'57	0.3	1.0	1.0	0.8	0.3	0.2	0.6																			
'58	0.3	0.9	0.9	0.7	0.3	0.2	0.5	0.3																		
'59	0.4	1.0	1.0	0.8	0.6	0.5	0.8	0.9	1.5																	
'60	0.7	1.3	1.3	1.2	1.1	1.2	1.5	1.8	2.6	3.7																
'61	0.9	1.4	1.4	1.3	1.2	1.3	1.6	1.9	2.4	2.9	2.1															
'62	1.0	1.4	1.5	1.4	1.3	1.4	1.7	1.9	2.3	2.6	2.0	2.0														
'63	1.0	1.4	1.5	1.4	1.3	1.4	1.6	1.8	2.1	2.3	1.8	1.7	1.4													
'64	1.1	1.5	1.6	1.5	1.5	1.5	1.8	1.9	2.2	2.4	2.0	2.0	2.0	2.7												
'65	1.2	1.5	1.6	1.5	1.5	1.6	1.8	1.9	2.2	2.3	2.0	2.0	2.0	2.3	1.8											
'66	1.2	1.6	1.6	1.6	1.5	1.6	1.8	1.9	2.1	2.2	2.0	2.0	1.9	2.1	1.8	1.9										
'67	1.3	1.6	1.6	1.6	1.6	1.6	1.8	1.9	2.1	2.2	2.0	2.0	2.0	2.1	1.9	2.0	2.1									
'68	1.3	1.6	1.6	1.6	1.6	1.6	1.8	1.9	2.0	2.1	1.9	1.9	1.9	2.0	1.8	1.8	1.7	1.3								
'69	1.2	1.5	1.6	1.5	1.5	1.6	1.7	1.8	1.9	2.0	1.8	1.8	1.7	1.8	1.6	1.5	1.4	1.1	0.8							
'70	1.4	1.7	1.7	1.7	1.7	1.7	1.9	2.0	2.1	2.2	2.0	2.0	2.0	2.1	2.0	2.1	2.1	2.1	2.5	4.1						
'71	1.5	1.7	1.8	1.8	1.7	1.8	2.0	2.1	2.2	2.2	2.1	2.1	2.1	2.2	2.2	2.2	2.3	2.3	2.7	3.6	3.0					
'72	1.4	1.7	1.7	1.7	1.7	1.8	1.9	2.0	2.1	2.2	2.0	2.0	2.0	2.1	2.0	2.1	2.1	2.1	2.3	2.7	2.1	1.1				
'73	1.3	1.5	1.5	1.5	1.5	1.5	1.6	1.7	1.8	1.8	1.7	1.7	1.6	1.6	1.5	1.5	1.4	1.3	1.3	1.4	0.6	−0.7	−2.4			
'74	1.1	1.3	1.3	1.3	1.3	1.3	1.4	1.4	1.5	1.5	1.3	1.3	1.2	1.2	1.1	1.0	0.9	0.7	0.6	0.5	−0.4	−1.5	−2.7	−3.0		
'75	1.1	1.3	1.3	1.3	1.2	1.3	1.4	1.4	1.5	1.5	1.3	1.3	1.2	1.2	1.1	1.0	0.9	0.7	0.6	0.6	−0.1	−0.9	−1.5	−1.1	1.0	
'76	1.1	1.4	1.4	1.3	1.3	1.3	1.4	1.5	1.5	1.5	1.4	1.3	1.3	1.3	1.2	1.1	1.0	0.9	0.9	0.9	0.3	−0.2	−0.5	0.1	1.7	2.5

Percent per annum, compounded annually.

Sources: Bond market data—Lawrence Fisher (compiler), CRSP Monthly Return File for U.S. Treasury Securities (magnetic tape). See Appendix A.
Consumer Price Index—U.S. Bureau of Labor Statistics.

139

Held Until	Purchased 12/25	12/26	12/27	12/28	12/29	12/30	12/31	12/32	12/33	12/34	12/35	12/36	12/37	12/38	12/39	12/40	12/41	12/42	12/43	12/44	12/45	12/46	12/47	12/48	12/49
12/26	3.9																								
12/27	3.5	3.2																							
12/28	3.5	3.2	3.3																						
12/29	3.9	3.9	4.2	5.1																					
12/30	3.8	3.8	4.0	4.3	3.5																				
12/31	3.4	3.3	3.3	3.3	2.5	1.5																			
12/32	3.4	3.3	3.4	3.4	2.8	2.5	3.5																		
12/33	3.0	2.9	2.9	2.8	2.2	1.8	1.9	0.4																	
12/34	3.0	2.9	2.8	2.7	2.3	2.0	2.1	1.5	2.6																
12/35	2.8	2.6	2.6	2.5	2.0	1.7	1.8	1.2	1.7	0.7															
12/36	2.6	2.4	2.4	2.2	1.8	1.6	1.6	1.1	1.3	0.7	0.7														
12/37	2.4	2.2	2.1	2.0	1.6	1.4	1.4	0.9	1.1	0.6	0.5	0.3													
12/38	2.2	2.1	2.0	1.9	1.5	1.3	1.2	0.9	1.0	0.5	0.5	0.4	0.5												
12/39	2.1	2.0	1.9	1.8	1.5	1.2	1.2	0.9	1.0	0.6	0.6	0.6	0.7	0.9											
12/40	2.0	1.9	1.8	1.7	1.4	1.1	1.1	0.8	0.9	0.6	0.6	0.5	0.6	0.7	0.4										
12/41	1.9	1.7	1.6	1.5	1.2	1.0	1.0	0.7	0.7	0.5	0.4	0.4	0.4	0.3	0.0	−0.4									
12/42	1.8	1.7	1.6	1.4	1.2	1.0	0.9	0.7	0.7	0.5	0.4	0.4	0.4	0.4	0.2	0.0	0.4								
12/43	1.7	1.6	1.5	1.4	1.1	0.9	0.9	0.7	0.7	0.5	0.5	0.4	0.4	0.4	0.3	0.3	0.6	0.7							
12/44	1.7	1.5	1.5	1.3	1.1	0.9	0.9	0.7	0.7	0.5	0.5	0.4	0.5	0.5	0.4	0.4	0.6	0.7	0.6						
12/45	1.6	1.5	1.4	1.3	1.1	0.9	0.9	0.7	0.7	0.5	0.5	0.5	0.5	0.5	0.4	0.4	0.6	0.7	0.6	0.7					
12/46	1.6	1.5	1.4	1.3	1.0	0.9	0.9	0.7	0.7	0.5	0.5	0.5	0.5	0.5	0.5	0.5	0.6	0.7	0.7	0.7	0.7				
12/47	1.5	1.4	1.3	1.2	1.0	0.9	0.8	0.7	0.7	0.5	0.5	0.5	0.5	0.5	0.5	0.5	0.6	0.7	0.7	0.7	0.7	0.7			
12/48	1.5	1.4	1.3	1.2	1.0	0.9	0.8	0.7	0.7	0.6	0.6	0.5	0.6	0.6	0.5	0.5	0.7	0.7	0.7	0.7	0.8	0.8	0.9		
12/49	1.5	1.4	1.3	1.2	1.0	0.9	0.9	0.7	0.7	0.6	0.6	0.6	0.6	0.6	0.6	0.6	0.7	0.8	0.8	0.8	0.8	0.9	1.0	1.1	
12/50	1.5	1.4	1.3	1.2	1.0	0.9	0.9	0.7	0.7	0.6	0.6	0.6	0.6	0.6	0.6	0.6	0.7	0.8	0.8	0.8	0.8	0.9	0.9	0.9	0.8
12/51	1.5	1.4	1.3	1.2	1.0	0.9	0.9	0.7	0.8	0.7	0.6	0.6	0.7	0.7	0.7	0.7	0.8	0.8	0.8	0.9	0.9	0.9	1.0	1.1	1.0
12/52	1.5	1.4	1.3	1.2	1.0	0.9	0.9	0.8	0.8	0.7	0.7	0.7	0.7	0.7	0.7	0.7	0.8	0.9	0.9	0.9	1.0	1.0	1.1	1.2	1.2
12/53	1.5	1.4	1.3	1.2	1.1	1.0	1.0	0.8	0.9	0.8	0.8	0.8	0.8	0.8	0.8	0.9	1.0	1.0	1.0	1.1	1.1	1.2	1.3	1.4	1.5
12/54	1.5	1.4	1.3	1.3	1.1	1.0	1.0	0.9	0.9	0.8	0.8	0.8	0.9	0.9	0.9	0.9	1.0	1.0	1.1	1.1	1.2	1.2	1.3	1.4	1.4
12/55	1.5	1.4	1.3	1.2	1.1	1.0	1.0	0.9	0.9	0.8	0.8	0.8	0.8	0.9	0.9	0.9	1.0	1.0	1.0	1.1	1.1	1.2	1.2	1.3	1.3
12/56	1.5	1.4	1.3	1.3	1.1	1.0	1.0	0.9	0.9	0.9	0.9	0.9	0.9	0.9	0.9	1.0	1.0	1.1	1.1	1.2	1.2	1.3	1.3	1.4	1.4
12/57	1.5	1.4	1.4	1.3	1.2	1.1	1.1	1.0	1.0	1.0	1.0	1.0	1.0	1.0	1.0	1.1	1.2	1.2	1.3	1.3	1.4	1.4	1.5	1.6	1.6
12/58	1.5	1.5	1.4	1.3	1.2	1.1	1.1	1.0	1.0	1.0	1.0	1.0	1.0	1.1	1.1	1.1	1.2	1.2	1.3	1.3	1.4	1.4	1.5	1.6	1.6
12/59	1.5	1.5	1.4	1.4	1.2	1.2	1.2	1.1	1.1	1.0	1.0	1.1	1.1	1.1	1.1	1.2	1.3	1.3	1.3	1.4	1.4	1.5	1.6	1.6	1.7
12/60	1.6	1.6	1.5	1.5	1.3	1.3	1.3	1.2	1.2	1.2	1.2	1.2	1.2	1.3	1.3	1.3	1.4	1.5	1.5	1.6	1.6	1.7	1.8	1.9	1.9
12/61	1.6	1.6	1.5	1.5	1.4	1.3	1.3	1.2	1.2	1.2	1.2	1.2	1.3	1.3	1.3	1.4	1.5	1.5	1.5	1.6	1.7	1.7	1.8	1.9	1.9
12/62	1.7	1.6	1.6	1.5	1.4	1.3	1.3	1.3	1.3	1.2	1.3	1.3	1.3	1.3	1.4	1.4	1.5	1.6	1.6	1.6	1.7	1.8	1.8	1.9	2.0
12/63	1.7	1.6	1.6	1.5	1.4	1.4	1.4	1.3	1.3	1.3	1.3	1.3	1.3	1.4	1.4	1.4	1.5	1.6	1.6	1.7	1.7	1.8	1.9	1.9	2.0
12/64	1.7	1.6	1.6	1.6	1.5	1.4	1.4	1.3	1.4	1.3	1.3	1.4	1.4	1.4	1.5	1.5	1.6	1.6	1.7	1.7	1.8	1.9	1.9	2.0	2.1
12/65	1.7	1.7	1.6	1.6	1.5	1.4	1.4	1.4	1.4	1.4	1.4	1.4	1.5	1.5	1.5	1.6	1.6	1.7	1.7	1.8	1.9	1.9	2.0	2.1	2.1
12/66	1.8	1.7	1.7	1.7	1.6	1.5	1.5	1.5	1.5	1.5	1.5	1.5	1.6	1.6	1.6	1.7	1.7	1.8	1.8	1.9	2.0	2.0	2.1	2.2	2.2
12/67	1.8	1.8	1.8	1.7	1.6	1.6	1.6	1.5	1.6	1.5	1.6	1.6	1.6	1.7	1.7	1.8	1.8	1.9	1.9	2.0	2.1	2.1	2.2	2.3	2.3
12/68	1.9	1.9	1.8	1.8	1.7	1.7	1.7	1.6	1.7	1.6	1.7	1.7	1.7	1.8	1.8	1.8	1.9	2.0	2.0	2.1	2.2	2.2	2.3	2.4	2.4
12/69	2.0	1.9	1.9	1.9	1.8	1.7	1.8	1.7	1.7	1.7	1.8	1.8	1.8	1.9	1.9	2.0	2.0	2.1	2.2	2.2	2.3	2.3	2.4	2.5	2.6
12/70	2.1	2.1	2.0	2.0	1.9	1.9	1.9	1.8	1.9	1.9	1.9	1.9	2.0	2.0	2.1	2.1	2.2	2.3	2.3	2.4	2.5	2.5	2.6	2.7	2.8
12/71	2.2	2.1	2.1	2.1	2.0	2.0	2.0	1.9	2.0	1.9	2.0	2.0	2.1	2.1	2.2	2.2	2.3	2.4	2.4	2.5	2.6	2.6	2.7	2.8	2.9
12/72	2.2	2.1	2.1	2.1	2.0	2.0	2.0	2.0	2.0	2.0	2.0	2.1	2.1	2.2	2.2	2.2	2.3	2.4	2.5	2.5	2.6	2.7	2.7	2.8	2.9
12/73	2.2	2.2	2.2	2.1	2.1	2.0	2.1	2.0	2.1	2.0	2.1	2.1	2.2	2.2	2.3	2.3	2.4	2.5	2.5	2.6	2.7	2.7	2.8	2.9	3.0
12/74	2.3	2.3	2.2	2.2	2.2	2.1	2.1	2.1	2.2	2.1	2.2	2.2	2.3	2.3	2.4	2.4	2.5	2.6	2.6	2.7	2.8	2.8	2.9	3.0	3.1
12/75	2.4	2.3	2.3	2.3	2.2	2.2	2.2	2.2	2.2	2.2	2.3	2.3	2.4	2.4	2.5	2.5	2.6	2.7	2.7	2.8	2.9	2.9	3.0	3.1	3.2
12/76	2.4	2.4	2.4	2.3	2.3	2.3	2.3	2.3	2.3	2.3	2.3	2.4	2.4	2.5	2.5	2.6	2.7	2.7	2.8	2.9	2.9	3.0	3.1	3.2	3.2

Table XLVIII

Time-Weighted Rates of Return* on Short-Term U.S. Treasury Securities:
  Interest Reinvested,
  Lower Tax Rate,
  Current Dollars

Held until	12/50	12/51	12/52	12/53	12/54	12/55	12/56	12/57	12/58	12/59	12/60	12/61	12/62	12/63	12/64	12/65	12/66	12/67	12/68	12/69	12/70	12/71	12/72	12/73	12/74	12/75
/51	1.3																									
/52	1.4	1.5																								
/53	1.7	1.9	2.3																							
/54	1.6	1.7	1.8	1.4																						
/55	1.4	1.5	1.5	1.0	0.7																					
/56	1.5	1.6	1.6	1.4	1.4	2.0																				
/57	1.7	1.8	1.9	1.8	1.9	2.5	3.0																			
/58	1.7	1.8	1.8	1.8	1.9	2.2	2.4	1.7																		
/59	1.8	1.8	1.9	1.8	1.9	2.2	2.3	2.0	2.2																	
/60	2.0	2.1	2.2	2.2	2.3	2.7	2.8	2.8	3.3	4.4																
/61	2.0	2.1	2.2	2.2	2.3	2.6	2.7	2.6	2.9	3.2	2.0															
/62	2.1	2.1	2.2	2.2	2.3	2.5	2.6	2.6	2.8	2.9	2.2	2.4														
/63	2.1	2.2	2.2	2.2	2.3	2.5	2.6	2.5	2.7	2.8	2.2	2.3	2.2													
/64	2.2	2.2	2.3	2.3	2.4	2.6	2.6	2.6	2.7	2.8	2.4	2.5	2.6	3.0												
/65	2.2	2.3	2.3	2.3	2.4	2.6	2.7	2.6	2.7	2.8	2.5	2.6	2.7	3.0	2.9											
/66	2.3	2.4	2.5	2.5	2.6	2.7	2.8	2.8	2.9	3.0	2.8	2.9	3.1	3.3	3.5	4.1										
/67	2.4	2.5	2.6	2.6	2.7	2.8	2.9	2.9	3.0	3.1	3.0	3.1	3.3	3.5	3.7	4.1	4.1									
/68	2.5	2.6	2.7	2.7	2.8	3.0	3.0	3.0	3.2	3.3	3.1	3.3	3.5	3.7	3.9	4.2	4.3	4.4								
/69	2.7	2.7	2.8	2.8	2.9	3.1	3.2	3.2	3.3	3.5	3.4	3.5	3.7	3.9	4.1	4.4	4.5	4.7	5.0							
/70	2.9	3.0	3.1	3.1	3.2	3.4	3.5	3.5	3.7	3.8	3.7	3.9	4.1	4.4	4.6	5.0	5.2	5.6	6.1	7.3						
/71	3.0	3.1	3.2	3.2	3.3	3.5	3.6	3.6	3.8	3.9	3.8	4.0	4.2	4.5	4.7	5.0	5.1	5.4	5.7	6.0	4.8					
/72	3.0	3.1	3.2	3.2	3.3	3.5	3.5	3.6	3.7	3.8	3.8	4.0	4.1	4.3	4.5	4.7	4.8	5.0	5.1	5.1	4.0	3.2				
/73	3.1	3.1	3.2	3.3	3.4	3.5	3.6	3.6	3.8	3.9	3.8	4.0	4.1	4.3	4.5	4.7	4.8	4.9	5.0	4.9	4.2	3.8	4.4			
/74	3.2	3.3	3.4	3.4	3.5	3.7	3.7	3.8	3.9	4.0	4.0	4.2	4.3	4.5	4.7	4.8	4.9	5.1	5.2	5.2	4.7	4.6	5.4	6.3		
/75	3.3	3.4	3.4	3.5	3.6	3.7	3.8	3.9	4.0	4.1	4.1	4.3	4.4	4.6	4.7	4.9	5.0	5.1	5.2	5.2	4.8	4.8	5.4	5.8	5.4	
/76	3.3	3.4	3.5	3.6	3.7	3.8	3.9	3.9	4.1	4.2	4.2	4.3	4.4	4.6	4.7	4.9	5.0	5.1	5.2	5.2	4.9	4.9	5.3	5.6	5.2	5.0

Percent per annum, compounded annually

Sources: Bond market data—Lawrence Fisher (compiler), CRSP Monthly Return File for U.S. Treasury Securities (magnetic tape). See Appendix A.
Income tax rates—Income levels estimated from U.S. Bureau of the Census, Current Population Reports, Series P-60, Nos. 101 and 103 and Historical Statistics of the United States. Tax rates were found in U.S. Internal Revenue Service, Statistics of Income and Your Federal Income Tax.

Held Until	12/25	12/26	12/27	12/28	12/29	12/30	12/31	12/32	12/33	12/34	12/35	12/36	12/37	12/38	12/39	12/40	12/41	12/42	12/43	12/44	12/45	12/46	12/47	12/48	12/49
12/26	5.4																								
12/27	5.4	5.4																							
12/28	5.0	4.8	4.3																						
12/29	5.0	4.9	4.6	4.9																					
12/30	6.0	6.2	6.4	7.5	10.2																				
12/31	7.0	7.3	7.8	9.0	11.1	12.1																			
12/32	8.2	8.6	9.3	10.6	12.5	13.7	15.4																		
12/33	7.1	7.3	7.7	8.3	9.2	8.9	7.3	-0.1																	
12/34	6.3	6.5	6.6	7.0	7.4	6.8	5.0	0.2	0.6																
12/35	5.5	5.5	5.5	5.6	5.8	4.9	3.2	-0.6	-0.8	-2.2															
12/36	4.9	4.9	4.8	4.9	4.9	4.0	2.4	-0.6	-0.7	-1.3	-0.5														
12/37	4.2	4.1	4.0	4.0	3.9	3.0	1.6	-1.0	-1.2	-1.8	-1.6	-2.7													
12/38	4.2	4.1	4.0	3.9	3.8	3.0	1.8	-0.3	-0.3	-0.5	0.0	0.3	3.3												
12/39	4.0	3.9	3.7	3.7	3.6	2.9	1.8	-0.0	-0.0	-0.2	0.4	0.6	2.4	1.4											
12/40	3.7	3.5	3.4	3.3	3.2	2.5	1.5	-0.1	-0.1	-0.2	0.2	0.4	1.4	0.5	-0.5										
12/41	2.8	2.6	2.5	2.3	2.1	1.4	0.4	-1.2	-1.3	-1.6	-1.4	-1.6	-1.4	-2.9	-5.0	-9.2									
12/42	2.1	1.9	1.7	1.5	1.3	0.6	-0.4	-1.9	-2.1	-2.4	-2.4	-2.7	-2.7	-4.2	-6.0	-8.7	-8.1								
12/43	1.9	1.7	1.5	1.3	1.0	0.3	-0.6	-1.9	-2.1	-2.4	-2.4	-2.7	-2.7	-3.8	-5.1	-6.6	-5.3	-2.3							
12/44	1.7	1.5	1.3	1.1	0.8	0.2	-0.7	-1.9	-2.0	-2.3	-2.3	-2.5	-2.5	-3.4	-4.4	-5.3	-4.0	-1.9	-1.4						
12/45	1.5	1.3	1.1	0.9	0.7	0.1	-0.7	-1.9	-2.0	-2.2	-2.2	-2.4	-2.4	-3.2	-3.9	-4.6	-3.4	-1.8	-1.5	-1.6					
12/46	0.7	0.5	0.2	-0.0	-0.3	-0.9	-1.7	-2.8	-3.0	-3.3	-3.4	-3.7	-3.8	-4.7	-5.6	-6.4	-5.8	-5.2	-6.1	-8.4	-14.8				
12/47	0.3	0.1	-0.2	-0.4	-0.7	-1.3	-2.1	-3.2	-3.4	-3.7	-3.8	-4.1	-4.2	-5.0	-5.8	-6.5	-6.1	-5.7	-6.5	-8.1	-11.3	-7.6			
12/48	0.2	-0.0	-0.3	-0.5	-0.8	-1.3	-2.1	-3.1	-3.3	-3.5	-3.6	-3.9	-4.0	-4.7	-5.4	-6.0	-5.5	-5.1	-5.6	-6.6	-8.2	-4.8	-1.8		
12/49	0.3	0.1	-0.1	-0.3	-0.6	-1.1	-1.8	-2.7	-2.9	-3.1	-3.2	-3.4	-3.5	-4.0	-4.6	-5.0	-4.5	-4.0	-4.2	-4.8	-5.6	-2.3	0.5	2.9	
12/50	0.1	-0.1	-0.3	-0.5	-0.8	-1.3	-2.0	-2.8	-3.0	-3.2	-3.3	-3.5	-3.6	-4.1	-4.6	-5.0	-4.5	-4.0	-4.3	-4.8	-5.4	-2.9	-1.2	-1.0	-4.7
12/51	-0.1	-0.3	-0.5	-0.7	-1.0	-1.5	-2.1	-2.9	-3.1	-3.3	-3.4	-3.5	-3.6	-4.1	-4.6	-4.9	-4.5	-4.1	-4.3	-4.7	-5.2	-3.2	-2.0	-2.1	-4.5
12/52	-0.0	-0.2	-0.5	-0.7	-0.9	-1.4	-2.0	-2.8	-2.9	-3.1	-3.1	-3.3	-3.3	-3.8	-4.2	-4.5	-4.0	-3.6	-3.8	-4.1	-4.4	-2.6	-1.5	-1.4	-2.9
12/53	0.0	-0.2	-0.4	-0.6	-0.8	-1.2	-1.8	-2.6	-2.7	-2.8	-2.9	-3.0	-3.0	-3.4	-3.8	-4.0	-3.6	-3.2	-3.2	-3.4	-3.7	-2.0	-1.0	-0.8	-1.7
12/54	0.1	-0.1	-0.3	-0.5	-0.7	-1.1	-1.6	-2.4	-2.5	-2.6	-2.6	-2.7	-2.7	-3.1	-3.4	-3.6	-3.2	-2.7	-2.8	-2.9	-3.1	-1.5	-0.6	-0.4	-1.0
12/55	0.1	-0.1	-0.3	-0.4	-0.6	-1.0	-1.6	-2.2	-2.3	-2.5	-2.5	-2.6	-2.6	-2.9	-3.2	-3.4	-2.9	-2.5	-2.5	-2.6	-2.7	-1.3	-0.5	-0.3	-0.8
12/56	0.1	-0.1	-0.3	-0.5	-0.6	-1.0	-1.5	-2.2	-2.3	-2.4	-2.4	-2.5	-2.5	-2.8	-3.0	-3.2	-2.8	-2.4	-2.4	-2.5	-2.6	-1.2	-0.5	-0.3	-0.8
12/57	0.1	-0.1	-0.3	-0.4	-0.6	-1.0	-1.5	-2.1	-2.2	-2.3	-2.3	-2.4	-2.4	-2.7	-2.9	-3.0	-2.6	-2.2	-2.2	-2.3	-2.4	-1.1	-0.5	-0.3	-0.7
12/58	0.1	-0.1	-0.3	-0.4	-0.6	-1.0	-1.4	-2.0	-2.1	-2.2	-2.2	-2.3	-2.3	-2.5	-2.7	-2.9	-2.5	-2.1	-2.1	-2.1	-2.2	-1.0	-0.4	-0.3	-0.6
12/59	0.1	-0.1	-0.2	-0.4	-0.6	-0.9	-1.3	-1.9	-2.0	-2.1	-2.1	-2.1	-2.1	-2.4	-2.6	-2.7	-2.3	-1.9	-1.9	-1.9	-2.0	-0.9	-0.3	-0.2	-0.5
12/60	0.2	0.0	-0.2	-0.3	-0.4	-0.8	-1.2	-1.7	-1.8	-1.9	-1.9	-1.9	-1.9	-2.1	-2.3	-2.4	-2.0	-1.7	-1.6	-1.6	-1.7	-0.6	-0.1	0.1	-0.2
12/61	0.2	0.0	-0.1	-0.2	-0.4	-0.7	-1.1	-1.6	-1.7	-1.8	-1.8	-1.8	-1.8	-2.0	-2.1	-2.2	-1.9	-1.5	-1.5	-1.5	-1.5	-0.5	0.0	0.2	-0.1
12/62	0.2	0.1	-0.1	-0.2	-0.3	-0.7	-1.0	-1.6	-1.6	-1.7	-1.7	-1.7	-1.7	-1.9	-2.0	-2.1	-1.7	-1.4	-1.3	-1.3	-1.3	-0.4	0.1	0.2	0.0
12/63	0.2	0.1	-0.1	-0.2	-0.3	-0.6	-1.0	-1.5	-1.5	-1.6	-1.6	-1.6	-1.6	-1.8	-1.9	-2.0	-1.6	-1.3	-1.2	-1.2	-1.2	-0.4	0.1	0.3	0.1
12/64	0.3	0.1	-0.0	-0.1	-0.3	-0.6	-0.9	-1.4	-1.4	-1.5	-1.5	-1.5	-1.5	-1.6	-1.8	-1.8	-1.5	-1.2	-1.1	-1.1	-1.1	-0.2	0.2	0.3	0.2
12/65	0.3	0.2	0.0	-0.1	-0.2	-0.5	-0.9	-1.3	-1.3	-1.4	-1.4	-1.4	-1.4	-1.5	-1.6	-1.7	-1.4	-1.1	-1.0	-1.0	-1.0	-0.2	0.3	0.4	0.2
12/66	0.3	0.2	0.0	-0.1	-0.2	-0.5	-0.8	-1.3	-1.3	-1.3	-1.3	-1.3	-1.3	-1.5	-1.6	-1.6	-1.3	-1.0	-0.9	-0.9	-0.9	-0.1	0.3	0.4	0.3
12/67	0.3	0.2	0.1	-0.0	-0.2	-0.4	-0.8	-1.2	-1.2	-1.3	-1.2	-1.3	-1.2	-1.4	-1.5	-1.5	-1.2	-0.9	-0.9	-0.8	-0.8	-0.1	0.3	0.4	0.3
12/68	0.3	0.2	0.1	-0.0	-0.2	-0.4	-0.7	-1.2	-1.2	-1.2	-1.2	-1.2	-1.2	-1.3	-1.4	-1.5	-1.2	-0.9	-0.8	-0.8	-0.8	-0.1	0.3	0.4	0.3
12/69	0.3	0.2	0.0	-0.1	-0.2	-0.4	-0.8	-1.2	-1.2	-1.2	-1.2	-1.2	-1.2	-1.3	-1.4	-1.4	-1.2	-0.9	-0.8	-0.8	-0.8	-0.1	0.2	0.3	0.2
12/70	0.3	0.2	0.1	-0.0	-0.1	-0.4	-0.7	-1.1	-1.1	-1.2	-1.1	-1.1	-1.1	-1.2	-1.3	-1.3	-1.1	-0.8	-0.7	-0.7	-0.7	-0.0	0.3	0.4	0.3
12/71	0.3	0.2	0.1	0.0	-0.1	-0.3	-0.6	-1.0	-1.0	-1.1	-1.1	-1.1	-1.0	-1.2	-1.2	-1.3	-1.0	-0.7	-0.7	-0.6	-0.6	0.0	0.3	0.4	0.3
12/72	0.3	0.2	0.1	-0.0	-0.1	-0.3	-0.6	-1.0	-1.0	-1.1	-1.0	-1.0	-1.0	-1.1	-1.2	-1.2	-1.0	-0.7	-0.6	-0.6	-0.6	0.0	0.3	0.4	0.3
12/73	0.2	0.1	0.0	-0.1	-0.2	-0.4	-0.7	-1.1	-1.1	-1.1	-1.1	-1.1	-1.1	-1.2	-1.3	-1.3	-1.1	-0.8	-0.8	-0.7	-0.7	-0.1	0.2	0.2	0.1
12/74	0.1	-0.0	-0.1	-0.2	-0.3	-0.5	-0.8	-1.2	-1.2	-1.2	-1.2	-1.2	-1.2	-1.3	-1.4	-1.4	-1.2	-1.0	-0.9	-0.9	-0.9	-0.3	-0.1	0.0	-0.1
12/75	0.1	-0.0	-0.1	-0.2	-0.3	-0.6	-0.8	-1.2	-1.2	-1.3	-1.2	-1.2	-1.2	-1.3	-1.4	-1.4	-1.2	-1.0	-0.9	-0.9	-0.9	-0.4	-0.1	-0.0	-0.2
12/76	0.1	-0.0	-0.1	-0.2	-0.3	-0.5	-0.8	-1.2	-1.2	-1.2	-1.2	-1.2	-1.2	-1.3	-1.4	-1.4	-1.2	-0.9	-0.9	-0.9	-0.9	-0.4	-0.1	-0.0	-0.1

Table XLIX

Time-Weighted Rates of Return* on Short-Term U.S. Treasury Securities:
Interest Reinvested,
Lower Tax Rate,
Deflated by the Consumer Price Index

Held until	12/50	12/51	12/52	12/53	12/54	12/55	12/56	12/57	12/58	12/59	12/60	12/61	12/62	12/63	12/64	12/65	12/66	12/67	12/68	12/69	12/70	12/71	12/72	12/73	12/74	12/75
/51	−4.3																									
/52	−1.9	0.6																								
/53	−0.7	1.1	1.7																							
/54	−0.1	1.4	1.8	1.9																						
/55	−0.0	1.1	1.3	1.1	0.3																					
/56	−0.1	0.7	0.8	0.5	−0.3	−0.8																				
/57	−0.1	0.6	0.6	0.3	−0.2	−0.4	−0.0																			
/58	−0.1	0.5	0.5	0.3	−0.1	−0.3	−0.0	−0.0																		
/59	−0.0	0.5	0.5	0.3	0.0	−0.0	0.2	0.3	0.7																	
/60	0.3	0.8	0.8	0.7	0.5	0.5	0.9	1.2	1.8	2.9																
/61	0.4	0.8	0.9	0.8	0.6	0.7	1.0	1.2	1.7	2.1	1.4															
/62	0.4	0.9	0.9	0.8	0.7	0.7	1.0	1.2	1.5	1.8	1.2	1.1														
/63	0.4	0.8	0.9	0.8	0.7	0.7	0.9	1.1	1.3	1.5	1.0	0.9	0.6													
/64	0.5	0.9	1.0	0.9	0.8	0.8	1.0	1.2	1.4	1.6	1.2	1.2	1.2	1.8												
/65	0.6	0.9	1.0	0.9	0.8	0.9	1.0	1.2	1.4	1.5	1.2	1.1	1.1	1.4	1.0											
/66	0.6	0.9	0.9	0.9	0.8	0.8	1.0	1.1	1.3	1.4	1.1	1.0	1.0	1.2	0.9	0.7										
/67	0.6	0.9	0.9	0.8	0.8	0.9	1.0	1.1	1.2	1.3	1.1	1.0	1.0	1.1	0.9	0.9	1.0									
/68	0.6	0.8	0.9	0.8	0.7	0.8	0.9	1.0	1.1	1.1	0.9	0.9	0.8	0.8	0.6	0.5	0.4	−0.3								
/69	0.5	0.7	0.8	0.7	0.6	0.6	0.8	0.8	0.9	0.9	0.7	0.6	0.5	0.5	0.3	0.1	−0.1	−0.6	−1.0							
/70	0.5	0.8	0.8	0.8	0.7	0.7	0.8	0.9	1.0	1.0	0.8	0.7	0.7	0.7	0.5	0.4	0.3	0.1	0.3	1.7						
/71	0.6	0.8	0.8	0.8	0.7	0.8	0.9	0.9	1.0	1.0	0.9	0.8	0.8	0.8	0.6	0.6	0.6	0.4	0.7	1.6	1.4					
/72	0.5	0.8	0.8	0.7	0.7	0.7	0.8	0.9	0.9	0.9	0.8	0.7	0.7	0.7	0.5	0.5	0.4	0.3	0.5	1.0	0.6	−0.2				
/73	0.3	0.6	0.6	0.5	0.4	0.4	0.5	0.5	0.6	0.6	0.4	0.3	0.2	0.2	0.0	−0.1	−0.2	−0.4	−0.4	−0.3	−0.9	−2.1	−4.0			
/74	0.1	0.3	0.3	0.2	0.1	0.1	0.2	0.2	0.2	0.2	−0.0	−0.1	−0.2	−0.3	−0.5	−0.7	−0.9	−1.1	−1.3	−1.3	−2.0	−3.2	−4.6	−5.3		
/75	0.0	0.2	0.2	0.1	0.1	0.0	0.1	0.1	0.1	0.1	−0.1	−0.2	−0.3	−0.4	−0.6	−0.8	−0.9	−1.2	−1.3	−1.3	−1.9	−2.8	−3.6	−3.4	−1.5	
/76	0.0	0.2	0.2	0.1	0.1	0.0	0.1	0.1	0.1	0.1	−0.1	−0.2	−0.3	−0.4	−0.5	−0.7	−0.8	−1.0	−1.1	−1.1	−1.6	−2.2	−2.7	−2.2	−0.7	0.2

Percent per annum, compounded annually

Sources: Bond market data—Lawrence Fisher (compiler), CRSP Monthly Return File for U.S. Treasury Securities (magnetic tape). See Appendix A.
Consumer Price Index—U.S. Bureau of Labor Statistics.
Income tax rates—Income levels estimated from U.S. Bureau of the Census, Current Population Reports, Series P-60, Nos. 101 and 103 and Historical Statistics of the United States.· Tax rates were found in U.S. Internal Revenue Service, Statistics of Income and Your Federal Income Tax.

Held Until	Purchased 12/25	12/26	12/27	12/28	12/29	12/30	12/31	12/32	12/33	12/34	12/35	12/36	12/37	12/38	12/39	12/40	12/41	12/42	12/43	12/44	12/45	12/46	12/47	12/48	12/49
12/26	3.8																								
12/27	3.5	3.2																							
12/28	3.4	3.2	3.3																						
12/29	3.8	3.8	4.2	5.0																					
12/30	3.8	3.7	3.9	4.3	3.5																				
12/31	3.4	3.3	3.3	3.3	2.5	1.5																			
12/32	3.4	3.3	3.3	3.4	2.8	2.5	3.5																		
12/33	3.0	2.9	2.8	2.8	2.2	1.8	1.9	0.4																	
12/34	3.0	2.9	2.8	2.7	2.3	2.0	2.1	1.5	2.6																
12/35	2.7	2.6	2.5	2.4	2.0	1.7	1.8	1.2	1.7	0.7															
12/36	2.5	2.4	2.3	2.2	1.8	1.6	1.6	1.1	1.3	0.7	0.7														
12/37	2.4	2.2	2.1	2.0	1.6	1.4	1.4	0.9	1.1	0.6	0.5	0.3													
12/38	2.2	2.1	2.0	1.9	1.5	1.3	1.2	0.9	1.0	0.5	0.5	0.4	0.5												
12/39	2.1	2.0	1.9	1.8	1.5	1.2	1.2	0.9	1.0	0.6	0.6	0.6	0.7	0.9											
12/40	2.0	1.9	1.8	1.7	1.4	1.1	1.1	0.8	0.9	0.6	0.6	0.5	0.6	0.7	0.4										
12/41	1.9	1.7	1.6	1.5	1.2	1.0	1.0	0.7	0.7	0.5	0.4	0.4	0.4	0.3	0.0	−0.4									
12/42	1.8	1.6	1.5	1.4	1.1	0.9	0.9	0.6	0.7	0.4	0.4	0.3	0.4	0.3	0.1	−0.0	0.3								
12/43	1.7	1.6	1.5	1.4	1.1	0.9	0.9	0.6	0.7	0.4	0.4	0.4	0.4	0.4	0.2	0.2	0.4	0.5							
12/44	1.6	1.5	1.4	1.3	1.0	0.9	0.8	0.6	0.6	0.4	0.4	0.4	0.4	0.4	0.3	0.2	0.4	0.4	0.4						
12/45	1.6	1.4	1.4	1.2	1.0	0.8	0.8	0.6	0.6	0.4	0.4	0.4	0.4	0.4	0.3	0.2	0.4	0.4	0.4	0.4					
12/46	1.5	1.4	1.3	1.2	1.0	0.8	0.8	0.6	0.6	0.4	0.4	0.4	0.4	0.4	0.3	0.3	0.4	0.4	0.4	0.4	0.4				
12/47	1.4	1.3	1.2	1.1	0.9	0.8	0.7	0.6	0.6	0.4	0.4	0.4	0.4	0.4	0.3	0.3	0.4	0.4	0.3	0.3	0.3	0.3			
12/48	1.4	1.3	1.2	1.1	0.9	0.8	0.7	0.6	0.6	0.4	0.4	0.4	0.4	0.4	0.3	0.3	0.4	0.4	0.4	0.4	0.4	0.4	0.6		
12/49	1.4	1.3	1.2	1.1	0.9	0.8	0.7	0.6	0.6	0.5	0.4	0.4	0.4	0.4	0.4	0.4	0.4	0.5	0.5	0.5	0.5	0.6	0.7	0.8	
12/50	1.4	1.2	1.2	1.1	0.9	0.8	0.7	0.6	0.6	0.5	0.4	0.4	0.4	0.4	0.4	0.4	0.5	0.5	0.5	0.5	0.5	0.5	0.6	0.6	0.5
12/51	1.3	1.2	1.2	1.1	0.9	0.8	0.7	0.6	0.6	0.5	0.5	0.4	0.5	0.5	0.4	0.4	0.5	0.5	0.5	0.5	0.6	0.6	0.7	0.7	0.6
12/52	1.3	1.2	1.1	1.1	0.9	0.8	0.7	0.6	0.6	0.5	0.5	0.5	0.5	0.5	0.4	0.4	0.5	0.5	0.5	0.6	0.6	0.6	0.7	0.7	0.7
12/53	1.3	1.2	1.2	1.1	0.9	0.8	0.8	0.6	0.7	0.6	0.5	0.5	0.5	0.6	0.5	0.5	0.6	0.6	0.6	0.7	0.7	0.8	0.8	0.9	0.9
12/54	1.3	1.2	1.2	1.1	0.9	0.8	0.8	0.7	0.7	0.6	0.6	0.6	0.6	0.6	0.6	0.6	0.6	0.7	0.7	0.7	0.8	0.8	0.9	0.9	1.0
12/55	1.3	1.2	1.1	1.0	0.9	0.8	0.8	0.6	0.7	0.6	0.6	0.5	0.6	0.6	0.5	0.5	0.6	0.6	0.6	0.7	0.7	0.7	0.8	0.8	0.8
12/56	1.3	1.2	1.1	1.0	0.9	0.8	0.8	0.7	0.7	0.6	0.6	0.6	0.6	0.6	0.6	0.6	0.6	0.7	0.7	0.7	0.7	0.8	0.8	0.8	0.9
12/57	1.3	1.2	1.1	1.1	0.9	0.8	0.8	0.7	0.7	0.6	0.6	0.6	0.6	0.6	0.6	0.6	0.7	0.7	0.7	0.8	0.8	0.9	0.9	0.9	1.0
12/58	1.3	1.2	1.1	1.1	0.9	0.8	0.8	0.7	0.7	0.6	0.6	0.6	0.7	0.7	0.7	0.7	0.7	0.7	0.8	0.8	0.8	0.9	0.9	1.0	1.0
12/59	1.3	1.2	1.1	1.0	0.9	0.8	0.8	0.7	0.7	0.6	0.6	0.6	0.7	0.7	0.7	0.7	0.7	0.7	0.8	0.8	0.8	0.9	0.9	0.9	0.9
12/60	1.3	1.2	1.2	1.1	1.0	0.9	0.9	0.8	0.8	0.7	0.7	0.7	0.8	0.8	0.8	0.8	0.8	0.9	0.9	0.9	1.0	1.0	1.1	1.1	1.1
12/61	1.3	1.2	1.2	1.1	1.0	0.9	0.9	0.8	0.8	0.8	0.8	0.8	0.8	0.8	0.8	0.8	0.9	0.9	0.9	0.9	1.0	1.0	1.1	1.1	1.1
12/62	1.3	1.2	1.2	1.1	1.0	0.9	0.9	0.8	0.8	0.8	0.8	0.8	0.8	0.8	0.8	0.8	0.9	0.9	0.9	1.0	1.0	1.0	1.1	1.1	1.2
12/63	1.3	1.2	1.2	1.1	1.0	0.9	0.9	0.8	0.8	0.8	0.8	0.8	0.8	0.8	0.8	0.8	0.9	0.9	0.9	1.0	1.0	1.0	1.1	1.1	1.1
12/64	1.3	1.2	1.2	1.1	1.0	1.0	0.9	0.9	0.9	0.8	0.8	0.8	0.8	0.9	0.9	0.9	0.9	1.0	1.0	1.0	1.0	1.1	1.1	1.2	1.2
12/65	1.3	1.3	1.2	1.2	1.0	1.0	1.0	0.9	0.9	0.8	0.9	0.9	0.9	0.9	0.9	0.9	1.0	1.0	1.0	1.0	1.1	1.1	1.2	1.2	1.2
12/66	1.3	1.3	1.2	1.2	1.1	1.0	1.0	0.9	0.9	0.9	0.9	0.9	0.9	0.9	0.9	1.0	1.0	1.0	1.1	1.1	1.1	1.2	1.2	1.3	1.3
12/67	1.4	1.3	1.3	1.2	1.1	1.1	1.0	1.0	1.0	0.9	0.9	1.0	1.0	1.0	1.0	1.0	1.1	1.1	1.1	1.2	1.2	1.2	1.3	1.3	1.3
12/68	1.4	1.3	1.3	1.2	1.1	1.1	1.1	1.0	1.0	1.0	1.0	1.0	1.0	1.0	1.0	1.1	1.1	1.2	1.2	1.2	1.2	1.3	1.3	1.4	1.4
12/69	1.4	1.4	1.3	1.3	1.2	1.1	1.1	1.1	1.1	1.0	1.0	1.0	1.1	1.1	1.1	1.1	1.2	1.2	1.2	1.3	1.3	1.3	1.4	1.4	1.5
12/70	1.5	1.4	1.4	1.3	1.2	1.2	1.2	1.1	1.1	1.1	1.1	1.1	1.2	1.2	1.2	1.2	1.3	1.3	1.3	1.4	1.4	1.4	1.5	1.5	1.6
12/71	1.5	1.4	1.4	1.4	1.3	1.2	1.2	1.2	1.2	1.1	1.2	1.2	1.2	1.2	1.2	1.3	1.3	1.3	1.4	1.4	1.4	1.5	1.5	1.6	1.6
12/72	1.5	1.5	1.4	1.4	1.3	1.2	1.2	1.2	1.2	1.2	1.2	1.2	1.2	1.2	1.2	1.3	1.3	1.4	1.4	1.4	1.5	1.5	1.6	1.6	1.6
12/73	1.5	1.5	1.4	1.4	1.3	1.3	1.3	1.2	1.2	1.2	1.2	1.2	1.2	1.3	1.3	1.3	1.4	1.4	1.4	1.5	1.5	1.5	1.6	1.6	1.7
12/74	1.6	1.5	1.5	1.4	1.4	1.3	1.3	1.3	1.3	1.2	1.3	1.3	1.3	1.3	1.3	1.4	1.4	1.4	1.5	1.5	1.6	1.6	1.6	1.7	1.7
12/75	1.6	1.5	1.5	1.5	1.4	1.3	1.3	1.3	1.3	1.3	1.3	1.3	1.3	1.4	1.4	1.4	1.5	1.5	1.5	1.6	1.6	1.6	1.7	1.7	1.8
12/76	1.6	1.6	1.5	1.5	1.4	1.4	1.4	1.3	1.3	1.3	1.3	1.3	1.4	1.4	1.4	1.4	1.5	1.5	1.6	1.6	1.6	1.7	1.7	1.8	1.8

Table L

Time-Weighted Rates of Return* on Short-Term U.S. Treasury Securities:
  Interest Reinvested,
  Higher Tax Rate,
  Current Dollars

Held until	Purchased					Purchased					Purchased					Purchased					Purchased					
	12/50	12/51	12/52	12/53	12/54	12/55	12/56	12/57	12/58	12/59	12/60	12/61	12/62	12/63	12/64	12/65	12/66	12/67	12/68	12/69	12/70	12/71	12/72	12/73	12/74	12/75
12/51	0.8																									
12/52	0.8	0.9																								
12/53	1.1	1.2	1.5																							
12/54	1.1	1.2	1.3	1.1																						
12/55	0.9	0.9	0.9	0.6	0.1																					
12/56	0.9	0.9	1.0	0.8	0.6	1.0																				
12/57	1.0	1.1	1.1	1.0	1.0	1.4	1.7																			
12/58	1.0	1.1	1.1	1.0	1.0	1.3	1.4	1.0																		
12/59	1.0	1.0	1.0	1.0	0.9	1.1	1.2	0.9	0.7																	
12/60	1.2	1.2	1.3	1.3	1.3	1.5	1.6	1.6	1.9	3.1																
12/61	1.2	1.2	1.3	1.2	1.3	1.5	1.5	1.5	1.6	2.1	1.1															
12/62	1.2	1.2	1.3	1.3	1.3	1.4	1.5	1.5	1.6	1.8	1.2	1.3														
12/63	1.2	1.2	1.3	1.2	1.3	1.4	1.4	1.4	1.5	1.7	1.2	1.2	1.1													
12/64	1.2	1.3	1.3	1.3	1.3	1.4	1.5	1.4	1.5	1.7	1.3	1.4	1.4	1.7												
12/65	1.3	1.3	1.3	1.3	1.3	1.5	1.5	1.5	1.5	1.7	1.4	1.5	1.5	1.7	1.8											
12/66	1.3	1.4	1.4	1.4	1.4	1.5	1.6	1.6	1.6	1.8	1.6	1.7	1.7	1.9	2.1	2.3										
12/67	1.4	1.4	1.5	1.5	1.5	1.6	1.7	1.7	1.7	1.9	1.7	1.8	1.9	2.0	2.1	2.3	2.3									
12/68	1.5	1.5	1.5	1.5	1.6	1.7	1.7	1.7	1.8	1.9	1.8	1.9	2.0	2.1	2.2	2.4	2.4	2.5								
12/69	1.5	1.5	1.6	1.6	1.6	1.7	1.8	1.8	1.9	2.0	1.9	1.9	2.0	2.2	2.3	2.4	2.4	2.5	2.5							
12/70	1.6	1.7	1.7	1.7	1.8	1.9	1.9	2.0	2.0	2.1	2.1	2.2	2.3	2.4	2.5	2.7	2.8	2.9	3.2	3.9						
12/71	1.7	1.7	1.8	1.8	1.8	1.9	2.0	2.0	2.1	2.2	2.1	2.2	2.3	2.4	2.5	2.7	2.7	2.8	3.0	3.2	2.6					
12/72	1.7	1.7	1.8	1.8	1.8	1.9	2.0	2.0	2.1	2.2	2.1	2.2	2.2	2.4	2.5	2.6	2.6	2.6	2.7	2.8	2.2	1.8				
12/73	1.7	1.7	1.8	1.8	1.8	1.9	2.0	2.0	2.1	2.2	2.1	2.2	2.3	2.4	2.4	2.5	2.6	2.6	2.6	2.7	2.2	2.1	2.4			
12/74	1.8	1.8	1.9	1.9	1.9	2.0	2.1	2.1	2.1	2.2	2.2	2.3	2.3	2.5	2.5	2.6	2.6	2.7	2.7	2.8	2.5	2.5	2.8	3.3		
12/75	1.8	1.9	1.9	1.9	2.0	2.1	2.1	2.1	2.2	2.3	2.2	2.3	2.4	2.5	2.6	2.7	2.7	2.7	2.8	2.8	2.6	2.6	2.9	3.2	3.0	
12/76	1.9	1.9	1.9	2.0	2.0	2.1	2.1	2.2	2.2	2.3	2.3	2.3	2.4	2.5	2.6	2.7	2.7	2.7	2.8	2.8	2.6	2.6	2.8	3.0	2.8	2.6

*Percent per annum, compounded annually

Sources: Bond market data—Lawrence Fisher (compiler), CRSP
Monthly Return File for U.S. Treasury Securities (mag-
netic tape). See Appendix A.
Income tax rates—Income levels estimated from U.S.
Bureau of the Census, Current Population Reports, Series
P-60, Nos. 101 and 103 and Historical Statistics of the
United States. Tax rates were found in U.S. Internal
Revenue Service, Statistics of Income and Your Federal
Income Tax.

Held Until	Purchased					Purchased					Purchased					Purchased					Purchased				
	12/25	12/26	12/27	12/28	12/29	12/30	12/31	12/32	12/33	12/34	12/35	12/36	12/37	12/38	12/39	12/40	12/41	12/42	12/43	12/44	12/45	12/46	12/47	12/48	12/49
12/26	5.4																								
12/27	5.4	5.3																							
12/28	5.0	4.8	4.3																						
12/29	5.0	4.8	4.6	4.8																					
12/30	6.0	6.1	6.4	7.5	10.2																				
12/31	7.0	7.3	7.8	9.0	11.1	12.1																			
12/32	8.1	8.6	9.3	10.6	12.5	13.7	15.4																		
12/33	7.1	7.3	7.6	8.3	9.2	8.9	7.3	-0.1																	
12/34	6.3	6.4	6.6	7.0	7.4	6.8	5.0	0.2	0.6																
12/35	5.4	5.4	5.5	5.6	5.8	4.9	3.2	-0.6	-0.8	-2.2															
12/36	4.9	4.8	4.8	4.8	4.8	4.0	2.4	-0.6	-0.7	-1.3	-0.5														
12/37	4.2	4.1	4.0	4.0	3.9	3.0	1.6	-1.0	-1.2	-1.8	-1.6	-2.7													
12/38	4.2	4.1	3.9	3.9	3.8	3.0	1.8	-0.3	-0.3	-0.5	0.0	0.3	3.3												
12/39	4.0	3.9	3.7	3.7	3.6	2.9	1.8	-0.0	-0.0	-0.2	0.4	0.6	2.4	1.4											
12/40	3.7	3.5	3.4	3.3	3.2	2.5	1.5	-0.1	-0.1	-0.2	0.2	0.4	1.4	0.5	-0.5										
12/41	2.8	2.6	2.4	2.3	2.1	1.4	0.4	-1.2	-1.3	-1.6	-1.4	-1.6	-1.4	-2.9	-5.0	-9.2									
12/42	2.1	1.9	1.7	1.5	1.3	0.6	-0.4	-1.9	-2.1	-2.4	-2.4	-2.8	-2.8	-4.2	-6.0	-8.7	-8.2								
12/43	1.9	1.7	1.4	1.2	1.0	0.3	-0.6	-2.0	-2.1	-2.4	-2.5	-2.7	-2.7	-3.9	-5.2	-6.7	-5.4	-2.6							
12/44	1.7	1.5	1.2	1.1	0.8	0.2	-0.7	-1.9	-2.1	-2.4	-2.4	-2.6	-2.6	-3.5	-4.5	-5.5	-4.2	-2.1	-1.7						
12/45	1.5	1.3	1.1	0.9	0.6	0.0	-0.8	-1.9	-2.1	-2.3	-2.3	-2.5	-2.5	-3.3	-4.1	-4.8	-3.6	-2.0	-1.8	-1.8					
12/46	0.6	0.4	0.1	-0.1	-0.4	-1.0	-1.8	-2.9	-3.1	-3.4	-3.6	-3.9	-4.0	-4.9	-5.7	-6.6	-6.0	-5.5	-6.4	-8.7	-15.1				
12/47	0.2	-0.0	-0.3	-0.5	-0.8	-1.4	-2.2	-3.3	-3.5	-3.8	-3.9	-4.2	-4.4	-5.2	-6.0	-6.8	-6.4	-6.0	-6.8	-8.5	-11.6	-8.0			
12/48	0.1	-0.1	-0.4	-0.6	-0.9	-1.4	-2.2	-3.2	-3.4	-3.7	-3.8	-4.1	-4.2	-4.9	-5.6	-6.2	-5.8	-5.3	-5.9	-6.9	-8.5	-5.1	-2.1		
12/49	0.2	0.0	-0.2	-0.4	-0.7	-1.2	-1.9	-2.9	-3.0	-3.3	-3.3	-3.6	-3.6	-4.2	-4.8	-5.2	-4.7	-4.2	-4.5	-5.1	-5.9	-2.6	0.3	2.6	
12/50	0.0	-0.2	-0.4	-0.7	-0.9	-1.4	-2.1	-3.0	-3.1	-3.4	-3.5	-3.7	-3.7	-4.3	-4.8	-5.2	-4.8	-4.3	-4.6	-5.1	-5.7	-3.2	-1.5	-1.3	-5.0
12/51	-0.2	-0.4	-0.6	-0.8	-1.1	-1.6	-2.2	-3.1	-3.2	-3.5	-3.5	-3.7	-3.8	-4.3	-4.8	-5.2	-4.8	-4.4	-4.6	-5.0	-5.5	-3.5	-2.4	-2.5	-4.9
12/52	-0.2	-0.4	-0.6	-0.8	-1.0	-1.5	-2.1	-2.9	-3.1	-3.3	-3.3	-3.5	-3.6	-4.0	-4.4	-4.8	-4.4	-4.0	-4.1	-4.4	-4.8	-2.9	-1.9	-1.8	-3.3
12/53	-0.1	-0.3	-0.5	-0.7	-1.0	-1.4	-2.0	-2.8	-2.9	-3.1	-3.1	-3.3	-3.3	-3.7	-4.1	-4.3	-3.9	-3.5	-3.6	-3.8	-4.1	-2.4	-1.4	-1.3	-2.3
12/54	-0.1	-0.3	-0.5	-0.6	-0.9	-1.3	-1.8	-2.6	-2.7	-2.8	-2.9	-3.0	-3.0	-3.4	-3.7	-3.9	-3.5	-3.1	-3.2	-3.3	-3.5	-1.9	-1.0	-0.8	-1.5
12/55	-0.1	-0.3	-0.5	-0.6	-0.8	-1.2	-1.8	-2.5	-2.6	-2.7	-2.7	-2.8	-2.9	-3.2	-3.5	-3.7	-3.3	-2.9	-2.9	-3.0	-3.1	-1.7	-0.9	-0.7	-1.3
12/56	-0.1	-0.3	-0.5	-0.7	-0.9	-1.3	-1.8	-2.4	-2.5	-2.7	-2.7	-2.8	-2.8	-3.1	-3.4	-3.6	-3.2	-2.8	-2.8	-2.9	-3.0	-1.7	-1.0	-0.9	-1.4
12/57	-0.2	-0.3	-0.5	-0.7	-0.9	-1.3	-1.8	-2.4	-2.5	-2.6	-2.6	-2.7	-2.7	-3.0	-3.3	-3.4	-3.1	-2.7	-2.7	-2.8	-2.9	-1.7	-1.0	-0.9	-1.3
12/58	-0.2	-0.4	-0.5	-0.7	-0.9	-1.2	-1.7	-2.3	-2.4	-2.5	-2.5	-2.6	-2.6	-2.9	-3.1	-3.3	-2.9	-2.6	-2.6	-2.6	-2.7	-1.6	-1.0	-0.9	-1.3
12/59	-0.2	-0.4	-0.5	-0.7	-0.9	-1.2	-1.7	-2.3	-2.3	-2.5	-2.5	-2.6	-2.5	-2.8	-3.0	-3.2	-2.8	-2.5	-2.5	-2.5	-2.6	-1.5	-1.0	-0.9	-1.2
12/60	-0.2	-0.3	-0.5	-0.6	-0.8	-1.1	-1.6	-2.1	-2.2	-2.3	-2.3	-2.4	-2.4	-2.6	-2.8	-2.9	-2.6	-2.3	-2.2	-2.3	-2.3	-1.3	-0.8	-0.7	-1.0
12/61	-0.1	-0.3	-0.5	-0.6	-0.8	-1.1	-1.5	-2.0	-2.1	-2.2	-2.2	-2.3	-2.3	-2.5	-2.7	-2.8	-2.4	-2.1	-2.1	-2.1	-2.1	-1.2	-0.7	-0.6	-0.9
12/62	-0.1	-0.3	-0.4	-0.6	-0.7	-1.1	-1.5	-2.0	-2.0	-2.1	-2.1	-2.2	-2.2	-2.4	-2.5	-2.6	-2.3	-2.0	-2.0	-2.0	-2.0	-1.1	-0.6	-0.5	-0.8
12/63	-0.1	-0.3	-0.4	-0.6	-0.7	-1.0	-1.4	-1.9	-2.0	-2.1	-2.1	-2.1	-2.1	-2.3	-2.5	-2.5	-2.2	-1.9	-1.9	-1.9	-1.9	-1.1	-0.6	-0.5	-0.8
12/64	-0.1	-0.3	-0.4	-0.5	-0.7	-1.0	-1.4	-1.8	-1.9	-2.0	-2.0	-2.0	-2.0	-2.2	-2.3	-2.4	-2.1	-1.8	-1.8	-1.8	-1.8	-1.0	-0.6	-0.5	-0.7
12/65	-0.1	-0.3	-0.4	-0.5	-0.7	-1.0	-1.3	-1.8	-1.8	-1.9	-1.9	-2.0	-1.9	-2.1	-2.3	-2.3	-2.0	-1.8	-1.7	-1.7	-1.7	-1.0	-0.5	-0.5	-0.6
12/66	-0.1	-0.3	-0.4	-0.5	-0.7	-1.0	-1.3	-1.8	-1.8	-1.9	-1.9	-1.9	-1.9	-2.1	-2.2	-2.3	-2.0	-1.7	-1.7	-1.7	-1.7	-1.0	-0.6	-0.5	-0.7
12/67	-0.2	-0.3	-0.4	-0.5	-0.7	-1.0	-1.3	-1.7	-1.8	-1.9	-1.8	-1.9	-1.9	-2.0	-2.2	-2.2	-1.9	-1.7	-1.6	-1.6	-1.6	-0.9	-0.6	-0.5	-0.7
12/68	-0.2	-0.3	-0.5	-0.6	-0.7	-1.0	-1.3	-1.8	-1.8	-1.9	-1.9	-1.9	-1.9	-2.0	-2.2	-2.2	-1.9	-1.7	-1.7	-1.7	-1.7	-1.0	-0.7	-0.6	-0.7
12/69	-0.3	-0.4	-0.5	-0.7	-0.8	-1.1	-1.4	-1.8	-1.8	-1.9	-1.9	-1.9	-1.9	-2.1	-2.2	-2.3	-2.0	-1.8	-1.7	-1.7	-1.7	-1.1	-0.8	-0.7	-0.9
12/70	-0.3	-0.4	-0.6	-0.7	-0.8	-1.1	-1.4	-1.8	-1.8	-1.9	-1.9	-1.9	-1.9	-2.1	-2.2	-2.2	-2.0	-1.8	-1.7	-1.7	-1.7	-1.1	-0.8	-0.8	-0.9
12/71	-0.3	-0.4	-0.6	-0.7	-0.8	-1.1	-1.4	-1.8	-1.8	-1.9	-1.9	-1.9	-1.9	-2.0	-2.1	-2.2	-1.9	-1.7	-1.7	-1.7	-1.7	-1.1	-0.8	-0.8	-0.9
12/72	-0.3	-0.5	-0.6	-0.7	-0.8	-1.1	-1.4	-1.8	-1.8	-1.9	-1.9	-1.9	-1.9	-2.0	-2.1	-2.2	-1.9	-1.7	-1.7	-1.7	-1.7	-1.1	-0.8	-0.8	-0.9
12/73	-0.5	-0.6	-0.7	-0.8	-0.9	-1.2	-1.5	-1.9	-1.9	-2.0	-2.0	-2.0	-2.0	-2.1	-2.2	-2.3	-2.1	-1.9	-1.8	-1.8	-1.8	-1.3	-1.0	-1.0	-1.1
12/74	-0.6	-0.7	-0.9	-1.0	-1.1	-1.3	-1.6	-2.0	-2.1	-2.1	-2.1	-2.2	-2.1	-2.3	-2.4	-2.5	-2.2	-2.0	-2.0	-2.0	-2.1	-1.6	-1.3	-1.3	-1.4
12/75	-0.7	-0.8	-0.9	-1.0	-1.2	-1.4	-1.7	-2.1	-2.1	-2.2	-2.2	-2.2	-2.2	-2.3	-2.4	-2.5	-2.3	-2.1	-2.1	-2.1	-2.1	-1.6	-1.4	-1.4	-1.5
12/76	-0.7	-0.8	-1.0	-1.1	-1.2	-1.4	-1.7	-2.1	-2.1	-2.2	-2.2	-2.2	-2.2	-2.3	-2.4	-2.5	-2.3	-2.1	-2.1	-2.1	-2.1	-1.6	-1.4	-1.4	-1.5

Table LI

Time-Weighted Rates of Return* on Short-Term U.S. Treasury Securities:
   Interest Reinvested,
   Higher Tax Rate,
   Deflated by the Consumer Price Index

Yield until	12/50	12/51	12/52	12/53	12/54	12/55	12/56	12/57	12/58	12/59	12/60	12/61	12/62	12/63	12/64	12/65	12/66	12/67	12/68	12/69	12/70	12/71	12/72	12/73	12/74	12/75
12/51	-4.8																									
12/52	-2.4	-0.0																								
12/53	-1.3	0.4	0.9																							
12/54	-0.6	0.8	1.3	1.6																						
12/55	-0.5	0.6	0.8	0.7	-0.2																					
12/56	-0.7	0.1	0.1	-0.1	-1.0	-1.8																				
12/57	-0.8	-0.1	-0.2	-0.4	-1.1	-1.5	-1.2																			
12/58	-0.8	-0.2	-0.2	-0.5	-1.0	-1.2	-1.0	-0.7																		
12/59	-0.8	-0.3	-0.3	-0.5	-0.9	-1.1	-0.9	-0.7	-0.8																	
12/60	-0.6	-0.1	-0.1	-0.2	-0.5	-0.6	-0.3	0.0	0.4	1.6																
12/61	-0.5	-0.0	-0.0	-0.1	-0.4	-0.4	-0.1	0.1	0.4	1.0	0.4															
12/62	-0.4	-0.0	-0.0	-0.1	-0.3	-0.3	-0.1	0.1	0.3	0.7	0.3	0.1														
12/63	-0.4	-0.1	-0.1	-0.2	-0.4	-0.4	-0.2	0.0	0.2	0.4	0.0	-0.2	-0.5													
12/64	-0.4	-0.0	-0.0	-0.1	-0.3	-0.3	-0.1	0.1	0.2	0.4	0.1	0.0	0.0	0.5												
12/65	-0.3	-0.0	-0.0	-0.1	-0.3	-0.3	-0.1	0.1	0.2	0.3	0.1	-0.0	-0.0	0.2	-0.2											
12/66	-0.4	-0.1	-0.1	-0.2	-0.3	-0.3	-0.2	-0.1	0.0	0.1	-0.1	-0.2	-0.3	-0.2	-0.6	-1.0										
12/67	-0.4	-0.1	-0.1	-0.2	-0.3	-0.4	-0.2	-0.1	-0.1	0.0	-0.2	-0.3	-0.4	-0.3	-0.6	-0.8	-0.7									
12/68	-0.5	-0.2	-0.3	-0.3	-0.5	-0.5	-0.4	-0.3	-0.3	-0.2	-0.4	-0.6	-0.7	-0.7	-1.0	-1.3	-1.4	-2.2								
12/69	-0.7	-0.4	-0.4	-0.5	-0.7	-0.7	-0.6	-0.6	-0.6	-0.5	-0.8	-0.9	-1.1	-1.2	-1.5	-1.8	-2.1	-2.8	-3.4							
12/70	-0.7	-0.5	-0.5	-0.6	-0.7	-0.8	-0.7	-0.6	-0.6	-0.6	-0.8	-1.0	-1.1	-1.2	-1.5	-1.8	-1.9	-2.4	-2.5	-1.5						
12/71	-0.7	-0.5	-0.5	-0.6	-0.7	-0.8	-0.7	-0.7	-0.6	-0.6	-0.8	-1.0	-1.1	-1.2	-1.4	-1.6	-1.7	-2.0	-1.9	-1.1	-0.8					
12/72	-0.7	-0.5	-0.6	-0.7	-0.8	-0.8	-0.7	-0.7	-0.7	-0.7	-0.9	-1.0	-1.1	-1.2	-1.4	-1.6	-1.7	-1.9	-1.8	-1.3	-1.2	-1.6				
12/73	-1.0	-0.8	-0.8	-0.9	-1.1	-1.1	-1.1	-1.0	-1.1	-1.1	-1.3	-1.4	-1.6	-1.7	-1.9	-2.1	-2.3	-2.6	-2.7	-2.5	-2.8	-3.8	-5.9			
12/74	-1.3	-1.1	-1.2	-1.3	-1.4	-1.5	-1.5	-1.5	-1.5	-1.6	-1.8	-2.0	-2.1	-2.3	-2.5	-2.8	-3.0	-3.4	-3.6	-3.6	-4.1	-5.2	-6.9	-7.9		
12/75	-1.4	-1.2	-1.3	-1.4	-1.5	-1.6	-1.6	-1.6	-1.6	-1.7	-1.9	-2.1	-2.2	-2.4	-2.6	-2.9	-3.1	-3.4	-3.6	-3.6	-4.0	-4.8	-5.9	-5.9	-3.7	
12/76	-1.4	-1.3	-1.3	-1.4	-1.5	-1.6	-1.6	-1.6	-1.7	-1.7	-1.9	-2.1	-2.2	-2.4	-2.6	-2.8	-3.0	-3.3	-3.4	-3.4	-3.7	-4.3	-4.9	-4.6	-2.9	-2.1

Percent per annum, compounded annually.

Sources: *Bond market data—Lawrence Fisher (compiler),* CRSP Monthly Return File for U.S. Treasury Securities *(magnetic tape). See Appendix A.*
Consumer Price Index—U.S. Bureau of Labor Statistics.
Income tax rates—Income levels estimated from U.S. Bureau of the Census, Current Population Reports, *Series P-60, Nos. 101 and 103 and* Historical Statistics of the United States. *Tax rates were found in U.S. Internal Revenue Service,* Statistics of Income *and* Your Federal Income Tax.

Appendix A

Definitions and Sources of Data

Scope of this Appendix

The 66,300 rates of return or rates of change in price that we have tabulated in this volume show the hypothetical result of having selected and followed the set of investment and book-keeping policies that applied to each particular table.

In the calculation process, which is summarized in Appendix B, we worked with the data for one security at a time as we followed the applicable policy. Our immediate sources of data were a special version of the *CRSP Monthly Return File for Common Stocks Listed on the New York Stock Exchange* (Stock Return File) and the *CRSP Monthly Return File for United States Treasury Securities* (Bond Return File). The original version of the Stock Return File was compiled by the first author in 1964.[1] Recent editions have been greatly improved through the use of more reliable computational algorithms worked out by Myron Scholes.[2] The Bond Return File was also compiled by the first author. These data files and the *CRSP Daily Return File for Common Stocks*,[3] which covers the period since July 2, 1962, have been used for a large fraction of the empirical research studies on the behavior of security prices and interest rates that have been published since 1965. They usually are casually referred to as "Chicago Tapes," "CRSP Tapes," or "data from CRSP" without further specificity or citation.

The stocks included in this study are issued by companies that continually change their names, merge with other companies, or go out of business. The Governments are offered for sale, quoted in the market for a period ranging from a few months to fifty years, and either disappear as they reach their agreed upon maturity dates or are called for early redemption by the Secretary of the Treasury. From its beginning date, each return file contains in summary form a month-by-month (or day-by-day) history of the effect of owning the security in question on the investor's wealth for the entire time that a stock was listed or a Government was publicly traded.

The calculations for a return file are made by applying a computer program to a "master file" in which coded raw data for each security have been collected. For example, in a month in which a particular stock pays no dividends and has no capital changes, the return for that month is simply the change in price of one share of the

---

[1] Cf. Lawrence Fisher, "Outcomes for 'Random' Investments in Common Stocks Listed on the New York Stock Exchange," Journal of Business 38 (April 1965): 149–161 and "Some New Stock-Market Indexes," op. cit.

[2] Myron S. Scholes, "Returns to Investing in Common Stocks Listed on the New York Stock Exchange," op. cit.

[3] The Daily Return File covers all common stocks listed on the NYSE (Consolidated A Ticker) and on the American Stock Exchange (Consolidated B Ticker) and the over-the-counter issues that are included in Standard & Poor's "Composite" Index (S & P 500). It was originally compiled by Professor Scholes under the sponsorship of Wells Fargo Bank.

stock since the last month divided by last month's price. However, if a dividend was paid during the month, the dividend on one share is added to the price change before dividing by last month's price. If there is a stock dividend rather than a cash dividend, last month's price is adjusted before calculating the return for the month. The adjustment is equivalent to dividing last month's price by the ratio of the number of shares after the stock dividend to the number of shares before the stock dividend. When there are both dividends and capital changes or several of either during a month, finding that month's return requires a complex computer program.

Once they have been compiled, the Return files are easy to use. The major work in constructing such files is the building of the underlying master file. That process consists of collecting information and compiling it into a file of coded raw data which can be corrected as errors are discovered and which is in a form from which the Return file may be calculated.

The major task of this Appendix is the description of the procedures by which data get into a master file. It will be a nontechnical description designed primarily to identify the data sources used by the CRSP staff.

The calculations reported in the tables required using some data that are not in the CRSP Master or Return files. These data will also be described in this Appendix.

Data in the CRSP Stock-Market Files

The Stock Return File used for this study covers the period from December 31, 1925 to December 31, 1976. It includes data for 2,655 common stocks. Five hundred three such stocks were listed on the NYSE on December 31, 1925. Their data begin at that time. For each of the remaining 2,152 stocks, data begin on the last day of the month in which it was first listed. Most of the issues used (1,540) were still listed on December 31, 1976. Their last entries are on that date. Four hundred eighty-one stocks were succeeded by others in mergers in which their owners received listed common stock. Their data end in the month of the merger. The remaining stocks have been stricken from the list or suspended from trading for other reasons. Their data extend through the month of delisting or suspension, if such action was announced in advance, or to a time at which the value after suspension could be determined.

Whenever the necessary underlying calcula-

tions could be made, the special Stock Return File used for this study contains

1. The closing price for the last business day of the month
2. The number of shares of the issue that were outstanding on the same date as the closing price
3. The total return for the month (as described above)
4. The return for the month excluding (i.e., ignoring) cash dividends.[4]

The Stock Return File was calculated from the *CRSP Monthly Master File for Common Stocks Listed on the New York Stock Exchange* (Monthly Master File).

The working version of the Monthly Master File is a merger of data from a *Base Monthly Master File*, which includes month-end prices from December 31, 1925 through June 29, 1962 and other data for the same period, and a *Daily Master File*, which contains daily closing prices and all other data from July 1962 to date.

Nearly all of the data in the *Base Monthly Master File* were collected by the CRSP staff and were used by us for "Rates (1964)," "Rates (1968)," "Variability," etc. Rights to the CRSP monthly files were sold to an outside agency after they had been updated through early 1966. The outside agency extended the base file through 1972 but the quality of the data after mid-1968 was too low for a study like this one.

Meanwhile, Myron Scholes, who was then at the Massachusetts Institute of Technology, compiled a forerunner of the present *Daily Master File*. He became the director of CRSP at about the same time that the Center recovered rights to the CRSP files. The present *Daily Master File* includes data from both sources as well as additions and corrections made during the past three years of intensive effort.

The *Working Monthly Master File* contains data on NYSE common stocks for the period they have been listed since December 31, 1925. It contains all of the data in the base file and all of the data on NYSE stocks in the daily file except for the omission of prices that are not for the last business day of a month.

[4]*The special version of the Stock Return File differs from the tapes labeled MSRA-76C.G006V05 that were distributed to subscribers to the file in March 1977. The special version was made in May 1977 after several errors in the underlying master file had been corrected and after extensive revision of the data on shares outstanding. The special version was the first copy of the file to contain monthly shares outstanding. These improvements will appear in the next files through June 1977 when they are distributed. In addition, returns for the 481 merged stocks referred to in the text have been carried through the end of the merger month.*

Coverage

To be included in the monthly files as a common stock, an issue must have been traded on the NYSE and it must not be preferred to any other issue that has a right to receive dividends. Included are almost all issues called "capital stock," "common stock," or "ordinary shares." Also included are some issues of "Class A stock," "Class B stock," shares of beneficial interest in land and real-estate trusts, capital shares of dual funds, American depository receipts for bearer shares issued by foreign companies, voting-trust certificates, "preferred" stock of the Great Northern Railway (which had never issued "common" until the preferred was renamed in the 1950s), and the Class B Debentures of the Green Bay & Western Railroad. Excluded are Class A stocks that were really preferreds, guaranteed railroad stocks (whose dividends were an obligation of the lessee), stock purchase warrants, and subscription rights.

Prices

The prices used for initial investment, for reinvestment of cash dividends, etc., are monthly closing prices, i.e., the last sale price on the last business day of the month. If the stock was not sold on the NYSE on the last day of the month, then the mean of the "bid" and "ask" quotations is used. If the mean does not exist, the price is treated as missing; and for our calculations, the next month-end price in the file is used.[5] In all, 615,474 month-end price quotations are used in this study.

Primary sources. These prices have come from the following primary sources:

A. December 1925–January 1928, the "Bank and Quotation Section" of the *Commercial and Financial Chronicle.*

B. February 1928–December 1960, the *Bank and Quotation Record,* an expansion of the "Bank and Quotation Section."

Both are monthly publications. Among other data, they show closing sale prices for the last day of each month for issues traded on the NYSE. During the periods for which they were our primary source, they also show bid and ask prices for NYSE stocks and a large number of other securities.

Data from these sources were hand coded and punched into computer cards. The process of coding, compilation, checking, and correction is described in "Rates (1964)."

After 1960 there were machine-readable data available for prices.

C. January 1961–June 1962. Cards punched by the Stock Exchange Clearing Corporation (a subsidiary of NYSE) and made available to NYSE members. These data were compiled into semi-annual or annual tapes of daily quotations by Merrill Lynch, Pierce, Fenner & Smith Inc. The prices on these tapes differ from those in other sources because they represent clearing-house transactions rather than what appears on stock tickers. For very active stocks, there are frequent fractional differences. These files contain high, low, close, volume, and number of transactions—a fact that makes checking for discrepancies within a single computer card fairly easy. The discrepancy rate for this source appeared to be about 3 percent. When an issue was not traded on a particular day, only the bid was shown and another source had to be consulted.

D. Since July 2, 1962, various forms of the computer data base now provided by Interactive Data Corporation (IDC) have been used. From July 1962–December 1972 quarterly ISL tapes were used. These files were originally compiled by the Investment Statistics Laboratory of Palo Alto, California. The ISL service was acquired by a subsidiary of Standard & Poor's Corporation (S & P) in 1966. It and other machine-readable portions of S & P's pricing and dividend services were acquired by Interactive Data Corporation in 1972. For a number of years the prices were collected from the *Wall Street Journal,* which took them from the Associated Press. The Associated Press read the prices from the stock ticker.[6] Interactive Data now receives prices directly from the "high-speed ticker" and, after processing, stores them on magnetic disks attached to a computer.

The Center for Research in Security Prices reads the disk records shortly

---

[5] *For "Rates (1964)" and "Rates (1968)" we used the bid or the ask if only one of them was available. The* Base Master File, *which covers the period when only-bid and only-ask quotations were most frequent, retains those data; but the* Daily File *does not. Inspection of data for firms for which such single quotations exist, e.g., American Express Co. in the 1930s, has convinced us that the next "good" quotation is generally a more reliable estimate of what the sale price would have been than the bid or ask alone. This policy does not apply when we must estimate the value of stocks that have been suspended or delisted. Then, we use the earliest relevant quotation that can be found.*

[6] *By clerks until 1963, by computer thereafter.*

after the end of each calendar quarter to obtain the prices.

The prices now used for NYSE stocks are those that come from the Consolidated A Ticker Service.

Secondary Sources. In the *Base Master File* for 1925–60, if the price quoted in the NYSE section of the *Bank and Quotation Record* or its predecessor is missing or suspect, the general quotations section in the back of the issue is consulted first. Then the next day's opening price, which is in the next issue, is checked. Occasional reference has been made to newspapers.

For January 1961–June 1962, the *Bank and Quotation Record* is the secondary source. It has been used whenever the month-end price from the Clearing Corporation is from an internally inconsistent record and whenever both bid and ask quotations are required.

The *Commercial and Financial Chronicle* has served as the chief secondary source of daily prices. The *Wall Street Journal, Barron's,* and the *Bank and Quotation Record* also have been consulted.

Checking and Correction. Although CRSP's waiting until the end of the quarter to collect prices from IDC's files allows IDC to correct many of the errors that appear in its files initially, waiting also allows the editing process to introduce still other errors. The primary checks on prices are made by looking for large changes—and especially for "reversals." A reversal occurs when the reported price rises or falls substantially one day and moves in the reverse direction the next. Reversals are often, but by no means always, the result of data errors. Large changes that are not reversals indicate that there may have been some substantial capital change. In those cases, the price has been checked with a secondary source. In recent years, most errors have involved bid and ask quotations. For these quotations, the *Commercial and Financial Chronicle* has been the only independent daily source.

Cash Dividends and Other Distributions to Stockholders

In theory at least, the only reason for a common stock to be worth anything is that the issuing company may eventually distribute something of value, e.g., cash, to its shareholders. In the period covered by our study, NYSE companies made distributions more than 175,000 times.

There are many kinds of distributions. The system of classification that we use depends on what is distributed, on the tax status of the distribution, and on the subsequent existence of the company.

The most frequent distribution is the cash dividend paid from the retained earnings of the corporation. *Moody's Dividend Record* has served as a primary source of information on cash dividends throughout the period 1926–76. From July 1962–December 1972 dividend data have also been taken from the ISL tapes, and, since 1973, from the IDC Dividend Service, which can be read in the same manner as the prices provided by IDC. Neither of these sources contains the date the dividend was declared. Hence, all data from the ISL and IDC services have been checked against those from *Moody's* and the declaration dates have been collected from *Moody's.* Conflicts are resolved by consulting the *Weekly Bulletin* of the NYSE. *Standard & Poor's Register of Corporations* is used as a second source of declared dates.

Many distributions do not transfer property from the corporation to its shareholders. Stock dividends, splits, and subscription rights are prime examples of such distributions. Other distributions are too complicated to be described clearly in the tabular format of the dividend services. These distributions are usually described in the Commerce Clearing House *Capital Changes Reporter.*

A substantial number of foreign companies are listed on the NYSE. Dividends in Canadian currency are converted by CRSP using exchange rates given by the *Bank and Quotation Record.* Dividends paid in other foreign currencies are usually converted to U.S. dollar equivalents in *Moody's Dividend Record.*

Cash dividends are treated as if they were available for reinvestment on the last day of the ex-dividend month. Stock dividends, splits, subscription rights, and other distributions that can readily be treated as if old shares had been exchanged for a larger or smaller number of new shares without making a purchase on the floor of the NYSE are converted to factors that are used to adjust the previous month's price for the computation of the net return for the month. Special procedures are used to make sure that any distribution whose ex-dividend or ex-distribution date is between the ex and payment dates of some other distribution is treated correctly.

Number of Shares

The number of shares actually outstanding is collected periodically. There have been a large number of sources. *Moody's Manuals* have been used throughout the period as a primary source. Data in the ISL tapes, from IDC, and from Standard & Poor's COMPUSTAT Service have been used for all or part of the period since 1946.

Between explicit share entries in the *Master File,* the number of shares outstanding is inferred by using an algorithm devised by Professor Scholes. The algorithm takes account of the effects of dividends, splits, and new offerings in which stockholders received pre-emptive subscription rights. The number of shares outstanding may also change for a large number of other reasons—mergers, conversions of bonds and preferred shares, exercise of purchase warrants and executive stock options, and operations of the company's treasury. At this time, entries of shares outstanding are complete from 1946 to date and sparse for earlier years, except that discrepancies between inferred and actual shares outstanding that could have affected the tables of rates of return on portfolios that were initially value-weighted have been checked and corrected. From 1926 to 1936 and since September 1975, *Listing Statements of the New York Stock Exchange* (current title *Listing Applications to the New York Stock Exchange, Inc.)* have been consulted. For other dates, checking has been done by consulting the appropriate volume of *Moody's Manuals* and still other sources.

Tax Status

Currently, the taxability of cash dividends is indicated in *Moody's Dividend Record.* For the entire period, dividends with special tax status have been described in the *CCH Capital Changes Reporter.* The tax status of all other distributions is also given in the *Capital Changes Reporter.* Prentice-Hall's *Capital Adjustments* is also consulted.

Delistings and Suspensions from Trading

When trading ceases for a substantial period of time, the series of price quotations in our primary source is also interrupted. If trading has ceased because of a merger, the merger terms normally can be entered into our data files from the *Capital Changes Reporter.* When trading ceases for some other reason, an investigation that is often time consuming is required. Sometimes the suspension of trading is announced in advance. Then the last sale price on the NYSE is taken as the final value. Sometimes the corporation is completely liquidated at or shortly after the time trading is suspended. Then the final price can be taken as zero, and the value to the investor at the delisting date is given by the value of whatever liquidating distributions may be pending.

The most difficult cases occur when dealings are suspended because of insolvency or fraud or other irregularity. Then no final price that takes account of the news that caused the suspension may be available for several months or years. When no value can be found or estimated, returns can be computed only to the end of the month before the suspension; and, temporarily, the stock is treated as if it had been delisted at that date. Fortunately the number of such cases is less than twenty, and, in most of those cases, the stock had little value at the date of the last usable price.

Data in the CRSP Files on U.S. Government Securities

The CRSP files on U.S. Government securities cover nearly all direct, marketable obligations of the United States Treasury. These issues include bonds, notes, certificates of indebtedness, and bills. The files covers about 3,000 issues (mostly Treasury bills) and includes about 40,000 monthly price quotations.

For each issue, the data currently in the files include a summary description and several series of monthly data.

At this time, the summary description includes an identifying number (assigned by CRSP and describing the terms of most issues), the maturity date, the first call date (and required notice) if callable, the month that notice of call was given, the coupon rate, the federal income-tax status of interest, the type of issue, the range of dates for which there is price information in the file, an indication of why data end, and indicators of flower-bond and bank-eligibility status.

The monthly data include end-of-month price, accrued interest, interest paid during the month, promised yield, return for the month, excess of return over last month's promised yield, duration, amount outstanding, amount in the hands of the public, and an indication of the source of that month's price quotations.

Definitions of Data

CRSP Number. The identifying number controls the order of data in the file and is designed to simplify use of the file by indicating the major terms of the issue—maturity date, type of issue, and coupon rate. These items are defined below.

Maturity Date. Unless it was callable, every issue has had a definite date it was payable by the Treasury. For interest-bearing securities, the maturity date also defines dates at which interest is due. All such securities that are in the file and were issued since 1917 pay interest semi-annually. One of the interest payments is due on the same month and day that the issue will mature.[7]

Call Date. Most bonds (and a few notes) have been callable for redemption at par before final maturity. Typically these bonds are callable after four months' notice at any interest date during the five years before the final maturity date. However, the period between the first call date and final maturity varied from two years to twenty years (and was infinite for the bond just noted). The required notice has varied from sixty days to six months.

Month of Notice. Many issues have been redeemed on the first call date; some have been called later; and many others have not been called at all. The month that notice was given both defines the actual redemption date for issues that have been called and shows when the issue changed from a callable bond to a very short-term bond due on the redemption date.

All but one of the called issues was called as a whole. The exception was the Fourth Liberty Loan 4¼s of October 15, 1933–38, which was about one-fourth of the total Federal public debt in 1933. It was called for redemption in four lots, depending on serial number, from April 1934 to October 1935. This action made it necessary to treat the Fourth Liberty Loan as four separate issues in the file.

Coupon Rate. The coupon rate states the annual interest in terms of the number of dollars a year per hundred dollars of par (face) value.

Tax Status of Interest. Federal taxation of interest on Governments has varied both with respect to time and with respect to the terms stated in the offering circular. Interest on some issues has been wholly tax-exempt; on others, partially tax-exempt; and on all domestic securities issued since March 1, 1941, fully taxable. Tax exemption was given to securities issued until shortly after the start of World War I, to all Treasury bills issued before March 1941, and to notes and certificates of indebtedness issued from about 1930 through 1940 (except for "Defense" notes issued in 1940). Partial tax exemption applied to all other securities issued before March 1941. Partial tax exemption meant that interest on the first five thousand dollars' worth of such bonds (more in the 1920s) was exempt

from all income taxes and that remaining interest was exempt from "normal" taxes. Through 1935, dividends paid on common stock were also exempt from the normal tax. Until that time, the normal tax was graduated. Hence, the value to the holder of both full or partial tax exemption depended on his total income. The last wholly and partially tax-exempt issues were outstanding until 1961.

Type of Issue. The following kinds of security have been issued:

- Bonds, both callable and noncallable. These are the longest term issues. Maturities have ranged as high as fifty years.

- Notes, noncallable except for a few issues in the early 1930s. Maturities range from about eighteen months to nine years.

- Certificates of indebtedness. Interest-bearing issues with maximum maturities of about one year. Last issued about 1960.

- Treasury bills. Discount notes. All gain or loss is "interest" for income-tax purposes. Maturities of one year or less.

Some of the bills and certificates have been issued in anticipation of taxes. They were acceptable at par for taxes due about a week before their ostensible maturity dates. This privilege affected the quoted yield.

Some bonds have had special features that cannot be reflected accurately in the machine-readable format used for the file—e.g., the Fourth Liberty Loan called and uncalled bonds, the "Consols" of 1930, and an issue whose coupon rate dropped from four percent to three percent after it was outstanding for one year.

The type of issue is shown both as a number, for data processing purposes, and as an abbreviated name, for use with printed sources.

Range of Dates. This item is for data processing purposes.

Stop Code. This item is both for data processing and research use. The code indicates whether the issue was still quoted on the latest date for the file. If it was not still quoted, the code shows whether the issue was called, had matured, or had been dropped by our data sources.

Flower Bond Status. Bonds have fallen into three categories: (1) no special privilege, (2) acceptable at par in payment of federal estate tax if owned by the decedent at the time of

---

[7] *The six bonds in the file that were issued before World War I paid interest quarterly. Only one issue, the Consolidated 2s of 1930, had no contractual final maturity date. It was callable on any interest date beginning April 1, 1930 and was called in 1935.*

death, (3) acceptable only if owned during the entire six-month period before death. Bonds with provisions (2) or (3) are popularly called flower bonds. Provision (2) was used for many bonds issued after 1941. Provision (3) applied to bonds with coupon rates of more than 4 percent per annum that were issued during and after World War I.

Bank Eligibility. A security is "bank eligible" if a commercial bank may own it. All securities in the file were bank eligible at all times except for some $2^{1}/_{4}$s and $2^{1}/_{2}$s issued during or immediately after World War II. The restrictions on bank eligibility were intended to and did restrict the negotiability of the bonds in question. The file shows the date on which each such restriction ended or was scheduled to have ended when the restriction on the last two such bonds was removed in 1956.

Price. Governments have generally been traded in the over-the-counter market during the period covered by the file. The exception is that, until about 1941, there was active trading in bonds on the New York Stock Exchange. As in other over-the-counter securities, both bid and ask prices are quoted; and these quotations for the last business day of each month appear in the file. From 1934 through 1941, our data source reported closing sale prices for most bonds rather than the bid and ask. Sometimes only the mean of the bid and ask was reported and sometimes only a bid price was available.

Accrued Interest. Governments and most other debt issues that are quoted on a price rather than a yield basis have prices to which accrued interest must be added. We show interest accrued through the last business day of the month.[8]

Interest Paid. The amount of interest paid since last month's quotation date is shown.[9]

Yield. If the issue is noncallable or if it is callable and the price (excluding accrued interest) is less than par, yield is computed to the maturity date. For other callable bonds, yield is computed to the nearest call date, taking account of the notice that is required for a call. Yield actually is presented twice: as a per diem rate compounded continuously and as a percent per annum compounded semi-annually and assuming a 365-day year.[10]

Return for the Month. The return for the month is found by dividing the net "income" for the month by last month's price. The net income for the month is the sum of the change in quoted price since last month, the change in accrued interest, and the amount of interest paid. The price used as the divisor includes accrued interest. Monthly returns computed in this manner are the precise analogs of returns including cash dividends provided on the *CRSP Monthly Return File for Common Stocks.*

Excess Return. Excess return is the difference between return for the month, as just defined, and "expected return." Expected return is the return that would have been calculated if yield had remained at last month's level for the entire month. Excess return is computed because finding expected return is substantially more complicated than setting it equal to one twelfth of the annual yield both because months vary in length and because of the policy of holding interest paid until the end of the month, which is implied by the method of finding return.

Duration. Duration is the average time to payment of principal and interest. For discount instruments such as Treasury bills and for issues that are due the next interest-payment date, duration is simply the number of days to maturity. For other securities, duration is a weighted average of the number of days until each interest payment and the number of days to the maturity or call date. Each number of days is given a weight equal to the present value of the interest or principal payment.[11] As we indicated in Chapter 12, the derivative of the logarithm of the price (including accrued interest) of a security with respect to the yield compounded continuously is equal to the negative of duration.[12]

Amount Outstanding. The principal amount of the security that is outstanding on, or shortly before, the quotation date.

Amount in the Hands of the Public. Substantial amounts of the gross public debt are held by federal agencies or trust funds for the benefit of the Social Security System, etc. The

---

[8] *Each month's accrued interest is not physically present on the magnetic tape containing the file. It is among the derived data that are added by a computer subroutine that should be called by programs that read the file. The subroutine does not take account of the fact that the initial coupon may cover a period that is longer or shorter than the usual six months between coupons. It treats the accrual and also the payment of interest as if the bond had been outstanding for an indefinite period before the first quotations appeared in the file. For securities that enter the file when quoted on a when-issued basis, there may be an error of about 2/100 of one percentage point in the first month's return. We believe that that error is negligible.*

[9] *We assume that interest is actually paid on the due date even if it is a Saturday, Sunday, or holiday. Interest paid is inserted by the same subroutine that inserts accrued interest and is consistent with the latter.*

[10] *The per diem rate is read from the tape. The annual rate is inserted by the subroutine.*

[11] *Duration is inserted by the subroutine.*

[12] *Interest and duration must be stated in equivalent units, e.g., per diem and days, per annum and years.*

amount in the hands of the public is an alternative measure of the amount outstanding.

Source Code. There were two chief sources and two main secondary sources of price data for the file. One of the important ways in which they varied was in the amount of redundancy in their quotations. The source code is an indication of reliability.

Data Sources

The chief sources of data have been the dealer's offering sheets issued daily by Salomon Brothers and a monthly publication of the Government Actuary. The offering sheets issued in 1947 or later are in the University of Chicago Library. The Government Actuary's publication was originally issued as Circular 2 in 1901. It continued under various titles and formats until February 1953. During the period 1947–52 we collected some data from one source, some from the other, and recorded about half of the data in duplicate.

The Government Actuary's data are more redundant than the Salomon Brothers' data, and therefore tests of the internal consistency of the former quotations for a security are more reliable. The contents and coverage of the Government Actuary's circular varied. However, the vast majority of quotations are presented both as bid and ask or sale prices and as a promised yield based on the mean of the bid and ask prices. Hence, checking the price implied by the yield against the mean of the bid and ask quotations assures that no single error in bid, ask, coupon rate, maturity (or call) date, quotation date, or yield goes undetected.

The Salomon Brothers quotation sheets present a yield that is based only on the ask price. Hence the bid price must be omitted from the list of things checked by the process of finding the price implied by the reported yield.

There were other sources of data. *Moody's Government Manual* was consulted for descriptions of the terms of many of the securities. The *Bank and Quotation Record* was used for checking prices. However, it was seldom our original source because yields were not sufficiently reliable or were omitted entirely and because, in the early years, quotations for notes and certificates of indebtedness appeared to be for the next-to-last day of the month. The *New York Times* microfilm edition was used for prices of securities that were omitted by the Government Actuary before 1934. The *Wall Street Journal* and several Treasury Department publications were also consulted.

Data on amounts outstanding appeared in convenient and fairly regular format only in the Salomon Brothers quotation sheets. When data for the month were collected from another source, the amount outstanding was estimated by the amount in the next (first) entry taken from Salomon Brothers.

Checking

Each month's quotation is initially treated as an independent record. When it has passed tests for internal consistency, it is merged with the data in a master file. The master file is similar to the file described earlier in this section except that only price, amount outstanding (both values), and source code are retained as monthly items.

After the master file has been checked for gaps and undesirable redundancies, the full monthly file described above is created. Then a check is made relating the computed excess returns to the value expected from running a monthly series of cross-sectional regressions of excess return for the month on duration. Separate regressions are run for each tax class. If the apparently inconsistent recorded data agree with what was actually given by the source, an alternative source is checked and the quotation is revised if the alternative source differs substantially from the original in either direction.

Issues Selected

Long-Term Bonds. The long-term bonds used to calculate Tables XXXIV through XXXIX had the following characteristics:

During 1926–41 ten different issues were held one at a time. All were both callable and partially tax-exempt. Coupons ranged from 2 percent to 4 percent. Assumed purchases, at year-end 1925–40, were at yields of from 1.61 percent per annum, compounded *annually,* to 4.09 percent. However, the range of differences between yield and coupon was −39 basis points (−0.39 percent per annum) to +16 basis points.

From 1942 through 1957 the 2½s of September 15, 1972, first callable in 1967, constituted the only issue held. It was fully taxable. Its promised yield was from 2.00 to 3.56 percent.

From 1958 through 1970 either the 3⅜s of November 15, 1974 or the 4s of May 15, 1980 were held. They were fully taxable, noncallable flower bonds. However, less than one and one half percent of the aggregate of either issue was redeemed during the thirteen-year period although yields ranged from 3.29 to 8.14 percent.

During 1971 the 3¼s of May 15, 1985 were held. That issue is a fully taxable, noncallable flower bond. Its yield was 6.54 percent in December 1970, which was 5 basis points higher than the yield of the 4s of 1980. About one fifteenth of the amount in the hands of the public appears to have been tendered to pay estate taxes during 1971.

From 1972 through 1976 the issues held were fully taxable, were noncallable, and were not flower bonds. They were the $6^1/8$s of November 15, 1986 and the $6^3/4$s of February 15, 1993.

Intermediate-Term. Thirty-one intermediate-term issues were held. From 1926 through 1941 the issues held were partially tax-exempt. The issues held in 1926–28 were flower bonds that sold at a premium during all three years. For nine of the sixteen years, the issue held was callable.

From 1942 through 1976 the issue held was fully taxable. In 1942 and from 1944 through 1952, the bond held was callable.

Short-Term. The number of issues held was 102. Initial terms to maturity ranged from a little less than seven months through twelve months. Notes, certificates of indebtedness, and Treasury bills were all held at various times. Through 1960 certificates were held most frequently. From 1961 through 1976 only bills were held. Interest was partially tax-exempt on the issue held from January 1926 through June 1930; wholly tax-exempt, July 1930–June 1942; but fully taxable, July 1942–December 1976.

Other Data

Some of the data used for the calculations of rates of return were not contained in CRSP Stock or Bond Files. This section reports the sources for data on brokerage commissions; the Consumer Price Index; and the tax rates applied to dividends, interest, and capital gains.

Commissions

The commission rates used for the cash-to-portfolio and cash-to-cash computations for NYSE common stocks were the rates that applied to transactions of 100 shares on the date the transaction was assumed to have taken place. From 1925 through April 1975, the rates used were the "minimum" rates specified by the NYSE rules.[13] The April 30, 1975 schedule was used for later transactions.

Early editions of the *CRSP Monthly Master File* contained both "price" and "price plus commission." In the current, more compact format the second variable is omitted. In the calcula-

tions of rates of return, our computer programs used a revised version of the same subroutine that had been used to find price plus commission for the early editions. The subroutine follows the NYSE rules.

The commission schedules that were in effect through 1965 were taken from a mimeographed summary of changes in commission rates issued by the NYSE. Later rate schedules were taken from various issues of *Standard & Poor's Stock Guide.*

The Consumer Price Index

The Consumer Price Index (CPI) was taken from a release issued by the U.S. Bureau of Labor Statistics, the compiling agency, for the period through March 1976. Later data were taken from issues of the *Monthly Labor Review* and the *Consumer Price Index,* which are published by the same agency.

Income Tax Rates

Compiling the set of income-tax rates used in our calculations of rates of return was a two-stage process. Since the marginal rate of tax depends on the level of income, the first step was estimating the investor's income for each year. The second step was to find the marginal tax rate that applied to a taxpayer with that income. Neither was a simple task.

Income Level. For "Rates (1964)," we assumed three income-tax categories—tax exemption; the rate that applied to a married person with an income of $10,000 in 1960 ("lower" tax rate); and the rates that applied to a married person with an income of $50,000 in 1960 ("higher" tax rate). Since both real income and the price level have varied substantially over the period studied, we decided that the tax rates should be applied to "equivalent" incomes in other years. This policy has been continued for "Rates (1968)" and the present study.

Over the fifty-one years covered by this study (and even the thirty-five years covered by "Rates [1964]") there have been large changes in the relative number of people in each age group, family size, and the number of wage earners per family. A real investor would have become substantially older between 1926 and 1976. Should the man with $50,000 in 1960 be assumed to have had a very successful paper route in 1926, a substantial salary or professional practice in 1960, and to have retired by 1976? What about the investor to whom the higher tax bracket applied and who bought his portfolio in 1975?

---

[13] *The rates specified for bonds were used for the Green Bay & Western Class B Debentures.*

Table A-1

Marginal Tax Rates Used for Calculations

<table>
<tr><td colspan="4" align="center">Marginal Tax Rate (percent)</td><td></td><td colspan="4" align="center">Marginal Tax Rate (percent)</td></tr>
<tr><td>Period
(1)</td><td>Dividends
(2)</td><td>Capital Gains
(3)</td><td>Interest
(4)</td><td></td><td>Period
(1)</td><td>Dividends
(2)</td><td>Capital Gains
(3)</td><td>Interest
(4)</td></tr>
<tr><td colspan="4" align="center">A. Lower Tax Rates</td><td></td><td colspan="4" align="center">B. Higher Tax Rates</td></tr>
<tr><td>1926–1939</td><td>0.0</td><td>0.0</td><td>0.0</td><td></td><td>1926–1930</td><td>1.0</td><td>6.0</td><td>1.0</td></tr>
<tr><td>1940</td><td>4.0</td><td>2.0</td><td>1.0</td><td></td><td>1931</td><td>0.0</td><td>5.0</td><td>0.0</td></tr>
<tr><td>1941</td><td>10.0</td><td>5.0</td><td>7.0</td><td></td><td>1932–1934</td><td>1.0</td><td>9.0</td><td>1.0</td></tr>
<tr><td>1942</td><td>13.0</td><td>6.5</td><td>13.0</td><td></td><td>1935</td><td>6.0</td><td>8.0</td><td>6.0</td></tr>
<tr><td>1943</td><td>22.0</td><td>11.0</td><td>22.0</td><td></td><td>1936–1937</td><td>11.0</td><td>6.6</td><td>8.0</td></tr>
<tr><td>1944–1945</td><td>25.0</td><td>12.5</td><td>25.0</td><td></td><td>1938–1939</td><td>10.0</td><td>5.0</td><td>7.0</td></tr>
<tr><td>1946–1947</td><td>24.7</td><td>12.4</td><td>14.7</td><td></td><td>1940</td><td>15.4</td><td>7.7</td><td>12.4</td></tr>
<tr><td>1948–1949</td><td>17.4</td><td>8.7</td><td>17.4</td><td></td><td>1941</td><td>36.0</td><td>15.0</td><td>33.0</td></tr>
<tr><td>1950</td><td>18.0</td><td>9.0</td><td>18.0</td><td></td><td>1942</td><td>42.0</td><td>25.0</td><td>42.0</td></tr>
<tr><td>1951</td><td>20.3</td><td>10.1</td><td>20.3</td><td></td><td>1943</td><td>58.0</td><td>25.0</td><td>58.0</td></tr>
<tr><td>1952–1953</td><td>22.1</td><td>11.1</td><td>22.1</td><td></td><td>1944–1945</td><td>62.0</td><td>25.0</td><td>62.0</td></tr>
<tr><td>January–July 1954</td><td>19.8</td><td>9.9</td><td>19.8</td><td></td><td>1946–1947</td><td>58.9</td><td>25.0</td><td>58.9</td></tr>
<tr><td>August 1954–December 1959</td><td>15.8</td><td>9.9</td><td>19.8</td><td></td><td>1948–1949</td><td>41.4</td><td>20.7</td><td>41.4</td></tr>
<tr><td>1960</td><td>18.0</td><td>11.0</td><td>22.0</td><td></td><td>1950</td><td>42.8</td><td>21.4</td><td>42.8</td></tr>
<tr><td>1961</td><td>18.0</td><td>11.0</td><td>26.0</td><td></td><td>1951</td><td>51.0</td><td>25.0</td><td>51.0</td></tr>
<tr><td>1962–1963</td><td>22.0</td><td>13.0</td><td>26.0</td><td></td><td>1952</td><td>56.0</td><td>26.0</td><td>56.0</td></tr>
<tr><td>1964</td><td>21.5</td><td>11.8</td><td>23.5</td><td></td><td>1953</td><td>59.0</td><td>26.0</td><td>59.0</td></tr>
<tr><td>1965–1967</td><td>22.0</td><td>11.0</td><td>22.0</td><td></td><td>January–July 1954</td><td>53.0</td><td>25.0</td><td>53.0</td></tr>
<tr><td>1968</td><td>26.9</td><td>13.4</td><td>26.9</td><td></td><td>August 1954–December 1955</td><td>49.0</td><td>25.0</td><td>53.0</td></tr>
<tr><td>1969</td><td>27.5</td><td>13.8</td><td>27.5</td><td></td><td>1956–1958</td><td>52.0</td><td>25.0</td><td>56.0</td></tr>
<tr><td>1970</td><td>25.6</td><td>12.8</td><td>25.6</td><td></td><td>1959–1962</td><td>55.0</td><td>25.0</td><td>59.0</td></tr>
<tr><td>1971</td><td>25.0</td><td>12.5</td><td>25.0</td><td></td><td>1963</td><td>58.0</td><td>25.0</td><td>62.0</td></tr>
<tr><td>1972–1974</td><td>28.0</td><td>14.0</td><td>28.0</td><td></td><td>1964</td><td>54.0</td><td>25.0</td><td>56.0</td></tr>
<tr><td>1975–1976</td><td>32.0</td><td>16.0</td><td>32.0</td><td></td><td>1965</td><td>53.0</td><td>25.0</td><td>53.0</td></tr>
<tr><td></td><td></td><td></td><td></td><td></td><td>1966–1967</td><td>55.0</td><td>25.0</td><td>55.0</td></tr>
<tr><td></td><td></td><td></td><td></td><td></td><td>1968</td><td>59.1</td><td>26.9</td><td>59.1</td></tr>
<tr><td></td><td></td><td></td><td></td><td></td><td>1969</td><td>63.8</td><td>27.5</td><td>63.8</td></tr>
<tr><td></td><td></td><td></td><td></td><td></td><td>1970</td><td>59.5</td><td>25.6</td><td>59.5</td></tr>
<tr><td></td><td></td><td></td><td></td><td></td><td>1971</td><td>60.0</td><td>25.0</td><td>60.0</td></tr>
<tr><td></td><td></td><td></td><td></td><td></td><td>1972</td><td>59.6</td><td>25.0</td><td>59.6</td></tr>
<tr><td></td><td></td><td></td><td></td><td></td><td>1973–1975</td><td>61.6</td><td>25.0</td><td>61.6</td></tr>
<tr><td></td><td></td><td></td><td></td><td></td><td>1976</td><td>63.6</td><td>25.0</td><td>63.6</td></tr>
</table>

These questions would make a fascinating study, but their answer was not the primary goal of this work. At best we can hope for only an approximate answer. Fortunately, the brackets to which particular rates apply are fairly broad.

To reduce the problem to a manageable one, we rather arbitrarily defined incomes for two years as equivalent if they bore the same ratio to the average income in the United States for their respective years. One complication was introduced. In examining averages of a variable whose distribution is highly skewed, e.g., income, the median is a better average than the arithmetic mean. Estimates of median money income for families are available for the years 1947 through 1975 in U.S. Bureau of the Census, *Current Population Reports,* Series P-60. These esti-

mates are the result of sample surveys made in March of each subsequent year. Since the median was $5,620 in 1960, estimates for 1947–75 were made by multiplying the reported median by 8.968 for the equivalent of $50,000 in 1960 and by 1.779 for the equivalent of $10,000. For the earlier years and for 1976, per capita personal income was used as an implicit estimator of median family income. Multipliers of personal income that would yield the same estimates of "equivalent" income as those from median income for 1947 (or 1975) were chosen and applied to the years 1926–46 (or 1976). The estimates of income equivalent to $50,000 in 1960 ranged from $9,000 in 1933 to $131,000 in 1976.

Applicable Rates. The marginal tax rates were found by a process equivalent to filling out income-tax returns for the years 1926 through 1976 for taxpayers at both income levels. The forms and instructions reproduced annually in U.S. Internal Revenue Service, *Statistics of Income* or *Your Federal Income Tax* were followed.

In finding the tax rates, a large number of assumptions about the taxpayer and the sources of his income had to be made, e.g.,

1. The "taxpayer" was a husband and wife filing a joint return. They were under sixty-five and sighted. They had no other dependents.

2. Only one of them had income.

3. Dividends barely exceeded the amount that could be excluded from gross income.

4. Interest, if partially tax-exempt, barely exceeded the amount that could be excluded from gross income.

5. Capital gains were small (in the mathematical sense).

6. Almost all income was "earned."

7. Dividends were all taxable and qualified for any dividend credit that was granted for the year in question.

8. Only the standard deduction was taken.[14]

9. For the cash-to-portfolio and U.S. Treasury-security cases: no capital gains or losses are realized.

10. For the cash-to-cash case: capital gains are taxed as if the holding period were between two and five years.

11. For the cash-to-cash case: there is other income against which capital losses may be offset.

Table A-1 shows all of the tax rates used for this study.[15]

[14] *This assumption may seem unrealistic to taxpayers who are in a substantial tax bracket. However, they should recall that we make no calculation of liability for state income or personal property taxes, which may be a major part of itemized deductions.*

[15] *Benjamin F. King, who is now Professor of Statistics at the University of Washington, made the estimates of income and the marginal tax rates used for "Rates (1964)." We have revised his estimates of capital gain tax rates because we changed an assumption. We also added the tax rates on interest. Income and all tax rates for 1961–75 were estimated by Peter Nicholson. We made the estimates for 1976.*

Appendix B
Computational Procedures

The data files described in Appendix A were used to calculate the rates of return reported in Tables I–XXX and XXXIV–LI. The calculations were made on an IBM 370 computer with programs written by the first author.

In this appendix, we describe the computational procedures in rather general terms. We present five sections. The first discusses finding time-weighted rates of return for portfolios of NYSE common stocks. The second discusses the similar procedures used to find internal rates of return. The third section reports the more important changes in procedure from those used for "Rates (1964)" and "Rates (1968)." Section four describes the procedures that we used to estimate rates of return on Governments. The last section is a note on the time-weighted rate of return.

Time-Weighted Rates of Return on Common Stocks

Finding the time-weighted rate of return on a buy-and-hold portfolio of NYSE common stocks for any particular one of the 1,326 holding periods reported in the tables is a three-stage process: (1) find the ratio of the end-of-period value of the investment in each stock (with dividends reinvested) to its cost at the beginning of the holding period, (2) average the individual wealth ratios to find the wealth ratio for the entire portfolio, (3) apply Equation 3.1 to obtain the annual rate of return.

The complexity of the procedure for estimating the wealth ratio for any particular stock depends on several factors, viz., whether the stock was still listed on the NYSE at the end of the holding period, whether our calculations take account of brokerage commissions on purchases and sales, and whether they allow for the payment of income and capital-gain taxes. We begin by describing the procedure for the simplest case, and then we tell how the complicating factors are taken into account. Finally, we point out how we made the computational process efficient by taking account of all 1,326 holding periods simultaneously.

The Simple Case

In the simple case, the stock is listed on the NYSE for the entire holding period; and taxes and commissions are ignored.

Recall that our special version of the *CRSP Monthly Return File for Common Stocks Listed on the New York Stock Exchange* contains the following data for each whole month that a stock was listed:

1. Month-end price (Price, P)
2. Number of shares outstanding at month-end (Shares, S)
3. Return for the month including cash dividends (Return, R)
4. Return for the month excluding cash dividends (Gain, G).[1]

---

[1] *Note that R and G are expressed as fractions of the value at the end of last month, e.g., R=.08 and G=.05 for a month show that the total return was 8 percent and price change (adjusted for stock dividends, etc.) was 5 percent. We infer that there was a cash dividend of 3 percent.*

In the simple case only "Return" for the months included in the holding period need be used. If we define the beginning of the holding period as month zero and the end of the holding period as month M, then for stock i, the wealth relative for the holding period is

$$W_i = \prod_{j=1}^{M} (1 + R_j). \qquad (B.1)$$

Equation B.1 says to consider all of the monthly returns of the stock during the holding period. Change the returns to ratios of end-of-month value this month to end-of-month value last month by adding one to each return. Then multiply all of the ratios together.[2]

The average value of W is found by applying either Equation B.2 (for equally weighted portfolios) or Equation B.3 (for portfolios that are initially weighted by value):

$$W = \left(\sum_{i=1}^{N} W_i \right) \Big/ N \qquad (B.2)$$

$$W = \left(\sum_{i=1}^{N} P_{0,i} S_{0,i} W_i \right) \Big/ \sum_{i=1}^{N} P_{0,i} S_{0,i}, \quad (B.3)$$

where N = number of stocks in the portfolio.

Equation B.2 says to add up the wealth relatives for all of the stocks and then divide by the number of stocks. Equation B.3 says to take a weighted average by multiplying each stock's wealth relative by the appropriate weight—the total market value of all of its shares at the beginning of the holding period—before adding. Then divide by the sum of the weights.

The time-weighted rate of return in percent per annum, compounded annually, is found from Equation 3.1.

Complex Cases

When there are complications, the procedures for using Equations B.2 or B.3 and 3.1 are not affected. However, Equation B.1 no longer describes the procedure for finding a stock's wealth relative.

When a stock does not remain listed until the end of the holding period, one of two alternative actions is taken.

Merged Stocks. If the stock disappeared because of a merger in which its holders received another listed common stock, the investment is followed by "splicing" the data for the successor stock onto the series of prices, returns, and gains for the stock in question (the shares of the successor are not needed because we are interested in shares outstanding only at the starting date of a holding period).

Stocks without Successors. When a stock ceases to be traded on the NYSE for any other reason, or when its last successor fails to remain listed until the end of the holding period, we assume that the proceeds up to the time of liquidation or sale are reinvested for the remainder of the holding period.

To find the stock's wealth relative for the entire holding period, we multiply its wealth relative for that part of the holding period from the beginning through the reinvestment month by the wealth relative for a new, equally weighted or value-weighted portfolio for the part of the holding period that began at the reinvestment month and ended at the end of the original holding period. For example, suppose we are computing the wealth relative for the holding period that begins in month zero and ends in month thirty-six—a three-year period—and that we are now considering a stock that was liquidated in month twenty. To find the wealth relative for the investment in the stock, we find its relative for the period month zero to month twenty and multiply that relative by the relative for a portfolio that was held from month twenty through month thirty-six.

The rates of return reported in this volume are based on portfolio wealth relatives for the 1,326 holding periods that began at the end of each year from 1925–75 and ended at the end of each subsequent year through 1976. However, because more than 600 stocks without successors stopped trading on the NYSE, wealth relatives for portfolios were actually found for holding periods beginning each month from December 1925 through November 1976 and ending each subsequent December. Hence, it was necessary to find portfolio wealth relatives for 15,912 holding periods although the final step of applying Equation 3.1 was carried out for only the 1,326 periods shown in the tables.[3]

Taxes on Dividends. When account is to be taken of either taxes or brokerage commissions, it is necessary to convert the series of returns (R) and gains (G) into series of dividends (D) and gains (G). The calculation is trivial

$$D_j = R_j - G_j. \qquad (B.4)$$

---

[2] If we were considering a stock that paid no dividends and had no capital changes during the entire holding period, the wealth relative would be equal to P_M/P_0.

[3] The final step is trivial for time-weighted rates of return. However, just as many holding periods are used for internal rates of return; and the process of calculating the rates of return from cash flows would not be trivial for 15,912 holding periods under ten sets of assumptions.

To take the income tax on dividends into account, we assume that the tax is paid immediately and subtract the tax from the dividend. Then we add the remainder of the dividend to the gain to obtain an adjusted return and proceed as we would have in the simple case.

Brokerage Commissions on Purchases. In the cash-to-portfolio case, we allow for brokerage commissions on the purchases at the beginning of the holding period and upon reinvestment of dividends.

To allow for the commission at the beginning of the holding period, we introduce an additional factor to the calculation of the wealth relative for the stock. This factor is the ratio of the price of the stock at the beginning of the holding period to the price plus commission as of that date. The wealth relative is multiplied by this initial commission factor.

To allow for commissions paid on reinvestment of dividends, we make a further adjustment to the dividend by multiplying the net dividend by the ratio of price to price plus commission for the date of reinvestment. This adjustment is not used for the last month in the holding period.

Brokerage Commissions on Sales. For the cash-to-cash case, we also assume payment of brokerage commissions at the end of the holding period. When there is no dividend the last month, the required adjustment is made by multiplying the wealth ratio by a sale-commission factor. This factor is found by dividing the price minus commission by the price. The sale commission is not charged on the cash held.

Capital-Gain Taxes. In order to find the capital-gain tax, we must first find out what the gain was. To find out, we must keep track of value and "cost," which includes the initial investment and the sum of dividends reinvested. For reasons that will become apparent when we discuss the problem of making the calculations efficient, this process requires computing value and what we call an "aboriginal cost." Value is the running product of the original investment ($100), the adjusted monthly ratios, and the initial commission factor. Aboriginal cost is the running sum of the original investment and the after-tax portions of dividends. The gain is the difference between the value (after any sale commissions) and the aboriginal cost.

Making the Programs Efficient

In the preceding discussion we wrote as if we made a separate calculation of each stock's wealth relatives for up to 15,912 holding periods.

In fact, we consider all 15,912 holding periods at the same time. To do so we convert the information in the four time series from the *Monthly Return File* into four other time series in a *CRSP Multiperiod Return File.* While the calculations take place we also maintain other time series in the computer.

The time series in the Multiperiod File are total market value, original cost, ending value, and aboriginal cost.

Total Market Value. Total market value is a monthly series. It is simply the product of shares and price for each month. It is used to provide weights for value-weighted portfolios.

Ending Value. Ending value is an annual series. However, it is the sum of year-end values of two monthly series, value of shares and cash.

Original Cost. For the first month a stock appears in the file, original cost is the assumed initial investment. The value is arbitrary. The program uses $100. At each subsequent month that the stock is still on the *Monthly Return File,* original cost represents the cost of acquiring the same interest in the stock that the investor on the initial date has. Value of shares plus cash is similar to the net-asset value of a mutual fund. Original cost is similar to the offering price of the fund except that the "sales charge" depends on the commission rate that applies to the shares actually held.

Value of Shares. Value of shares is the running product of the initial investment, the initial commission factor, the monthly ratios implied by the adjusted return through last month, and a factor equal to one plus this month's gain.

Cash. Cash is each month's dividend (after taxes).

Aboriginal Cost. Aboriginal cost is the running sum of the initial cost and dividends reinvested, as defined above. It shows the cost (for tax purposes) of the investment from the first possible holding period to each date. The cost for any holding period that began at a later date is the "original cost" at that date plus the *change* in the aboriginal cost between the beginning of the later holding period and the date in question.

Computation Process. To produce a cash-to-portfolio wealth relative for a stock, we make a Multiperiod File with the appropriate assumptions about commissions and taxes. Then we merely divide the value for the end of the holding period by the cost at the beginning of the holding period.

To find the cash-to-cash wealth relative for a stock requires reducing the ending value by the capital-gain tax for the holding period before we perform the calculation just described. The reduction depends on the gain to the end of the holding period if the stock or its successor was still listed. Otherwise the reduction is by a factor that depends on the capital gain through the date that proceeds were reinvested in a new portfolio.

Internal Rates of Return

In this study, we report internal rates of return only on a cash-to-portfolio basis. In processing data the aboriginal cost series was omitted and the cash series was saved instead. After the first nonzero value, the cash series was different from that of the time-weighted rate-of-return calculations because dividends were not reinvested.

Whenever a stock was liquidated and the proceeds reinvested, both the ending value and the cash series were affected.

For holding periods that had the same beginning date, the only difference in the monthly series of ratios of dividend to cost was the length of the series. Hence many of the elements of the cash flow were shared by a number of holding periods.

To apply Equation 3.2, "An Algorithm for Finding Exact Rates of Return," op. cit., was used. On the IBM 370, the cost was approximately one cent per rate of return for cash flows that had 213 elements, on average.

Changes of Procedure

The computer programs used for this study almost all differ from those used for our earlier studies, "Rates (1964)" and "Rates (1968)." In the new programs there are several differences in the assumed investment policy and a number of simplifications in bookkeeping.

The effects of these changes on rates of return for portfolios are small. For example, the vast majority of the 771 comparable estimates of rates of return in Table I and in Part A of Table 1 of "Rates (1968)" are within 0.1 percent per annum of each other.

However, the changes may have had substantial effects on the returns for some stocks.

The major procedural change was in working from the special version of the *CRSP Monthly Return File for Common Stocks Listed on the New York Stock Exchange,* described in Appendix A, rather than directly from the *Monthly Master File for NYSE Stocks.*

The other important change was in the way we reinvested proceeds from the liquidation of stocks that had been suspended or delisted without being exchanged for other NYSE common stock at the time trading ceased.

Also, a minor change is noted.

Use of Monthly Return File

Use of the *CRSP Monthly Return File for Common Stocks,* and making the changes in assumptions that were thereby required, allowed us to avoid the time and cost of rewriting the rather complex computer program that would have been required to maintain the bookkeeping standards that were used for "Rates (1964)" and "Rates (1968)." We had planned to do the rewriting; but comparison of the rates of return in a preliminary, test version of Table XXIX with an unpublished table (that had been developed from the computer output used for "Rates [1968]" and "Variability") showed that the differences were far too small to make the rewriting worthwhile.[4]

Simplifications. Use of the monthly returns required us to introduce the following bookkeeping simplifications that did not have to be made with the old procedures:

1. (Time-weighted rates of return) *New:* Dividends are assumed to be available for reinvestment at the end of the ex-dividend month even though many dividends are not paid until the following month or even later.

   Old: Dividends were not available for reinvestment until the end of the month in which they had been paid.

2. (Internal rates of return) *New:* Dividends are assumed to be received at the end of the ex-dividend month.

   Old: Dividends were assumed to have been received at the middle of the month in which they were paid.

3. *New:* All cash dividends are taxed as if they were dividends paid out of the retained earnings of a domestic corporation, i.e., as ordinary "unearned" income, exempt from normal tax (1926–35), eligible for tax credit (August 1954–December 1964).

---

[4] *Production of the test table did reveal a number of discrepancies in the* Master File. *Moreover, substantial clerical effort was required to splice the time series of returns for merged stocks to those of their successors. In addition, the test version of the computer programs had to be greatly altered to allow the other tables, which have more complicated assumptions than Table XXIX, to be produced.*

Old: Dividends with special tax characteristics were taxed accordingly, e.g., foreign dividends were always ordinary "unearned" income, many utilities and mines paid dividends that were partially "return of capital," investment companies distributed realized capital gains.

4. *New:* Capital gains or losses that had to be recognized at the time a distribution was made are treated as if they were not realized until all holdings were sold and, then, only in the "cash-to-cash" case.

Old: Such distributions were taxed as the gain or loss was realized.

Investment Policy. The use of the *Monthly Return File* also required a change in the treatment of spin-offs, which are distributions of the stock of another firm, usually in reorganization. In the new policy, the shares are assumed to be disposed of at their fair market value and used immediately to buy more shares of the distributing company. Under the old policy, such shares were kept if they were NYSE common stock.

Treatment of Liquidations

Three different methods have been used to estimate the returns on stocks after they were delisted.

For "Rates (1964)," we arranged the *Master File* so that all stocks that were delisted without their owners' receiving other listed common had their data at the beginning of the file and in the order that they had been delisted. Then, as the file was processed, the proceeds of each liquidation were allocated among the stocks that were listed in the liquidation month. That method allowed exact account to be taken of the returns after the liquidation date. However, it also made the stock-by-stock return data unsuitable for further analysis because they were affected both by the return on the original investment in the stock and by the reinvestment of liquidation proceeds.

For "Rates (1968)," we reinvested proceeds from liquidations in a fictitious stock that had the same monthly returns and dividends as the *ad hoc* "Combination" Investment Performance Index discussed above.[5] That method allowed us to use the stock-by-stock return data for "Variability," but the returns on liquidated stocks were only approximations. By 1965, about one-fifth of the assets of the portfolio assumed to have been purchased in January 1926 were represented by

the index. We thought that continuing to rely on an index for a substantially longer period would be pressing our luck too much.

In this study, we have had the advantage of using a computer that has about ten times as much storage capacity as the one we used for the earlier studies. It was feasible to sort stocks in descending order by the last date on which one of their holding periods began. Then, when a stock that had been liquidated was processed, we already had available the actual results for portfolios that were acquired in the liquidation month and held to each subsequent December.

Other Changes

The only other change that was important (other than correcting errors in the data) was to assume that the holding period for capital gains was at least two but less than five years, rather than at least one but less than two years. This change reduced the effective tax rate on capital gains that were realized between 1936 and 1941. Only Tables XXVII and XXVIII were affected by this change.

Effects of the Changes

As we noted at the beginning of this section, the net effects of all of these changes were very small. Comparison of corresponding rates of return from tables other than Table I indicates that the simplified assumptions about the timing and taxation of dividends had small effects, which sometimes raised and other times reduced the computed rates of return. We suspect that most of the differences between corresponding rates of return reported in "Rates (1968)" and in this study are due to revisions of the raw data in the *Master File*.

Rates of Return on Governments

Once the selection criteria for securities, the algorithm for finding after-tax returns, and the tax rates to apply had been decided upon, four steps were required to find the rates of return reported for Governments in Tables XXXIV through LI:

1. Selecting the issue to be held for each portfolio (long, intermediate, or short) for each year or half year

2. Extracting data for the selected issues

3. Constructing an index for each table

4. Finding rates of return from the indexes.

---

[5] *Lawrence Fisher, "Some New Stock-Market Indexes," op. cit.*

Selecting Issues

The selection criteria were given in Appendix A. For each portfolio a program was run that, for each December or each June and December, listed the relevant characteristics of the securities in the *CRSP Monthly Return File for U.S. Treasury Securities* that met the criterion of time to first call or to maturity. For a given date and portfolio, the list included between zero and about twelve issues. We examined each of the 204 lists and picked the security that appeared to meet the selection criteria best. The issue, date, and portfolio were entered into a card-image file on the computer.

Extracting Data

Another program was run. It selected issues and data for the appropriate months under control of the card-image file. Unmatched control cards and securities with missing data were reported.

When the card-image file had been perfected, the data on the selected issues were formed into a group of time series for each portfolio.

Constructing Indexes

An index of portfolio value was constructed for each of Tables XXXIV through LI. First, an index with values measured in current dollars was constructed for a portfolio. From it, a table of rates of return was constructed. Then an index that was deflated by the Consumer Price Index was found. It was used for the next table of rates of return.

The index with values measured in current dollars was constructed by subtracting tax liability from total return for the issue for the month. As described in Chapter 12, the tax liability was found from "return" or the difference between "return" and "excess return" for the month, depending on whether the security was a Treasury bill or some other type of issue.

After the return had been adjusted for tax liability, the index was constructed by applying Equation B.1 from December 1925 (as month 0) through the end of each subsequent December.

The indexes deflated by the CPI were constructed from the indexes in current dollars by dividing each value by the ratio of the current month's CPI to the CPI for December 1925.

Finding Rates of Return

The annual rates of return, compounding annually, were found by defining W as the ratio of the value of the index at the end of the holding period to the value at the beginning of the holding period. Then Equation 3.1 was applied.

Note on Time-Weighted Rates of Return

By definition, the time-weighted rate of return, compounded continuously, is

$$i = \sum_{j=1}^{n} i_j L_j \Big/ \sum_{j=1}^{n} L_j, \qquad (B.5)$$

where i_j is the rate of return of a subperiod

L_j is the length of a subperiod

n is the number of subperiods

The equivalent rate of return compounding annually is

$$r = e^i - 1, \qquad (B.6)$$

where e is the base of natural logarithms (2.71828 . . .).

Let V_{bj} = beginning valuation for a subperiod (after any investment or dividend withdrawal at the start)

V_{ej} = ending valuation for a subperiod (before any dividend withdrawal).

Then

$$i_j = \ln(V_{ej}/V_{bj})/L_j. \qquad (B.7)$$

Hence

$$i = \sum_j \ln(V_{ej}/V_{bj})/(t_e - t_b). \qquad (B.8)$$

But if there are no additions or withdrawals (i.e., if dividends are reinvested) between t_b and t_e,

$$i = \ln(V_e/V_b)/(t_e - t_b). \qquad (B.9)$$

Hence, when dividends are reinvested, Equation 3.1 provides the time-weighted annual rate of return, compounded annually.

Appendix C
Interest Tables

This appendix presents two interest tables. Table C-1 is a conventional table that shows the amount of one at various effective rates of interest for periods ranging from one to fifty-one years. Its only novel feature is that the rates of return range from −19 percent per annum to +40 percent per annum.

Table C-2 shows the effective rates of interest that are required if $100 grows to the value shown at the head of each column of the table in the time shown in the stub.

These tables are offered as an aid in converting the rates of return in the text tables to index values, which may be of interest in themselves or for comparing investment performance of portfolios that contain only a small number of stocks.

Table C-1 was constructed by applying the formula

$$W = (1 + r)^T. \qquad (C.1)$$

The rate of interest (or return), r, appears at the head of each column, the length of the time period, T, appears in the stub, and the amount, W, appears in the body of the table. The rate of return is stated as percent per annum, compounded annually.

Table C-2 was constructed by applying the formulas

$$W = V_e/100, \qquad (C.2)$$

$$(t_e - t_b) = T, \qquad (C.3)$$

and Equation 3.1. V_e appears at the head of each column, T appears in the stub, and r (in percent per annum) is in the body of the table.

ble C-1

tios of Ending Market Value to Beginning Market Value, W,
Rates of Return, r, between −19 Percent per Annum, Compounded Annually,
+40 percent and Holding Periods, T, of 1 to 51 years

gth of riod T	Annual Rate of Return, r																			
	−19%	−18%	−17%	−16%	−15%	−14%	−13%	−12%	−11%	−10%	−9%	−8%	−7%	−6%	−5%	−4%	−3%	−2%	−1%	0%
1	.8100	.8200	.8300	.8400	.8500	.8600	.8700	.8800	.8900	.9000	.9100	.9200	.9300	.9400	.9500	.9600	.9700	.9800	.9900	1.000
2	.6561	.6724	.6889	.7056	.7225	.7396	.7569	.7744	.7921	.8100	.8281	.8464	.8649	.8836	.9025	.9216	.9409	.9604	.9801	1.000
3	.5314	.5514	.5718	.5927	.6141	.6361	.6585	.6815	.7050	.7290	.7536	.7787	.8044	.8306	.8574	.8847	.9127	.9412	.9703	1.000
4	.4305	.4521	.4746	.4979	.5520	.5470	.5729	.5997	.6274	.6561	.6857	.7164	.7481	.7807	.8145	.8493	.8853	.9224	.9606	1.000
5	.3487	.3707	.3939	.4182	.4437	.4704	.4984	.5277	.5584	.5905	.6240	.6591	.6957	.7339	.7738	.8154	.8587	.9039	.9510	1.000
6	.2824	.3040	.3269	.3513	.3771	.4046	.4336	.4644	.4970	.5314	.5679	.6064	.6470	.6899	.7351	.7828	.8330	.8858	.9415	1.000
7	.2288	.2493	.2714	.2951	.3206	.3479	.3773	.4087	.4423	.4783	.5168	.5578	.6017	.6485	.6983	.7514	.8080	.8681	.9321	1.000
8	.1853	.2044	.2252	.2479	.2725	.2992	.3282	.3596	.3937	.4305	.4703	.5132	.5596	.6096	.6634	.7214	.7837	.8508	.9227	1.000
9	.1501	.1676	.1869	.2082	.2316	.2573	.2855	.3165	.3504	.3874	.4279	.4722	.5204	.5730	.6302	.6925	.7602	.8337	.9135	1.000
10	.1216	.1374	.1552	.1749	.1969	.2213	.2484	.2785	.3118	.3487	.3894	.4344	.4840	.5386	.5987	.6648	.7374	.8171	.9044	1.000
11	.0985	.1127	.1288	.1469	.1673	.1903	.2161	.2451	.2775	.3138	.3544	.3996	.4501	.5063	.5688	.6382	.7153	.8007	.8953	1.000
12	.0798	.0924	.1069	.1234	.1422	.1637	.1880	.2157	.2470	.2824	.3225	.3677	.4186	.4759	.5404	.6127	.6938	.7847	.8864	1.000
13	.0646	.0758	.0887	.1037	.1209	.1408	.1636	.1898	.2198	.2542	.2935	.3383	.3893	.4474	.5133	.5882	.6730	.7690	.8775	1.000
14	.0523	.0621	.0736	.0871	.1028	.1211	.1423	.1670	.1956	.2288	.2670	.3112	.3620	.4205	.4877	.5647	.6528	.7536	.8687	1.000
15	.0424	.0510	.0611	.0731	.0874	.1041	.1238	.1470	.1741	.2059	.2430	.2863	.3367	.3953	.4633	.5421	.6333	.7386	.8601	1.000
16	.0343	.0418	.0507	.0614	.0743	.0895	.1077	.1293	.1550	.1853	.2211	.2634	.3131	.3716	.4401	.5204	.6143	.7238	.8515	1.000
17	.0278	.0343	.0421	.0516	.0631	.0770	.0937	.1138	.1379	.1668	.2012	.2423	.2912	.3493	.4181	.4996	.5958	.7093	.8429	1.000
18	.0225	.0281	.0349	.0434	.0536	.0662	.0815	.1002	.1227	.1501	.1831	.2229	.2708	.3283	.3972	.4796	.5780	.6951	.8345	1.000
19	.0182	.0230	.0290	.0364	.0456	.0569	.0709	.0881	.1092	.1351	.1666	.2051	.2519	.3086	.3774	.4604	.5606	.6812	.8262	1.000
20	.0148	.0189	.0241	.0306	.0388	.0490	.0617	.0776	.0972	.1216	.1516	.1887	.2342	.2901	.3585	.4420	.5438	.6676	.8179	1.000
21	.0120	.0155	.0200	.0257	.0329	.0421	.0537	.0683	.0865	.1094	.1380	.1736	.2178	.2727	.3406	.4243	.5275	.6543	.8097	1.000
22	.0097	.0127	.0166	.0216	.0280	.0362	.0467	.0601	.0770	.0985	.1256	.1597	.2026	.2563	.3235	.4073	.5117	.6412	.8016	1.000
23	.0079	.0104	.0138	.0181	.0238	.0312	.0406	.0529	.0685	.0886	.1143	.1469	.1884	.2410	.3074	.3911	.4963	.6283	.7936	1.000
24	.0064	.0085	.0114	.0152	.0202	.0268	.0354	.0465	.0610	.0798	.1040	.1352	.1752	.2265	.2920	.3754	.4814	.6158	.7857	1.000
25	.0052	.0070	.0095	.0128	.0172	.0230	.0308	.0409	.0543	.0718	.0946	.1244	.1630	.2129	.2774	.3604	.4670	.6035	.7778	1.000
26	.0042	.0057	.0079	.0107	.0146	.0198	.0268	.0360	.0483	.0646	.0861	.1144	.1516	.2001	.2635	.3460	.4530	.5914	.7700	1.000
27	.0034	.0047	.0065	.0090	.0124	.0170	.0233	.0317	.0430	.0581	.0784	.1053	.1409	.1881	.2503	.3321	.4394	.5796	.7623	1.000
28	.0027	.0039	.0054	.0076	.0106	.0147	.0203	.0279	.0383	.0523	.0713	.0968	.1311	.1768	.2378	.3189	.4262	.5680	.7547	1.000
29	.0022	.0032	.0045	.0064	.0090	.0126	.0176	.0245	.0341	.0471	.0649	.0891	.1219	.1662	.2259	.3061	.4134	.5566	.7472	1.000
30	.0018	.0026	.0037	.0054	.0076	.0108	.0153	.0216	.0303	.0424	.0591	.0820	.1134	.1563	.2146	.2939	.4010	.5455	.7397	1.000
31	.0015	.0021	.0031	.0045	.0065	.0093	.0133	.0190	.0270	.0382	.0537	.0754	.1054	.1469	.2039	.2821	.3890	.5346	.7323	1.000
32	.0012	.0017	.0026	.0038	.0055	.0080	.0116	.0167	.0240	.0343	.0489	.0694	.0981	.1381	.1937	.2708	.3773	.5239	.7250	1.000
33	.0010	.0014	.0021	.0032	.0047	.0069	.0101	.0147	.0214	.0309	.0445	.0638	.0912	.1298	.1840	.2600	.3660	.5134	.7177	1.000
34	.0008	.0012	.0018	.0027	.0040	.0059	.0088	.0130	.0190	.0278	.0405	.0587	.0848	.1220	.1748	.2496	.3550	.5031	.7106	1.000
35	.0006	.0010	.0015	.0022	.0034	.0051	.0076	.0114	.0169	.0250	.0369	.0540	.0789	.1147	.1661	.2396	.3444	.4931	.7034	1.000
36	.0005	.0008	.0012	.0019	.0029	.0044	.0066	.0100	.0151	.0225	.0335	.0497	.0733	.1078	.1578	.2300	.3340	.4832	.6964	1.000
37	.0004	.0006	.0010	.0016	.0024	.0038	.0058	.0088	.0134	.0203	.0305	.0457	.0682	.1013	.1499	.2208	.3240	.4735	.6894	1.000
38	.0003	.0005	.0008	.0013	.0021	.0032	.0050	.0078	.0119	.0182	.0278	.0421	.0634	.0952	.1424	.2120	.3143	.4641	.6826	1.000
39	.0003	.0004	.0007	.0011	.0018	.0028	.0044	.0068	.0106	.0164	.0253	.0387	.0590	.0895	.1353	.2035	.3049	.4548	.6757	1.000
40	.0002	.0004	.0006	.0009	.0015	.0024	.0038	.0060	.0095	.0148	.0230	.0356	.0549	.0842	.1285	.1954	.2957	.4457	.6690	1.000
41	.0002	.0003	.0005	.0008	.0013	.0021	.0033	.0053	.0084	.0133	.0209	.0328	.0510	.0791	.1221	.1876	.2868	.4368	.6623	1.000
42	.0001	.0002	.0004	.0007	.0011	.0018	.0029	.0047	.0075	.0120	.0190	.0301	.0475	.0744	.1160	.1800	.2782	.4281	.6557	1.000
43	.0001	.0002	.0003	.0006	.0009	.0015	.0025	.0041	.0067	.0108	.0173	.0277	.0441	.0699	.1102	.1728	.2699	.4195	.6491	1.000
44	.0001	.0002	.0003	.0005	.0008	.0013	.0022	.0036	.0059	.0097	.0158	.0255	.0410	.0657	.1047	.1659	.2618	.4111	.6426	1.000
45	.0001	.0001	.0002	.0004	.0007	.0011	.0019	.0032	.0053	.0087	.0144	.0235	.0382	.0618	.0994	.1593	.2539	.4029	.6362	1.000
46	.0001	.0001	.0002	.0003	.0006	.0010	.0017	.0028	.0047	.0079	.0131	.0216	.0355	.0581	.0945	.1529	.2463	.3948	.6298	1.000
47	.0000	.0001	.0002	.0003	.0005	.0008	.0014	.0025	.0042	.0071	.0119	.0199	.0330	.0546	.0897	.1468	.2389	.3869	.6235	1.000
48	.0000	.0001	.0001	.0002	.0004	.0007	.0013	.0022	.0037	.0064	.0108	.0183	.0307	.0513	.0853	.1409	.2318	.3792	.6173	1.000
49	.0000	.0001	.0001	.0002	.0003	.0006	.0011	.0019	.0033	.0057	.0098	.0168	.0286	.0482	.0810	.1353	.2248	.3716	.6111	1.000
50	.0000	.0000	.0001	.0002	.0003	.0005	.0009	.0017	.0029	.0052	.0090	.0155	.0266	.0453	.0769	.1299	.2181	.3642	.6050	1.000
51	.0000	.0000	.0001	.0001	.0003	.0005	.0008	.0015	.0026	.0046	.0081	.0142	.0247	.0426	.0731	.1247	.2115	.3569	.5990	1.000

Table C-1 (Continued)

Ratios of Ending Market Value to Beginning Market Value, *W*,
for Rates of Return, *r*, between −19 Percent per Annum, Compounded Annually,
and +40 percent and Holding Periods, *T*, of 1 to 51 years

Length of Period T	\\ Annual Rate of Return, r																			
	1%	2%	3%	4%	5%	6%	7%	8%	9%	10%	11%	12%	13%	14%	15%	16%	17%	18%	19%	20%
1	1.010	1.020	1.030	1.040	1.050	1.060	1.070	1.080	1.090	1.100	1.110	1.120	1.130	1.140	1.150	1.160	1.170	1.180	1.190	1.2
2	1.020	1.040	1.061	1.082	1.102	1.124	1.145	1.166	1.188	1.210	1.232	1.254	1.277	1.300	1.323	1.346	1.369	1.392	1.416	1.4
3	1.030	1.061	1.093	1.125	1.158	1.191	1.225	1.260	1.295	1.331	1.368	1.405	1.443	1.482	1.521	1.561	1.602	1.643	1.685	1.7
4	1.041	1.082	1.126	1.170	1.216	1.262	1.311	1.360	1.412	1.464	1.518	1.574	1.630	1.689	1.749	1.811	1.874	1.939	2.005	2.07
5	1.051	1.104	1.159	1.217	1.276	1.338	1.403	1.469	1.539	1.611	1.685	1.762	1.842	1.925	2.011	2.100	2.192	2.288	2.386	2.4
6	1.062	1.126	1.194	1.265	1.340	1.419	1.501	1.587	1.677	1.772	1.870	1.974	2.082	2.195	2.313	2.436	2.565	2.700	2.840	2.9
7	1.072	1.149	1.230	1.316	1.407	1.504	1.606	1.714	1.828	1.949	2.076	2.211	2.353	2.502	2.660	2.826	3.001	3.185	3.379	3.5
8	1.083	1.172	1.267	1.369	1.477	1.594	1.718	1.851	1.993	2.144	2.305	2.476	2.658	2.853	3.059	3.278	3.511	3.759	4.021	4.3
9	1.094	1.195	1.305	1.423	1.551	1.689	1.838	1.999	2.172	2.358	2.558	2.773	3.004	3.252	3.518	3.803	4.108	4.435	4.785	5.1
10	1.105	1.219	1.344	1.480	1.629	1.791	1.967	2.159	2.367	2.594	2.839	3.106	3.395	3.707	4.046	4.411	4.807	5.234	5.695	6.19
11	1.116	1.243	1.384	1.539	1.710	1,898	2.105	2.332	2.580	2.853	3.152	3.479	3.836	4.266	4.652	5.117	5.624	6.176	6.777	7.4
12	1.127	1.268	1.426	1.601	1.796	2.012	2.252	2.518	2.813	3.138	3.498	3.896	4.335	4.818	5.350	5.936	6.580	7.288	8.064	8.9
13	1.138	1.294	1.469	1.665	1.886	2.133	2.410	2.720	3.066	3.452	3.883	4.363	4.898	5.492	6.153	6.886	7.699	8.599	9.596	10.
14	1.149	1.319	1.513	1.732	1.980	2.261	2.579	2.937	3.342	3.797	4.310	4.887	5.535	6.261	7.076	7.988	9.007	10.15	11.42	12.8
15	1.161	1.346	1.558	1.801	2.079	2.397	2.759	3.172	3.642	4.177	4.785	5.474	6.254	7.138	8.137	9.266	10.54	11.97	13.59	15.4
16	1.173	1.373	1.605	1.873	2.183	2.540	2.952	3.426	3.970	4.595	5.311	6.130	7.067	8.137	9.358	10.75	12.33	14.13	16.17	18.4
17	1.184	1.400	1.653	1.948	2.292	2.693	3.159	3.700	4.328	5.054	5.895	6.866	7.986	9.276	10.76	12.47	14.43	16.67	19.24	22.
18	1.196	1.428	1.702	2.026	2.407	2.854	3.380	3.996	4.717	5.560	6.544	7.690	9.024	10.58	12.38	14.46	16.88	19.67	22.90	26.
19	1.208	1.457	1.754	2.107	2.527	3.026	3.617	4.316	5.142	6.116	7.263	8.613	10.20	12.06	14.23	16.78	19.75	23.21	27.25	31.
20	1.220	1.486	1.806	2.191	2.653	3.207	3.870	4.661	5.604	6.727	8.062	9.646	11.52	13.74	16.37	19.46	23.11	27.39	32.43	38.
21	1.232	1.516	1.860	2.279	2.786	3.400	4.141	5.034	6.109	7.400	8.949	10.80	13.02	15.67	18.82	22.57	27.03	32.32	38.59	46.
22	1.245	1.546	1.916	2.370	2.925	3.604	4.430	5.437	6.659	8.140	9.934	12.10	14.71	17.86	21.64	26.19	31.63	38.14	45.92	55.
23	1.257	1.577	1.974	2.465	3.072	3.820	4.741	5.871	7.258	8.954	11.03	13.55	16.63	20.36	24.89	30.38	37.01	45.01	54.65	66.
24	1.270	1.608	2.033	2.563	3.225	4.049	5.072	6.341	7.911	9.850	12.24	15.18	18.79	23.21	28.63	35.24	43.30	53.11	65.03	79.
25	1.282	1.641	2.094	2.666	3.386	4.292	5.427	6.848	8.623	10.83	13.59	17.00	21.23	26.46	32.92	40.87	50.66	62.67	77.39	95.4
26	1.295	1.673	2.157	2.772	3.556	4.549	5.807	7.396	9.399	11.92	15.08	19.04	23.99	30.17	37.86	47.41	59.27	73.95	92.09	114
27	1.308	1.707	2.221	2.883	3.733	4.822	6.214	7.988	10.25	13.11	16.74	21.32	27.11	34.39	43.54	55.00	69.35	87.26	109.6	137
28	1.321	1.741	2.288	2.999	3.920	5.112	6.649	8.627	11.17	14.42	18.58	23.88	30.63	39.20	50.07	63.80	81.13	103.0	130.4	164
29	1.335	1.776	2.357	3.119	4.116	5.418	7.114	9.317	12.17	15.86	20.62	26.75	34.62	44.69	57.58	74.01	94.93	121.5	155.2	197
30	1.348	1.811	2.427	3.243	4.322	5.743	7.612	10.06	13.27	17.45	22.89	29.96	39.12	50.95	66.21	85.85	111.1	143.4	184.7	237
31	1.361	1.848	2.500	3.373	4.538	6.088	8.145	10.87	14.46	19.19	25.41	33.56	44.20	58.08	76.14	99.59	129.9	169.2	219.8	284
32	1.375	1.885	2.575	3.508	4.765	6.453	8.715	11.74	15.76	21.11	28.21	37.58	49.95	66.21	87.57	115.5	152.0	199.6	261.5	341
33	1.389	1.922	2.652	3.648	5.003	6.841	9.325	12.68	17.18	23.23	31.31	42.09	56.44	75.49	100.7	134.0	177.9	235.6	311.2	410
34	1.403	1.961	2.732	3.794	5.253	7.251	9.978	13.69	18.73	25.55	34.75	47.14	63.78	86.05	115.8	155.4	208.1	278.0	370.3	492
35	1.417	2.000	2.814	3.946	5.516	7.686	10.68	14.79	20.41	28.10	38.57	52.80	72.07	98.10	133.2	180.3	243.5	328.0	440.7	590
36	1.431	2.040	2.898	4.104	5.792	8.147	11.42	15.97	22.25	30.91	42.82	59.14	81.44	111.8	153.2	209.2	284.9	387.0	524.4	708
37	1.445	2.081	2.985	4.268	6.081	8.636	12.22	17.25	24.25	34.00	47.53	66.23	92.02	127.5	176.1	242.6	333.3	456.7	624.1	850
38	1.460	2.122	3.075	4.439	6.385	9.154	13.08	18.63	26.44	37.40	52.76	74.18	104.0	145.3	202.5	281.5	390.0	538.9	742.7	1,0
39	1.474	2.165	3.167	4.616	6.705	9.703	13.99	20.12	28.82	41.14	58.56	83.08	117.5	165.7	232.9	326.5	456.3	635.9	883.8	1,2
40	1.489	2.208	3.262	4.801	7.040	10.29	14.97	21.72	31.41	45.26	65.00	93.05	132.8	188.9	267.9	378.7	533.9	750.4	1,052	1,4
41	1.504	2.252	3.360	4.993	7.392	10.90	16.02	23.46	34.24	49.78	72.15	104.2	150.0	215.3	308.0	439.3	624.6	885.4	1,251	1,7
42	1.519	2.297	3.461	5.193	7.762	11.56	17.14	25.34	37.32	54.76	80.09	116.7	169.5	245.5	354.3	509.6	730.8	1,045	1,489	2,1
43	1.534	2.343	3.565	5.400	8.150	12.25	18.34	27.37	40.68	60.24	88.90	130.7	191.6	279.8	407.4	591.1	855.1	1,233	1,772	2,5
44	1.549	2.390	3.671	5.617	8.557	12.99	19.63	29.56	44.34	66.26	98.68	146.4	216.5	319.0	468.5	685.7	1,000	1,455	2,109	3,0
45	1.565	2.438	3.782	5.841	8.985	13.76	21.00	31.92	48.33	72.89	109.5	164.0	244.6	363.7	538.8	795.4	1,170	1,717	2,510	3,6
46	1.580	2.487	3.895	6.075	9.434	14.59	22.47	34.47	52.68	80.18	121.6	183.7	276.4	414.6	619.6	922.7	1,369	2,026	2,986	4,3
47	1.596	2.536	4.012	6.318	9.906	15.47	24.05	37.23	57.42	88.20	135.0	205.7	312.4	472.6	712.5	1,070	1,602	2,390	3,554	5,2
48	1.612	2.587	4.132	6.571	10.40	16.39	25.73	40.21	62.59	97.02	149.8	230.4	353.0	538.8	819.4	1,242	1,875	2,821	4,229	6,3
49	1.628	2.639	4.256	6.833	10.92	17.38	27.53	43.43	68.22	106.7	166.3	258.0	398.9	614.2	942.3	1,440	2,193	3,328	5,033	7,5
50	1.645	2.692	4.384	7.107	11.47	18.42	29.46	46.90	74.36	117.4	184.6	289.0	450.7	700.2	1,084	1,671	2,566	3,927	5,989	9,1
51	1.661	2.745	4.515	7.391	12.04	19.53	31.52	50.65	81.05	129.1	204.9	323.7	509.3	798.3	1,246	1,938	3,002	4,634	7,127	

Table C-1 (Continued)

Ratios of Ending Market Value to Beginning Market Value, W,
or Rates of Return, r, between −19 Percent per Annum, Compounded Annually,
and +40 percent and Holding Periods, T, of 1 to 51 years.

Length of Period T										Annual Rate of Return, r										
	21%	22%	23%	24%	25%	26%	27%	28%	29%	30%	31%	32%	33%	34%	35%	36%	37%	38%	39%	40%
1	1.210	1.220	1.230	1.240	1.250	1.260	1.270	1.280	1.290	1.300	1.310	1.320	1.330	1.340	1.350	1.360	1.370	1.380	1.390	1.400
2	1.464	1.488	1.513	1.538	1.562	1.588	1.613	1.638	1.664	1.690	1.716	1.742	1.769	1.796	1.823	1.850	1.877	1.904	1.932	1.960
3	1.772	1.816	1.861	1.907	1.953	2.000	2.048	2.097	2.147	2.197	2.248	2.300	2.353	2.406	2.460	2.515	2.571	2.628	2.686	2.744
4	2.144	2.215	2.289	2.364	2.441	2.520	2.601	2.684	2.769	2.856	2.945	3.036	3.129	3.224	3.322	3.421	3.523	3.627	3.733	3.842
5	2.594	2.703	2.815	2.932	3.052	3.176	3.304	3.436	3.572	3.713	3.858	4.007	4.162	4.320	4.484	4.653	4.826	5.005	5.189	5.378
6	3.138	3.297	3.463	3.635	3.815	4.002	4.196	4.398	4.608	4.827	5.054	5.290	5.535	5.789	6.053	6.328	6.612	6.907	7.213	7.530
7	3.797	4.023	4.259	4.508	4.768	5.042	5.329	5.629	5.945	6.275	6.621	6.983	7.361	7.758	8.172	8.605	9.058	9.531	10.03	10.54
8	4.595	4.908	5.239	5.590	5.960	6.353	6.768	7.206	7.669	8.157	8.673	9.217	9.791	10.40	11.03	11.70	12.41	13.15	13.94	14.76
9	5.560	5.987	6.444	6.931	7.451	8.005	8.595	9.223	9.893	10.60	11.36	12.17	13.02	13.93	14.89	15.92	17.00	18.15	19.37	20.66
10	6.728	7.305	7.926	8.594	9.313	10.09	10.92	11.81	12.76	13.79	14.88	16.06	17.32	18.67	20.11	21.65	23.29	25.05	26.92	28.93
11	8.140	8.912	9.749	10.66	11.64	12.71	13.86	15.11	16.46	17.92	19.50	21.20	23.03	25.01	27.14	29.44	31.91	34.57	37.43	40.50
12	9.850	10.87	11.99	13.21	14.55	16.01	17.61	19.34	21.24	23.30	25.54	27.98	30.64	33.52	36.64	40.04	43.72	47.70	52.02	56.69
13	11.92	13.26	14.75	16.39	18.19	20.18	22.36	24.76	27.39	30.29	33.46	36.94	40.74	44.91	49.47	54.45	59.89	65.83	72.31	79.37
14	14.42	16.18	18.14	20.32	22.74	25.42	28.40	31.69	35.34	39.37	43.83	48.76	54.19	60.18	66.78	74.05	82.05	90.85	100.5	111.1
15	17.45	19.74	22.31	25.20	28.42	32.03	36.06	40.56	45.59	51.19	57.42	64.36	72.07	80.64	90.16	100.7	112.4	125.4	139.7	155.6
16	21.11	24.09	27.45	31.24	35.53	40.36	45.80	51.92	58.81	66.54	75.22	84.95	95.86	108.1	121.7	137.0	154.0	173.0	194.2	217.8
17	25.55	29.38	33.76	38.74	44.41	50.85	58.17	66.46	75.86	86.50	98.54	112.1	127.5	144.8	164.3	186.3	211.0	238.8	269.9	304.9
18	30.91	35.85	41.52	48.04	55.51	64.07	73.87	85.07	97.86	112.5	129.1	148.0	169.6	194.0	221.8	253.3	289.0	329.5	375.2	426.9
19	37.40	43.74	51.07	59.57	69.39	80.73	93.81	108.9	126.2	146.2	169.1	195.4	225.5	260.0	299.5	344.5	396.0	454.7	521.5	597.6
20	45.26	53.36	62.82	73.86	86.74	101.7	119.1	139.4	162.9	190.0	221.5	257.9	299.9	348.4	404.3	468.6	542.5	627.5	724.9	836.7
21	54.76	65.10	77.27	91.59	108.4	128.2	151.3	178.4	210.1	247.1	290.2	340.4	398.9	466.9	545.8	637.3	743.2	865.9	1,008	1,171
22	66.26	79.42	95.04	113.6	135.5	161.5	192.2	228.4	271.0	321.2	380.2	449.4	530.6	625.6	736.8	866.7	1,018	1,195	1,401	1,640
23	80.18	96.89	116.9	140.8	169.4	203.5	244.1	292.3	349.6	417.5	498.0	593.2	705.6	838.3	994.7	1,179	1,395	1,649	1,947	2,296
24	97.02	118.2	143.8	174.6	211.8	256.4	309.9	374.1	451.0	542.8	652.4	783.0	938.5	1,123	1,343	1,603	1,911	2,276	2,706	3,214
25	117.4	144.2	176.9	216.5	264.7	323.0	393.6	478.9	581.8	705.6	854.6	1,034	1,248	1,505	1,813	2,180	2,618	3,140	3,762	4,500
26	142.0	175.9	217.5	268.5	330.9	407.0	499.9	613.0	750.5	917.3	1,120	1,364	1,660	2,017	2,447	2,965	3,587	4,334	5,229	6,300
27	171.9	214.6	267.6	333.0	413.6	512.9	634.9	784.6	968.1	1,193	1,467	1,801	2,208	2,703	3,304	4,032	4,914	5,980	7,268	8,820
28	208.0	261.9	329.1	412.9	517.0	646.2	806.3	1,004	1,249	1,550	1,921	2,377	2,937	3,622	4,460	5,484	6,733	8,253		
29	251.6	319.5	404.8	512.0	646.2	814.2	1,024	1,286	1,611	2,015	2,517	3,138	3,906	4,853	6,021	7,458	9,224			
30	304.5	389.8	497.9	634.8	807.8	1,026	1,301	1,646	2,078	2,620	3,297	4,142	5,195	6,503	8,129					
31	368.4	475.5	612.4	787.2	1,010	1,293	1,652	2,106	2,681	3,406	4,319	5,468	6,909	8,715						
32	445.8	580.1	753.3	976.1	1,262	1,629	2,098	2,696	3,458	4,428	5,658	7,217	9,189							
33	539.4	707.7	926.5	1,210	1,578	2,052	2,664	3,451	4,461	5,756	7,412	9,527								
34	652.7	863.4	1,140	1,501	1,972	2,586	3,383	4,417	5,755	7,483	9,710									
35	789.7	1,053	1,402	1,861	2,465	3,258	4,297	5,654	7,424	9,728										
36	955.6	1,285	1,724	2,308	3,081	4,105	5,457	7,237	9,577											
37	1,156	1,568	2,121	2,862	3,852	5,173	6,930	9,263												
38	1,399	1,913	2,609	3,548	4,815	6,517	8,801													
39	1,693	2,334	3,208	4,400	6,019	8,212														
40	2,048	2,847	3,946	5,456	7,523															
41	2,479	3,473	4,854	6,765	9,404															
42	2,999	4,238	5,971	8,389																
43	3,629	5,170	7,344																	
44	4,391	6,307	9,033																	
45	5,313	7,695																		
46	6,429	9,388																		
47	7,779																			
48	9,412																			

Table C-2

Annual Rates of Return*, *r*, Required for $100 To Grow (or Shrink)
to a Given Value in 1 to 51 Years

Length of Period T	$30	$40	$50	$60	$70	$80	$90	$100	$110	$120	$130	$140	$150	$160	$170	$180
								Ending Value (W × $100)								
1	−70.00%	−60.00%	−50.00%	−40.00%	−30.00%	−20.00%	−10.00%	0.00%	10.00%	20.00%	30.00%	40.00%	50.00%	60.00%	70.00%	80.00%
2	−45.23	−36.75	−29.29	−22.54	−16.33	−10.56	−5.13	0.00	4.88	9.54	14.02	18.32	22.47	26.49	30.38	34.16
3	−33.06	−26.32	−20.63	−15.66	−11.21	−7.17	−3.45	0.00	3.23	6.27	9.14	11.87	14.47	16.96	19.35	21.64
4	−25.99	−20.47	−15.91	−11.99	−8.53	−5.43	−2.60	0.00	2.41	4.66	6.78	8.78	10.67	12.47	14.19	15.83
5	−21.40	−16.74	−12.94	−9.71	−6.89	−4.36	−2.09	0.00	1.92	3.71	5.39	6.96	8.45	9.86	11.20	12.47
6	−18.18	−14.16	−10.91	−8.16	−5.77	−3.65	−1.74	0.00	1.60	3.09	4.47	5.77	6.99	8.15	9.25	10.29
7	−15.80	−12.27	−9.43	−7.04	−4.97	−3.14	−1.49	0.00	1.37	2.64	3.82	4.92	5.96	6.94	7.88	8.76
8	−13.97	−10.82	−8.30	−6.19	−4.36	−2.75	−1.31	0.00	1.20	2.31	3.33	4.30	5.20	6.05	6.86	7.62
9	−12.52	−9.68	−7.41	−5.52	−3.89	−2.45	−1.16	0.00	1.06	2.05	2.96	3.81	4.61	5.36	6.07	6.75
10	−11.34	−8.76	−6.70	−4.98	−3.50	−2.21	−1.05	0.00	0.96	1.84	2.66	3.42	4.14	4.81	5.45	6.05
11	−10.37	−7.99	−6.11	−4.54	−3.19	−2.01	−0.95	0.00	0.87	1.67	2.41	3.11	3.75	4.37	4.94	5.49
12	−9.55	−7.35	−5.61	−4.17	−2.93	−1.84	−0.87	0.00	0.80	1.53	2.21	2.84	3.44	3.99	4.52	5.02
13	−8.85	−6.81	−5.19	−3.85	−2.71	−1.70	−0.81	0.00	0.74	1.41	2.04	2.62	3.17	3.68	4.17	4.63
14	−8.24	−6.34	−4.83	−3.58	−2.52	−1.58	−0.75	0.00	0.68	1.31	1.89	2.43	2.94	3.41	3.86	4.29
15	−7.71	−5.93	−4.52	−3.35	−2.35	−1.48	−0.70	0.00	0.64	1.22	1.76	2.27	2.74	3.18	3.60	4.00
16	−7.25	−5.57	−4.24	−3.14	−2.20	−1.38	−0.66	0.00	0.60	1.15	1.65	2.13	2.57	2.98	3.37	3.74
17	−6.84	−5.25	−4.00	−2.96	−2.08	−1.30	−0.62	0.00	0.56	1.08	1.56	2.00	2.41	2.80	3.17	3.52
18	−6.47	−4.96	−3.78	−2.80	−1.96	−1.23	−0.58	0.00	0.53	1.02	1.47	1.89	2.28	2.65	2.99	3.32
19	−6.14	−4.71	−3.58	−2.65	−1.86	−1.17	−0.55	0.00	0.50	0.96	1.39	1.79	2.16	2.50	2.83	3.14
20	−5.84	−4.48	−3.41	−2.52	−1.77	−1.11	−0.53	0.00	0.48	0.92	1.32	1.70	2.05	2.38	2.69	2.98
21	−5.57	−4.27	−3.25	−2.40	−1.68	−1.06	−0.50	0.00	0.45	0.87	1.26	1.62	1.95	2.26	2.56	2.84
22	−5.33	−4.08	−3.10	−2.30	−1.61	−1.01	−0.48	0.00	0.43	0.83	1.20	1.54	1.86	2.16	2.44	2.71
23	−5.10	−3.91	−2.97	−2.20	−1.54	−0.97	−0.46	0.00	0.42	0.80	1.15	1.47	1.78	2.06	2.33	2.59
24	−4.89	−3.75	−2.85	−2.11	−1.48	−0.93	−0.44	0.00	0.40	0.76	1.10	1.41	1.70	1.98	2.24	2.48
25	−4.70	−3.60	−2.73	−2.02	−1.42	−0.89	−0.42	0.00	0.38	0.73	1.05	1.35	1.64	1.90	2.15	2.38
26	−4.53	−3.46	−2.63	−1.95	−1.36	−0.85	−0.40	0.00	0.37	0.70	1.01	1.30	1.57	1.82	2.06	2.29
27	−4.36	−3.34	−2.53	−1.87	−1.31	−0.82	−0.39	0.00	0.35	0.68	0.98	1.25	1.51	1.76	1.98	2.20
28	−4.21	−3.22	−2.45	−1.81	−1.27	−0.79	−0.38	0.00	0.34	0.65	0.94	1.21	1.46	1.69	1.91	2.12
29	−4.07	−3.11	−2.36	−1.75	−1.22	−0.77	−0.36	0.00	0.33	0.63	0.91	1.17	1.41	1.63	1.85	2.05
30	−3.93	−3.01	−2.28	−1.69	−1.18	−0.74	−0.35	0.00	0.32	0.61	0.88	1.13	1.36	1.58	1.78	1.98
31	−3.81	−2.91	−2.21	−1.63	−1.14	−0.72	−0.34	0.00	0.31	0.59	0.85	1.09	1.32	1.53	1.73	1.91
32	−3.69	−2.82	−2.14	−1.58	−1.11	−0.69	−0.33	0.00	0.30	0.57	0.82	1.06	1.28	1.48	1.67	1.85
33	−3.58	−2.74	−2.08	−1.54	−1.07	−0.67	−0.32	0.00	0.29	0.55	0.80	1.02	1.24	1.43	1.62	1.80
34	−3.48	−2.66	−2.02	−1.49	−1.04	−0.65	−0.31	0.00	0.28	0.54	0.77	0.99	1.20	1.39	1.57	1.74
35	−3.38	−2.58	−1.96	−1.45	−1.01	−0.64	−0.30	0.00	0.27	0.52	0.75	0.97	1.17	1.35	1.53	1.69
36	−3.29	−2.51	−1.91	−1.41	−0.99	−0.62	−0.29	0.00	0.27	0.51	0.73	0.94	1.13	1.31	1.48	1.65
37	−3.20	−2.45	−1.86	−1.37	−0.96	−0.60	−0.28	0.00	0.26	0.49	0.71	0.91	1.10	1.28	1.44	1.60
38	−3.12	−2.38	−1.81	−1.34	−0.93	−0.59	−0.28	0.00	0.25	0.48	0.69	0.89	1.07	1.24	1.41	1.56
39	−3.04	−2.32	−1.76	−1.30	−0.91	−0.57	−0.27	0.00	0.24	0.47	0.67	0.87	1.05	1.21	1.37	1.52
40	−2.97	−2.26	−1.72	−1.27	−0.89	−0.56	−0.26	0.00	0.24	0.46	0.66	0.84	1.02	1.18	1.34	1.48
41	−2.89	−2.21	−1.68	−1.24	−0.87	−0.54	−0.26	0.00	0.23	0.45	0.64	18.82	0.99	1.15	1.30	1.44
42	−2.83	−2.16	−1.64	−1.21	−0.85	−0.53	−0.25	0.00	0.23	0.44	0.63	0.80	0.97	1.13	1.27	1.41
43	−2.76	−2.11	−1.60	−1.18	−0.83	−0.52	−0.24	0.00	0.22	0.42	0.61	0.79	0.95	1.10	1.24	1.38
44	−2.70	−2.06	−1.56	−1.15	−0.81	−0.51	−0.24	0.00	0.22	0.42	0.60	0.77	0.93	1.07	1.21	1.34
45	−2.64	−2.02	−1.53	−1.13	−0.79	−0.49	−0.23	0.00	0.21	0.41	0.58	0.75	0.91	1.05	1.19	1.31
46	−2.58	−1.97	−1.50	−1.10	−0.77	−0.48	−0.23	0.00	0.21	0.40	0.57	0.73	0.89	1.03	1.16	1.29
47	−2.53	−1.93	−1.46	−1.08	−0.76	−0.47	−0.22	0.00	0.20	0.39	0.56	0.72	0.87	1.01	1.14	1.26
48	−2.48	−1.89	−1.43	−1.06	−0.74	−0.46	−0.22	0.00	0.20	0.38	0.55	0.70	0.85	0.98	1.11	1.23
49	−2.43	−1.85	−1.40	−1.04	−0.73	−0.45	−0.21	0.00	0.19	0.37	0.54	0.69	0.83	0.96	1.09	1.21
50	−2.38	−1.82	−1.38	−1.02	−0.71	−0.45	−0.21	0.00	0.19	0.37	0.53	0.68	0.81	0.94	1.07	1.18
51	−2.33	−1.78	−1.35	−1.00	−0.70	−0.44	−0.21	0.00	0.19	0.36	0.52	0.66	0.80	0.93	1.05	1.16

ble C-2 (Continued)

nual Rates of Return*, r, Required for $100 To Grow (or Shrink)
a Given Value in 1 to 51 Years

,th of riod T								Ending Value ($W \times 100$)								
	$190	$200	$210	$220	$230	$240	$260	$280	$300	$330	$360	$400	$450	$500	$600	$700
1	90.00%	100.00%	110.00%	120.00%	130.00%	140.00%	160.00%	180.00%	200.00%	230.00%	260.00%	300.00%	350.00%	400.00%	500.00%	600.00%
2	37.84	41.42	44.91	48.32	51.66	54.92	61.25	67.33	73.21	81.66	89.74	100.00	112.13	123.61	144.95	164.58
3	23.86	25.99	28.06	30.06	32.00	33.89	37.51	40.95	44.22	48.88	53.26	58.74	65.10	71.00	81.71	91.29
4	17.41	18.92	20.38	21.79	23.15	24.47	26.98	29.36	31.61	34.78	37.74	41.42	45.65	49.53	56.51	62.66
5	13.70	14.87	16.00	17.08	18.13	19.14	21.06	22.87	24.57	26.97	29.20	31.95	35.10	37.97	43.10	47.58
6	11.29	12.25	13.16	14.04	14.89	15.71	17.26	18.72	20.09	22.02	23.80	25.99	28.49	30.77	34.80	38.31
7	9.60	10.41	11.18	11.92	12.64	13.32	14.63	15.85	16.99	18.60	20.08	21.90	23.97	25.85	29.17	32.05
8	8.35	9.05	9.72	10.36	10.97	11.56	12.69	13.74	14.72	16.10	17.36	18.92	20.68	22.28	25.10	27.54
9	7.39	8.01	8.59	9.16	9.70	10.22	11.20	12.12	12.98	14.19	15.30	16.65	18.19	19.58	22.03	24.14
10	6.63	7.18	7.70	8.20	8.69	9.15	10.03	10.84	11.61	12.68	13.67	14.87	16.23	17.46	19.62	21.48
11	6.01	6.50	6.98	7.43	7.87	8.28	9.07	9.81	10.50	11.46	12.35	13.43	14.65	15.76	17.69	19.35
12	5.49	5.95	6.38	6.79	7.19	7.57	8.29	8.96	9.59	10.46	11.26	12.25	13.35	14.35	16.10	17.60
13	5.06	5.48	5.87	6.25	6.62	6.97	7.63	8.24	8.82	9.62	10.36	11.25	12.27	13.18	14.78	16.15
14	4.69	5.08	5.44	5.79	6.13	6.45	7.06	7.63	8.16	8.90	9.58	10.41	11.34	12.18	13.65	14.91
15	4.37	4.73	5.07	5.40	5.71	6.01	6.58	7.11	7.60	8.28	8.91	9.68	10.55	11.33	12.69	13.85
16	4.09	4.43	4.75	5.05	5.34	5.62	6.15	6.65	7.11	7.75	8.34	9.05	9.86	10.58	11.85	12.93
17	3.85	4.16	4.46	4.75	5.02	5.28	5.78	6.24	6.68	7.28	7.83	8.50	9.25	9.93	11.12	12.13
18	3.63	3.93	4.21	4.48	4.74	4.98	5.45	5.89	6.29	6.86	7.38	8.01	8.72	9.35	10.47	11.42
19	3.44	3.72	3.98	4.24	4.48	4.72	5.16	5.57	5.95	6.49	6.97	7.57	8.24	8.84	9.89	10.78
20	3.26	3.53	3.78	4.02	4.25	4.47	4.89	5.28	5.65	6.15	6.61	7.18	7.81	8.38	9.37	10.22
21	3.10	3.36	3.60	3.83	4.05	4.26	4.66	5.03	5.37	5.85	6.29	6.82	7.42	7.97	8.91	9.71
22	2.96	3.20	3.43	3.65	3.86	4.06	4.44	4.79	5.12	5.58	6.00	6.50	7.08	7.59	8.49	9.25
23	2.83	3.06	3.28	3.49	3.69	3.88	4.24	4.58	4.89	5.33	5.73	6.21	6.76	7.25	8.10	8.83
24	2.71	2.93	3.14	3.34	3.53	3.72	4.06	4.38	4.68	5.10	5.48	5.95	6.47	6.94	7.75	8.45
25	2.60	2.81	3.01	3.20	3.39	3.56	3.90	4.20	4.49	4.89	5.26	5.70	6.20	6.65	7.43	8.09
26	2.50	2.70	2.89	3.08	3.26	3.42	3.74	4.04	4.32	4.70	5.05	5.48	5.96	6.39	7.13	7.77
27	2.41	2.60	2.79	2.96	3.13	3.30	3.60	3.89	4.15	4.52	4.86	5.27	5.73	6.14	6.86	7.47
28	2.32	2.51	2.69	2.86	3.02	3.18	3.47	3.75	4.00	4.36	4.68	5.08	5.52	5.92	6.61	7.20
29	2.24	2.42	2.59	2.76	2.91	3.06	3.35	3.61	3.86	4.20	4.52	4.90	5.32	5.71	6.37	6.94
30	2.16	2.34	2.50	2.66	2.82	2.96	3.24	3.49	3.73	4.06	4.36	4.73	5.14	5.51	6.15	6.70
31	2.09	2.26	2.42	2.58	2.72	2.86	3.13	3.38	3.61	3.93	4.22	4.57	4.97	5.33	5.95	6.48
32	2.03	2.19	2.35	2.49	2.64	2.77	3.03	3.27	3.49	3.80	4.08	4.43	4.81	5.16	5.76	6.27
33	1.96	2.12	2.27	2.42	2.56	2.69	2.94	3.17	3.39	3.68	3.96	4.29	4.66	5.00	5.58	6.07
34	1.91	2.06	2.21	2.35	2.48	2.61	2.85	3.07	3.28	3.57	3.84	4.16	4.52	4.85	5.41	5.89
35	1.85	2.00	2.14	2.28	2.41	2.53	2.77	2.99	3.19	3.47	3.73	4.04	4.39	4.71	5.25	5.72
36	1.80	1.94	2.08	2.21	2.34	2.46	2.69	2.90	3.10	3.37	3.62	3.93	4.27	4.57	5.10	5.55
37	1.75	1.89	2.03	2.15	2.28	2.39	2.62	2.82	3.01	3.28	3.52	3.82	4.15	4.45	4.96	5.40
38	1.70	1.84	1.97	2.10	2.22	2.33	2.55	2.75	2.93	3.19	3.43	3.72	4.04	4.33	4.83	5.25
39	1.66	1.79	1.92	2.04	2.16	2.27	2.48	2.68	2.86	3.11	3.34	3.62	3.93	4.21	4.70	5.12
40	1.62	1.75	1.87	1.99	2.10	2.21	2.42	2.61	2.78	3.03	3.25	3.53	3.83	4.11	4.58	4.99
41	1.58	1.70	1.83	1.94	2.05	2.16	2.36	2.54	2.72	2.95	3.17	3.44	3.74	4.00	4.47	4.86
42	1.54	1.66	1.78	1.90	2.00	2.11	2.30	2.48	2.65	2.88	3.10	3.36	3.65	3.91	4.36	4.74
43	1.50	1.63	1.74	1.85	1.96	2.06	2.25	2.42	2.59	2.82	3.02	3.28	3.56	3.81	4.25	4.63
44	1.47	1.59	1.70	1.81	1.91	2.01	2.20	2.37	2.53	2.75	2.95	3.20	3.48	3.73	4.16	4.52
45	1.44	1.55	1.66	1.77	1.87	1.96	2.15	2.31	2.47	2.69	2.89	3.13	3.40	3.64	4.06	4.42
46	1.41	1.52	1.63	1.73	1.83	1.92	2.10	2.26	2.42	2.63	2.82	3.06	3.32	3.56	3.97	4.32
47	1.38	1.49	1.59	1.69	1.79	1.88	2.05	2.21	2.37	2.57	2.76	2.99	3.25	3.48	3.89	4.23
48	1.35	1.45	1.56	1.66	1.75	1.84	2.01	2.17	2.32	2.52	2.70	2.93	3.18	3.41	3.80	4.14
49	1.32	1.42	1.53	1.62	1.71	1.80	1.97	2.12	2.27	2.47	2.65	2.87	3.12	3.34	3.72	4.05
50	1.29	1.40	1.49	1.59	1.68	1.77	1.93	2.08	2.22	2.42	2.59	2.81	3.05	3.27	3.65	3.97
51	1.27	1.37	1.47	1.56	1.65	1.73	1.89	2.04	2.18	2.37	2.54	2.76	2.99	3.21	3.58	3.89

percent per annum compounded annually

Table C-2 (Continued)

Annual Rates of Return , r, Required for $100 To Grow (or Shrink)
to a Given Value in 1 to 51 Years

Length of Period T	Ending Value ($W \times \$100$)															
	$800	$900	$1,000	$1,200	$1,500	$2,000	$2,500	$3,500	$5,000	$7,000	$10,000	$15,000	$20,000	$25,000	$30,000	$40,0
1	700.00%	800.00%	900.00%	1,100.00%	1,400.00%	1,900.00%	2,400.00%	3,400.00%	4,900.00%	6,900.00%	9,900.00%	14,900.00%	19,900.00%	24,900.00%	29,900.00%	39,900
2	182.84	200.00	216.23	246.41	287.30	347.21	400.00	491.61	607.11	736.66	900.00	1,124.74	1,314.21	1,481.14	1,632.05	1,900
3	100.00	108.01	115.44	128.94	146.62	171.44	192.40	227.11	268.40	312.13	364.16	431.33	484.80	529.96	569.43	636
4	68.18	73.21	77.83	86.12	96.80	111.47	123.61	143.23	165.91	189.25	216.23	249.96	276.06	297.64	316.18	347.
5	51.57	55.18	58.49	64.38	71.88	82.06	90.37	103.62	118.67	133.89	151.19	172.41	188.54	201.71	212.91	231.
6	41.42	44.22	46.78	51.31	57.04	64.75	71.00	80.86	91.94	103.01	115.44	130.51	141.83	150.99	158.73	171.
7	34.59	36.87	38.95	42.62	47.24	53.41	58.38	66.18	74.87	83.48	93.07	104.58	113.17	120.07	125.88	135.
8	29.68	31.61	33.35	36.43	40.29	45.42	49.53	55.96	63.07	70.07	77.83	87.07	93.92	99.41	104.00	111.
9	25.99	27.65	29.15	31.80	35.11	39.50	43.00	48.44	54.45	60.33	66.81	74.50	80.16	84.69	88.47	94.
10	23.11	24.57	25.89	28.21	31.10	34.93	37.97	42.69	47.88	52.94	58.49	65.05	69.86	73.70	76.89	82.
11	20.81	22.11	23.28	25.35	27.91	31.30	33.99	38.16	42.71	47.14	51.99	57.70	61.88	65.19	67.95	72.
12	18.92	20.09	21.15	23.01	25.32	28.36	30.77	34.48	38.54	42.48	46.78	51.82	55.51	58.43	60.85	64.
13	17.35	18.41	19.38	21.06	23.16	25.92	28.10	31.45	35.11	38.65	42.51	47.03	50.32	52.92	55.08	58.
14	16.01	16.99	17.88	19.42	21.34	23.86	25.85	28.91	32.24	35.45	38.95	43.03	46.00	48.35	50.29	53.
15	14.87	15.78	16.59	18.02	19.79	22.11	23.94	26.75	29.80	32.74	35.94	39.66	42.36	44.50	46.27	49.
16	13.88	14.72	15.48	16.80	18.44	20.59	22.28	24.88	27.70	30.41	33.35	36.77	39.26	41.21	42.83	45.
17	13.01	13.80	14.50	15.74	17.27	19.27	20.85	23.26	25.87	28.39	31.11	34.28	36.57	38.37	39.87	42.
18	12.25	12.98	13.65	14.80	16.24	18.11	19.58	21.84	24.28	26.62	29.15	32.10	34.23	35.90	37.28	39.
19	11.57	12.26	12.88	13.97	15.32	17.08	18.46	20.58	22.86	25.06	27.43	30.18	32.16	33.72	35.01	37.
20	10.96	11.61	12.20	13.23	14.50	16.16	17.46	19.45	21.60	23.67	25.89	28.47	30.33	31.79	33.00	34.
21	10.41	11.03	11.59	12.56	13.76	15.33	16.57	18.45	20.48	22.42	24.52	26.95	28.70	30.07	31.21	33.
22	9.91	10.50	11.03	11.96	13.10	14.59	15.76	17.54	19.46	21.30	23.28	25.58	27.23	28.53	29.60	31.
23	9.46	10.02	10.53	11.41	12.50	13.91	15.02	16.72	18.54	20.29	22.17	24.34	25.91	27.13	28.14	29.7
24	9.05	9.59	10.07	10.91	11.94	13.29	14.35	15.97	17.70	19.37	21.15	23.22	24.70	25.87	26.83	28.3
25	8.67	9.19	9.65	10.45	11.44	12.73	13.74	15.28	16.94	18.52	20.23	22.19	23.61	24.71	25.63	27.0
26	8.33	8.82	9.26	10.03	10.98	12.21	13.18	14.65	16.24	17.75	19.38	21.25	22.60	23.66	24.53	25.9
27	8.01	8.48	8.90	9.64	10.55	11.73	12.66	14.07	15.59	17.04	18.60	20.39	21.68	22.69	23.52	24.8
28	7.71	8.16	8.57	9.28	10.15	11.29	12.18	13.54	14.99	16.38	17.88	19.60	20.83	21.80	22.59	23.8
29	7.43	7.87	8.26	8.95	9.79	10.88	11.74	13.04	14.44	15.78	17.21	18.86	20.05	20.97	21.74	22.9
30	7.18	7.60	7.98	8.64	9.45	10.50	11.33	12.58	13.93	15.21	16.59	18.18	19.32	20.21	20.94	22.1
31	6.94	7.35	7.71	8.35	9.13	10.15	10.94	12.15	13.45	14.69	16.02	17.54	18.64	19.50	20.20	21.3
32	6.71	7.11	7.46	8.07	8.83	9.81	10.58	11.75	13.00	14.20	15.48	16.95	18.01	18.83	19.51	20.5
33	6.50	6.88	7.23	7.82	8.55	9.50	10.25	11.38	12.59	13.74	14.98	16.40	17.42	18.21	18.87	19.9
34	6.31	6.68	7.01	7.58	8.29	9.21	9.93	11.02	12.19	13.31	14.50	15.88	16.86	17.63	18.27	19.27
35	6.12	6.48	6.80	7.36	8.04	8.94	9.63	10.69	11.83	12.91	14.06	15.39	16.34	17.09	17.70	18.67
36	5.95	6.29	6.61	7.15	7.81	8.68	9.35	10.38	11.48	12.53	13.65	14.93	15.86	16.58	17.17	18.1
37	5.78	6.12	6.42	6.95	7.59	8.43	9.09	10.09	11.15	12.17	13.25	14.50	15.40	16.09	16.67	17.58
38	5.62	5.95	6.25	6.76	7.39	8.20	8.84	9.81	10.84	11.83	12.88	14.09	14.96	15.64	16.19	17.08
39	5.48	5.80	6.08	6.58	7.19	7.98	8.60	9.54	10.55	11.51	12.53	13.71	14.55	15.21	15.75	16.6
40	5.34	5.65	5.93	6.41	7.00	7.78	8.38	9.30	10.27	11.21	12.20	13.35	14.16	14.80	15.33	16.16
41	5.20	5.51	5.78	6.25	6.83	7.58	8.17	9.06	10.01	10.92	11.89	13.00	13.79	14.42	14.93	15.74
42	5.08	5.37	5.64	6.09	6.66	7.39	7.97	8.83	9.76	10.64	11.59	12.67	13.45	14.05	14.55	15.33
43	4.95	5.24	5.50	5.95	6.50	7.22	7.77	8.62	9.52	10.38	11.30	12.36	13.11	13.70	14.18	14.95
44	4.84	5.12	5.37	5.81	6.35	7.05	7.59	8.42	9.30	10.14	11.03	12.06	12.80	13.37	13.84	14.59
45	4.73	5.00	5.25	5.68	6.20	6.88	7.42	8.22	9.08	9.90	10.78	11.78	12.50	13.05	13.51	14.24
46	4.62	4.89	5.13	5.55	6.06	6.73	7.25	8.04	8.88	9.68	10.53	11.51	12.21	12.75	13.20	13.91
47	4.52	4.79	5.02	5.43	5.93	6.58	7.09	7.86	8.68	9.46	10.29	11.25	11.93	12.47	12.90	13.60
48	4.43	4.68	4.91	5.31	5.80	6.44	6.94	7.69	8.49	9.25	10.07	11.00	11.67	12.19	12.62	13.29
49	4.34	4.59	4.81	5.20	5.68	6.30	6.79	7.53	8.31	9.06	9.85	10.77	11.42	11.93	12.34	13.01
50	4.25	4.49	4.71	5.10	5.57	6.17	6.65	7.37	8.14	8.87	9.65	10.54	11.18	11.68	12.08	12.73
51	4.16	4.40	4.62	4.99	5.45	6.05	6.51	7.22	7.97	8.69	9.45	10.32	10.95	11.43	11.83	12.47

Bibliography

I. Printed Matter

Bank Administration Institute. *Measuring the Investment Performance of Pension Funds for the Purpose of Interfund Comparisons.* Park Ridge, Illinois: Bank Administration Institute, 1968.

Bank and Quotation Record, 1928–date.

"Bank and Quotation Section." *Commercial and Financial Chronicle,* 1926–1928.

Barron's.

Capital Adjustments. Englewood Cliffs, N.J.: Prentice-Hall.

CCH Capital Changes Reporter.

Commercial and Financial Chronicle.

Fisher, Lawrence. "Outcomes for 'Random' Investments in Common Stocks Listed on the New York Stock Exchange." *Journal of Business* 38 (April 1965): 149–61.

———. "An Algorithm for Finding Exact Rates of Return." *Journal of Business* 39 (January 1966, Part 2): 111–18.

———. "Some New Stock-Market Indexes." *Journal of Business* 39 (January 1966, Part 2): 191–225.

Fisher, Lawrence, and Lorie, James H. "Rates of Return on Investments in Common Stocks." *Journal of Business* 37 (January 1964): 1–21. ("Rates [1964]")

———. "Rates of Return on Investments in Common Stocks: The Year-by-Year Record, 1926–65." *Journal of Business* 41 (July 1968): 291–316. ("Rates [1968]")

———. "Some Studies of Variability of Returns on Investments in Common Stocks." *Journal of Business* 43 (April 1970): 99–134. ("Variability")

Fisher, Lawrence, and Weil, Roman L. "Coping with the Risk of Interest-Rate Fluctuations: Returns to Bondholders from Naïve and Optimal Strategies." *Journal of Business* 44 (October 1971): 408–31.

Jensen, Kenneth R. "An Analysis of Various Rules for Determining Expenditures from Endowment Funds." Ph.D. dissertation, Graduate School of Business, University of Chicago, 1973.

Levy, Haim, and Sarnat, Marshall. *Investment and Portfolio Analysis.* New York: John Wiley & Sons, 1972.

Listing Applications to the New York Stock Exchange, Inc.

Listing Statements of the New York Stock Exchange.

Macaulay, Frederic R. *Some Theoretical Problems Suggested by the Movement of Interest Rates, Bond Yields and Stock Prices in the United States since 1856.* New York: National Bureau of Economic Research, 1938.

Moody's Dividend Record.

Moody's Manual of Investments.

The New York Times.

"Rates (1964)." See Fisher and Lorie, 1964.

"Rates (1968)." See Fisher and Lorie, 1968.

Redington, F. M. "Review of the Principles of Life-office Valuations." *Journal of the Institute of the Society of Actuaries* (England) 78 (1952): 286–340.

Salomon Brothers. *Quotation Sheets.*

Scholes, Myron. "Returns to Investing in Common Stocks Listed on the New York Stock Exchange." *Proceedings: Seminar on the Analysis of Security Prices* 20 (May 1975): 127–30.

———. "Predicting Betas and Variances Using Daily Data." *Proceedings: Seminar on the Analysis of Security Prices* 21 (May 1976): 205–34.

Sharpe, William F. "Capital Asset Prices: A Theory of Market Equilibrium under Conditions of Risk." *Journal of Finance* 39 (September 1964): 425–42.

Standard & Poor's Register of Corporations.

Standard & Poor's Stock Guide.

U.S. Bureau of Labor Statistics. *BLS Handbook of Methods* (BLS Bulletin 1711, revised 1972).

————, *Chartbook on Prices, Wages, and Productivity.*

————. *Consumer Price Index.*

————. *Monthly Labor Review.*

U.S. Bureau of the Census. *Current Population Reports Series P-60.*

U.S. Department of the Treasury, Government Actuary. *Circular 2.*

U.S. Internal Revenue Service. *Statistics of Income* (Annually).

————. *Your Federal Income Tax* (Annually).

"Variability." See Fisher and Lorie, 1970.

The Wall Street Journal.

Weekly Bulletin of the New York Stock Exchange.

II. Machine Readable Data Files

Fisher, Lawrence, compiler. *CRSP Monthly Return File for U.S. Treasury Securities.* Chicago: Circulated privately by the Center for Research in Security Prices (Sponsored by Merrill Lynch, Pierce, Fenner & Smith Inc), Graduate School of Business, University of Chicago (CRSP), 1976–.

Fisher, Lawrence, and Scholes, Myron, compilers. *CRSP Monthly Master File for Common Stocks Listed on the New York Stock Exchange.* Chicago: Circulated privately by CRSP, 1977. (Earlier editions have been circulated since 1964.)

————. *CRSP Monthly Return File for Common Stocks Listed on the New York Stock Exchange.* Chicago: Circulated privately by CRSP, 1977. (Earlier editions have been circulated since 1964.)

Scholes, Myron, compiler. *CRSP Daily Return File for Common Stocks.* Chicago: Circulated privately by CRSP, 1977. (Earlier editions have been circulated since 1970.)